Modernism and Fascism

Also by Roger Griffin

The Nature of Fascism (1991)

Fascism (in 'The Oxford Readers Series', 1995)

International Fascism: Theories, Causes, and the New Consensus (1998)

Fascism: Critical Concepts in Political Science edited with Matthew Feldman (2004)

Modernism and Fascism

The Sense of a Beginning
under Mussolini and Hitler

Roger Griffin

First published 2007 by
PALGRAVE MACMILLAN

Palgrave Macmillan in the UK is an imprint of Macmillan Publishers Limited, registered in England, company number 785998, of Houndmills, Basingstoke, Hampshire RG21 6XS.

Palgrave Macmillan in the US is a division of St Martin's Press LLC, 175 Fifth Avenue, New York, NY 10010.

Palgrave Macmillan is the global academic imprint of the above companies and has companies and representatives throughout the world.

Palgrave® and Macmillan® are registered trademarks in the United States, the United Kingdom, Europe and other countries.

ISBN-13: 9781403987839 hardback
ISBN-10: 1403987831 hardback
ISBN-13: 9781403987846 paperback
ISBN-10: 140398784X paperback

This book is printed on paper suitable for recycling and made from fully managed and sustained forest sources. Logging, pulping and manufacturing processes are expected to conform to the environmental regulations of the country of origin.

A catalogue record for this book is available from the British Library.

A catalog record for this book is available from the Library of Congress.

Transferred to Digital Printing in 2014

This ain't no time for doubting your power
This ain't no time for hiding your care
You're climbing down from an ivory tower
You've got a stake in the world we ought to share
This is the time of the worlds colliding
This is the time of kingdoms falling
This is the time of the worlds dividing
Time to heed your call
Send your love into the future
Send your precious love into some distant time
And fix that wounded planet with the love of your healing
Send your love into the future
Send your love into the distant dawn

'Send Your Love'. Words and music by Sting © 2003
Reproduced by permission of
Steerpike (Overseas) Ltd/EMI Music Publishing Ltd, London WC2H 0QY

This book is dedicated to the memory of my mother
And to the future of my son

Contents

List of Illustrations

Acknowledgements

This book could not have been written without the generous period of sabbatical leave made possible by an AHRC Research Leave award for one semester combined with a Brookes Research Leave award for two. I hope the final outcome goes some way towards justifying the trust placed in me by the various anonymous assessors of my grant applications. I also owe an enormous debt to several key members of the School of Arts and Humanities at Oxford Brookes University who gave me moral or practical support to progress with this project at various points in its long gestation when it was needed, and to the hundreds of its students who have taken my history courses over the years who became unwitting guinea-pigs for the interpretations and theories that culminated in this metanarrative, some of them showing the sort of spontaneous enthusiasm for my approach to history which is the life-blood of a teaching career. The process of writing the book and assembling the illustrations for it over the last 18 months has also revealed the remarkable generosity and humanity retained by some academics and para-academics despite the mounting temporal, bureaucratic, and financial stress inflicted on this particular global community.

So many people have played a role in the genesis or completion of this project that the list resembles the credits that roll unseen down the screen as people leave the cinema. To explain the unique contribution of each one would swell further the dimensions of a tome already full to bursting. I thus propose simply to list everyone democratically in alphabetical order of their first name. They all know what they have done for me, in some cases reading a whole draft, proofreading the entire manuscript, suggesting key books of which I was oblivious, writing an inspiring article, or simply, in a timely moment, pointing me in the right direction academically or emotionally in my own wrestling match with Cronus and modernity. I hope that in their different ways those who are still with us can all find something in the final result that makes them pleased to be acknowledged in this understated way: Alice Demartini, Alfred Schobert, Andreas Umland, Aristotle Kallis, Cassie Watson, Claudio Fogu, Clotilde D'Amato, Cyprian Blamires, David Baker, David Luke, David Nash, David Robertson, Detlef Mühlberger, Emilio Gentile, Francesco Innamorati, George Mosse, Gillian Hooper, Gregory Maertz, Ian Kershaw, Jeffrey Schnapp, John Perkins, John Stewart, Josephine Reynolds, Library staff in the Bodleian Library (upper reserve), Karla Poewe,

Marco Demartini, Marco Medicina, Marius Turda, Mark Antliff, Mary Chamberlain, Matthew Feldman, Michael Golston, Michael Strang, Mitch Sedgwick, Modris Eksteins, Orietta Rossini, Orietta Panicelli, Paul Hooper, Paul Jackson, Paul Weindling, Peter Fritzsche, Peter Harbour, Peter Osborne, Peter Pulzer, Quinto Demartini, Reginald Cave, Richard Evans, Rob Pope, Robert Murray, Roberto Ventrone, Robin Mowat, Roger Eatwell, Rosalba Demartini, Samuele Demartini, Siegfried Jäger, Stan Mathews, Stanley Payne, Steve King, Sue Neale, Susanne Baackmann, Susan McCrae, Tudor Georgescu, Walter Adamson, Werner Loh, Zygmunt Baumann, and last, but far from least, Mariella, without whom nothing would have been possible.

This book is about the quest for transcendence under the conditions of Western modernity, and about the human need to draw from the past to give meaning to the future. If it is to be dedicated to anyone, then it is to the person from my past who did most to instil a search for 'higher' values and an appreciation of life's fragile beauty, Joan Griffin, and to the person in whom the best of what I have learnt will, I hope, live on in a different way in the future, Vincent Griffin. On 11 December 2005 while I was writing this book his precocious grasp of the principles of academic life was illustrated by the following exchange: *Vincent* (aged 6, looking at the overflowing shelves in my study) 'Did you make all these books?'; *Roger Griffin*: 'No, I read them to write mine'; *Vincent*: 'But that's cheating, Rog.'

Introduction
Aufbruch

'Then you know your destination', he asked. 'Yes', I said 'I have
already said so, "Away-From-Here" that is my destination.' 'You
have no provisions with you', he said. 'I don't need any', I said. 'The
journey is so long that I will die of hunger if I do not get something
along the way. It is, fortunately, a truly immense journey.'

Franz Kafka, *Der Aufbruch* [A New Beginning] (1922)[1]

The sense of an ending [...] has not diminished, and is as endemic
to what we call modernism as apocalyptic utopianism is to political
revolution.

Frank Kermode, *The Sense of an Ending* (1966)[2]

Tomorrow has become today: the feeling that the world is ending
has given way to the sense of a new beginning. The ultimate goal
now stands out unmistakably within the field of vision now opening
up before us, and all faith in miracles is now harnessed to the active
transformation of the present.

Julius Petersen, *The Longing for the Third Reich* (1934)[3]

NEW HORIZONS

This book is a sustained attempt to explore the profound kinship that exists
between modernism and fascism. These two concepts are still widely assumed
to be antithetical and oxymoronic when combined in the phrase 'fascist
modernism', especially within the context of the regimes led by Mussolini
and Hitler. Nevertheless, the second part of the book will present them as
outstanding examples of the 'modernist state'. The Leitmotif of the book is
that a key element in the genesis, psychology, ideology, policies, and praxis
of fascism was played by the 'sense of a beginning', the mood of standing on
the threshold of a new world. It is a mood of heady expectancy which is the
dialectical twin of the obsession with the closing of an era explored by the

1

English literary historian Frank Kermode in his seminal text on modernism, *The Sense of an Ending*, four decades ago. Whereas his focus was the significance of 'apocalyptic time' as a central topos of the modernist imagination, the theme of this book is the way the belief that transcendence can be achieved through cultural, social, and political transformation leaves its stamp on the ideology, policies, and practice of Fascism and Nazism.

The germ of the undertaking can be found in a passage written some 15 years ago in *The Nature of Fascism*, my bid to offer historians and political scientists a more useful definition than those currently available for investigating such issues as the relationship of Italian Fascism to Franco's Spain, Hitler's Germany, the Romanian Iron Guard, or the prospects of fascism's post-war revival in old or new forms. In one section I spelled out the implications of seeing in the rebirth myth (the myth of 'palingenesis') not just the key definitional component of fascism, but the element that in the extreme conditions of inter-war Europe could endow some variants of nationalism and racism with extraordinary affective and destructive power. It contains the assertion that, far from being intrinsically anti-modern, fascism only rejects 'the allegedly degenerative elements of the modern age', and that its 'thrust towards a *new* type of society' means that 'it represents an *alternative modernism* rather than a rejection of it'.[4]

In order to unpack this cryptic statement my original plan for a slim volume on fascist culture surveying 'successful' and abortive movements, both inter-war and post-war (such as Third Positionism and the European New Right), proved utopian. Instead, it has been necessary to devote considerable attention to re-conceptualizing 'modernism' (Part One), and to limit my detailed application of the resulting ideal type to the regimes of Mussolini and Hitler (Part Two), chosen both because of profound differences in their conception of the new national culture, and because they alone offer case studies not only in fascism's utopian aspirations as a revolutionary project but its praxis as a regime. The aim is to cast fresh light not just on fascism, but on the nature of modernity and modernism as well, thereby providing the basis for future work, particularly by other specialists whose work impinges on some of the many aspects of this vast topic which have been necessarily omitted or neglected here.

Incongruously enough, a 'kitsch' image flitted through my mind on the day when after months of planning, grant applications, and draft proposals I finally embarked on 'realizing' this venture through the magic lantern of the computer screen. It was that of Leonardo Di Caprio and Kate Winslet perched precariously on the prow of the *Titanic*. They stand atop a structure as tall as a skyscraper, with a powerful breeze ruffling their hair, both enraptured by the dizzy sensation of ploughing a thin white line through the grey-blue vastness of the Atlantic. We are encouraged to feel that with every fibre of their being they feel they are living at the cutting edge of time and space, surrendering themselves to the part metaphysical, part erotic sensation of imbibing with each gulp of air a foretaste of unlimited freedom and possibility, of becoming the master and mistress of their communal destiny.

The lovers-to-be are standing on the threshold of an unimaginable New Time, racing headlong towards the New World, an America more utopian myth than geographical reality. The poignancy of the scene, underscored by the tear-jerking Irish love-song that accompanied the closing credits, derives from the tragic-ironic gap between the exhilarating but drastically foreshortened 'field-of-vision' available to the young pair, and the spectator's knowledge that a horrendous fate awaits them just over the horizon. Yet there are other ways of interpreting this event.

When the actual ship went down on the 15 April 1912 it was a knee-jerk response for some evangelical Christians to interpret the disaster as a sign of the hubris of modern man, and some contemporary artists instinctively endowed it with more free-floating apocalyptic significance. Even a century on it is still tempting to see the sinking as presaging the imminent fate of Western civilization as a whole as it speeds on its maiden voyage headlong into two decades of catastrophic wars, dictatorships, and mass killing which so cruelly exposed the myth of unlimited progress on which liberal-capitalist-imperialist civilization was being built in the *belle époque*.[5] Doubtless, still more cosmic layers of symbolism contribute to the perennial fascination emanating from the ocean liner's fate. In the present context, though, the fact that my psyche plucked this scene from a film which so unashamedly transmutes a historical disaster into Hollywood melodrama suggests two alternative readings, both of which have an immediate bearing on the following 12 chapters.

One might be the subliminal acknowledgement that setting out to rethink the relationship between modernism and fascism is a 'high risk venture', not least because it involves constructing what once was a standard product of academic research but which is now regarded with considerable suspicion, namely a 'master narrative' of a vast and an intrinsically multivalent topic. I will return to this aspect of the book shortly. More importantly, the ecstatic moment on the prow of the *Titanic* can be seen as a *tableau vivant* for a particular way that human beings can experience time 'mythically' as pregnant with exhilarating potential for renewal and purification. Apart from my own sense of 'setting sail' which informed the composition of this preface, an important subtext of this study is the catastrophic impact on modern history that such an experience of time can have once translated from the realm of personal relationships and poetry into political and social aspirations to build a new society at all costs.

It is this mood that helped convince the revolutionaries of the French National Assembly they were not just changing the political and social regime in France, but regenerating history, creating a new type of 'man', and starting time anew.[6] It is the state of mind that seduced Friedrich Nietzsche into believing his books were intellectual 'dynamite', blowing a hole in the oppressive rock walls trapping his contemporaries in the existing phase of cultural evolution, and thus opening up a portal into an entirely new kind of human history based on a 'transvaluation of all values'.[7] It is a moment of higher consciousness captured in the Futurist Manifesto, when Filippo Marinetti, a decade before becoming a member of the first *Fascio*, claimed to be 'standing on the last promontory of the centuries' and announced the death of 'Time and Space'. Indeed, one of the poetic symbols which he offers for the new consciousness was 'adventurous steamers that sniff the horizon'.[8]

It will be argued in this book that – at least for its most committed, idealistic activists – fascism in the inter-war period was the vehicle for realizing the heady sense, not of impotently watching history unfold, but of actually 'making history' before a new horizon and a new sky. It meant breaking out of the ensnarement of words and thoughts into deeds, and using the power of human creativity not to produce art for its own sake, but to create a new culture in a total act of creation, of *poesis*. Fascism for its most ardent believers promised to be literally epoch-making.

In the event, the two movements that managed to place themselves at the helm of political power catastrophically failed to achieve the permanent trans-formation of society they craved, let alone bring about a sea-change in History itself. Mussolini's Third Rome lasted only two decades compared with the 500 years of the Roman Empire, while the Reich that Hitler intended to last for a whole millennium lay in ruins after a mere 12 years. The Axis they formed led directly or indirectly to the deaths of millions, eventually leaving their nations in the rubble of broken promises and shattered dreams. Yet their ambitions, failures, and crimes against humanity remain unintelligible if due weight is not given to the role played in mobilizing their troops, both military and civilian, by consciously inducing a revolutionary experience of standing on the edge of history and proactively changing its course, freed from the constraints of 'normal' time and 'conventional' morality.

THE QUEST FOR A 'BIGGER PICTURE'

As the allusions to Nietzsche and Marinetti imply, the premise of this enquiry is that the 'visions of the world' (*Weltanschauung*, or *visione del mondo*) which conditioned the policies of the two very different fascist dictatorships established in inter-war Europe were both deeply bound up with intellectual and artistic modernism, but in ways that defy simplistic equations or reductionist formulae. Despite over half a century of sustained academic effort and countless publications which have a direct bearing on this subject, a number of basic issues about how the states created by Mussolini and Hitler 'fit into' modernity are still far from being resolved to the satisfaction of most experts working in this area.

This book aims to provide a new analytical framework within which to resolve them more satisfactorily. Yet ironically, one of the factors threatening the credibility of this attempt to gain a synoptic grasp of the subject is that the type of 'big picture' this requires has generally become taboo in academic circles, and in some quarters is associated with the very 'totalitarianism' that fascisms embodied in their drive to remake society and history in their image.[9] However dubious such an association, the paradox remains that the staggering proliferation since 1945 of scholarship, secondary sources, and theoretical perspectives on every conceivable aspect of social reality, past and present in all branches of the humanities has not culminated in comprehensive explanations. Instead, a mood of growing self-consciousness has come to prevail within each discipline of the impossibility of achieving definitive inter-pretations. This, combined with the 'cultural turn' triggered by postmodernism and poststructuralism, has resulted in the delegitimization of all accounts of reality offered by earlier generations of experts which imply reductionism, essentialism, or 'totalizing narratives'. As a result even works which display profound scholarship in their drive for an overview of a vast topic, such as Hannah Arendt's *The Origins of Totalitarianism* (first published in 1951) or Karl Popper's *The Open Society and its Enemies* (1945), now seem to belong to a different era.

Against this background the self-appointed mission to rethink the socio-psychological dynamics and scope of 'modernism', an extensively contested term, and then explore the relevance of its redefinition to two regimes whose praxis is assumed – though even this is a contentious assumption in the case of the Third Reich – to embody the world-view of 'fascism', another highly problematic term, is to go against the grain of the prevalent academic *Zeitgeist*. If not reckless, it is certainly what is known in German as 'unzeitgemäß' – 'untimely', or 'unmodern' – the term used by Nietzsche to characterize a series of essays which he knew were out of tune with the spirit of his age.[10]

Nevertheless, let it be stated at the outset that this work, though undoubtedly speculative in its drive to syncretize different areas of the humanities into an overarching interpretative framework, has none of the totalizing pretensions of a 'metanarrative'. The overarching interpretation it offers draws attention to its own constructedness, and the contested nature of its theoretical foundations, like a modernist building that deliberately exposes its lifts, supportive structures, and the tubing that supplies its power and plumbing. It is based on the premise that not only is there room in the human sciences for 'lumpers' as well as 'splitters',[11] but that they are indispensable to all fields of specialist research. It is in this spirit that the pioneer of reconstructing daily life under the Third Reich, Detlef Peukert, wrote: 'Everyday experience never tallies exactly with large analytical or systematic hypotheses. At the same time, if experience is to be understood at all, *it cannot do without synoptic interpretation either.*'[12] Indeed, it seems to me self-evident that the constant dialectic between attempts to synthesize knowledge 'nomothetically' into big pictures – though not one big picture – identifying broad patterns in phenomena, and research that focuses on understanding particular aspects of reality 'idiographically' guarantees progress towards greater knowledge and understanding.

FASCISM AS THE OFFSPRING OF MODERNISM

It is thus in an anti-totalizing, anti-essentialist mode of academic narration that this book explores its 'synoptic interpretation' of the intimate but complex relationship between modernism and the regimes of Mussolini and Hitler. It will be not be framed as a 'hypothesis', which implies criteria of testability and falsification, for as Karl Popper points out 'historical approaches' or 'points of view' *cannot be* tested. He adds soberingly that 'they cannot be refuted, and apparent confirmations are of no value, even if they are as numerous as the stars in the sky'. For the 'thesis' that informs this book we will adopt the term that he proposes for 'a selective point of view or focus of historical interest, if it cannot be formulated as a testable hypothesis': namely 'a *historical interpretation*'.[13]

At the core of our synoptic historical interpretation lies the proposition that, not only were Fascist Italy and Nazi Germany both concrete manifestations of a generic political ideology and praxis that has come to be termed 'fascism', but that fascism itself can be seen as a political variant of modernism. This peculiar genus of revolutionary project for the transformation of society, it will be argued, could only emerge in the first decades of the twentieth century in a society permeated with modernist metanarratives of cultural renewal which shaped a legion of activities, initiatives, and movements 'on the ground'. In its varied permutations fascism took it upon itself not just to change the state system, but to purge civilization of decadence, and foster the emergence of a new breed of human beings which it defined in terms not of universal categories but essentially mythic national and racial ones. Its activists set about their task in the iconoclastic spirit of 'creative destruction' legitimized not by divine will, reason, the laws of nature, or by socio-economic theory, but by the belief that history itself was at a turning point and could be launched on a new course through human intervention that would redeem the nation and rescue the West from imminent collapse.

Whereas the night-time slumber of reason produces only imaginary monsters, the extreme actions that fascism's 'dreamers of the day' were prepared to take in order to realize their fantasies of a new epoch found expression in edifices of stone, technological inventions of steel, and the flesh and minds of would-be 'new men' ready to exact the 'sacrifice' – especially the sacrifice of the 'other' – demanded by the process of regeneration. In this context the poem by one artist exposed to the storm of modernity, William Butler Yeats, acquires a clairvoyant quality. Composed when he felt simultaneously drawn to and repelled by the apocalyptic yearnings for a 'new dawn' that spread throughout European society in the aftermath of the First World War, one section in particular adumbrates the horrors of the Second. Having famously evoked the anarchy of contemporary history where 'things fall apart' and 'the centre cannot hold' he gives vent both to his blend of hope and fear so characteristic of the modernist *imaginaire*:

> Surely some revelation is at hand;
> Surely the Second Coming is at hand.
> The Second Coming! Hardly are those words out
> When a vast image out of the Spiritus Mundi
> Troubles my sight: somewhere in sands of the desert
> A shape with lion body and the head of a man,
> A gaze blank and pitiless as the sun,
> Is moving its slow thighs, while all around it
> Reel shadows of the indignant desert birds.
> The darkness drops again; but now I know
> That twenty centuries of stony sleep
> Were vexed to nightmare by a rocking cradle,
> And what rough beast, its hour come round at last,
> Slouches towards Bethlehem to be born?[14]

Such lines have a bearing on an important distinction drawn by Frank Kermode in *The Sense of an Ending*. He stresses the difference between the poetic *fictions* used by artists to illuminate or articulate elusive aspects of contemporary reality, and politicized *myths*, which become incorporated into the ideological rationale for attempts to engineer radical transformations of that reality. To illustrate this distinction he cites Yeats, the bulk of whose visionary poetry is 'safely' confined to the realm of apocalyptic fiction, but who, when the political animal in him overpowered the artist, slipped over the invisible border into the realm of political, or rather metapolitical myth. This helps explain why the pioneer of the Celtic Revival also became 'enthusiastic for Italian fascism, and supported the Irish fascist movement' – the Blue Shirts.

It might be added as evidence of his openness to *scientized* fictions as well as politicized myths that in 1937 he joined the British Eugenics Society, a fact which assumes considerable significance in the light of the conception of modernism explored in this book.

Kermode calls Yeats a prime example 'of that correlation between early modernist literature and authoritarianism which is *more often noticed than explained*: totalitarian theories of form matched or reflected by totalitarian politics'.[15] Forty years on, the correlation may have been noticed more widely academically, but both explanations and, more importantly, the synoptic interpretive frameworks needed to make sense of them, are still thin on the ground. It is the purpose of this book to help rectify this situation. It seeks to clarify the linkage between poetic and political modernism to which Kermode alluded in 1965, but which as a Professor of English he did not consider part of his brief to explore in any great depth.

In contrast, my own expedition into the terrain of the 'modern apocalypse' deliberately sets out to excavate the relationship that exists at an ideological and psychological level between two areas of reality that have for so long been dealt with by separate departments of the humanities. On the one hand, the role played in literary and cultural modernism by 'apocalyptic' fictions concerning the decadence of the contemporary world, its sense of permanent transition and crisis, and its need for renovation. On the other, the correlatives of such fictions in the ideologies of modern social and political movements bent on healing society from its alleged corruption and decadence.

These myths arguably play a central role in any form of political ideology, left or right,[16] which posits the radical socio-political renewal from a state of decadence, not just as a rhetorical device, but in a genuinely revolutionary spirit geared to permanent change and the improvement of society. However, this book focuses exclusively on the projects of national, social, racial or cultural cleansing and rebirth subsumed under the term 'fascism' and given concrete expression in the regimes of Mussolini and Hitler. They were myths that generated policies and actions designed to bring about collective redemption, a new national community, a new society, a new man. Their goal was rebirth, a 'palingenesis' brought about not through suprahuman agency, but engineered through the power of the modern state.[17]

If it can be brought to a convincing conclusion – though not, of course, closure – *Modernism and Fascism* should have the effect of complementing Kermode's pioneering lecture series on 'the sense of an ending' in modern visionary literature. It offers an account of the complex links which this literary mood had to the powerful sense of inaugurating a *new epoch* expressed in the visionary schemes spawned by fascism in the first half of the twentieth century. This politicized, historicized 'sense of a beginning' will in turn be implicitly linked with endings of a very different type than the one Kermode was concerned with. These are the agonizingly unfictional and unmythical endings, the shattering of hopes, lives, and bodies that particularly in the twentieth century some currents of social and political modernism – once implemented as the basis of state policy – have inflicted with such extraordinary physical and psychological ruthlessness on entire categories of human life in the pursuit of the regeneration of history and the inauguration of a new era.

AUFBRUCH

It should by now be clear that this project is exploratory or 'heuristic' in the fullest sense of the term. It is posited on the need for regular attempts to break out of established conceptual frameworks so as to discover fresh horizons within which to 'revisit' even the most extensively scrutinized and obsessively documented episodes in modern history. It is an adventurous mood associated in German with the term '*Aufbruch*' with its connotations of literally 'breaking up', 'breaking out', and 'breaking open', a word which can refer both to the ending of a meeting when it 'breaks up', and 'irruption' or breaking *into* a new phase or situation, and hence a 'new departure'. It is the term used by Kafka as the title of the unpublished short story cited in the epigraph to this Introduction.

At the same time *Aufbruch* can also refer to the state of expectancy induced by the intuitive certainty that an entire phase of history is giving way to a new one. This meaning will prove to be crucial to our twin investigations of modernism and fascism. The premise of this book is that the two fascist regimes of inter-war Europe cannot be understood without taking into account the wide-spread conviction that the upheavals of contemporary history were the death throes of the modern world under the aegis of Enlightenment reason and liberal capitalism. But this was no 'cultural despair'. In the immediate aftermath of the First World War not just the avant-garde, but millions of 'ordinary people' felt they were witnessing the birth pangs of a new world under an ideological and political regime whose nature was yet to be decided. What the cultural historian Siegfried Kracauer claimed about the 'mood' of Germany in the early years of the Weimar Republic has a profound resonance throughout the Europeanized world wherever the experience of breakdown and need for transformation was particularly acute. As he says himself, it was a mood that

> can best be defined by the word *Aufbruch*. In the pregnant sense in which it was used at the time, the term meant departure from the shattered world of yesterday towards a tomorrow built on the grounds of revolutionary conceptions. [...] People suddenly

grasped the significance of *avant-garde* paintings and mirrored themselves in visionary dramas announcing to a suicidal mankind the gospel of a new age of brotherhood. [...] They believed in international socialism, pacifism, collectivism, aristocratic leadership, religious community, life, or national resurrection, and frequently presented a confused mixture of these variegated ideals as a brand-new creed.[18]

A major premise of this book is that the mood of *Aufbruch* described here is to be seen as a defining component of a particular form of modernism, of a sense of breaking through to new beginnings no longer experienced by cultural elites or restricted to the realm of art and thought. Part One, 'The Sense of a Beginning in Modernism', will establish that even before the First World War imparted it with powerful populist and revolutionary impetus, the drive towards a new vision and a new era was expressing itself with increasing intensity throughout European society, not just in the sphere of avant-garde aesthetics, but in the realms of intellectual and cultural speculation about finding a new foundation for meaning or reality, social movements, popular initiatives to bring about a renewed sense of rootedness, community, and health, as well as revolutionary politics of both the left and right. Our analysis will seek to establish the premodern and 'primordial' ideological and sociological forces precipitating extremely heterogeneous modernist longings for *Aufbruch*, and to show how they were unleashed by a perceived crisis not just in contemporary society, but in the experience of history and time itself. On the basis of this characterization of modernism as a cultural, social, and political force born of a Western modernity in profound subjective and (after 1914) objective structural crisis, Part Two, 'Fascism's Modernist State', will consider the aspects of the Fascist and Nazi regimes illuminated by the account of modernism offered in Part One.

It is a journey which means criss-crossing traditional frontiers between disciplines, sometimes juxtaposing or syncretizing discrete areas of specialist knowledge and academic theory. Towards the end of the book many aspects of the relationship of Fascism and Nazism to modernity, still widely perceived as a flight from or assault on the modern world, should seem disturbingly 'natural' expressions of Western modernity at a certain point in its evolution. It will also be more intelligible why some of the most 'barbaric' acts of modern history were carried out by activists who felt they were at the cutting edge of history, pioneers of a new age driven on not by nihilism or cruelty, but by visionary idealism, a brand-new creed of redemption, purification, and renewal.

The process of elaborating the conceptual framework needed to explore fascism's modernism has demanded an entire part to itself. Though hopefully of intrinsic interest as a contribution to the conceptualization of modernism and modernity, its six chapters are primarily conceived as an elaborate analytical framework with which to explore the peculiar permutations of modernity embodied in the regimes led by Mussolini and Hitler in Part Two. The litmus test of the book's value will be how far the policies and acts of these regimes in various spheres of society become more intelligible, more historically explicable as the argument unfolds without 'normalizing' them morally, let alone rationalizing them or diminishing the crimes against humanity they committed in pursuit of their dreams.

Given these goals, the focus of this Introduction should thus now move decisively away from the mood of *Aufbruch* bound up with the hazardous nature of the whole undertaking in an academic context, and shift to the sense of a new beginning cultivated by fascism itself in both its 'movement' and 'regime' aspect. In cinematic terms images from the Hollywood blockbuster evoking the Romantic, illusory 'new beginning' felt so passionately by the star-crossed pair on the prow of the *Titanic* could now dissolve into fascist ones. The sequence could start with the closing scene in Giovacchnio Forzano's *Camicia Nera* [Black Shirt] (1933) which shows Mussolini inaugurating the

Figure 1 The opening frame of Leni Riefenstahl's *Triumph of the Will* has been seen as a subliminal evocation of the pagan sky-god Wotan descending to earth. But it can also be seen as the opening of a new historical era for Germany under Nazism.

Produced by Leni Riefenstahl Studio-Film, Berlin, 1935, Distribution UFA-Filmverleih.

reclamation ('bonifica') of the Pontine Marshes where a new city will soon arise, a symbol of the modernizing and modernist plans for the *bonifica* of the whole of Italy. This could fade to the moment in Alessandro Blasetti's *Vecchia Guardia* [The Old Guard] (1935) where Blackshirts set off for the March on Rome, the first steps to a New Italy, which in turn could merge into the closing moments of *Hitlerjunge Quex* when serried ranks of banner-carrying Hitler Youth march heroically into the new Germany in which the ultimate sacrifice of one of their comrades in the war against Bolshevism will be redeemed.

The closing shot could be the opening frames of *Triumph of the Will* (see Figure 1) with their famous images of Hitler descending from the clouds like a latter-day sky-God to land at Nuremberg where he will preside over the 1934 Party Congress. It follows these portentous words:

> On September 5, 1934, 20 years after the outbreak of the World War, 16 years after the beginning of our suffering, 19 months after the beginning of Germany's rebirth, Adolf Hitler flew again to Nuremberg to muster the columns of his faithful followers.

Part One

The Sense of a Beginning in Modernism

1
The Paradoxes of 'Fascist Modernism'

It appears, in fact, that modernist radicalism in art – the breaking down of pseudo-traditions, the making new on a true understanding of the nature of the elements of art – this radicalism involves the creation of fictions which may be dangerous in the dispositions they breed towards the world.

Frank Kermode, 'The Modern Apocalypse' (1967)[1]

Modernism appears less as the denial of the realist project and a denial of history, than as an anticipation of a new form of historical reality, a reality that included, among its supposed unimaginable, unthinkable, and unspeakable aspects, the phenomenon of Hitlerism, the Final Solution, total war, nuclear contamination, mass starvation, and ecological suicide.

Hayden White, 'Historical Emplotment
and the Problem of Truth' (1992)[2]

The slogan of the First Futurist Manifesto of 1909 – *'War is the world's only hygiene'* – led directly [...] to the shower block of Auschwitz-Birkenau.

Paul Virilio, *Art and Fear* (2003)[3]

REVOLTING AGAINST THE MODERN WORLD

On 2 February 1938 a certain K. Weisthor sent Reichsführer Heinrich Himmler his report on a lecture presented to SS circles entitled 'The Restoration of the West on the Basis of the Original Aryan Spirit'. In it he expressed some reservations about aspects of the talk. Nevertheless, he enthusiastically endorsed its central thesis, namely that 'the bearers of the Aryan heritage in our Aryan Europe must consider the Spiritual aspect, namely the Solar conception' crucial to the actualization of the 'Aryan Imperial Idea'. This was because 'matter, in itself, is merely the visible manifestation of Eternity or of the eternal cycle, which can be dominated and guided only with the help of the force of Spirit'.[4]

K. Weisthor was in fact Karl Wiligut, aka 'Himmler's Rasputin',[5] member of the 'Central Bureau for SS Race and Settlement' and head of the 'Department for Pre- and Early History'. Until his fall from grace later that year, he exerted a major influence on the esoteric beliefs, liturgy, and symbolic paraphernalia that Himmler devised for the SS, and was probably behind the decision to convert the seventeenth-century castle at Wewelsburg into its ritual headquarters. The lecturer was Baron Julius Evola, author of *Revolt against the Modern World*, which had been published in German in 1935.[6] On the basis of his intense research into the world's occultist and mystical traditions carried out in the 1920s, he now sought to convince his specially invited audience that the vitality of a civilization was determined by the degree to which it followed the precepts of the perennial 'Tradition'. Having neglected its moral laws for over two millennia, the West was now reaching the nadir of its cycle of cultural decay and the climax of what is known in Hindu cosmology as the Kali Yuga – the 'Black Age' of dissolution. As a result the West now stood on the threshold of a new Krita Yuga, the 'Age of Purity', but only on condition that the leaders of Fascism and Nazism recognized the metaphysical dimension of their mission, namely to carry out a total material and *spiritual* revolution against the putrefying world of modernity epitomized in materialism, individualism, egalitarianism, the loss of hierarchy, and the erosion of higher values.

Once back in Italy, the Baron set about encouraging the leaders of Fascism to be mindful of its ultimate mission to regenerate the entire modern world with two extensive expositions of racial theory based on 'Traditionalist' principles, *Sintesi di dottrina della razza* [Synthesis of the doctrine of race] and *Indirizzi per un'educazione razziale* [Guidelines for a racial education], both published in 1941. These stressed that the 'Aryan' New Man (the inverted commas will be used throughout to indicate the entirely mythical nature of this racial category) must be based on the combination of body, mind, and soul, and not primarily on biological or genetic qualities as Nazi eugenicists claimed, thereby betraying the corrupting influence of modern materialism and the materialistic science of Darwinism.[7] In the event, Evola had no perceptible influence on mainstream Nazism or Fascism, which, at least exoterically, flowed along ideological channels far removed from the shadowy worlds of occultist racism dreamed up by 'ariosophists',[8] and 'Traditionalists'.[9]

It was not Evola's highly idiosyncratic racism, but his virulent attacks on what he saw as an increasingly soulless democratic and communist Europe after 1945 that made him the guru of a new generation of post-war extreme right-wing intellectuals seeking a 'vision of the world' to the point where Giorgio Almirante, leader of the neo-Fascist *Movimento Sociale Italiano* could refer to him as 'our Marcuse only better'.[10] Nevertheless, his involvement with inter-war fascism seems to provide ample corroboration of what has often been taken for its fundamentally reactionary and radical *anti-modernism*, its concern to take refuge from a modernity experienced as psychologically threatening. Yet a decade before Evola turned to the study of 'magic idealism' and began assessing the chances that a new elite of 'warrior-priest' would arise to regenerate the decadent West, he had been an active member of the pre-war Florentine avant-garde associated with the journals *Leonardo* and *Lacerba*, cultural reviews that – as we shall see in Chapter 7 – played a significant role in the genesis of Fascism. Though he was for a time associated with the futurist painter Giacomo Balla, he stayed aloof from the interventionist enthusiasm of these circles, drawn more to the Prussian cult of discipline than the decadence of Britain and France. When he does surface again within the Italian avant-garde it is as one of Italy's foremost representatives of Dadaism (see Figure 2), an art movement widely assumed to be essentially incompatible with any form of political commitment, especially with extreme forms of nationalism and racism.[11]

Figure 2 'Abstraction' (1920), Dadaist painting by Julius Evola, who would later become famous in right-wing circles as the author of *Revolt against the Modern World*.

To complicate the issue of Evola's anti-modernism and relationship to fascism further, the German translation of *Revolt against the Modern World* was enthusiastically received by none other than Gottfried Benn, one of Germany's foremost Expressionist poets. In the 1920s Benn had drawn on his professional experience as a doctor and pathologist to conjure up haunting biological metaphors for a steady flow of hallucinatory verse expressing his obsession with physical and psychological degeneration. His personal campaign to combat the progressive 'cerebralization of the world' which was allegedly draining it of primordial energy led to his enthusiastic conversion to the 'vitalism' of National Socialism, and he used his election in 1932 to one of Germany's most venerable cultural institutions, the Prussian Academy of Arts (founded in 1696) to promulgate his vision of the Third Reich's mission, namely to bring about the cultural and *anthropological* revolution needed to save the nation from dissolution.[12] He also was one of the most high-profile supporters of the campaign to have the works of fellow Expressionists and Nationalists such as Ernst Barlach and Emil Nolde included within the Nazi canon of 'Aryan art'. This honeymoon was rudely interrupted in May 1936 when an article in the SS newspaper, *Das schwarze Korps* attacked an anthology of his poetry as 'widernatürliche Schweinereien' ('unnatural obscenities'), thereby signalling his imminent fall from grace. After his exclusion from the Reich Writers' Chamber in 1938 Benn retreated into 'inner emigration' until it was safe for him to relaunch his career as an authority on Expressionism after the war. Henceforth his once eloquent passion for the Nazi transformation of world history would be conveniently euphemized or airbrushed over in official biographies.

FASCISM AND MODERNISM: 'APORIA' OR PARADOX?

On the basis of these two examples the task of making sense of the relationship of modernism to fascism 'as a whole' is far from straight-forward. The careers of Evola and Benn allow contradictory inferences to be drawn about it. A term to which continental intellectuals in particular are drawn when discussing phenomena generated by modernity that are anomalous or defy simple explanations is 'aporia'. Literally meaning 'no way through' or 'cul-de-sac', it was used in Greek philosophy to refer to the intellectual conundrum or *impasse* that can result from attempts to encapsulate within neat definitions or logical categories an elusive aspect of phenomenal reality. Since fascism is still widely associated with the forces of reaction and the flight from 'the modern world', its relationship with modernity can easily come across as bristling with aporias.

To take Mussolini's Italy, for example, how did a regime dedicated to destroying the 'progressive' forces of socialism and renewing Italy's Roman heritage attract the active collaboration of so many of its most prominent modern artists, architects, designers, and technocrats? What brought Mussolini – initially a prolific socialist activist and intellectual, though widely perceived in his years as *duce* as a megalomaniac without a shred of genuine ideological commitment heading a reactionary regime – to succumb to the vociferous campaign for national reawakening fought in the pages of *La Voce* by leading Florentine artists and intellectuals – all passionate modernists – in the decade before the First World War?[13] What led Filippo Marinetti,[14] the founder of one of the most radical forms of aesthetic modernism, to see Mussolini's peculiar brand of nationalism as the vehicle for his Futurist war on the decadence of 'pastism'? Why were other prominent figures of Italian culture such as Gabriele D'Annunzio, Giuseppe Prezzolini, and Giovanni Papini able to betray what is often assumed to be the avant-garde's natural allegiance to the 'true' revolution of the left in order to promote the 'pseudo-revolution' proposed by the right?

The contradictions do not end there. How was it that the same regime could contemporaneously host Giuseppe Bottai's modern art competition for the Bergamo Prize and sponsor some of the boldest experiments in modernist town-planning and civic buildings, while also promoting the 'ultra-ruralist' painting of the *strapaese* movement. Thus it came about that, in direct opposition to Bottai, the pro-Nazi Fascist 'hierarch', Roberto Farinacci, set up the Cremona Prize for non-modernist art. How could it launch initiatives to revitalize local customs and traditions such as the *sagra*,[15] promote the return to the highly mythicized rural traditions extolled in Alessandro Blasetti's film *Terra Madre* (Mother Earth, 1931), make enormous efforts to instil in the entire population a sense of awe for the glory that was once Rome, lovingly restore the treasures of the country's rich medieval, Renaissance, and ecclesiastical heritage to promote national pride and the domestic and foreign tourist industry, yet at the same time build motorways, drain marshes, electrify railways, and turn Italian aviators into national, and – after Italo Balbo's transatlantic flight to Chicago – international heroes?

Balbo's epic feat provides a case-study in Fascism's anomalous relationship to modernity. He left Italy with a squadron of 24 Savoia-Marchetti SM.55X flying boats, built at the cutting edge of aviation technology, on 30 June 1933. Six weeks later he landed on Lake Michigan near the fairgrounds of Chicago's 'A Century of Progress' exposition, a highly popular exhibition which, in spite of, or rather because of the terrible social effects of the Great Depression attracted some 39 million visitors from all over the world. Yet to commemorate this achievement – which provoked rapturous scenes of public acclaim in the US – Mussolini ordered a 1,700-year-old column excavated from a portico near the harbour of Ostica Antica, the ancient port of Rome, to be shipped to Chicago. It was duly erected in front of the Italian pavilion, an ancient monument deployed to celebrate the triumph of modernity.

Such glaring contradictions are also suggested by the contrast between the Giuseppe Terragni's bold, ultra-modern use of rationalist design in the Casa del Fascio, ceremonially opened in Como in 1936, and the building designed by Vittorio Morpurgo – an ardently pro-Fascist Jew later barred from entering his own building – and erected at great, cost-cutting haste, to house the Ara Pacis (see Figures 3–5). This heavily restored Roman monument, built by August Caesar, assumed central importance within the bimillennial celebrations of the birth of the emperor staged at enormous state expense to anoint Mussolini as the modern incarnation of Caesarean qualities. (There is a certain irony that a frieze of right-handed – and hence non-Nazi – Swastikas runs round this 'altar to peace' which Hitler was shown on his state visit to Rome in May 1938, an irony that may have eluded the Führer.)[16] Morpurgo's structure, blending the modernist use of steel and glass construction with the 'rootedness' familiar from the 'stripped' neo-classicism of Nazi monumentalism, would doubtless have made the Führer feel much more at home than Terragni's building.

Figure 3   Elevation of Giuseppe Terragni's Casa del Fascio, the Fascist headquarters completed in Como in 1936, one of the most famous modernist buildings of the time.[17]

Figure 4 Vittorio Morpurgo's building erected to house the Ara Pacis (completed 1938). Note blend the of classical symmetries with a modern emphasis on glass.[18] It is reproduced with the kind permission of Orietta Rossini who has used the image in her book *Ara Pacis Augustae* (Rome: Electa, 2006).

© Sovraintendenza del Comune di Roma, Museo di Roma, Archivio Fotografico Comunale.

Figure 5: Mussolini opening the building to house the Ara Pacis on 23 September 1938. Note the classical swastikas on the frieze. My thanks to Orietta Rossini for supplying this photo and giving me permission to use it.

© Sovraintendenza del Comune di Roma, Museo di Roma, Archivio Fotografico Comunale.

STRATEGIES FOR RESOLVING THE APORIAS OF FASCIST MODERNISM

On the basis of such examples there seems little point in trying to read any sort of consistent pattern into Fascism's relationship with modernism, which sometimes generated curious idiosyncrasies. For example, the Foro Mussolini, the capital's brand new sports stadium opened in 1928, was built in a modernized classical style and adorned with classical statues. It also displayed a mosaic depicting not scenes from Roman mythology, but, in what an art historian has described as a 'bizarre dichotomy',[19] flag-waving *squadristi* setting off on a truck, presumably to attack a communist headquarters or join the March on Rome. It was a truck similar to the one that provided the central character of *BL 15*, a vast outdoor experiment in mass theatre staged in Florence in the spring of 1934 dramatizing the birth of Fascism from the trench-warfare of the First World War and the Black Shirts' struggle (as they saw it) to quell communism and subversion in the *biennio rosso*, the 'red two years' of 1919 to 1920. Were such cultural artefacts and events examples of totalitarian 'kitsch', or was something more profound going on?

Certainly on the basis of such examples, it is understandable that many historians of Fascism have treated its art as peripheral to the regime, its lack of a coherent aesthetic confirming the image of a personal dictatorship in which spectacle, rhetoric, and the illusion of permanent revolution were more important than the substantial transformations in Italian society. Taken this way they endorse the sweeping judgement which Norberto Bobbio – an egregious anti-Fascist intellectual – once made in an interview with *L'Espresso*: 'Where there was culture, there was no Fascism, where there was Fascism there was no culture. There never was a Fascist culture.'[20] On this premise the quest to establish a coherent affinity between modernism and Fascism is futile since they are essentially incompatible phenomena, the one genuinely creative and innovative, the other an elaborate act to camouflage a reactionary response to the challenges of modernity.

In the course of his 2006 documentary series *Marvels of the Modern Age*, the British architectural historian Dan Cruickshank took viewers on a guided tour of the 'extraordinary building' which the Italo-German Fascist writer and intellectual Curzio Malaparte (Kurt Suckert) had built atop a rugged promontory on an isolated stretch of Capri's coastline just before the outbreak of the Second World War (see Figure 6). Cruickshank must have confirmed the preconceptions of most educated viewers when he asserted in his commentary that this 'eccentric but brilliant' statement, both personal and social, 'defied the times' since it embodied 'modernism at its wildest and most solitary'. After all, he went on, 'Mussolini, like Hitler had suppressed modernism', yet 'unaccountably this building slipped through the net'.[21]

Figure 6   Adalberto Libera's highly modernist house built for Curzio Malaparte on Capri.

It is even more unaccountable, given Cruickshank's profession, that he should have omitted to mention the decisive role played in the whole conception of the Casa Malaparte by its architect, Adalberto Libera. One of Europe's most visionary architectural modernists, Libera's career flourished under Fascism and, had the war not intervened, would have been crowned by the construction of the audaciously modernist arch he designed to dominate the vast site of EUR '42, the Exhibition of the Universality of Rome planned for 1942. It was this arch that was chosen for the stunning poster which adorns the front cover of this book and which was realized after the war over 5,000 miles away in the St Louis' Gateway Arch pictured on the back cover. In fact, all Libera's work for the regime was a triumphalist celebration of the regime's futural spirit, and as such an eloquent refutation of any notion that Mussolini had a deep animus against aesthetic modernism. It is consistent with this misreading of his topic that in his documentary Cruickshank devotes a whole sequence to illustrating the productive synergy between architectural modernism and Bolshevik state planning in the first 15 years after the Revolution. The effect is to only entrench further the prejudice that, whereas modernism and socialism go hand in hand, modernism and fascism are like oil and water, or perhaps like one of the surreal encounters that André Breton compared to an umbrella and a sewing machine juxtaposed on an operating table.

If a deeper intellectual rationale is sought for the apparently irrational art policies of Mussolini's regime and its considerable investment of resources in cultural projects, some defiantly modernist in conception, then a far more sophisticated approach is to hand. This has emerged from a lengthy tradition of fleshing out the skeletal theory sketched in a now famous essay bequeathed by one of fascism's victims, Walter Benjamin. It basically argues that the regime, in order to preserve the capitalist system from socialist revolution, cynically embarked on the wholesale 'aestheticization of politics' and the manipulation of cultural symbology to bring about the pervasive nationalization of intellectual, academic, and artistic life. Under both Mussolini and Hitler, therefore, culture was exploited as a tool of social engineering and state aesthetics so as to become a form of political anaesthetic. Their combined effect was supposed to depoliticize and disempower the masses by generating the outward trappings of cultural and hence social revolution but without the substance. Thus even in cases where Fascism tolerated, and even embraced modernism, it was for cynical, reactionary, and hence anti-modernist ends.[22]

A fascinating variation on this theme is Igor Golomstock's highly scholarly and impressively illustrated monograph expounding his thesis concerning the 'Law of Totalitarianism'. According to this thesis the impact of the avant-garde, though crucial to creating the ethos of dynamism and transformation needed to establish a new totalitarian regime, even a communist one, quickly wanes once power is securely in the hands of the new ruling elite, who promptly begin to persecute any compliant modernists once they have outlived their usefulness.[23] Another explanatory approach altogether is proposed by the veteran of radical cultural theory, Paul Virilio who, as the epigraph to this chapter shows, claims to perceive a direct lineage between Futurism and Auschwitz. This connection is posited on a latent nexus that links the cold-hearted experimentalism evident in some variants of modernism – particularly those which apparently reduce the human body to an object to be manipulated for the amoral purposes of aesthetic pleasure – to the episodes of mass murder, state torture, and systematized cruelty that litter modern European history. Such atrocities, he is at pains to stress, have been committed not just by fascist, communist, and nationalist regimes, but take place in so-called 'liberal' democracies as well.

When in 1998, 200 plastinated human corpses were displayed at 'The World of Bodies' exhibition held at the Mannheim Museum of Technology and Work, Virilio was profoundly struck by the sound-bite provided by their 'creator', Günter von Hagens: 'It's about breaking the last taboo.' He commented: 'It will not be long before we are forced to acknowledge that the German Expressionists who called for murder were not the only avant-garde artists. By the same token so were people like Ilse Koch.' He goes on:

> The woman they would call 'the Bitch Dog of Buchenwald' actually enjoyed aesthetic aspirations pretty similar to those of the good Dr von Hagens, for she had certain detainees sporting tattoos skinned so that she could turn their skins into various objects of *art brut*, as well as lampshades.[24]

With such comments Virilio turns on its head the assumption that a truly avant-garde art-form such as Futurism can have no genuine affinity with a fascist regime. Instead the wholesale aestheticization of reality allegedly advocated by modernists is seen as both symptomatic of and contributing to the failure of compassion and erosion of *pity* – 'pitié' is a key concept in Virilian world-view – which makes modern states capable of wholesale crimes against humanity for the 'good of the people'.

Such an argument has distant echoes of George Lukács' indictment of Expressionism in the 1930s as preparing the ground for Nazism through an orgy of irrationalism. But in case this refreshingly pre-postmodern variant of Marxism seems a fruitful line of investigation for resolving some of the many aporias of modernism's relationship to fascism, it should be remembered that Lukács' position provoked intense dissent from fellow Marxists, notably Ernst Bloch and Walter Benjamin. In the spirit of Bertolt Brecht and the master of anti-fascist photomontage, Hermut Herzfelde (aka John Heartfield), these defended experimental art precisely because of its capacity to subvert the 'bourgeois' realist tradition born of the classical humanism through which capitalism had been so extensively mystified and legitimized in modern times. Only when it had been sufficiently defamiliarized and exposed to critical engagement could the social and political system be rethought in a progressive direction.[25]

In short, wherever we turn for expert insight into Fascism's convoluted relationship with modernism we find not a harmonious chorus but a cacophony. Even a work with the promising title *Fascist Modernism*, despite its sophisticated postmodernist cultural apparatus and sustained analytical verve, does not take us very far. Its author, Andrew Hewitt, proceeds to reduce the entire topic – which in principle embraces the entire history of Nazism as well – to little more than a single empirical case-study, Marinetti's Futurism (un-coincidentally the same example Benjamin cited in his ground-breaking essay). Moreover he investigates it on the premise of the fundamentally reactionary nature of fascism's response to modernity. Its 'aestheticization of politics', we are assured, was 'inscribed from the very outset in the bourgeois construction of the public sphere', and hence an integral part of 'capitalism's libidinal project of self-destruction'.[26] No genuine modernism or revolution here.

NAZISM'S CONVOLUTED 'ANTI-MODERNISM'

The sense that academic expeditions towards modernity's heart of darkness are continually generating fresh conundrums in the context of fascist studies is confirmed when we follow up the allusion which both Virilio and Lukács make to Expressionism, the principal form assumed by early twentieth-century aesthetic modernism in Germany. The first problem to be confronted is the acute lack of academic consensus about whether the Third Reich is to be included within the scope of a study of 'modernism and fascism' in the first place. For one thing, Hitler's New Germany exhibited so many areas in which state policies, and especially the manner of their execution, contrast with Mussolini's regime that several major academics – notably Renzo de Felice, Zeev Sternhell, and A. James Gregor – have adamantly rejected its credentials for being classified as a manifestation of generic fascism at all. It is a position tacitly agreed with by the many (non-Marxist) German historians of the Third Reich convinced that the application of any generic term – with the partial exception of totalitarianism – dilutes its 'uniqueness', possibly betraying a relativizing and hence apologetic intent.

Renzo de Felice, for example, argues the two regimes created entirely different habitats for modernity, asserting that Fascism aimed at the creation of 'a new kind of man' and 'wanted to achieve the transformation of society and the individual in a direction that had never been attempted or realized in the past'. By contrast 'Nazism sought a *restoration* of values and not the creation of new values. The idea of the creation of a new kind of man is not a Nazi idea.'[27] At first sight the Third Reich's violent campaign against aesthetic modernism, which assumed the ferocity of a full-scale witch-hunt after 1936, would appear to bear this out. The genocidal crimes with which its cultural policies are indelibly associated make it even more difficult to conceive Nazism as hosting anything genuinely modernist, a term that still tends to have progressive or liberating connotations.

Such assumptions about the contrasting relationship of Nazism and Fascism to modernity help explain the contrasting history of the way they have been 'marketed' since the Second World War. In 1982, 50 years after the Exhibition of the Fascist Revolution held in Rome, one of the most successful exercises in regime propaganda in history, Milan staged 'The 1930s: Art and Culture in Italy'. As the sanitized title suggests, the cumulative impact of what was on display was effectively a celebration not just of the tumultuous creativity, vitality, and innovativeness of Italian (Fascist?) society and culture under Mussolini, but of its all-pervasive *modernity*, particularly its passionate affair with modernism in painting, architecture, photography, technology, and design.[28]

Six decades after the defeat of the Third Reich it would be still unthinkable to stage an equivalent exhibition called laconically 'The 1930s: Art and Culture in Germany' without inviting the charge of revisionism, and scrupulous care would have to be taken by the organizers not to be accused of surreptitiously 'normalizing' Nazism by using the exhibits and catalogue notes to emphasize the modernity of life under the regime without drawing attention to its attendant horrors for those excluded from the new 'national community'. What is branded on the collective memory instead is the Nazis' vilification of aesthetic modernism in the 'Degenerate Art Exhibition' held in Munich of 1937 – in terms of official visitor figures still the world's most 'successful' exhibition of modern art ever mounted. This monstrous 'anti-exhibition' is naturally associated with the regime's other ritual acts of iconoclasm, such as the burning of 'decadent' books presided over by Goebbels on 10 May 1933, or the order given by the Degenerate Art Commission on 20 March 1939 for over 1,000 paintings and almost 4,000 watercolours and drawings to be burned at Berlin's central fire station. It is further symptomatic of the essentially nihilistic image of Nazi cultural policy that, while no comprehensive exhibition of its state-approved art and architecture has been staged, the public was given the chance to see the modernist art it condemned when in 1993 the Los Angeles County Museum of Art mounted 'Degenerate Art: The Fate of the Avant-Garde in Nazi Germany'. (The acute distortions in our understanding of Nazi culture resulting from official policy both sides of the Atlantic to bury most of its painting in inaccessible deposits will be considered in due course.)

Such events reinforce the image of a regime that was determined to seal itself hermetically from the modern world, producing an anti-culture that defies conventional analysis. For example, the premise to Peter Adam's survey of 'the art of the Third Reich' is that:

> It is difficult, complex, and controversial. Whether it be in the form of fine arts, architecture, film literature, or music, it cannot be considered the same way as the art of other periods. It must be seen as the artistic expression of a barbaric ideology. One can only look at the art of the Third Reich through the lens of Auschwitz.[29]

According to the conceptual framework that shapes Adam's investigation, then, the Nazis were bent solely on denying modern art *Lebensraum* [vital space] and replacing it with propagandistic kitsch[30] to euphemize the atrocities to be committed in the creation of the racial state. Their regime's relationship to modernism is thus one of vandalism, persecution, and 'culture-cide', a direct corollary in the arts of its eugenic politics and the genocidal campaigns they led to. Yet, as with Fascism, the brute but not always brutal facts of Nazism's cultural history defy reduction to such temptingly simplistic formulas. It is true that when Hitler delivered an address on art at the 7th Party Congress of September 1935 – the same one at which the infamous Nuremberg Race Laws were promulgated – he attacked those who defended Dadaism, Cubism, and Futurism 'on the grounds that such effusions are examples of primitive forms of expression', reminding them of 'the purpose of art', namely 'to strive to overcome symptoms of degeneration by directing the imagination to what is eternally good and beautiful'.[31] Yet when Hitler spoke these words the ultra-modernist poet Gottfried Benn was still enjoying the privileges of an elite member of the Prussian Academy of Art. Indeed, it may be more than coincidence if a significant omission from the Führer's hate-list of degenerate 'isms' is Expressionism, whose Aryan credentials – as we shall see in Chapter 9 – were still the subject of a bitter dispute among loyal Nazis. In fact, even after the anathema had finally been placed officially on such pro-Nazi German Expressionists such as Ernst Barlach and Emil Nolde in July 1937, elements of aesthetic modernism continued to survive to an astonishing degree, and overtly modernist industrial design in consumer durables actually thrived under Hitler.

Thus it is no 'aporia', but a paradox to be gradually resolved in the course of this book that Wassili Luckhardt, who had designed a vast, crystalline 'Monument to Labour' in 1920 epitomizing architectural modernism at its most utopian, proposed a diamond-like glass structure for the Deutsche Arbeiterfront (DAF, or German Workers' Front) in 1934. Moreover, it was not until 1938 that Mies van der Rohe, the personification of the architectural modernism epitomized by the American skyscraper, felt the walls closing in to the point where he felt forced to emigrate to the US from the Third Reich. Before that he had proactively sought the regime's patronage, and entered the competition to build the new Reichsbank under the regime,[32] despite the pre-eminent position he had held in the ultra-left-wing Bauhaus, which the Nazis rushed to close down immediately after seizing power in one of the first shots fired by the regime in the war against 'cultural Bolshevism'. (This highly symbolic act did not deter Walter Gropius, the founder of the Bauhaus, from submitting projects both for the DAF and the new Reichsbank in Berlin. See Figure 7.)

One way for academics to deal with alleged aporias of this kind encountered in the history of the Third Reich is to resort to euphemism or denial. The web-bio of van der Rohe published on the occasion of the MOMA 2001–02 Exhibition 'Mies in Berlin' sums up the circumstances of his emigration to the US with the laconic phrase 'By the mid-1930s, the architect realized he had few prospects under the increasingly oppressive Nazi regime.'[33] Dan Cruickshank's 2006 television documentary *Marvels of the Modern Age*, though it dwells on van der Rohe's relationship to the left-wing Bauhaus and the legacy of his career as a modernist architect in the cityscapes of New York and Chicago,

Figure 7 Walter Gropius' uncompromisingly modernist competition entry for the Reichsbank in Berlin, 1933.

took the easier option of ignoring altogether the awkward matter of this former socialist's sustained collusion with Hitler's regime before his voluntary exile.[34] However, a subsequent article by Tom Dyckhoff puts this 'non-issue' in a somewhat different light:

> Starved of work, Mies tried to ingratiate himself with this new, powerful and rich state patron, signing a motion of support for Hitler in the August 1934 referendum and joining Goebbels' Reichskulturkammer, a progressive alternative to Rosenberg's ministry, which asked for 'fresh blood' and new forms to give 'expression to this age'. Mies was shortlisted to build the state's new Reichsbank, with a fiercely modern, abstract design; and Goebbels even pressed him to design the 'Deutsches Volk, Deutsche Arbeit' exhibition. Things were on the up.[35]

The image of the Reichsminister for Propaganda and Enlightenment, Joseph Goebbels, encouraging Mies van der Rohe to tender for prestigious regime projects encourages us to 'revisit' the whole subject of Nazism's famed jihad against modernism.

An even more striking example of the recurring incongruities in Nazism's interactions with Western modernity is Joseph Goebbels' weakness for Jazz, officially lambasted as the epitome of 'degenerate music'. This foible accounts for a remarkable moment on the evening of 15 February 1938 when he went backstage with Hermann Goering at the Scala Theatre, Berlin, to congratulate the internationally acclaimed English band-leader, Jack Hylton, whose tour was breaking all Germany's box-office records that spring. (Apparently Hitler had attended the concert but gone straight home.) This was no lapsus on

Goebbels' part, for the event had been 'cleansed' in advance. His own censors had axed a Shirley Temple routine by Maureen Potter as 'too American' and ensured there were no Jews playing in the orchestra.[36] Moreover, Goebbels' patronage was officially portrayed as showing his support not for Jazz (which was classified 'decadent') but Swing (which was 'life-asserting'): more on this anon. Nevertheless, whatever the official gloss put on the occasion, the brief encounter at the Scala flew ideologically in the face of the adulation that Jack Hylton had previously enjoyed in modernist circles located far beyond the Nazi pale, one example of which was Igor Stravinsky's invitation to collaborate with him on the comic opera *Mavra* in 1931.

Goebbels' almost surreal presence in Hylton's dressing room can be seen in a fresh light after reading his semi-autobiographical diary novel, *Michael: A German Destiny* (1926), a work bearing the unmistakable stamp of Expressionism in both style and structure. One passage recounts a visit to an exhibition of modern painting in which a solitary 'star' shone out amidst all the trash on display: Vincent van Gogh. His canvases prompt Goebbels' *alter ego* to reflect on the nature of modernity, which he describes as 'a new way of experiencing the world':

> Modern man is necessarily a seeker after God, perhaps a Christ-Man. Van Gogh's life tells us more than his work. He combines the most important elements in himself: he is teacher, preacher, fanatic, prophet – he is mad. When it comes down to it, we are all mad when we have an idea. [...] What makes up the modern German is not so much cleverness and intellect as the new spirit, the willingness to become one with the people, to devote oneself and sacrifice oneself to it unstintingly.[37]

Such a declaration calls into question the deeply entrenched preconceptions about Nazism's hostility to modernity which make it 'self-evident' that the austere rectilinear geometry and stripped neo-classicism of Paul Troost's Haus der deutschen Kunst in Munich symbolize the Nazis' urge to take refuge in an idealized past. This assumption seems corroborated by the building's declared purpose, namely to display the 'organic' artistic products of the nation's ongoing social and political renaissance. The new collection would showcase the steady stream of 'healthy' paintings and sculptures spontaneously filling the yawning gaps in the national heritage resulting from the ruthless slash and burn tactics that the Nazis applied to the self-appointed mission to purge Germany of cultural decadence. Yet the extended cohabitation of Gottfried Benn, Emil Nolde, and van der Rohe with the regime, not to mention Goebbels' enthusiasm for Van Gogh, suggest that even such apparently irrefutable semiotic demonstrations of the regime's visceral anti-modernism as Troost's German art gallery may warrant reappraisal.

Re-evaluating modernism's relationship to fascism means more than just acknowledging how aesthetic modernism flourished under Mussolini or retained some enthusiastic proselytes under Hitler. It means creating an entirely different 'lens' through which to observe Fascist and Nazi culture than that offered by Norberto Bobbio or Peter Adam, one that at least makes it possible to contemplate the possibility that there was more than 'totalitarian propaganda' involved in the regime's cultural production. Take, for example the speech which Hitler made on 17 July 1937 at the opening ceremony for the House of German Art. In it he claimed that Troost's building was 'to be the turning point, putting an end to the chaotic and botched architecture of the past', the symbol of the State's effort to lay 'the basis for a new and mighty flowering of German art'.[38] The address leaves no doubt that the new art gallery's purpose was to display art that rejected the experimentalism of modernist aesthetics in order to celebrate instead 'eternal values'. Yet once we entertain the possibility that the building genuinely represented for Hitler a 'new beginning', an *Aufbruch* into a new era, certain passages in the catalogue published to commemorate the occasion assume fresh significance, such as the boast that the structure incorporated the latest gas-fired central heating, an air-conditioning system, and a modern air-raid shelter. Thinking in the old groove leads us to dismiss the modern elements in buildings such as the House of German Art, the Casa del Fascio in Como, or the construction of entire new towns such as Sabaudia in areas of the Pontine Marshes that had once bred malaria, simply as symptoms of fascism's cynicism in the manipulation of culture. Any unmistakable elements of modernization appropriated are dismissed as serving solely to realize its fundamentally reactionary, regressive vision of the future, its 'utopian anti-modernism'.[39] But approaching the issue from the perspective which is beginning to open up here invites us at least to entertain the possibility that in strikingly different ways both the Fascists and Nazis were not rejecting modernity, but using the built environment to lay the cultural foundations of an *alternative* modernity. They were thus seeking to realize an alternative *modernism*.

This at least is the perspective offered by Hitler himself in the closing passage of his speech, even if he naturally avoids referring to 'modernity' or 'modernism', both terms replete with decadent connotations for Nazis. He tells his audience that, though great new tasks had been assigned to art – an assertion that would have been enthusiastically endorsed by many early twentieth-century modernists – 'it is not art that creates new ages'. These only come about when the life of entire peoples assumes new forms and searches for new expression.[40] In such a speech the Nazi rejection of artistic modernism is clearly bound up with what Frank Kermode calls the 'creation of fictions' needed to 'make new'. It also chimes in with what Hayden White calls the 'anticipation of a new form of historical reality', and announces a variant of modernism in a totalizing sense that transcends the realm of 'pure' art.

A 'SYNOPTIC INTERPRETATION' OF FASCIST MODERNISM?

Hitler's speech in July 1938 announced the task he had set German art, to both manifest and inspire the process of national rebirth, its triumphal recovery from the Weimar years of decadence that preceded the Third Reich. The task I have set myself in this book is fortunately considerably less epoch-making. It is to establish a new conceptual framework within which to investigate modernism's relationship to fascism, one that may prove useful to historians in numerous specialisms which impinge on the dynamics of modern history, especially in its more extreme, uncompromisingly irrational or destructive manifestations. It aims to resolve not only the tensions and ambivalence constantly encountered in the history of fascist culture, but the blatant paradoxes persistently generated by so much scholarship on the topic, such as Henry Turner's insistence on fascism's 'anti-modern utopianism' and Jeffrey Herf's investigation of the 'reactionary modernism' which allegedly resulted when hardcore Nazi conservatives wholeheartedly embraced the modern technocracy.

The need for greater conceptual clarity and rigour in this area is underlined by a scintillating collection of scholarly essays written for the catalogue of the 'Modernism – Designing a New World 1914–1939' exhibition held at the Victoria and Albert Museum in London in 2006. As the subtitle suggests, it marks a radical break with much earlier work in the way the eleven essays cumulatively build up a powerful picture of aesthetic modernism's thrust towards historical *Aufbruch*, its aspiration to harness the power of art and design to supply a new vision to a modern world urgently in need of social and metapolitical renewal. Yet at the same time they perpetuate the taxonomic confusions that led Dan Cruickshank to see Malaparte's Capri house as profoundly un-Fascist in spirit, rather than made conceivable precisely by the caesura Fascism had brought about with Italy's history under liberalism in the mind of genuine converts to the new era.

Thus, while Christina Lodder's essay 'Searching for Utopia' highlights the central role played by modernism in the pioneering days of the Russian Revolution, it passes over in silence Le Corbusier's close association with French fascism.[41] Similarly, David Crowley's chapter on 'national modernisms' makes only the briefest of allusions to the tumultuous but protracted relationship between Futurism and Fascism,[42] with no attempt to identify the underlying ideological matrix that enabled powerful currents of artistic and architectural modernism to thrive under Mussolini alongside apparently 'reactionary' ones. At first sight the section on Nazism is more promising, since van der

Rohe's persistent attempts to win patronage from the Third Reich are for once documented without retouching the historical record, and the extensive adoption of Bauhaus design principles in the sphere of Nazi consumer goods and technology is fully acknowledged. Yet, Crowley also betrays considerable uncertainty about the appropriate 'analytical framework' to account for the presence of such 'bizarre dichotomies' within a regime notorious for its calculated acts of barbarism against modernism and humanity. He is content to describe the vexed issue of Nazism's modernity as one 'which has taxed historians', referring readers anxious to probe deeper both to Jeffrey Herf's theory of 'reactionary modernism' and Peter Fritzsche's far more radical theory of Nazism as a 'totalitarian version of the modern', making no attempt to resolve the considerable tensions between the two.[43]

This book sets out to move beyond the unsatisfactory state of modernist studies where they impinge on fascism that is illustrated by the exhibition catalogue – which in other respects clearly represents the 'state of the art' in this field of cultural history – by offering what we referred to in the Introduction, after Detlef Peukert, as a 'synoptic historical interpretation' of the relationship between modernism and fascism. Drawing on existing secondary literature, ideal types of both 'isms' will be constructed that when applied to Fascist Italy and Nazi Germany suggest a deep structural kinship between the two, one which dissolves the paradoxes and awkward silences which arise when the cultures of Fascist Italy and Nazi Germany are assumed to be fundamentally anti-modern or anti-modernist. It will seek to demonstrate instead that for intelligible historical reasons an elective affinity existed between both phenomena, with the result that, in this area as Marcel Proust says in *The Remembrance of Things Past*, 'every "although" is a misunderstood "because of"'. For example, it is precisely *because* fascism was an intrinsically modernist phenomenon that it could host some forms of aesthetic modernism as consistent with the revolutionary cause it was pursuing, *and* condemn others as decadent, as well as imparting a modernist dynamic to forms of cultural production normally associated with backward looking 'reaction' and nostalgia for past idylls. In the light of what follows, a regime that celebrates the past in the name of the future, or where occultists daily rub shoulders with engineers and scientists in pursuit of racial regeneration, should come to seem fully compatible with modernism, no matter how vehemently it rejects the particular permutations of modernity promoted as progressive by liberal or 'Enlightenment' humanism.

The construction of this 'synoptic historical interpretation' involves a sustained inquiry into the nature of modernism as a reaction to the condition of Western modernity, which will be the main subject of Chapters 2–4. But before we can embark on this first stage in the process of finding a way out of the impasse of modernism's convoluted relationship to fascism, it is necessary to break through another impasse, this time of a methodological nature. The first obstacle that a would-be researcher has to overcome to construct a panoramic account of this relationship of the type undertaken here is not just the sheer vastness of historical phenomena it potentially embraces and the highly contested nature of every key concept and putative relationship it subsumes. It is the highly questionable nature of the ambition to create a synoptic interpretive framework in the first place.

THE BABEL EFFECT IN ACADEMIA

There is nothing exceptional about the welter of particular phenomena subsumed under the terms 'modernism' and 'fascism', since most of the 'isms' embrace areas of empirical facts far beyond the ken of any one individual human mind, no matter how zealous. Moreover, each generic concept – and not only those ending in 'ism' – has spawned its own ongoing academic debate over what the definitional properties of the term are, the demarcation line separating it from adjacent terms, or how it relates to overlapping ones. In fact one of the hallmarks of any serious scholarly investigation into a generic phenomenon is that it starts with an extended discussion of definition and methodology in order to establish the scope and remit of the undertaking.

Thus Malcolm Bradbury and James McFarlane's introduction to their admirable anthology of essays on many aspects of modernism stresses how hard it has been for critics to 'find a date or a place' for Modernism, and emphasize that it has been subject to 'extreme semantic confusion'.[44] In his introduction to the no less groundbreaking catalogue of the V&A Modernism exhibition that we have already cited, Christopher Wilk states that the term's 'ubiquity hides a surprising vagueness and ambiguity of meaning', and points out that even within the circumscribed area of the visual arts 'it has different, sometimes contradictory, meanings'.[45] A directly parallel situation inevitably exists within fascist studies, where most academics go to considerable trouble to establish the way their usage of the term relates to or differs from that of other experts, sometimes with a considerable element of vitriol reserved for those they disagree with.[46] As with modernism, entire monographs and collections of essays have been dedicated to defining the term[47] or to rehearsing the debate over its semantics.[48]

This is not the place to go into the technical epistemological reasons why unanimity can never be achieved among specialists on such issues, or why it would be a utopia with sinister implications for scholarly enquiry if it were ever realized. It is perhaps worth pointing out, however, that despite the 'Babel effect' generated among experts by each irreducibly polysemic term in the human sciences, real progress is still achieved in every field of studies, and not just through the continual accretion of empirical knowledge or 'facts' through primary research. Its main driving force is the never-ending dialogue between specialists with contrasting conceptual frameworks, hypotheses, and points of view – as long as this dialogue is carried out in a collaborative collegial spirit. The kernel of what Clifford Geertz claimed over 40 years ago for social anthropology is surely true of all disciplines concerned with human phenomena: 'Cultural analysis is intrinsically incomplete. [...] Anthropology, or at least interpretive anthropology, is a science whose progress is marked less by a perfection of consensus than by a refinement of debate. *What gets better is the precision with which we vex each other.*'[49]

THE METHODOLOGICAL CRISIS IN THE HUMANITIES

The present book will doubtless vex many experts in the various disciplines onto which it trespasses, but it is carried out, at least as far as its conscious authorial intentions are concerned, with a view both to refining the debate and to encouraging more precisely the formulation of the issues being contested. However, it also sets out to offer a new 'synoptic interpretation', one that shifts or renegotiates some of the conventional demarcation lines between disciplines dealing with fascism, modernism, and their relationship. This has become a particularly thorny issue since the twentieth century's 'fin-de-siècle'. In the two decades that have ensued since Geertz carried out his own cultural expeditions to establish the crucial role played by cosmology, symbolism, and ritual not just in legitimating political power but constituting the *raison d'être* of the state, a remarkable cultural process has transformed the very ground on which human scientists walk and the intellectual air they breathe. Known by the shorthand 'the cultural turn' (CT),[50] and fuelled at least partly by a triple alliance of formidable 'isms' (postmodernism, poststructuralism, and deconstructionism), a sustained methodological self-consciousness has installed itself – some might say with the insidiousness of computer spyware – within every field of research. All would-be experts have become gleefully or painfully aware of the subjectivity that conditions all human understanding, the constructed nature of the key concepts used to explore the world, and hence the radical incompleteness and arbitrariness intrinsic to any bid to formulate definitive 'truths' or supply the 'big picture' on any topic.

This methodological excursus is itself typical of the oppressive climate of reflexivity under which academic research is now pursued, forcing experts to become adept at wrestling with their own shadow. It is a climate of self-doubt and introspection which frequently acts as a powerful prophylactic against all 'metanarratives', and in the present instance calls into grave doubt the wisdom of setting out in the first place on the search for a 'synoptic historical interpretation' of the relationship between two such potentially vast areas of empirical phenomena as modernism and fascism. The ferocity of postmodern attacks on the hubris of a more naïve age has forced entire disciplines 'onto the back foot'. Thus a major historian such as Richard Evans felt duty-bound to write a book in defence of his discipline,[51] while a group of anthropologists put their minds to formulating strategies for 'recapturing' their specialism[52] in the face of accusations that all academics are now caught in a trap of 'total relativism' laid by poststructuralist theory. Their works are attempts to engineer a break-out – perhaps more *Ausbruch* than *Aufbruch* – from a conceptual autism in which 'the boundaries between history and fiction dissolve', and 'the demarcation line between history and historiography, between historical writing and historical theory is erased'.[53] The alleged result is to make it impossible to communicate anything objective, definitive, or significant to the rest of society.

One inference that could be drawn now that the effects of the methodological seism of the late twentieth century have worked their way through the humanities, is that henceforth only humble, quake-proof, one-storey – or rather 'no-story' – constructions are permissible. Towering edifices of speculation, let alone overarching 'grand récits', can now look as grotesque and taboo as the high-rise solutions for low cost housing that scarred the townscape of the 1960s (and for related reasons). However this book is posited on another premise, a way out of the apparent cul-de-sac which consists in insisting on the need for narration despite awareness of its intrinsic flaws as a means to capture or convey truth. It involves a paradoxical state of mind on the part of the writer adumbrated in a passage in Virginia Woolf's remarkable modernist novel, *The Waves* (1931), in which at one point Bernard articulates the dilemma of recognizing the deceptive quality of all stories, while yet at the same time realizing the need for stories in order to communicate lived reality:

> But in order to make you understand, to give you my life, I must tell you a story – and there are so many – stories of childhood, stories of school, love, marriage, death, and so on; and *none of them are true* [...] How I distrust neat designs of life that are drawn upon half-sheets of note-paper. I begin to long for some little language such as lovers use, broken words, inarticulate words, like the shuffling of feet on the pavement.[54]

'REFLEXIVE HUMANITIES' AND THE ITINERARY OF THIS BOOK

The next ten chapters do not formulate a testable hypothesis about modernism's complementary relationship to fascism under Mussolini and Hitler, but rather offer a fresh overarching interpretation' of this relationship that challenges

– but cannot 'refute' – many prevailing assumptions about its nature. It has been implied in some attacks on 'metanarratives' in historiography that postmodernist epistemology has somehow refuted the possibility of the progressive rational understanding of reality aspired to by 'the Enlightenment project'. In other words, once properly understood, the reflexivity of human cognition thwarts all attempts to produce synoptic interpretations even before they leave the drawing-board. The axiom of this book instead is, once its implications for knowledge are worked through, reflexivity becomes a methodological principle that actually contributes positively to the bid to bring about *Aufbruch* in the investigation of complex and contested issues such as the correlation of modernist to fascist studies. It suggests a tactic for confronting the problem of reflexivity which avoids entering a state of denial – whether founded on ignorance or sheer hubris – about the subjective, constructed component hard-wired into the very process of acquiring knowledge. At the same time it makes it unnecessary to resort to the expedient of 'thinking small' in an act of damage limitation.

The methodology adopted in this book means, 'sleeping with the enemy', by *self-consciously* and *deliberately*[55] – perhaps even passionately – acknowledging the reflexivity imposed by the protracted cultural turns that have taken place in art history, and intellectual, social, and political history, thus making it integral to the formulation and application of the central thesis structuring any research monograph. At this point the narrative template or 'Gestalt' shaping the reconstruction and analysis of the segment of reality under investigation ceases to present itself as the 'controlling metanarrative' smuggled surreptitiously – sometimes even unbeknown to the author – into the analysis for the discerning critic to ferret out. Instead it becomes a *reflexive* metanarrative, a self-consciously exploratory and *heuristic*, overtly constructed one that dissolves the sinister subliminal, myth-making connotations of the prefix 'meta'. It may even be (as here) a *systematic* synoptic interpretation, a full-blown *grand récit*, but one which never makes 'totalizing' claims.

Callum Brown, a Professor in Religious and Cultural History, has written a useful first-aid manual for historians who may have just woken up to the degree to which postmodernism has been silently eating away like dry rot at the solid foundations of the 'empirical fact' and 'objectivity' of traditional historical analysis. He claims that 'most historians are rarely as reflexive as scholars in other disciplines, such as anthropology',[56] and warns that 'the more complex the hypothesis of the historian, the closer it comes to the sweep and breadth and disconcerting certainty of the metanarrative'.[57] It is perhaps an example of the debilitating impact of postmodernism on the professional ethos in which historians now work that he ignores the possibility that bold, overarching, highly speculative, really *big* hypotheses ('historical interpretations') are still legitimate as long as they are cogently formulated (rather than being implicit), scrupulously substantiated – not 'proved' – through references to a wide range of secondary sources (rather than being plucked out of thin air), and applied as rigorously as possible to the interpretation of concrete historical phenomena. By becoming reflexive the deliberately *non-totalizing* historiographical metanarrative can surely cease to be 'disconcerting' even to historians who have 'turned', and may even be left to resume its original function of being *illuminating*, of stimulating fresh debate, new research, and deeper understanding of 'how things actually were'.

The thesis explored in this book is unrepentantly 'big'. It maintains that a fundamentally homogeneous and uniform psycho-cultural matrix generates not just the bewildering proliferation of heterogeneous aesthetic, cultural, and social forms of modernism, but conditions – without *determining* them – the ideologies, policies, and praxis of generic fascism as well. In short, it claims that fascism can be usefully, but not exclusively, analysed as a *form of modernism*. Hopefully, even historians tormented by the abyss of bottomless relativism will find its constructed nature sufficiently conspicuous, its empirical corroboration sufficiently rigorous, and its heuristic value sufficiently strong to justify the unfashionably epic scale of its metanarrative. For readers who still need further convincing of the theoretical solidity of the present work I have provided an appendix with some further methodological reflections.

The romantic image conjured up in the Introduction of setting sail adventurously towards a new horizon of understanding may already seem like a distant memory of more innocent days. It should soon become clear, however, that the epic voyage has merely been briefly delayed for technical reasons, namely to firewall the 'totalizing' analysis that follows from charges of methodological naivety or sheer folly. Now this issue has been addressed we are finally in a position to provide a clearer outline of the itinerary. Part One (Chapters 2–4) constructs a 'systematic synoptic interpretation' of the nature of modernism. It is one which stresses the importance to its dynamics of a primordial human need to erect elaborate psycho-social defences against the prospect – or rather certainty – of personal extinction, the mind-numbing realization not just that 'we' shall 'all' die, but that 'I shall die' explored so powerfully Leo Tolstoy's haunting short story *The Death of Ivan Illych* (1886). Chapter 5 then applies this theory to exposing a fundamental kinship that exists between scores of apparently unrelated cultural and social initiatives undertaken between 1850 and 1914 whose common goal was to banish decadence and revitalize modern society, even if only locally rather than globally. Chapter 6 argues that an identical bid for cosmological and societal regeneration informs *political* modernism, a term subsuming a number of different political reactions to the destructive impact of modernization on a personal sense of 'transcendence' and 'belonging' compounded by particular configurations of the historical crisis brought about by modernity. It then focuses on the principal form of political modernism that concerns us here, namely fascism, and offers an ideal type of this much contested term. Part Two is then devoted to applying the models of modernity, modernism, and fascism that have emerged to understanding aspects of the ideology, policies, and praxis of Fascism and Nazism.

The theoretical edifice that results can be conceptualized as a modular construct made up of several interlocking and extensively elaborated ideal types: an ideal type of 'human nature' in its confrontation with mortality in a world without 'objective' transcendence; a cluster of ideal types associated with 'the modern': modernization, and modernism, as well as modernity and postmodernity as period concepts; plus an ideal type of fascism. Together these form the belvedere from which modernism's relationship with fascism can be constructed – though the metaphor is misleading to the extent that it implies passive viewing, rather than a proactive process of interpretive reconstruction.

JULIUS EVOLA REVISITED

If these methodological reflections have given our narrative a disconcerting change of direction away from the 'facticity' of modernism and fascism, we can rapidly reconnect empirically with our subject matter, while also providing a trailer for the argument that will unfold in the following chapters, by citing the case of Julius Evola. Even in its present raw, embryonic state, our thesis helps resolve into simple paradoxes the contradictions otherwise implied by his transition from pre-war Futurist circles to being Italy's foremost exponent of Dadaism between 1920 and 1923; a major expert on esotericism by the late 1920s; and the formulator by the mid-1930s of his own totalizing philosophy of history, Traditionalism, on a par with Oswald Spengler's *Decline of the West*. By 1941 he had morphed into a vociferous pro-Nazi Fascist as well as becoming a 'spiritual' – but still profoundly anti-Semitic – racist by 1941. He went on to be the guru of 'black terrorism', Eurofascism, and the New Right in post-war Italy and beyond. In every phase he stayed true to the quest for a 'cure' to the crisis of modernity.

This book argues that there is a common matrix behind modernism in the bewildering heterogeneity of concrete manifestations with which historians have grappled for decades. It argues that this matrix is usefully seen as the search for transcendence and regeneration, whether confined to a personal quest for ephemeral moments of enlightenment or expanded to take the form of a cultural, social, or political movement for the renewal of the nation or the whole of Western civilization. The drive towards renewal may even seek to regenerate an entire historical epoch experienced as 'decadent' – but not terminally and *inexorably* decadent – by identifying a portal within linear time that opens onto the prospect of rebirth.

Some evidence for this interpretation's applicability to Evola's long and winding road through mid-twentieth-century Europe is provided by his 'spiritual' autobiography, *The Cinnabar Path* – a title connoting alchemical transformation. In it Evola explains the importance of the Dada movement for him in the immediate aftermath of the First World War:

> Dadaism did not just want to be a new trend in avant-garde art. Rather it asserted a general vision of life in which the impulse towards an absolute emancipation which threw into disarray all logical, ethical, and aesthetic categories manifested itself in paradoxical and disconcerting ways.[58]

By his own account Evola was attracted to Dada by the 'thrill of reawakening' instilled in its campaign to embark on 'a great negative work of destruction' necessary to 'clean up the filth' of modernity. In other words, he was drawn by the archaic logic of what we will encounter later under such terms as 'active nihilism' and 'destructive creation'. Spurred on by an acute sense of the imminent collapse of civilization, he desperately sought *Aufbruch* into a new reality beyond the one offered by the official culture and politics of Giolittian Italy. By the time he published *Revolt against the Modern World* in 1934, he had convinced himself that Traditionalism provided the most comprehensive diagnosis of the decadence of the modern world. He was also confident that it offered the ethical and cosmological foundations for the process of socio-political renewal to which he looked to save it from total collapse by inaugurating the rebirth of (European) civilization, its *palingenesis*.[59] This was 'a more radical Fascism, more fearless, a really absolute Fascism, made of pure force, impervious to any compromise'.[60] It was also deeply *racist*.[61]

In his illuminating essay on Evola's intense affair with Dada, Jeffrey Schnapp argues that, though brief, it sowed 'the seeds of that subsequent wholesale revolt against modernity, founded on the advocacy of elitism, spiritual racism, and pagan imperialism that propelled Evola – alone among the fascist theorists – beyond the catastrophe of Benito Mussolini and Adolf Hitler into postwar prominence'.[62] The cult of self-contradiction it fostered served 'as a tool for dismantling the stranglehold of logic over everyday existence, for freeing the self from logic's gravitational pull, for demolishing the destructive core of a fallen world'.[63] On the other side of this destruction, however, Evola was able to forge a palingenetic vision of the world process that opened onto a new modernity beyond the 'actually existing one'. This he achieved through an orgy of unbridled eclecticism – Schnapp identifies scores of sources welded together to form the 'Traditionalist' world-view – thereby producing a true metanarrative, one undiluted by an academic sense of relativism, reflexivity, or the heuristic status of all theory. It was deliberately forged as a source, not of infinitely contestable scholarly knowledge but of *gnosis*, the visionary knowledge that allows its holder to *act* on the world and achieve a sense of meaning and belonging beyond the abyss of paralysing pluralism and nihilism.

It was this literally *epoch-making* concept of knowledge as *vision*, so important to modernism as we shall define it, which forms the subterranean link between Evola's Dadaism and his Traditionalism, and makes it more comprehensible why he later dedicated a whole essay to extolling the brilliance of Ernst Jünger's philo-Nazi prediction of the coming of *homo technologicus* in *Der Arbeiter* (1932), of the emergence of 'The Worker' as a new human type, even though the German's futuristic élan may seem far removed from the mental world of Traditionalism.[64] It also accounts for the enthusiasm that the deeply un-Expressionist *Revolt against the Modern World* aroused in the Expressionist Gottfried Benn. In his review of the book that he wrote for *Die Literatur* in 1935 he singled out for praise Evola's recognition that both Fascism and National Socialism were turning their 'racially religious axiom' about the basis of human society into historical reality. They were thus creating the premises

> for a new connection of nations with the Tradition, for the production of authentic history, and for a new legitimation of the relationship between spirit and power (indeed it is against the background of Evola's teaching that *the epoch-making nature of these movements stands out clearly*). [...] Here we see in whose name we will have lived: in the name of the Tradition, of the handing down of values from deeper worlds of existence, of remote historical cycles, of the great Empire [Reich]. Thus we were and so we shall be.[65]

So was Virilio right after all? The examples of Evola and Benn certainly point to a nexus of some sort between extreme forms of aesthetic modernism and fascism, even in its most radical Nazi permutation, raising the spectre that Futurism and Expressionism are linked directly to Auschwitz. In the course of the following chapters it will be argued such a connection exists, but that it is of an oblique, mediated kind which also accommodates a host of *anti-*fascist manifestations of aesthetic modernism. To bring out this point in more concrete terms it is fitting to close this chapter with the example of Giuseppe Pagano, whose fate discloses the gruesome contradiction that can occur in the relationship of modernism to fascism. Pagano was one of the leading exponents of an anti-monumental, rationalist form of architectural modernism that flourished under Fascism, perhaps the most familiar example of which is in Rome's Città Universitaria. Having poured his creativity into forging what he hoped would become the official modernist aesthetic of Fascism, he became increasingly alienated once Mussolini embarked on his fatal alliance with Hitler, and when the armistice of September 1943 led to the Nazi occupation of what remained of Fascist Italy, he joined the partisan movement. Arrested by Mussolini's 'republicchini' as leader of the Matteotti group of partisans, he escaped from prison, but was re-arrested, tortured and sent to the Nazi concentration camp in Melch. He died in April 1945 in the death camp of Mauthausen just days before its liberation.

The camp's specialized form of torture and execution was in its use of slave labour for producing blocks of granite earmarked for the vast architectural programmes to be carried out in the extensive reconstruction of cities such as Linz, Munich, Nuremberg, Weimar, and Berlin as symbols of Germany's reawakening, projects which, we will argue, symbolize Nazism's own chilling dialect of cultural modernism.[66] Its most infamous site of suffering and death was the Wiener Graben or 'staircase to hell', where prisoners were forced to walk up a long flight of rough hewn steps carrying blocks of stone, and sometimes to leap to their deaths once at the top in the 'parachute jump'.[67]

Pagano was just one of thousands of intellectuals and artists, modernist and non-modernist, branded as 'degenerate' by the canons of Nazism, and worked to death in the camp alongside many more alleged enemies of racial purity such as gypsies, homosexuals, and Russian prisoners of war. They were all victims of the Nazi regime's sustained attempt to use the resources of an entire continent to turn fiction into reality and lay the foundations of a new historical epoch, at whatever human cost. This utopian undertaking was born of an extreme form of what Kermode calls in the epigraph to this chapter the 'disposition' to 'make new' the world at the core of modernism. Their fate was determined by the readiness of convinced Nazis to collaborate in creating 'the new, unimaginable forms of historical reality' to which Hayden White refers in his epigraph, thereby forcing untold millions into the roles of henchmen or victims in the 'modern apocalypse' that ensued. The first step towards understanding how Pagano could become both protagonist and victim of this apocalypse is to clarify the first of the concepts at the core of our investigation: modernism.

2
Two Modes of Modernism

> And whoever must be a creator of values in good and evil: verily, he must first be an annihilator and shatter values.
>
> Friedrich Nietzsche, *Thus Spoke Zarathustra* (1883)[1]

> Modernity [...] pours us all into a maelstrom of perpetual disintegration and renewal, of struggle and contradiction, of ambiguity and anguish.
>
> Marshall Berman, *All that is Solid Melts into Air* (1982)[2]

> Because [...] the modern world is distinguished from the old by the fact that it opens itself to the future, the epochal new beginning is rendered constant with each moment that gives birth to the new.
>
> Jürgen Habermas, 'Modernity's Consciousness of Time and Its Need for Self-Reassurance' (1987)[3]

MODERNISM'S 'DIALOGIC' (DIRE LOGIC?)

The centre comes into being as it dissipates. Modernity's grand narratives institute their own radical dismantling. The lifeblood of modernity's chaos is its order. The impulse to order is the product of chaos. Modernism requires tradition to make it new. Tradition comes into being only as it is rebelled against.[4]

This is – at least for those who have just entered the labyrinth of modernist studies – the somewhat cryptic conclusion arrived at by Susan Friedman, a leading expert on the theory and practices of literary modernism, after a 'definitional excursus' on the meanings of 'modern', 'modernity', and 'modernism' that appeared in 2001 in *Modernism/Modernity*, the foremost academic journal devoted to the study of these topics. The article follows a self-consciously postmodern logic in refusing to satisfy any ingenuous expectations of a succinct definition awakened in traditional minds by the title. Instead it applies the technique known as 'ironic deconstruction' used by modernists such as Franz Kafka or the Dadaists to underscore the impossibility of achieving 'closure' in investigations of the term's semantics. Rather than resolve the issue of modernism's definition, Friedman chooses to highlight the way the 'grammatical/philosophical and political/cultural routes' that she has escorted readers down 'suggest that the oppositional meanings of *modern/ modernity/ modernism* point to the contradictory dialogic running through the historical and expressive formations of the phenomena to which the terms allude'.[5]

At least her essay points to a sustained concern with wresting meaning from the concept, for as Christopher Wilk observes in his insightful essay 'What was Modernism?', even when it is used in the title, 'vast numbers of articles and books – including very good ones – use the term Modernism without the authors ever explaining what they mean', seemingly content to stress the intrinsic difficulty of defining it.[6] Thus the introduction to one anthology is reluctant to go beyond the observation that the term 'comprises numerous, diverse and contesting, theories and practices which first flourished in a period that knew little of the term as it has now come to be understood'. The reader is left none the wiser about how it is 'now understood'.[7]

Nevertheless, some recurrent motifs emerge in the various synoptic treatments of the topic which suggest it is possible to progress to something more solid and substantial than the Dali-esque self-dissolution of any definite conceptual frame of reference in a nexus of paradoxes with which Friedman regales the reader. In particular there are recurrent references to how culture, under the dispensation of 'high' *modernity* in the West, entered an acute state of flux, its social and ideological cohesion being degraded and fractured to a point where reality itself was increasingly experienced as breaking down, dissolving, or losing its mythic 'centre'. There is also a wide consensus that *modernism* is somehow intimately bound up with the radically disorienting, atomistic experience of modernity that results. However, superimposing the different accounts creates a fuzzy interference pattern reminiscent of an abstract painting rather than a lucid conceptual framework, as if the term has somehow taken on by osmosis characteristics of the very topic it is being used to investigate.

In her analysis of this situation Friedman describes it in terms of a 'contradictory dialogic', an allusion to the literary theory of the Russian philosopher Mikhail Bakhtin who has had a major influence on modernist studies. Whereas a 'monologic' work is a largely self-contained universe, the dialogic one is engaged in a continual dialogue with other works of literature, thereby altering the reading of earlier works just as they in turn influence how it is read. Every academic debate about a topic is necessarily 'dialogic', and hence there can be no closure in defining what is meant by a key generic 'ism'. However, rather than highlight the impossibility of closure in the tradition of postmodernism – a paradoxical phrase in itself – the next three chapters approach the lexicographical conundrum posed by 'modernism' in the spirit of reflexive historiography discussed in the last chapter, with a drive towards imposing clarity on the tangle of issues surrounding it and offering a coherent narrative within which to locate its use.

To enable some order to be put in the conceptual chaos surrounding the term, this chapter will thus construct a provisional – and to a postmodernist mindset probably distinctly 'old-fashioned' – ideal type of modernism to be further expanded and refined in the two chapters that follow. It subsumes three components: the view of 'modernization' as a secularizing and disorienting force that tends to erode a stable sense of 'tradition' and promotes the rise of 'reflexivity'; the identification of 'modernity' with a qualitative change in the experience of time resulting from the reflexive experience of history and its 'temporalization', so that it seems continually to open out onto potentially new futures; and the recognition of the growing tendency after the mid-nineteenth century for modernity to be perceived no longer through the trope of progress but of 'decadence', thereby provoking countervailing projects to enact alternative modernities.

THE MALAISE OF MODERNITY

Since our ideal-typical construction of modernism approaches it as a product of and response to the peculiar conditions of Western modernity, it is as well to outline the specific connotations which the process of 'modernization' itself acquires in this context. This is, of course, yet another highly value-laden term in a field of studies where every key concept is contested to the point where one academic's purportedly 'neutral' use of the word can seem charged with provocative value-assumptions to academics applying a more politically radical perspective – for example, Marxist, feminist, Third World, or ecological.[8] It is being used here as a collective noun or 'blanket term' for a nexus of processes within Western society triggered by partly discrete and coincidental, partly interrelated and self-reinforcing ideological, political, cultural, sociological, institutional, and technological developments. These combined to bring about change in the value systems (the way people thought about their place in the world, their cosmology, their morality) and lives (the material conditions and patterns of existence) of human beings living in 'the West' at every level in the social hierarchy, change associated in text book history with such phrases as the 'birth of the modern world'.[9] These include – the list is obviously far from exhaustive – the spread of rationalism, liberalism, secularization, individualism, and capitalism,[10] the cult of progress, expanding literacy rates and social mobility, urbanization and industrialization, the emergence of the urban middle (capitalist) and working (rural and proletarian) classes

from a feudal structure of society, the growth of representative government
and bureaucratization, revolutionary developments in communications and
transport, geographical discoveries and imperial expansion, the advance of
secular science and ever more powerful technology and technocracy. Such
factors interact in an irreducibly complex way to form a synergy which
transforms material realities and human relations not just at a highly varied
pace, but in a geographically and socially highly 'uneven' manner.[11] Between
the sixteenth and twentieth centuries they impacted on traditional societies
within the Europeanized world with increasingly irresistible and pervasive
force in such a way as to produce 'modernity'.

In case such a simplistic overview suggests the lurking presence of a totalizing
interpretation of history, it must be stressed that determining what factors are
subsumed under 'modernization', their causal relationship, when 'it' took place
– it is, of course, a multiple phenomenon – the particular role played in it by
any one element such as secularization, the rise of technology, individualism,
or urbanization, is the highly contested subject of an entire field of specialist
studies in several disciplines. 'Modernization' is a construct like all other
concepts, and any attempt made here to offer a concise definition of it or
suggest how it should be periodized would raise a cluster of thorny issues which
fortunately do not concern us. What can be stated dogmatically is that we are
dealing with an ongoing, multi-factorial process which does not 'start' *ex nihilo*
at any particular point or in any particular place. As the evocative English
mistranslation of the title that the Dutchman Johan Huizinga chose for his
study of Burgundian court society reminds us, the 'Middle Ages' did not come
to an abrupt end: 'they' waned.[12] Slowly mutating, structures and phenomena
classifiable as 'medieval' continued for centuries after the fourteenth century to
coexist and interact with new forms of urban society, culture, and economics
associated with 'the Renaissance' – another highly contested term – to produce
what can now be construed as the first stirrings of 'modernity' and hence of
'early modern Europe'.

In fact, the whole idea of a static, closed, homogeneous 'traditional'
('premodern', 'medieval', 'feudal') Europe being transformed through a single
cohesive process into a dynamic, heterogeneous, open, progressive 'modern'
one is the fruit of mythic not historiographical thinking: a 'master narrative',
in fact. 'Tradition', for example, is to be considered not as a static, timeless
entity but as a dynamically evolving, in some cases historically recent, set
of beliefs and practices. Its hallmark as a mobilizing myth is that it tends
to be constructed by those who feel thrown into an age of chaos or decline
– especially when the stability of their society or their class is threatened
by objective forces of rapid change – as a 'given' or 'natural' state of order
now under threat, a proposition legitimated by invoking unbroken continuity

with the no less mythicized 'past'. At whatever pace they change, all societies continually spawn new traditions in an endless interplay of transformation and stabilization – or what Henri de Saint-Simon called 'critical' and 'organic' phases – which modulates the syncretization of old and new.

However European modernization's impact on tradition since the eighteenth century is modelled, there is considerable unanimity on the generally disorienting, destabilizing nature of its end result. Thus David Harvey, in his seminal book *The Condition of Postmodernity* emphasizes how Marx depicts modernization in terms of social processes engendered by capitalism conducive to 'individualism, alienation, fragmentation, ephemerality, innovation, creative destruction, speculative development, unpredictable shifts in methods of production and consumption (wants and needs), a shifting experience of space and time, as well as a crisis-ridden dynamic of social change'.[13] Such materialist accounts need complementing, however, by giving due weight to the impact that the break-up of rural communities, the rise of science, and particularly the impact of Darwinism had on traditional Christian beliefs and the 'cosmology' of ordinary people.

'Modernity' has further subtleties of its own. The exclusively chronological identification of the component 'modern' with 'contemporary' would make it a neutral period concept whose starting point moves forward as the calendar of our civilization ratchets itself inexorably onwards, like a Swiss mountain railway locomotive. But, as Theodor Adorno asserted, 'modernity is a qualitative, not a chronological category'.[14] In other words, at least in the context of Western history, it has come to denote the effects of the modernization process as a social force, both objective and subjective, rather than a period. It has a chronology, of course, but a disputed one impossible to chart with precision, so that cases can be made for it starting in the seventeenth century[15] and eighteenth century,[16] while some historians focus on the nineteenth century.[17] What it is possible to assert with some certainty, however, is that, like modernization, 'it' did not have a starting point but 'waxed', with the result that European societies in the eighteenth century still presented an extraordinarily variegated mixture of elements deriving from different phases in socio-economic, technological, and political evolution, its precise constitution in any one time or place conditioned by the specific cultural, religious, economic, ethnic, regional, national, imperial context of each locality.

It is obviously a situation that precludes simple definitions. As one of the foremost experts on the subject, Zygmunt Bauman, points out:

'How old is modernity?' is a contentious question. There is no agreement on dating. There is no consensus on what is to be dated. And once the effort of dating starts in earnest, the object itself begins to disappear. Modernity, like all the other quasitotalities we want to prise off from the continuous flow of being, becomes elusive: we discover the concept fraught with ambiguity, while its referent is opaque at the core and frayed at the edges.[18]

Thankfully, no attempt needs to be made here to resolve such ambiguities either. What we propose to do instead is focus on one aspect of modernity where there is a pocket of scholarly consensus, namely that is defined at least in part by a qualitative change in the experience of time itself. This can be characterized as the tendency for an increasing number of inhabitants of European culture to experience the erosion of external reality's self-evident 'givenness',[19] the attrition of its *phenomenological* solidity previously *unreflexively* underpinned by socially and institutionally reinforced beliefs in a 'higher' metaphysical or 'natural' order ('tradition'). The process by which ontological certainties came to be undermined can be modelled in a variety of ways. In *Modernity and Ambivalence* Bauman highlights the degree to which modernization has so fragmented the relative cohesion of premodern society that stability under modernity paradoxically lies in its very instability, and the 'dysfunctionality of modern culture is its functionality'.[20] The experience of the world's coherence prevalent in earlier centuries has been replaced by dynamic configurations of order and chaos, which he terms 'modern twins' because they are the co-dependent products of a history no longer perceived through the lens of shared overarching belief-systems.

This portrait of modernity as an ongoing sense-making crisis is broadly convergent with the accounts of it offered by other leading experts. Anthony Giddens, for example, identifies as one of the most important 'consequences of modernity' its 'disembedding' impact that 'empties out' time and space.[21] Fredric Jameson writes of modernity as a 'catastrophe' that 'dashes traditional structures and lifeways to pieces, sweeps away the sacred, undermines immemorial habits and inherited languages, and leaves the world as a set of raw materials to be reconstructed rationally'.[22] Stephen Kern documents the way the bounded universe of 'traditional' Newtonian space and time underpinned by a relatively stable Christian cosmology was blown apart by the growing momentum of technological innovation and scientific discovery in the late nineteenth century. This not only produced a revolution in art and architecture, but simultaneously intensified both the optimistic belief in the infinite malleability of the future, and nebulous fears of degeneration and decline.[23] Other investigations of modernity focus on the way 'modern' human beings feel permanently exiled from some primordial existential 'home' that was available for earlier generations[24] in a way that alienates them from official Christian and Enlightenment values as well as any overarching teleology of progress or redemption.

The precursors of this rich vein of cultural analysis are several intellectuals who at the end of the nineteenth century sought to devise sociological models to explain the profound psychological and sociological dilemmas that were emerging under modernity, acting both as the victims of the 'sickness' of modernity and its physicians. Max Weber, for example, concentrated on the role played by the process of 'rationalization' that derived its impetus from the Enlightenment cult of reason, the rise of capitalism, technology, science, and the centralization of power. He saw it as draining magic from the world to produce the 'disenchantment' of all aspects of reality that once had a metaphysical or supernatural aura. A text on the sociology of religion he wrote during the First World War puts it thus:

> The unity of the primitive image of the world, in which everything was concrete magic, has tended to split into rational cognition and mastery of nature, on the one hand, and into 'mystic' experiences, on the other. The inexpressible contents of such experiences remain the only possible 'beyond', added to the mechanism of a world robbed of gods.[25]

Weber's observation is broadly compatible with several other penetrating sociological analyses of modernity being offered at the time, notably Émile Durkheim's theory of the breakdown of 'mechanical solidarity' that bound together traditional religious communities and the spread of *anomie*,[26] Ferdinand Tönnies's thesis that the relatively cohesive organic 'community' (*Gemeinschaft*) was being replaced by a loose-knit, atomized 'society' (*Gesellschaft*),[27] and Georg Simmel's investigation of the dire spiritual consequences of the rise of materialism and urban living.[28] It was in this very modern 'tradition' that in 1930 Sigmund Freud analysed contemporary society in terms of an all-pervasive 'malaise',[29] and Carl Jung explored the dilemma of 'modern man' as a being cut off from healthy sources of spirituality.[30]

MODERNITY AS 'DECADENCE'

One diagnostic approach to the conceptualization of modernity that has a particular bearing on the ideal type of modernism we are seeking to construct focuses on the intimate relationship between two features of the qualitative change it has brought about in the way the world is experienced: first, the growth of 'reflexivity', in which human beings first become aware of themselves as historical agents living within a unique constellation of historical forces (a particular epoch), and second, the resulting 'temporalization of history'. For example, in *The Philosophical Discourses of Modernity* (1987) Jürgen Habermas identifies Enlightenment modernity with a new temporality resulting from a growing consciousness of time. In a book exploring the growing divide between 'lifetime' and 'worldtime',[31] Hans Blumenberg postulates that a defining feature of the Enlightenment was that progress was no longer an inevitable consequence of the past but could be 'advanced by method, organization and institution, and condensed by speeding it up'.[32] These were all symptoms of a new consciousness of being the protagonists of historical change, though it was only in the nineteenth century that human beings began to believe that they could make history from scratch. Anthony Giddens sees the growth in personal and institutional reflexivity as a major symptom and consequence of late modernity with its roots in the nineteenth-century changes in consciousness.[33] Similarly, Zygmunt Bauman suggests 'we can think of modernity as a time when order – of the world, of the human habitat, of the human self, and of the connection between all three – is *reflected upon*; a matter of thought, of concern, of a practice that is aware of itself, conscious of being a conscious practice'.[34]

One of the most influential historians to have concerned himself with these aspects of modernity is Reinhardt Koselleck, whose sustained work on European intellectual history since the Enlightenment has convinced him that since the second half of the eighteenth century a new concept of time which he calls 'Neuzeit' – 'New Time', or 'modernity' – took root in the West. Its hallmark is that

> [t]ime does not just remain the form in which all histories take place, but time itself gains a historical quality. History no longer takes place in time, but through time. Time is metaphorically dynamized into a force of history itself.[35]

This makes the future no longer a neutral temporal space for what destiny or providence will bring, but a site for realizing transformative cultural, social, or political projects through human agency. As a result, periods of intense historical upheaval under modernity foster the feeling that 'the "newest time" is not only one's own time, but it is more: *the beginning of a new epoch*'.[36]

Koselleck singles out two eloquent symptoms of this sea-change in the experience of history: first, the publication in 1770 of Louis-Sébastien Mercier's futuristic novel *The Year 2440*, in which he sees evidence of 'the metamorphosis of utopia into the philosophy of history, [...] in short, the temporalization of utopia';[37] second, the creation during the French Revolution of a new calendar aimed at supplanting the hegemony of Christianity with the principles of Enlightenment humanism. For Koselleck, 'what was really new about it is the idea of *being able to begin history anew* by accounting for it in terms of a calendar'.[38]

In an investigation of time under modernity which draws extensively on Koselleck, Helga Nowotny draws attention to the way the growing pace of change under modernization eventually altered the 'space of experience' and increased a general sense of 'expectation [...] directed towards the open horizon of the future', so that, by the late nineteenth century, history could mean 'a constant opening up into something better'.[39] In her account of contemporary society, the temporalization of history underwent a further stage of radicalization in the twentieth century with the result that 'the temporal category of the future is being abolished and replaced by that of the extended present', a process that precipitates the emergence of the postmodern consciousness of time.[40] Koselleck's theory is also central to the account of modernity as a qualitatively 'different time' that provides the premise to Peter Osborne's sustained investigation into the 'politics of time'. This analyses the fundamental change brought about to political projects once human beings see themselves reflexively as belonging to a particular epoch in the open-ended unfolding of history. It is an experience that empowers them to create a new epoch that deliberately makes a caesura with what has gone before. He dates modernity from the decades around 1800 in which 'the modern is no longer simply opposed either to the ancient or to the medieval, but to "tradition" in general'.[41]

On the basis of such works it seems relatively uncontentious to identify modernity with the localized emergence in late eighteenth-century Europe of the reflexive mode of historical consciousness which legitimated the French revolutionaries' fundamentalist war against tradition and their deliberate attempt to replace it lock, stock, and barrel with an entirely new epoch. It was the presumption that such a *self-conscious* act of historical regeneration was possible that so incurred the wrath of Conservative thinkers such as Edmund Burke and Joseph de Maistre. It was when the alliance between the temporalization of history and Enlightenment, liberal, and Revolutionary myths of progress broke down that a further qualitative change in the experience of history occurred that forms the precondition for the emergence of 'modernism'.

By the mid-nineteenth century the practical effects on European society of what Eric Hobsbawm calls the Dual Revolution (the French and industrial revolutions) had undermined the myth of progress to a point where for many among its cultural elites modernity lost its utopian connotations and began to be constructed as a period of decline, decay, and loss. David Harvey, in his superb exploration of the impact of modernization on European consciousness, pin-points the capitalist crisis and revolutionary upheavals of 1847–48 as provoking a 'radical readjustment in the sense of time and space in economic, political, and cultural life', and in particular a breakdown in the Enlightenment sense of 'time pressing forward', that precipitated 'the rise of modernism as a cultural force'.[42] The general shift to an awareness of the disorienting aspects of an increasingly temporalized history had been articulately anticipated by what has been called 'negative Romanticism',[43] or what Nietzsche calls in another context 'Romantic pessimism',[44] with its dark moods of nihilism and existential anguish. However, it was not until the mid-century that modernity itself started to be experienced in biological, moral, and aesthetic categories of degeneration, corruption, and effeteness.

This line of thought brings us to the lynch-pin of 'our' ideal type of modernism. It maintains that modernism comes into being as a cultural phenomenon unique to modernity at the point[45] at which the contemporary age is both experienced and expressed (constructed) by a critical mass of artists and intellectuals as an epoch not of progress and evolution, but of regression and involution: in a word, of *decadence*. Three decades ago Stuart Hughes' analysis of 'the reorientation of European consciousness' helped popularize the expression 'the revolt against positivism'.[46] The thesis put forward here suggests that modernism can be treated as 'the revolt against decadence'. It was a revolt which in some of its permutations embraced elements of both the visceral revolt against positivism and a passionate commitment to positivism in a way that would call for a Venn diagram of overlapping circles to portray its unique ideological configuration in individual cases.

In the decades after the largely abortive 1848 revolutions, in marked contrast to the French Revolutionary period that had made them possible, the quint-essentially modern experience of contemporary history as opening out into an as yet undefined future, as permanently pregnant with an 'epochal new beginning', began to run *against* the grain of actually existing modernity and the way post-Revolutionary society was visibly developing. In this profoundly *uncoordinated*, heterogeneous, polycentric countermovement the orthodoxy of political and technocratic progress came to be rejected as constituting in itself a superseded and moribund 'tradition' that urgently demanded to be transcended in order to find new sources of meaning, spirituality, and communality. In the most utopian forms of modernism, concerted attempts were made to establish an entirely new ideological and social basis for the progress of Western civilization.

Whereas Susan Friedman's 'excursus' on the meanings of 'modern', 'modernity', and 'modernism' deliberately beguiles the reader with an act of semantic striptease, David Harvey offers an enviably succinct, impeccably dressed, pre-postmodern formulation: 'Modernism is a troubled and fluctuating aesthetic response to conditions of modernity produced by a particular process of modernization.'[47] 'Unpacked' this can be taken to mean that by the early-to-mid nineteenth-century modernization had created particular configurations of modernity in certain milieux of Europeanized society which fostered the reflexive temporalization of history. Once optimism about the historical process gave way to a generalized mood of pessimism exacerbated by the increasingly destructive impact of the Dual Revolution on traditional society in some regions – a mood which could be further exacerbated locally by profound socio-political upheavals and rapid change – a growing number of artists and intellectuals became convinced that modernization was leaching modernity of elements vital to a healthy civilization and a vital culture. Even the many millions who lacked the heightened capacity of the avant-garde for introspection and self-awareness were nevertheless prone to feel they were living through perhaps the last days of an entire epoch of civilization which was materially progressing while spiritually regressing. Contemporary history thus became a permanent paradox of exponential growth in productivity, technology, knowledge, middle-class wealth, imperial power, and national (capitalist) self-assertion, social mobility, but at the cost of beauty, meaning, and health, both spiritual and physical. It was rushing nowhere ever faster.

The condition of modernity generated myriad countervailing bids by artists and non-artists not just to find ways of expressing the decadence of modernity, but to assert a higher vision of reality, to make contact with deeper, eternal 'truths' – or even to inaugurate an entirely new epoch. Their creative acts, initiatives, and projects to reverse the tide of anomy and re-embed time and space have come to be known to cultural historians collectively as 'modernism', which, as the product of an unevenly experienced cultural crisis, is naturally 'troubled and fluctuating'. Modernism expresses the striving for *Aufbruch*, the drive to break through established normality to find unsuspected patterns of meaning and order within the encroaching chaos, to turn crepuscular twilight into a new dawn, to inaugurate a new beginning beyond the ongoing dissolution, and achieve, if not an alternative modernity, at least a lasting spiritual refuge, or even just a temporary night-shelter, from its devastating effects. It is the twin of 'decadence', not in the sense of the late nineteenth-century art movement of that name, but because it articulates the urgent need for contemporary society to be regenerated and for history itself to be renewed. It turns modernity itself into a trope for decadence, one that we will distinguish from the more 'value-neutral' uses of the term with the upper case 'Modernity'. Thus modernism can be seen as an attempted rebellion against Modernity carried out in order to inaugurate a new modernity.

In a footnote on the term modernity, Zygmunt Bauman describes modernism as 'an intellectual (philosophical, literary, artistic) trend' in which 'modernity turned its gaze upon itself' in the attempt to attain 'clear-sightedness and self-awareness'.[48] The thesis we have been arguing suggests instead that modernism is to be seen as the fruit of a modern reflexivity *in crisis*, the product of a temporalized self-awareness that, responding to the perceived decay of history itself, is thus driven in extreme cases to envisage its 'total' regeneration through an unprecedented process of creative destruction. This impulse may have been articulated most lucidly in the artistic and intellectual spheres of cultural production, but in the decades before 1914 it also expressed itself in social and political phenomena apparently far removed from the sphere of philosophy, literature, and art. This makes modernism overflow the boundaries of the 'aesthetic' category to which Harvey's aphoristic formulation seems to confine it. It is significant, however, that his book documents in impressive detail that modernism is not primarily an aesthetic, but rather a *cosmological* phenomenon inextricably bound up with upheavals in the perception of time and space.

AN IDEAL TYPE OF MODERNISM

On the basis of such reflections it is possible to formulate a succinct ideal type of modernism, one which will undergo further refinements as our argument unfolds in the course of the next two chapters:

MODERNISM: *the generic term for a wide variety of countervailing palingenetic reactions to the anarchy and cultural decay allegedly resulting from the radical transformation of traditional institutions, social structures, and belief systems under the impact of Western modernization. These reactions were fostered by the growth of reflexivity and its concomitant, the progressive temporalization of history characteristic of modernity, one consequence of which was the trend towards re-imagining the future as a permanently 'open' site for the realization of utopias within historical time. Modernism gained momentum in the second half of the nineteenth century when liberal, capitalist, and Enlightenment myths of progress lost the partial cultural hegemony they had attained during the French Revolution and early industrial revolution, with the result that the manifold changes that society was undergoing became increasingly identified by intellectual and artistic elites with decadence, so that modernity itself became a trope for degeneration (Modernity).*

Between the 1860s and the end of the Second World War, modernism acted as a diffuse cultural force generated by the dialectics of chaos and (new) order, despair and hope, decadence and renewal, destruction and creation, manifesting itself in countless idiosyncratic artistic visions of how new representations of reality could act as the vehicle to revitalize ignored or forgotten principles of a redemptive vision of the world, and even help it regenerate itself socially and morally. Beyond the sphere of aesthetics and 'high' culture, the palingenetic dynamics of modernism have also shaped numerous personal projects and collective movements to establish a healthier social and ethical basis for society, or inaugurate an entirely new socio-political order. This order is conceived as an alternative *modernity which holds out the prospect of putting an end to political, cultural, moral, and/or physical dissolution, and sometimes looks forward to the emergence of a new type of 'man'.*

In considering how this definition relates to existing ones, the first point to note is that it is a recurrent theme in secondary literature to stress the paradoxical, 'Janus-headed' aspect of modernism which enables it to express both cultural pessimism and optimism, moods of despair and celebration. Frank Kermode, for example, sees archetypal features of 'apocalyptic thinking', notably the concern with 'Decadence and Renovation', as a common denominator of the 'fictions' that characterized early modernism.[49] This insight is elaborated in Malcolm Bradbury and James McFarlane's introduction to their pioneering collection of essays on literary modernism:

> In short, Modernism was in most countries an extraordinary compound of the futuristic and the nihilistic, the revolutionary and the conservative, the naturalistic and the symbolistic, the romantic and the classical. It was a celebration of a technological age and condemnation of it; an excited acceptance of the belief that the old régimes of culture were over, and a deep despairing in the face of that fear; a mixture of convictions that the new forms were escapes from historicism and the pressures of time with convictions that they were precisely the living expressions of these things.[50]

Similarly, Peter Childs detects in it 'paradoxical if not opposed trends towards revolutionary and reactionary positions, fear of the new and delight at the disappearance of the old, nihilism and fanatical enthusiasm, creativity and despair'.[51] Even Jane Goldman, who like Susan Friedman has her heart post-modernistically set on denying closure in the search for a definition, recognizes the importance of modernism's palingenetic aspect when she chooses Ezra Pound's slogan 'Make it New' for the title of her introduction – a call 'answered in a myriad ways'[52] – and dedicates the whole final section of her book to the theme of Apocalypse, which again subsumes elements of 'collapse' and a new world.[53]

It should be noted that, apart from Kermode's reference to the apocalyptic tradition underlying modernist thought – a theme explored at some length in his book – none of these characterizations of modernism, including my own provisional one, allude to any underlying psychodynamics or premodern sources of modernist quests for renewal and innovation. This lacuna will be remedied in the following two chapters. The reason for my periodization of modernism which portrays it as becoming a dominant force between the 1860s and 1945 will also become clearer as the argument unfolds. More than by what is missing, what might strike some readers particularly is its extension to include phenomena outside the aesthetic and cultural spheres. Fortunately, as with the emphasis it places on the 'temporalization of history', some major authorities can be invoked to corroborate this argument.

For example, Walter Adamson, in a book seminal to the topic of modernism's relationship to Italian Fascism, makes the *socio-political* dimension of its response to modernity central to his account of the formative role played by Florentine modernism in the genesis of Fascism. Furthermore, he endorses a crucial element of my thesis by arguing that 'modernism was an "adversary culture" or "other modernity" that challenged the "modernizing forces" of science, commerce, and industry, usually in the name of some more "spiritual" alternative'. This led European modernists to stress 'the importance of recreating the mythic, legendary, and "primal" forces of cultural life' in a 'messianic mood of frenzy, despair, and apocalyptic hope'. Central to this hope was their belief that their intellectual and artistic efforts would play a 'central role [...] in the creation and organization of a regenerated culture'.[54]

A similarly 'maximalist' concept of modernism also underlies Marshall Berman's *All that is Solid Melts into Air*, his classic attempt to recapture 'the experience of modernity', and probe into 'the dialectic' of its ephemerality. In it he talks of the 'paradoxical unity' of modernity, 'a unity of disunity: it pours us all into a maelstrom of perpetual disintegration and renewal, of struggle and contradiction, of ambiguity and anguish'. It is a maelstrom created and maintained in a 'state of perpetual becoming' by 'world-historical processes' fuelling 'an amazing variety of visions and ideas that aim to make men and women the subjects as well as the objects of modernization, *to give them the power to change the world that is changing them, to make their way through the maelstrom and make it their own.*' Over the past century, these visions and values have come to be loosely grouped together under the name of 'modernism'.[55]

Another authority who makes the socio-political aspect of modernism explicit, though in a more circumspect, historically grounded exposition of its effects, is Modris Eksteins. His *Rites of Spring* treats the concept of modernism as central not just to the understanding of modern art, but 'the birth of the modern age'. He is fully aware of the contentiousness of such an expansion, however, commenting: 'Few critics have extended the idea of avant-garde and modernism to the social and political as well as artistic agents of revolt, and to the act of rebellion in general, in order to identify a broad wave of sentiment and endeavour.'[56] Peter Osborne also offers an 'overarching' theory of modernism, seeing it as a manifestation of a constant tension between actuality and (utopian) expectations of radical transformation, between the 'temporality of the old' and the possibility of a radically different future temporality which is born of the self-reflexive temporalization of history. In this context modernism can be conceived as 'the affirmative cultural self-consciousness of the temporality of the new',[57] expressing itself not just in art, but in philosophy and, above all, in political movements that seek to realize alternative temporalities to resolve the perceived crisis of history. Peter Fritzsche puts this position succinctly. The hallmark of modernism is that 'it breaks with the past, manufactures its own historical traditions, and imagines alternative futures'. As a result, 'though it has usually been conceived in literary or artistic terms', modernism has 'remarkable social and political implications'.[58]

The key witness to call for a testimony on modernism that broadly substantiates the maximalist definition we have proposed, however, is Ronald Schleifer. In the course of his penetrating investigation of the relationship between modernism and time, he makes four points that have a direct bearing on our thesis. First, he argues that a precondition of modernism is the devastating impact of modernization on traditional society, the most important component of which for him is the 'overwhelming multiplication of commodities in the second Industrial Revolution'. The effects of this were further intensified by 'the vast multiplications of knowledge', and the 'vast multiplications of populations' in Europe and North America in the nineteenth century. Second, he emphasizes the way such momentous changes brought about 'dislocations in time and space' leading to the subject of experience being 'temporalized'. In other words, 'the temporal situation of the subject of experience – situated within the contours of his or her own life and within the "events" of history more generally conceived – is a constituent element in the nature of that experience'.[59]

Third, he confirms that it was in the last decades of the nineteenth century, when Enlightenment and liberal myths of progress or revolution had long since surrendered any mass credibility and industrialization was creating seismic social and psychological upheavals, that a 'crisis consciousness arose'. The sense of historical time as accelerating, in conjunction with the general 'collapse of ontological continuity', helped generate the apocalyptic sense of the 'new' which Schleifer sees as one of the hallmarks of modernism.[60] This palingenetic element is also bound up with the diffusion of what he calls 'the logic of abundance' resulting from the proliferation of new experiences and perspectives on the world that could not be accommodated within 'traditional' frames of reference. Fourth, his book explores evidence of 'modernist time' not in the artistic sphere alone, but in cultural and scientific narratives that would a few decades earlier have assumed the homogeneity of time and the neutrality of the narrator/observer, but in which conventional accounts of objective reality were now subverted or transformed. This involved refracting external events through a variety of techniques such as analogical thinking, the invocation of non-Newtonian, 'cyclical' time, and the contrivance of collisions between past and present so as to produce a redemptive sense, not of an atemporal plane of existence outside history, but of a 'new time' accessible *within* historical time. [61]

NIETZSCHE'S MODERNIST REVOLT

It will put some much needed flesh on these steadily accumulating bones of 'idealizing abstraction' if we illustrate some of the main features of the ideal type of modernism we have assembled so far with one of the outstanding figures of the revolt against Modernity-as-Decadence, Friedrich Nietzsche. In an essay written shortly after the creation of the Second Reich in 1871 on the lessons to be drawn from the philosophy of Arthur Schopenhauer, an outstanding specimen of 'negative Romanticism' in the realm of ideas, he warns of the catastrophic spiritual drought that the West was facing now that its vast reservoirs of collective values and meaning once provided by 'culture' were drying up so rapidly:

> How, then, does our philosopher view the culture of this age? Very differently, of course, from those professors of philosophy who are so delighted with the new state and the present state of affairs.[62] If he reflects on the universal frenzy and the accelerating tempo, the disappearance of contemplation and simplicity, it almost seems to him as if he were seeing the symptoms of the complete destruction, the total extirpation of culture. The flood of religion recedes, leaving swamps or puddles behind; the nations veer apart once again in the most violent hostility, impatient to massacre one another.[63]

Nietzsche lists further symptoms of cultural decadence: the fragmentation of academic disciplines, the unbridled materialism of the educated classes, the growing worldiness and lovelessness of society. The conclusion he draws is that: 'Everything, contemporary art and scholarship included, serves the approaching barbarism. The educated man has degenerated into culture's greatest enemy by denying the general malaise with lies and thereby impeding the physicians.'[64]

As the last phrase makes clear, this is no world-weariness, but a mood of passionate outrage at the state of a European society whose myth of progress seems to be propelling it towards the abyss of nihilism. The ideas put forward in the collection of essays – *Untimely Meditations* or *Unmodern Observations* (1874) – from which this passage is taken are thus not simple 'meditations' or 'observations' from the side-lines of history. Rather they are calls for a spiritual awakening, for a rebellion against prevailing reality launched from the mythic centre of a future society based on a revolutionary set of *healthy* values, one that Nietzsche is striving to bring into existence through the power of ideas. This is why he calls his observations 'unzeitgemäss' – 'untimely', 'out of step with the age', not 'anti-' but 'un-modern'. They rail against the present because, anticipating the central theme of the major works that are to follow such as *Thus Spoke Zarathustra* (1883–85) and *Beyond Good and Evil* (1886), they are *reflexively* laying the foundation for a different time, a new age, an alternative modernity, for a new type of man, the superior human being, the *Übermensch*.

This is certainly 'cultural pessimism' or 'cultural despair', but they have been radicalized to a point where cynicism is transformed into utopian hopes of imminent metamorphosis, of *Aufbruch*, of palingenesis. At this point it conforms to the 'pessimism as strength' referred to by Nietzsche in the notes he wrote for a projected book entitled *The Will to Power*. It is a pessimism that has overcome the 'pessimism as decline' associated with refined cosmopolitan sensibility and the 'decay of cosmological values' to become 'strong'. A lucid expression of this aspect of the activist, life-affirming mode of pessimism, which does not give in to nihilism but seeks to triumph over it, occurs in Nietzsche's description of his struggle to defeat his 'inner Wagner', whom he eventually came to identify not with the salvation of culture, but with a 'sick' variant of Romanticism which insidiously deepened decadence while appearing to transcend it:

> What does a philosopher demand of himself first and last? To overcome his time in himself, to become 'timeless'. With what must he therefore engage in the hardest combat? With whatever marks him as the child of his time. Well, then! I am, no less than Wagner, a child of this time; that is, a decadent: but I comprehended this, I resisted it. The philosopher in me resisted. [...] For such a task I required a special self-discipline: to take sides against everything sick in me, including Wagner, including Schopenhauer, including all modern 'humaneness'. [...] My greatest experience was recovery. Wagner is merely one of my sicknesses.[65]

This drive to ('will to') self-healing led Nietzsche to make a crucial distinction between two types of nihilism, passive and active. When 'passive nihilism' prevails in society '[t]he strength of the spirit may be worn out, exhausted, so that previous goals and values have become incommensurate and no longer are believed; so that the synthesis of values and goals (*on which every strong culture rests*) dissolves and the individual values war against each other: disintegration'. On the other hand, on a personal level nihilism can be a sign of the capacity 'to posit for oneself, productively, a goal, a why, a faith', expressing itself as 'a violent force of destruction – as active nihilism'.[66] Employed in this way nihilism is endowed with a dialectical, self-overcoming component which is implicit in the description of Russian anarchists bent on overthrowing the Tsarist system as 'nihilists'. It now acquires a constructivist, futural thrust diametrically opposed to its connotations when it is used to refer to the absolute denial that life has any transcendent value or purpose (or what will be called in Chapter 3 'nomos' and 'logos').

As we have seen, Nietzsche's intense experience of the decadence of late nineteenth-century modernity, of a contemporary history feverishly progressing on the surface, but corroded from within by *passive* nihilism or 'Romantic pessimism', provoked his personal crusade against Modernity in the spirit of 'Dionysian pessimism' and 'active nihilism'. Hence the recurrent motif in his works of the theme of 'creative destruction' epitomized, for example, in the epigraph to this chapter or his assertion in *Ecce Homo* (1888): 'Yes-saying life: negating *and destroying* are conditions of saying Yes'.[67] He conceived his writings not as commentaries on the age, but as the manifestos of a cultural rebellion that would one day be powerful enough to overthrow the present decadent order and institute a new society based on the new 'tablets of values' that he had formulated. This far-reaching *metapolitical* – and ultimately socio-political – goal of his 'philosophy' is made explicit in the preface to his projected book *The Will to Power*:

> For one should make no mistake about the meaning of the title that this *gospel of the future* wants to bear. 'The Will to Power: Attempt at a Revaluation of All Values' – in this formulation a *countermovement* finds expression, regarding both principle and task; a *movement* that in some future will take the place of this perfect nihilism – but presupposes it, logically and psychologically, and certainly can come only after and out of it.[68]

According to the ideal type we have constructed it is Nietzsche's drive to provide a 'gospel of the future' that would inspire a successful revolt against decadence that makes him paradigmatic of *modernism* in the maximalist sense we are using it. It is a line of interpretation extensively corroborated by the Nietzsche expert, Robert Gooding-Williams, who explores the will to trans-formation that forms the central theme of *Thus Spoke Zarathustra* under the term 'Dionysian Modernism', an impassioned attempt to re-enchant the world, to break out of the 'iron cage' which Max Weber saw modernity assembling around the human soul. It is consistent with our definition that Gooding-Williams uses modernism in this context to mean 'novelty-engendering interruptions of received practices and traditions', which he sees as bound up with the fantasy of an 'aesthetic purity that initiates artistic beginnings unstained by the past, [...] beginnings from ground zero'.[69] He thus presents Zarathustra as 'the personification of a modernist will to cultural change',[70] and as embodying the 'modernist ambition' to entice others to join him in surrendering to, in *going under* to 'passional [sic] Dionysian chaos' and so collectively revalue human passions and produce 'new values that stymie the perpetuation of the rationalistic culture of the last and small man'.[71] This is clearly a project whose scope extends far beyond the renewal of art and literature, and envisages new beginnings that are far from being exclusively 'artistic' (unless the transformation of the world is itself seen as the ultimate aesthetic event!).

EPIPHANIC AND PROGRAMMATIC MODERNISM

In the poem 'Between Birds of Prey' Nietzsche warned: 'If you love abysses you must have wings, and not just hang there'.[72] Modernism is not just the awareness of falling from a dizzy height into the ravine of contemporary nihilism. It is also the attempt magically to sprout wings and pull out of the stall before the crash, and if possible fly off into a new sky and a new sunrise. However, while we have emphasized Nietzsche's struggle to understand and *cure* the sickness of Modernity by inspiring a countermovement *against* decadence, his work contains glimpses of another side to his 'strong pessimism'. There is an intriguing passage in *Thus Spoke Zarathustra*, the sacred text of his 'Dionysian Modernism', which evokes the experience in which in 'the blinking of an eye' – the literal meaning of the German word for 'moment' – the prophet realizes that the 'infinitesimally *small*' is the source of the greatest joy. Upon realizing this he '*instantly*' falls 'into the fountain of eternity'.[73] Another such moment seems to have occurred in his mountain retreat in Sils-Maria:

> Here I sat, waiting, waiting – but for nothing. / I was beyond good and evil, / Enjoying the whole play of light and shade, / Nothing but lake, noon, and *aimless* time / Then suddenly, my sweet friend, one became two / And Zarathustra walked past.[74]

These lines conjure up what in his investigation of mystic experience Rudolf Zaehner terms a 'panenhenic' experience, where the interconnectedness, the 'oneness' of all Being dramatically reveals itself.[75] It is a meditative state in which the self feels enclosed within a 'higher' reality and which is complete in itself: it is 'aimless'. It requires no further action to be realized. Nietzsche is rudely awakened from this state of grace by the figure of Zarathustra, his fictional alter ego symbolizing the prophetic, activist, rebellious aspect of his work, his desire to covert those who read him into 'fellow-creators' charged with the mission to 'inscribe new values on new tables'.[76] Nietzsche's acute experience of the encroaching nihilism of Modernity makes it impossible for him to accept that meditation can be an end in itself. Instead, it must serve the cause of bringing about a truly 'great event', of endowing the empty happenings of modernity with purpose and a soul:

> The greatest events – they are not our noisiest, but our stillest hours. The world revolves, not around the inventors of new noises, but around the inventors of new values, it revolves *inaudibly*. And just confess! Little was ever found to have happened when your noise and smoke dispersed. What did it matter if a city had become mummified, and a statue lay in the mud![77]

Gooding-Williams stresses that, in contrast to the unbridled optimism with which he wrote *The Birth of Tragedy*, Nietzsche is not confidently promulgating a new gospel in *Thus Spoke Zarathustra*. Rather, he is exploring the proposition that social reality might be transformable through a trans-valuation of values, harbouring considerable doubts about the feasibility of such an undertaking: 'Nietzsche's doubts: his scepticism as to the viability of Zarathustra's modernism, animates and organizes the plot of *Zarathustra*'.[78] In Kermode's terms, Nietzsche was therefore walking a tight-rope stretched between palingenesis as a social and metapolitical (but ultimately also *political* and *revolutionary*) project and palingenesis as a 'fiction', as a literary trope, a utopian metaphor with which to investigate reality without any concrete strategy or even desire to intervene directly in the historical process in order to realize it.[79]

I would go further by suggesting that this scepticism indicates an unresolved tension in Nietzsche's creative response to modernity between two poles discernible within the modernist sensibility, the modernist '*imaginaire*'. The one we have been concerned with so far is 'programmatic' modernism, in which the rejection of Modernity expresses itself as a mission to change society, to inaugurate a new epoch, to start time anew. It is a modernism that lends itself to the rhetoric of manifestos and declarations, and encourages the artist/intellectual to collaborate proactively with collective movements for radical change and projects for the transformation of social realities and political systems. Charged with programmatic modernism an artist/intellectual may deliberately set out directly to inspire such movements and act as the catalyst which precipitates historical transformation.

However, in Nietzsche's evocation of 'aimless time' we catch a glimpse of another form that can be assumed by the modernist rejection of Modernity, namely the cultivation of special moments in which there is *Aufbruch* of a purely inner, spiritual kind with no revolutionary, epoch-making designs on 'creating a new world'. In this case the decadence of Modernity induces a protracted sense of disorientation and unreality, punctuated by fleeting episodes of spiritual union with something 'higher' – what T. S. Eliot called 'the unattended Moment, the moment in and out of time'.[80] We propose to call the type of artistic modernism that gravitates around unexpected and unsustainable experiences of the lightness of being[81] 'epiphanic', after James Joyce's use of the term 'epiphany' to describe such moments of this-worldly revelation.[82]

A host of modern novelists, poets, painters, and thinkers have dedicated their creativity to giving form to the unexpected suspension of Modernity's anomy, for the sudden sensation of 'standing outside' normal time – 'ecstatically' in its etymological sense. In the terminology proposed by Frank Kermode, for example, they are moments in which the soul-destroying *chronos* of 'waiting time' magically gives way to *kairos*, 'a point in time filled with significance, charged with meaning derived from its relation to the end'.[83] Such transient moments are the cornerstone of the vast architectural edifice of Marcel Proust's *In Remembrance of Things Past*, a profoundly modernist work in conception however much the style is devoid of Expressionistic experimentation. In a famous passage the narrator describes the sudden rush of ecstasy induced by eating a Madeleine bun – or rather by the 'involuntary memory' of the same sensation in his youth – as a revelation of 'the essence of things [...] outside time', which briefly turned him into an 'extra-temporal being'.[84] It is an experience which Zaehner describes as a spontaneous example of the 'natural mystic experience' described by Zen Buddhists as *satori*.[85] It was a sensation familiar to Virginia Woolf who distinguished between the part of life 'not lived consciously', but wrapped in 'a kind of nondescript cotton wool', and 'moments of being' which reveal that all human beings are connected within a much greater scheme of things. In such moments it is as if – or perhaps, if the claims of mystics are true, the higher reality becomes apprehendable through the realization that – 'the whole world is a work of art; that we are parts of the work of art'; 'we are the words; we are the music; we are the thing itself'.[86] As one critic explains, in such a moment an individual

> is not only aware of himself [sic] but catches a glimpse of his connection to a larger pattern hidden behind the opaque surface of daily life. Unlike moments of non-being, when the individual lives and acts without awareness, performing acts as if asleep, the moment of being opens up a hidden reality.[87]

It is possible to take Kafka as paradigmatic of 'epiphanic modernism', inhabiting a creative universe utterly remote from the panoramic vision of the human condition that Zarathustra enjoyed from his mountain-peaks. It was a universe of tortured reflexivity, of profound, tragi-comic ambivalence, of being both enraptured and tormented by the existence of a higher, purely spiritual world he could only tantalizingly glimpse. Zygmunt Bauman remarked that 'Kafka's life, like modern life, is an in-between life: in between in space, in between in time, in between all fixed moments and settled places that, thanks to their fixity, boast an address, a date, or a proper name'.[88] His extraordinary creative energies were channelled into exploring metaphorically, and with almost total disregard for the public success or impact of his work, the aporias of a daily existence in which he felt trapped – though in a cage with bars wide enough for him to get through had he wanted.[89]

Meanwhile he stayed on a constant vigil for those ephemeral moments when a hidden harmony or higher purpose mysteriously revealed itself to him. Kafka could not conjure 'miracles' or 'illuminate' things on the stage-set of contemporary life, since 'everyday life is already a miracle': 'The stage is not in darkness. In fact it is flooded with daylight. That is why human beings close their eyes and see so little.'[90] When he was overtaken by 'moments of being' he was able to live the 'happy times' or 'good moments' he referred to in a diary entry of 1922 when his tuberculosis was already at an advanced stage. In it he discusses (with himself) his sense of abandonment and isolation from his fellow human beings, a plight which he attributes to the fact that he draws his main source of nourishment ('Hauptnahrung') not from society, but from 'other roots breathing another air', defiantly commenting that 'even if these roots are shrivelled, they are still more hardy'. This means he is caught between the attraction of 'his world' and that emanating from 'the world of human beings'. Most of the time, however, he is 'elsewhere', so that the prospect of being dependent on others for a sense of reality would mean being totally lost, an 'immediate execution'. In fact, those who love him do so precisely because he is 'abandoned'. They feel that 'in my good times I enjoy the freedom of movement that I am totally lacking here *on another level*'.[91]

One such 'good time' is evoked in the last of Kafka's 'observations on sin, suffering, hope, and the true way':

> It is not necessary that you leave the house. Remain at your table and listen. Do not even listen, only wait. Do not even wait, be wholly still and alone. The world will offer itself up to you so as to reveal itself: it cannot help it. It will writhe before you in ecstasy.[92]

THE POROUS MEMBRANES OF MODERNISMS

When cultural historians talk about what we have identified as the 'programmatic' and 'epiphanic' permutations of modernism they can easily seem to be talking about unrelated phenomena. Thus Malcolm Bradbury and James McFarlane claim at one point that 'the Movement principle was an essential constituent of Modernism' and that its spirit was thus summed up in the tendency of artists to promulgate their aesthetic principles in 'a programme and a manifesto'.[93] Yet their own collection of essays includes Richard Sheppard's analysis of the 'crisis of language' which lies at the heart of so much modernist poetry and which is epitomized in Hugo von Hofmansthal's *The Lord Chandos Letter*.[94] Here, through an alter ego, the poet expresses 'real pessimism about the possibility of revivifying language' and hence the very possibility of art. It is in the context of a brooding sense of being condemned to live in an age in which the unity of the world has become irretrievably lost, of being born too late, that

> Eliot, Yeats, and Rilke seem, like Hofmansthal, to be intent on preserving the sense of eternity which inhabits a few fragments left to them by the past, and without which, they suggest, all would be blackness, boredom and despair.[95]

Once reality has fragmented – as it did for such writers – to a point where language loses its capacity even to express it adequately then the basis for programmatic modernism disappears. Kafka certainly belongs in their company, but, apart from illustrating how ecstatically the 'sense of eternity' could still be experienced when the veil lifted, he also underlines how erroneous it would be to treat 'epiphanic modernism' as hermetically sealed from the compartment represented by its 'programmatic' counterpart. As will become clear in the course of this book, the divide between them resembles the bars of what he described as his open cage, with artists in one category sometimes displaying elements of the other, or even shifting from one pole to another. It is a pattern we have already encountered in the case of Julius Evola, who moved from Dada to an idiosyncratic form of fascism, and his admirer Gottfried Benn, who after converting to Nazism belatedly returned to the safe haven of apolitical poetry.

It is consistent with the permeability of the membranes separating the two spheres of modernist activity that unattended 'moments of being' formed the eye of the storm of ideas that Nietzsche hurled against the bastions of Modernity in an outpouring of literature designed to bring about a revolution in Western consciousness. By the same token even Kafka could fleetingly entertain in his diary the possibility that at the core of his intense experience of unreality lay the kernel of a Jewish outlook on Modernity that had much wider potential resonance, and that, 'but for Zionism', might have 'developed into a new esoteric doctrine, a Kabbala'. He immediately reins in this audacious thought by conceding it would take 'an almost inconceivable genius to drive his roots deep into former centuries to create the old ones [of faith] anew'.[96]

What nipped in the bud any initiative to form or even join a movement for change in Kafka's case, however, was the yawning gulf not just between 'lifetime' and 'worldtime' explored by Hans Blumenberg, but between his inner and outer times. In a diary entry written three days before his reference to a new Kabbala, Kafka describes how he has been going through something like a nervous breakdown, with his internal and external realities utterly out of sync and tearing apart from each other: 'The watches do not agree. The inner one races on in a diabolical or demonic, or in any case inhuman way, while the outer one haltingly goes at its normal pace.' Nevertheless, he feels that if the 'smallest part of him' can keep from going under, he may be able to let himself be carried along by this 'chase', this 'assault against the last earthly frontier'.[97] Significantly, this assault on the material world is not only that of an outsider, but it is not under his command: instead, he is swept along by it.

The ambition of programmatic modernists is made of sterner stuff. They project the new vision, the new temporality contrived deep inside their inner world onto 'history', planning utopian ways in which society can be harmonized and synchronized with it, and leading assaults not against earthly frontiers, but citadels of decadence. The architect Walter Gropius may have stated in the immediate aftermath of the First World War that 'Today's artist lives in an era of dissolution without guidance. He stands alone. The old forms are in ruin.' But these lines are part of a speech made to the congress of the World Council for Art in Berlin which made it clear that he had utter faith in his own mission to help formulate the 'new form' of the 'old human spirit' invalidated by History, and the 'new order' destined to arise from ashes of the old.[98] The pessimism that informs his manifesto-like declaration is 'strong', the nihilism 'active', the destructiveness is 'creative'. They stem from Gropius' visionary brand of socialism that convinced him of the possibility of regenerating society through the power of architecture and design, and would turn him, as head of the Bauhaus, into the foremost visionary architect of his age, the very stuff that exhibitions on Modernism are made of.

EXPLORING THE MODERNISM OF FASCISM

Perhaps the difference between the epiphanic and programmatic modernist is ultimately one of temperament. In another diary entry Kafka uses a hallucinatory metaphor to evoke the extreme differences in the way individuals can react to the 'disaster' of Modernity:

> Seen with the impaired vision of a purely earthly perspective, we are in the situation of some passengers whose train has had an accident in a long tunnel at a point where the light of the entrance can no longer be seen, and the light of the end of the tunnel

is so faint that we have to keep looking for it, for we keep losing sight of it, and we are not even sure which is the entrance and which is the exit. But all around us we can see, because of the confusion of our senses or the extreme sensitivity of our senses, unearthly creatures, and a kaleidoscopic play of images which, according to the mood and the degree of injury of the individual, is either entrancing or exhausting. 'What shall I do?', or 'Why should I do it?' are not questions to ask in these parts.[99]

Programmatic modernists were more prone than epiphanic ones to be entranced rather than exhausted by Modernity, and to feel spurred on to formulate projects for its transcendence within an alternative modernity the other side of decadence at the end of the tunnel. Until 1914 both groups were vastly outnumbered by millions of apparently ontologically secure human beings, who, like the servant in Kafka's short story *New Beginning*,[100] heard no trumpets summoning them on a 'truly awesome journey' whose destination could only be designated as 'away-from-here'. From a modernist perspective they were Nietzsche's somnambulistic 'modern men'[101] or 'last men'. 'Hopping like a flea on a shrinking earth',[102] they somehow managed to live lives outwardly attuned to modernity, oblivious of the deepening cultural crisis that modernists of all varieties believed was undermining its spiritual and social foundations.

By now aspects of our own project should be coming into focus and certain knots of aporia and paradox should be starting to loosen. If the juxtaposition of 'modernism' with 'fascism' still sounds surreally discordant it has much to do with the way historians have tended to concentrate on the artistic mani-festations of modernism's revolt against decadence in a way that ignores their profound links to wider social and political phenomena. This tendency was encouraged by the fact that, especially in the field of poetry and literature, this revolt frequently took the form of cultivating sublime aesthetic or spiritual moments which stood out like flashes against a darkened sky, expressing a sensibility which was generally – though with some outstanding exceptions – utterly alien to the ethos of Fascism and Nazism. Much of the secondary literature on Modernism thus constructs it as an apolitical topic replete with ambivalences stemming from its 'dialogic' nature.

As we shall see in Chapters 5 and 6, some historians of painting and architecture and numerous cultural historians have extended the depth of field sufficiently to keep in focus the multi-plane nexus connecting modernist art, especially in its programmatic mode, to non-artistic movements of renewal, both social and political. However, even here there has been a general tendency to concentrate on the socialist or communist affiliations of artists and ignore the abundant evidence of collusion of modernists with ultranationalist and racist forms of politics. Thus, even in the most 'cutting edge' publications on the subject, modernism is still constructed as a cultural phenomenon having a natural affinity with (left-wing) socio-political phenomena. In contrast, we are presenting it in these pages as a palingenetic force that can express itself directly in revolutionary social and political movements, left and *right*, without aesthetic mediation.

This point can be illustrated by the description of the movement which is offered by Christopher Wilk in the introduction to the catalogue of the major exhibition on modernism which he staged in London in 2006. He states that modernism was 'a loose collection of ideas' covering a range of movements and styles in many countries, especially those flourishing in key cities in Germany and Holland, as well as in Paris, Prague, and, later, New York.

> All these sites were stages for an espousal of the new and, often an equally vociferous rejection of history and tradition; a utopian desire to create a better world, to reinvent the world from scratch; an almost messianic belief in the power and potential of the machine and industrial technology. [...] All these principles were frequently combined with social and political beliefs (largely left-leaning) which held that art and design could, and should, transform society.[103]

Two things stand out. First, Wilk's definition clearly reaches across disciplines to converge with those of Eksteins, Berman, and Osborne on the conceptualization of modernism as a force that bursts asunder the narrow confines of the aesthetic, even if it still presents modernism as a *primarily* aesthetic and cultural phenomenon. Second, it suggests a predominant association of modernist creativity with the politics of the Left. Christina Lodder's article on modernist utopianism follows Wilk's introduction and is clearly based on similar premises. She argues that modernism 'straddles the divides between affirmations and rejections of modernity within spiritual visions, Dionysian and rationalistic attitudes towards the Machine Age, and communist and socialist versions of a radical political ideology'.[104] Again, the Right is left out of the picture, and it is *utopianism* that is treated as the common denominator between, say, Constructivism and Bolshevism, not modernism.

The task this book has set itself is to present an alternative synoptic interpretation to the currently available ones sampled here. It presents modernism as capable of not just collaborating with socio-political movements, but of expressing itself directly in them unmediated through art, and liable to manifest itself in the values and politics of the Right no less than the Left. It argues that the modernists involved in right-wing ultranationalist social and political projects of renewal were usually – the Italian Futurists and Ernst Jünger are exceptions – at pains precisely *not* 'to reinvent the world from scratch', but to build on what they saw as healthy elements of the past in order to construct their utopia. Once reconfigured ideal-typically in this way, 'modernism' can provide a tool for understanding why fascism could attract the allegiance of some avant-garde artists, namely because a powerful elective affinity could arise between artistic and political revolutionaries who radically rejected the present and longed for the dawning of a new age. Far more importantly, it allows fascism to be interpreted as an expression of modernism in its own right, despite the aggressive stance some of its advocates can adopt to some forms of *aesthetic* modernism when they condemn it as an expression of Modernity's degeneracy rather than its cure.

Before we reach this stage in the argument, however, we must introduce a lengthy excursus to consider the deeper psychological and social dynamics of modernism, both in its search for epiphanic release from the curse of Modernity and in its quest for programmatic utopian solutions capable of putting an end to decadence once and for all. Such quests involved not just temporally lifting the veil of History to glimpse a transcendent reality, but diverting its flow as if it were a mighty river to be tamed so as to inaugurate a new era and a new modernity. The next chapter will thus be devoted to probing into modernism's relationship to an ancient paradox – or perhaps the ultimate aporia: the longing for immortality in the face of what human reflexivity, in a *negative* epiphany peculiar to our species, reveals to be the certainty of our physical death within individual, linear time. The starting point for our new itinerary will not be in the world of art or thought, but the realm of social and political ritual, apparently far removed from the agonies and ecstasies of modernism's 'creative destruction'. However, as will become clear, it is the persistence of liturgical behaviour into the modern age, the way social crises seem to intensify ritual activities rather than eradicate them, that can supply vital clues to the nature of the existential 'homelessness' generated by the maelstrom of modernity. It also helps us understand the mechanisms through which 'modern' human beings set about satisfying what Habermas calls 'the need for reassurance' stemming from our unique consciousness of time, and sense of vulnerability it induces, by finding alternative shelter.[105]

3
An Archaeology[1] of Modernism

The Terrors and Decadence are two of the recurring elements in the apocalyptic pattern: Decadence is usually associated with the hope of renovation.

Frank Kermode, *The Sense of an Ending* (1966)[2]

Regardless of the site we choose for our excavation, we shall always hit the same ancient underground river which feeds the springs of all art and discovery.

Arthur Koestler, *The Act of Creation* (1964)[3]

From the Neolithic era has come clear evidence of ideas of space, number, life, death, and rebirth, which have preserved the same symbolic forms through subsequent millennia.

Anthony Stevens, *Ariadne's Clue* (1998)[4]

THE RITUALS OF MODERNITY

In one of the first non-Marxist attempts to make sense of Fascism as a new political phenomenon, the future American professor of religion and philosophy, Herbert Schneider, writing shortly after Mussolini inaugurated the Fascist era, drew attention to the extraordinary energy that the new regime was pouring into creating a 'new religion'.[5] It was an observation to be amply confirmed over the next decade. On 18 December 1935, for example, at the height of international tensions over Italy's invasion of Ethiopia, the *duce* presided over a carefully orchestrated display of national solidarity in the 'Giornata della fede' – a refined pun meaning both 'Day of the Wedding Ring' and 'Day of Faith' – on which hundreds of thousands Italian women, led by the Queen herself, publicly sacrificed their wedding rings as a contribution to the campaign to recreate the Roman Empire in the Horn of Africa. In return they received a token ring of base metal, whose symbolic value in hindsight was certainly not the one intended by the regime's propagandists.

Once in power the Third Reich eclipsed even the Third Rome in its capacity to stage a constant flow of ritual events participated in by hundreds of thousands and communicated to millions more through the growing power of radio and cinema. One of the high points of the annual Nuremberg rally of the NSDAP was the moment when Adolf Hitler solemnly touched Nazi banners with the 'Blutfahne', the Swastika flag allegedly stained with the blood of fellow-conspirators who fell in the abortive Munich putsch of November 1923. The 'Fahnenweihe', or 'consecration of the flags', was just one of countless newly invented rituals that together constituted the continuous liturgy of the elaborate 'political religions' presided over by Mussolini[6] and Hitler.[7]

How the conspicuous ritualistic, liturgical aspect of fascism is to be located into modernity is a highly contentious topic.[8] 'Empirical' historians of a liberal persuasion tended in the past to dismiss such episodes as little more than totalitarian – and hence according to the received wisdom of the day 'reactionary' – propaganda (or simply as 'brainwashing'). Marxist scholarship on the other hand has traditionally approached it as a rich case-study in the phenomenon described by Walter Benjamin as the 'aestheticization of politics', a concept which has given rise to a whole cottage industry of its own exploring the way art was cynically used to camouflage reaction in right-wing regimes.[9] An important twist in the story of the Left's engagement with fascism's special brand of spectacular politics, however, comes in the book *Society of the Spectacle* when the Situationist Marxist, Guy Debord, describes its 'immensely irrationalist' rationalism as

> a violent resurrection of *myth* which demands participation in a community defined by archaic pseudo-values: race, blood, the leader. Fascism is *technically-equipped archaism*. Its decomposed *ersatz* of myth is revived in the spectacular context of the most modern means of conditioning and illusion.[10]

This astute – though from our point of view misconceived – comment could be taken as the starting point for the next stage in our definitional expedition into the conceptual jungle of 'modernism'. The 'synoptic historical interpretation' we are gradually piecing together in these chapters radically reinterprets the fusion of the archaic with the modern under fascist regimes Debord believed he was observing, locating it in a quite different causal nexus. It is transported from a Marxist context in which it is seen essentially as a function of reactionary *capitalism* – in its 'terroristic' rather than liberal and 'progressive' incarnation – to a new conceptual framework centred on revolutionary *modernism* understood as a force that perpetuates archaic elements of human consciousness. Its revised definition places considerable weight on the crucial role played by the 'resurrection of myth' and other apparently backward-looking, regressive elements within Western modernity in its revolutionary *left*-wing manifestations as well. After all, by the time Italian housewives were donating their wedding rings to sustain Fascism's murderous occupation of Abyssinia, Soviet Russia had long been staging increasingly elaborate, bellicose, and symbolically multi-layered May Day parades in Moscow, keying into primordial associations of spring with cyclic renewal and strength no less energetically than the Third Reich.[11] Stalin's purges and show-trials also had their share of age-old ritualistic and spectacular elements.

It is no less wrong-headed to approach the modern enactment of overtly mythic spectacles steeped in religious symbolism as a monopoly of totalitarian regimes. June 2005, for example, saw the staging off England's south coast of 'Nelson 200', the largest international 'regatta' of warships in history, assembled to commemorate the victory of the British over the French at Trafalgar and the death of its principal architect and martyr. The pageant included the 'Drumhead Ceremony', a traditional religious service of remembrance for those fallen in battle in which soldiers parade on three sides of a hollow square, the fourth consisting of drums being piled up in the form of an altar draped with regimental colours. At the climax of the version of this militaristic mortuary rite that had been specially choreographed for the day, three torches were lit beneath Portsmouth's Naval War Memorial, symbolizing – so the press release informed us – 'remembrance, service, and hope'.

A 'PRIMORDIALIST' THEORY OF MODERNISM

The Fascist Day of Faith in Rome, the Blood Flag ritual at the 1938 Nuremberg rally, and the Drumhead Ceremony in Portsmouth are all examples of the 'rites of power' studied in detail by the social anthropologist David Kertzer. His research makes a powerful case for recognizing the central role played in modern societies no less than in premodern, 'traditional' ones by ritual practices and public liturgies which serve the function of enacting political ideas, whether by legitimizing the status quo or challenging its hegemony. At the heart of such liturgies lie symbols which constitute an essential part 'of the tissue of myth that helps structure an understanding of the political world'.[12] In performing this role they are only a specialized form of the symbol systems that provide a 'primary means by which we give meaning to the world around us; they allow us to see what we see, and, indeed, what we are'. It is through symbols that human beings 'confront the experiential chaos that envelops us and create order', objectifying and reifying the symbolic categories we construct to the point of seeing them as 'the product of nature rather than as human creations'.[13]

In this respect there is fundamental kinship and unbroken historical continuity between the elaborate rituals and symbols that celebrated the divinity of the Pharaohs or guaranteed the continued revolutions of the sun for the Aztecs, and the theatrical, cultic politics deliberately employed by the Fascist and Nazi regimes to create their new order. Both were states based on 'spectacular politics' in which ritual was inextricably linked to power, however, not to dupe the exploited masses into passivity as Guy Debord implies. Rather their function was to transform into a lived reality for their population and enemies the cosmological myths underpinning Fascism's 'total' experiment in injecting the mythic legacy of Rome into contemporary Italy, and the bid by the Nazis to create an Aryan empire at the heart of twentieth-century Europe, both regimes availing themselves of the latest technology at their disposal.

Kertzer's observations point to the need to revisit the whole issue of the 'modernity' or 'anti-modernity' of the activist revolt against decadence launched by what we have called 'programmatic modernism', and consider how far its thrust towards renewal is to be relocated within archetypal, perennial aspects of human culture. The *telos* towards which we are working in this phase of our 'reflexive metanarrative' is the reformulation of the ideal type of modernism offered in the last chapter in a way that integrates the 'archetypal' component of human symbolic behaviour whose existence we are attempting to establish here. Our argument posits an innate human faculty for projecting onto the 'brute facts' of external reality an infinite abundance of significant patterns, of symbolic meanings, of ultimate purposes, all rooted in a higher order, whether immanent or supernatural. It will be argued that this archaic faculty has continued to shape historical events despite the apparently hostile conditions created by increasing secularization and materialism that prevailed in the Europeanized world after the eighteenth century.

In arguing that existing theories of modernism can be complemented by recognizing the determining role played in it by mythopoeic forces whose origins are lost in the mists of time, we are seeking to establish in the broad field of academic studies concerned with modernity/modernism the equivalent of what Anthony Smith calls the 'primordialist' approach to nationalism. Those theorists he terms 'modernists' – a term shorn of all the connotations it acquires in the present book – insist on the comparative recentness of the nation state and of the mass allegiance it has commanded in key moments of modern history. By contrast, proponents of 'primordialist' theory argue that the many variants of populist nationalism that have come to dominate contemporary history are direct descendants of the powerful affective ties of ethnic and cultural belonging engendered by social groupings (tribes, peoples, civilizations etc.) in *premodern* times, groupings which with hindsight can be seen as embryonic 'nations'. Smith himself adopts a version of primordialism, for example, when he states that 'nations are linked by the chains of memory, myth and symbol to that widespread and enduring type of community, the *ethnie*, and this is what gives them their unique character and the profound hold over the feelings and imaginations of so many people'.[14]

It should be emphasized that in reconstructing the primordial (perennial, universal, archetypal) psycho-social mechanisms subsumed in modernism, we have no intention of presumptuously formulating an overarching anthropological theory about 'man', something which, as we have seen, would be completely out of step with anthropology in its present extremely reflexive and self-critical state. Nor is this a throwback to the discredited pseudo-positivist theories of an 'archetypal unconscious' associated with Carl Jung and Joseph Campbell. Instead, in the spirit of 'transdisciplinarity'[15] we propose to syncretize a composite ideal type from theses on human culture propounded by experts working in several different specialisms. Their point of convergence lies in postulating the presence of an innate human drive to achieve transcendence and create new cultural worlds, a drive which becomes particularly active whenever an established order is threatened by collapse.

THE NEED FOR A 'SACRED CANOPY'

There are several possible starting points for our syncretic ideal type of the primordial human need to create 'culture' which played such a formative role in shaping modernism. The one chosen here is the theory developed by the highly influential sociologist, Peter Berger, who, long before poststructuralists started painstakingly deconstructing human realities – as well as attempts by anthropologists to conceptualize them – became fascinated by the cognitive and ritual techniques through which our species fashions 'society' in its countless permutations. Written over four decades ago, *The Sacred Canopy* offers what is by modern standards a remarkably unreflexive and un-self-critical meta-narrative of 'man' as 'out of balance' with 'himself' and forced to engage in sustained communal work, both material and symbolic, to complete the biological processes that bring 'him' into being.

For Berger the 'human world' is a natural birthright that has to be created artificially.[16] The resulting complex of beliefs, practices, and rituals subsumed under the term 'culture' serves not only to provide the basis for physical survival, but to guarantee to members of society the experiential certainty that their lives are an integral part of a higher reality, one whose cohesion stems from a cosmic, suprahuman ordering principle which he terms 'nomos'. At least in premodern societies, culture takes the form of a relatively homogeneous, stable, normative cosmology expressed in infinitely variegated and nuanced patterns of belief and practice. Though this culture has been 'made' by collective human agency, it is experienced by those immersed in it as a lived reality as handed down by a 'tradition' originating in an eternal metaphysical reality whose meaningfulness is usually not conceived in anthropocentric terms at all, but 'cosmocentrically'.

Berger locates the most important function of each cultural nomos in its ability to act as a 'shield against terror'[17] – a phrase also used by David Kerzter in his analysis of the importance of political ritual.[18] Perhaps it is because modern European culture was palpably losing its protective properties that Rainer Maria Rilke portrayed the beauty of an Angel's embrace as 'nothing but the beginning of terror' in the famous opening lines of *The Duino Elegies* – one of the most powerful poetic accounts ever written of the human quest for transcendence in a secularizing world. Premodern culture offers existential shelter from a cosmos devoid of intrinsic spiritual purpose and which, if contemplated without the protective lens of myth, makes nonsense of all human efforts to create anything of lasting value. More importantly, each cultural nomos – and there have been countless thousands of them in the course of human history – creates the illusion that personal death can be overcome by locating 'the individual's life in an all-embracing fabric of meanings that, by its very nature, transcends that life'.[19] Separation from society is the ultimate human nightmare since it submerges human beings 'in a world of disorder, senselessness and madness', making 'anomy unbearable to the point where the individual may seek death in preference to it'.[20] According to Berger's 'synoptic interpretation' of the human condition, religion in its manifold forms originated when the socially constructed nomos was 'cosmicized' and projected communally onto the universe as a higher order, thus forming a 'sacred canopy' over the abyss of meaninglessness. The opposite of the sacred is thus not just the profane but, at a deeper level, chaos, the intimation of nothingness. The recurrence in premodern cosmologies of the theme that the sky or the heavens are a vault held in place by a cosmic ordering principle to serve as a 'firmament' for existence thus expresses a longing for metaphysical rather than astronomical certainties.[21]

It is appropriate that among the copious notes that Samuel Beckett took on his own ontological state can be found one of the most lucid articulations of the difference between transient, rationalized, objectivized terror of something and the primordial angst of the void, of finitude, of cosmic absurdity on which it draws:

This is how angst starts growing and [begins] to be transformed once more into the old, familiar physical pain. How translucent this mechanism now seems to me: at its core lies the principle that it is better to be afraid of something than of nothing. In the first case only a part of you is threatened, in the second case the whole of you, not to mention the monstrous quality that is an intrinsic and inseparable part of the incomprehensible, one might even say the boundless. And that angst is truly completely incomprehensible, for its causes lie in the depths of the past, and not just in the past of the individual (in this case the task would perhaps not be insoluble and life would not necessarily be tragic), *but of the family, the race, the nation, human beings, and of nature itself.*[22]

THE EROSION OF OUR 'SHELTERING SKY'

On the basis of his 'grand récit' Peter Berger offers his own version of what Koselleck was later to call the 'temporalization' of history. He sees the breaking up of the sacred canopy in the West as leading inevitably to the 'revolutionary transformation of consciousness' associated with modernity. When growing numbers could no longer experience history as a 'theodicy' – the vindication of God's benign plan for humanity whatever evils it seems to cause or accommodate – 'an age of revolutions' was inaugurated in which what he calls 'nomization' was for the first time conceived as occurring through 'human actions in history'.[23]

Berger's interpretation of the impact of modernization on the human need for a shield against anomy imparts fresh significance to the extensive research carried out by Carl Jung and his acolytes – however flawed their own inter-pretation of their findings – to demonstrate the existence of 'archetypes' of symbology and mythopoeia that structure the human bid to make sense of the world. Another 'Jungian', the psychiatrist Anthony Stevens, makes the premise of this type of enquiry explicit in the introduction to *Ariadne's Clue*, a panoramic 'Guide to the Symbols of Humankind': 'Everything that constitutes a core experience of human life has been put into symbols and tales which, for all their manifold variety, often share striking resemblances to each other, wherever on this planet they have been brought into being.' Thus 'symbolism is a language that transcends race, geography, and time. It is the natural Esperanto of humanity.'[24] On the basis of the impressive empirical evidence not just for the universality of certain motifs in religious symbolism, legends, and folk tales, but for common mythic denominators in the social organization of all human culture, Stevens claims that 'it is hard to escape the conclusion that the propensity to create them is implicit in the mind-brain of humanity'.[25]

The methodological assumptions on which Jung's theory of archetypes is based, especially in its original Aryanized version,[26] are now almost as discredited within professional anthropology as the methodology used by Sir James Frazer in his encyclopedic survey of universal mythological patterns relating to death and rebirth, *The Golden Bough* (1890). Nonetheless, there seems to be impressive evidence from ethnography, social anthropology, and cultural history for an evolutionary propensity of the human 'mind-brain' to 'nomize' the potentially psychologically devastating facts of biological existence and so construct elaborate symbolic fictions of life's significance. Furthermore, it is a faculty that continues to imbue life with transcendent meaning and find strategies for re-enchanting the world, no matter what inroads secularization has made into the dominant world-view, even if it means erecting the nomic canopy within and not above the historical process.[27]

My first, somewhat rudimentary attempt to explore this factor in the 'psycho-dynamics' of fascism which I proposed in *The Nature of Fascism* centred on Arthur Koestler's theory of transcendence propounded in *The Ghost in the Machine* (1970).[28] The heuristic value of Koestler's profoundly secular approach to the issue is complemented by the theological analysis of Richard Fenn, who argues that the steady erosion of a once largely homogeneous 'temporal matrix'[29] in the West has left contemporary human beings increasingly 'exposed' to the passage of secular time. The resulting loss of the suprahistorical dimension means that they now live 'in an indefinite duration in which even the traditional symbols of transcendence are clearly temporal', and 'liturgies and expectations of a millennial transfusion of grace are merely a matter of time'. Modern human beings continue to make sacrifices and pilgrimages, but for most they are sacrifices to 'human deities' and pilgrimages to 'earthly cities'.[30]

An even deeper resonance with Berger's analysis of the existential plight of contemporary humanity is encountered in the prolific writings of the Romanian intellectual, Mircea Eliade. His own search for transcendence led him to support the Romanian Iron Guard and dedicate himself to yoga before moving to the US soon after the war. Here he quickly established himself as one of the world's most influential experts on the universal patterns of symbology exhibited by the world's cornucopia of religious myths and rituals. Central to his own 'synoptic interpretation' – which has been widely criticized for its totalizing, metanarrative sweep[31] – is the recognition that the fundamental generative impetus behind human culture is the ontological imperative to ward off the 'Terror of History'[32] by maintaining the belief in a sacred time, space and history scrupulously demarcated from the profane world of human mortality. According to Eliade, the mythopoeic needs of '*homo religiosus*' have not changed, despite the intensive secularization promoted by modernity. As a result, even if consciously 'modern man' has largely lost touch with or consciously denies the world of suprahistorical, timeless realities on which the stability and cohesion of 'premodern' societies is/was founded, 'he still retains a large stock of camouflaged myths and degenerated rituals':

> Strictly speaking, the great majority of the irreligious are not liberated from religious behaviour, from theologies and mythologies. They sometimes stagger under a whole

magico-religious paraphernalia, which however has degenerated to a point of caricature and hence is hard to recognize for what it is.[33]

Such accounts of modernity confirm T. S. Eliot's observation in *The Four Quartets* that 'Human kind cannot bear very much reality.'[34] The universality of the rich symbolic worlds associated with 'religion' and 'myth' conjured up out of cultural activity throughout human history suggests – at least to disenchanted eyes – that the purposefulness of human existence has always depended on the power of collective mythopoeia and ritual to construct the viable material and spiritual 'home' needed to make bearable the otherwise intolerable human condition. From the perspective of evolutionary ethics (which is only one perspective among many), human beings appear to be culturally, or even genetically, 'programmed' to erect an essentially fictitious 'sheltering sky'[35] to conceal the metaphysical emptiness of the heavens. After all, a sense of cosmic purpose has considerable survival value, providing protection from what would otherwise be experienced as a negative epiphany of 'man's' utter isolation and finitude.[36] Long before Darwinism tore down the ontological divide separating human beings from the primates and consigned religion to the recycle bin of human culture, such a negative revelation appears to have been recorded by the Catholic philosopher Blaise Pascal in his *Thoughts* (1660) when he wrote 'The eternal silence of these infinite spaces fills me with dread'.[37]

Within Berger's master narrative, the drive to fabricate cosmological meaning so as to drown the metaphysical silence is to be considered as much a defining property of our species of the genus 'homo' as *erectus, faber, economicus, familiaris,* or *sapiens*. Indeed, if the curiously named sub-species 'sapiens, sapiens' (i.e. our 'race' of human beings) is taken to imply 'aware of knowing', and hence a euphemism for 'knowing we are dying' (*sapiens moriens*), then the sense of tautology evaporates. It becomes a synonym for what has also been called *homo reflexivus*, and by extension *homo religiosus, homo symbolicus,*[38] *homo ritualis,*[39] *homo sacer,*[40] *homo utopicus,* or, most important of all in the present context, *homo transcendens*.[41] In short, human beings are endowed with a species-defining need – a drive, an instinctive will – to transcend their inexorable personal mortality, a feat they are able to achieve, if only symbolically, through mind power, the extraordinary creativity of their mythopoeic, ritual, and symbolic consciousness.

THE SEARCH FOR TRANSCENDENCE

A number of alternative accounts of the human condition might have served equally well as the starting point for our deliberations on the primordial basis of modernist, palingenetic reactions to Modernity. One is the 'logotherapeutic concept of man'[42] propounded by the professional psychoanalyst Viktor Frankl. After the war he drew on his experience of survival and death in Auschwitz and Dachau – which encompassed the murder of members of his own family – to give his therapy a new focus. The result, 'logotherapy', sets out to reactivate the capacity of every suffering individual to endow life with meaning ('logos') through a conscious act of 'self-transcendence' that can rise above the most profound temptation to utter nihilism and self-destruction.[43] In the course of his own investigations into the anthropological foundations of his therapy, published as *Logos und Existenz* (1951), he coined another defining epithet for 'man': '*homo patiens*' to signal the paradox of persistent human attempts to find a justification of existence through suffering, or what he termed a 'pathodicy'.[44]

Frankl's therapeutic system is based on a deep faith – a faith tested by the unimaginable physical and emotional pain of his own life – in the capacity of human beings who have been 'disinherited'[45] by modernity to create a substitute source of meaning for themselves, despite being deprived of their natural 'birth-right' to a traditional nomos. It implies a concept of meaning that seems close to what Kafka had in mind when he observed to his friend Gustav Janouch:

> Truth is what everyone needs in order to live, and yet cannot be obtained or acquired from anyone else. All human beings must continually produce it out of their own inwardness, otherwise they will perish. Life without truth is impossible. Perhaps it is truth itself.[46]

Working at least on partially convergent premises to those of Berger and Frankl, the social psychologist Ernest Becker devoted enormous intellectual energy to synthesizing wide-ranging theories of human culture in a deliberately 'transdisciplinary' manner to construct a cohesive view of the 'human animal'. The metanarrative he assembled stresses the deep ambivalence of our unique self-awareness. Our power and importance as the only species able to shape its own world, and hence be a cultural as well as a social animal, comes at the cost of the knowledge of our mortality, so that 'despair and the death of meaning are carried by man in the basic condition of his humanity'.[47] With Berger, Becker believes that in order to ward off the terror that would otherwise be induced by the certainty of personal death, human beings have – in a creative act unique in the animal kingdom – constructed 'hero systems' which turn mortals into actors living out their destinies within a suprahuman, metaphysical order. The result has been the countless mythological, cosmological, and religious systems of human history which Becker sees as the 'fictions' which 'have from prehistoric times hung like a flimsy canopy over his world'.[48] Thus he characterizes all cultures as 'basically styles of heroic death denial', their essential project being to make possible the transcendence of mortality.[49] It is 'man's innate and all-encompassing fear of death' that 'drives him to attempt to transcend death through culturally standardized hero systems and symbols'.[50]

Two decades later, despite the fact that the deconstruction of the humanities was by then in full swing, Zygmunt Bauman, whom we have already encountered as one of the world's foremost sociologists of modernity, undertook what he himself calls the 'immodest' task of investigating various 'life strategies' through which human beings contrive to suppress the realization of death. It is a realization that he associates with the primordial moment of human reflexivity which the Judeo-Christian tradition locates in the mythic moment when 'humans tasted of the Tree of Knowledge', and were immediately expelled from the paradise of being fully at home in the world enjoyed – though enjoyed *unreflexively* – by other animals.[51] From then on we have been condemned to ex-ist, to stand outside, rather than to 'be'. Bauman too sees culture as a means of providing nature's outsiders with a sense of 'transcendence', the 'permanence and durability which life, by itself, so sorely misses'. It is the certainty of personal death that 'makes permanence into a task, into an urgent task, into a paramount task – a fount and a measure of all tasks – and so it makes culture, that huge and never stopping *factory of transcendence*'.[52]

What is common to all such accounts of human existence is that they posit a sense of a transcendent purpose and meaning as a literally *vital* necessity – a necessity of a visceral, biological nature – in order to keep at bay the paralysing, life-threatening ontological terror that would immediately set in if reality was experienced without a 'nomos', a sense of transcendence. It is this possibility that Kafka was presumably alluding to when he talked in his diaries of the 'immediate execution' that would take place for him were there not another – suprapersonal, spiritual – level to existence.[53] The object of this primordial terror and fear is not just physical non-being, but the subjective, *phenomenological* collapse of the meaningful 'world' that each person is condemned either to inherit or to contrive in order to live out fully his or her biological existence.

THE TERROR OF CRONUS

It will have become obvious that accounts of culture as the product of the human bid to survive not just physically but psychologically in an indifferent cosmos imply qualitative distinctions in the experience of time. More precisely, they recognize a dual temporality at the experiential core of human existence. A definitional property of transcendence, after all, is that the mythopoeic faculty enables individuals to 'climb beyond' the linear temporality of a single, ephemeral, unrepeatable life rushing headlong towards eternal extinction, at which point they subjectively enter another type of time. From a secular perspective at least, for it is one that admits any number of religious and mystic interpretations, the resulting experience appears to be a remarkable 'trick' of reflexivity. Like a self-induced out-of-body experience, a sense of transcendence allows us to see our own life as part of a larger reality or pattern of existence that will outlive us and in which we are subsumed, neutralizing, or at least numbing the pain induced by the prospect of total loss.

In his *The Sense of an Ending* Frank Kermode dwelt on the distinction between three notions of time: ordinary, 'clock-time' (*chronos*); a 'point of time filled with significance, charged with meaning derived from its relationship to the end' (*kairos*);[54] and *aevum*, a time 'neither temporal nor eternal' 'in which things can be perpetual'. He points out that Romans used *aevum* to translate the scholastic Greek *aion* meaning 'the new order of time', a new historical dispensation.[55] However heuristically useful this tripartite scheme in the context of his own inquiry into the apocalypticism of modern literature, it better suits our own heuristic investigation into the temporality of modernism if we replace the God Chronos (Xronos), the father of Zeus and personification of cosmic time, with Cronus (Kronos), known to the Romans as Saturn, the monstrous incarnation of human time.[56] It was a scene from the popular mythology surrounding this Titan that inspired Francisco de Goya's famous portrait painted in 1815 of an obscene ogre-like creature devouring his own children (see Figure 8), an image which brings out the full terror of an all-consuming, mortal, *Cronic* time that denies any escape route to transcendence. This we propose, following Kermode's recommendation, to contrast with *aevum*, used as a generic term for transcendental time in its many modes. These include and subsume the moments of '*kairos*' that from Kermode's description clearly correspond to what we have called 'epiphanic' time, as well as to the far more protracted but nonetheless historical, *sub*-eternal concepts of immortality fostered by a temporalized history. It is particularly when the concern with reinstating aeval time opens up the prospect of a 'new age' that its affinity with the time of 'programmatic modernism' and social or political rebirth becomes palpable.

Though Kermode muses on whether *kairos* and *aevum* are just 'a rootless fantasy rather than a heuristic fiction', i.e. an ideal type, it is worth noting that there is some basis for such a distinction in anthropology. The possibility that inhabitants of non-Western cultures experience time differently is a topic which has naturally fascinated Western ethnographers, and a vast amount has been written on the contrasting temporalities encountered all over the world wherever globalization has not completely eradicated 'traditional society'. This is difficult terrain, however, on which interlopers from other disciplines

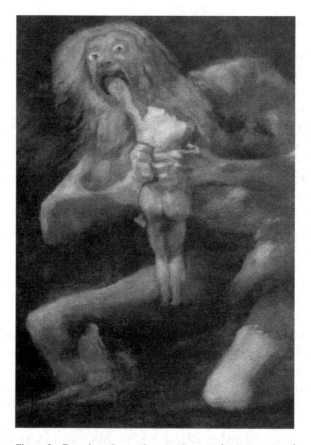

Figure 8   Francisco Goya, 'Saturn (Cronus) devouring one of his sons' (c. 1815).

© The Prado Museum, Madrid. Reproduced with kind permission of the Prado Museum.

should tread with caution. Some years ago the social anthropologist Andrew Gell wrote a devastating critique of the differing schemes of qualitatively different temporalities postulated by such luminaries as Émile Durkheim, Edward Evans-Pritchard, Claude Lévi-Strauss, Edmund Leach, Jean Piaget, and Henri Bergson (which would apply even more to the likes of Carl Jung, Joseph Campbell, and Mircea Eliade). In the conclusion of *The Anthropology of Time* he issued a stern warning to those who would like to formulate a dualistic or tri-partite model of human time experience of the sort proposed by Frank Kermode and myself:

There is no fairyland where people experience time in a way that is markedly unlike the way in which we do ourselves, where there is no past, present, and future, where time stands still, or chases its own tail, or swings back and forth like a pendulum.[57]

Gell insists that experts are constantly confusing particular events occurring within 'physical', 'biological', 'social' or 'psychological' processes with objectively different phenomenological *times*, whereas it is time – intrinsically homogeneous, unitary, and unifying – that actually coordinates such processes. I should stress, therefore, that I am not arguing that concepts such as 'Cronus' and 'aevum' have any scientific basis as terms referring to objective properties of time as a physical property. What legitimates their use as ideal-typical constructs – and not as pseudo-scientific or philosophical categories – is the abundant evidence for the existence of social and psychological events and processes which can be associated with two contrasting and perfectly 'normal' perceptions (*experiential* 'constructs' or 'imaginings') of existence: in the first it is lived from the individual, atomistic, egocentric point of view as entropic, linear, unidirectional time leading inexorably to a personal death; from the second, it is viewed from an imagined suprapersonal social, anthropocentric, or cosmocentric perspective in which each individual life and death, even one's own, is seen as part of a suprapersonal, transcendent scheme of things. Both these perspectives are sanctioned by empirical reality, for our lives are objectively both unique *and* simultaneously an integral part of wider – often *repeated* and *cyclic* – social and biological patterns common to all humanity.

This dualism may even have some deep-seated correlation to a distinction made by philosophers of time to which the arch-sceptic, mercilessly positivistic Gell nevertheless attaches considerable importance.[58] This is between the dynamic, open 'A-series' of time which moves from the past to the future via an ever moving present, and the static, closed 'B-series' in which past events are fixed in chronological sequence having 'for all time' occurred either before or after each other. Perhaps the unique reflexivity of *homo transcendens* has enabled us not only to commute between a personal and social experience of life, but between a present-oriented vision and one projected forward to a future where our lives have already occurred and can be seen within the metaphorical and symbolic consciousness part of a greater pattern of social meaning or higher cosmic order. This would certainly make sense of the universal aspiration to 'leave a mark' or 'bequeath a legacy' for those who come after or in some other way give life a transcendent purpose, even if it is only to write a book about transcendence or modernity which temporally modifies the academic paradigm.

The complexities of human time are – on a human temporal scale at least – open to infinite speculation by human beings attempting to make sense of their manifold subjective experience of it and the 'reality' that underlies them. What *can* be stated as a matter of record is that there is considerable ethnographic data – however contestable or scientifically dubious the generic temporal matrix within which they are interpreted – to demonstrate the universal importance to human societies throughout history of a *belief* in transcendent modes of time and of *experiences* of different temporalities, whatever their 'objective' scientific or philosophical foundation. 'Premodern' societies are/were dominated either by the ritually reinforced belief that the meaningfulness of society continues after the death of any one individual, or that personal life itself has a supreme value independent of society. It is thus a value that outlives physical death through the continued symbolic importance of the deceased to the society that survives them, or through the communal belief that after death they pass to a metahistorical realm in which their life will continue, if not physically then spiritually. In one way or another, religious rituals celebrate the symbolic triumph of what we are calling in this book 'aeval' time over 'Cronic' time.

It is consistent with the simplistic model of human temporality we are positing that in their introduction to a collection of essays on the remarkable diversity of the world's mortuary rituals in non-Christian societies, the social anthropologists Maurice Bloch and Jonathan Parry see the common denominator between them in the way each ceremony enacts the triumph of the forces of *collective* life over personal death. The need to hold such ceremonies stems from the fact that 'individuality and unrepeatable time are major existential problems which must be overcome if the social order is to be represented as "eternal"', in other words *aevum* must prevail over Cronus. They contrast this imperative with the situation in 'contemporary western cultures' where it is the individual who is given a 'transcendental value' and the ideological stress is on each person's 'unique and *unrepeatable* biography' (another strategy for guaranteeing a sense of transcendence).[59] In the present context what stands out is that, whether the emphasis is on the renewal of society and the irrelevance of the individual, or on the unique importance of the individual and the unimportance of the worldly plane, funerals defiantly enact the triumph of regeneration in the face of death. In premodern cultures they help keep in place and intact the sacred canopy which threatens to come apart at the seams for all those affected by the death of a loved one or the member of a community.

A glimpse into the supreme importance of transcendent time to traditional societies, though within the orbit of life rather than death can be gleaned from Angela Hobart's detailed investigation of the Galungan festival in Bali. In this (to Western eyes) astonishingly elaborate 'healing ceremony', the processions carry statues representing cosmic spirits called Barongs and the Lord of the

Forest Rangda so as to 'demarcate a sacred orbit, a mandala, an expanded social universe'.

> The regenerative power that these figures embody draws humans, gods, and benign spirits into the 'magic circle of creation'. In this protected space participants are progressively imbued with the ordering and purifying qualities of the cosmos. The integrating, centring, dynamic underlying the festivals enables humans to remake their realities in line with the moral and social norms of the village community. The corollary of this is that the person extends his or her consciousness of responsibility to the spirits, the forces of nature, in the environment. As a result, the land prospers and plants flourish.[60]

Hobart argues that such rituals ensure traditional medical systems remain 'embedded in cultural assumptions regarding the association between body, society and cosmos'.[61] The entire Galungan ceremony can thus be seen as the symbolic re-enactment and re-energizing of the nomos of Bali culture, a vitalistic celebration of the 'world' created to complete and underpin biological survival on the island which reinforces the role of healers in 'bridging' the seen and unseen.[62] It dramatizes the perpetual presence of a supra-individual and suprahuman realm in which the entropic, Cronic, 'A-series' time of personal mortality is ecstatically defeated and transcended not just symbolically but *phenomenologically*, however much icy water of scepticism is thrown on the *objective* reality of such an experience by Gell's postmortem. Indeed, from the perspective of Hobart's book, his demystifying analysis of the anthropology of time unwittingly illustrates what Carl Jung called the 'unparalleled impoverishment of symbolism' presided over by modernity that has led to gods being reduced simply to 'psychic factors' and 'archetypes of the unconscious': 'Since the stars have fallen from heaven and our highest symbols have paled, [...] heaven has become for us the cosmic space of the physicists, and the divine empyrean a fair memory of things that once were.'[63]

TMT

Another relevant interpretation of the peculiar cultural dilemma faced by the inhabitants of the West's disenchanted modernity is provided by a group of social psychologists whose work is informed by Terror Management Theory (TMT). It originated in the 1980s as a means of formulating answers to the question 'why do humans seem to have such a desperate and pervasive need to view themselves as valuable (i.e. to have self-esteem)?'[64] Its starting point was Ernest Becker's analysis of self-esteem implicit in such books as *The Birth and Death of Meaning* (1962) and *The Denial of Death* (1973), where he presented it as the product of the uniquely human capacity 'for symbolic, temporal, and self-reflective thought'. This, he argues, has 'greatly enhanced our ability to survive in a wide variety of environments', but its considerable downside is our awareness of personal mortality. As a result 'we have the capacity to wonder why we exist and consider the possibility that the universe is an uncontrollable, absurd setting in which the only inevitability is our own ongoing decay toward absolute annihilation'. In this perspective self-esteem can be interpreted as an existential defence mechanism, integral to the 'cultural world that imbued the universe with order, predictability, meaning, and permanence'. It is part of an instinctive mechanism of denial without which we would be *'paralyzed with terror'*.[65]

The full relevance of TMT to understanding modernity emerges in a more recent refinement of the model in an article which concentrates on 'group reification and social identification as immortality strategies'.[66] In other words, it investigates empirical evidence for the hypothesis – and its theorists go to considerable lengths to test it empirically *as* a hypothesis – that the self-esteem derived from identification with social groupings or movements which are perceived to be successful helps 'defeat death' symbolically and counteract existential malaise ('depression'). It does this by supplying a powerful phenomenological, subjective sense of belonging to a 'higher' temporality that in a modern secular society, though not suprahistorical and metaphysical, is still suprapersonal, and *transcendent*. This is underlined by the epigraph chosen for the article. Taken from a study of the 'murderous' aspect of social and cultural identities, it singles out two fundamental human drives: first, 'the striving for a vision of the world that transcends our existence, our suffering, our disappointments, which gives meaning – however illusory – to life and death'; second, the need for people 'to feel connected to a community which accepts them, which recognizes them, and within which they can be quickly understood'.[67]

In the course of developing their argument its authors make three points that have a direct bearing on our own synoptic interpretation of the human need for transcendence. First, contemporary behaviour, such as the rise in self-esteem when the national football team does well in the World Cup, is a function of *primordial* (archetypal) patterns of behaviour stemming from the imperative to create a cultural 'world' as a shield against the terror of non-existence. In their exposition of this thesis they stress that individuals have different temperamental 'needs for closure', so that the drive to take refuge in transcendent cosmologies varies in potency from person to person.

Second, they relate the driving force behind the modern quest for transcendence in its myriad disguised forms to the 'weak symbolization' that prevails under modernity. This they see emerging with the diffusion of 'new, revolutionary ideas about the nature of man and his place in the universe' by Enlightenment thinkers, the culmination of over two centuries of growing conflict between a theological, humanistic, and a scientific world-view. They claim that the attempt of the *philosophes* to replace the theocentric, transcendental teleology of Christianity with an anthropocentric, historicizing one precipitated a dysfunction in the culturally embedded mechanisms of terror management.

Third, the authors imply that as a direct result of this dysfunction, modernity acquired its definitional properties as an era of *permanently* fragmented, weakened symbolization, thereby causing a perpetual crisis in the capability of Western culture to meet its inhabitants' primordial need for a cohesive 'vision of the world' and a sense of communal belonging. This explains the never-ending proliferation under modernity of strategies for anaesthetizing existential pain, a situation alluded to in Becker's cynical observation (expressed in singularly inappropriate gendered language) that 'Modern Man is drinking and drugging himself out of awareness, or he spends his time shopping.'[68] By relating the obsession with 'killing time' or numbing the emotional pain it induces with strategies to 'manage' the terror of the void, the article confirms Richard Fenn's analysis of secularized modern human beings as often 'waiting in quiet helplessness',[69] constantly vulnerable to a sudden attack of angst that bursts through the fragile coastal defences they have thrown up to preserve a small hinterland of personally constructed meaning they have colonized. For as Peter Berger observed, the new *nomoi* of modernity, the myriad modern tents and gazebos 'we' erect to ward off 'the terror of anomy' are 'forever threatened by the forces of chaos, and finally by the inevitable fact of death'.[70]

The way of imagining the 'modern' human condition proposed by TMT is explored with considerable creative power in Jean-Paul Sartre's *Nausea* (1938). This novel shows how the palliative against metaphysical suffering which Antoine Roquentin has subliminally sought in researching the part played by the Marquis de Rollebon in the French Revolution first loses its effectiveness and then evaporates entirely, exposing him to increasingly sustained attacks of existential anguish. The TMT article has further relevance to our argument by exploring one of the major human strategies for symbolically 'defeating death'. This consists of identifying with 'collective ideologies' which foster 'forms of experiential transcendence that extend into much of existence'.[71] Their case study in this way of managing terror is nationalism, 'an ideology particularly well-suited to buffer death-anxiety, since the national group is usually highly reified'. As a result the nation is seen as 'a timeless entity, and even in the absence of a state and an essence, is thought to characterise and unite all fellow nationals'.[72] Such an interpretation of the appeal of nationalism under the impact of modernity is corroborated by Zygmunt Bauman, who in the course of his investigation of human 'life strategies' devotes a whole section to analysing the power of nationalism to engineer the symbolic transcendence of death. This it does by encouraging the masses to participate in the ongoing project of the nation's 'immortality', an illusion readily manipulated to their own political ends by ruling elites.[73]

Anthony Smith also underlines the power of nationalism as a source of the transcendence needed to offset the peculiarly anomic conditions of modernity. He argues that 'the modern nation has become what ethno-religious communities were in the past: communities of history and destiny that confer on mortals a sense of immortality through the judgement of posterity rather than divine judgement in an afterlife'. Despite its 'dark side', Smith sees national identity as satisfying the needs of many modern human beings for 'cultural fulfilment, rootedness, security and fraternity', their 'craving for immortality'.[74] At this point the mythic 'homeland' at the heart of the nationalists' vision of the world has become the primordial 'home' discussed by Berger, their shield against ontological terror, their sheltering sky.

TEMPORALIZATION REVISITED

The convergent elements in the approach to modernity proposed by Becker, Bauman, and the proponents of TMT allow us to suggest a transdisciplinary model of modernity that renders the underlying dynamics of modernism less elusive. Such factors as the Renaissance, urbanization, religious schism, geographical discoveries, and the rise of literacy, science, and secular humanism formed a configuration of cultural forces in what came to be known as the 'Early Modern Period' which brought about a gradually intensifying 'symbolic crisis', as the sacred canopy fashioned by Christianity became ever more 'flimsy' and inadequate for the nomic needs of a growing educated elite. This crisis was considerably deepened by the joint impact of the Enlightenment and the American and French revolutions on the viability of the ancien régime not just as a political system, but also as a cosmological system and metaphysical shield.

According to some historians, the nomic crisis precipitated in the 4th century BC by Alexander the Great in the Middle East was resolved by the rise of Christianity, a totalizing suprahistorical world-view which provided what was to prove for centuries a durable and effective shield against ontological terror.[75] By contrast, the Enlightenment's solution to the threat of spiritual homelessness resulting from the erosion of Christianity's sacred canopy – a process it had done so much to accelerate – was to offer a vision of *secular* historical time as the site in which human nature could perfect itself through its own agency so as to create a collective *nomos* and a *logos* of its own making.

This process of temporalization added a new dimension to human reflexivity by making humanity a project to be realized in the future, thus channelling cultural, social, and political energies towards the realization of what Koselleck calls a 'temporalized utopia'. The many variants of this new cosmology – which became increasingly identified with 'progress' – underpinned and legitimated developments in liberalism, individualism, capitalism, rationalism, science, and industrial technology, and formed a new cosmological canopy, coexisting and partially overlapping with traditional religious and absolutist values, which for the first time was profane rather than sacred. Its presence helped alleviate the growing nomic crisis that in Early Modern Europe had been externalized in the wave of social pathology that fuelled the 'wars of religion' and 'witch-crazes' of the sixteenth and seventeenth centuries, and found symbolic expression in the canvases of Hieronymus Bosch.[75] However, the existential canopy provided by the myth of progress soon turned out to be made of inferior, even defective, material.

For one thing not all those disaffected with Christianity felt comfortable in the new mythic 'home' provided by rationalism. One thinker who achieved considerable influence by articulating his doubts about the progressiveness of contemporary civilization and fears of a coming age of anomy was Jean-Jacques Rousseau. He played a major role simultaneously in the Enlightenment, the 'counter-enlightenment',[77] and pre-Romanticism thanks to his realization that any revolution setting out to replace the ancien régime with a society based on reason would have to take steps to address the resulting nomic crisis, something that was beyond the scope of rationalism alone. As early as 1762 his theory of the 'social contract' advocated the deliberate manufacture of 'sentiments of sociability' and the institution of a 'civic religion' to maintain a sense of transcendence.

It was with an even greater sense of urgency that the Romantics trained their creative and intellectual powers on finding a remedy for the symbolic breakdown and loss of transcendence precipitated by the secular humanism of the Enlightenment. The result was an extraordinary outpouring of literature, poetry, paintings, and essays, some of which express visionary optimism about the possibility of restoring through the power of the creative imagination the spiritual wholeness of the world destroyed by materialism, rationalism, and science. Others are dominated by black moods of melancholy, despair, evil, and madness, evocations of an ontological terror too profound to be resolved by imagination and inspiration. Vivid testimonies to both the transcendent, 'panenhenic'[78] and the anguished, anomic poles of the Romantic experience of modernity are found in the works of such poets as William Blake, William Wordsworth, Guy de Maupassant, and Heinrich Heine.

In a passage of the travel diary he kept in 1829 Heine provides a memorable testimony to how the 'sacred canopy' no longer afforded shelter against terror to those with 'artistic' sensibilities and heightened metaphysical needs. Prompted by talk of the distraught state of Lord Byron's soul, he exhorts readers not to lament the poet's *Zerrissenheit*, – literally 'a state of being ripped to pieces' – a key term in the context of German Romanticism for extreme psychological stress and anomy. He insists they should instead direct their pity at 'the way the world itself has been rent asunder'. Being 'the centre' of that world, it is inevitable that the poet's heart should be 'pitifully torn apart' since it is impossible for it to 'stay whole' in a fragmented age. Indeed, those who do feel whole are only demonstrating their spiritual shallowness. Far from aspiring to be healed, Heine takes it as a sign of his higher calling as an artist that the Gods let his heart be 'rent by the great tear in the cosmos [Weltriss]':

> Once the world was whole, in classical times and the Middle Ages, and in spite of external battles there was still a basic unity in the world, and there were whole poets. We should honour these poets and enjoy their works; but all imitation of them is a lie, a lie that every healthy eye can see through and merits only scorn.[79]

In such a testimony to modernity as a phenomenological force, 'progress' has been recoded as regress, fragmentation, breakdown – in a word as 'decadence'. It was not until the 1850s, however, when the myth of progress was more widely undermined by a generalized sense of social malaise under the intensifying impact of modernization in some urban centres of the Europeanized world, that modernity entered a perceptibly new phase. It was signalled by the emergence of a critical mass within the West's intelligentsia of individuals who had what TMT experts call a high temperamental 'need for closure', but who could not find a 'home' in Christianity, traditional values, myths of progress, or the Romantic cult of the sublime. At this point aestheticism became a *counter-movement* to progress, the cult of beauty turned into an act of defiance in an age of mediocrity and vulgarity now felt to be beyond hope of redemption. For the new generation of the 'disinherited', art's function was to serve as a reminder of the spiritual world being lost. Their task was either to suspend Cronus through the evocation of epiphanic moments of revelation, or, for those whose pessimism was 'stronger', to overcome it permanently by contributing directly to the new visionary programmes needed to regenerate society and inaugurate a new historical age beyond decadence.

In *Madame Bovary* (1857), for example, Gustave Flaubert, driven by an obsession with the aesthetics of composition and style unprecedented in the history of the novel, explores the tragic consequences for a woman attempting to live out literary fantasies of passion and beauty imprisoned in a society dominated by the soul-destroying values of 'progress' and the spiritual emptiness of those around her. Her confused bid for transcendence delivers her into the hands of Monsieur Homais, the apothecary in the provincial town of Yonville where she lives, whose blind belief in medical progress contributes to Bovary's moral and physical destruction. Flaubert's entire literary career can be seen – indeed, it has been seen[80] – as the fulfilment of a self-appointed mission to weave a new sacred canopy out of the poetic, world-creating, power of language and so transcend the 'dead time' that was corrupting society from within. The novel explores vicariously, through the heightened but transferred reflexivity facilitated by fiction, the 'quintessential malady of modernity, the inability to incorporate time into experience'.[81] It sublimated into art the author's own 'temporal disorders' and their concomitant pathologies and neuroses, the very act of writing it offering a refuge from all-consuming Cronus.

THE BIRTH OF AESTHETIC MODERNISM

It was the conjuncture of the temporalization of history with the erosion of the myth of progress and the illusions of Romanticism in the second half of the nineteenth century that brought forth 'aesthetic modernism'. It has now emerged from our reflexive master narrative as a generic term for myriad coun-tervailing attempts by individual artists to resolve the deepening nomic crisis caused paradoxically by the growing societal power and material 'progress' of European civilization. In different ways and with varying degrees of self-awareness and creative power, modernists were seeking a sense-making, transcendent, *healing* 'vision of the world', as well as a community with which to share it, if only of fellow artists. According to 'the mood and the degree of injury' of individuals affected by the 'train accident' of Modernity described by Kafka, they either cultivated epiphanic moments in which the dark clouds parted to reveal, however briefly, a sky radiant with transcendent meaning, or, if more optimistically disposed, threw their energies 'programmatically' into the inauguration of a new world, a society with a reconditioned or brand new canopy, erected defiantly in the face of cosmic absurdity to protect the human gaze from the void.

In their idiosyncratic ways all modernists thus became an 'Angel of History'. In a famous 'thesis on history' Walter Benjamin describes this angel as seeking refuge from 'the storm of progress' which unlike mortals he is able to see as 'one single catastrophe, which keeps piling wreckage upon wreckage and hurls it at his feet'. The Angel strives to 'make whole what has been smashed'. But the storm blowing from Paradise has 'got caught in his wings' and 'drives him irresistibly into the future'.[82] Benjamin himself dedicated his creative energies not to restoring the wholeness of the past, but to finding the formula for 'exploding the continuum of history', thereby making room for a new nomos replete with shards of suprahistorical 'Messianic time'.[83] This is just one example of the countless ways that modernists sought 'new forms' of art in the hope that 'there were escapes from *historicism and the pressures of time*'.[84]

One expert on modernity who intuitively recognizes the defining role played by the quest for *temporal* transcendence in modernism is David Harvey. In *The Condition of Postmodernity* he states: 'Much of the aesthetic thrust of modernism [...] is to strive for [the] sense of eternity in the midst of flux.'[85] In support of this assertion he then cites an article by the philosopher Karsten Harries which, deeply under the influence of Mircea Eliade, argues that certain forms of architecture are to be seen as the symbolic expression of the human need to erect a defence against anomy by constructing symbols of a timeless reality: 'If we can speak of architecture as a defense against the terror of space, we must also recognize that from the very beginning it has provided defenses against the terror of time.'[86]

To substantiate this view he cites his mentor's assertion that in premodern societies 'a "new era" opens with the building of every house. Every construction is an absolute beginning; that intends to restore the instant, the plenitude of a present that contains no trace of history.'[87] In a purple passage of wilfully paradoxical prose, Harries claims that the modernist view of architecture leads to a concept of the beautiful as something that

> lifts us out of the life world, out of reality, carries us to a man-made paradise that, like every paradise, has no need for a house. Man now turns to beauty not to illuminate temporal reality so that he may feel more at home in it, but to be relieved of it: *to abolish time within time, if only for a time.*[88]

THREE CASE STUDIES IN CULTURAL MODERNISM

To bring alive this excessively abstract schema we propose briefly to consider three creative individuals whose work exemplifies salient aspects of the modernist revolt against decadence. Considerable critical attention has been devoted to Charles Baudelaire by historians of modernism. In 'The Painter of Modern Life' (1863) he became one of the first Europeans to combine the description of modernity as a world that has lost its ordering principle and mythic centre – a world of 'the transient, the fleeting, the contingent' – with the recognition that the artist's task is to wrest from it a sense of transcendence: 'the eternal, the immutable'.[89] It is consistent with this vision of transcendence that the draft epilogue to the second edition of *The Flowers of Evil* portrays the transformative process involved in poetry as that of a 'perfect alchemist' who extracts the quintessential 'gold' from the 'mud' of reality, thereby reversing the disenchanting impact of modernity and endowing the increasingly 'fallen' world with its own *aesthetic* sublimity, and hence this-worldly immortality, a simulacrum of the divine. He calls as witnesses to his triumph over 'dead time' suprahuman beings, 'angels dressed in gold, purple and hyacinth', metaphors that reveal how far art itself had become for Baudelaire the only available realm of nomos, a poetic world created through his artistic imagination that endowed his existence with a 'higher' meaning.[90]

The mainspring of Baudelaire's creativity seems to have been epiphanic 'moments of being'. These provided the temporalized suprapersonal perspective needed to evoke through sustained bouts of creative destruction the terror of Cronus, reconfigured as the 'evil' to be transformed into flowers of beauty. The result was a series of painstakingly crafted verses describing human life alternatively as cursed by *ennui*, by the tyranny of clock-time, or by the feeling of being eternally damned and punished, of being sucked under by a material world that has nightmarishly turned into a viscous quicksand. Yet such sonnets contrast with others recording times when, like Virginia Woolf in her 'moments of being', he glimpsed his 'connection to a larger pattern hidden behind the opaque surface of daily life'.[91] One such privileged moment is 'immortalized' in the famous poem 'Correspondences'. It describes a synaesthetic union of human beings with nature of the sort celebrated in the Bali festival of healing, in which 'Man passes through the forests of symbols/ Which watch him with familiar gazes'. Yet an abyss of historical time separates the traditional participant in the Bali rituals from the 'cursed' nineteenth-century poet surprised by the momentary joy of a panenhenic experience of unity with the world.

The most relevant trope in his poetry in the present context, however, is the theme of the blue sky, 'l'azur'. The metaphor of the albatross who is taunted by sailors for its ungainliness on the deck of the ship, and 'prevented from walking'[92] by wings designed to soar in the heavens, points to Baudelaire's profound urge to escape his 'exile on earth' and rise above the modern age of decadence to inhabit a celestial world which corresponds to his own faculty for transcendence. A study of the significance of the sky to his creative universe reveals the extraordinary degree to which his 'modernist' writings were drawing on archetypal imagery linked to the *topos* of the 'firmament', the metaphysical vault of heaven that paradoxically provides the solid basis of reality and which 'gathers together the dimensions of time and space and creates an accord between them'.[93]

In *The Marriage of Heaven and Hell* William Blake reminds us: 'The hours of folly are measur'd by the clock, but of wisdom: no clock can measure.' Both for Flaubert, whose *Madame Bovary* appeared in 1857, and for Baudelaire, whose 'Flowers of Evil' were published in the same year, art was generated by temporal *Zerrissenheit*, by the creative tension between the transcendent, nomic, aeval, primordial time of 'being' and the 'modern' clock time of rationalized, disenchanted 'existence'. It is consistent with this primordialist approach to their work that one of the most pre-eminent theorists in the field of the cultural theory of modernism, Fredric Jameson, cites 1857 as the 'crucial year' in the emergence of modernism. He portrays the art of Baudelaire and Flaubert as a response to the temporal crisis of modernity. Phenomenologically for those with their temperament, time had fallen asunder into 'chronometric' time on the one hand and on the other 'the deep, bottomless vegetative time of Being itself, no longer draped and covered with myth or inherited religion'. For Jameson, the crisis was a direct result of the disenchanting, disembedding impact of modernization we considered in the last chapter:

> Modernization, by stripping away the traditional representations with which human temporality was disguised and domesticated, revealed for one long stark moment *the rift in existence* through which the unjustifiability [sic] of the passing of time could not but be glimpsed.[94]

The echoes of the great rip that Heine saw being torn in the fabric of the cosmos are audible from such a passage.

Zerrissenheit was also the air that Nietzsche lived and breathed. We saw in the last chapter how in his writings the critique of Modernity moves beyond the sphere of aestheticism and contemplative philosophy to the realm of cultural criticism and metapolitics, the antechamber to social and political action. The relevance of the primordialist perspective on modernism to understanding his crusade to achieve transcendence becomes particularly apparent in those passages where he contrasts the nihilism of the modern world with previous ages when the 'sacred canopy' was still intact.

One such passage occurs in *The Birth of Tragedy*, which can be seen as the manifesto of a programmatic modernist convinced that the art of Richard Wagner heralds the stirring of mythic forces that will resolve the moral crisis of Europe caused by the breakdown of its mythic shield against terror. This becomes explicit when he declares that 'only a horizon defined by [or "framed by"] myth completes the unity of an entire cultural movement'. 'Images of myth' act as 'the omnipresent but unnoticed daemonic guardians' necessary to nurture a 'young soul': 'even the state knows no more powerful unwritten laws than the mythical foundation that provides its connection to religion.' By contrast, the West has degenerated to a point where its culture 'has no fixed and sacred primordial seat', and its inhabitants are thus deprived of a life-giving nomos. The fate of modern 'man' is thus to be 'eternally starving', always 'digging' and 'rummaging' in 'search of roots, even in the most remote of the most ancient worlds'. The West's obsession with the cultures and histories of non-European peoples reveals 'the loss of myth, the loss of the mythic homeland, of the maternal womb'.[95]

The same theme is taken up again in Nietzsche's *Unmodern Observations*. He laments the debilitating effects of the surfeit of historical knowledge flooding the West which 'by continually shifting perspectives and horizons, by eliminating the surrounding atmosphere, prevents man from acting *unhistorically*. From the infinity of this horizon, he then retreats into himself, into the smallest parish of his egoism, and there is doomed to arid sterility.'[96] The antidote he prescribes to this 'historical sickness' is immersion in the 'suprahistorical' forces of art and religion which cultivate the 'unhistorical' power that derives from voluntary seclusion 'within a limited horizon'.[97] In this context, the figure of Zarathustra can be seen as what Becker calls 'a heroic fiction' whose role is to inspire contemporary Europeans to transcend the decadence of Modernity and restore the mythic centre and limited horizon needed for a strong culture to re-emerge in Europe, even if it means ripping down once and for all the sacred canopy supplied by Christianity. Zarathustra's insistence on 'self-overcoming'[98] and of liberating the 'superior being' in us all is thus symptomatic of the primordial human need to neutralize the terror of nihilism, and to complete biological existence by the deliberate creation of a new nomic 'world' and a mythic 'home', in other words a new *culture*.

The highly idiosyncratic Marxism of the intellectual Ernst Bloch provides yet another permutation of the 'revolt against the modern world' thrown into relief by the primordialist perspective on modernism we have sketched. Though famous for his courageous Marxist stand against Nazism under Weimar, a study of *The Spirit of Utopia* composed at the height of the First World War shows the young Bloch taking a Dionysian, Zarathustran stand against the decadence of the world. He has absolute faith in his mission to act as midwife for the new world being born out of the death-throes of the old: 'In us alone the light still burns while earth and heaven collapse all around: the supreme creative, philosophical moment has arrived.'[99]

Bloch's longing to renew the transcendence of a world that has lost its transcendence cries out from the concluding chapter 'Karl Marx, Death and the Apocalypse'. Here he portrays himself as part of an elite working 'toward the *external* divination of the waking dream, toward the *cosmic* implementation of utopia'. History has assigned him his task: 'to cut new, metaphysical paths towards a new order, to summon up what is not there, to build into the blue that circumscribes the world, building ourselves into the blue, there to seek the true, the real, where the merely factual disappears – *incipit vita nova*.'[100] It is not cold facts but feverish dreams that will regenerate the world.

This theme is exhaustively explored in the three encyclopaedic volumes and 55 chapters of Bloch's *magnum opus*, *The Principle of Hope*, the fruit of a decade's scholarly research to document the omnipresence of utopianism in human history which he carried out in the US while in exile from Nazi Germany. It compiles a vast thesaurus of historical and cultural facts to demonstrate that the utopian thrust towards a better world is an integral component of every expression of human cultural activity: from fairy tales and poetry to totalizing philosophies of history and revolutionary ideologies, from daydreams and jokes to the music and drama of high culture, from religion and philosophy to technological inventions and geographical discoveries. It is latent in even the most tragic or negative portraits of reality.

The ubiquitous 'principle of hope' is the manifestation of a drive as fundamental for Bloch as the Unconscious was for Freudian psychoanalysis: 'the Not-Yet-Conscious'. The challenge of modernity is to turn utopia into a collective project for the construction of a better world. The last lines read:

> The root of human history is the working, creating human being who reshapes and overhauls the given facts. Once he has grasped himself and established what is his, without expropriation and alienation, in real democracy, there arises in the world something that shines into the childhood of all and in which no one has yet been: homeland.[101]

In such a scenario 'utopia' becomes synonymous with Berger's 'nomos', Frankl's 'logos', Baudelaire's 'sky', and Nietzsche's 'home', the 'maternal womb' of myth.

THE PRIMORDIAL DYNAMIC OF MODERNIST MOVEMENTS

The premises of a primordialist theory of modernism should by now have become, if not uncontentious, then at least clear. As Guy Debord intuited, the elaborate aestheticization of politics under Fascism and Nazism is indeed an 'archaism' in which mythic forces have been deliberately conjured up and spectacles calculatedly stage-managed in order to 'condition' the masses. However, this is no reactionary ploy to tighten the stranglehold of a capitalism fighting to the death against the attempted socialist revolution. Though manipulative and 'brainwashing' on one level, it *also authentically* expresses a quintessentially primordial human drive to resolve the unprecedented socio-political and *nomic* crisis through which European history was passing after the First World War by constructing a new order which would provide 'healthy' Italians and Germans with a new homeland, both material and mythic.

The primordial aspect of modern social and political movements for change has often been recognized. Norman Cohn points out in the conclusion of *The Pursuit of the Millennium* that though the 'old religious idiom has been replaced by a secular one, [...] stripped of their original supernatural sanction, revolutionary millenarianism and mystical anarchism are still with us'.[102] He presents the attempts by Marxists, Nazis, and the 1960s counter-culture to bring about a new age as precipitated by the same psychodynamic factors that drove marginalized groups in Early Modern Europe to hasten the end of a corrupt age and trigger the immediate winding up of History in the Apocalypse. Evil would finally be expunged from the world in God's ultimate act of 'creative destruction'.

Mircea Eliade also sees the primordial instincts of *homo religiosus* conspicuously at work in 'the various political movements and social utopianisms whose mythological structure and religious fanaticism are visible at a glance'. As an example he cites not only Marxism, but causes 'that openly avow themselves to be secular or even anti-religious', such as 'nudism or the movement for complete sexual freedom, ideologies in which we can discern traces of the "nostalgia for Eden", the desire to re-establish the paradisial state before the Fall'.[103]

We have seen that Terror Management Theory, Zygmunt Bauman, and Anthony Smith all interpret modern nationalism as providing a metaphysical refuge from mortality. Ernest Becker goes further, arguing that a chilling continuity can be detected in human violence and tyranny throughout history stemming from 'transference mechanisms', hero systems, and saviours, whether suprahuman or all-too-human, desperately needed 'in order to be able to stand life' now that we have made 'death conscious'. They serve to identify, localize, and demonize the mythic evil that threatens us, so transposing our instinctual drive to overcome the 'terror' born of reflexivity onto the fight to combat a temporalized 'enemy':

> From the head-hunting and charm-hunting of the primitives to the holocausts of Hitler, the dynamic is the same: the heroic victory over evil by a traffic in pure power. And the aim is the same: purity, goodness, righteousness – immunity. Hitler Youth were recruited on the basis of idealism. [...] Men cause evil by wanting heroically to triumph over it.[104]

It is the task of Part One of this book to show that the period between 1850 and 1945 saw the appearance of a host of European movements for cultural, social, and political renewal, all driven at least in part by the primordial *logos* of 'purity, goodness, and righteousness'. However 'religious' their dynamics, the secular ethos of modernity ensured that they now took the form of temporalized utopias constructed to immunize society against decadence and the terror of nihilism. They thus operated as permutations of what we have termed 'programmatic modernism'. Having completed our exposition of this argument in the next three chapters, Part Two will then explore the ways the two fascist regimes established after the First World War exhibited this species of modernism in the doctrines, political rituals, policies, and praxis through which they attempted to create a new order. The socio-political revolution they sought to achieve therefore exhibits an 'apocalyptic pattern' akin to the one that Frank Kermode identified in literary modernism, namely the conjunction between 'terror', 'decadence', and 'the hope of renovation'. This chapter has attempted to show that it is a pattern that spontaneously forms when the 'Not-Yet-Conscious' is thrown into frenzied activity by the primordial terror induced by modernity once its temporalized utopias break down and its mechanisms for 'killing time' lose their narcotic effect. A modern political movement born of nomic as well as socio-economic crisis is thus the manifestation of the collective search for a new nomos, a new community living under a new sky.

In the context of such speculations a passage in *Mein Kampf* about the vital role played by 'ethical-moral principles' in human existence assumes fresh significance. In it Adolf Hitler states that 'by helping to raise man above the level of bestial vegetation, faith contributes in reality to the securing and safeguarding of his existence'. Indeed, 'not only does man live to serve higher ideals, but [...] these higher ideals also provide the premise to his existence'. However, in itself 'a philosophy of life' [*Weltanschauung*] 'even if it is a thousand times correct and of the highest benefit to humanity, will always be irrelevant to the practical shaping of a people's life'. For this to occur its principles must 'become the banner of a fighting movement' which must secure 'the victory of its ideas' so that 'party dogmas' become 'the new state principles of a people's community, the *Volksgemeinschaft*'.[105]

In such passages the future leader of the Third Reich recognizes that the strength of a state depends on what Nietzsche from the standpoint of his Dionysian modernism called 'powerful unwritten laws'. He understands that the strength of a culture depends on a community bound together under a limited horizon, a horizon 'defined' and framed by myth. In the next chapter we will consider the insights offered by anthropology into the factors that enable a new movement and a new community to emerge at the height of a social and symbolic crisis. This will enable us to complete the ideal type of modernism to be used to resolve one of the fundamental aporias posed by fascism's relationship to modernism: its momentum towards realizing the utopia of a homeland conceived in mythic terms which are at one and the same time anti-modern and hypermodern, futuristic yet arch-conservative. In its various forms, fascism did not just operate like the twin-headed God Janus. Rather it resembled a single head with two pairs of eyes, one facing forwards, the other backwards, like the spectacle that faces Harry Potter when the evil Quirrell, masquerading as a school-teacher, takes off his turban and turns round:

> Harry would have screamed, but he could not make a sound. Where there should have been a back to Quirrell's head, there was a face, the most terrible face Harry had ever seen. It was chalk white with glaring red eyes and slits for nostrils, like a snake.[106]

4
A Primordialist Definition of Modernism

> Innocence the child is and forgetting, a beginning anew, a play, a self-propelling wheel, a first movement, a sacred Yea-saying.
>
> Friedrich Nietzsche, *Thus Spoke Zarathustra* (1885)[1]

> The very *fact* of modernism raises the question of whether cultural renewal is any longer possible at all. This is a paradox of large dimensions, for modernism identifies itself with renewal, and transforms transition into a constant state. *Die Brücke*, the bridge to tomorrow celebrated by various avant-gardes, is also a bridge into the unknown, or rather the never-to-be-known.
>
> David Weir, *Decadence and the Making of Modernism* (1996)[2]

THE MYTH OF TRANSITION

'One sheep-fold, one flock, one King.' It was under this unlikely slogan that in 1534 a militant group of besieged Anabaptists led by the new King David, former apprentice tailor Jan Bockelson, got to work transforming the German town of Münster into the earthly Jerusalem, having hitherto successfully defied all attempts of the Papal armies to prevent them from fulfilling their 'sacred task to purify the world of evil in preparation for the Second Coming'. The pamphlet *Announcement of the Vengeance* declared that 'Revenge without mercy must be taken of all those who are not marked with the Sign [of the Anabaptists].'[3] Such slogans were preludes to terrible atrocities committed by those who believed they were hastening the advent of the millennium, and to worse atrocities committed by their enemies who treated such fanaticism as an evil heresy to be brutally extirpated.

For Norman Cohn, who has documented this episode in Early Modern History in copious detail, the millenarians' beliefs, and particularly the episodes of revolutionary violence and counter-violence they led to, adumbrate the horrors of twentieth-century totalitarianism in both its elitist and egalitarian forms which often condemned to unspeakable suffering those who could not display the right 'sign'. He explains the waves of chiliasm that spread across parts of Europe from the thirteenth century as the product of a society in crisis. The combination of acute socio-economic instability with repeated bouts of plague and famine that followed the epidemics known collectively as the Black Death, itself a historical event of traumatic proportions, disseminated anxieties and anomic forces, especially among those who did not have a firm social or economic foothold in society. As a result 'revolutionary millenarianism drew its strength from a population living on the margin of society'.[4]

> As social tensions mounted and the revolt became nation-wide, there would appear, somewhere on the radical fringe, a *propheta* with his following of paupers, intent on turning this one particular upheaval into the apocalyptic battle, the final purification of the world.[5]

In his investigation of the 'sense of the end' in modern literature, Frank Kermode adds a 'cosmological' dimension to this sociological explanation by emphasizing the pivotal role played in the apocalyptic imagination by the 'myth of Transition'. This convinced fanatics such as the Anabaptists to believe that they were literally living in the *eschaton*, the last days of a doomed world, and hence standing on the threshold of a historical transformation 'in a period which does not properly belong either to the End or to the *saeculum* preceding it'.[6] Following this line of thought, it makes sense that the eschatological myth of the imminent inauguration of a new era first originates among those who are the most marginalized and hence the most disaffected with the existing order. The readiness to commit acts of extreme violence stems from the millenarian fantasy that, paradoxically, by intensifying the chaos and violence of the present dispensation, they are bringing to a head the crisis of the old order and accelerating the advent of the new one of peace, harmony, and justice. The millenarian revolt against existing society thus assumes the cathartic, cleansing quality of a 'holy war' against a sinful world fought by those charged with a divine mission to be the interpreters of divine will now that the Church itself has become corrupt.

This interpretation of millenarianism informs Kermode's account of the renewed importance assumed by 'the myth of Transition' in early twentieth-century literature against the background of an age haunted by a particular variant of 'the sense of an ending', namely a belief in the decline of the West brought about by its spiritual decay. As an example of the modern version of the 'apocalyptic paradigm' he cites the two versions of W. B. Yeats' *A Vision* (1925 and 1937), which together express 'a deep conviction of decadence and a prophetic confidence of renovation' stemming from the artist's belief that 'his moment was the moment of the supreme crisis, when one age changed into another'. Particularly revealing in the context of the discussion of the First World War in chapter 5 is the poet's conviction of the need, in his own words, to 'love war because of its horror', so that 'belief may be changed, civilization renewed'.[7] Even though Yeats was no Christian millenarian, the 'myth of Transition' inspired in him moods in which he felt he was living on the cusp of a new era betokened by the very intensity of the world's spiritual anarchy and self-destructive violence, manifestations of the 'last days' of history in its present, unsustainable constitution, the modern *eschaton*.

Kermode suggests that the myth of transition originates in the three-and-a-half year reign of the Beast described in The Book of Revelation, but credits the twelfth-century Calabrian monk Joachim of Floris with providing its first explicit articulation as a historical prophecy, one which he believes exerted a 'remarkably enduring'[8] influence both on Christianity's millenarian tradition and on literary modernism. For him 'the Joachite "transition" is the historical ancestor of the modern crisis'.[9] However, one of the foremost experts on modernity in its many conceptual and ideological intricacies, Jürgen Habermas, has warned against interpreting vast sweeps of human history in the narrow terms of Judeo-Christian eschatology.[10] It is a warning to be wary of attributing 'the myth of transition' and 'the apocalyptic paradigm' which began to take such a hold on both literary and political mythopoeia in fin-de-siècle Europe to the resurfacing in modern aesthetic and ideological garb of an arcane mystical tradition that had grown up within the Christian exegesis of human history.[11] Once we look beyond the parameters of Christian history to make sense of apocalypticism, we soon recognize the relevance of a specialist field of studies within cultural and social anthropology that is concerned precisely with the 'myth of transition' that Kermode refers to, but in one of its most ancient and universal ritualized forms: the rite of passage. It is a phenomenon that proves to have a direct bearing on modernism in the extended sense we have given it.

THE RITE OF PASSAGE

The ethnographical study of rites of passage was pioneered by Arnold van Gennep in his classic text of 1909.[12] Here he defined them as 'rites which accompany every change of place, state, social position and age',[13] and showed they were characterized by a threefold (triadic) progression of stages, which a contemporary expert summarizes thus: '(1) separation or the *pre-liminal* (after *limen*, Latin for threshold), when a person or group becomes detached from an earlier fixed point in the social structure or from an earlier set of social conditions; (2) margin or the *liminal*, when the state of the ritual subject is ambiguous; he is no longer in the old state and has not yet reached the new one; and (3) aggregation or the *post-liminal*, when the ritual subject enters a new stable state with its own rights and obligations'.[14] Inevitably, a vast amount of anthropological literature has grown up since van Gennep's research documenting the rites of passage peculiar to the numerous major civilizations and countless tribal cultures that flourished before the globalization of modernity. The volume of collected essays on mortuary rites cited in the last chapter is one of many hundreds of publications that have a bearing on the topic.[15] Inevitably, too, his original ideal type has been modified.

In the course of his extensive research into the function of ritual in premodern societies carried out in the 1950s and 1960s the Anglo-American anthropologist, Victor Turner, offered a particularly incisive refinement of von Gennep's original schema. He saw the first phase of separation or disaggregation as one that 'demarcates sacred space-time from mundane space-time' – or what we have called *aevum* from Cronus – and drew particular attention to the display of 'symbols of birth and renewal' that accompany the concluding rites of reaggregation. In the 1990s the eminent British social anthropologist, Maurice Bloch, added a further refinement to the model that adds a fresh component to the theory of modernism under construction. The premise of his modification to Turner's model was 'the startling quasi-universality of the minimal religious structures' that shape human cultures and which manifest themselves in the recurrence of the 'same structural pattern in ritual and other religious representations at many times and in many places'. In an argument profoundly compatible with theories postulating the universal human need for access to a suprapersonal, aeval temporality discussed in the last chapter, Bloch attributes such regularities to the fact that 'the vast majority of societies represent human life as occurring within a permanent framework which transcends the natural transformative process of birth, growth, reproduction, ageing and death'.[16]

For Bloch the key to the paradoxical process of accessing transcendence involved in rites of passage lies in the psycho-symbolic process that occurs in the stage of separation from society. Initiates enter a liminal 'world beyond process' and are able to see themselves and others 'as part of something permanent, therefore life-transcending'. Thus empowered and transformed by their experience of liminality, they change into 'a permanently transcendental person who can therefore dominate the here and now' to which they originally belonged before their ritually induced schism from it. In the third stage of post-liminal re-aggregation 'vitality is regained, but it is not the home-grown native vitality which was discarded in the first part of the rituals that is regained'. Instead it is 'a conquered vitality obtained from *outside* beings, usually animals, but sometimes plants, other peoples or women'. Thus the outcome of the *rite de passage* is 'not seen as a return to the condition left behind in the first stage, but as an aggressive consumption of a vitality which is *different* in origin from that which had originally been lost'.[17]

This analysis leads Bloch to conceive the central function of triadic initiation ceremonies not as the initiate's transformation, but society's regeneration, the replenishing of its supply of transcendence. Their ultimate purpose is to keep anomy and entropy at bay for the collectivity, which is why rites of passage play a key role in the elaborate 'cosmogonic' processes by means of which tribes or peoples revitalize themselves by symbolically re-enacting 'the creation of moral life'. The liminal stage of transitional rites enables human beings to nourish themselves with metaphysical energy unavailable in 'normal' phases of reality, and thus refuel society with transcendence on their symbolic return to it. Rites of passage rewind a society's cosmic clock while renewing the bonds between individual life, community, culture, state power, and the cosmos.[18] We saw in the last chapter that meticulous ethnographic research suggests the main function of mortuary rituals is to revitalize and re-legitimize both the cultural nomos and the social and political system it underpins. They can now be seen as symptoms of an even more 'archetypal' regenerative pattern in ritual behaviour, one fully consistent with Richard Fenn's claims about the universal role of ritual in regenerating time and purifying the world.[19]

THE REVITALIZATION MOVEMENT

In *From Prey to Hunter* Maurice Bloch focuses on liminal transitions which result in the restoration or invigoration of existing society. We do not learn how his refinement of conventional rite of passage theory applies to the second type of ritual transition which Turner identifies, namely one that leads to a new society, either by the radical transformation of the old society or collective secession from it to form a new culture. The conditions that produce revolutionary rather than restorative transitional states Turner describes as 'liminoid'. It is a concept which Mathieu Deflem explains thus: 'the liminoid originates outside the boundaries of the economic, political, and structural process, and its manifestations often challenge the wider social structure by offering social critique on, or even suggestions for, a revolutionary re-ordering of the official social order'.[20]

In other words, the liminoid transition to a new order takes place when a society undergoes a crisis sufficiently profound to prevent it from perpetuating and regenerating itself through its own symbolic and ritual resources. Such crises can occur as a result of natural calamities – such as plagues, droughts, floods, or changes in habitat – or may be due to the eruption of internecine socio-economic and political tensions, or to occupation, colonization, or acts of aggression inflicted on it by other societies. The ability of human beings to take collective action to resolve such crises by creating a new society with a new nomos is obviously crucial to the evolution of all human cultures over time, and to their capacity to adapt to the new environments and situations that are constantly emerging to threaten the existing social system. 'Liminoidality' and adaptive, innovative, *revolutionary* social reactions to it which create a *new* order and a 'new world', have certainly been as constitutive of human history as the evolving but conservative liminal processes that maintain and regenerate the status quo.

It seems safe to infer from such considerations that what Bloch argued in the case of liminal situations also holds true for liminoid ones. The rituals they produce are performed in order to regenerate society rather than the lives of the individuals, to ensure collective rather than personal survival, to maintain eternal transcendence in spite of personal mortality. The main differences are that in the case of liminoid rites of passage, it is society as a whole that enters the stage of liminal separation, and the outcome is not society's reaggregation but its rebirth in a new form. This explains why the new community that emerges from the breakdown of the old society is often described in palingenetic terms, appearing 'in the guise of an Edenic, paradisiacal, utopian or millennial state of affairs, to the attainment of which religious or political action, personal or collective, should be directed. Society is pictured as a *communitas* of free and equal comrades – of total persons'.[21] In terms of Peter Berger's theory encountered in the last chapter, such mythic self-representation is the sign that the sacred canopy has not been repaired, but replaced by a new one, albeit one that generally recycles a lot of the original material.

Turner has described the way the embryonic new society arises from a liminoid situation:

> People who are similar in one important characteristic [...] withdraw symbolically, even actually, from the total system, from which they may in various degrees feel themselves 'alienated' to seek the glow of *communitas* among those with whom they share some cultural or biological feature they take to be their most signal mark of identity. Through the route of 'social category' they escape the alienating structure of a 'social system' into '*communitas*' or social anti-structure.[22]

Such a 'social anti-structure' operates as something that is familiar to anthropologists by another name: the 'revitalization movement'. Anthony Wallace, who pioneered research into this phenomenon,[23] identified as a crucial element in formulating the nomos of the new society the appearance of a 'prophet' who has 'an ecstatic vision or revelation', on the basis of which, now 'personally rejuvenated' he (or she) undertakes the salvation of the community by imposing through preaching and proselytizing 'a syncretism of both ancient and new-fangled elements'. The crisis of the old society is thus resolved 'by a reaffirmation of identification with some definable cultural system' which has been created through the agency of the leader.[24] In *Dramas, Fields and Metaphors*, Victor Turner similarly talks of liminoid situations giving rise to 'a new 'visionary' within the embryonic community who 'experiences a radical change in personality, assumes a new role in society, devises a new plan for reorganizing society and proposes a new order that promises new meaning and purpose for living'.[25] The formulation of the nomos of the new society is a syncretic process of 'ludic' or 'mythic' recombination, synthesis, and 'reaggregation' in which 'many of the features found in liminal and liminoid situations come to dominate the new religion, drawing sustenance from many hitherto separate tribal conditions'.[26] Wallace terms this process a 'mazeway resynthesis', the concept of the mazeway subsuming connotations of 'world-view', 'cognitive map', and 'life space'.[27] Under his influence, Kenneth Tollefson talks of cultural revitalization as an 'adaptive social response whereby the past and present values, customs, and beliefs – which produce dissonance arising from the distortions that exist between them – are analyzed and recombined into a new synthesis, a new mazeway, or a new Gestalt'.[28]

The term 'mazeway', with its archaic connotations of finding a path through a labyrinth, has caught the attention of some psychiatrists studying new religious movements. John Price, for example, identifies it with

> the change in belief system which occurs in prophets, the mazeway being to the individual what culture is to society, so that the prophet awakes to a new reality which he or she then tries to impart to followers; if successful, the prophet becomes the leader of a new religious movement; otherwise, he or she is alienated from the parent group and is likely to be labelled as mentally ill.[29]

Such a passage has obvious relevance to Norman Cohn's description of the *propheta* who arises to lead the revolt of the marginalized against the corrupt age and build the New Jerusalem. Clearly, millenarian fantasies of inaugurating a new *aevum* have origins long predating Joachim of Floris and even Christianity: the chiliastic movements that Cohn has studied with such impressive scholarship are surely to be seen as relatively modern Western manifestations of the *archetypal* revitalization movement that has been driving the adaptation and evolution of human culture ever since *homo reflexivus* first walked this marvellous and terrifying planet. The Anabaptists were the natural product of the acute liminoid conditions that he documents so fully, living out a ritualized pattern of behaviour as old as humanity itself, just as Jan Bockelson's self-appointed role as the prophet reshaping society in the light of divine revelations was an adaptive response to their crisis which led not to a new *aevum* but mass slaughter.[30]

Frank Kermode was thus misguided when he looked for the origins of the modernist 'myth of transition' in the Christian Middle Ages. The 'apocalyptic' theme of decadence and renewal that he discerns as the Leitmotif of W. B. Yeats' poetic universe is instead to be seen as a permutation of an archetypal pattern brought to the surface by what a growing number of Europeanized human beings experienced after 1850 as an indefinitely protracted phase of *liminoidality* brought on by a Western society that was seen by a growing number of artists and intellectuals as sliding towards the abyss of nihilism.

PROGRAMMATIC MODERNISM REVISITED

When the primordialist approach to modernism outlined in the last chapter takes into account the elements from the social anthropology of rites of passage introduced into this one, what we identified in Chapter 2 as 'programmatic modernism' takes on a new aspect. The more intimate and diaphanous 'epiphanic' form of modernism seeks transcendence by 'immortalizing' glimpses of the lost nomos in art, prose, painting, or song. Meanwhile, its more robust, sanguine cousin can be seen at work in countless personal and collective initiatives to resolve the liminoid conditions caused by the impact of modernization. All of these tend naturally to assume characteristics of contemporary 'revitalization movements' pitted against the forces of Modernity, even if it means no more than assuming the Zarathustran stance of a would-be *propheta*, a seer come before his time, ignored by those who would flock to become his followers if only they could grasp the gravity of the situation.[31]

Approaching programmatic modernisms in this way highlights several features they share with premodern revitalization movements that will prove to have a particular relevance to our analysis of modernism's relationship to fascism in Part Two. An obvious one is the way they often form round a charismatic leader or prophet figure who takes charge of the values, tactics, and world-view ('mazeway') needed for the transition to the new order. This is a feature that will assume particular significance when we consider the leader cults common to the two fascist regimes. Another is the mythically constructed exclusiveness and superiority of the new *communitas* as it secedes from, or attempts to take charge of, the failing society. Following the logic of creative destruction and active nihilism, the primary aim of such a movement is, in Turner's words, 'to revitalize a traditional institution, while endeavouring to eliminate alien persons, customs, values, even material culture from the experience of those undergoing painful change'.[32] Political revitalization movements thus tend to demonize both the old order and any groups in society who can be identified as the cause of its decadence or as threats to the process of rebirth. It is a feature that has obvious relevance to the (highly contrasting) ethnocentric concepts of the national community officially adopted under Mussolini and Hitler.

The two commonly acknowledged features of revitalization movements that will concern us in this chapter, though, are first, the intense syncretism involved in the creation of the new 'mazeway' needed to guide the search of the embryonic *communitas* for a new mythic home; and second, the fact that they appear 'during epochs of marked cultural change and its accompanying personal distress'.[33] The syncretism of revitalization movements stems not only from the practical impossibility of making *tabula rasa* of the traditional nomos in order to create an entirely new one, but also from the instinctive need to incorporate all healthy elements of the traditional apparatus of transcendence, all 'eternal values', in the establishment of a viable communal new order. How 'mazeway resynthesis' and its attendant 'ludic recombination' operates within the orbit of cultural modernism will become clearer when in the concluding section of this chapter we consider the fusion of aesthetics with social and political ideals in a small sample of avant-garde art movements which illustrate the tendency of modernism to assemble collages of meaning by integrating ideological elements of extreme heterogeneity. The second feature is bound up with appreciating the peculiar nature assumed by liminoidality under modernity, which helps explain the unique features of modernist revitalization movements compared with traditional ones. Before we proceed to examine this topic, however, it may be helpful to give a concrete example of a premodern revitalization movement to throw into relief points of difference and comparison.

In the last decade of the nineteenth century the millennial culture of indigenous tribes living in the northern plain states of the US now known as South Dakota was being rapidly destroyed under the impact of the occupation of their homelands by the 'White Man'. The response was the spontaneous spread of hopes and rumours that coalesced into a utopian vision of emancipation bearing all the archetypal hallmarks of eschatological myth. A saviour was said to be living beyond the mountains who would restore the Indians' traditional way of life in a new homeland beyond the reach of the White Man, where they would one day live reunited with the dead of their tribes. Two delegations sent by local tribes travelled to make contact with the new Messiah in Western Nevada and reported back that the stories were true. In the spring of 1890 the first 'Ghost Dance' was performed by Sioux Indians at Pine Ridge, a spectacular ceremony that spiritual leaders assured their tribes would make the bodies of the dancers invulnerable to bullets and hasten the fulfilment of the prophecy. The dance was soon taken up by other tribes in the area, becoming the focal point for an emancipation movement which briefly whipped up a frenzy of religious fervour among Indians convinced that they would soon be entering the promised land, their way of life and culture safe for ever.

What stands out from Victor Turner's account of the Ghost Dance is that it represented a fusion of traditional and innovative ritual elements of Indian culture presided over by medicine men in the name of an invisible Saviour who acquired charismatic qualities reminiscent of the ones which the Anabaptists projected onto Bockelson. By 'ludically combining' invocations of tribal foundation myths with ritualized representations of the war against the White Men, the dance became 'a symbolic restoration or re-enactment of the creative or generative past when creation was, so to speak, new-minted and unpolluted'. In it the tribe's 'painful present' was symbolically '"washed" or "blown" or "burned" away by the natural forces of water, wind, and fire'.[34] However, the symbolic forces of sacred time were no match for the latest instruments of death carried by American soldiers. By January 1891 an attempted revolt had been put down by 3,000 troops in the massacre at Wounded Knee. With the death of the old chief Red Cloud in 1909 the last living link to the Indian past was severed.

MODERNITY AND THE LIMINOID

The Ghost Dance was a typical premodern revitalization movement. It emerged spontaneously as a remedy to a temporary liminoid crisis whose outcome was closure, either in the total destruction of the *communitas* and the old order from which it had seceded, or its transformation into a viable new culture lived out under a new sacred canopy. Under the peculiar conditions of Western modernity, however, the quality of liminoidality changes in one crucial respect. It becomes a perpetually open-ended condition which denies closure for society 'as a whole', however many individual initiatives to restore transcendence may be realized at the microcosmic level. Under the thrall of modernity, individual cultures have become locked in the second, liminal stage of the passage to a new order. Frank Kermode senses this when he draws attention to the modern experience of existing in an 'in between time', an age of 'perpetual transition in technological and artistic matters', and hence 'understandably an age of perpetual crisis in morals and politics'.[35] Zygmunt Bauman explored the same dilemma from a different angle when he probed into the intimate relationship between 'modernity and ambivalence'. There is an obvious connection between what he identifies as the instinctive 'horror of indetermination'[36] which can drive individuals, groups, and governments to adopt draconian solutions to 'put an end' to ambivalence artificially, and the archetypally human 'terror of anomy' posited by Berger, Becker, and the social scientists of TMT. An equally obvious relationship exists between the experience of modernity as an age of protracted liminoidality and the temporalization of history considered in the last chapter. (I say 'protracted' rather than 'permanent' because the social *experience* of modernity is not always liminoid, and there have been situations where modernity's very instability can paradoxically provide a nomos in its own right, notably in the case of postmodernism.)

Once utopias, mythic homelands, and sacred canopies are relocated from suprahistorical, extra-temporal realms to become projects realizable within the historical process they partake of the open-endedness of perpetual becoming. As Richard Fenn puts it, modern human beings are condemned to be pilgrims whose journey has no destination, so that 'limbo thus becomes a chronic social condition rather than a temporary condition'.[37] He too cites Turner's theory of the liminoid to explain what is happening – or rather what is not happening – under modernity. Though he makes no reference to Turner's taxonomy or any other anthropological sources, Reinhart Koselleck comes to a similar conclusion about modernity's denial of closure when he argues that modern human beings constantly feel that they are living in 'the "newest time" which is simultaneously the beginning of a new epoch'.[38] He documents one of the first articulations of this unprecedented cultural situation in Rousseau's prediction of 1762 that Europe was moving into an age of 'permanent crisis', a perpetual dynamism and instability that imparted modern history with permanent *revolutionary* potential. It is consistent with this that the term 'crisis' henceforth became particularly current among *philosophes* drawn to a cyclic view of history. Conceiving history cyclically is a symptom of the subterranean link between a sense of cultural breakdown and the possibilities this opens up of rebirth and renewal once cultural pessimism becomes Dionysian rather than Romantic, and the Blochian 'principle of hope' swings into action.

The precondition for modernity to be increasingly experienced as decadence (Modernity) after 1850 was the end of a cosmological process in which the mazeway provided by Christianity overlapped with sources of nomos based on the myths of rational, scientific, liberal, industrial, and imperial progress that were emerging in Rousseau's day. As the crisis of the credibility of both Christianity and the progress myth as stable sources of transcendence deepened, a situation began to crystallize towards the mid-nineteenth century where ever greater numbers of artists and intellectuals expressed pessimism about the course taken by history, and the extreme spiritual cost of the spectacular material advances being made. At this point the liminal gave way to the liminoid, a shift articulated in a process we commented on in Chapter 2, namely the growing tendency of those 'alienated from the total system' to equate modernity with decadence and moral chaos. It is at this point that new forms of art first appear that pit the creative faculty, not against reason or the Enlightenment, but against *decadence*. Aesthetic modernism was born. It is thus no coincidence that modernist artists have left us some of the most powerful evocations of the modern experience of the liminoid.

One of these we have encountered already, namely Kafka's metaphor of the rail-crash in a tunnel where it is difficult to tell the entrance from the exit, a disaster inducing moods of either terror or ecstasy. Writing at the turn of the century, the Czech decadent artist Jiří Karásek expressed a less ambivalent sense of historical crisis when he referred to '*the horror of* transition, the uncertainty of this age which has cast out everything old but has not yet created anything of its own to replace it, an age with nothing to lean on, in which the anxieties of someone drowning are to be heard'.[39] August Strindberg was no less bleak in his assessment of the times in his comment about the characters he created for his play *Miss Julie* (1888). They were 'modern', and hence 'split and vacillating', 'conglomerations of past and present'. The reason for this is that they were 'living in an age of transition more urgently hysterical at any rate than the age that preceded it'.[40]

The experience of modernity as permanently unresolved ambivalence informs some of the most iconic images of modernist art: Edvard Munch's silent scream at the prospect either of the dusk of one day or the dawn of a new one; Giorgio de Chirico's eerily 'metaphysical' townscapes where transcendence itself has become a menacing pall that hangs over civic spaces devoid of life; Salvador Dali's watches melting like ice-cream; K.'s futile struggle to gain admission to the Law or the Castle in two of Franz Kafka's novels whose fragmentary state only accentuates their modernism; and, a generation later, the heavenless purgatory of Jean-Paul Sartre's *Huis Clos*, and the rule-less, unwinnable contest of Samuel Beckett's *Endgame*. All convey an aporic sense of a permanently unfolding future where transcendence, by becoming excessively temporalized, often seems to have become suffused with neurasthenia, one of the fashionable 'temporal disorders' of the late nineteenth century. If the sublime manages to retain its suprahistorical, numinous aura, it simply recedes tantalizingly and inaccessibly from those who seek it, like a rainbow chased across open fields.

Despite his general confidence in his mission to formulate the life-asserting values on which the nomos of the post-nihilist age would be based, Nietzsche also knew moments of anguish when his voyage of discovery became imprisonment aboard the *Flying Dutchman*, condemned to drift on the shoreless oceans of the liminoid, gazing at its shifting, mythless horizons for ever:

I cry out, 'Land ho!' Enough, and more than enough of this passionate, wandering journey on dark and alien seas! Landfall at last! No matter where it is, we must disembark; even the poorest haven is better than being swept back into the infinity of hopeless scepticism. Our first task is to make land. Later we will find good harbours and help others who come after us to put into shore.[41]

Within the broader context of his writings, Nietzsche's maritime metaphor to convey anomy expresses not despair but the desperation to *transcend* despair, to reach landfall even if it has to be an artificial harbour. In terms of the anthropological analyses of Turner and Wallace, the task he had set himself was to use his intellectual alienation from his age to drive his mind forward to the final stage of the modern crisis of nihilism where Romantic pessimism became Dionysian and the liminoid was resolved by a new mazeway resynthesis. It was a situation which called forth the image of Zarathustra, the prophet who has come too soon, but who might yet usher in a new form of modernity in which 'European man' was effectively shielded from the terror of the abyss by a new nomos. This *dialectical* 'moment' in pessimism conceived as a reaction to anomy, turning it from a negative state of mind to the wellspring of a regenerative process – from the weakness of the Last Man to the strength of the New Man – is found at the core of the creativity of all the artists just cited. The hypothesis under construction posits a deep structural link between the 'permanent transition' ascribed to modernity by some cultural historians and the archetypal 'transition stage', or liminal phase in rituals of regeneration recognized by some anthropologists. This results in a 'primordialist' interpretation of modernism that offers a new perspective both on its internal dynamics as a cultural phenomenon, and on its relationship to fascism.

The premise of this interpretation – speculative but sustainable through transdisciplinary research – is that the 'permanent crisis' of the temporalized history that became the hallmark of Western modernity once it was equated with decadence, tends to activate a no less permanent human faculty integral to the 'nature' of *homo sapiens*. It is a faculty at least as old as our species' reflexive awareness of immortality, and has been essential to 'our' capacity for social adaptation and for the creation of culture throughout 'our' evolution. This is the largely subliminal capacity and – to use a Nietzschean expression – *will* to overcome the terror induced by the prospect of personal death through a mythopoeically elaborated, cosmologically grounded, and communally configured belief in some form of suprapersonal *renewal*. It is this primordial palingenetic instinct that drives the 'active nihilism' advocated by Friedrich Nietzsche, the perennial 'principle of hope' believed in by Ernst Bloch, the human instinct to create a mythic world of culture and nomos postulated by Peter Berger, the perpetual construction of 'fictional hero-systems' hypothesized by Ernest Becker, the projection of life into a transcendent world-view identified by Maurice Bloch as a 'quasi-universal religious structure', and the 'palingenetic myth' which in *The Nature of Fascism* I claimed to be an 'archetype of the human mythopoeic faculty'.[42]

When 'liminoid' acquires the dialectical connotations *both* of 'perpetual crisis', 'permanent transition', the impossibility of closure *and* of cultural regeneration, the renewal of humanity, the inauguration of a new era, it assumes particular heuristic value in the interpretation of modernism. This paradoxical 'coincidence of opposites' resolves the paradox identified by David Weir when he points out that, because modernism 'identifies itself with renewal as well as transforming transition into a constant state', the 'bridge' it builds to a new social reality can never be completed, so that 'the very *fact* of modernism raises the question of whether cultural renewal is any longer possible at all'.[43] From the standpoint of the sceptical outsider or historian this is objectively true. But for those who feel thrown by history into the maelstrom of modernity and who experience the full force of the anomy generated by its liminoid condition, the will to create a new nomos can become so urgent that the *programmatic* modernist may enter a utopian, ecstatic, and ultimately delusory state of mind in which it seems possible to disembark, to make a *new world*, or at least inspire others to do so. It is the self-delusion of an idealist vision of reality and of all temporalized utopias when they provide a refuge from cosmic despair, a self-delusion that can have catastrophic historical consequences if ever enacted as a political programme that aims to induce the total rebirth of society.

A window into this extreme mental state is provided by Ernst Bloch in *The Spirit of Utopia* written in 1916. In a passage written as the 'old world' collapsed around him in the catacombs of the trench warfare, he declared that what would help visionaries like himself to cut 'new metaphysical paths towards a new order' and fulfil the 'supreme creative, philosophical moment' was 'the constant concentration of our waking dream on a purer, higher life, on a release from malice, emptiness, death and enigma, on communion with the saints, on all things turning into paradise'.[44] In the midst of such a waking dream the somnambulists of programmatic modernism soar on the wings of *kairos* high on their private privileged moment. They see a new *aevum* approaching through the magic portal of opportunity that has suddenly opened up in the soul-crushing walls of history, offering a path 'up' to a higher reality beyond the endless transition of linear time. In this state of false transcendence, the visionary artist or ideologue synthesizes the roles that Joseph Goebbels saw combined in Vincent van Gogh: 'teacher, preacher, fanatic, prophet … and madman', and attempts to embody a redemptive 'idea' which will transform the future. In such a 'higher state', sceptical questions about the sanity or feasibility of the palingenetic mission to be undertaken have no place, for, as Goebbels himself recognized, 'when it comes down to it, we are all mad when we have an idea'.[45]

With the exception of Arpad Szakolczai,[46] sociologists seems to have generally ignored the relevance of the cultural anthropology of rites of passage to the study of modernity. However, the significance of Turner's concept of the liminoid for understanding aspects of contemporary society has been fully grasped by the Jungian psychoanalyst, Anthony Stevens. In the course of cataloguing the archetypes of symbolism and myth he presents the mythopoeic mechanisms by which new symbolic communities (cultures) are born out of liminoid conditions as crucial to the evolution and diversification of human society. Moreover, he recognizes the vital role played by charismatic leaders in the formation and viability of the new communities that eventually emerge, making a direct link between what he calls tribal 'shamans',[47] and modern figures who have inspired fanatical loyalty in their followers, such as David Koresh, Jim Jones, Charles Manson, and, crucially in the present context, Adolf Hitler. The Führer's rise to power demonstrates for Stevens 'the power of liminoid symbolism arising from the unconscious of a charismatic leader to inspire his people to collective action with incalculable consequences'.[48]

A PRIMORDIALIST DEFINITION OF MODERNISM

We return from our lengthy expedition through the luxuriant undergrowth of social psychology, reflexive sociology, conceptual history, social philosophy, the history of ideas, and social anthropology weighed down with samples of paradigms and fragments of explanatory strategies which offer fresh clues to the dynamics of modernism. As a result, some existing theories on the topic we have already encountered in Chapter 2 lend themselves to new readings. Thus when Bradbury and McFarlane claim that a 'feature of Modernist sensibility' is 'the audacious attempts to discern a moment of transition' in terms of 'significant time', evoking the 'intersection of an apocalyptic and modern time',[49] they are alluding in our terms to the activist experience of the epiphanic moment, the *kairos* encountered in the writings of programmatic modernists such as Nietzsche. A previously invisible door appears in the endless corridor of Cronic time allowing those bent on changing the world to envisage a way out from the continuum of history. The relevance of this conception of time to the theory of revolution propounded in Walter Benjamin's *Theses on the Philosophy of History* is obvious.[50]

Ronald Schleifer identifies even more clearly the pattern we have construed as the 'dialectic of the liminoid' when he portrays modernism's 'apocalyptic sense of the "new"' as a product of the 'crisis consciousness' and the general 'collapse of ontological continuity'.[51] Modris Eksteins too implicitly recognizes the dialectic when he writes that the post-WWI 'craving for newness was rooted in what was regarded by radicals as the bankruptcy of history and by moderates as at least the derailment of history', precisely the metaphor Kafka used for Modernity.[52] The dialectic is also implicit in Peter Osborne's identification of modernism with 'the affirmative cultural self-consciousness of the temporality of the new'.[53]

What is also thrown into relief by applying the primordialist perspective to existing theories of modernism is the cogency of the maximalist usage that both these experts exemplify. This rejects attempts to restrict it artificially to the narrow confines of art by severing the experimental aesthetic phenomena of the period 1850–1945 from the forces of social transformation and political renewal with which they were so intricately linked. For example Schleifer traces the impact of the temporalization of history under modernity on the representation of reality in literature, music, physics, economics, philosophy, and political theory, showing how the human quest for the transcendence of anomic time was refracted through the new reflexivity to produce modernist modes of configuring meaning and purpose in all these fields. Peter Osborne, too, applies his ideal type to scrutinizing the complex links between modern forms of politics, literature, and thought exhibiting the reflexive affirmation of a new temporality that he sees as the hall-mark of modernism.

Both these historians are examples of the exceptions whom Modris Eksteins had in mind when, as we saw in Chapter 2, he referred to the 'few critics' prepared to use the concepts 'avant-garde' and 'modernism' to describe 'the social and political as well as artistic agents of revolt, and to the act of rebellion in general, in order to identify a broad wave of sentiment and endeavour'.[54] His *Rites of Spring* is a sustained exploration of the 'general rebellion' of turn-of-the-century Europe which he portrays as a quest for liberation, innovation, and renewal in every field of artistic, cultural, social, technological, and political activity driven by a common ethos of cultural crisis and palingenetic longings. All these wide-lens perspectives on modernism take on a deeper resonance in the context of Peter Berger's anthropological schema in which existential imperatives drive human beings to create their own 'world' through culture. The use of 'world' to denote not the planet Earth, but our own cognitive, social, and moral universe is what Richard Etlin calls a 'base-metaphor', a metaphor literally constitutive of the human experience of reality.[55]

The quest of programmatic modernism to establish a new nomos and alternative modernity for a decadent civilization – to make a 'new world' – is totalizing. It bursts apart any artificial academic segmentations of human creativity and activity into separate compartments. To the dispassionate ear of the academic mind it may well sound wildly utopian and megalomaniacal when a modernist artist claims that the visionary faculty endows the universe itself with meaning and beauty, as if the 'world' depended on them. Yet if we see the nomos of every functional culture as the product of human mythopoeia and creativity, of poetic and artistic forces working at a collective rather than an individual level, then there is an element of anthropological fact in the sweeping claim made by Guillaume Apollinaire in his eulogy of Pablo Picasso written on the eve of the First World War:

> Without poets, without artists, men would soon weary of nature's monotony. The sublime idea men have of the universe would collapse with dizzying speed. The order which we find in nature, and which is only an effect of art, would at once vanish. Everything would break up in chaos. There would be no seasons, no civilization, no thought, no humanity; even life would give way, and the impotent void would reign everywhere.[56]

With none of the Dionysian pessimism and Zarathustran self-confidence that pervades Apollinaire's pronouncement, we are finally in a position to complete the discursive ideal type of modernism we proposed in Chapter 2.

MODERNISM is a generic term for a vast array of heterogeneous individual and collective initiatives undertaken in Europeanized societies[57] in every sphere of cultural production and social activity from the mid-nineteenth century onwards. Their common denominator lies in the bid to achieve a sense of transcendent value, meaning, or purpose despite Western culture's progressive loss of a homogeneous value system and overarching cosmology (nomos) caused by the secularizing and disembedding forces of modernization. The modernists' rejection of or revolt against contemporary modernity was shaped by innate predispositions of the human consciousness and mythopoeic faculty to create culture, to construct utopias, to access a suprahuman temporality, and to belong to a community united by a shared culture. All these are vital to providing a refuge from the potentially life-threatening fear of a personal death bereft of any sort of transcendence, even an extensively humanized, secularized, and historicized one.

Modernism can assume an exclusively artistic expression, often involving extreme experimentation with new aesthetic forms conceived to express glimpses of a 'higher reality' that throw into relief the anomy and spiritual bankruptcy of contemporary history ('epiphanic modernism'). Alternatively, it can focus on the creation of a new 'world', either through the capacity of art and thought to formulate a vision capable of revolutionizing society as a whole, or through the creation of new ways of living or a new socio-political culture and praxis that will ultimately transform not just art but humankind itself, or at least a chosen segment of it (programmatic modernism).

The modernist search to counteract the threat of nihilism first took shape once Western myths of progress lost their credibility and modernity entered a protracted period of liminoidality. This process was intensified by the growing temporalization of history since the Enlightenment and further accelerated by the social disruptions and rise of materialism promoted by the industrializa-tion of society under new capitalist classes. This caused ever more of Europe's avant-garde artists and intellectuals to construct modernity discursively as 'decadence', and to assume the mission either of replenishing the aquifers of transcendence that were rapidly running dry, or of providing the inspiring vision needed to create an alternative, healthy modernity. Using an extreme variety of values and techniques, modernists thus sought to bring closure to the psychologically distressing liminoid conditions of contemporary reality, and offer solutions for, or at least life-changing diagnoses of, the deepening cultural and spiritual crisis of the West. This crisis was experienced primarily within creative elites before 1914, and more widely, though less reflexively, by the general public after the cataclysm of the First World War.

True to the logic of 'mazeway resynthesis' found in all revitalization movements, the hallmark of modernism in both its epiphanic and programmatic permutations is a tendency to syncretism, so that conflicting values and principles, sometimes drawn from quite different spheres of society and history, are combined in the search for the founding principles and constitutive values needed for a new world to be constructed out of the decadence or collapse of the old one. Within some variants of programmatic modernism this can lead to the paradoxical appropriation of elements found in the premodern, mythic, 'reactionary' past to serve the revolutionary task of creating a new order in a new future. A second paradox is that some forms of aesthetic modernism find a source of transcendence in the artistic exploration and expression of decadence rather than in focusing on utopian remedies to it. However, even though some forms of modernism may seem concerned with reviving tradition or conveying a sense of cultural decay, its overall momentum is futural and optimistic. In whatever medium it operates it works towards – or at least points to the need for – the erection of a new canopy of mythic meaning and transcendence over the modern world, a new beginning.

BEYOND THE 'DECAY OF VALUES'

It will hopefully help to 'bring alive' this highly abstract, possibly still abstruse definition of modernism if we illustrate it at some length with an example of a modernist diagnosis of Modernity. It is the analysis of the 'decline of the West' and the need for total cultural renewal which the Austrian novelist Hermann Broch interpolated – in typical modernist fashion – into his trilogy *The Sleepwalkers*. Broch lived in Vienna from his birth in 1886 until he escaped to the US shortly after Austria's annexation by Hitler in 1938. He thus experienced at first hand the cultural and historical turbulence of the early twentieth century from one of the epicentres both of the crisis of the West and of modernism.[58] *The Sleepwalkers* portrays the period 1880–1918 through three central characters, the Romantic von Pasenow, the anarchist Esch, and the realist Hugenau, whose unwittingly intersecting lives epitomize different phases and aspects of the accelerating plunge of modern society into dissolution and anomy.

Using a technique of *Verfremdung* or defamiliarization typical of aesthetic modernism, Broch interweaves into the narrative episodes from the life of a Salvation Army girl, as well as a ten-part excursus on the history of ideas, 'The Decay of Values'. The essay analyses the powerful spiritual, cultural, and historical processes that, unbeknown to the three men, have shaped their fates as ineluctably as the shifts in tectonic plates that cause entire continents to move over time. The essay is, of course, a speculative 'master narrative' and no claim can be made for its historiographical objectivity. Yet, given the fact that it was composed by someone experiencing 'on his skin' the collapse of all stable socio-psychological realities in the heart of inter-war Europe just when modernity's liminoidality was reaching its climax with such 'incalculable consequences', its numerous points of correspondence with the primordialist ideal type of modernism we have constructed are illuminating.

The essay opens with the discursive construction of modernity as fragmented, as decadent, as 'Modernity'. The world has become 'cancerous', and is 'losing its contours' so that 'man' is forced to grope his way 'with the help of a small, frail thread of logic through a dream landscape that he calls reality and that is nothing but a nightmare to him'.[59] The rhyme and reason of modern existence escapes us: 'We know too well that we are ourselves split and riven, and yet we cannot account for it.' Rather than examine the disorder of our inner lives, we prefer to see contemporary history itself as 'mad' or 'great' while continuing to think 'we are normal because, in spite of the split in our souls, our inner machinery seems to work on logical principles'.[60]

In contrast, Broch's anonymous narrator detects a deeper logic to modern lives, but it is a perverse one. In the Middle Ages Christianity still provided Europe with 'the ideal centre of values [...] to which all other values were subordinate: the belief in a Christian God'.[61] This nomos acted as 'the point of plausibility in which every line of enquiry ended'. It was 'what enforced logic and gave it that specific colouring, that style-creating impulse, which expresses itself not only in a certain style of thinking, but continues to shape a style characterizing a whole epoch for so long as the faith survives'.[62] It was with the Renaissance, 'a criminal and rebellious age', that the Christian scheme of values 'was broken in two halves, one Catholic and the other Protestant'. With the 'falling asunder of the medieval organon, a process of dissolution destined to go on for five centuries was inaugurated and the seeds of the modern world were planted'.[63] The human reaction to this schism, this tear in the sacred canopy, this fissure in the primordial firmament – what Heine called the 'Weltriss' – was an instinctive 'fear of approaching loneliness and isolation'. The ensuing social, political, and ontological crisis opened up the way for the Counter-Reformation to take upon itself 'the gigantic task [...] of attempting a new synthesis of the world and all its values under the guidance of the new Jesuit scholasticism, of once more striving towards the lost medieval wholeness'.[64]

Anticipating existentialist and postmodernist analyses of contemporary relativism, Broch argues that the loss of modern culture's animating style and 'ideal centre of values' means that it is threatened with the disappearance of the symbolic, *transcendent* dimension [nomos] without which 'the visible world would fall asunder into unnameable, bodiless, dry layers of cold and transparent ash'.[65] The decay of values has progressed to a point where modern reality now has no overarching meaning, or in Frankl's terminology no 'logos', beyond 'the non-meaning of a non-existence'.[66] It thus afflicts all human lives with 'the curse of the casual, of the fortuitous, that spreads itself over things and their relations to each other, making it impossible to think of any arrangement that would not be equally arbitrary and fortuitous'.[67] The instinctive horror of a totally disenchanted time – what we have called the terror of anomy, of Cronus – drives 'modern' human beings to act feverishly in *space*. They are continually obeying the dictates of private goals that are no longer organically bound to a meaningful cultural whole. The result is a relentless, purposeless purposefulness that conceals the subliminal dread of dissolution and death, their lives following the 'brutal and aggressive logics' that structure the myriad 'values and non-values' hosted by modern society.

Broch contrasts the logics of the soldier, army, business man, painter, revolutionary, and the bourgeois *arriviste*. It is the ceaseless proliferation of these conflicting logics, each with its own value-system, that Broch sees as constituting the intrinsically aporic experience of life under modernity. 'Modern man', once the 'image of God, the mirror of a universal order *created by himself*, has fallen from his former estate'. He may have some 'dim remembrance' of the security, the mythic womb, he once had, but he is now, 'driven out into the horror of the infinite', doomed, in the absence of a total cosmology to be 'helplessly caught in the mechanism of the various autonomous value systems' of modernity, 'a specialist, eaten up by the radical logic of the value into whose jaws he has fallen'.[68]

As a result, a 'modern' citizen such as Hugenau, his heart frozen and his consciousness oblivious of any 'higher' spiritual calling or 'deeper' ontological needs, is subliminally driven to pursue the ruthless logic of profit and loss in both his commercial and moral life, the same logic that helps provide the metaphysical underpinnings of capitalism. Yet even he 'cannot help but feel the icy breath sweeping over the world, freezing it to rigidity and withering all meaning out of the things of the world'. Thus in all social gatherings he senses a 'dread zone of silence' that separates him from his fellow human beings. When, like them, he reads newspapers it is only so that 'the mass of facts may fill the emptiness of a world that has fallen silent: in their hearts is the terror that comes every morning from wakening to loneliness, for the speech of the old community life has failed them and that of the new is too faint to hear'.[69]

The generation that came of age in the Europe of the early twentieth century is thus portrayed by Broch as 'sleepwalking'. Its members are cut off from any reflexive insight into the illogical logic, rootless roots, de-centred centre, mazeway-less maze, homeless home, and symbol-less symbolic world that determine their own lives. Buffeted by 'the icy hurricane' of modernity,[70] each individual remains 'an outcast from his epoch, and an outcast from Time', and if 'he' ever becomes 'aware of his isolation [...] he is flung back into the deepest animal anguish, the anguish of the creature that suffers violence and inflicts violence, flung back into an overwhelming loneliness'. However the dialectic of cultural pessimism born of the liminoid ensures that the alarm system of the Not-Yet-Conscious is activated, and the 'principle of hope' begins to glow:

> In the fear of the voice of the judgement that threatens to issue from the darkness, there awakens within him the doubly strong yearning for a Leader to take him tenderly and lightly by the hand, to set things in order and show him the way; [...] the Leader who will rebuild the house so that the dead may come to life again; [...] the Healer who by his actions will give meaning to the incomprehensible events of the Age, so that Time can begin anew.[71]

The redemptive power that seems to emanate from such a leader stems from the way 'his' private value-system and world-view seems to make sense of the anomy of the age, imparting it with a 'significant shape' and a rationale which provides 'the motivation for events that in his absence we can only characterize as insane'.[72]

That the novel is the fruit of Broch's own search for a nomic shield against absurdity, his own magic canopy, becomes clear in the closing pages of the novel. Here a remarkable *peripeteia* takes place, the shift from 'Untergang' to 'Aufbruch', from Romantic to Dionysian pessimism. An epiphanic mode of modernism steeped in 'cultural pessimism' mutates into a metaphysical variant of programmatic modernism of the overtly 'apocalyptic' variety that so fascinated Frank Kermode. The narrator now portrays the acute cultural fragmentation of modernity as the liminal phase of separation in a rite of passage, and hence the sign of an imminent 'vertical transition'[73] to the final stage in the triad: a new, 'absolute' era of history in which the liminoid condition of Modernity will be finally transcended: 'The transition from any value-system to a new one must pass through that zero-point of atomic dissolution, make its way through a generation destitute of any connection with either the old or the new system.'[74] It is now revealed that the curse of temporalization is set to be lifted in a final palingenetic act 'of self-elimination and self-renewal, the last and greatest ethical achievement of the new, the moment when time is annulled and history radically formed in the pathos of absolute zero'.[75]

In the final paragraphs Broch's narrator assumes the persona of the millenarian *propheta* whose breathless flow of visionary pronouncements are the outward sign that Truth is being revealed. He declares that even if the coming Leader fails to fulfil the expectations of redemption he has aroused, 'the hope that the Absolute will one day fulfil itself on earth' and that 'a Messiah will lead us to it' remains 'imperishable':

> inviolable the brotherhood of humble human creatures, from whose deepest anguish there shines inviolable and inviolate the anguish of a divine grace, the oneness of all men, gleaming in all things, beyond all Space and all Time.[76]

THE SEARCH FOR TRANSCENDENCE IN MODERN ART

The Sleepwalkers offers a forensic diagnosis of the decadence of modernity between the world wars as it was experienced by a novelist with a modernist temperament. It also provides a highly textured case-study in the 'dialectic of the liminoid' that transformed the experience of transition from the anomic 'horizontal' one of an endless continuum to the epiphanic 'vertical' sense of *Aufbruch* towards a new world. Through this radical re-imagining of modernity's 'permanent crisis', pessimism became strong, nihilism became active, the principle of hope became Nietzschean in intensity.[77] This powerful act of mythopoeic magic provides the precondition for modernism's attempts to renew transcendence, whether in the epiphanic suspension of Cronus momentarily achieved by passing through 'the still point of the turning world',[78] or in the striving towards a human future finally purged of chaos, ambivalence, and dysfunctionality, a dream in which visionary artists and thinkers could sometimes join forces with modernist architects, town planners, social engineers, technocrats, or experts in racial hygiene and eugenics.

Either way Roger Shattuck seems to have put his finger on a profound aspect of Western modernity, or rather the revolt against it, when, in the context of his investigation of the French avant-garde he sees in Alfred Jarry's fantasy project to build a 'Machine which isolates us from time', the epitome of modernist longing for 'absolute stillness in our physical and spiritual system'. This experiment in applied 'Pataphysics' (Jarry's imaginary technology) – conceived on the very threshold of the twentieth century – poetically expresses, with a pseudo-facticity that anticipates the fantasy world of the Surrealists, what we would term the longing of the epiphanic modernist to escape from the realm of Cronus and partake of *aevum*, or in Shattuck's words the feeling that

> [t]hrough all the whirl of contradiction and dream and nonsense we can reach the still centre, and from there we can behold the world at once and for all time as revolving around us and as indistinguishable from us.[79]

(Programmatic modernists also longed for the world to revolve around them, but in the external, physical meaning that involved the wholesale transformation of outer reality.)

Hermann Broch's novel also throws into relief how deeply bound up the aesthetic experimentation so typical of modernism was with the search for higher or deeper levels of transcendence, and with the impulse of artists to assume the role of *propheta* in the process of renewing the 'world'. There has been a tendency of the more purist art historians to play down this metaphysical and metapolitical dimension of modernism, thus implicitly reaffirming the very 'autonomy' of art from society from which modernist artists themselves were so concerned to break free. Fortunately, there are exceptions. A number of specialists have uncovered the profound nexus between aesthetic modernism and the quest for transcendence in all its sumptuous complexity. In doing so, they amply confirm the tendency of modernists seeking the revitalization of society to syncretize potentially conflicting values and to burst out of the cultural space to which art had been safely confined by the nineteenth century into the realm of movements for social renewal and political change.

One exceptionally rich source of insight into this topic is the catalogue published to accompany the exhibition 'The Spiritual in Art: Abstract Painting 1890–1985' held in Los Angeles County Museum in 1986–87. It lavishly documents the readiness with which the generation of artists that pioneered abstraction turned their canvases into what T. S. Eliot calls an 'objective correlative' of the occult dimension they believed to be latent in reality and crucial to supply the transcendence so urgently needed to regenerate a society dissolving into matter. Thus Wassily Kandinsky, František Kupka, and Piet Mondrian were all deeply influenced by Theosophy, the dominant form of the occultist revival of the day, while Kazimir Malevich was drawn to the theory of a fourth dimension popularized by Petyr Ouspensky. The highly conceptual canvases of the Futurists Giacomo Balla and Gino Severini, too, bear the unmistakable imprint of spiritualist notions of a supramundane reality. This conflicts with the conventional image of futurism as employing only 'materialist' – physicist and mathematical – conceptions of speed and dynamism with which to 'break down the mysterious doors of the impossible', conceptions which in any case produced monist, scientistic imaginings of transcendence in their own right. Occultist notions of a higher reality had an important influence too on the Cubism of Pablo Picasso, Henri Matisse, Hilma af Klint, and on the Dadaism of Hans Arp, Kurt Schwitters, and Marcel Duchamp, all of whom created their own cocktail of spiritually-oriented aestheticism.[80]

In his manifesto *On the Spiritual in Art* (1911) and *The Blaue Reiter Almanac* (1912), Kandinsky, assuming the guise of 'a Moses leading his people to the promised land', articulated his belief in the primary role of art in counteracting the decadence, anxiety, and insecurities bred by Modernity.[81] That he adopted the archetypal guise of 'seer' takes on renewed significance in the context of the primordialist approach to modernism we have been proposing. We have seen that Maurice Bloch interprets the communal function of initiates in a rite of passage as that of soaking up transcendence during the liminal stage so that they can replenish society's reservoirs of it upon their 'reaggregation' and so regenerate society. The sociologist Edward Tiryakian has suggested revivals of occultism and mysticism normally occur when 'cultural paradigms are shifting', and thus at a time of 'loss of confidence in established and cognitive models of reality, in the exhaustion of institutionalized collective symbols of identity'. Translated into 'our terms', they arise at a time when a nomic and symbolic crisis places society in a 'liminoid' state. Tiryakian portrays the artist's retreat into occultism is as a retreat 'in the religious sense, a temporary withdrawal for inspirational meditation *which provides a restoring of psychic energy to be used in re-entering everyday life with greater vigour*'.[82] Kandinsky himself alludes to such a process when he states in his manifesto of 1911 that 'Every man *who steeps himself in the spiritual possibilities of his art* is a valuable helper in the building of the spiritual pyramid which will one day reach to heaven.'[83]

In the light of such considerations it is possible to suggest – reflexively and heuristically, of course – that the more 'programmatically' inclined modernist artists seem to have instinctively used their spiritual and social marginalization (liminality) within an increasingly materialist, 'philistine' society to take on the role of both initiate and *propheta*. Their 'mission impossible' from the late nineteenth century onwards was to locate fresh sources of transcendence in the increasingly desertified wastes of Modernity, and channel the resulting outpouring of creativity into slaking the raging spiritual thirst of society – or even help it put an end to the nomic drought for good. In this respect the modernist artist thus can be likened to those molluscs in which the nanotechnology of nature has implanted sophisticated circadian pacemakers, and who continue to open and close in time with the changing tides of invisible seas even when they are transported far inland. The inner clocks of modernists are set to cosmic rhythms and calendars imperceptible to those who persuade themselves they are comfortable in an 'interpreted world'[84] without transcendence, Nietzsche's 'ultimate men'.

August Strindberg's extensive research into occultism and Edvard Munch's contacts with spiritualist and Theosophist circles while in Berlin are to be seen as manifestations of this modernist behavioural syndrome. However, the pattern is exhibited particularly clearly by cofounder of the Berlin Dada movement, Raoul Hausman. He read eclectically in Western and Eastern mysticism in his attempt to synthesize Christianity, Buddhism, and Taoism into a harmonious vision of transcendence. This was no private search for enlightenment. Having sated himself on the esoteric knowledge and mystic wisdom of which he felt the West was starved, he came to see the purpose of Dada as providing a 'communal form of transition which could aid in man's "practical self-decontamination", the premise to the rediscovery of an immediate experience of wholeness, a "living presence"', 'the mystery of existence'.[85] His redemptive mission required him to ludically combine various sources of transcendence into a new mazeway. The syncretism that Kandinsky embarked on was even more pronounced. He eagerly exchanged ideas with the occultists, mystics, anarchists, socialists, and pacifists who congregated in Munich's Bohemian quarter, Schwabing, at the turn of the century, though the main ingredients of his own totalizing vision were anarchism welded together with theosophy.

The common denominator of all the many different sources of transcendence to which modernists turned was that they were almost always compatible with the radical temporalization of history under modernity that since the Enlightenment had discredited the notion of suprahistorical, preternatural realities. Being supraindividual but not suprahistorical, modernist transcendence could be conceived as woven immanently into the woof of life itself. In this respect Henri Bergson's theories of an alternative temporality latent in all organic life but invisible to positivists or materialists, performed the same role in supplying a sense of transcendence for a whole generation of French modernists as occultism, mysticism, spiritualism, or Eastern philosophy did for avant-garde artists in Paris, Moscow, Vienna, Prague, and Amsterdam. Once blended with judicious elements of anarchism, Nietzscheanism, or nationalism, Bergsonianism could exert a crucial influence on artists, scientists, and revolutionary ideologues seeking to escape the clutches of a literally soul-destroying materialism, and break the thrall of Cronus with which it was identified.[86]

We shall see in the next chapter how Wagnerism, Freudian and Jungian psychoanalysis, and the scientific Monism of Ernst Haeckel could all be converted within the modernist mindset into rich deposits of transcendent meaning, thus providing the momentum necessary to break free from the gravitational pull exerted by materialism, anomy, ambivalence, and nihilism. It is consistent with the quest for this-worldly transcendence that Surrealists, in their 'collective desire for action, bearing both on the surpassing of literature and of art and on the social transformation of the world',[87] drew extensively on Freud's materialist theories, though extra ingredients could be supplied by elements drawn from the wider anti-materialist revolt, such as metaphysical philosophy, the mathematics of chance, occultism, and spiritualism. The 'death-defeating' impulse behind Surrealism became explicit in the piece that Robert Desnos wrote for the second issue of *La Révolution Surréaliste*, in January 1925:

> Death is a material phenomenon. To have God intervene is to materialize him. Death of the mind is an absurdity. I live in eternity in spite of the ridiculousness of such a declaration. I believe I live, therefore I am eternal. Past and future serve matter. Spiritual life, like eternity, is conjugated in the present tense.[88]

During the Nazi occupation of France Desnos worked for the French Resistance, which eventually led to his transportation to Auschwitz, and then on to Theresienstadt where his physical death was caused by typhus shortly after the camp's liberation.

The two most pervasive active ingredients to be found in the modernist rebellion against a world without transcendence, however, was Nietzscheanism and anarchism. Both granted artists a flexible licence to fight a holy war against established institutions in order to create a new world, as long as 'the rebellious and nihilistic passion for destruction served a spiritual end'.[89] However, whereas Nietzsche's creative destruction stayed on the printed page and his 'dynamite' remained metaphorical, the bombs of political anarchists were, for their victims, frighteningly real. In contrast to Nietzscheanism, anarchists hoped that the 'purifying orgy of destruction' precipitated by their terrorist acts would 'create the conditions for the eventual era of harmony'. They 'played on the desire to escape historical time in a moment of apocalyptic revolutionary fury and to enter the future paradise that would cyclically return men and women back to their primal innocence and goodness'.[90] Such ideals point to anarchism's deep structural affinity with the revitalization movements of premodernity that, as we have seen, also sought to deliver society back to an Edenic, prelapsarian state. It is an affinity directly acknowledged by Richard Sonn when he compares anarchism to the revitalization movements of American Indians under the threat of extinction, citing the Ghost Dance as an outstanding example.[91]

Anarchism's elective affinity with the modernist quest for a new temporality can be seen not just in the way it suffuses the work of a cubist painter such as Pablo Picasso,[92] but the 1912–21 diaries of the Dadaist Hugo Ball which were published in 1927 as *Die Flucht aus der Zeit* (Flight out of Time), revealing the influence of both Catholicism and Mikhail Bakunin. It set forth the mission of Dada, both redemptive and world-creating (cosmogonic), 'to cure the madness of the age' and establish 'a new order of things that would restore the balance between heaven and hell'.[93] This palingenetic vision of contemporary history ensured that anarchism was osmotically absorbed by the French avant-garde, exerting a particular influence on Symbolists, since they too 'desired the transformation of the world as the material counterpart of their goal of spiritual transcendence'. Sonn sees the Symbolists' 'passionate urge for destruction' as the expression of 'a religious desire to transcend the temporal flow of history, to affect a great break [Aufbruch] out of which a new millennium would emerge'.[94] One testimony to the palingenetic fervour of some Symbolists is the prose-poems of *Ballades rouges* (1901). In one passage their author, Émile Bans, promises that a 'great red night' will engulf the evils of society and that 'the new dawn, in gilding the infinity of a better world, will pour out its light, benevolent Anarchy will awaken the desired city of happiness, of harmony'.[95]

Both Nietzscheanism and anarchism left their mark on German Expressionism, a blanket term covering an extraordinary outpouring of poetry, drama, painting, and graphic art attacking the spiritual bankruptcy of Modernity. The Expressionists' quest for a new temporality and nomos beyond the confines of aestheticism is clear from the characterization of Expressionist literature offered by Douglas Kellner. He stresses that 'one cannot really separate the formal, the ethical-political, and the thematic dimension without violating the work's intent and spirit', so that it has to be seen as 'part of a broader project of artistic-social rebellion'. In its 'drive for transcendence and trans-formation' it fuses 'a rather unique "worldliness" and "other-worldliness"' that seek 'to transcend conventional life for a "new life" and higher reality'. The insights it offers into existing reality are 'contrasted with provocative ideals of human liberation and a "new humanity", embodied in the topos of the "New Man"'.[96]

A MODERNIST EVALUATES MODERNISM

We have seen that Pablo Picasso was the incarnation of the New Man, at least as far as the Surrealist poet Guillaume Apollinaire was concerned when he wrote *The Cubist Painters*. In the hyperbolic rhetoric familiar since *Thus Spoke Zarathustra* he describes the painter as the embodiment of the nomos-creating power of the poet who was to 'make the world his new representation of it', leading to an 'enormous conflagration'.[97] By the time he wrote this, Picasso was the most famous modernist artist in the world, so it is significant that he exemplifies the pattern we have been postulating: extreme syncretism in seeking out new sources of transcendence, and an axiomatic sense of the corruption of the world in its present state, both combined with the embrace of a Nietzschean (Dionysian) anarchism in his vision of art as a vehicle for moral and social renewal. Though not given to programmatic manifestos, in private he could at times express a vision of the role of the artist that fully bears out the hypothesis of Peter Berger about the existential need for 'myth'. A well known example is the explanation he offered his partner Françoise Gilot for his fascination with the Negro masks he saw in the Trocadéro ethnographical museum in 1907 which inspired *Les Mademoiselles d'Avignon*, a defining moment in the history of modernist art. By his own account it was a 'moment of being' of '*kairos*' in which Picasso saw clearly the cosmological, nomos-creating function of art:

> Men had made those masks and other sacred objects for a sacred purpose, a magic purpose, as a kind of mediation between themselves and the unknown hostile forces that surrounded them, in order to overcome their fear and horror by giving it a form and image. At this moment I realized that this was what painting was all about. Painting isn't an aesthetic operation; it's a form of magic designed as a mediator between this strange hostile world and us, a way of seizing the power by giving form to our terrors as well as our desires. When I came to that realization, I knew that I had found my way.[98]

From Berger's more disenchanted point of view, though, the mediation provided by human culture is more of a safety curtain, given the absolute silence that this 'strange, hostile world' keeps in all our attempts to wrest from it a sense of the numinous.

Perhaps the most telling corroboration of a primordialist reading of aesthetic modernism comes not from the study of any one of its bewildering number of permutations, but from a social critic who was himself a modernist intellectual and *propheta* and who offered an extra-European perspective to its wider historical significance. Ananda Coomaraswamy was of an Anglo-Tamil background and emerged from his education in Britain having absorbed the influence of both Indian and European cultures, as well as a concern with the ongoing spiritual crisis of modernity typical of the fin-de-siècle in which he had come of age. Synthesizing insights drawn from Hinduism, Buddhism, the utopian socialism of William Morris, Peter Kropotkin's 'anarchist communism', and Nietzsche, as well as latter day mystics such as William Blake and Walt Whitman, he developed a master narrative which portrayed the rise of aesthetic modernism as betokening a sea-change in the history of the West. The anti-materialism and quest for transcendence in a painter such as Van Gogh signified for him a crisis in the materialism that had driven European colonization, imperialism, and the First World War, and heralded the dawn of an age of idealistic individualism which would allow both the West and the East to heal from the trauma of modern history. Like the medieval Rajput school of Indian painting, modernist art was 'metaphysical and saturated with ideas', and sought to 'interpret the absolute as a dynamic unity, a motionless but ever burning flame, a stillness which embraces an infinity of ceaseless movement'.[99] It was therefore destined to play a major role in providing the transcendent values of the coming revolution.

Coomaraswamy campaigned tirelessly in the first two decades of the twentieth century to encourage Indians to be empowered by awareness of their own cultural identity, to foster mutual understanding of Eastern and Western cultures, and to make Europeans and Americans conscious of the velvet revolution of values being carried out in front of their eyes by their own avant-garde artists. Despite what was claimed by the major academic pundits of the day, he believed modernism was not animated by an attempt to escape from the world, but the will to change it. Modernists had spontaneously 'rediscovered' an ancient vision of reality capable of erecting a new canopy woven from a fabric of a strictly monist, this-worldly sacrality. Just as Apollinaire and all self-respecting programmatic modernists themselves believed, Coomaraswamy saw them as the creative driving force behind a process that would resolve the decadence of modernity and fashion a better world for all humankind. They would collectively supply a new nomos for a decadent society, reinstating what Broch would later call in *The Sleepwalkers* 'the ideal centre of values, to which all other values were subordinate'.

With Coomaraswamy we have moved far beyond the invisible frontier dividing cultural modernism from social modernism. Like his heroes, Nietzsche and Peter Kropotkin, and William Morris, he looked not just to art, but to the power of the written and spoken word to overcome Modernity. He became well known in India and Ceylon for his efforts to raise popular awareness of ethnic and cultural identity in the revitalizing spirit of 'national idealism'. In Britain he wrote articles for the radical modernist magazine *The New Age* announcing the era of 'idealistic individualism', and became an associate of Arthur Penty, follower of William Morris, guild socialist, anarchist, and prophet of the 'postindustrial' era. In the US his ideas exerted considerable influence on anarchist modernists such as Carl Zigrosser and Rockwell Kent.

It was a sign of his impact that he was regarded with grave suspicion by both the British and American authorities for his subversive politics.

In 1905 Coomaraswamy had co-founded the Ceylon Social Reform Society. One of its first guest lecturers was Annie Besant, president of the International Theosophical Society who addressed the issue of 'national reform'. Her support for Indian independence was bound up with the Theosophical movement's axiomatic belief 'that the world was undergoing a universal "awakening" in which humanity's spiritual consciousness would overcome all social, cultural, and political divisiveness'.[100] The next chapter explores how the modernist revolt against decadence manifested itself in non-artistic movements for cultural and social renewal, an important step towards appreciating modernism's intimate relationship with fascism.

5
Social Modernism in Peace and War
1880–1918

Yes, I recognize Zarathustra. His eyes are clear and no disgust lurks
about his mouth. Does he not go along like a dancer?
>   Friedrich Nietzsche, Zarathustra's Prologue 2 (1883)[1]

Why is it our age that is overflowing with both destructive and creative
forces? Why is it pregnant with such awesome expectations? For even
if much may perish of fever, in a thousand retorts things are brewing
over the same flame which speak of a wondrous future.
>   Ernst Jünger, *Battle as Inner Experience* (1922)[2]

PAST MASTERS

Those attending a workshop run by the Theosophical Society in Tekels Park
on the outskirts of London nowadays will be impressed by the lushness of
the grounds and the dedication of its staff to promoting awareness of non-
European religions. However, few could suspect that it was once the British
hub of a powerful international movement of spiritual regeneration. The first
centre was opened in New York by Helena Blavatsky in 1875, and branches
quickly spread throughout North America, Europe, and India. By the eve of
the First World War the Society numbered several hundred thousand members
world-wide, many keen to be initiated further into the ultimate truths revealed
to Blavatsky in trance states by invisible Mahatmas or 'Masters', and set out
for all to read in the international bestsellers, *Isis Unveiled* (1877) and *The
Secret Doctrine* (1888). In countless lectures and pamphlets they would learn
ever more aspects of the karmic laws allegedly governing the progress both
of the individual soul and of the 'root races', notably the Aryans who had
started life on the lost continents of Lemuria and Atlantis. They would also

be encouraged to encounter every conceivable religious, mystic, and occult tradition that conserved a fragment of the 'perennial philosophy'.[3]

Members of the public keen to probe further into the esoteric could receive basic training in clairvoyance and teleportation, or learn to communicate directly with their personal gurus beyond the veil of mortality. It was in Theosophy's hey-day that Ananda Coomaraswamy encountered the movement in India and felt encouraged to pursue his own spiritual quest for ecumenical solutions to the world's spiritual crisis. As we saw in the last chapter, Theosophical wisdom had a major impact on a number of abstract painters, notably Kandinsky and Mondrian, but it also exerted some influence on other artists seeking to break the thrall of materialism, such as Lord Tennyson, Paul Gauguin, Constantin Brancusi, Theo van Doesburg, Walter Gropius, Robert Delauney, Aleksandr Skryabin, Arnold Schoenberg, Paul Klee, Franz Marc, Boris Pasternak, Katherine Mansfield, W. B. Yeats, Gustav Mahler, and Aleksandr Blok. Another famous figure who at one point was fascinated by its non-materialist vision of reality and universal harmony was Mahatma Gandhi.[4]

Theosophy's wildfire success cannot be understood by scrutinizing the authenticity of any of the cosmic insights or occult techniques it offered, but by understanding its social dynamics as a modern revitalization movement. In terms of Nietzsche's analysis of the plight of the West in *The Birth of Tragedy*, it offered metaphysically 'starving' Westerners a steady supply of the 'roots' resulting from 'digging' and 'rummaging' in 'even the most remote of the most ancient worlds'. It provided a horizon once more 'framed by myth'.[5] To its followers it guaranteed a source of transcendence, one flexible enough to create a personalized sense of 'nomos' whatever their original cultural or religious background. Theosophy linked this personal redemption to a collective vision of the rebirth of humanity from the decadence of materialism and Western science. The luminaries of the art world who were drawn to it were symptomatic of a much more diffuse longing for spirituality which created the demand for a new 'mazeway' among those for whom Christianity no longer maintained the 'sacred canopy' aloft. In fabricating one for mass consumption, Theosophy took ludic recombination to unprecedented heights, syncretizing ingredients culled from the world's religions and hermetic traditions with elements of Western humanism, occultism, spiritualism, cultural anthropology, ethnography, and evolutionary theory, endowing its leaders Blavatsky and Annie Besant with the aura of prophets showing a way out of the spiritual desert.

In terms of the ideal type of cultural processes we have elaborated, Theosophy not only had an impact on aesthetic modernism – Kandinsky's *Concerning the Spiritual in Art* is unthinkable without its influence – but was itself a form of modernism, one we propose to call *social modernism*. As the career of Coomaraswamy demonstrates, this often overlaps or intersects with aesthetic and cultural modernism, but places peculiar emphasis on the need to regenerate society not through a soul-nourishing 'vision' alone, but through some sort of collective social *action* or behaviour that is supposed to pioneer a new source of health, spiritual or physical. Its characteristic expression is thus in the activities of associations and institutions with a modernist mission, rather than through the medium of art or ideas alone. One aspect of social modernism that Theosophy illustrates particularly clearly is the principle that for a new nomos to emerge for the modern West it was necessary to turn to lost sources of spirituality, to go 'back to the future' in a process which the Conservative Revolutionary Moeller van den Bruck was to call a 'reconnection *forwards*'.[6] It was by reconnecting with the most ancient strata of human wisdom and belief interred by Modernity that the West was to be saved from itself. This *topos* of modernism is encountered in a wide range of forms: the primitivism of Picasso and Gauguin; the importance to both Nietzsche and Heidegger of the pre-Socratic Greeks and the world of myth generally before the curse of modern reflexivity; the cult of sub-rational, 'primitive' energies in such movements as Fauvism and Expressionism, or the key role played in Surrealism and Dada by the 'primitive' unconscious as postulated by Freud; Walter Benjamin's theory of the role of mythicizing memory in the revolutionary moment; Jung's belief in the liberating power of the 'archetypal unconscious'; Mircea Eliade's concern with the need to overcome the spiritual impoverishment of modern life through the power of myth and ritual.

OCCULTIST SOCIAL MODERNISM

Theosophy was only one variant of the wave of interest in recharging the spiritual batteries of an increasingly materialistic world through esoteric knowledge and practices that erupted in late nineteenth-century Europe and America. The 'occult revival' led many educated Westerners to search for 'Eastern' wisdom, attempt communication with 'the beyond', or even dabble in the 'Black Arts'. Though only the latest in several 'epidemics' of occultism that have periodically swept through Europe in periods of high liminoidality ever since the latter stages of the Roman Empire, the nineteenth-century one was unique because it became so intertwined with modernist literature, poetry, painting, and science, and assumed a deeply ambivalent role as both the symptom and cure of Modernity's decadence. Its symbolic starting point was the publication of Eliphas Lévi's *Le Dogme et Rituel de la Haute Magie* (1855), an exact contemporary of Baudelaire's *Les Fleurs du Mal*. Anticipating the claims of Theosophy to global truths, Lévi 'revealed' the presence of a doctrine hidden in all the world's religious, mystic, and esoteric traditions which, as the introduction to his book asserted, 'is everywhere the same and everywhere carefully hidden'. A profusion of obscure movements, societies, clubs, and periodicals devoted to different branches of occultism then mushroomed, some of the more famous being the Hermetic Order of the Golden Dawn, the New Knights Templar, the Brotherhood of Luxor, Ancient Mystical Order Rosae Crucis, Societas Rosicruciana, and Ordo Templi Orientis. The movement also had its cult figures such as Aleister Crowley and Papus (Gérard Encausse).[7]

As a practice rather than a literary phenomenon, the mythic starting point of modern occultism can be dated to the public sensation caused by the direct experiences of the beyond claimed by the Fox sisters in 1847. The resulting vogue for a modern form of the ancient practice known as 'spiritualism' soon spread from the US to Europe, becoming so popular that by 1900 the number of Westerners who had participated in at least one séance, whether through a professional medium or of the 'do-it-yourself' kind with a simple Ouija board, has been put at hundreds of thousands. Major personalities such as William James, Houdini, and Carl Jung, took the phenomenon of trance and mesmerism seriously, and Thomas Edison even worked on a mechanical device to enable communication with the spirit world. Edison was also drawn to Theosophy, and it is significant that Blavatsky herself enjoyed a notable reputation as a medium before founding her movement. The upsurge of interest in mediumnic phenomena led to the founding of the Society for Psychical Research (SPR) in London in 1882. Astrology, phrenology, palmistry, and other forms of divination also underwent a renaissance at the time.

Another aspect of the upsurge of interest in accessing a metaphysical reality beyond personal mortality was an increased openness to Eastern thought. Theosophy was the main vehicle for the dissemination of knowledge of non-Christian religions, but the high international profile of Coomaraswamy and the success of Swami Vivekananda's first World Parliament of Religions held in Chicago, an epicentre of American modernism, in 1893 are symptoms of a search for non-Western enlightenment that extended beyond the lure of arcane knowledge. Within a few years the Swami had started Vedantic centres in New York City and London, lectured at major universities, and helped kindle Western interest in Hindu philosophy. It was in this special climate that in 1911 Annie Besant, Blavatsky's successor as leader of the Theosophical Society, made the 14-year-old Jiddhu Krishnamurti the leader of what she intended to be a new global religious movement, the Order of the Star of the East. A further 'sign of the times' was the spread in the West of the Bahai faith as a result of two successful tours made between 1911 and 1913 by its founder Abdu'l-Bahá to North America, Great Britain, France, Germany, and Hungary.

In the light of our ideal type of cultural dynamics, the demand for occultist and mystical ideas and what would now be called 'New Religions' is an unmistakable symptom of the spiritual or nomic crisis of Modernity, the corollary of the success of Western industrialization, technology, science, capitalism, and imperialism in transforming Europe, still largely feudal, rural, and Christian in the eighteenth century, with such dizzying speed in the nineteenth. The Dual Revolution[8] severely compromised the metaphysical protective power first of the traditional Christian nomos, and then that of the initially successful secular substitutes it found in myths of progress. This is not to equate this occultism with modernism as such. Though esotericism played a major role in literary and artistic Decadence, turning Joris Karl Husyman's *Là Bas* (1891) into a canonical text, it only becomes a manifestation of *modernism* – at least in the primordialist understanding of the term – where the world-weary pessimism acquires a 'strong', Dionysian, palingenetic momentum towards social regeneration.[9] Bram Stoker's *Dracula* (1897), for example, visibly lacks the futural thrust which endows Edward Bulwer-Lytton's *Vril: The Coming Race* (1871) with a modernist aura. In this novel cultural pessimism, esotericism, and utopianism blend into the evocation of a cultural and anthropological revolution made possible by drawing on an occult form of energy, *vril*, an idea which was to exert irresistible fascination on post-war occultist Nazis.[10]

By the same token most currents of Europe's new occultism, mysticism, and religion were not forms of modernism in themselves, but merely symptoms of the cultural crisis that produced it. When they did become part of a regenerative movement they were usually no more than ingredients within a particular variant of the modernist vision of social transformation. Nevertheless, the recourse to occultism in this regenerative spirit became so widespread that the cultural historian Frances Saunders can claim that 'From *fin de siècle* Paris to 1950s' New York a fascination with magic, the occult, and the supernatural were *integral* to the Modernist spirit.'[11] Thus we should find nothing the least peculiar in the fact that in the last decade of the nineteenth century modernist architects could be as susceptible to theosophy in the 1920s as abstract artists,[12] or that in 1921 Walter Gropius, synonymous with modernism in architecture and design, employed Georg Muche and Johannes Itten to introduce students of the newly formed Bauhaus to the New Age cult of Mazdaznan.[13]

It is when occultism serves as the principal vehicle for regenerating a civilization allegedly dying from the poison fruits of progress that it can be seen as a form of social modernism in its own right (though this means suspending deeply entrenched preconceptions that identify modernism exclusively with the stance of an avant-garde of artists and intellectuals experimenting with new ways of seeing and thinking). According to this criterion Theosophy in the original conception of Blavatsky and Besant certainly operated as a form of social modernism, and was responded to as such by the many aesthetic and social modernists of the time who blended its core ideas into their own mazeway. It is also true of the most important offshoot from Theosophy, Anthroposophy, founded by Rudolf Steiner in 1923, who attempted to perpetuate his esoteric view of the universe through the international network of Steiner Schools and (in the US) Waldorf Schools that still exists today. Their curriculum is designed to replace the dehumanizing, spiritually desiccating impact of orthodox education, and foster the creativity and spirituality needed by the new generations if they are to save civilization from total collapse.

MODERNITY'S 'CULTIC MILIEU'

Both Theosophy and Anthroposophy were forms of ecumenical humanism based on the existence of perennial laws allegedly governing life revealed in the world's mystic and esoteric traditions. As such they were, at least within the syncretizing mindset of modernist 'mazeway resynthesis', compatible with the wide array of utopian socialisms and visionary humanisms that flourished in the liminoid conditions of late nineteenth-century Europe. This blend is exemplified in the rampant eclecticism discernible in Wassily Kandinsky's *Concerning the Spiritual in Art*, and in an even more elaborated version in Ananda Coomaraswamy's intellectual synthesis in which Theosophical ideas were conjoined seamlessly with an enthusiasm for anti-colonialism, Kropotkinite anarchist syndicalism, the utopian socialism of the Arts and Crafts movement pioneered by William Morris and John Ruskin, and the 'post-industrial' theory of Arthur Penty, as well as elements of Hindu and Buddhist idealism.[14]

How fluid distinctions between left and right became in the luxuriant greenhouse climate of the time where ideological hybrids thrived so easily is shown by Coomaraswamy's role in promoting a visionary leftist reading of Nietzsche which found considerable resonance in US avant-garde circles. He also published articles in Alfred Orage's *The New Age* (1907–22) whose combination of socio-political radicalism with avant-garde cultural theory made it for at least a decade the most important Anglophone organ for disseminating the 'modernist mindset' in the widest, maximalist sense it has acquired in this book. There his articles appeared alongside those of rightist modernists such as critic Thomas Hulme, Catholic economic modernist Hilaire Belloc, founder of Futurism Filippo Marinetti, and right-wing cultural critic and poet Wyndham Lewis, who incarnated the turbulent ideological energies of the time and also launched his own brand of modernist aesthetic, Vorticism, just after the outbreak of the First World War.

Coomaraswamy, Marinetti, and Lewis illustrated different ways in which artists and intellectuals campaigning for radical social change absorbed elements of Nietzscheanism, often an adulterated form of the thinker's own brand of 'Dionysian modernism' which in lesser hands reduced it to a vague call for the re-evaluation of all values and the iconoclastic destruction of fallen idols. As such it was appropriated by 'politicians, theologians, anarchists, philosophers, psychiatrists, psychoanalysts, sexual libertarians, promoting the "new ethic" – indeed anyone seeking change, renewal, or rebirth',[15] and could seep into the critiques levelled at the status quo by Social Democrats, Anarchists, and bourgeois feminists alike. Paradoxically, given the Nazis' later eagerness to find him a place within the Pantheon of the Third Reich, Nietzsche's contempt for German nationalism and his ambivalent verdict on Jewish culture exposed him before 1914 to contempt from extreme nationalists and anti-Semites in Germany.[16] Bergsonism was a similar phenomenon. Henri Bergson's dethroning of the linear, rational, Newtonian perception of time, his celebration of *l'élan vital* and the temporality of duration (*durée*) lent themselves to legitimizing diverse socio-political agenda, both leftist and rightist, to inaugurate a new vision of reality and a new historical era which spurned the checks and balances of rationalism,[17] all formulated in the characteristic palingenetic key of social modernism.

The spread of Nietzscheanism and Bergsonism was just one index of the transformation of the intellectual and artistic climate of turn-of-the-century Europe into a powerful incubator for what Colin Campbell has called the 'cultic milieu',[18] where groups of like-minded intellectuals collaborated in promoting ideas of change with a fervour that caused their main sources of ideas to be treated as revered prophets. The extreme syncretism that is a feature of such milieux is symptomatic of the modernist ideological process of ludic recombination at work typical of revitalization movements. It is consistent with this that Karla Poewe points out in her study of the *völkisch* subculture in Germany that in their bid to regenerate society the leaders of different groupuscules would typically 'take or reject opportunistically bits and pieces of Yogic and Abrahamic traditions' and mix in 'popular notions of science – or rather pseudo-science – such as concepts of "race", "eugenics" or "evolution"', and so create a synthesis of ideas that 'nourish[ed] new mythologies of would-be totalitarian regimes'.[19] Fin-de-siècle Europe hosted countless cells and currents of palingenetic ideological activity symptomatic of the West's deepening nomic crisis. Collectively they formed a diffuse counter-cultural environment where personality cults and radical ideas of imminent historical transformations could prosper outside the political process.

The general search for what Hermann Broch described as a 'Healer' to 'give meaning to the incomprehensible events of the Age', led to the cults that grew up not just around Indian gurus such as Swami Vivekananda and Jiddhu Krishnamurti, but outstanding creative figures such as Fyodor Dostoevsky, Leo Tolstoy, Henrik Ibsen, Gabriele D'Annunzio, and Johann Goethe – whose memory was celebrated in the temple-like Goetheanum which Rudolf Steiner built at the Anthroposophical headquarters in Switzerland. Before acquiring guru status within the fin-de-siècle (especially after his collapse into insanity), Nietzsche himself had fallen victim of a cult, namely the one that developed around the figure of Richard Wagner. For some the act of attending the performance of his operas itself became an initiatic experience, the Bayreuth festival serving as a pagan Lourdes for thousands of 'pilgrims' anxious for direct contact with the numinous, transcendental power of myth summoned up through the 'total work of art'. For more nationalistically inclined Germans, like Leopold von Schröder, an Indologist working at Vienna University, the opera house there became the geographical and symbolic site in which for the first time in 5,000 years the 'Aryan tribes' could 'contemplate the ancient mysteries fulfilled in a new form'. His book *The Fulfilment of the Aryan Mystery at Bayreuth* (1911) declared that the town had become 'the centre of all the Aryan peoples', a fact guaranteeing 'an astonishing supremacy to Germany and the Germans'.[20]

RIGHTIST SOCIAL MODERNISM

The cults of both Nietzsche and Wagner were later appropriated by the Nazis and perverted into legitimation of the Third Reich. This fact alone might in some eyes disqualify them from being considered as forms of modernism given the marked tendency in the past to equate the politics of modernism, in so far as they were recognized at all,[21] with left-wing radicalism. It is a stance whose concomitant is to insist on the reactionary, and hence anti-modern, nature of the right that lurks under its aestheticized sheen.[22] Approached on the basis of such ingrained prejudice, there is, for example, nothing at all contradictory about Coomaraswamy's blend of Nietzschean anarchism with the promotion of art and crafts socialism and a celebration of Van Gogh. In contrast, Ezra Pound's presence alongside him in the pages of *The New Age* is anomalous, particularly given the poet's later fanatical espousal of Fascism. It is thus important to stress unequivocally that, just as modernity has its dark side masterfully explored by Zygmunt Bauman in *Modernity and the Holocaust* (1991), so modernism has its dark side too. It is exemplified in the emergence of a cultic milieu which worked towards a *new* modernity, but which was itself based on a variant of occultism that saw communist and liberal or anarchist ideas of universal social justice – nowadays condemned by the New Right as a decadent 'one-worldism' – as symptoms of degeneracy, rather than the cure.

This dark side is illustrated by the very context in which Coomaraswamy came to promulgate the *philosophia perennis* as the basis of an ecumenical, pacifist vision of human solidarity deeply indebted to Theosophy. It was a vision taken up independently in the inter-war period by Aldous Huxley (e.g. *The*

Perennial Philosophy, 1938) and, after the cataclysm of another world war, by Fritjof Schuon (*The Transcendent Unity of Religions*, 1948). However, this 'Traditionalism', which bore all the hallmarks of a revitalization movement in the realm of modern ideas, had already become politically ambiguous in the works of René Guénon. In the 1920s he called for a return to the spiritual tradition to resolve the decline of the West (*La crise du monde moderne*, 1927) in a condemnation of materialism that contained a conspicuous component of elitism, anti-liberalism, anti-communism, and anti-democracy. With Julius Evola 'Traditionalism' allied itself overtly to totalitarianism, misogyny, anti-Semitism, racism, imperialism, and biopolitics, and hence became the accomplice to the most elitist, uncompromising, and terroristic forms of Fascism and Nazism. Even Mircea Eliade's Traditionalism only assumed a reassuringly 'democratic' countenance after he had placed out of sight and out of mind (at least of others) the passionate commitment to the Romanian Iron Guard he displayed so openly in the 1930s.[23]

Rather than approach Coomaraswamy as a *progressive* modernist and Evola as a *reactionary* anti-modernist, it is argued here that they should be seen as representing left- and right-wing forms of modernism, each with their own futural, palingenetic agenda to erect a new sacred canopy in a decadent world. This line of argument leads to the proposition that, just as Theosophy should be seen as a form of social modernism, so should its racist and anti-Semitic perversions, some of which played a well-documented role in the genesis of Nazism. The most notorious example of this perversion was the work of a contemporary of Rudolf Steiner, the Austrian Lanz von Liebenfels. He carried out yet another feat of mazeway synthesis so typical of the age, fusing Blavatsky's belief in the Aryans as humanity's root race with other strands of esotericism, extreme German nationalism, and a rabid hatred of Jews, and cemented this amalgam with a newly invented panoply of symbolism and ritual. The totalizing world-view that resulted was known as Ariosophy, a diagnosis of the ills of Modernity based on a theory of evolution conceived in Manichean terms as an ongoing battle between healthy and evil forces operating in an invisible metaphysical realm, a clash of cosmic cultures. Ariosophy became the official ideology of the Order of the New Templars, founded by von Liebenfels in 1915. Despite its pronounced anti-modernity, Ariosophy derived a *futural* momentum from the assumption that the occult truth about the demonic contamination of the Aryan race not only explained the decadence of contemporary Europe, but in particular the tribulations of the German race, deprived of its own homeland and at the mercy of dysgenic, *inhuman* racial forces. It thus fanatically promoted the creation of a *new* Germany uniting all Aryans in a single nation purged of the metaphysical evil incarnated in racial degeneracy.

Von Liebenfels had been influenced by another racist who had also adapted Theosophical ideas to the cause of Germany's regeneration, Guido von List. It was his brand of racist mysticism that helped shape the version of Ariosophy – here a generic term for occultist variants of Aryanism – devised by Rudolf von Sebottendorf, who became a leader of the Germanenorden (founded 1912) before setting up the Thule Society as a Munich branch of the Order of the Germans in August 1917. It was members of this society that formed the Deutsche Arbeiter Partei in 1919.[24] Ariosophical influence may explain Rosenberg's cryptic reference to the 'Nordic-Atlantean' master race in his *The Myth of the Twentieth Century*.[25] More importantly it encouraged those Nazis familiar with the Ariosophical diagnosis of Modernity to see the task of creating the new, post-Versailles Germany in Manichean terms of eradicating an enemy who embodied the decadence of Modernity, the Jews. The political struggle was only the outward form of a fight to the death between decadent and healthy races in a war that was not just apocalyptic in a millenarian sense, but *cosmogonic*: its task was the creation of a new world out of contemporary chaos.

It is in the context of a cultic milieu which produced both left- *and* right-wing variants of social modernism that we should see the late nineteenth-century rise of *völkisch* nationalism. This was a polycentric revitalization movement made up of hundreds of associations, magazines, books, and a highly variegated ideology, but bent on the common goal of bringing about the birth of a new Germany purged of the symptoms of decadence identified with the Second Reich. We will have reason to consider it again in the context of political modernism in the next chapter. For the moment it is sufficient to establish that the *völkisch* movement operated primarily as a campaign for cultural and metapolitical revitalization, something that emerges clearly from two of its most influential texts. Thus in his bestselling *Deutsche Schriften* (1878) Paul Lagarde preaches the need for the awakening of a Germanic faith, a synthesis of nationalism with Christianity and anti-Semitism, to overcome the materialism of the age. It falls to 'true' leaders endowed with a vision that rises above the vulgar sphere of power politics to preserve the spiritual essence of the organic German nation, whose rebirth naturally involved a process of cleansing:

> We cannot achieve authenticity ourselves: governments must do their part for us by conscientiously ridding us of everything that has been created artificially, and by promoting with the steady gaze of expert love the growth of what will sprout up out of the old soil once it has been cleansed of rubbish: the roots of our being are still alive.[26]

Similarly Julius Langbehn in *Rembrandt as Educator* (1890), which ran to 80 editions before 1945, depicted Germany's rebirth in terms of the awakening of the German creative genius embodied in the Dutch painter: 'Rembrandt is a genuine Aryan; if the still and powerful breath of the Rembrandtian spirit infuses the quality which is uniquely Germanic, then its life can be renewed once more.'[27] The solution is in the rebirth of German culture, in the re-education of Germans in a way that cures them of decadence. Langbehn's vision of the regenerative process was shaped by the theosophy not of Madame Blavatsky, but of Emanuel Swedenborg, a Swedish mystic who constructed a monistic version of Christianity that stressed the organic interconnectedness of human life with the cosmos.[28]

In both texts a mythicized Germany becomes the physical and metaphysical antidote to the threat of nihilism so as to resolve 'the crisis raised by modernity',[29] namely Modernity. The ethnic nation re-embeds time and space and re-enchants the world. It supplies a limited horizon framed by myth, the canopy of faith needed to exorcise the horror of anomy. Within this mythic discourse the *Volk* in its present state becomes the point of intersection of a cluster of metaphors evoking decadence: the loss of transcendence (spirit), metaphysical homelessness, uprootedess, chaos, fragmentation, sickness, physical degeneracy, and pollution. It must thus be sacralized, restored as homeland, re-rooted, founded on a new order, united within a single community, healed of sickness, and purged of pollution. A mythicized Germany itself became for *völkisch* thinkers and artists the nomos, the sacred canopy, but they were responding to the same cultural forces that made 'the fascination with magic, the occult, and the supernatural' and the imperative 'to clean up, to sterilize, to re-order, to eliminate chaos and dirt'[30] the twin fulcrum around which programmatic modernism revolved not just in Germany, but *internationally*.[31]

Seen from this perspective, *völkisch* nationalism is an outstanding form of socio-political modernism, a product not just of the crisis of *German* ideology – the title of Mosse's book – but of the ideological and ontological crisis of modernity itself. There has been much attention lavished on Germany's *Sonderweg* to nationhood, but perhaps not enough to the bigger *Sonderweg*, the 'special', dysfunctional path of Western civilization in which Germany's history was embedded. It is indeed important to see *völkisch* nationalism emerging as a response to the particularly liminoid conditions created by the impact of modernization on Wilhelmine Germany combined with its 'belated' nationhood. But it is no less important to see this crisis in turn as one permutation of a phenomenon that was taking place throughout the Western world wherever fault lines opened up between modernity and 'traditional' culture once the combined scientific, capitalist, technological, liberal revolutions gathered pace. It is thus no coincidence if contemporaneously with the spread of the *völkisch* subculture, the late nineteenth century witnessed the rise of cultural and political nationalism in Ireland, the spread of political anti-Semitism in Germany, Austria and France, and the emergence of powerful currents of ultra-nationalism in Eastern Europe as well as in Catalonia, where Barcelona was the confluence of powerful currents of both aesthetic and political modernism as the sense of cultural and historical distinctiveness from Castilian Spain gathered strength.

Behind intensely futural projects centred on national rebirth lurked archetypes of pristine, Edenic, unalienated, homile states of human community *in illo tempore* where the firmament was still solid, where the cosmic order was intact, where Gods were near, where harmony, rootedness, and physical health reigned, where human beings lived in a harmonious state of being, rather than in the permanent exile of existence. Nor did the impulse to regain the lost paradise in defiance of Modernity need to express itself artistically, ideologically, or through the bizarre cultic behaviour of a new religion based on the worship of race. In fact, an even more natural outlet was to adopt a healthy life-style, or impose health on a decadent age.

MODERNIST BODY POLITICS

In the first of his discourses Zarathustra reveals the final metamorphosis of the spirit. In the desert the camel bearing the full weight of an age of decadence suddenly changes into a lion capable of the fierce courage needed to utter the 'sacred No' necessary to defy the nihilism of prevailing social norms. Finally the lion mutates into the child of innocence and forgetfulness needed for 'a new beginning' and 'sacred Yes'. Robert Gooding-Williams comments, 'the essence of this affirmation, the child-spirit's "yes" to the game of creation, is the transformation of passional chaos into a newly integrated body'. It is a concept that betrays the belief 'shared with many of his contemporaries – scientists, physicians, and novelists among them' – that 'modern civilization was fast succumbing to the forces of physical fatigue', and that 'physical exhaustion' was a symptom of 'cultural decay'.[32]

Had Nietzsche followed through this epiphany and taken up yoga or an oriental martial art, then the history of Western philosophy might well have taken a different turn, even if the cultural crisis that he was trying to resolve through his writings would have certainly continued to summon forth 'Nietzschean' reactions of Dionysian pessimism. Others, however, were more prepared than him to embrace fully the idea of the body as the site of personal and social transformation, and actively lived out this ideal in one or other of the groups or organizations attempting the total re-evaluation of modern human beings' relationship to their body that spread throughout northern and central Europe in the late nineteenth century. The result was an upsurge of interest in such practices as gymnastics, body building, callisthenics, and various types of dietetics, each with their own philosophy and ethic, some based on esoteric or religious traditions, others intensely 'scientized'. A famous instance of this new form of social modernism was the efficient digestion rhapsodically promoted as cure-all by the vegetarian fundamentalist, anti-sex crusader, and inventor of the breakfast cereal, John Kellogg. His religious zeal – enforced with militaristic precision – about creating a holistic new world through alternative therapies such as colonic irrigation and abstinence is mercilessly parodied in Alan Parker's 1994 film, *The Road to Wellville* set in Kellogg's appropriately named Battle Creek Sanatorium.

The same period also saw the appearance of the first communes in which small groups of civilized Westerners deliberately 'dropped out' of the decadent West to find a healthy balance between mind, body, and nature denied them in the cities.[33] One was the Eden Association, founded by 18 vegetarians in 1893 north of Berlin. Its seed-oil margarine was first manufactured in 1908 and sold as 'Eden Reform Butter'. Having been Nazified under Hitler and then 'Communized' under the GDR, the community was then 'Capitalized' after the German unification in 1991 and underwent a further transformation reflecting a more ecologically sensitive age in 2000 when it became Eden Naturbau Gmbh specializing in organic and environmentally friendly products. In 2006 it was chosen as one of 365 places symbolizing Germany as Land of Ideas in the context of the World Cup Finals. Eden was once again under new management.

However, the foremost utopian community of the pre-1914 period was the Swiss Monte Verità community, located on the mountain above Ascona overlooking Lake Maggiore, which between 1900 and the early 1920s was the unrivalled Mecca of the so-called Lebensreform or 'life reform Movement'. The link between aesthetic, social, and political modernism and this movement is underscored by the list of just some of the more famous personalities to have participated briefly in the vegetarian life-style at 'Mount Truth': notably Hermann Hesse, Carl Jung, Erich Maria Remarque, Hugo Ball, Else Lasker-Schüler, Stefan George, Isadora Duncan, Paul Klee, Rudolf Steiner, Mary Wigman, Ernst Toller, Otto Gross, and Gustav Stresemann. All such counter-cultural projects in alternative living in the first decades of the twentieth century can be seen as practical manifestations of the utopianism that was such a powerful feature of the modernist revolt against decadence.[34] They literally 'embodied' the simultaneous search for restored health and for renewed roots through the discovery, on behalf of a modern humanity sinking ever further into a morass of decadence, of a new *arche* to modern life, a basic ordering principle on which to build an alternative, cosmologically and *biologically* regrounded future. 'Life reform' pursued a politically ambiguous agenda. The racist counterpart to Monte Verità, whose ethos was distinctly libertarian, was the colony of Nueva Germania set up by Nietzsche's brother-in-law, Wilhelm Förster, in 1896 to breed pure-blooded Christian Aryan peasants in Paraguay, far away from the moral and racial corruption of urban Europe.

The vegetarianism adopted by some of these utopian communities was symptomatic of the new relationship between mind and body cultivated in what Christopher Wilk, the organizer of London's 2006 exhibition on modernism, calls the 'Healthy Body Culture'. He gives a fascinating panoramic account of this culture in an article which opens with the statement, 'the entire Modernist enterprise was permeated by a deep concern for health'.[35] It traces the roots of this pre-eminently *social* project of renewal to a point in the nineteenth century where not just avant-garde artists but city-dwellers began identifying modernity with dysgenic living, and could feel the polluting, dehumanizing consequences of 'progress' not just mentally but on and in their bodies. Though vegetarianism was an extremely ancient practice, the 'fin-de-siècle' obsession with the degeneracy of an entire civilization provided the essential precondition for it to become a form of programmatic modernism. Within a few years enough national vegetarian societies had sprung up for them to hold their first world Congress in Dresden in 1908. It was also attended by the Esperanto Vegetarian Society three years after the first International Congress of Esperanto, yet another example of a form of modernist utopianism attempting to counteract the divisiveness and fragmentation of human society. Some of the more famous personalities attracted to vegetarianism were Leo Tolstoy, Annie Besant, George Bernard Shaw, and Franz Kafka,[36] not to mention the countless disciples of yoga, for whom it is integral to the discipline.[37]

Another symptom of the modern West's rediscovery of the ancient precept of 'mens sana in corpore sano' was the promotion of yoga by Swami Vivekananda's Vedantic centres to complement a purely intellectual understanding of Hinduism. Meanwhile, the growing awareness of Taoism led to greater openness to Chinese traditions such as acupuncture, herbalism, holistic medicine, martial arts, and macrobiotics. The same period saw a wave of interest in complementary therapies such as homeopathy and physiotherapy, whose first professional body was founded in London in 1894 – Freud was using massage to treat hysteria a year later.

The current of thought that underpinned, or at least complemented, this aspect of the revolt against materialism was a phenomenon sometimes known as 'vitalism', and known in German cultural history as 'life-mysticism' ('Lebensmystik'). In radically undermining the metaphysical claims of Christianity, Darwinism had also created the cultural space for a cult of biological life. Darwinism could provoke a deep sense of the utter irrelevance of human life in the cosmic scheme of things, a negative epiphany glimpsed in the last pages of H. G. Wells' *The Time Machine* (1895). A diametrically opposed temperamental reaction was to 're-enchant' the disenchanted universe, and approach it as the physical manifestation of a mysterious life-force newly revealed by science to be transforming itself – through natural selection and not the intervention of God – into myriad diverse organisms, all living out their unique cycle of life and death and integral to an evolutionary process of which humans were the latest stage. The sense of awe at the mystery of life itself, of the entire biosphere, crystallized in the vitalism that the literary historian Wolfdietrich Rasch has shown to be a common denominator between late nineteenth-century European artists of such disparate aesthetics as naturalism, symbolism, and realism. In avant-garde circles it represented 'a conspiracy of counter-forces' determined to resist 'the disintegration of the world into unrelated facts'. In a world now '*entgöttert*' – literally 'stripped of its gods' – to a point where human beings were being reduced 'to units of work or of purchasing power, to a calculable and exchangeable entity', poetry's mission was to reconstitute the lost spirit (nomos) by 'turning individual objects into symbols of the universal'.[38] This 'secularized, immanent mysticism without God', is a *topos* not just of the philosophy of Nietzsche, the poetry of Rainer Maria Rilke, and the early novels of Thomas Mann, but recurs throughout the literature, poetry, painting, and philosophy of European culture at the turn of the century, from Ibsen to Yeats, from Zola to D'Annunzio.

The call for a vegetarian life-style, for a new relationship with the body, for sexual emancipation,[39] for 'natural remedies', for enhancing the 'life-spirit' was deeply bound up with less philosophically reflexive, more physical longings to get 'back-to-nature' and find an escape from the degenerate aspects of modernity epitomized in the squalor of polluted, overcrowded, dysgenic cities. The middle-class fashion for holidays in seaside resorts, mountains, or spa towns, the new popular interest in cycling, swimming, seaside, lake-side, mountain village and spa holidays, mountaineering, rambling, and hiking was not just a function of the rise of leisure, but of a sea-change in the attitude to 'civilization', partly stimulated by the prevalence of contagious diseases, notably tuberculosis. This is the period when scouting quickly grew from Baden-Powell's first camping expedition on an island in Poole Harbour in 1908 to an international movement that held its first jamboree in 1924. The manual *Scouting for Boys* became the all-time bestseller in the English language after the Bible.

Contemporaneously the German youth movement was taking off through the extraordinary success of the Wandervogel organization founded in 1896, a forerunner of the 50,000 strong 'bündische Jugend' (Federated Youth) movement formed in 1923 that eventually was absorbed into the Hitler Youth. The 'world-view' of the German youth movement fused health, nature, life, and the fatherland into a single cultic entity, and was epitomized in the solemn declaration made by the Free German Youth after its mass ascent of the peak of North-East Hessen's Hohe Meissner mountain in 1913. It declared the resolve of German youth, now standing 'at a historical turning point', to contribute a 'rejuvenating current to the spiritual life of the people' by encouraging the young to develop an 'inner relationship to nature and the Volk'. Its members saw themselves as the nucleus of a new type of German, courageous, active, healthy – drinking and smoking were banned at all Free Youth meetings – and ready to sacrifice himself (and by implication herself) to the nation in both war and peace. Stuart Hughes's groundbreaking study of the turn-of-the-century's 'reorientation of European social thought' in *Consciousness and Society* (1979) presents this 'melodramatic pledge' as epitomizing the way younger men everywhere in Europe 'were in search of an ideal and a faith'.[40] In fact, all the intellectual phenomena that Hughes explored under the heading 'the revolt against positivism' were deeply bound up with a more generalized 'revolt against decadence' expressed through action rather than images or words.

Perhaps the outstanding expression of this international, socially *modernist* concern for health was the 'Free Body Movement' ('Freikörperbewegung') that emerged in Germany in the 1890s. It is an expression that significantly embraces not just naturism ('Freikörperkultur'), but experimental forms of dance where social and aesthetic modernism become inextricable. Evidence that the naturist movement is to be associated with the revolt against decadence and the search for temporalized forms of transcendence, is provided by the campaigns on behalf of naturism fought by Richard Ungewitter. In *Nudity and Morality* (1907) and *Nudity and Culture* (1913) he spread the gospel of nudism as an emancipating force that would 'free' the body from the pernicious effects of a soft, over-cerebral, and hypocritical civilization. In 1913 he was calling upon Ariosophists to incorporate nudism in their war against the decadence epitomized in Jews, communists, and feminists.[41] The loss of the war did not dampen his ardour. In the 1920s he wrote increasingly fanatical accounts of the key role to be played by nudism in national regeneration and the recapturing of the national essence.[42]

It was thus symptomatic of a cultural mood that had spread far beyond the confines of art that modern dance exploded onto the scene in the early 1900s in Germany and the US. Its effects were felt not just in the dance companies that formed in Moscow, Paris, London, and New York, or in the revolutionary type of ballet that modernist composers such as Stravinsky or Prokoviev and the choreographers Sergei Diaghilev and Vaslav Nijinsky felt compelled to stage, but in a transformed relationship between dance, self-expression, physical athleticism, sensuality, and the spectator. For Karl Toepfer, whose *Empire of Ecstasy* is an encyclopaedic history of the intimate relationship between life reform and Modern Dance, the revolution in movement 'signified the most powerful (and therefore ecstatic) claim of the body, fusing mystical transcendence of material illusions and modern fearlessness at looking at human identity with optimum nakedness and materiality'.[43] At its most experimental, 'expressive dance' (Ausdruckstanz) also had obvious links with the rebellious ethos of Expressionism, enacting the longing to stage *kinetic* representations of the 'new man' and 'new woman' who had broken free from decadence and celebrated a new modernity.[44]

The modernist dynamic of dance's revolutionary break-away from the classical ballet tradition can be sensed strongly in the 'eurhythmics' developed by Rudolf Steiner as an Anthroposophical exercise. It is also perceptible in the trip taken to Russia by Isadora Duncan, the pioneer of 'free dance', an aesthetic form directly inspired by Nietzsche's 'Dionysian modernism', to make her personal contribution to the creation of a new socialist world then in its infancy. It is also apparent in the highly influential summer workshops in expressive dance held from 1910 in the Monte Verità commune by the Hungarian-born Rudolf von Laban, the 'Picasso of modern dance'. One of the pupils who fell under the spell of the new art form at one of the Ascona workshops was Mary Wigman, who went on to become the most influential choreographer of her day. They collaborated on staging the elaborate dance spectacles of the 1936 Berlin Olympics immortalized in Leni Riefenstahl's *The Triumph of the Will*. (Goebbels cancelled the Dance Olympics that Wigman planned as a parallel event to the Games, perhaps because he anticipated Hitler's displeasure at their subtext of pacifistic internationalism.)[45]

SCIENTISTIC 'NARRATIVES OF CHANGE'

It was not only in avant-garde dance and the new 'body culture' that the modernist search for health found expression. It permeated the creative imagination of professionals in every sphere of activity that impinged on the well-being of modern society, such as doctors, engineers, designers, architects, town planners, pedagogues, educational theorists, and the pioneers of what has now become familiar as the 'welfare state'. It also created a new climate for research in the natural and behavioural sciences, one in which the ethos of the revolt against decadence became integral to what Hermann Boch called in *The Sleepwalkers* the 'radical logic' into the jaws of which the most forward-looking specialists of the time were liable to fall.[46] The result was 'scientism', the blend of positivist science with palingenetic myths of societal regeneration or creating a new world.[47]

The obsession with finding cures for neurotic conditions previously regarded as irreversible in an age that itself was 'mad' ensured that Freud's development of a therapeutic technique based on his theory of the unconscious had an impact far outside the confines of clinical medicine. According to Richard Noll, psychoanalysis was turned by the more ardent converts to the therapy into a movement for 'totalizing cultural revitalization', to the point where in 1907 Max Weber expressed concern that Freudian analysts were becoming a 'quasi-mystical charismatic group based on the personality and ideas of a charismatic leader who was considered to have almost divine qualities'.[48] In 1930 Freud would publish his own account of the 'malaise of modernity',[49] and the concern with societal decadence as manifested in neurosis is the Leitmotiv of his life's work. However, he retained much more scepticism about the potential of psychoanalysis to resolve the psychological dysfunctionality of Modernity than his more fanatical followers.

In the decade before the First World War the most prominent of these had been Carl Jung who for a time campaigned fervently for psychoanalysis to develop into an 'irresistible mass movement'[50] of redemption and rebirth. In his eyes it had the potential not only to offer a personal path to overcoming degenerative neurosis, but to substitute the cosmology of a moribund Christianity. At the same time it would contribute to the revival of the Aryan legacy in Europe, and hence the renewal of history itself.[51] Until well into the 1930s the driving force behind Jung's ceaseless psychological experiments with human mythopoeia and research into the archetypal symbols of religious, mystic, and occultist traditions was his personal sense of mission to help modern human beings – or at least their Aryan component – to access once more the archetypal symbols which he saw as supplying the psychic life-blood of all societies before Modernity destroyed the sacred canopy.

The outstanding example of the scientistic currents of social modernism in this period, however, is the 'Monistic Alliance' founded by the vitalistic life-scientist Ernst Haeckel, which within a few years of its formation in 1906 had chapters all over central Europe. 'Monism' was based on a vitalistic interpretation of Darwinism which derived a sense of a higher metaphysical order from the 'miraculous' intricacies of organic life being revealed every day by the secular natural sciences, then in a phase of rapid expansion. True to the pervasive spirit of the life-mysticism of the time, *uncreated* Life itself became the source of the numinous, providing every organism with an envelope of sacrality. Haeckel and his followers saw this awe-struck perception of the natural world as 'ample compensation for the anthropistic ideals of "God, freedom, and immortality" which we have lost'. In 1877 he used a lecture to point out that 'the soul and body of man' were formed from a particular combination of elementary chemicals, mostly carbon. 'With this single argument the mystery of the universe is explained, the Deity is annulled and a new era of infinite knowledge is ushered in.'[52] Haeckel's own interpretation of Monism developed in an increasingly racist rather than humanist direction. The impact that it could have on those who already had racist convictions is illustrated by Vacher de Lapouge, the main ideologue of Aryanism and political anti-Semitism in France,[53] who 'aspired to nothing less than the birth of a new spiritual age, a religious reformation that civilization in the twentieth century was fated to inaugurate, [...] rooted in the "behaviour of life" itself'.[54]

Significantly, Richard Noll himself uses the anthropological model of the *rite de passage* to explain the process that brought converts to Monism, though it would apply to the conversion of any anomic individual to a current of social modernism in this period:

> In a secular rite of passage, the monist is thus reborn through the rejection of the tenets of organized religion (separation), an initiation into the proof of the essential unity of matter and spirit (a period of liminality), and then participation in local societies promoting monistic ideas (reincorporation).[55]

The paradoxical transformation of positivist science – the main vector of 'disenchantment' – into a source of transcendence was the precondition for the rise of 'eugenics'. When Francis Galton, who coined the term in 1883, gave his paper on its 'definition, scope, and aims' to the Sociological Society at London University in May 1904, he specifically presented it as what we have termed a new mazeway to be inculcated by the state:

> It must be introduced into the national conscience, like a new religion. It has, indeed, strong claims to become an orthodox religious tenet of the future, for eugenics co-operate with the workings of nature by securing that humanity shall be represented by the fittest races.

Galton concludes: 'Then let its principles work into the heart of the nation, which will gradually give practical effect to them in ways that we may not wholly foresee.'[56] With hindsight his words have a chilling air of prescience.

A number of cultural historians have recognized the influence of eugenics on the imagination of artistic modernists.[57] However, once it is seen as a form of social modernism in its own right,[58] its dramatic rise to prominence in early twentieth-century history can be seen attributable, not to disinterested scientific curiosity or even humanist idealism, but to the prospect it offered of purging society of its degeneracy through an unprecedented alliance between modern science and the power of the modern state. It is thus no coincidence if the first recorded use of the term 'biopolitics' not only seems to have occurred in this period (1911), but in the leading modernist periodical of the day, *The New Age*.[59] Scientized racism exerted a particular appeal to educated circles where the impact of Social Darwinism encouraged the subliminal social anxieties fuelled by modernity to be 'biologized' into the conviction that civilization was being destroyed from within by the forces of physiological 'degeneracy' and racial decay. Eugenics thus represents a supreme example of what Koselleck calls 'the temporalization of utopia', a fact illustrated by Galton's brief sketch of a society called Laputa which uses social control to promote hard work.[60] The unholy alliance of science with projects to create an ideal society emerges even more clearly from the uncompleted novel *Kantsaywhere* that he started shortly before his death. It describes a land in which reproduction and migration are strictly controlled by the state to preserve the purity of the race, and where university degrees are awarded to the most genetically gifted.[61]

The history of eugenics is highly complex,[62] with each European country following its own *Sonderweg* and hosting unique blends of Social Darwinism, physical and cultural anthropology, and genetics, with elements of demography, racial hygiene, organic nationalism, anti-Semitism, occultism, and particular political agendas, both left-wing and right-wing. In Britain, for example, eugenicist ideas were taken up by a pre-1914 radical right concerned with the impact that racial decay would have on the strength of the Empire,[63] but also by left-wing intellectuals such as H. G. Wells and George Bernard Shaw, as well as the Fabian socialist leaders Sidney and Beatrice Webb. Meanwhile in Germany the eugenic climate was shaped by such pivotal works as Alfred Ploetz's *Principles of Racial Hygiene* (1895), Ernst Haeckel's *The Riddle of the Universe at the Close of the Nineteenth Century* (1899), and Houston Stewart Chamberlain's *The Foundations of the Nineteenth Century* (1899) all written against the background of increasingly powerful currents of *völkisch* nationalism and political anti-Semitism. It was also in this period that Eastern Europe saw the rapid emergence of biopolitics as a discourse for legitimizing projects of national self-assertion, ethnic division, and racial prejudice.[64] In every case, social modernism was being rationalized through science to create palingenetic projects driven by the spectre of decadence and nebulous longings for transcendence.

Though the focus of this chapter is the rise of social modernism between 1880 and 1918, it is worth illustrating the way the prevalent concern with degeneracy and decadence before 1914 went on to feed concrete projects aimed at effecting radical change in society after the war even in countries where liberal democracy was intact. In this case the prevailing ethos was reformist and pragmatic, mercifully free of the strident tones of creative destruction and Dionysian pessimism intrinsic to the totalizing rhetoric of the modern political *revolutions* being carried out under Hitler and Stalin. In

her study of the attempts by philanthropists and enlightened state authorities
in inter-war Britain to counteract the dire impact of unplanned modernization
on the poorest groups in society, Elizabeth Darling devotes one chapter to
considering the 'new landscape of health' that emerged in the aftermath of
victory. It focuses on two projects to enhance communal welfare in London,
the Peckham Experiment and the Finsbury Plan, both of which she claims can
be understood as 'having been enacted by *programmatic modernists*', and
'exemplify the way in which modernist reformers in complementary fields
– health, housing, architecture – came together to form an alliance to create
and promote narratives of change'.[65] It was an alliance that, in the fullest sense
of the title used for the exhibition on modernism held in London in 2006, set
about 'designing a new world'.

Darling traces the origins of these schemes to a new conception of individuals
as both 'biological and social beings', as simultaneously 'corporeal and social'
became 'intertwined with the ideological field of another branch of Social
Medicine, that of reform eugenism'.[66] This was a left-wing current of social
hygiene driven by widespread Edwardian anxieties about the high degree of
'physical deterioration' and 'devitalization' revealed by the Boer War, anxieties
intertwined in their turn both with the scientistic concerns of eugenicists about
the urgent need, as Cecil Chesterton put it in 1906, to breed the right 'kind of
race', and with the perceived task of government to increase 'national efficiency'
so that Britain would not be 'overtaken' by Germany and the US.[67] The two
projects carried out in London in the 1930s anticipate the most progressive
post-1945 theories of the 'welfare state' in the way they deliberately set out
to create a synergy between medicine, architecture, town planning, interior
design, aesthetic modernism, and the state's capacity to structure the leisure
of the masses and integrate them into the body of the nation. The resulting
schemes were thus imbued with a visionary ethos about the enormous potential
for a *reformist* state to apply the growing power of modern technocracy in an
enlightened, humanistic spirit to improve the lot of its citizens. They exhibit
a distant but unmistakable kinship with the projects being realized under
Fascism to create an entirely new order through large-scale state intervention
in social housing, social hygiene, demography, and the structuring of mass
leisure (i.e. in the mass organizations of 'Dopolavoro', or 'after work', and
the sustained state-led campaign for increasing the nation's health and birth
rate). However, even the explicitly revolutionary and totalitarian measures
of reform adopted in Italy were little more than a strong breeze compared to
the violent hurricanes of change that raged in these spheres in contemporary
Germany and Russia.

If Darling's book provides a glimpse of the new social realities that fin-
de-siècle European angst about society's 'devitalization' and 'racial decay'

could lead to under liberal forms of social modernism, the specific ideological dynamics of *fascist* social modernism are illuminated by considering the impact similar fears of social degeneracy had on the life of Max Nordau. He achieved international fame with two bestsellers, *The Conventional Lies of our Civilisation* (1883), a scathing indictment of the moral bankruptcy of modern society, and *Degeneration* (1892), an exhaustive catalogue of the symptoms of contemporary decadence. The extraordinary success of these books points to a diffuse sense of decay and degeneracy among the general reading public that extended far beyond creative elites.[68] At the end of *Degeneration* the pervasive sense of cultural pessimism is only relieved by the prospect of the eventual eradication – actually 'clubbing to death' – of the most decadent human specimens to ensure the survival of a fitter generation. However, he was soon to find a nobler outlet for his palingenetic longing: Zionism.

Fresh from his prolonged wrestling match with degeneracy, Nordau placed at the core of the Zionist mission his vision of a 'muscular Judaism', the counterpart to the highly influential 'muscular Christianity' movement of the day. In his study of the debt of Nordau's Zionist vision to the all-pervasive obsession with life reform that characterized the period, Todd Presner has drawn particular attention to its link with other manifestations of the contemporary revolt against decadence:

> This emphasis on corporeal regeneracy should come as no surprise since Zionism emerged from the same fin de siècle culture that had spawned numerous other body reform movements, ranging from the women's and the homosexual emancipation movements to the youth, sport, fitness, and nudist movements, all of which were striving to gain social recognition and political momentum.[69]

Nordau's reification of the Jewish 'body politic', of national redemption achieved not just through a New Homeland but by being inscribed within each Jewish body, was entirely consistent with 'Modernist depictions of men's and especially women's bodies' in which the body became 'a site of preoccupation, alteration, transformation and even reinvention'.[70]

WARNING SHADOWS

A deep-seated, primordial impulse to stave off the threat of anomy brought on by the liminoid conditions of early twentieth-century Europe linked Nordau's campaign for a muscular Zionism to such diverse modernist phenomena as the attempts of Les Fauves use painting to tap into the primitive energies of 'wild beasts'; and to Diaghilev's conception of art as a 'life force' with 'the invigorating power of religion'.[71] It was also related to the congress held by the 'International Society for Racial Hygiene' at the International Hygiene Exhibition in Dresden in 1911 to plan the eradication of the dysgenic from the modern world, a campaign that was gathering particular momentum in Germany at the time.[72] The modernist landscape of the future was nearly always conceived as 'a New Old Land', the title of the 1902 utopian novel (*Altneuland*) by Theodor Herzl, founder of Zionism. The new society would emerge once modernity had sloughed off the physical and metaphorical dirt of Modernity and returned to pristine, primaeval sources of purity and transcendence. Thus, when Theobald Scholem set up the Blue-White in 1912 as a Zionist youth organization,[73] he saw as its founding principle the hope that 'in the forests and fields, in rain or sun, the Jew will get to know what he has lost for millennia, namely the love of mother earth'.[74]

The necessity for the modern world to restore human contact with the primal, revitalizing constituents of life even in the construction of the modern metropolis resonates through Paul Scheerbart's plea for an architecture that 'allows the light of the sun, the moon and stars to enter not merely through a few windows set in the wall, but through as many walls as possible', the 'walls of coloured glass' creating a milieu from which would arise not just 'a new culture' but 'paradise on earth'.[75] Yet in the words of Goethe, the avatar of Rudolf Steiner's Anthroposophy, 'where there is much light, there is much shadow'. A deep penumbra was cast over European culture when patriotic longings to reconnect with ethnic roots conjoined with dreams of hygiene, the numinous, and national resurrection. It could predispose intellectuals and 'ordinary people' alike to devote their capacity for fanaticism to a cult of war as a process of cleansing and a source of transcendence, as a total solution to the malaise of Modernity.

We have encountered this *topos* already in the Nietzschean celebration of 'active nihilism', as well as in the anarchists' longing to precipitate a 'purifying orgy of destruction', and the symbolist dream of a 'great red night' to engulf a corrupt world. The same fearsome mythopoeic logic permeates one of the most influential manifestos of pre-WWI social modernism, Georges Sorel's *Reflexions on Violence*, published in 1908, which called for revolutionary movements to arise inspired by utopian myths in order to regenerate a decadent, effete civilization.[76] A similar mindset caused the cultural modernist Giovanni Amendola to announce four years before the interventionist campaigns that brought Italy in to the First World War that what was needed to complete the Risorgimento was 'collective effort, popular sacrifice, bloodshed, and sanguinary affirmation of the national will to rise'.[77] In 1914 Ernst Stadler published the collection of poetry *Der Aufbruch*, 'New Beginning', the same title as Kafka's prose fragment written in 1922 which we encountered in the Introduction to this book. Its poems are replete with mythic correspondences between the primal forces of spring renewing the earth and the stirring of chthonic forces quickening the vital energies of the human heart. In the title poem, soldiers strike their tents and ride into battle. In October of the same year Stadler was killed by a grenade at Ypres.

Goethe also said that 'great events cast their shadow before them'. When Filippo Marinetti celebrated war in the Futurist Manifesto as 'the sole hygiene in the world' he was in tune with a diffuse undercurrent of modernist mythopoeia that saw bloody conflicts between human beings as a ritual act of collective cultural catharsis. Emilio Gentile alludes to the primordial echoes of such a vision when he suggests that Marinetti's use of the term 'conflagration' in his interventionist speeches of 1913 implies that fighting the Austrians and Germans would 'actualize the Stoic myth of the palingenetic "great fire" from which Great Italy was to rise'.[78] In 1913 the Irish nationalist leader Pádraic Pearse declared in a no less sanguinary vein: 'Bloodshed is a cleansing and sanctifying thing, and the nation which regards it as the final horror has lost its manhood.'[79]

In 1914 the 'impending European war' predicted by W. B. Yeats in 1896 ceased to be one of the harmless 'fictions' generated by what Frank Kermode calls the modernist's 'apocalyptic imagination'. Instead, it took concrete historical form as a four-year conflict of unprecedented political, social, technological, and human totality, thrusting to the surface the dangers inherent 'in the dispositions' such fictions 'breed towards the world'.[80] In the cauldron of a palingenetic vision supercharged by the increasingly liminoid conditions of history, a fatal axis was thus forged between ritual killing and cosmic renewal. It was a primordial alliance that made Stravinsky's *Sacre du printemps*, with its dramatic enactment of the sacrifice of a virgin who immolates herself 'in the presence of old men in the great holy dance',[81] appear to Modris Eksteins such a powerful symbolic harbinger of the outbreak of the First World War. It also adumbrated the cosmological significance that the war would acquire within the development of modernism.

1914: THE BEGINNING OF A BEGINNING

In *Redemption by War* (1982) Roland Stromberg attempted to address the inadequacy of existing historical explanations for the 'almost manic bellicosity of the European intellectuals, writers, artists, scientists at the crucial beginning of the terrible war of 1914–18'.[82] He confirms that not only the avant-garde, but ordinary people from every class were 'eager to witness a "cultural rebirth" unfolding in an age of machines and masses rather than popes and princes'.[83] Angelo Ventrone, one of the foremost Italian experts on the significance of the First World War for the genesis of Fascism, states that 'The age of nationalism had powerfully promoted the "war ethic": namely the conviction that the war experience fulfilled the task of rejuvenating and regenerating a civilization now in steep decline.'[84]

The bellicose 'mood' that resulted had by 1914 become an essential factor in the origins of the First World War.[85] In Berlin, Vienna, Paris, and London (though not in Rome or Moscow) a 'storm of war feeling broke', and the assumption took hold on segments of the collective mythopoeia in Europe that 'destroying a contemptible society would open the way to a better one'. Within this mindset the brief bout of ruthless slaughter of the enemy this demanded was perceived as a ritual act of purification, 'a cleansing fire'.[86] For once the avant-garde really proved to be the 'advanced guard' of a popular army, as a war-fever descended on the crowds of the pro-war movements whose enthusiasm destroyed any chance of negotiated peace, and marked what Thomas Mann would later describe as 'the beginning of much that was still in the process of beginning', as the West marched joyfully into labyrinthine mental catacombs of its own making. It would only finally emerge from them in 1945 after over 70 million combatants and civilians had died as a direct result of war, persecution, or genocide – a mere fraction of the survivors whose lives were devastated.[87]

Stromberg seeks the explanation for the 'August madness' in the powerful 'revolt against intellect' and longing for community that had arisen at the turn of the century as a result of modernity's attrition of traditional society: 'The 1914 spirit was an antidote to anomie, which had resulted from the sweep of powerful forces of the recent past – urban, capitalistic, and technological forces tearing up primaeval bonds and forcing people into a crisis of social relationships.'[88] Such an account bears out the thesis that the 'primitive instinct to do battle against a common foe' which seized so many educated, civilized Europeans at the time expressed what we have called an instinctive search for a transcendent nomos and sense of belonging as an antidote to Modernity. Both of these crystallized in 1914 in precisely the kind of myth-driven populist regeneration movement Sorel had speculated about a decade earlier. In the event, it was a rebirth triggered not by the image of the general strike bringing down capitalism to establish social justice, but by that of 'the fatherland in danger', the last bulwark against the loss either of 'civilization' or 'culture', according to who were judged to be the barbarians. It is no coincidence if the war was often referred to at the time as a contemporary 'Armageddon', a battle occurring at the end of time, the prelude to a new era.

The international crisis which came to a head in July 1914 thus turned millions of Nietzsche's passive 'last men' into myth-hungry 'modern men'. However, they spurned everything Zarathustra had preached by looking to the *nation* to provide the 'womb', the 'home', and the 'horizon-framing myth' whose loss he had mourned in *The Birth of Tragedy*. Certainly Europeans did not throng to become Dionysian vitalists finding creative, peaceful, compassionate ways to affirm the value of life in the face of cosmic absurdity. Instead they rushed lemming-like over the cliff of civilization into mechanized barbarism. The sacralization of the nation that resulted from a vulgarized, nationalized Nietzscheanism was epitomized when Maurice Barrès, the artist-politician of French organic nationalism,[89] announced that 3 August 1914, the day of Germany's declaration of war on France, had been not just a 'historic' day – since every day is historic 'in this era which is seeing the start of a new world' – but a 'sacred day'.[90]

War-fever was thus both an elite and mass movement of *modernist* reactions to the historical crisis, now no longer a brooding 'malaise' or a refined aesthetic sense of the putrefaction of culture under the cosmetic sheen of progress. It was now the concrete, palpable implosion of the entire social, political, and moral order of the post-Napoleonic political system, the self-destruction of the Age of Progress. In this special sense the First World War can be approached as a modernist event, not just experienced by millions as the harbinger of a new temporality demanding self-sacrifice and destruction, but precipitating paroxysms of despair and palingenetic expectation far beyond the confines of the avant-garde.[91] Robert Wohl observed that what led 'many young men and women' to believe 'they were about to witness the dawning of a new age', was the sensation of being 'in the throes of a cultural transmutation'.[92] When our primordialist ideal-type of modernism is applied to such a statement it means that the sudden collapse of the nineteenth-century political system in Europe brought decades of European society's growing liminoidality to the surface. The acute insecurity this unleashed activated in millions the archetypal human faculty for projecting daydream and utopias onto what now seemed a blank future. As a result, the primordial logic of the rite of passage took control, filling many with adamant certainty that the war represented a process of 'cultural demolition' vital 'to lay the foundations for the culture of the New'.[93]

It would be logical to assume from a humanist perspective that the infernal realities of industrialized warfare that unfolded over the next four years would shatter such great illusions. Certainly, the poetry of Wilfred Owen and Erich Remarque's *All Quiet on the Western Front*, the outstanding bestseller of the inter-war period, spoke for untold thousands for whom the experience of combat was hell on earth, and whose only new community was the international but largely silent one of fellow survivors for whom promises of redemption rang lugubriously hollow. Yet, as the prospects of a short war evaporated and the death toll from the 'war of position' grew ever higher, powerful psychological processes continued to be activated, thereby ensuring the war would remain for millions a catalyst to experiencing transcendence.

It was as if the fantasy of redemption through sacrifice, a fantasy stubbornly entertained by both the fighters and the onlookers, was fuelled rather than quenched by the blood of the fallen, like pouring oil on flames.

In the section 'Liminality and War', Eric Leed addresses this paradox by analysing the experience of No Man's Land from the perspective of anthropological theories of the 'rite of passage' that we encountered in the last chapter. He argues that 'the moments of collective transition such as mobilization of a nation for war, open a gap in historical time that is filled with images of "something new"'.[94] This is why many combatants, rather than feel crushed by nihilism, came to feel they belonged to a 'secret' community, and were participating in a 'moral revolution' leading to a 'new order', 'a synthesis of traditional values'.[95] For some the 'new order' was an unprecedented experience of the nation's sacralization into a site for the enactment of Christian imaginings of self-sacrifice and redemption. Allen Frantzen, for example, has explored the deep nexus between 'chivalry, sacrifice, and the Great War' which emerges in poems, diaries, and essays where the soldier's death is pictured as a gesture of 'purification' and 'love'.[96]

By extension the whole war could be seen as a collective act of redemptive self-sacrifice, attributing to the relentless flow of blood the transcendent meaning evoked in the passage of May Sinclair's novel, *The Tree of Heaven* (1917) when the central character suddenly realizes 'how the war might grab hold of you like a religion':

> It was the Great War of Redemption. And redemption meant simply thousands and millions of men in troop-trains coming from the ends of the world to buy the freedom of the world with their bodies.[97]

However, the religion that revealed itself to combatants broke the vessel of orthodox Christianity. Michael Burleigh's analysis of religion's symbiosis with politics in the Great War stresses that 'exposure to tremendous displays of material might and the imminence of death turned minds to an unseen power and the awakening of an elemental faith that most of the men were ill equipped to articulate in terms familiar to the Church'.[98]

The use of Christian discourse in the celebration of war should therefore not be taken at face-value as an assertion of religious faith. On one level it was no more than the articulation in the conventional language of the dominant religion of archetypally human impulses to 'redeem' individual human lives in the face of a squalid, degrading, meaningless death. It was, in other words, an elaborate *euphemism*: 'the medieval language of Christian redemption and warrior honour' worked to 'gloss the world of blood, filth, and futility',[99] an abuse of faith, a blasphemy even, that seems to occur in the history of every religion held hostage by war.[100] But in the context of the First World War this discourse expresses a fundamentally *modernist* urge to conjure up the prospect of historical renewal, to turn the obscenely meaningless mechanized slaughter into a holocaust, a 'burnt sacrifice' that would infuse a decadent age with a new sense of transcendence. In short, mythic responses were triggered by the combination of the brooding liminoidality of modernity, the acute liminality of trench warfare, and the imminent prospect of death, a psychological defence-mechanism that long pre-dated Christianity.

This line of argument is corroborated by the American social psychologist Richard Koenigsberg, who in a series of essays has explored the 'sacrificial fantasy' that the death of the soldier is essential to the revitalization of the community, or more precisely the 'body politic'. This is a literalized, reified metaphor configured as a suprapersonal, 'magic' organism of flesh, blood, and spirit, whether in the form of the tribe, a distinctive ethnic culture, or in a modern context, the nation. He argues that the all-consuming sacralization of death in the First World War points to the survival into modern times of the same primordial logic that drove the elaborate social and ritual life of the Aztecs, which was entirely constructed round the myth that war was a sacred necessity.[101] The logic was simple: If no enemy warriors were captured in combat to immolate atop the pyramid-altar, no sacrificial blood could run down the steps to keep the sun alive. As Barak Rahimi puts it, 'the sacrificed blood of a soldier bestows [...] a new life for the community, as it identifies the reality of the nation displayed with the destruction of each body on the battle field'.[102]

By the twentieth century international forces of *völkisch* nationalism generated throughout Europe by the revolt against Modernity had led to the theological obscenity of God's conflation with 'country', and the perversion of the Christian concept of sacrifice into a patriotic duty.[103] This was no rhetorical flourish of state propaganda. For some it was a phenomenological reality. The Italian historian Emilio Gentile records that

> many combatants lived the experience of the trenches as the sanguinary rite of initiation to a new life, the entrance into a world apart, [...] a sacred world which in the course of the war, became ever more distinct from the *profane* world of the rear guard of the civilians. With the baptism of fire occurred the *metanoia*[104] of the old man into the fighter or the new man.[105]

Thus it was that millions of 'ordinary' soldiers, once they found themselves members of the community of the front-line, experienced the war not as absurd, but as a 'second birth', filled with enthusiasm by 'a new sentiment of national communion imbued with lay religiosity'.[106]

Figure 9   Paul Nash, 'We are making a New World' (1918), now shown in the Imperial War Museum, London.

© The Imperial War Museum, London. Reproduced with kind permission of the Imperial War Museum.

According to the 'explanatory strategy' offered by the primordialist theory of modernism as a social as well as an aesthetic force, the extraordinary tolerance of the daily slaughter generally shown by combatants, their families, and their 'mother' nations on all sides for four years, was far from being the sign of a collective 'death wish' as some historians have claimed.[107] Instead it was deeply bound up with the contemporary avant-garde 'revolt against decadence', and with the archaic myth that 'fighting and dying for one's country' are the 'means through which a society is cleansed, purified, and indeed resurrected'. The spectacular eruption of this religious belief to become a myth that dominated the historical imagination and political policies of an entire civilization for four years cannot be dissociated from the fact that 'On the eve of World War 1, many European countries feared what they saw as the degeneration and degradation of their societies, linked to the loss of virile, manly values.'[108]

The mindset that generally prevailed for the first three years of the conflict was that the greater the losses suffered in the war, the greater its cleansing power. It is the paradox that illuminates the 'anomaly' identified in Paul

Fussell's classic *The Great War and Modern Memory*, that 'a war representing a triumph of modern industrialism, materialism, and feeling' could give rise to a 'myth-ridden world' made up of 'conversions, metamorphoses, and rebirths'.[109] For those whose chauvinism was turbocharged by the war, the identification of death with 'spring and resurrection, the forest of oaks, nature symbolizing the nation' formed 'a tradition which made it possible for wartime nature to be viewed as a transcendent reality supporting the Myth of the War Experience'.[110] It was a myth that would make the aftermath of the war an incubator for palingenetic myths of social transformation which would take on a revolutionary, totalizing, populist, uncompromisingly *political* dynamic unthinkable before 1914.

6
The Rise of Political Modernism
1848–1945

The most spectacular displays of modernism are not to be found in a museum of expressionist art or a collection of prose poetry, but in the avant-garde political collaborations that sought to come to terms with a brand new world regarded as unstable or dangerous.

Peter Fritzsche, 'Nazi Modern' (1996)[1]

The consideration of fascism and modernism from the perspective of modernity underscores the need for art historians to treat fascism not as an isolated political phenomenon or as an aberration in the modernist march towards abstraction, but as a form of cultural politics in dialectical (or dialogic) relationship to other anti-Enlightenment movements, both left and right.

Mark Antliff, 'Fascism, Modernism, and Modernity' (2002)[2]

CREATIO EX PROFUNDIS

For Europe as a whole the title that Paul Nash gave his painting of the front-line at dawn, 'We are making a new world', lost none of its bitter irony in the days following the armistice of 11 November 1918. The one place where the irony was inappropriate was Russia. Here the rapid disintegration of the war effort after March 1917 created the conditions for Lenin's seizure of power a year before hostilities ceased on the Western front. On one level the Bolshevik Revolution was the application of the Marxist-Leninist theory of revolution. However, as we shall argue below, it also makes sense to see the frenzied construction of the Soviet Union as the final stage of the triadic movement from one stage of society to another via an intensely liminoid phase of separation and disaggregation, namely the anarchy into which absolutist Russia was thrown when events overtook the Tsarist regime in 1916–17.

160

Currents of political modernism, the attempt to create a new sacred canopy through the comprehensive political restructuring of modern society, had played a role in European history ever since the mid-nineteenth century, as a study of anarchism, revolutionary syndicalism, and Marxism will show. Nevertheless, it was only in the October Revolution that it formed its first state. We will devote considerable attention in this chapter to considering the modernism of the Bolshevik Revolution in order to establish the hallmarks of political modernism as a generic category, an exercise that should make it easier to detect the modernist features of fascism explored in Part Two.

However, in the Western homeland, at least outside Marxist circles, the Soviet Revolution could easily be construed as yet another morbid symptom of the deepening crisis of civilization and the swamping of order by the forces of chaos. Unless historically aware individuals were safely ensconced within an alternative belief-system that had survived the war, they were prone to experiencing acute bouts of anomy and anxiety about the state of things to come. Even in the Entente nations the Pyrrhic nature of their victory left a legacy of objective socio-political problems and subjective traumas which compounded the acute personal suffering, physical and psychological, inflicted on countless millions by the war. The peace settlements could not settle the malaise. No amount of wreaths, monuments, or ceremonies of remembrance could heal the wounds or exorcise the nightmares of the survivors and the bereaved who were immune to the palliative of jingoism. There could be no closure.

Inevitably, even in the hands of the best narrative historians the academic register used in most accounts of the impact of the First World War fails to convey the *phenomenological* impression of a world in ruins, and tends to take on an unintended euphemistic flavour. References in conventional academic discourse to 'the destabilization of the liberal cultural synthesis of the nineteenth century and the discrediting of the leadership' identified with the 'liberal cultural synthesis of the nineteenth century, already increasingly questioned before the war', and the 'profoundly altered political and cultural landscape which resulted',[3] inevitably come across as curiously disembodied, given the depth of a nomic crisis that the most spiritually wounded experienced as a cosmological *tabula rasa*, a historical *catastrophe*. David Harvey probes deeper into the *emotional* facts of the time when he gives 'some credence' to Stephen Kern's statement that 'in four years the belief in evolution, progress, and history itself was wiped out' as the war 'ripped up the historical fabric and cut everyone off from the past suddenly and irretrievably'.[4]

Harvey goes on to illustrate the truth of this statement – at least for those with a 'high need for closure' – by citing the impact the war had on the work of the German Expressionist Max Beckmann who, as the fighting wore on, felt the need to use his painting to conceal what he described as the 'black hole' opening up in front of him 'with some sort of rubbish'. After a nervous breakdown his post-war canvases then started expressing an 'almost unimaginably strange dimension' in 'quasi-mystical works of transcendent generality which responded to no actual events'.[5] Clearly Beckmann's mythopoeic, culture-generating creative faculty was still intact, but cut off from any sort of sacred canopy or community it could only express isolation and anomy in an unspecific religious register as the last line of defence against the terror of the void.

Significantly, two cultural historians who are equally keen to engage with the war as an existential reality seize on the same metaphor for acute liminality that we have already encountered in Kafka to evoke the subjective catastrophe and temporal caesura that accompanied the sudden breakdown of the nineteenth-century 'world' outside Russia, or rather the rapid disintegration of the pre-war nomos compounded by the slow realization that after such horrendous birth-pangs the long awaited 'new world' was still-born. For Peter Fritzsche, '[h]istory had truly become a delinquent. Derailed by war and revolution it no longer seemed to run along the straight and predictable tracks of the nineteenth century.'[6] For Modris Eksteins too there had been a 'derailment of history' in 1918.[7] The history of the inter-war period was not to be determined by leaders alone, but also by the new historical subject, the masses, whose palingenetic reflexes had been awakened by this intense subjective experience of 'the end of the world', a brooding sense of catastrophe that was no longer the morbid conceit of a cultural avant-garde but a palpable social reality. Decadence had been democratized.

In short, the effect of the war was to have objectified the liminoid nature of modernity previously self-evident only to Europe's intelligentsia. As a result, it was not despair, or 'cultural pessimism' – except in the 'strong', Nietzschean, *Dionysian* sense of 'active' nihilism – that shaped and misshaped post-WWI Europe. Instead, it was the confluence and sometimes violent interaction between a proliferation of utopian projects, revitalization movements, and ideological communities called into being by the urgent need of many millions of human beings who, in the words of Hermann Broch, risked in their own way becoming 'outcasts from Time' and 'flung back into an overwhelming loneliness'.[8] This existential isolation awakened a deep-seated human urge to 'manage' the looming terror of anomy and of time running out by 'imagining' a new temporality.[9] Four years of total war had ruthlessly stripped the West bare of conventional myths affirming its inherent progressiveness and revealed its underlying ontological void. Yet the unprecedented depth that disenchantment had reached created a vast potential constituency of post-war individuals eager to re-erect the sacred canopy, 'rebuild the house' on the rubble of the nineteenth-century world devastated by the war, so that time 'could begin anew'.[10]

Such responses found expression in what historians have described as the 'apocalyptic expectations about the end of time',[11] and the 'craving for newness' which became 'a universal preoccupation in the west after the war' in the face of history's 'bankruptcy'.[12] In other words, acute anomy and spiritual disorientation intrinsic to early twentieth-century modernity turbocharged by the conjuncture of the First World War, the Russian Revolution, the collapse of three absolutist regimes and a powerful monarchy, with an influenza pandemic that killed as many as 100 million people world wide[13] had made the modernist drive to ward off the terror of the void – cultural, social, and political – a phenomenon of mass culture. The new era would be a *creatio ex profundis*, an act of creativity defying the void.[14] The ambivalence of the resulting mood where nihilism was so closely bound up with hope and pessimism with a rebellious vitalism was captured in Wyndham Lewis's editorial for the first issue of a new cultural periodical *The Tyro*, launched in April 1921. There he states that 'we are at the beginning of a new epoch, the creatures of a new state of human life as different from nineteenth-century England as the Renaissance was from the Middle Ages'. However, the contours of the future are still unclear, the post-war generation existing 'in a sort of No Man's Land atmosphere', now that there is 'no mature authority, outside of creative and active individual men, to support the new and delicate forces bursting forth everywhere today'.[15]

The contours of the post-war horizon were even hazier for a modernist such as Virginia Woolf who eschewed programmes and manifestos. At the end of *The Waves* (1931) her alter ego Bernard observes that:

> The canopy of civilization is burnt out. The sky is dark as polished whalebone. But there is a kindling in the sky whether of lamplight or dawn. […] There is the sense of a break of day. I will not call it dawn. […] Dawn is a sort of whitening in the sky; some sort of renewal.[16]

A few lines later he finds his own solution to the ambivalence and nomic crisis of the age that had blighted his own life by committing suicide in an act of vitalistic defiance. The final words of the novel are: 'Against you I will fling myself, unvanquished and unyielding, O Death!' Writing these words triggered an intense 'moment of being' for Woolf. They were used by Woolf's husband for her epitaph after her own suicide in 1941.

The prevailing *Zeitgeist* was one of acute crisis, of a deep cultural despair relieved only by illusory intimations of new beginnings, of the possibility that a new era was dawning. It was a mood that turned the two volumes of Oswald Spengler's *The Decline of the West* into international bestsellers. It also inspired Ernst Jünger, who had served on the Western front continuously from December 1914 until he was hospitalized with serious wounds in August 1918, to write of 'a new constellation' that had appeared over the horizon since the armistice 'betokening a turning point in world history, just as it once did for the kings from the East':

> From this point on the surrounding stars are engulfed in a fiery blaze, idols shatter into shards of clay, and everything that has taken shape hitherto is melted down in a thousand furnaces to be cast into new values.[17]

HOMO FABER AS PROMETHEAN MODERNIST

In the course of his study of how the intense liminality of the First World War experience impacted on the combatants, Eric Leed underlines the primordial symbolic repercussions of what were – except in Russia – its inconclusive political and *psychological* consequences as a historical event in narrative terms. For those who returned 'no "rites of reaggregation" could efface the memory of utter defencelessness in the face of authority and technology. No ceremonial conclusion to the war could restore the continuities it had ended.' He then focuses attention on the core myth underlying Ernst Jünger's account of the war as an 'inner experience' that induced such widespread 'millenarian' longings. The years of relentless combat and mechanized slaughter had gouged out a deep psychic space where 'those still capable of a solution' would be transformed into 'the revolutionary type in postwar politics', a type of human being prepared to execute the imperatives of the new order with utter ruthlessness in what was the 'prosecution of war by other means'.[18]

Jünger's 'myth of the new *Gestalt* fashioned in war' is seen by Leed as 'an extremely important fiction [...] for the many young men who had fought the war, or stood waiting helplessly on the sidelines and who wanted to retain some belief that the war had not been *merely* a meaningless orgy of destruction but an event creative of personality, a rebirth and regeneration of the nation'.[19] Within this myth he detects the persistence of the 'very old dream of Homo Faber: collaboration in the perfecting of matter while at the same time securing perfection for himself'.[20] It is a dream that takes us to the very heart of the faculty for the creation of human culture and the ritual erection of the sacred canopy that we have argued is a defining property of '*homo sapiens sapiens*'. The process exemplified in Jünger's writings of forging images of the New Culture, the New Man, and the New Order out of the memories of the slaughter and the post-war spectacle of a civilization in ruins exhibits a *modernist* alchemy now at work for the first time in mass psychology. It is cognate with the demiurge's mission to transform 'evil' matter into transcendent spirit that was lived out within the creative imagination of a single poet, Charles Baudelaire, when he composed *Flowers of Evil*. However, the metamorphosis advocated by Jünger is not one in which decadence is changed by art into 'timeless' beauty. Rather the process of cultural dissolution is envisaged as giving birth to a new social and political order, renewing historical time itself. Here *homo faber* reveals 'his' true identity as *homo transcendens*. In 'his' hands modernism becomes not just Dionysian but *Promethean*, awakening ancient dreams of humankind wresting from the Gods technological mastery over its terrestrial home.

It is by tapping into this primordial logic that the First World War came to be personified by Jünger as another ancient symbol of alchemical transformation, the blacksmith.[21] His war memoirs portrayed the conflagration as a modern Vulcan, hammering the white-hot fragments of the old world into a new order in which the lives lost would find redemption, thus bringing closure to Modernity's protracted rite of passage. These writings culminated in his vision of the next stage in human evolution set forth in *Der Arbeiter* (1932), which showed how the war had brought forth a new type of human being, 'the Worker', a hybrid of soldier and technocrat, to whom would be entrusted the construction of a new Germany and a new civilization. Yet Jünger himself stayed aloof from politics, reluctant to abandon the heights of his metapolitical outposts from which he could live out his self-appointed role as the spokesman of the war generation. Many other artists shrank from activism and political *engagement* altogether in the prevailing cultural limbo and withdrew deep into the realm of epiphanic modernism. In approaching the cultural production of the 1920s it is thus worth bearing in mind Kafka's own metaphor of the train crash, and his observation that the whirl of kaleidoscopic sensations caused by the disaster was, according to the degree of injury of the individual – and the situation and temperament through which they experienced the conflict – either 'entrancing or exhausting', leading to many permutations of despair blended with hope, horror with ecstasy.

Max Beckmann, for example, once he was over the worst of the trauma, dedicated himself to developing his own fusion of Gothic and Cubist aesthetics in which to paint cryptic allegories of spiritual disorientation.[22] Other German Expressionists such as Ernst Toller, Fritz von Unruh, and Georg Kaiser, seeing their hopes 'that a new order would arise, phoenix-like, from the holocaust' dashed by actual events, now wrote plays dramatizing 'the shattering of these utopian dreams'.[23] In fact all the iconic works of aesthetic modernism produced in the aftermath of 1918 express in distinctive ways the deep wounds inflicted by four years of mass destruction on the faculty of human beings living under modernity to achieve transcendence and community, whether we think of the radical 'anti-aesthetics' of Surrealism and Dada, Pirandello's *Six Characters in Search of an Author* (1921), T. S. Eliot's *The Waste Land* (1922), Virginia

Woolf's *Jacob's Room* (1922), Rainer Maria Rilke's *The Duino Elegies* (1923), Italo Svevo's *The Conscience of Zeno* (1923), Franz Kafka's *A Hunger Artist* (1924), or W. B. Yeats' *A Vision* (1925).

A revealing example of the reaction to the First World War of countless artists who, unlike Jünger and Lewis, had no pretensions of being prophet of the New Era, is offered by Romain Rolland. A prolific novelist, playwright, biographer, essayist, and pacifist before 1914, he was awarded the Nobel Prize for literature in 1915 in what was clearly a pointed anti-war gesture on the part of the Swedish judges. Deeply disturbed rather than inspired by four years of total warfare, in 1924 he wrote the preface to the collection of essays on Indian culture, *The Dance of Shiva*, by Ananda Coomaraswamy whom we met in Chapter 4. It was published by the Sunwise Turn bookstore and study centre, which had established itself as the focal point for New York's burgeoning subculture of 'anarchist modernism' ever since its foundation in 1916.[24] Rolland uses the preface to express his anguish at the spiritual blindness with which 'the Western races find themselves trapped deep in a blind alley, and are savagely crushing each other out of existence'. He rails at the myopia of the 'average European' who 'cannot see beyond the boundaries of his individual life, or the life of his class, of his country or his party', and pursues the chimera of 'social Paradises realized on earth, with Maxim guns and ruthless edicts'.[25]

The importance of Coomaraswamy's essays for Rolland is that they remind the West of an alternative perspective on reality, of a temporality peculiar to the 'philosophy of Brahma' that 'does not expect that the world will be suddenly and miraculously transformed by a war or a revolution, or an act of God. [...] It knows that there is time. [...] It watches the turn of the wheel and waits', in the knowledge that eventually the 'soul will escape from Time and its vicissitudes'.[26] To 'snatch our souls from the bloody rout' Europeans must 'climb back to the high plains of Asia'.[27] A decade later T. S. Eliot, now the foremost modernist poet in the English language, would evoke just such a possibility of transcending Cronus:

> At the still point of the turning world. Neither flesh nor fleshless;
> Neither from nor towards; at the still point, there the dance is.[28]

Within the imaginaire of artists such as Rolland and Eliot the higher self could complete its final metamorphosis into the child and dancer alluded to in Nietzsche's prologue to *Thus Spoke Zarathustra*, and might finally utter a 'sacred Yes', though only at the cost of creating an unbridgeable distance between their inner world and History. But such poetic voices would be drowned out by the far more strident tones of a new breed of artistic, social, and political modernist. They called not for new insight, but a new world, a world not just spiritual but realized through history itself.

DIONYSIAN SOCIALISM

Outside the studies, studios, and ivory towers of fine art and literature, the war had triggered a flood of programmatic, constructivist social modernism expressed in a remarkable outpouring of creativity and inventiveness throughout Europe in the applied arts, architecture, civil engineering, the creation of living spaces, furniture, household objects and gadgets, private homes, housing estates, factories, sanatoria, sports stadiums, bridges, cars – in short, of everything *designable*. Europe had now become a powerful incubator for 'temporalized utopias' of every description. A new breed of artists and technocrats had arisen who, even if they lacked the Promethean qualities of Jünger's Worker, were nonetheless bent on creating a new post-war world through the power of design, planning, and technology. They thus threw themselves into visionary projects that gave concrete form and historical substance to the nebulous pre-war daydreams of Expressionists and Futurists about the dawn of a new era of humanity.

It is thus within the heightened *modernist* socio-political ethos created by the war that we should locate the aspirations of the Bauhaus to redesign the modern world from bottom up, and the 'Purist' schemes of urban renewal proposed by Le Corbusier whose palingenetic fantasies embraced 'clearing away from our cities the dead bones that putrefy in them'.[29] Whatever practical purposes their designs and projects served or material needs they were meant to satisfy, they also were a response to generalized longings for transcendence, for hope, for a new horizon. A symptom of this primordial dimension of much technocratic modernism was the 'compelling new imperative' that it obeyed 'to clean up, to sterilize, to re-order, to eliminate dirt and dust'.[30] The rational agendas of urban regeneration and social hygiene were shaped by mythic rites of purification and catharsis. In their different ways all programmatic modernists after the First World War, from Dadaists to Bauhaus designers, sought a symbiosis between aesthetic, social, and political renewal. Instinctively they set about creating the 'new centre of order' and laying the 'new spiritual and physical foundations' that according to Arthur Penty, Coomaraswamy's political ally in the campaign for a post-industrial society and a regular contributor to *The New Age*, had to be established so as to replace modern civilization which was so obviously 'an experiment that has failed'. It was a process that on the eve of the Second World War he called 'modernism in politics'.[31]

Initially such a symbiosis could only occur in Russia, the one country that in the immediate aftermath of the war seemed to be triumphantly completing the rite of passage from the 'permanent transition' of Modernity to 'a New Age'. The dramatic change of cultural ethos this could involve at an individual level from Romantic to Dionysian pessimism, and from epiphanic, purely cultural modernism to programmatic and socio-political forms of *engagement* is epitomized in the remarkable career of Aleksandr Blok (1880–1921). The paper he gave to the Religious-Philosophical Society of St Petersburg on 30 December 1908 when he was Russia's most famous Symbolist poet shows him keenly aware of living through seismic changes in the history of the West. Its immediate emotional backcloth was the catastrophic earthquake in Sicily that had occurred two days earlier, almost totally destroying Messina and taking some 100,000 lives – almost half the death-toll caused by the Asian tsunami of December 2004. Blok used it as a vivid metaphor for the 'terrible crisis' of contemporary history. White-hot magma was bursting out from under the mountains of black rock, though it was not clear to him whether it was destructive fire of the sort that had devastated Calabria, or instead 'a *purifying* fire':

> We still do not know exactly what awaits us, but in our hearts the needle of the seismograph is already deflected. Already we see ourselves, as if against the background of a glow, flying in a light, rickety aeroplane, high above the earth; but beneath us is a rumbling and fire-spitting mountain, and down its sides, behind clouds of ashes, roll streams of red-hot lava.[32]

By the eve of the First World War he was cultivating the type of aestheticized esotericism that had enjoyed such a vogue in the European Decadent movement 20 years earlier. The most famous product of this phase was *The Rose and the Cross*, conceived as the libretto first of a ballet and then of a Symbolist opera, whose allusions to Rosicrucianism, astral projection, aura reading, hypnotism, and meditation express Blok's quest to tap into hidden wellsprings of illumination in an age rushing towards social and spiritual collapse.[33]

Yet within four years he was pursuing redemption of less ethereal variety. In the turbulent aftermath of the October Revolution, he was employed on the Commission for the Reorganization of Theatres and Spectacles, and in rapid succession became representative of the People's Commissariat for Education, director of the Bolshoi Drama Theatre, co-founder of the Free Philosophical Association, and chairman of the Petrograd division of the All-Russian Union of Poets. He also somehow found time to be editor of the literary journal *Zapiski Mechtatelei* ('Dreamers' Notes'), in which capacity he expressed a fervent belief in the poet's revolutionary task in preparing society for a new beginning:

> A poet must realize that Russia as she was no longer exists, and will never return [....] A new era is opening for the world. The old civilization, the old social ideas,

the old religion are dead. Of course there are those trying to revive the corpse of the old world, but a poet must be inflamed by a holy anger against all those who wish to reinvigorate such a corpse. [....] A poet must prepare for the even greater events still to come, and he must know how to bow before them.[34]

An extraordinary set of events had catapulted Blok from the periphery of society to its centre, from decadent avant-garde to the forefront of populist currents of change where he felt called upon to establish the ideal centre of values needed to usher in the new Russia.

Blok was no isolated case. His enthusiasm for the new regime is symptomatic of a tide of programmatic modernism – elitist and populist, aesthetic and social, agrarian, and technocratic – whose history has been reconstructed in detail by Richard Stites in his investigation of 'utopian vision and experimental life in the Russian Revolution'. He quotes the testimony of Isaak Steinberg, leading member of the Socialist Revolutionary Party and the first Soviet Commissar for Justice, about the intense climate of rebirth and renewal in which the regime set about its task to make a new society rise from the ruins of the old order:

All aspects of existence – social, economic, political, spiritual, moral, familial – were opened to purposeful fashioning by human hands. Ideas for social betterment and progress that had been gathering for generations in Russia and elsewhere, seemed to wait on the threshold of the revolution ready to pour forth and permeate the life of the Russian people. The issues were not only social and economic reforms and thoroughgoing political changes: with equal zeal the awakened people turned to fields of justice and education, to art and literature. Everywhere the driving passion was to create something new, to effect a total difference with the 'old world' and its civilization.[35]

The result was that the formative years of the revolution hosted an intense and largely spontaneous ethos of extreme technocratic modernism under Lenin and Stalin, the spirit of which can still be sensed in the pages of a propaganda publication such as *The USSR in Construction*. This monthly was published in Russian, English, French, German, and Spanish to showcase the Promethean achievements realized at breakneck speed by Russia's Five Year Plans which were illustrated using unmistakably modernist graphics, despite the contemporary Stalinist persecution of 'formalism'.[36]

The Bolshevik Revolution is thus to be interpreted not just as an attempted Marxist transformation of an absolutist system into a socialist regime, but also as a *modernist* experiment in designing and building a new society carried out on an unprecedented scale of social, economic, cultural, and political transformation and regenerative zeal. Bolshevism provided the mazeway for the *communitas* of socialists – known appropriately enough as communists

– who formed a revolutionary revitalization movement led by a new *propheta*, Vladmir Lenin. It quickly hardened into a totalizing nomos imposed with increasingly fanatical ruthlessness by Russia's new rulers. This heuristic line of interpretation helps make sense of a number of features of Russian society between 1917 and 1930 that, though apparently disparate, can all be seen as symptoms of a common palingenetic matrix. One is the enthusiasm with which so many aesthetic – and hence deeply *anti*-materialist – modernists followed the example of the major Futurist poet Vladimir Mayakovsky in spontaneously dedicating their creative energies to the revolutionary cause.[37]

The relevance of the maximalist definition of modernism we have constructed becomes palpable when we examine the programmatic declarations made in 1923 by the Constructivist poet and playwright – destined to fall victim to Stalin's purges in 1937 – Sergei Tretyakov, in a brand new Soviet art magazine published in 1923 in his article, 'From where to where (Futurism's perspectives)'. He emphasizes society's need for what Peter Berger calls a nomos: 'No Weltanschauung could be vital if it was not alloyed to a world-sense, if it had not become the driving force which determines all actions of the human being, his everyday physiognomy.' He celebrates the way Futurist poetry from the very beginning 'was criss-crossed by agit-prop explosions about the human being sensing the world anew'.[38] He underlines the pivotal revolutionary role of the artist in providing the frame for the new horizon: 'The task of the poet is to produce the living, concretely useful language of his time.'[39] He presents art as 'the religion of eternal youth and renewal in persistent work on the appointed task', a constituent factor in the anthropological revolution undertaken by Bolshevism: 'The new human being in reality, in his everyday actions, in the construction of his material and mental life – this is what Futurism must be able to demonstrate.'[40]

Other features illuminated by recognizing the modernist dynamics of the Russian Revolution are the eagerness with which countless architects, scientists, educators, academics, and technocrats flocked to Bolshevism as the midwife of a Promethean new world; the spontaneous acts of cathartic violence and iconoclasm carried out against symbols of the old regime and its human and institutional embodiments; the generation, part spontaneous and part orchestrated, of popular festivals and liturgical ceremonies which provided Marxism-Leninism with all the trappings of a 'spectacular state' in which politics was extensively aestheticized and sacralized; the radical measures taken by the regime to devise new forms of urban and rural communal living; the enthusiastic deployment of modernist aesthetics in the service of the new regime before Stalin's imposition of 'socialist realism'; the cult of technology and the machine; the communitarian and agrarian projects to base the new Russia on an idyllic state of harmony with nature; the leader cults that grew up around Lenin and Stalin portraying them as 'healer', 'saviour', *propheta*, the New Man.

Such an interpretive strategy is fully consistent with Bernice Rosenthal's impressively documented thesis that Bolshevism in both its Leninist and Stalinist phases was pervaded by the 'active nihilism' of Nietzsche. She claims that by 1921 'the "hard" aspects of his thought fused with and reinforced the Bolsheviks' ruthlessly voluntarist, mercilessly cruel, and radically future-oriented interpretation of Marxism'.[41] The remarkable syncretism of dialectical materialism with Dionysian and Promethean currents of social modernism was a feat only possible within the white-hot ethos of total renewal and 'ludic recombination' created by the collapse not just of the Tsarist order but of an entire temporality and nomos, a catastrophe that insistently called forth a new temporality and nomos.

This helps explain the seminal importance of the myth of the 'New Soviet Man', 'New Woman', 'New Cult', and 'New Morality' under Lenin. Rosenthal shows how the injection of Nietzscheanism into Bolshevism also sheds light on the savage 'will to power' that enabled the new regime to liquidate the Kulak class, ruthlessly implement the first Five Year Plans, force through draconian cultural policies and educational reforms, and create within a few years and at horrendous social and human cost a Soviet science, technocracy, industry, and modernity. Even the purges of the 1930s were carried out in a climate shaped by (perverted) Nietzschean notions of a morality beyond good and evil that had infected Stalin's own vision of his historical role.[42] 'Nietzschean Marxism' even contributed to rationalizing the Socialist Realism that finally ousted avant-garde theories of art and modernist aesthetics. For its proponents it 'reconstituted the horizon broken by futurism on a new basis, pulled together a new world, and restored ontological wholeness, partly by means of language'.[43]

The portrait of Bolshevism that emerges from Rosenthal's book is fully consistent with seeing it as a modern 'revitalization movement'. Once in power it had no interest in simply repairing the damage caused by the train-crash of Modernity, but set about placing History on a larger gauge railway track altogether, where it would be pulled by locomotives of a revolutionary design. The ideological fuel was provided by Lenin's powerful 'mazeway resynthesis' blending Marxism with a Nietzschean cult of the will and the higher morality of the superman. An extraordinary conjuncture of historical circumstances precipitated by the First World War and the collapse of the ancien régime meant that the Bolshevik movement was not crushed like the Sioux Ghost Dance rebellion or simply marginalized like the Parisian anarchist counterculture. Instead, it had a unique opportunity to 'explode the continuum' of history and start time anew.

MARXISM AS MODERNISM

It would be understandable if some readers found it disconcerting, or infuriating, to see Bolshevism treated as a form of modernism. It should thus be stressed that this is not an attempt to depoliticize and 'aestheticize' revolutionary socialism or ignore the charge of genuine socialist humanism and idealism that fuelled the revolutionary zeal of Lenin and his followers. Instead, it seeks to illuminate another causal layer to the Russian Revolution, which was not solely a revolutionary response to the iniquities of the Tsarist state and the social injustice endemic to capitalist liberalism, but also a response to the crisis of modernity. The enormous energy poured by the revolutionaries under Lenin and Stalin into the construction of a total new order cannot be understood simply in terms of total commitment to a modern political theory. Deeper, archaic psychological forces were unleashed within the revolutionary leadership and its most fervent followers by the crisis of the old regime and the acute liminoid social conditions that ensued. Whatever utopian goals they consciously pursued, at a psycho-dynamic level they were being partly compelled by primordial fears of Cronus to erect a new sacred canopy and construct a new community which would ward off the terror of anomy. Moreover, the fanatical energy needed to fulfil this utopian goal arguably stemmed partly from a 'will to transcendence' integral to revolutionary socialism itself.

To substantiate this line of interpretation it is worth revisiting Marx's own political theory. This has specifically been construed as a form of modernism by Peter Osborne, a philosopher who approaches the temporal aspects of modernity from a radically *socialist* perspective. As we saw earlier,[44] he identifies (programmatic) modernism in *The Politics of Time* with projects to create an alternative modernity through 'the affirmative cultural self-consciousness of the temporality of the new'.[45] In a subsequent monograph, *Philosophy in Cultural Theory*, he builds on this position by arguing for an 'expansive' – what we have called a 'maximalist' – concept of modernism, insisting that its remit 'in its most basic or core temporal sense [...] cannot be restricted in advance either to the social domain of the arts, or to some chronologically bounded historical period'.[46] Though the 'affirmations of the new' implicit in different political ideologies and programmes vary significantly, their implementation in concrete forms of praxis always involves 'a rupturally *futural* sense of the present as an (always, in part, destructive) transition to a (temporary) new order'.[47]

On the basis of his definition, Osborne devotes an entire chapter to the exegesis of the *Communist Manifesto* as a modernist text which embodies not only 'a historical futurity of qualitative newness, independent of its penultimate narrative act (proletarian revolution), in the historical dimension of its cultural form', but also an 'openly socially critical modernist art'.[48] In the course of his analysis, Osborne takes to task Marshall Berman who, as we saw in Chapter 2, took the title for his monograph, *All that is Solid Melts into Air*, from a passage in the Manifesto. He convincingly shows how Berman has remade Marx's modernism in his own image, stripping this seminal document of its revolutionary significance as an anti-capitalist tract in order to celebrate the vitality and open-endedness of liberal modernism in its American permutation. This significance lies in its powerful articulation of a radical *alternative* to capitalism destined to create a *new* modernity in which social justice and the common good of humanity will one day prevail over systemic alienation and exploitation.

In Osborne's hands *The Communist Manifesto* is lovingly restored to its pristine state as 'the founding text of an internationalist political modernism',[49] namely communism. The Marx who emerges from Osborne's analysis is the same sort of epoch-making, transcendence-seeking political visionary that becomes the protagonist of Tom Stoppard's play *Salvage*, and declares:

> Everything that seemed vicious, mean, and ugly, the broken lives and ignoble deaths of millions, will be understood as part of a higher reality, a superior morality, against which resistance is irrational – a cosmos where every atom has been striving for the goal of human self-realization and the culmination of history.

To which the anarchist Alexander Herzen replies soberingly: 'But history has no culmination. There is always as much in front as behind.'[50]

The primordialist perspective on modernism we are proposing may contribute a further element to Osborne's interpretation. It throws into relief the causal link which exists at a mythopoeic level between Marx's drive to construct a grounded future for humankind and his acute sense of the evanescent, anomic quality of modern reality. It was this sensation that was immortalized in the reference in the Manifesto to the solid world 'melting into air' that so impressed Berman. The same disorienting experience of Modernity also forms the subtext of the brief but famous speech Marx delivered at a banquet held in London on 14 April 1856, to mark the fourth anniversary of the *People's Paper*, the main organ of the Chartist movement in Britain. In it he stressed the deep ambivalence of a modern age in which unprecedented scientific and technological advance coexisted with 'symptoms of decay, far surpassing the horrors recorded of the latter times of the Roman Empire'. It is an age in which 'everything seems pregnant with its contrary'. In a seismological analogy that directly anticipates the imagery used by Aleksandr Blok 50 years later, he refers to the 'so-called revolutions of 1848' as 'small fractures and fissures in the dry crust of European society' which nevertheless point to 'the abyss' below:

'Beneath the apparently solid surface, they betrayed oceans of liquid matter, only needing expansion to rend into fragments continents of hard rock.'

In a remarkable metaphorical leap, Marx then evokes the intense revolutionary pressures exerted by such an age on every individual, addressing to his audience the pointed question, 'But, although the atmosphere in which we live weighs upon every one with a 20,000 lb. force, do you feel it?'[51] As the consummate propagandist of a political vision, Marx at a conscious level is inviting his audience to share his sense of revolutionary urgency. However, *subliminally* the metaphor also functions as a powerful evocation of the dramatically increasing 'liminoidality' of a society caught in the throes of an open-ended process of change. 'History' was now accelerating to a point where the transitional and ephemeral had become a permanent condition, precisely as Baudelaire was to state in his seminal document of modernism, the essay 'The Painter of Modern Life' published in 1863.

Ontologically the 'atmospheric pressure' which Marx evokes results from the collapse of the primal firmament that once shielded individuals from the incursion of Cronus ('the abyss') and guaranteed a certain lightness of being. The metaphorical 'weight' Marx refers to stems from the visceral terror that magic and meaning are evaporating from the world so fast that it will soon be reduced to inanimate, meaningless matter. The particular strategy Marx found to relieve this *existential* pressure was to work towards the realization of a new community, its solidity restored and horizon reframed by an economically rationalized utopian myth ('Marxism') after a revolution that would establish communism as the sole nomos of the new world.

It is the anomy-transcending *modernism* of Marxism originating in the existential needs of Marx himself that is indirectly acknowledged by those non-socialist historians who have treated it as a modern version of millenarianism,[52] political religion,[53] or Gnosticism.[54] Each is a different reading of what is being presented here as Marxism's attempt to re-erect a sacred canopy appropriate to the age of secularizing modernity, one based on the revolutionary ethic of social justice and human compassion. In fact what is known as 'Marxist revisionism' can be seen as the adoption of Marxism by a host of different socio-political modernisms, all of which made him the principal, but far from exclusive ingredient, in the mazeway resynthesis of a would-be revitalization movement. It is a pattern exhibited in the various forms of syndicalism that sprang up in the late nineteenth century, the Nietzschean Marxism of the young Ernst Bloch and of Lenin himself,[55] and the blending of Marx with aesthetic modernism and Jewish mysticism in Walter Benjamin.

Perhaps the most striking example of the incorporation of Marxism into a thinly disguised form of programmatic modernism, both cultural and social, was the 'God-building movement' founded by the Russians Maxim Gorky and

Anatoly Lunacharsky in the 1890s. This attempted to turn 'scientific socialism' into a fully fledged secular religion by, among other things, selecting exceptional human beings for worship in specially created sacred sites modelled on Bayreuth – Lunacharsky was also the main promoter of Wagnerism in Russia. Predictably, Lenin was elected the first socialist deity by the movement in 1924.[56] By this time Lunacharsky was Commissar of Enlightenment, in which position he oversaw the creation both of a Soviet educational system which massively improved literacy rates, and of the state-controlled censorship apparatus. He also helped his former colleague, Aleksandr Bogdanov, to found the highly influential and semi-autonomous proletarian art movement, Proletkult. Though Proletkult was anti-experimentalism and anti-abstraction, the concept of the plastic arts it promoted was influenced initially by constructivism and its literary and musical aesthetics by futurism. Moreover, its axiomatic belief in the regenerative power of art was quintessentially modernist. Whenever an aspect of Bolshevism is examined in detail, it reveals its modernist kernel.

THE MODERNISM OF ORGANIC NATIONALISM

Widespread assumptions about the progressiveness of Marxism and Bolshevism in their utopian stages mean that few would find it counter-intuitive to associate them with modernism when it is defined by Peter Osborne as 'the cultural condition of possibility of a particular, distinctively future-oriented series of forms of experience of history as temporal form'.[57] Equally well-entrenched pre-conceptions make the terms fascism and modernism seem to point in opposite temporal directions. Yet, once the modernist dynamics of revolutionary Marxism are recognized, only the smallest of steps is required to reach the crux of our argument in Part One. This is that fascism, despite the connotations of regression, reaction, and flight from modernity it retains for some academics, is to be regarded as an outstanding form of political modernism.

We have already seen in the last chapter how the *völkisch* nationalism that emerged in late nineteenth-century Germany took the form of a social revitalization movement. Crucial evidence for regarding it as a form of *political* modernism as well is provided by George Mosse's *The Nationalization of the Masses*. Here he locates the *völkisch* cult of Germanness within the context of a groundswell of illiberal nationalism, whose relationship to modernity he conceptualizes in *anthropological* terms profoundly akin to the primordialist perspective adopted in this book. Citing Claude Lévi-Strauss' account of the primal human sense of 'cosmic rhythm' so severely disrupted by modernity,[58] he describes the spectacular nineteenth-century rise of liturgical nationalism as a reaction to the increasing 'isolation' and 'acceleration of time' stemming from an age of rapid industrialization and historical change. These forces worked against and frustrated 'timeless longings' for 'wholeness', 'the totality of life', the 'holy', and for 'permanence and fixed reference points in a changing world', all of which are subsumed in Berger's concept of the 'sacred canopy'. The reaction was a susceptibility of broad swathes of the German public to the invocation of a mythicized history so as 'to preserve order within the ever faster flow of time'.[59]

Once again, the terror of anomy had driven sections of the public exposed to modernity to find a new wellspring of temporalized transcendence, this time in an overtly *political* movement of revitalization. Precisely the same 'synoptic framework' can be applied to Zionism, which as we saw in the last chapter, though intensely political, also bears the hallmarks of a unique form of socio-cultural modernism that sought a 'reconnection forwards' with primordial Biblical, corporeal, and natural realities as the basis of a new future for the Jews. The *völkisch* movement and Zionism are just two of a plethora of illiberal forms of identity politics known as 'organic', 'tribal', 'integral', or 'redemptive' nationalism that came to prominence in late nineteenth-century Europe, and which by common academic consensus was destined to contribute vital ingredients to fascism. The crucial role played by primordial religious energies in fuelling the ultranationalist mindset emerges forcefully from James Billington's *Fire in the Minds of Men: Origins of the Revolutionary Faith*, which reminds us that for most of the nineteenth century nationalism, not socialism, was the dominant revolutionary creed.[60]

The organic conception of the nation, far from being peculiar to Germany, is encountered in intellectual milieux throughout *Europeanized* society as a whole in the late nineteenth century. A revealing case-study in the modernist aspect of its dynamics is provided by Maurice Barrès, whose prolific literary output allows a detailed reconstruction of his itinerary from decadent poet to the foremost ideologue of French ultranationalism. By his late twenties he had come close to being swallowed in the vortex of narcissism and despair that spread within the French intelligentsia after the nation's crushing defeat in the Franco-Prussian War.[61] This period of intense introspection in his life bore artistic fruit in the trilogy of novels which appeared under the title 'The Cult of the Self: Under the Eyes of the Barbarians' (1888–91). Looking back on this phase in his life Barrès observed, 'If I have moved from the "Me-cult" to a taste for social psychology, it is thanks to my expeditions into history and the poetry of history, and above all because of the necessity to extract myself from the lethal and decidedly unsustainable fad for nihilistic contemplation.'[62] In Nietzschean terms his Romantic pessimism had become Dionysian.

As a result of his own healing process, Barrès came to see the decadent state of the nation and the consequent lack of roots in modern existence as the ultimate cause of the deep malaise that affected not just his life but the whole of society. He wrote: 'Our profound sickness stems from the fact that we are divided, troubled by a thousand individual desires and imaginations. We are fragmented, we lack a shared understanding of our goal, our resources, our *centre*. Lacking moral unity, a common definition of France, we have contradictory words, different flags.'[63] He explored this theme in a new trilogy of novels, 'The novel of national energy' (1897–1902), the first of which, *Les Déracinés* [The Uprooted] depicts the search for identity of seven young Lorrainers.

Following his own muse, Barrès threw himself into politics to become the advocate of a viscerally chauvinistic – and instinctively anti-Semitic – French nationalism, based on a heightened sense of belonging to a unique cultural tradition and regional geography. The title of the lecture he gave to La Ligue de la Patrie Française in 1899 on this new brand of nationalism, 'la Terre et les Morts', became one of the most famous slogans of organic nationalism. Rejecting any nostalgia for feudal society, he saw a rekindled historic (but actually modern) sense of Frenchness as the key to a 'national socialism' that would heal class divisions and secure social justice for all 'true' Frenchmen. By then he was a Deputy, having successfully fought an electoral campaign the year before on the basis of the 'Nancy Programme' which turned the values of re-rootedness extolled in his novels into a political manifesto.

Barrès' vision of a regrounded, reintegrated nation was just one of a plethora of illiberal nationalisms which arose spontaneously to put an end to the increasingly liminoid conditions of fin-de-siècle France and the profound public crisis of national identity which crystallized in the Dreyfus Affair. Far from being cohesive, the anti-Dreyfus camp was rent by divisions over which ethnic group constituted the 'root race' of the French (the Aryans, the Celts, the Romans, the Franks), over which aesthetic was associated with health or decadence (classicism, medievalism, modernism),[64] over the role attributed to monarchism, Catholicism, socialism, and anti-Semitism in the process of national regeneration, and over the attitude to be adopted to urbanization, technology, and rural life.[65] The study of the 'integral nationalism' advocated by Charles Maurras, for example, reveals another exercise in ludic recombination undertaken in the war against decadence. Maurassian nationalism in turn was further hybridized with Sorelian syndicalism to produce another form of 'national socialism' that influenced Georges Valois, the founder of France's first fascist party, Le Faisceau.[66]

FUTURAL REACTION

Peter Osborne's *The Politics of Time* provides a sophisticated conceptual framework on which to base the identification of organic forms of nationalism as both futural and modernist. He too is at pains to stress the varied reactions to the temporal crisis of modernity, contrasting Baudelaire's purely aesthetic response, namely the attempt 'to distil the eternal from the transitory' in verse[67] – what we have called '*epiphanic* modernism' – with the drive to *change* history – our '*programmatic* modernism'. This latter he sees conditioning the engagement with modernity of not just the 'progressive' Walter Benjamin but also 'reactionary' thinkers such as Martin Heidegger.

Osborne argues that, even though they remained poles apart in their reaction to Nazism, both these intellectual giants applied their philosophical powers to the diagnosis of modernity's all-consuming decadence after the cataclysm of the First World War with a view to *transcending* it, each looking to a mythicized past as the source of the inspiration needed to inaugurate a new, revitalized, nomic society. For Osborne, it is the fact that their contrasting projects of historical transformation contain their own distinctive temporality that 'leads to the idea of a *politics* of time'.[68] Following through this line of thought, he turns his attention to the taxonomic problems posed by German cultural critics such as Edgar Jung, Moeller van den Bruck, Ernst Jünger, Oswald Spengler, Carl Schmitt, and Martin Heidegger himself, all of whom represent extreme rejections of socialism and democracy. He points out that the two labels commonly applied to their politics, 'conservative revolution' or 'reactionary modernism', are widely assumed to be paradoxical. They denote an unresolved tension at the heart of world-views that celebrated some aspects of modernity, such as technology or the power of the modern state, while espousing viscerally anti-socialist, anti-liberal, and racist forms of nationalism which are assumed to be intrinsically backward-looking and 'anti-modern(ist)'.

It is this approach that Osborne insists is wrong-headed. Instead, the response of such thinkers to modernity is to be seen as a 'novel, complex, but *integral* form of modernism in its own right'.[69] The so-called 'conservative revolution' is thus 'modernist in the full temporal sense of affirming the temporality of the new': 'Its image of the future may derive from the mythology of some lost origin or suppressed national essence, but its temporal dynamic is rigorously futural.' Both 'conservative' and 'reactionary' acquire their *revolutionary* dynamic from the impact of Modernity's 'storm of progress' which makes it impossible to restore the past or retain eternal values in their pristine state. Conservative revolution 'understands that what it would "conserve" is already lost (if indeed it ever existed, which is doubtful), and hence must be created anew. It recognizes that under such circumstances the chance presents itself to fully realize this "past" *for the first time*.'[70] Similarly, '[r]eactionary modernism is not a hybrid form (modernism + reaction). Rather it draws attention to the modernist temporality of reaction *per se* once the destruction of traditional forms of social authority has gone beyond a certain point'.[71] The battle between socialism and fascism is thus not between 'revolution' and 'reaction' but between 'the revolutionary temporality intrinsic to socialist projects for the overthrow of capitalism'; and the 'counter-revolutionary temporality of a variety of reactionary modernisms'.[72]

FASCISM AS POLITICAL MODERNISM

The inference that Osborne draws from this analysis for the classification of fascism is striking in its succinctness: 'From the standpoint of the temporal structure of its project, fascism is a particularly radical form of conservative revolution.' As such it is 'neither a relic nor an archaism', but a *'form of political modernism'*.[73] Osborne refrains from delivering a succinct definition of fascism, and wisely so, since even the proposition that some degree of workable consensus is emerging among scholars on fascism's core definitional traits can provoke howls of dissent.[74] Nevertheless, if we sample core elements in the definitions proposed by prominent Anglophone specialists in comparative fascist studies since the early 1990s a pattern of convergence is surely discernible even by the most sceptical observers. Here are a few:

'Fascist ideology is a form of thought which preaches the need for social rebirth in a holistic-national radical Third Way.' (Roger Eatwell, 1995)[75]

'Fascism may be defined as a form of revolutionary ultra-nationalism for national rebirth that is based on a primarily vitalist philosophy.' (Stanley Payne, 1995)[76]

Fascism 'is a tortured, enraged, and passionate demand for national renewal'. It is 'unqualifiedly nationalist, redemptive, renovative, and aggressive'. (A. James Gregor, 1999)[77]

The core of fascism's ideas and myths is 'the belief in a national and/or racial revolution embodying rebirth from an existing condition of subjection, decadence or 'degeneracy' leading to the 'creation of [...] a "new fascist man"'. (Martin Blinkhorn, 2000)[78]

'Fascism is an authoritarian populist movement that seeks to preserve and restore premodern patriarchal values within a new order based on communities of nation, race, or faith.' (Steven Shenfield, 2001)[79]

'In a climate of perceived national danger and crisis, [fascist movements] sought the regeneration of their nations through the violent destruction of all political forms and forces which they held to be responsible for national disunity and divisiveness, and the creation of a new national order based on the moral

and "spiritual" reformation of their peoples, [and] a "cultural revolution".'
(Philip Morgan, 2003)[80]

Fascism is a 'form of political behaviour marked by obsessive preoccupation
with community decline, humiliation, or victimhood and by compensatory
cults of unity, energy, and purity, in which a mass-based party of committed
nationalist militants [...] pursues with redemptive violence [...] goals of internal
cleansing and external expansion'. (Robert Paxton, 2004)[81]

'Fascism is the pursuit of transcendent and cleansing nation-statism through
paramilitarism.' (Michael Mann, 2004)[82]

In their various ways all these definitions, several proposed by academics
scornful of any notion of a 'new consensus' in fascist studies, not only
acknowledge the *futural* dynamic of fascism, something generally denied for
decades, but imply that its core goal was to overcome decadence and create
a healthy new nomos, a new form of transcendence for the modern age. The
definition of another major expert, Zeev Sternhell, stands out from these in
several respects, not least in his insistence on the role played by anti-materialist
Marxism in the fascist synthesis and his denial of Nazism's fascist credentials.
Nonetheless, his extensive account of fascist ideology highlights its claim to
be inaugurating a 'new century', 'a new civilization', 'a revolution of morals',
a 'revolution of souls', a 'new type of society', and a 'new type of man'. In
their 'revolt against decadence' fascists were attempting to regenerate a Europe
whose 'morals' were 'in decay' and whose 'faith' was 'debased'. They sought
to impose 'the cult of the body, health, and the outdoor life' to replace the
degenerate man of 'stay-at-home civilization'. Fascism for Sternhell was thus
an ideology of 'life', of 'vitalism', of 'organic community', proposing a totalitarianism bent on creating 'a new social and human order' which 'constituted
an extremely violent attempt to return to the social body its unity, integrity,
and totality'.[83] The resonance with our maximalist definition of modernism
is obvious.

Even if it runs *against* the conscious intention of their authors, all these
approaches corroborate Osborne's thesis that fascism can for heuristic purposes
be seen as a form of *political modernism* seeking to establish an alternative
modernity within a new temporality. In terms of our own primordialist conceptualization of modernism, the resulting 'new order' is inseparable from
fascism's temporalized utopia of turning the reborn nation (as nation-state
or *ethnie*) into the basis of a sacred canopy in order to transcend what after
the First World War its activists saw as a period of profound cultural and
physical degeneracy and social disintegration. As such it is to be approached
as a modernist revitalization movement on a par with Bolshevism. It sought

to provide a radical solution to the liminoid state of modernity by providing a 'horizon framed by myth' in which a strong culture could once again emerge capable of providing the comprehensive nomos in the age of technology and the masses that liberalism had failed to deliver. Its goal was the reintegration of the nation within a new mazeway combining elements of the past and present into a composite myth which would enable the national *communitas*, purged of decadence, to make the transition to a new historical era. Even if the fascist cult of the past makes it for Osborne a 'counter-revolution', it is still a *revolutionary counter-revolution*, reacting not just against socialism, but conservatism and liberal modernity as well in the pursuit of new temporality. Fascism set out literally to 'make history'. Its belief that a doomed form of modernity was ending was dialectically related to a heightened sense of a new beginning.

These considerations place us in the position to offer a discursive definition of generic fascism. It retains the salient elements of the one offered in *The Nature of Fascism*,[84] but incorporates new elements drawing on our investigation into the nature of modernity and modernism.

FASCISM is[85] a revolutionary species of political modernism originating in the early twentieth century whose mission is to combat the allegedly degenerative forces of contemporary history (decadence) by bringing about an alternative modernity and temporality (a 'new order' and a 'new era') based on the rebirth, or palingenesis, of the nation. Fascists conceive the nation as an organism shaped by historic, cultural, and in some cases, ethnic and hereditary factors, a mythic construct incompatible with liberal, conservative, and communist theories of society.[86] The health of this organism they see undermined as much by the principles of institutional and cultural pluralism, individualism, and globalized consumerism promoted by liberalism as by the global regime of social justice and human equality identified by socialism in theory as the ultimate goal of history, or by the conservative defence of 'tradition'.

The fascist process of national regeneration demands radical measures to create or assert national vitality and strength in the spheres of art, culture, social cohesion, the economy, politics, and foreign policy. In the acute crisis conditions which prevailed in Europe after 1918, fascists saw the natural vehicle for this regeneration, once a critical mass of popular support was achieved, in a nationalist movement with both a mass base and paramilitary cadres that in the transition to the new nation would use propaganda and violence to create the new national community. The charisma of fascist leaders depended on their success in performing the role of a modern propheta *who offered his followers a new 'mazeway' (world-view) to redeem the nation from chaos and lead it into a new era, one that drew on a mythicized past to regenerate the future.*

Fascism can thus be interpreted on one level as an intensely politicized form of the modernist revolt against decadence. Its modernist dynamics in the inter-war period are manifested in the importance it attached to culture as a site of total social regeneration, its emphasis on artistic creativity as the source of vision and higher values, its adherence to the logic of 'creative destruction' (which in extreme instances could foster genocidal persecutions of alleged racial enemies), its conviction that a superseded historical epoch was dying and a new one was dawning, and the virulence of its attacks on materialism, individualism, and the loss of higher values allegedly brought about by modernity. They also condition the way it operates as a modern revitalization movement, the extreme syncretism of its ideology, and its draconian acts designed to bring about the cleansing, regeneration, and sacralization of the national community, and create the new fascist man.

Constructed in this way the distinctiveness of fascism can be encapsulated in the shorthand definition: 'fascism is a form of programmatic modernism that seeks to conquer political power in order to realize a totalizing vision of national or ethnic rebirth. Its ultimate end is to overcome the decadence that has destroyed a sense of communal belonging and drained modernity of meaning and transcendence and usher in a new era of cultural homogeneity and health.'

Part Two of this book will assume this ideal type of fascism in analysing how the sense of a new beginning cultivated by its ideology and politics can be understood as manifestations of its nature as a revolutionary form of political modernism. Rather than range far and wide within the extended family of inter-war and post-war fascist movements, the focus will be exclusively on Fascism and Nazism. In an essay on the problem of objectivity in historiography John Passmore has harsh words for titles that imply an impossibly large undertaking of historical reconstruction, and warns that 'History books ought commonly to be more, not less, selective than they are; greater selectivity would be a step *towards* objectivity, not away from it.'[87] Karl Popper identifies another element crucial to the search for objectivity when he recommends that we 'consciously introduce a *preconceived selective point of view* into [our] history; that is, to write *that history which interests us*'.[88]

It is thus as a step towards objectivity that Fascism and Nazism have been selected as case-studies in the vast topic of generic fascism, and that they have been analysed solely from a 'preconceived selective point of view' that interests me, namely the relationship of fascism to modernism.[89] The exclusive concentration on (according to our criteria) the only two fascist regimes not only makes the topic more manageable, but, more importantly, allows fascism's modernism to be explored both as ideology and movement, and as the praxis of a state system. The fact that the two regimes displayed such radical differences in nearly every sphere of official policy, whether on art, architecture, imperialism, religion, or race means that the heuristic value of the approach we have adopted can be submitted to a particularly stringent test.

Whatever the advantages of the 'case study' approach, the coverage of the topic of fascism's relationship to modernism is necessarily incomplete. Fortunately, there is an abundance of excellent secondary literature available to fill the vast gaps left in the necessarily fragmentary histories of the two regimes offered in Part Two of this book. No less fortunately, Mark Antliff has recently carried out a major investigation of fascism's relationship to modernism in France in a study that supplies independent corroboration of the heuristic value of our general thesis and thus complements our findings with respect to Fascism and Nazism.[90] Hopefully in due course monographs will appear in English on other examples of fascism which uncover the vitality and complexity of the relationship between the political, aesthetic and social currents of modernism they exhibit, a point to which we will return in the concluding chapter.

Before we proceed to our own, highly *partial* study of Fascism and Nazism in Part Two, it will help prepare the ground for what follows if we draw attention to two aspects of fascism that are thrown into relief when our ideal type of modernism is applied to the sole instances where it completed the transition from countermovement and anti-party to state and regime.

THE FASCIST REGIMES AS 'GARDENING STATES'

The first aspect relates to the investigation carried out by Zygmunt Bauman in *Modernity and Ambivalence* into the horror of the indeterminacy generated by modernity. This we have suggested is cognate with the 'terror of anomy' that constitutes the driving force behind modernism as an elaborate, culture-constitutive, form of 'terror management'. An important section of the book is dedicated to tracing how modern political regimes have resorted to it as part of their mission to fight 'a war against ambivalence, identified with chaos and lack of control, and hereby frightening and marked for extinction'.[91] The Leitmotif he uses to explore this theme is 'the gardening state', one of the earliest instances of the modern use of this metaphor being Frederick the Great's description of the state's duty to 'cultivate' and 'breed' healthy varieties of human beings.

The use of this organic and eugenic discourse by an eighteenth-century 'enlightened despot' underlines the fact that the Enlightenment not only intensified the temporalization of history characteristic of modernity. It also adumbrated the *modernism* of the second half of the nineteenth century by generating in the historical imagination schemes to compensate for the erosion of religious transcendence and its disembedding impact on human culture. At the height of its sustained orgy of creative destruction, the French Revolution could already hatch plans for the purification of society expressed in a discourse that directly anticipates the twentieth-century discourse of biopolitics and social hygiene. Thus in 1793 the famous grammarian François-Urbain Domergue urged the Committee of Public Instruction to purge the nation's books of false doctrines:

> Let us amputate all the gangrenous members from the bibliographic body. Let us remove from our libraries the swelling that presages death; let us leave only the plumpness which is a sign of health.[92]

However, the Enlightenment dream of founding a civic religion and creating a new breed of men 'purged of doubt'[93] was the product of a war on the irrationality of absolutism, and not a rebellion against the decay of a supposedly organic nation as it would be a century later in the age of 'Decadence'. Nevertheless it already incorporated the temporalization of utopia that plays such a key role in the modernist trend towards treating society as a legitimate object of what Bauman calls 'design, manipulation, management, engineering'.[94]

It was the nineteenth century – when science, social modernism, politics, and Dionysian pessimism began to enter such dangerous liaisons – that laid the scientistic foundations not just for the extensively planned, controlled, and engineered society of Fascism, but for the Nazi vision of a national community culturally and eugenically purged of all symptoms of deviancy and degeneracy. Bauman emphasizes that the fantasy of political 'gardening' was not exclusive to Nazi Germany and Soviet Russia, but was nurtured by elements within the scientific, academic, political, and cultural elites of early twentieth-century 'liberal' democracies as well, notably in Britain and the US. It even crops up occasionally in the utopian musings of H. G. Wells and T. S. Eliot. However, thanks to the subjective and objective crisis of liberalism, a conjuncture was able to form in the wake of the First World War between the growing power of the *modernized* state and the *modernist* image of society as a defective, decaying organism to be revitalized through draconian social and political measures of 'improvement'. At that point catastrophic human consequences were bound to ensue. What resulted were the 'most extreme and well documented cases of "social engineering" in modern history', namely those 'presided over by Hitler and Stalin', both 'legitimate offspring of the modern spirit'.[95]

According to our thesis both regimes were simultaneously offspring of the *modernist* spirit that arose from the cataclysm of the First World War. Freed of the moral and institutional constraints of liberalism, democracy, Christianity, and humanism, both dictators attempted to use the unprecedented concentration of state power to enact primordial longings for a rooted, *ordered* world, its horizon once more fixed and framed by myth, its population cleansed of the cultural, social, and human embodiments of chaos, ambivalence, and degeneracy. The Concentration Camps, Death Camps, Gulags, and Killing Fields of totalitarian states are thus to be approached not as products of irrationality, regression, and barbarism, for in reality they enact the ultimate logic of a *hyper*-modernity – an intensified, supercharged modernity. Its goal is to establish not only the new political and metaphysical *order* stressed by Bauman, but, as Osborne argues, a new, redemptive temporality, beyond anomy, degeneracy, and the liminoid of an incoherently modernized world. It is a project that against the background of the apparent collapse of the West turned swathes of politicians, scientists, academics, teachers, cultural critics, and social visionaries, along with millions of citizens who longed for a new beginning, into the accomplices, executives, and executioners of political modernisms, both left and right.

Totalitarian gardening was not only a eugenic activity. The proposed anthropological revolution undertaken by the new states required every aspect of social activity, from art to warfare, from work to personal relationships, to be retooled and coordinated, though in practice what it achieved depended on how far the state was able and willing to go to achieve its ends. Fascist Italy was restricted both politically and morally in this respect. Stalin's Russia and Hitler's Germany knew no bounds. The very radicalness of the utopia and scale of mass destruction its realization demanded seems to have 'cleansed' both dictators and their followers of the 'normal' conscience which upheld values that they associated with decadence, thus placing them, true to their Nietzschean heritage, in a moral orbit 'beyond good and evil'.

Following this logic Nazism became for its most fanatical followers a more *sublime* ethical system than religious or secular humanism. This insight led the modernist writer Luis Borges to place in the mouth of a concentration camp guard about to be executed the following chilling words: 'Essentially, Nazism is an act of morality, a purging of corrupted humanity, to dress him anew.'[96] Another glimpse into this 'higher morality' and 'higher conscience' is afforded by Hitler himself, who even compared with Stalin, Mao Zedong, and Pol Pot can be seen as the ultimate gardener of twentieth-century totalitarianism, at least in terms of the sheer scale of the ritual slaughter he unleashed. He writes in *Mein Kampf*:

Only when an epoch ceases to be haunted by the shadow of its own consciousness of guilt will it achieve the inner calm and outward strength brutally and ruthlessly to prune back the wild shoots and tear out the weeds.[97]

POLITICAL MODERNISM AND THE GORGON'S GAZE

If the primordialist theory of modernism illuminates the rationale behind the 'gardening state' and the concomitant crimes against humanity that fascism would have inevitably committed in the pursuit of its own logic wherever it seized power, it also adds a new aspect to the inevitable failure of any fascist state to achieve its ultimate objectives. It is the province of idiographic historians to produce empirically grounded arguments to show *how* Fascism and Nazism failed to achieve their own goals, but the 'modernist' interpretation of fascism can throw at least some light on *why* their projects were intrinsically unrealizable *a priori*. For one thing, all undertakings that seek to realize temporalized utopias on a vast scale inevitably flounder on the contradiction that they confuse historical with mythic time. In particular, fascism attempts/ attempted to realize within intrinsically evolutionary and plural societies degrees of cultural homogeneity and unity of purpose that are essentially poetic fantasies. All attempts to inaugurate a new historical era involve projecting onto the actually existing state of society the redemptive – soteriological – narratives of religion and the transformative metaphors of mysticism. Modern societies stubbornly resist modernist experiments in imposing on them visions of the new order originally conceived in the terror of anomy, a flight not towards but *from* the objective realities of human existence.

Anthropology itself bears out the ultimate futility of efforts made by modern political regimes to bring about any 'anthropological revolution'. David Kellner, for example, praises David Kertzer, whose insights into the primordial basis of modern political ritual we encountered in Chapter 4, for recognizing the limits imposed on any elite seeking to manipulate the symbology of a society. Not only is ritual 'equally important both to those who dominate and those who resist domination',[98] but as Kertzer himself says, 'the best an elite can hope to do is shore up a predominant symbolic construction of how society should work', since 'they can never eliminate all vestiges of alternative symbolic systems'.[99] Not only is total cultural hegemony, and total 'semiotic territorialization'[100] therefore an impossibility – so that any regime that pursues them ruthlessly rapidly degenerates into a terror state – but the activation of the 'principle of hope' in those who inwardly rebel against their subjugation under the new, the artificially imposed nomos will instinctively create their own cosmologies and rituals which resist *Gleichschaltung*. In this sense freedom from tyranny is anthropologically inscribed into our humanity. It is the birthright of a reflexive consciousness which leaves open the possibility that each individual's mythopoeic faculty will triumph over the psychopathologies of totalitarian leaders, whatever horrors they inflict on the bodies of those who do not conform. Like the dominant class for Marxists, totalitarian dictators create their own gravediggers.

Frank Kermode devotes an important section to this issue in *The Sense of an Ending* where he introduces the distinction between the 'fictions' of modernist mythopoeia in the realm of art and the 'myths' pursued by the leaders of totalitarian regimes. He states that 'The eschatological fictions of modernism are innocent as ways of reordering the past and present of art, and prescribing for its future', citing as an example the lines from W. B. Yeats' *Among School Children* 'Plato thought nature but a spume that plays / Upon a ghostly paradigm of things'. He goes on:

> But to clear the paradigm of natural spume is one thing in poetry or a theory of poetry; another when the encumbrances can be removed, the spume for ever blown away by a police and a civil service devoted to this final solution.[101]

The example of modernist architects such as Le Corbusier and Walter Gropius show that programmatic modernism is constantly criss-crossing the invisible boundary Kermode draws between fiction and myth, and that the 'innocence' of cultural modernism as a revolt against 'actually existing history' is constantly being compromised by political affiliations, as the examples of Richard Wagner, Friedrich Nietzsche, Martin Heidegger, Ernst Jünger, Drieu La Rochelle, Ezra Pound and other 'reactionary modernists' illustrate so clearly.

Nevertheless, Kermode's basic point stands: the attempt by a state to realize the modernist fiction of 'the world's' total regeneration by imposing a new nomos, by fixing the horizon, by creating a new man and a new world, and purging society of decadence can in the long run only create human disasters and destroy from within the very society it claims to save. Within our schema Himmler's SS can thus be seen as the henchmen of a potentially lethal form of political modernism, fascism, in its most virulent variant imaginable, Nazism. It was one which once in power specialized in reifying metaphors, projecting tropes of degeneracy and purification onto the flesh of living human beings, and turning fictions into myths to be actualized through the ruthless execution of state policies.

The 'anthropological' component of our theory further reinforces Kermode's point by suggesting that the 'eschatological' aspect of totalitarianism derives subliminally from the longing to resolve the liminoid character of modern history in the early twentieth century by establishing the final stage of a triadic rite of passage. However, in premodern societies this is one of reaggregation within a sustainable new order that puts an end to the acute instability of the second, liminal stage. Even Bolshevism at least looked forward in its theory to a point where future generations could enjoy such an 'endpoint', one where the constructive phase of socialism would finally give way to communism. Fascism knows no such terminus. By creating a cult of permanent expansion, dynamic change, and creative destruction under the leadership of an inspired *propheta*, fascism effectively 're-imagines' the third stage of the ritual triadic process as a permanent second stage, as perpetuated liminality. Driven by the terror of anomy and personal mortality, it is in denial even about the mortality of its leader, so that neither Fascism nor Nazism made effective plans for a post-revolutionary state where the birth pangs of the new nation would cease, the crusade against decadence would be over, and the leader had passed on his authority to a non-charismatic replacement.

By now the aporias of modernism's relationship with fascism reviewed in Chapter 1 have hopefully been transformed into a series of resolvable *paradoxes*, such as how a revolutionary political project can become obsessed with the mythic past; why some of the most creative architects would want to provide new buildings for totalitarian states; why so much destruction could take place in the name of a new order. Part Two will explore in more detail the complex relationship that resulted in practice between modernism and fascism when Mussolini and Hitler set out to use their power to realize their contrasting visions of a new order, and a new era.

In his video-poem *The Gaze of the Gorgon* Tony Harrison has bequeathed powerful verbal and visual images to help us comprehend the human consequences of the mission of political modernists to 'prune back the wild shoots' and 'tear out the weeds' in a world experienced as degenerate, and contemplate the horrors that ensue when the chrysalis of a revitalization movement metamorphosizes into the 'gardening state' bent on eliminating decadence. However idealistic, the fanaticism needed to execute projects of cleansing and total renewal can only augment the totality of social chaos and human suffering, trapping both henchmen and victims within 'the gaze of the Gorgon':

The Gorgon worshippers unroll/ The barbed-wire gulags round the soul.
The Gorgon's henchman try to force/ History on a straighter course/
with Gorgonisms that impose/ fixities on all that flows,
with Führer fix and crucifix/ and Freedom-freezing politics.
Each leader on his monstrous plinth/ waves us back into the labyrinth
Out of the meander and the maze/ Straight back into the Gorgon's gaze.[102]

Part Two

Fascism's Modernist State

7
The Birth of Fascism from Modernism

We stand on the last promontory of the centuries! [...] Why should
we look back, when what we want is to break down the mysterious
doors of the Impossible? Time and space died yesterday.

Filippo Marinetti, *The Futurist Manifesto* (1909)[1]

History as it is made, not as it is abstractly imagined – the only history
that really exists – is not in time but in thought and of thought; it is
eternal.

Giovanni Gentile, 'Time in History' (1936)[2]

DEATH IN FLORENCE

On 15 April 1944, Giovanni Gentile, who by the end of the First World War
had established himself as one of Europe's most eminent academic philosophers,
was brutally assassinated in his car outside the villa Montalto al Salviatino
where he had been staying as a guest of the bibliophile, Tammaro De Mariniis.
His assassins were communist partisans of GAP (Gruppi di azione patriottica)
who possibly carried out the attack with the collusion of Republican Fascists
keen to punish him for protecting anti-Fascists.[3] What is beyond doubt is that
he was returning from the Prefecture of Florence, where he had been negotiating
the release of professors charged with anti-Fascist activities by the authorities
of the Italian Social Republic, the steadily shrinking puppet state created by
the Nazis after the kingdom's surrender to the Allies in September 1943. He
thus paid the ultimate price for his continued loyalty, not to Mussolini, but
rather to his self-appointed mission to mould the Fascist regime into a new
type of state capable of repairing the havoc wrought by 'decadent' liberalism,
a goal he had been pursuing long before joining the National Fascist Party
(PNF) in June 1923.

Gentile's high-profile commitment to Fascism,[4] which followed eight months
as Minister of Education under Mussolini's administration, was the logical

consequence he drew from a philosophical system first fully elaborated in 1916 at the height of the war in his *Teoria generale dello spirito come atto puro* ['General theory of the spirit as pure act']. Written in the uncompromising technical register of neo-idealist philosophy, it unveiled a new ethical system called 'actualism', according to which 'pure acts', actions impregnated with ethical self-awareness resolved the tension between subjective and objective, mind and body, inner and outer reality. They opened the way to 'overcoming' the status quo in a new, ideally configured historical reality. Though his mainstream sources were Kant, Fichte, and Hegel, all of which reinforced the primacy of the mind over the material forces of existence, Gentile had also been influenced by Marx and the diagnoses of contemporary decadence proposed by Henri Bergson, Friedrich Nietzsche, and Georges Sorel which were mediated to him through *La Voce*. This Florentine periodical was fighting a vociferous campaign for a comprehensive reawakening of the nation through the forces of culture conceived in a way that melded aesthetic, cultural, social, and political visions of renewal to a point where they were indistinguishable.

In short, Gentile merits the title 'philosophical modernist' no less than fellow idealist Martin Heidegger when measured by Peter Osborne's yardstick for modernism. Both imbued their thought with what he calls 'the temporality of the new' in their intellectual striving to transcend an acutely liminoid historical situation. Gentile's search for a philosophy of transcendence predisposed him several years before the First World War to a palingenetic reading of contemporary history as an age in which the moral decadence of the liberal system had to be overcome in a new political and moral order. By 1910 he was already moving on a different tectonic plate from his fellow 'neo-idealist' Benedetto Croce. Croce too saw the problem of modernity as a religious problem, the 'need for an orientation concerning life and reality'.[5] However, he poured his no less formidable intellectual, philosophical, and polemical energies into renewing liberal humanism and reforming liberal politics rather than 'transcending' them dialectically in a new type of ethical system and a new state.

The watershed for relations between the two philosophers was the outbreak of the First World War, for while Croce opposed the interventionist campaign to persuade the government to side with the Entente powers, Gentile instinctively supported it. Through his own highly philosophical vision of national reawakening,[6] he saw Italy's participation in the war as a formative moment in the completion of the Risorgimento, a position fully articulated in *Politics and Philosophy*, written soon after the armistice.[7] This synthesized the spirit of avant-garde cultural criticism, interventionism, and actualism by offering an interpretation of contemporary history as a conjuncture of conditions in which Giuseppe Mazzini's dream of a populist 'national religion' to bind Italians together – so cruelly betrayed by the Cavourian liberal tradition – could finally become reality in an 'ethical state' in which the atomization and egoism of modern society would be transcended. Once Fascism had made its decisive shift to the right in the course of 1921 by abandoning negotiations for a 'pacification pact' with socialists along with its anticlericalism and republicanism, Gentile convinced himself it offered the historical vehicle necessary for the realization of his vision of a new ethical order. This conviction was further strengthened when in October 1922 Mussolini was appointed head of state after his threatened coup against liberal Italy as leader of the black-shirted 'Action Squads', the 'March on Rome'.

The highly public conversion to Fascism of one of Italy's two most famous philosophers was rewarded with a series of key positions in Fascist cultural politics that earned him the (misleading) reputation of 'the philosopher of Fascism'. As Minister of Education, member of the Fascist Grand Council, and director of numerous cultural initiatives and institutions – notably the *Enciclopedia Italiana* and the National Fascist Institute of Culture – Gentile campaigned tirelessly for Italy to become a truly 'totalitarian' state in which Fascism functioned as a secular theology. The 'political religion' he propounded would provide the basis of Italy's cultural renaissance by spiritually forming a generation of 'New Men' whose lives embodied the transcendent ethical principles of the state, thus enabling the New Italy to fulfil its civilizing mission on behalf of humankind.

THE MODERNISM OF THE 'PURE ACT'

In *The Historic Imaginary* Claudio Fogu attaches considerable importance to Gentile's actualism as the philosophical rationalization of what he identifies as one of the outstanding features of Fascism. This is its conception of history as a dynamic, living, futural reality that is to be proactively 'made' through the exertion of effort, vision, and will-power, and not just reconstructed *post hoc* in the university library. Its nature is thus not historiographic but *historic*. From this follows an activistic, interventionist, vitalistic approach to contemporary reality as the stuff of which 'great' history is made, thus transforming the past from something 'cut and dried' into a reservoir of regenerative myths. This is a familiar *topos* of late nineteenth-century thought, found in different permutations in such contrasting political contexts as the thought of Friedrich Nietzsche, Georges Sorel, Martin Heidegger, and Walter Benjamin. Within the 'historic imaginary' the value for both Giovanni Gentile, and later for the Fascists, of Mazzini's vision of a united Italy as a sacral entity was not the objective role it played in the Risorgimento, but its power to inspire the heroic campaign fought by Garibaldi's Thousand to liberate the South from despotism, bequeathing a memory that could still serve to mobilize social energies of transformation under the new regime.

Gentile's actualism provides an intellectual rationale for this wilfully 'interventionist', 'decisionist' approach to history – epitomized in Mussolini's March on Rome – by underpinning it with the concept of reality as the product of continuous *autoctisi* or 'self-creation'. For Fogu this is the key not only to his sustained liaison with Fascism but to his *modernism,* for he sees actualism's stress on the possibility of 'making oneself' and 'making history' as 'the quintessentially modernist utopia', one which shares the same 'intellectual horizon' as Futurism, Italy's outstanding expression of modernist aesthetics.[8] Arguing along lines congruent with the concept of modernist time as 'temporalized history' we have already encountered in the theories of Reinhardt Koselleck, Peter Osborne, and Peter Schleifer, Fogu cites T. S. Eliot's *The Sacred Wood: Essays on Poetry and Criticism* (1922). In this essay the poet suggested that a particular 'historical sense' characterized the 'modernist sensibility', namely 'the perception, not only of the pastness of the past but of its presence'.[9] It is a line of thought that leads Fogu to argue that by the time he published *Politica e filosofia* in 1920 Gentile had 'completed his modernist philosophy of historical experience'.[10] It resolved – at least on paper – the deep sense of historical crisis induced by the Bolshevik Revolution and the Italian army's calamitous defeat at Caporetto by proposing an actualist interpretation of the First World War and its successful outcome for Italy as a metapolitical 'new beginning', the *Aufbruch* into a new era.

Giovanni Gentile's attempt to found a secular religion on which to base a new Italian modernity by transforming the nation state itself into the source of an ethical,[11] metapolitical nomos is an outstanding example of the 'temporalization of utopia' discussed in Chapter 2. His philosophical evolution, recorded in a continuous flow of published texts, provides a remarkably detailed documentation of how one man's mind and personality, living through a period of extraordinary historical upheaval and liminoidality, could use abstract thought itself to 'manage' the terror of Cronus. In a period of acute historical crisis he harnessed his academic specialism to the subliminal drive to achieve spiritual transcendence, spending his whole life translating the primordial *topoi* of mythopoeia into the linguistic register of modern philosophy.

Actualism thus can be seen as Gentile's existential survival strategy. Evidence for this interpretation is provided by his 1936 essay 'The Transcending of Time in History', and again in his posthumously published *Genesis and Structure of Society.* Its concluding chapter, 'Transcendental society, death and immortality', written under the immediate impact of the loss of his son in September 1943, vividly evokes the 'fear of death' that 'turns the blood to ice until the pulse of life almost stops' once the realization strikes home that our own existence 'can be plunged into oblivion'. At this point 'an abyss opens before our feet and waits there to engulf us'. Yet even this 'terror of nothingness' is 'susceptible of redemption and can be illumined by an ideal light' when it is 'grafted onto the sense of society which makes us feel that our own existence is bound up with that of others, so that our life is not wholly our own'.[12]

From such passages it is clear that Gentile's actualism did indeed share a common cultural matrix not just with Futurism, but with the myriad contemporary forms of aesthetic, cultural, and social modernism being produced throughout the West during his life-time to counteract an exposure to nothingness due to the 'decay of values' and the erosion of the sheltering sky of culture by instilling a new nomos into society. All such cultural programmes exhibited the need to realize temporalized utopias in which 'actually existing' history would be not transcended, but itself transformed into the sustained *aevum* of a higher time. Gentileanism offered a vision of the world, a sacralizing canopy of suprapersonal meaning, in which ethically self-aware social action, by synthesizing inner and outer reality, individual and society, mind and history, will and world, held out the prospect of 're-embedding' and restoring a spiritual, suprapersonal dimension to the increasingly atomized and materialistic modern world. Moreover, Gentile specifically conceived the ethical state as replacing a dying religious tradition with a secular moral and metaphysical, but not meta-historical, creed. After the March on Rome he accepted the key role of Minister of Education in which he could apply his actualism to school reform. His career as the 'philosopher of Fascism' had begun, but also his growing collaboration with a regime for whom his system of thought was just one modernism among many all vying to become its sole ideological consort; a regime which remained inveterately promiscuous to the end. Gentile remained in stubborn denial about the one-sidedness of his relationship with Fascism, his actualism seeming to cut him off from actuality while it also sealed his fate.

THE PALINGENETIC CLIMATE OF POST-RISORGIMENTO ITALY

It was presumably his overweening idealist confidence in the primacy of ethical thought in determining external reality that caused Gentile to misjudge drastically the influence that a thinker could have on the course of Italian Fascism, let alone on the entire historical process. This was particularly naive given the profusion of rival projects to create an alternative modernity prompted by the convulsions of Italy's evolution as a society and nation-state at the turn of the century. To advance beyond the clichéd metaphor of 'roots' beloved of organic nationalists, Fascism's ideological root-system was not only extensive but lacked the taproot system characteristic of 'dicots'. Instead, its roots were of the adventitious variety encountered in the fibrous root system of monocots, in which no one root was more important than any other. Thus, as he might have known had he cultivated his garden more assiduously, even when Gentile achieved a dominant position within the regime's cultural institutions, Gentileanism could never establish itself as the hegemonic discourse.

Abandoning treacherous horticultural analogies, it is important to recognize how extensively Fascism's character was shaped by the diffuse, polycentric, and largely leaderless counter-cultural or 'cultic' milieu of cultural modernists who well before the First World War were calling for Italy's renewal. As we have indicated in Part One, fin-de-siècle Europe hosted many variants of palingenetic ultranationalism, each uniquely adapted to its ideological microclimate and still lacking the dynamics of a populist movement. Notable examples were the *völkisch* movement in Germany[13] and the many political formations intent on going beyond 'left and right' that mushroomed in France,[14] but there were also less virulent equivalents in countries as far flung as Ireland, Finland, and Romania. A particular conjuncture of circumstances made Italy an especially productive incubator of ultranationalist energies in the first decade of the twentieth century.

The factors that generated the acute malaise of the Italian fin-de-siècle are familiar from any standard text book on the Risorgimento and its aftermath: the diverse histories, traditions, cultures, and dialects of Italy's component regions; its deeply entrenched social divisions; the acute poverty, anarchy, and feudal conditions of large areas of the South; the rapid and poorly planned industrialization and wild capitalism of the North West corner of the country (the 'industrial triangle'), out of step with economic conditions elsewhere; the comparative weakness of the technocratic, industrial classes and 'new bourgeoisie' within the political class; the widespread illiteracy; the rudimentary educational system, and inadequate social infrastructure in much of the peninsula and especially in the islands; the arch-conservatism of the Catholic Church, still a major source of social cohesion and norms, and its alienation from the new state; the endemic egoism and corruption of a 'political class' out of touch with the living conditions and needs of the growing masses; the state's repressive use of the police and the military to quell public disorder and its refusal to address the underlying causes of the unrest. The cumulative effect was a yawning gap between the 'legal' and 'real' Italy which hampered the nationalization and democratization necessary to make the 'actually existing' nation an effective source of personal and collective identity.

In primordialist terms, the Risorgimento never became the liminal stage in the peaceful transition from the pre-unification state of Italy as a 'geographical expression' to a sustainable new state with an embedded sense of collective nationhood. Instead, its story was denied closure. Italians tended to feel they belonged to an ancient nation yet were unable to identify with the newly formed nation-state. The resulting 'liminoidality', which only intensified the growing liminoidality of modernity, was summed up in the way Massimo d'Azeglio's famous remark after Cavour's victory concerning the need to 'make Italians' continued to be invoked decades later as a shorthand expression for the incompleteness of the unification process. The reference of modern historians to the Risorgimento as an 'unfinished story'[15] expresses the same predicament. What spread among the educated elites was therefore a deep sense, not just of Italy's chronic backwardness and weakness in relation to the European 'Great Powers', but of the failure of the liberal system as a whole to provide, a failure adequate basis for modern civilization in Italy or elsewhere. It was a feeling exacerbated for the political right by the nation's failure as an imperial power, a failure epitomized in the humiliating defeat of Italian troops at the hands of Ethiopian forces at Adowa in 1896, and for the left by the state's refusal to tackle fundamental issues of inadequate infrastructure and social injustice.

Once the liminoid condition of Giolittian Italy is conceived as a *dialectical* phenomenon, it was inevitable that the brooding sense of deepening historical decline – compounded by the subliminal terror of anomy this induced – created a backlash, proliferating schemes to inaugurate an alternative modernity and a 'new world'. Luisa Mangoni pinpoints the shift from cultural pessimism to palingenetic hope among some of the more cosmopolitan of Italy's intelligentsia to the mid-1890s, but such a shift had been in the air ever since unification.[16] Emilio Gentile has traced how 'the myth of national regeneration' came to occupy 'a central place in Italian political and cultural history, from the Risorgimento to Fascism', a process that led to ideologues of every political persuasion assigning 'a palingenetic function to both culture and politics as important means to realize a national revolution'.[17] In *La Grande Italia* he reconstructs the intensely polemical ideological battle fought over different imaginings of the nation in the first years of the twentieth century between several factions who were themselves internally factionalized.

A major source of such imaginings was an artistic avant-garde that saw itself as central to supplying the visionary energies needed to revitalize Italy, but split into the several distinct cultural currents associated with Gabriele D'Annunzio, the Florentine circle that formed round such figures as Giovanni Papini and Giuseppe Prezzolini and their journals *Leonardo* and *La Voce*,[18] plus a wide constituency of Futurists loosely affiliated to Marinetti (not all of whom were destined to become Fascists).[19] Other important sources of political radicalism were ideologues of revolutionary syndicalism 'particularly sensitive to myths of power in their vision of a new society of the producers based on mixing elements of Marx and Nietzsche',[20] as well as a new breed of 'liberal professionals', technocrats, and industrialists drawn to the Associazione Nazionalista Italiana. The ANI was formed in Milan in 1910 as a lobby which 'aspired to the moral renovation and rehabilitation of the Italians, the palingenesis of the nation, and resistance to the impostures of the "plutocracies" of the modern world'.[21] Nor should we forget the contribution to the general climate of palingenetic expectancy made by a modernizing strand of Catholicism that promoted its own versions of national renewal.

All were concerned in their conflicting ways with reversing the decline of Italy constructed through a wide range of conflicting narratives. As a result an 'ideologization of the nation'[22] took place before the First World War spawning a rich variety of ultranationalisms all of which rejected the status quo as incapable of providing the sense of national identity and historical greatness needed to put an end to the liminoidality of a Giolittian era[23] experienced as increasingly 'decadent'. The result was the currency of several tropes indicative of the quest for a new suprapersonal nomos: the 'two Italies' (old and new), the 'new Italy',[24] the 'true Italy', 'the Great Italy', 'the 'Third Italy', 'the new State',[25] 'completing the Risorgimento', 'making Italians', creating the 'new civilization' and the 'new man' (or rather the 'new Italian'). Emilio Gentile subsumes the nationalism implied by this discourse under the term 'Italianism', which he defines as 'the project of making the culture, the consciousness, and the politics of the nation adequate to the new social reality created by industrialization and modernization', a 'new cultural synthesis between nationalism and modernity' that demanded a 'total spiritual revolution'.[26] Thus defined, Italianism is clearly to be considered a form of *political modernism*.

A revealing case study in the shift from a hedonistic pessimism to Italianist modernism in the heady palingenetic climate that prevailed in Italy before the outbreak of the First World War is Gabriele D'Annunzio. Having established himself as the nation's foremost novelist of 'decadentism' with his portrait of the effete Andrea Sperelli in *Il Piacere* (1889), the discovery of Nietzsche transformed his outlook on life to Dionysian vitalism infused with the 'ideologization of the nation'. The metamorphosis is heralded in a passage in *La vergine della roccia* (1896) when the hero expresses his longings for a new Italy, but even more clearly in *Il fuoco* (1900) in which the central character becomes conscious of the higher mission to use his creative gifts to mobilize the masses for the rebirth of Italy. This was no mere rhetorical gesture.[27] D'Annunzio took up a brief parliamentary political career, allied first with the right, then with the left, which would be followed some years later by a series of 'heroic' acts carried out at considerable personal risk to open a gaping breach in the defences of Giolittian liberalism through which the forces of revolutionary nationalism could storm.

The death in 1907 of Giosué Carducci, after Giuseppe Mazzini one of the main nineteenth-century prophets of the rejuvenated, 'young' Italy, prompted him to deliver a funeral oration that captures the ethos of palingenetic expectancy that characterized Italianism:

> Here is the new world, here is the divine comedy of new transfigurations, an extraordinary quantity of spiritual energy that is about to burst out of the tumult to form itself into unknown postures of beauty: out of modern mines and workshops of game and war new images and rhythms are being formed. [...] And everywhere the struggle for markets, the struggle for wealth brings with it the danger of martial conflagrations [...] the whole of the world is being stretched like a bow ready to release its arrow.[28]

Remote from the circles of aristocratic aestheticism, revolutionary socialists were also succumbing to the increasing gravitational pull of Italianism. In 1909 the newspaper run by the socialist and irredentist nationalist, Cesare Battisti, *Il Popolo*, published the text of a speech given in Trento celebrating the signs that the nation was finally 'losing the characteristics of the cemetery': 'Where once lovers day-dreamed and nightingales sang, factory sirens now blow. [...] Heroes have made way for producers and the pick-axe is ripping the heart out of the city. Italy is getting ready to inaugurate a new era in the history of humankind.'[29] It had been delivered by Benito Mussolini, who in November 1914, as the interventionist campaign for Italy to enter the First World War gathered momentum, would launch his own organ of Italianism, *Il Popolo d'Italia*.

ITALIANIST MODERNISM

According to our 'reflexive metanarrative' of modernism's dialectical relationship with modernity, the ardent craving for a new spirituality and a new temporality that drives what Emilio Gentile calls Italianism expresses primordial longings for a new nomos, a new canopy of temporalized sacrality generated by a contemporary reality experienced as anomic, as decadent. In other words, its rise to prominence under Giolitti betrays the presence of a powerful subculture of aesthetic, social, and political *modernism* bent on overthrowing a liberal system identified with the 'old Italy' whose utter inadequacy to address the forces of modernization irrevocably sealed its fate. For modernist nationalists it had to split apart to allow the chrysalis of the new Italy to metamorphize.

Such an interpretation has a profound resonance with the analyses of several historians who steadfastly resist reducing the history of Fascism to a banal chronicle of personalized events and anecdotes unilluminated by intelligent curiosity about the wider ideological and cultural motivation for the phenomena they are so painstakingly reconstructing. Walter Adamson, for example, devoted a major monograph to establishing the formative influence that the pre-war Florentine avant-garde exerted on the genesis of Fascism, using an ideal type of 'modernism' clearly congruent with the one we have constructed. He argues that 'modernism' was the bid of an 'adversary culture' or 'other modernity' to bring about 'cultural regeneration through the secular-religious quest of "new values"', challenging 'the "modernizing forces" of science, commerce, and industry, usually in the name of some more "spiritual" alternative'. This led European modernists like the Florentine artists he examines to stress 'the importance of recreating the mythic, legendary, and "primal" forces of cultural life' in a 'messianic mood of frenzy, despair, and apocalyptic hope'. Central to this hope was their belief that their intellectual and artistic efforts would play a 'central role [...] in the creation and organization of a regenerated culture'.[30] However, like Stephen Spender, who provided the template for this concept of modernism, Adamson sees Fascism not as a political form of modernism itself, but rather as a political movement *influenced* in its formative period by cultural modernism.

As we have seen, Claudio Fogu extends the term significantly beyond the sphere of the artistic avant-garde. He identifies it with the revolutionary way in which history itself was perceived by the regime, namely as an unfolding project to be shaped by the heroic new generation of Italians being formed in its schools, in its mass organizations, and through the constant presentation of history to the masses as a living, renewable, 'remakable' entity in museums, monuments, exhibitions, and anniversary commemorations. An aspect of his theory of considerable potential significance to the theory of fascism is the way he conceives Fascism's 'historic imaginary' as the linchpin between the 'aestheticization of politics' – the central focus of so much Marxist scholarship intent on demonstrating the reactionariness of Fascism – and the 'sacralization of politics' that Emilio Gentile considers central to its revolutionary dynamic.

What has encouraged Fogu to attempt the reconciliation of two such diametrically opposed schools of thought is the formative influence of the thesis set forth in Georges Bataille's 1933 essay 'The Psychological Structure of Fascism'.[31] This argued that Fascism was shaped, not solely by capitalist reaction, but by an 'appropriation of the sacred'[32] mediated by a specifically Catholic Mediterranean type of modernity and secularization whose unique quality eludes the theories of religion proposed by Max Weber or Émile Durkheim. As a result, Fogu sees in the regime's public displays of 'historicized' history sites 'where image- and ritual politics, Mussolini and the masses, fascist present and Risorgimental past, and modernist aesthetics and Catholic rhetorical codes effectively met'.[33] It is an interpretation that attributes to

Giovanni Gentile's philosophical writings 'a central role in the formation of fascist modernism':[34] 'If, as Zeev Sternhell has repeatedly argued, the principal ideological roots of Italian fascism were planted in the intellectual humus of the "anti-materialist revision of Marxism", in Italy this humus was fertilized by actualism.'[35]

The image of fascist modernism that emerges from Fogu's ludic recombination of existing paradigms of modernity still makes it primarily a cultural, intellectual, aesthetic, and semiotic force most clearly expressed through forms of political liturgy. While far from 'minimalist', this definition is still more restrictive than the one proposed by Emilio Gentile, which avoids the reductionism involved in attributing a monopoly of influence over early Fascism to any one form of Italianism. His concept of modernism emerged – practically unscathed by the upheavals of the 'cultural turn' and the lure of Benjaminian theories of political aestheticization[36] – from his exhaustive empirical investigations of 'Italianism' resulting from 'confrontation between national myth and modernity that took place at the end of the nineteenth century'. It was the struggle to give shape and direction to, and find a way out of, the growing chaos of post-Risorgimento modernity that gave rise to variegated forms of 'modernism'. This he defines as

> an ideology, a culture, a *movement* that, starting out from the perception of modern reality as an age of irreversible changes, wants to address and resolve the human, cultural, and political problems produced by industrial civilization and modernization by elaborating solutions consistent with its own vision of modernity.[37]

Modernism for Emilio Gentile thus manifests itself as both a cultural *and* a political force.

THE MAXIMALIST CONCEPT OF NATIONALIST MODERNISM

The crucial factors of convergence between Gentile's concept of modernism in the context of Italian Fascism and the generic ideal type we have constructed are threefold: its maximalist remit in embracing aesthetic, cultural, social, technological, political, ideological, and ritual forces, as well as entire movements; the stress it lays on the bid by modernists to restore the communal, spiritual, religious, *nomic* dimension of modern life being eroded by modernization; and the recognition that the invocation of the glories of bygone eras had nothing to do with nostalgia: the past – Roman, Renaissance, risorgimental – was a reservoir of revitalizing myths needed to construct an alternative modernity for Italy, a point we will return to in the next chapter.

Gentile is at pains to stress the pluralism of modernism's bids to bring about *Aufbruch* in Giolittian Italy. He thus talks of varieties of 'modernist nationalism', all of which insisted on the need for the industrial revolution and the massification of society to be accompanied by a *revolution of the spirit*, a 'religion of the nation' capable of shaping the sensibility, character, and conscience of a 'new Italian'.[38] The different forms it assumed varied in the emphasis placed on the use of historical tradition to underpin the patriotic identity and activism of the new Italy – which in the case of Futurism was zero – but all keyed into the Europe-wide redemptive, regenerative myth of war we considered in Chapter 5. Its advocates thus regarded international conflict and violence as accelerators of modernity, the producers of new elites, and the generators of a cult of heroism and self-sacrifice that would allow a new generation to transcend the materialism, hedonism, and atomization of the present. Thus in 1911 *La Voce* published an article with the terse headline 'War'. In it Giovanni Amendola, a fierce anti-Giolittian who went on to be an equally outspoken anti-Fascist, argued that what was needed to complete the Risorgimento was 'collective effort, popular sacrifice, bloodshed, and sanguinary affirmation of the national will to rise'. The ultimate goal of the resulting revolution was 'to found, in the granite of moral life, through a religion which links us to the most profound and total motives of humanity, the solid ethical edifice of the new Italian history'.[39]

Gentile's account of how he conceptualizes modernism underscores its kinship with the 'primordialist' approach we have adopted. Citing Marshall Berman's *All that is Solid Melts into Air*, he presents the term as applicable to political ideologies that 'seek to render human beings capable of mastering the processes of modernization in order not to be overwhelmed by the "vortex of modernity"' – what we have called the horror of anomy, of Cronus, of ambivalence. This endows them with 'the power to change the world that is changing them, to make their own way within the vortex and make it their own'.[40] Gentile goes on to stress the proliferation of alternative visions of a better society that have resulted from the striving to 'conquer modernity', observing that the political antagonism between them was 'perhaps one of the most disquieting, ambiguous, and tragic features of the twentieth century'.

It follows from this analysis that Gentile sees the tendency towards the aestheticization of politics in modernist nationalism as stemming 'directly from the sacralization of politics, the process of institutionalizing a secular religion necessary for the spiritual unity of a mass society that wished to confront the challenges of modernity',[41] a position that underlines the nomos- and community-creating dimension of political modernism. Furthermore, he highlights the futural thrust behind the bid to 'conquer modernity':

Modernist nationalism was not conservative, nor did it harbour nostalgia for a pre-industrial world, nor did it dream of turning back the clock of history. Its principal characteristic was the frank acceptance of modern life as an era of irreversible transformations that were affecting society, consciousness, and human sensibility, and that were preparing conditions for the rise of new forms of collective life, a new civilization.[42]

In short, Gentile refuses to see the driving force of the new forms of ultra-nationalism that had such a decisive impact on Italian history in the first two decades of the twentieth century in the need of ruling elites to prolong the death-agonies of capitalism, as generations of Marxists have postulated. Instead, it is to be sought in 'the typically modernist demand to formulate a response to the "death of God"':

In this sense all the avant-garde movements that arose in Italy prior to Fascism aspired to be religious movements, to elaborate a new sense of life and the world, to propagate it through modern myths for the masses and their integration into the national State, to give them the collective conscience of the nation as a community of values and destiny.[43]

It is this search for a new spirituality, a new nomos, and a new community that provides a common modernist matrix to such apparently disparate phenomena as Kandinsky's turn to a theosophically based abstraction in painting and the quest for a new Italy in early twentieth-century politics. Under the influence of Benjaminian theories of aesthetic politics and postmodernist concern with semiotic texts there has been a tendency for a recognition of Fascism's modernism to skew the study of its history towards an exclusive concern with its 'spectacular', religious, aesthetic aspects.[44] Such a distortion is precluded by the fully historiographical approach adopted to modernist nationalism by Emilio Gentile, who stresses how important it is 'to avoid letting emphasis on the "aestheticization of politics" lead to a kind of "aestheticization" of Fascism itself, privileging only its literary, aesthetic, and symbolic aspects while losing sight of motivations and matrices that are essentially political in nature'. For him this risks 'trivializing the fundamentally political nature of Fascism, its culture, its ideology, and its symbolic universe' to a point 'where it obscures Fascism's other important feature, its "politicization of aesthetics"'.[45]

In the light of the ideal type elaborated in Part One, the modernism of early twentieth-century Italy becomes an even more extended and less 'artistic' family than it does for Gentile, for it embraces not just various forms of aestheticized politics but 'Nietzschean', Dionysian forms of Marxism – notably the revolutionary syndicalism that Zeev Sternhell makes so central to his insufficiently reflexive metanarrative of the birth of Fascism.[46] It also recognizes the kinship of cultural with scientistic projects for purging modern society of degeneracy or stimulating national renewal.[47] From this perspective Vilfredo Pareto's 'proof' of Italy's need for new elites, the modernizing efforts to improve Italy's demographic and physical strength proposed by the demographer and statistician Corrado Gini[48] and by the social hygienist Giuseppe Sanarelli, one of the forces behind the International Exposition of Social Hygiene held in Rome in 1912,[49] were in their own way no less 'modernist' than Gentile's actualism. This suggests it might be useful to term scientistic attempts at national revitalization 'social modernist nationalism' while using 'cultural modernist nationalism' for the projects of avant-garde artists such as Marinetti and cultural commentators such as Giovanni Gentile.

THE SEARCH FOR A MAZEWAY OF ONE POLITICAL MODERNIST

The powerful eddies of social and political modernism, modernist nationalism, and politicized aesthetics coursing through pre-war Giolittian Italy were to have a formative impact on the morphing of Benito Mussolini from socialist agitator to the leader of a new revitalization movement called Fascism. He came of age intellectually just as the storm of modernism was reaching gale-force within Europe's intelligentsia, a symptom of which was the radicalness and extreme eclecticism with which revolutionary socialists all over the continent were adapting Marx to the dynamically changing historical situation that confronted them. Starting out from the relatively orthodox classical Marxism that dominated his socialist upbringing, he was soon absorbing the ethos of what was, after Leninism, the most significant current of revisionism of the day, that of revolutionary syndicalism. This was a variant of revolutionary socialism – in some respects the Western European equivalent of Marxism-Leninism – whose strategy for gaining power was influenced by Georges Sorel's cult of voluntarism, the role of heroic 'mobilizing' myths in bringing about change, and the regenerative function of violence: yet another example of the symbiosis between Nietzsche and Marx we encountered in Chapter 6. By 1903 Mussolini's political tracts were showing a sustained interest in elite theory and the psychology of crowd behaviour drawn from the works of theorists such as Gabriel Tarde, Gustave Le Bon, Gaetano Mosca, and Vilfredo Pareto. Over the next few years he constantly elaborated his revolutionary theory, becoming increasingly drawn to the possibility that the new society would be brought about not through the autonomous maturing of the international proletariat into the 'historical subject', but by a vanguard of dedicated revolutionaries operating within their national context to create their own historical subject.

It was against the background of a political culture in which both the left and the right were formulating projects of renewal in the discourse of Italianism that a major turning point in his ideological development took place. In 1908 he became a regular reader of *La Voce*, the organ of a Florentine avant-garde that at the time was the epicentre of modernist nationalism in Italy. It had been launched by Giovanni Papini, who in 1904 published with Giuseppe Prezzolini the highly influential 'Nationalist Programme'. This sought to address the urgent need 'to escape from this sad depression and feverish vacuum in which our country is struggling', and to 'restore a deeper meaning to our life, a full meaning to the life of the nation' by offering a 'unity of vision' and a 'programme of action'.[50] The metapolitical, cosmological, anti-anomic thrust of the document – so revealing of its fundamental *modernism* in the primordialist sense – emerges clearly from the evocation of the cultural renaissance that will ensue once the nation is 'aroused from its slumber': 'Then heroic deeds and superhuman passions, nature in all its light and all its mystery, proud thoughts that wreathe the world with iron bonds, will once more reappear in the drama and poetry and the metaphysics of a rising generation.'[51] Two years later Papini launched his campaign for the 'forced' awakening of Italian national consciousness in the pages of the periodical *Leonardo*, the principal journal of political modernism before *La Voce*.

Mussolini encountered the Vocian campaign for a total revolution of the nation's artistic, ethical, and political culture at a critical stage in his own quest for a coherent strategy to awaken the slumbering revolutionary forces of contemporary society. The paper's Dionysian rhetoric of the transvaluation of values persuaded him to cast himself in the leading role of the unfolding drama of political transformation, imparting to his vision of mass mobilization a specifically *nationalist* agenda. Renzo de Felice is hardly being an 'apologist' for Fascism when his exhaustive study of the 'revolutionary' phase of Mussolini's ideological development uncovers the fact that he was a reader of *La Voce* 'from the beginning' (i.e. December 1908). His study of the text of Mussolini's unpublished review of Prezzolini's *La teoria sindacalista*, submitted to *La Voce* in 1909, demonstrates that under the magazine's influence he now conceived himself as one of the Nietzschean *homines novi* called upon to transform morality, create new values, and lead the social revolution needed to overcome Italy's decadence.[52] Contact with the Vociani also intensified his awareness of the futural temporality of the imminent metamorphosis. In an interview he gave in 1935 the *duce* openly acknowledged this debt: 'I first had the feeling of being called upon to announce a new era when I started corresponding with the *Voce* group.'[53] It was after this political epiphany that he gave the speech in Trento referred to earlier (later published in *Il Popolo*) announcing that Italy would soon arise from its 'cemetery' to give birth to a new era.

It is important to note that when Mussolini and other left-wing revolutionaries embraced modernist nationalism, they did not abandon the myth of revolution but *Italianized* it. As Emilio Gentile points out:

> The new revolutionary nationalism reworked, using Mazzinian thought and myths of national radicalism, a conception of revolution as a process of *national palingenesis* that had to radically renew not only the political, economic, and social order, but also culture, mentalities, characters, leading to the construction of a new state and the creation of a New Italian without abandoning the universalist vocation, one that was now transferred from socialist internationalism to the myth of the Great Italy.[54]

The crucial Vocian stage in Mussolini's evolution as an ideologue and activist has been peculiarly neglected by generations of his more facile biographers to this day, who choose to interpret his transition from socialism to nationalism as no more than the whim of an ideologically vacuous opportunist.[55] Nevertheless, thorough documentation by Renzo de Felice, James Gregor, and Emilio Gentile shows unequivocally that five years before the outbreak of the First World War Mussolini was a rebel *with* a cause, no matter how utopian and mythic, namely to play a leading role in bringing about Italy's rebirth as the prelude to the inauguration of a new epoch in Western history. It was a cause to which he was to stay more faithful than the glaring contradictions between many of his subsequent tactics, policies, and rhetorical pronouncements would suggest.

At least in his early, idealistic years, the rampant syncretism of his thinking, its constantly evolving contents, the tensions between his positions over time, and even simultaneously, should not be dismissed rashly as symptoms of a pathological personality. Rather they are to be approached as the characteristics of an intensely politically and *pragmatically* oriented individual anguished at the state of the 'world' and desperately searching for an alchemical formula that will put an end to the liminoid conditions of the time, a nomos that after *La Voce* he projected not onto the international proletariat but the Italian nation. The modernist nationalism of Vocianism thus provided a vital component to his personal 'mazeway resynthesis'. What was still missing was the mobilizing myth that would trigger the national reawakening at a populist level. This would finally be supplied by the prospect of a European 'conflagration'.

THE POLITICAL MODERNISM OF THE FIRST 'FASCISTS'

The decision of Giolitti's government to remain neutral in the autumn of 1914 was indirectly responsible for the second great turning point in Mussolini's ideological development. He decided to break with the Partito Socialista Italiano (PSI) that still upheld the principle of neutrality, and became an interventionist, responding to the same ethos that caused Giovanni Gentile to support intervention on the grounds of what would become his philosophy of 'actualism'.

While there was little sociological basis for populist war fever in Italy, the acute alienation of its intelligentsia from Giolittian Italy meant that the redemptive connotations of war bred no less feverish utopian imaginings within the Italian avant-garde than it did within its French or German counterparts. Thus it was that '[f]or many interventionists the European War was the great event they had waited for to precipitate the Italian revolution, the transformation of the state and the regeneration of the nation'.[56] As a result, both the extreme left and extreme right overwhelmingly experienced the crisis over Italy's participation as the watershed between the 'old' and 'new' Italy, as the providential opportunity for Italy to become 'Great'. Political and cultural modernists of every persuasion 'knew' that fighting alongside France and Britain would precipitate the 'national palingenesis [...] necessary for the formation of a modern Italian conscience'.[57] The common denominator of their hopes was expressed in the famous speech, 'Il Discorso della Sagra dei Mille', delivered by D'Annunzio on 5 May 1915 to the vast crowds gathered at the port of Quarto just outside Genoa. They were there to inaugurate the monument commemorating the departure 55 years earlier of Garibaldi's 1,000 red-shirted troops on their expedition to liberate the South. The theme of the speech was summed up in a single phrase that resounded through the country's press the next day: 'Here a Greater Italy is being born.'[58] Within three weeks Italy had declared war on the Austro-German alliance.

D'Annunzio was speaking as part of a powerful, if ephemeral, coalition of modernist nationalisms united by the prospect of imminent redemption through war. For Filippo Marinetti events were rapidly realizing the dream of a cathartic, revitalizing war expressed in his Futurist manifesto of 1909 in the famous declaration: 'We will glorify war – the world's only hygiene – militarism, patriotism, the destructive gesture of freedom-bringers, beautiful ideas worth dying for and the scorn of women.'[59] He now described the violent events unfolding at the front as 'the most beautiful Futurist poem that has ever seen the light of day',[60] allowing 'artists, finally alive, and no longer perched high up on the peaks of disdainful aestheticism' to 'collaborate as workers and soldiers to world progress'.[61] The war would 'develop gymnastics, sport, practical schools of agriculture, commerce, and industry'. It would 'reinvigorate Italy, enrich its men of action, oblige her to stop living in the past amid ruins and a sweet climate, and force her to use her own national forces'.[62] The Futurists were the first to organize pro-war protests, and the sheer dynamism of their demonstrations could win the admiration of ideologues politically poles apart, such as the revolutionary syndicalist Angelo Olivetti who saw a kindred spirit animating the palingenetic zeal of their bellicose and *modernist* nationalism.

Inevitably the Florentine avant-garde had also become fervent interventionists. Giovanni Papini collaborated with Alfredo Soffici in 1913 to launch *Lacerba*, which soon rivalled *La Voce* as the main avant-garde organ of modernist nationalism with its merger of 'Florentine' with 'Milanese' – i.e. Futurist – cultural nationalism.[63] Soon after the war broke out in August 1914 with Italy helplessly looking on, Papini devoted the front page of *Lacerba* to the hot-headed – and chilling – declaration that:

> At last the *dies irae* has arrived after the long dusks of fear. At last they are paying the tithe of souls for the re-cleansing of the earth. We needed a hot bath of black blood after so many lukewarm ones of mother's milk and brotherly tears. We needed a good shower of blood for the heat of August. [...] There are too many of us. The war is a Malthusian operation.[64]

Equally spontaneously the Nationalists of the ANI welcomed it, interpreting it through the lens of their own version of Social Darwinism as a chance for nations to 'feel themselves what they are in fact: armies; armies in the universal struggle for selection and improvement'. Thanks to the war Italy would be transformed into a fully industrialized, imperial nation-state unified through the forces of patriotism.[65] Less predictable was the reaction of many revolutionary syndicalists. Some remained neutralists, while several of their leading spokesmen deepened the growing divide between them and the still adamantly neutralist PSI by throwing their weight behind interventionism in the hope that it would be a 'war of redemption', not only warding off the forces of reaction, but 'making it fit for socialism'.[66]

Mussolini's conversion to interventionism was made manifest by the dramatic decision to resign as editor of *Avanti!*, the newspaper of the PSI's revolutionary faction, and throw his weight behind the interventionist cause with the foundation of a new daily, *Il Popolo d'Italia*. The headline of its first editorial on 15 November 1914 was simply 'Audacia!' [Daring!] printed in block capitals. It addressed itself to 'a youth belonging to a generation charged by destiny to "make" history', exhorting them, 'in an age of general dissolution' to abandon the ranks of the 'eternally motionless mummies always facing the same horizon', and side instead with 'the living forces' of 'the new Italy' by responding enthusiastically to the 'dreadful and fascinating' word he was shouting: 'War!' Significantly, leading members of the Florentine avant-garde greeted *Il Popolo d'Italia* as a perpetuation of the spirit of *La Voce* and began treating Mussolini as the '*homo novus*' called upon to create the new Italy,[67] precisely the way he saw his own mission ever since his contact with

La Voce. The departure from *Avanti!* had cleared the way for an even closer rapprochement with modernist nationalism now that he was free to treat 'the people' not as a proletarian but a national entity comprising the youthful, productive, heroic forces of the new Italy born of war. This was their message to the public when Mussolini and Marinetti held a joint meeting in Milan on 31 March 1915, and were arrested in Rome the following month for organizing an interventionist demonstration.

In was thus in a climate of heightened palingenetic expectations and ecumenical Italianist idealism that on 10 October 1914, eight days before Mussolini's conversion to the pro-war lobby, a group of Milanese revolutionary syndicalists led by Filippo Corridoni founded the *Fascio rivoluzionario d'azione internazionalista* (FRAI: the Revolutionary League for Internationalist Action), to coordinate left-wing pressure on the government. According to Angelo Ventrone, whatever Mussolini claims in his posthumously published autobiography *La mia vita* (1947), it was only in January 1915 that he became the dominant force in the successor to FRAI, the Fasci d'azione rivoluzionaria (FAR), when it held its first congress in Milan that month. Leading FAR strengthened Mussolini's ties with revolutionary syndicalists, some of whom, notably Michele Bianchi and Cesare Rossi, would become founding members of Fascism after the war. It also ensured that the term *fascio*, originally a politically neutral term for a 'league', became widely identified with interventionism and the celebration of the regenerative power of war. By the end of 1915 '*Fascisti*' was already being used in the pages of *Il Popolo d'Italia* with the connotations of the heroic pioneers of a new Italy.[68]

However, FAR was destined never to be more than an ephemeral campaign of 'single-issue politics'. The goal it set itself, to force the government to intervene on the side of the Entente, was short-termist and it never aspired to become the nucleus of a 'rainbow alliance' between interventionist liberals and a deeply divided radical right made up of Nationalists, Futurists, and *vociani*. Nor did the now 52-year-old D'Annunzio, despite his charismatic presence as a speaker, show any sign of welding the disparate ideological values represented by the interventionists into a cohesive revitalization movement. In fact, the war had still whipped up none of the popular enthusiasm that led young Frenchmen, Germans, and Englishmen to volunteer to fight in their thousands. Nevertheless, Mussolini's experience of the interventionist campaign had provided him the 'clue' he needed to find his way out of the Giolittian labyrinth. He had seen how even a loose alliance between conflicting different strands of political modernism could generate a powerful revolutionary synergy.

THE BIRTH OF FASCISM AS A REVITALIZATION MOVEMENT

Though the masthead of *Il Popolo d'Italia* carried the motto 'A revolution is an idea that has found bayonets', initially Mussolini's own synthetic idea of revolution was too nebulous to find a significant readership, let alone bayonets, particularly in a situation where most 'ordinary' Italians were resigned to or opposed to war. However his brief time on the Italian front before he was wounded and returned to his journalism, only convinced him further of the role of war in national awakening.[69] It was the military disaster suffered at Caporetto between 24 October and 12 November 1917 that paradoxically transformed the situation in the direction Mussolini hoped by finally rallying Italians *en masse* behind the national war effort. The unexpectedness, extreme rapidity, and unprecedented scale of the defeat[70] created a very real sense that the nation was in 'mortal danger', turning the war for the first time into a disturbing mythic – and hence affectively 'real' – event for millions of ordinary Italians far from the sound of cannon.

In his investigation of the evolution of Fascism's 'historic imaginary' Claudio Fogu draws attention to the importance of the investigation by the Italian social psychiatrist Elvio Fachinelli into the psychological dynamics of the collective trauma inflicted by the defeat at Caporetto, high up in the Italo-Slovenian mountains, and by the spectre of total catastrophe it conjured up. He suggests that the prospective death of the mythic fatherland for which so much had been already sacrificed had the effect of triggering a mass response of denial. This took the form of transposing 'the ideal of the fatherland onto an absolute plane' in which it was endowed with immortality, thereby bringing about an 'archaic annulment of time': the 'arrow of time stopped'.[71] Translated into the discourse we have constructed in Part One, Fachinelli is arguing that the prospect of Italy 'running out of [historical] time' triggered the countervailing urge to overcome the devouring work of Cronus by making the fatherland/motherland – 'patria' is feminine in Italian – a temporalized utopia, reconfiguring it as the cosmic firmament or sacred canopy, a suprapersonal community inviolable by the ravages of time. The collective mythopoeic act of elevating the nation above profane time to rescue it from history was accompanied by palingenetic images of national renewal and rebirth that in turn spawned rituals of sacralization, sacrifice, and celebration symbolically imbuing history with renewed 'historic' meaning in a way that finally struck a chord with 'the masses'. In this way the mythic cessation of Cronus automatically started the clock of *aevum* ticking.

It was in this sense that Caporetto accelerated what George Mosse called the 'nationalization of the masses'. For at least a segment of the 'people' Italy became sacralized in conditions of acute national crisis into a living entity capable of being destroyed or reborn, demanding love and self-sacrifice as a vessel of transcendence. This dramatized and made 'real' the mythic image of the organic nation first cultivated by the Mazzinian tradition of the Risorgimento and then further refined through the projections of modernist nationalism and of the various interventionist factions seeking redemption through war. As Fogu himself implies, the sudden wave of chauvinism that followed Caporetto was a populist correlative to Giovanni Gentile's abstruse intellectual project to sacralize and 'ethicize' the nation through 'actualism'. In our 'primordialist' terms, by bringing to a head and crystallizing the liminality of Italy's whole war experience – one that only exacerbated the already acutely liminoid state of its historical situation – Caporetto ensured that the modernist fiction of 'making history' previously intelligible only to the avant-garde suddenly became a populist, 'democratic' – though still latent – source of support for revolutionary change. For the first time it made significant numbers of ordinary citizens susceptible to the myth that the Risorgimento *could* be completed, that after over half a century of decadence the second stage of the rite of passage to Italian nationhood, that of 'disaggregation', could finally be completed.

One political modernist who instantly recognized that Caporetto had blasted a major breach in the continuum of Giolittian history was Mussolini. Barely a month after the disaster, when its political fallout was at its height, he published an article in *Il Popolo d'Italia* under the title 'Trenchocracy'.[72] In it he portrays veterans as the nucleus of a new ruling elite. 'The trenchocracy is the aristocracy of the trenches. It is the aristocracy of tomorrow! It is the aristocracy in action.' He compares it with the bourgeoisie in the years immediately preceding the French Revolution, 'sweeping aside' the old political system once the war is over. Evoking the temporality of the new – 'the music of tomorrow will have another tempo' – Mussolini indicates that the inauguration of the 'Italy of tomorrow' involves a 'transvaluation of values': 'The words republic, democracy, radicalism, liberalism, the word "socialism" itself, have no sense any longer: they will have one tomorrow, but it will be the one given them by the millions of "those who returned".' With remarkable prescience about the rise of fascism in a number of countries in the 1920s, he adds 'it could, for example, be *an anti-Marxist and national socialism*'.[73]

Mussolini has no doubt that at long last the moment of palingenesis has arrived. A new Italy will arise spontaneously from the depths of the people once enough demobilized soldiers can be organized into the embryo of a new ruling elite who will take command of a new, post-Giolittian society. Though the contents of its new nomos are still to be defined, he conceives its core ideology specifically in terms of a 'ludic recombination' of left and right. As for the man of destiny, the *propheta* whose task it is to embody the new mazeway, turn disaffection and pessimism into a powerful revitalization movement, and lead the *communitas* of reborn Italians into a new era, it is of course none other than Mussolini himself. Thanks to the war, a freak conjuncture of historical events had finally granted him the chance to fulfil the mission revealed to him through his contact with *La Voce* a decade earlier: he was to be a 'new man' creating 'Great Italy'. After Caporetto Mussolini thus spontaneously played the part he had been rehearsing since 1909, the one performed by what studies of premodern revitalization movements call the 'visionary' who 'experiences a radical change in personality, assumes a new role in society, devises a new plan for reorganizing society and proposes a new order that promises new meaning and purpose for living'.[74] He now assumed the persona of a charismatic leader.

Mussolini's mazeway for the new post-war order would have remained yet another modernist pipe-dream had not Italy, despite being on the victorious side, been plunged into an even deeper structural crisis after the cessation of hostilities.[75] Its acute socio-political and economic problems were exacerbated by the shoddy treatment of Italy by the Allies in the Paris Peace Conference, by the insensitivity of the Giolittian government to the mood of a population that expected tangible rewards for its 'sacrifices', and by powerful currents of agitation by radical socialists who felt in the wake of the Bolshevik Revolution that their time had come. The subjective sense of breakdown and dysfunction was deepened by the seismic political changes occurring in a Europe ravaged by war, and by an influenza pandemic claiming between 20 and 40 million lives. These disseminated a mood of crepuscular gloom that turned Oswald Spengler's turgid *Decline of the West*, with its epic metanarrative of how the sun of an entire civilization was setting, into an international bestseller.[76]

It was a conjuncture of factors which provided the ideal conditions for propagating the myth of the Two Italies that had dominated avant-garde circles of modernist nationalism before the war. The 'old' Italy of a spineless, effete, morally bankrupt liberalism that had wanted to stay out of the war now had to make way for the 'new' youthful Italy that now emerged from the war invigorated by sacrifice, and open to undreamt adventures. Mussolini's response to the new situation was to launch a new *Fascio* on the model of the Fascio di Azione Rivoluzionaria founded four years earlier. On 23 March 1919, in a conference hall in Piazza San Sepolcro in Milan, he launched his new movement with a motley gathering of 118 founding members which included intellectuals, workers, war veterans, syndicalists, former Socialists, nationalists, five Jews, two women, and Filippo Marinetti, the Futurist leader, with nothing in common other than the common vision of a new Italy born of the war. The movement's astutely chosen title, *Fasci di combattimento*, invoked not just the interventionist *Fasci*, but the values of 'combattentismo', a term which refers both to the idealization of war and violence as a basic human and historical necessity, and the celebration of the spirit of solidarity among war-veterans as a moral and political force. The only two absolute principles on which the movement was to be based were 'anti-Bolshevism' and 'the nation', which Mussolini described as 'a tangible and intangible truth [...] which is feeling the first stirrings of a new life which is about to explode into a greatness that only the Italian genius can conceive in its conquest of humanity'.[77]

In short, what became known as San Sepolcro Fascism was intended as the first step to perpetuating the revolutionary momentum attributed by modernist nationalists to the war from the very beginning. The idea was to launch not a political party but what we have seen cultural anthropologists describe as an 'anti-structure', the embryo of the new *communitas*. As Mussolini put it in the section 'Political and Social Doctrine' of the article on Fascism written for Giovanni Gentile's *Enciclopedia Italiana* (1932): 'Fascism was not the nursling of a doctrine previously drafted at a desk; it was born of the need of action, and was action; it was not a party but, in the first two years, *an anti-party and a movement*.'[78] He intended the *Fasci* to form the cells of revolutionary national consciousness that were the first stage towards realizing his vision of the 'trenchocracy', a new elite infused with modernist resolve to inaugurate a new world, led not by a politician but by a 'healer' who would 'build the house again and start time anew'.

A CONFLUENCE OF MODERNISMS

In its first months of life the first *Fascio* remained largely ignored on the fringes of Milanese political life. The sign that Mussolini had correctly read the runes of the post-war situation came not from any dramatic expansion of his own movement, which seemed to be withering on the vine, but from the widespread public support for D'Annunzio's own modernist experiment in inaugurating the new era of Great Italy through a Dionysian act of 'making history'. In September 1919 he led a small force of *Arditi* (the crack troops of the Italian army) into the small port-city of Rijeka/Fiume on the Dalmatian coast while the Paris Peace Conference was still trying settle the rival claims to sovereignty of Italy and the future Yugoslavia. He proceeded to rule the town until he was forced out by the Italian army in 'the Christmas of Blood' in December 1920 amidst a storm of public protest throughout Italy against the government's 'unpatriotic' intervention. D'Annunzio's 'aesthetic' vision of politics ensured that the animating force of his microcosmic new order, the prototype of the New Italy, was supplied not by conventional politics, but by a blend of patriotism, militarism, corporatism, poetry, music, and spectacular 'happenings'. The state was now a 'total work of art', its modernist ethos underlined when, having committed himself to adopting the model of corporatism proposed by the revolutionary syndicalist Alceste De Ambris – in itself an extraordinary act of syncretism for the former artist of aristocratic decadence – he symbolically dedicated one of the corporations to the 'new man', 'il nuovissimo uomo'.[79]

In the event it was Fascism, not 'Dannunzianism', that won the day for 'combattentismo'. The threat – real or imaginary – of a total paralysis or even civil war provoked by the revolutionary left in the 'red two years' of 1919–20 caused the veteran-led violence of *squadre d'azione* to spread spontaneously in the North and Centre of Italy, underlining the government's impotence to restore law and order. Since each squad created its own *Fascio*, Fascism was turned, almost by proxy, into a genuine paramilitary and populist force comprising numerous paramilitary revitalization movements nominally under the Fascist umbrella, all pursuing nationalist aspirations that went far beyond merely crushing the left. The history of Fascism's spectacular growth from the paltry membership of the first *Fascio* in March 1919 to a movement powerful enough to enter government in October 1922 has been reconstructed in impressive empirical detail by historians.[80] What has received less attention is the key role played even in this phase of its rise to power by political modernism.

Squadrismo has been generally dismissed as an outburst of reactionary violence directed at the progressive forces of Catholic and Marxist socialism, which is doubtless true in the case of some opportunists or anti-communist thugs. Yet a closer study of texts relating to the motivation of the *squadristi* themselves reveals a powerful palingenetic vision at work, both in the mindset of its most ardent activists and in its mythic legacy to the regime. The sense of being called upon to carry through to fruition the national revolution that started when Italy entered the war is reflected not just in the memoirs and history of Fascism written by the most famous *squadrista* leader (known by the Ethiopian term for a chief, *ras*) of all, Roberto Farinacci,[81] but the accounts of several minor figures who were part of the rank and file.[82]

The spate of squadrista novels published in the 1930s, which enjoyed considerable success under the regime, reveal a significant mythic pattern. Their basic plot is 'the protagonist's path to redemption'. For example, the hero shakes off the 'bestial torpor' of life after demobilization and awakens to find a corrupt Italy in which the bourgeoisie hold parties while socialists desecrate national symbols. At that point he consciously severs his link with the past by turning to Fascism, and his life becomes filled with a sense of higher 'mission' which he shares with the demobbed comrades with whom he is reunited. Enrolment in an action squad 'purifies them, as they end the immoral life they led previously' and slough off their bourgeois self to become the incarnation of the 'new Italian'. As one novel put it, this did not mean proving yourself through some 'spectacular aviation or sporting feat', since 'even civil servants or shopkeepers can and must be "new Italians". It was all about giving yourself to the nation.'[83] It is well established that the *squadrista* myth of sacrifice for the new-born nation was incorporated into Fascism's sacralization and ritualization of politics. What is less well appreciated is how far the *squadrista* experience lent itself to this mythicization by living out the principle of cathartic destruction central to Ernst Jünger's vision of war as the 'blacksmith' of new values we saw in Chapter 6.[84]

The ability of Fascism to assimilate conflicting currents of revolutionary ideological energy on its path to state power is also inseparable from its essentially syncretic dynamic as a revitalization movement. David Roberts reminds anyone seeking to reduce Fascism to a single ideological entity such as Sorelian syndicalism or Vocian modernism of the fact that ideologically speaking it was 'a messy mixture, and its centre of gravity changed as the regime evolved'.[85] This is equally true of Fascism's five years of life before achieving power. However, its shifting centre of gravity had a relatively stable core in the protean myth of national palingenesis. What assured the movement sufficient cohesion and dynamism to form first a government and then a regime was that Mussolini welcomed all currents of cultural and political modernism to Fascism's fold as long as the new nomos they aspired to and the horizon they sought to fix were framed within the core myth of Italianism, the imminent creation of a 'New', 'Great' Italy.

The syncretism already apparent at the meeting that founded Fascism steadily grew, as ever more individuals – Futurists, revolutionary syndicalists, *squadristi*, war veterans, artists, architects, civil servants, social scientists, Catholic clergy, trade unionists, Dannunzians – threw in their lot with Mussolini's movement between 1921 and 1925, all projecting onto it their own 'Italianist' diagnosis of the current crisis and their own agenda for change. When in the section 'Political and Social Doctrine' of the Encyclopedia article on Fascism Mussolini referred to 'the great river of Fascism'[86] made up of numerous tributaries, his metaphor applied not just to his own ideology, but to the essentially pluralist nature of Fascism as a whole. It is against this background that we must see the ANI's decision to merge with what was now the National Fascist Party five months after the March on Rome of October 1922. This brought leading Nationalists such as Alfredo Rocco, Luigi Federzoni, and Enrico Corradini into positions of considerable influence in a government that had also won the allegiance of major revolutionary syndicalists such as Sergio Panunzio, Agostino Lanzillo, and Paolo Orano. Though originally from diametrically opposed ends of the conventional left–right spectrum they were able to coexist in the new, highly commodious political space 'beyond right and left'[87] filled with diverse imaginings of the reborn nation or Italy-led civilization.

For example, Rocco, the new regime's Minister of Justice, justified the abolition of free collective bargaining in the new laws governing industrial relations by invoking the life cycle of all societies from barbarism to civilization and back again. In outlining this organic concept of society he cited not Oswald Spengler but the law of ebb and flow in the lives of civilizations – *corsi* and *ricorsi* – postulated by the Renaissance philosopher, Giovan Battista Vico. Fascism was inaugurating 'a new phase in the eternal and reciprocal struggle between organization and the principle of dissolution'.[88] Vico was also the authority invoked by Sergio Panunzio in outlining his rival theory of the new state based on a nationalized version of revolutionary syndicalism. He portrayed Fascism as a '*ricorso* of pristine, healthy barbarian energies – so different from an influx of barbarity and decadence', 'the greatest guarantee of the perpetuation and vital process of human Society'.[89]

FASCISM AS THE ROHRSCHACH TEST OF ITALIAN MODERNISM

The psychological Rohrschach test is based on gleaning insight into the patient's fixations and state of mind from the way he or she interprets a shape that is deliberately designed to be ambiguous and 'polysemic'. Similarly it was Fascism's multivalent, multifaceted nature as a utopian project of historical change that allowed any number of rival political visions to be projected onto it as long as they were permutations of the core vision of Italian society's imminent rebirth from decadence. As the basic common denominator of all Italianism this vague *topos* could enlist fervent support by the protagonists of many permutations of modernist nationalism or nationalist modernism. It also encouraged collaboration from the representatives of ideological currents that were nationalistic for conservative reasons, notably civil servants, industrialists, or were motivated by anti-anarchist or anti-Bolshevik forms of monarchist, aristocratic, bourgeois, militarist, feudal, or Catholic reaction, none of whom could espouse Fascism wholeheartedly without compromising their own ideological principles.[90]

As Fascism gained political momentum in the 1920s it became a magnet to an ever wider gamut of modernists in one way or another keen to feel part of a dynamic, ongoing, open-ended process of cultural transformation that seemed to be heading with the inexorable force of destiny towards a 'new order' which would replace the bankrupt Giolittian system. Growing numbers of Italians could feel that – like Marinetti himself when he founded Futurism – they were standing on the 'last promontory of the centuries' where the Time and Space of the decadent past was actively being transcended, and History was being made. It was from this bridgehead in the battle for the future that ideologues as far apart politically as the Nationalist Alfredo Rocco and the Syndicalist Sergio Panunzio could both fight for their conflicting versions of *ricorso* or renewal. Alongside them in the arena were increasing numbers of academics, intellectuals, and educated elites converted to the cause of social and national regeneration in just the way that the *vociani* had been calling for in their pre-war campaigns for national reawakening.

Some of the Florentine avant-garde were now following their own itinerary, such as Ardengo Soffici, who came to embrace a cult of regional values that was anti-Futurist in aesthetic terms but still pro-modernist in ethos, and Giovanni Papini, who converted to a highly evangelistic Catholicism before writing *Italia Mia*, a chauvinistic evocation of the reborn Italy published in 1939, the same year he was honoured with the title 'Academic of Italy'. Yet they too sooner or later found themselves cohabiting Fascist cultural space with the luminaries of a new generation of politico-cultural modernists such as Curzio Malaparte, Massimo Bontempelli, and 'second generation' Futurists such as the architect Virgilio Marchi and the artists of 'aeropittura' (aviation painting),[91] Giacomo Balla and Fortunato Depero – not to mention Julius Evola and Filippo Marinetti, both of whose relationships with Fascism remained turbulent. All succumbed to the illusion they could help steer the ongoing Fascist Revolution towards the realization of their idiosyncratic longings for a new civilization.

Ezra Pound, one of the most famous modernist poets of the age, was drawn to Mussolini's regime for the same generic reason. However, the elements ludically recombined in his highly idiosyncratic world-view included the 'alternative' economic theory of Social Credit which he had discovered as one of the inner circle of contributors to Alfred Orage's *The New Age*,[92] Vorticism, a passionate interest in Chinese poetry, Dante, a fascination with the capacity of the latest sound recording technology, the phonoscope, to reveal primordial rhythms of race,[93] and, of course, a virulent form of anti-Semitism focused on the Jews' alleged economic parasitism, which could express itself at times with a eugenic ferocity: 'USURY is the cancer of the world, which only the surgeon's knife of Fascism can cut out of the life of nations.'[94]

Given Fascism's radically heterogeneous nature as an *essentially* syncretic form of political modernism, it follows that when Giovanni Gentile symbolically donated his 'actualist' programme of national renewal to Mussolini's movement by joining the PNF in June 1923, he did not become its 'prime ideologue' as is sometimes assumed, let alone provide the intellectual template of its doctrine. As Minister of Public Instruction and President of the National Institute of Fascist Culture he worked as part of a broad alliance of partially convergent, partially conflicting, cultural, social, and political schemes for completing the Risorgimento. Their ideologues and activists were loosely yoked together by Fascism's curious blend of authoritarianism and laissez-faire in an ever-growing team of ideological horses pulling in several different directions. They nevertheless provided enough forward momentum in the crucial period 1922–30 to enable Fascism to establish itself as the 'New State' improvised by a new ruling elite 'manning' the strategic positions of political and cultural power, all convinced that they were the architects of 'Great Italy'.

Gentile himself seems never to have abandoned his belief that he could provide the theoretical foundations for Fascism's 'spiritual government', even after opposition to his cultural and educational policies became too vociferous for Mussolini to ignore. Following the collapse of the Fascist regime he was still prepared to become president of the Royal Academy of Italy under the Nazis' puppet regime, the Italian Social Republic, thereby becoming a living symbol of intransigent Fascism and a natural target of Partisans. The fatal consequences of his 'ethical' decision to stay faithful to the regime were 'actualized' in his assassination in April 1944. Within a year the entire Fascist experiment in 'making history' to save a world from decadence had collapsed for the second time, this time irrevocably, amidst Nazi occupation, escalating state terror, mass-deportations, and a ferocious civil war. The next chapter will consider in more detail the modernist nature of Mussolini's regime during the 'ventennio fascista', during which it acted as an incubator to so many variants of cultural, social, and political modernism, sometimes with equally fatal personal consequences for its protagonists.

8
The Fascist Regime as a Modernist State

> The Fascist Party [...] started to become, like Mazzini's Young Italy, the faith of all Italians contemptuous of the past and longing for renewal. A faith like any faith that comes up against an established reality to be broken up and melted down in the crucible of new energies and recast to accommodate the burning zeal and intransigence of a new ideal. It was the same faith that had matured in the trenches and in intense reflection on the sacrifice made in the battle fields directed towards the only end that could justify it: the life and greatness of the Fatherland.
>
> Giovanni Gentile, *The Manifesto of Fascist Intellectuals* (1925)[1]

FASCISM'S 'CHALLENGE TO TIME'

What has emerged from the – necessarily highly condensed – narrative of Fascism's genesis offered in the last chapter is that it is not just to be approached as the *offspring* of cultural modernism, whether Futurism, Vocianism,[2] or Gentilean actualism, or as the derivative of Sorelian, revolutionary syndicalist currents of political modernism.[3] Rather it is to be regarded as a highly syncretic, synergetic form of political modernism *in its own right*. As Claudio Fogu observes, 'The modernist character of Fascism resided neither in the "spiritualization of technology", nor solely in its appropriation of avant-garde techniques, but rather in its self-presentation *as a modernist political movement for the age of the masses*.'[4] The many unresolved ideological tensions, inconsistencies, and contradictions gleefully documented both in Mussolini's personality and the regime as a whole by some historians[5] are thus not to be taken as symptoms of a personal dictatorship driven solely by megalomania, an obsession with the monopoly of power for its own sake, or aestheticized political reaction. Rather they stem to a large extent from the *revolutionary* bid to translate – in rapidly changing objective conditions – a loose alliance of often contradictory modernist projects for the regeneration of history and the creation of a new Italy into the *praxis* of a new political system able to meet the demands of a modern nation-state with as broad a consensus as possible.

The numerous practical problems that Fascism faced in doing this were exacerbated by the fact that the new regime was to be constructed not *ex nihilo*, but by transforming an existing state system with no agreed historical precedent or doctrine to go on, something which, given the small number of convinced Fascists as a percentage of the population, required as much collaboration as possible from existing elites, political, social, and cultural. The alarming cracks that appeared in the totalitarian edifice from the outset point not to the spurious nature of its totalitarianism implied by the term 'façade',[6] but to the fundamentally utopian – and hence essentially unrealizable – nature of the whole Fascist undertaking to create a modernist state capable of changing the course not just of Italian but world history *for the better*. There are thus good grounds for taking at face value the passage in Mussolini's autobiography, published in 1928 when the parabola of his career was still in the ascendant, in which he pours vitriol on the political parties under the Giolittian system.[7] He says that he was compelled to create the fascist movement because 'Their ideas had grown tawdry and insufficient – unable to keep pace with the rising tide of unexpected political exigencies, unable to adjust to the formation of new history and developments and new conditions of modern life.' It was thus vital

> to imagine a wholly new political conception, adequate to the living reality of the twentieth century, overcoming at the same time the ideological worship of liberalism, the limited horizons of various spent and exhausted democracies, and finally the violently Utopian spirit of Bolshevism. In a word, I felt the deep need for an original conception capable of bringing about a more fruitful rhythm of history in a new period of history. It was necessary to lay the foundation of a new civilization.[8]

Though it does not use the term 'modernist' to describe such aspirations, Angelo Ventrone's history of the genesis of Fascism in the First World War also corroborates the cogency of seeing the eventual regime as the concrete embodiment of political modernism as we have characterized it. He claims that after the war 'the project that Fascism made its own' was 'to institutionalize and make permanent the myth of the nation'. Mussolini's dictatorship undertook an experiment which, 'by refining political instruments constructed and elaborated in the course of the war', set out to overcome the domination of society under existing modernity by 'technology, finance, decadence and feminization, sensual desire and atomization, equality and entropy that was now threatening Italy as well'. Thus the new state was rooted in the search for 'a modernity capable of spiritualizing the masses',[9] its revolution aiming to comprehensively transform into politics the 'essentially literary' desire 'to give a new meaning to individual and collective life'.[10]

Alluding specifically to Marshall Berman's theory of modernism, Ventrone argues that Fascism arose 'from the confluence of different political projects to give back to reality that aura of sacrality and absoluteness that the processes of secularization and laicization had taken away from it'. Its real enemies were thus 'deracination, the indeterminate, heterogeneity, confusion, bastardization, and the complexities and afflictions that characterized bourgeois modernity'.[11] In the terminology used by Frank Kermode in *The Sense of an Ending*, Fascism tried to translate '*fictions*' of resurrection from decadence into *myths* that could serve as the legitimation of an entire political system and generate the living experience that overcoming the decadence of the Giolittian system signalled the dawning of a new world. In the discourse of Peter Berger, Fascism attempted to create a new nomos and erect a new sacred canopy to ward off the terror of anomy. In terms of Peter Osborne's theory it aspired to the inauguration of a new temporality in the spirit of a radical conservative revolution, activating a mythic past to produce a collective futural dynamic. In each reading, Fascism emerges as resolutely modernist.

It is Emilio Gentile who, by combining impeccable archival research with sophisticated conceptualization, makes the most authoritative pronouncements on Fascism's 'modernist' credentials, and in so doing explicitly imparts the term connotations that corroborate our primordialist perspective. He asserts that 'Fascist modernism sought to realize a new synthesis between tradition and modernity, without renouncing modernization in order to realize the nation's goals of power'. It was through the 'sacralization of politics and the institutionalization of the cult of the fasces' that Fascism attempted to fulfil the key ambition of modernist nationalism, 'the construction of a lay religion for the nation'.[12] Fascism's futural dynamic and civilizing mission emphasized by both Ventrone and Gentile is amply borne out by Pier Giorgio Zunino's comprehensive account of the matrix of Fascist ideology as inferred from the torrent of publications that poured forth from the new regime. He documents the way that for most Fascists the new state's mission to 'lead Italy out of its humiliating condition of marginalization' was linked to a much more ambitious goal, namely to 'spread the seeds of a new civilization in which the main problems inflicting contemporary society had been finally resolved'.[13] Under Mussolini Italians were encouraged to feel they were living on the threshold of 'a new civilization whose essence as yet no-one can know', a 'third time', a 'new epoch', a 'new cycle'. Zunino insists that the countless texts, speeches, events, and rituals mass-produced under Mussolini aimed not to 'manufacture consensus', but to fill his most fervent supporters with a 'longing for tomorrow' and 'thirst for [making] history'.[14]

By 1930 convinced Fascists at every level of society were now crowding onto the craggy outcrop of rock where once only Marinetti and a small artistic elite once stood enjoying the heady Nietzschean experience of standing 'on the last promontory of the centuries'. The experience of *Aufbruch* lauded by Expressionist poets had been democratized, the sense of an ending replaced by the heady sense of a beginning. Emilio Gentile himself draws attention to this factor when he claims that 'the principal impulse of fascism stemmed from its "movementist" and Dionysian feeling for existence, from the myth of the future, and not from a static contemplation of the past'. This futural dynamic is only apparently belied by the cult of Romanness (*romanità*) that came to assume such importance under the regime,[15] for it too was 'celebrated modernistically as a myth of action for the future'.[16] In the words of Giuseppe Bottai, the most technocratically minded of the Fascist *gerarchia*, the regime's fascination with Rome sprang 'not from erudition, not from books, not from so-called "dead history"', but above all from its capacity to inspire action in the present.[17] Fascism meant to carry out 'not a restoration but a renovation, a revolution in the idea of Rome'.[18]

By the late 1930s the centrepiece of the state's full-scale resuscitation of imperial glories and its extraction of the historic from the merely historical was the systematic exploitation of Italy's classical Roman heritage to convey mythic legitimation onto Mussolini's dictatorship so as to manufacture an aura of providential destiny and timelessness. Integral to this was the use of cultural and political ritual to identify *il duce* explicitly with Augustus Caesar to the point where the bimillennial celebrations of his birth were transformed into Mussolini's secular apotheosis as a reborn Roman emperor – an identification sanctioned by Cardinal Schuster on behalf of the Vatican.[19] It was the historicizing, modernizing, *futural* dynamic behind the bimillennium that Vittorio Morpurgo expressed in the judicious blend of neo-classicism with aesthetic modernism he incorporated into the design of the building constructed to house the Ara Pacis we encountered in Chapter 1. Semiotically the building implied that an illustrious part of the Augustean legacy could be restored and conserved so that after 2,000 years of fragmentation and dispersal the 'altar of peace' could now serve as a reservoir of revitalizing mythopoeic and ritual energies for the reborn Italy. As one scholar puts it: 'Rome was a dynamic, vital force, not a buried legacy to be exhumed. By reclaiming and restoring this essence, the regime and its collaborators sought to enact ancient values in the modern world and forge a direct and unmediated link between the past, present and future.'[20]

The cult of *romanità* was thus deeply bound up with the 'actualist' will to 'make history' central to Fogu's reading of the 'Fascist imaginary'. It would thus be glib – a glibness to which not a few historians have succumbed in the past – to dismiss as vacuous rhetoric Benito Mussolini's declaration in a speech made six months before the March on Rome that the 'history of tomorrow, which we assuredly want to create' would be no 'parody of the history of yesterday', since the Romans were not only fighters, but also powerful constructors who could '*challenge Time*'.[21] In fact the phrase takes us to the heart of Fascist conception of itself as the creators of an alternative modernity. We have seen that Elvio Fachinelli observed in his analysis of the temporal dimension of Fascism that the new regime 'transposed the fatherland under the mythic sky of its Roman origins'.[22] It did so not just to annul a 'real' historical time which was becoming psychologically intolerable. In the Fascist mindset 'challenging time' was the diametric opposite of the withdrawal from external reality into a meditative state of contemplation of the sort recommended by the idealist philosopher Arthur Schopenhauer (1788–1860). After all, it was his exhortations to renounce 'the will' that precipitated the intense vitalism of Nietzsche's assault on Western modernity.

Likewise, Fascism, in its own imaginary at least, was a *Dionysian* act of defiance, an irruption into a dynamic, sacralized, *historic* time, into the *aevum* of national life in which the anxieties of the present would be ritually assuaged. By constantly reminding modern Italians of their Roman heritage, Fascism was summoning them to make the same daring 'tiger's leap into the past' that Walter Benjamin argued was made by French Revolutionaries when they forged a symbolic link between the overthrow of the ancien régime and the ousting of the kings from Ancient Rome. By anchoring a new future in the mythic remembrance of things past, Fascists put themselves in the position to 'blast a specific era out of the homogeneous course of history' as much as any Bolshevik revolutionary.[23] Even the cult of traditional rural values under Fascism manifested in the *strapaese* art movement, or the regime's lavish restoration of Renaissance buildings and civic spaces, are to be read in modernist key, as the attempt, not to take refuge from the modern world, but to realize an 'Italian modernity'.[24]

In this context, the regime's introduction of a new calendar to run alongside the Gregorian one which established 1922, the year of the March on Rome, as Year I of the Fascist Era, is a gesture pregnant with symbolic significance. It parallels the adoption of the decimal year and decimal day[25] in the French Revolutionary Calendar (or 'Republican Calendar') on 24 October 1793, which was abolished on 1 January 1806 by Emperor Napoleon I, but, in an eloquent symbolic gesture, briefly revived under the Paris Commune in 1871. The mathematical manipulations of the measurement of time under Mussolini point to a profoundly mythic will to create a new type of state capable of realizing a new order in which *chronos* will be suspended and historical time will *literally* be made anew. It is a will that we have shown in the context of the early twentieth-century obsession with decadence to be quintessentially modernist.

FASCISM'S TECHNOCRATIC MODERNISM

In 1933 four artists, including Carlo Carrà and Mario Sironi, two of Italy's most famous aesthetic modernists, published a 'Manifesto of Mural Painting'. It celebrated the achievement of Fascism in returning to art its original social purpose. By 'giving unity of style and greatness of line to *communal life*' art had once more become '*a perfect instrument for spiritual government*'.[26] Under Fascism art was to no longer express the individual artist's 'originality' or 'inner world', but the restored nomos of the reborn community of Italians.

Since 1945 the policies and actions undertaken by the Fascist regime in the spheres of culture, society, and politics have been exhaustively reconstructed by historians, bequeathing researchers oceanic empirical data about the dismantling of the liberal system and its replacement by the 'totalitarian state'. What tends to get lost sight of in the sheer wealth of facts concerning *what* Fascists did once in power is *why* they did it. It is an issue which, if discussed at all, has in the past been frequently reduced implicitly to the whims of a personal dictator, a reactionary war on socialism, or the totalitarian pursuit of the monopoly of power for its own sake by a corrupt ruling elite. By contrast, it should be clear by now that the perspective proposed by our analysis is that the Fascist regime is to be seen as a *modernist state*, on a par with the modernist state being created in Bolshevik Russia at the time, and with the one to be constructed later in the Third Reich. It sought to perpetuate the palingenetic dynamics of Fascism as the extra-systemic revitalization movement that had 'marched on Rome' by creating a political system without historical precedent. It would purge the present decadence by realizing the temporalized utopia of a society uniquely appropriate to meeting the material and spiritual needs of the masses. In doing so Fascism revealed the close affinity between 'political modernism' as we have defined it and 'the gardening state' described by Zygmunt Bauman, one that undertakes to weed out decadence and rear a new breed of human beings in 'its war on ambivalence',[27] or the 'surgical state' prepared to wield scalpels to remove gangrenous tissue.

The relevance of the gardening or surgical metaphor is highlighted by the following passage on the term *bonifica* – literally 'making good' and hence 'land reclamation' as in the act of draining marshes – in Ruth Ben-Ghiat's study of the alternative 'modernities' pursued by Fascism. Making no explicit reference to Bauman's analysis, she writes:

> The concept of *bonifica*, or reclamation was central to many discourses of fascist modernity. [...] Land reclamation merely constituted the most concrete manifestation of the fascists' desire to purify the nation of all social and cultural pathology. The campaigns for agricultural reclamation (*bonifica agricola*), human reclamation

(*bonifica umana*), and cultural reclamation (*bonifica della cultura*), together with the anti-Jewish laws, are seen here as different facets and phases of a comprehensive project to combat degeneration and radically renew Italian society by 'pulling up the bad weeds and cleaning up the soil'.[28]

It was in this socially modernist spirit that under the regime draining the Pontine Marshes to remove a source of malaria and create land for development was presented to Italians as an archetypally Fascist act. Indeed, under Mussolini the verb *bonificare* came to denote 'the technocratic social planning impulses and mode of scientific thinking that [...] approached human society as "an organism to be manipulated by means of a vast surgical operation"'.[29]

The accounts of the Fascist regime offered by Claudio Fogu, Angelo Ventrone, Pier Giorgio Zunino, and Ruth Ben-Ghiat, though written using different conceptual frameworks, all exhibit a deep affinity with the way Emilio Gentile conceptualized 'totalitarianism'. This he defines as 'an experiment in political domination undertaken by a revolutionary movement', that, 'after having secured power, whether by legal or illegal means, destroys or transforms the previous regime and constructs a new state based on a single-party regime'. It does so to carry out 'the integral politicisation of existence, whether collective or individual, interpreted according to the categories, the myths and the values of a palingenetic ideology, institutionalised in the form of a political religion'. This aims 'to shape the individual and the masses through an anthropological revolution in order to regenerate the human being and create the new man', with the ultimate goal of creating 'a new civilisation along ultra-nationalist lines'.[30] In short, the Fascist regime, no less than the contemporary Bolshevik regime, is to be seen as a vast enterprise to carry out the *bonifica* of (a section) of humanity through the use of the unprecedented cultural, social, institutional, technocratic, and *revolutionary* power that the modern state had revealed so dramatically in the First World War. Though not on the scale of Bolshevik Russia or the Third Reich, it embodied the constructive power of modernism at its most programmatic, utopian, and Promethean.

In the first years of its existence the modernist state created by Fascism represented for its most fanatical believers, not least for Mussolini himself, a heroic attempt to complete the Risorgimento by integrating all Italians within a dynamically modernizing, demographically and territorially expanding, technologically powerful, culturally vital Great Italy. Viewing the world with the sense of ontological security and 'roots' afforded by the narratives of organic nationalism, Fascists looked forward expectantly to the day where, with its new-found strength and cohesion, Italy would once more take up the civilizing mission that the Roman/Italian 'race' had once performed for 'the world' in creating the Roman Empire, the Catholic Church, and the Renaissance. The collective 'principle of hope' it promulgated in totalitarian fashion was that the tattered canopy of Giolittian liberalism was day by day being replaced with a new sacred canopy which, unlike Bolshevism's, was to be a patchwork of materials woven from the unique religion, history, and culture of the nation. Fascism's 'action plan' to realize these goals demanded a highly advanced form of technocratic government, something seen clearly on a theoretical level only by a minority of Fascist hierarchy – notably Giuseppe Bottai – but instinctively understood by broad swathes of Italy's burgeoning technocratic elite. Fascism's technocracy took to its logical conclusion the readiness shown by all the states involved in the First World War – even purportedly 'liberal' ones – to commit ever more of their economic, cultural, and human resources to an accelerating programme of 'total mobilization' in order to achieve victory at all costs.

This totalizing vision underlay the rafts of radical legislation and institutional reforms introduced after 1925 designed to replace political pluralism with a single-party state which soon conferred on Mussolini almost total legislative and executive power.[31] It undertook major overhauls of the educational system,[32] the press,[33] and the arts,[34] and instituted an elaborate process by which everything associated with the politics of the new regime itself was sacralized.[35] Under Fascism an elaborate, in theological terms fundamentally secular and pagan, 'political religion' was instituted alongside Catholicism through a constant stream of ritual events, large-scale cultural projects, and the imposition of an official rhetorical discourse with an overt religious register of language. These were intended to infiltrate both public and private spheres in such a way that the ethos of society would be transformed into the incubator of 'the new Italian'.[36] In this process Mussolini himself became the centre of an extensive personality cult, as the embodiment of the New Man and *propheta* of a revitalization movement that had now taken command of state power, turning the *communitas* of Blackshirts into the ruling elite of an entire nation.[37] Far from resting on its laurels, the new regime engaged in a tide of new legislation in order to put in place the structures and launch the initiatives needed to carry out the Fascistization of society, only some of which can be briefly considered in this chapter. Whether it was in the cultural, social, or technocratic sphere, all authentically Fascist elements – in contrast to the many fellow-travellers whose 'commitment' instead was to inertia, opportunism, and corruption – strove to make Italy a modern, efficient, powerful state and a healthy, productive, and socially cohesive nation. 'Authentic' Fascism saw itself charged with the mission to create the technocracy of 'spiritual government' through a process of creative destruction in which violence became 'a rhetorical trope and a mystique': 'Through a series of mythical transformations and discursive reconfigurations, Fascist representations of violence glorified force and identified it with renewal and rebirth.'[38]

By humanistic or liberal democratic standards the regime that resulted from such aspirations, and the praxis forged from such tropes, was a catalogue of inconsistencies, dysfunctions, and disasters: proliferating ideological contradictions and policy failures, pervasive corruption and inefficiency, compromises with the monarchy, the Vatican, the conservative bourgeoisie, and big business, the widening gap between rhetoric and reality, daily acts of repression and coercion taken against its own people, violent war against socialism, the assault on the rights of women not to be mothers, of children not to be grown-ups, of men not to be warriors, war-crimes committed behind the scenes in occupied Ethiopia and Greece,[39] collaboration with General Franco's murderous military rebellion against the left-wing government, the supine alliance with Adolf Hitler, and the sickening collusion with anti-Semitism, the Nazi *Endsieg*, and the Final Solution which ensued. Yet in all this the Fascist regime was neither reactionary nor anti-modern, but *modernist*, its fundamental failure due to the impossibility of translating fictions into myths, palingenetic discourse into historical reality.

To follow through this alternative – and still *reflexive* – metanarrative of Fascism as a modernist state comprehensively it would be necessary to see how the pattern of creative destruction, utopian goal and failure, worked itself out in every one of the regime's policy areas. This would involve a totalizing project of historiographical reconstruction of the sort that Fascists themselves were prone to undertaking, but which has no place within the more limited, anti-utopian agenda of liberal academia, let alone in a single chapter of a wide-ranging monograph. There is space here only to consider a few episodes which illustrate how Fascist modernism informed the praxis of Mussolini's regime, first in its 'cultural production' and then in the sphere of social reform.

THE 'VORACIOUS AMOEBA' OF FASCIST CULTURE

Even before the March on Rome a number of artists, aesthetes, and intellectuals had publicly associated themselves with Fascism whose aesthetics conflicted, such as Gabriele D'Annunzio, Filippo Marinetti, and Giovanni Papini. Under the regime ever more artistic styles and currents of art prospered as a result of the deliberately non-interventionist state policy on artistic matters – at least as far as High Art was concerned – which Emily Braun sums up as leaving artists 'free to create but obliged to serve'.[40] Not only was there no officially prescribed Fascist style, but no proscribed style either. Mussolini resisted the pressure from individual factions to have certain aesthetics banned as un-Fascist or make theirs the official state aesthetic. As a result variants of ruralist realism (e.g. Ottone Rosai), and abstraction (e.g. Carlo Belli), all vied to the bitter end with the many permutations of Novecento's modernized neo-classicism (e.g. Mario Sironi) to encapsulate the essence of the Fascist revolution.

Meanwhile buildings sprang up that exhibited the remarkable range of permutations possible when classicism was blended with different percentages of Rationalism, or was supplanted by it altogether. This was not limited to the heyday of the regime's apparently laissez-faire approach to cultural matters in the late 1920s and early 1930s, as is often assumed, and even asserted as a positivist fact by Igor Golomstock in his determination to see in events in Fascist Italy the working out of his specious 'law of totalitarian art'.[41] Notwithstanding the rise of a semi-official late-Roman-Imperial architectural style called 'stile littorio', the vast Mostra delle terre d'oltremare (MTO, Exhibition of Foreign Lands) staged in Naples in 1940 showed that architectural eclecticism could still be favoured for official state exhibitions even though Italy was now at war as the ally of the Third Reich. Moreover, the aesthetic principle of a 'surprise architecture' adopted by the MTO organizers to impart a semblance of unity to the highly disparate styles of the exhibition was lifted straight from Futurist manifestos of the 1930s. In this respect, the MTO also proved that although it never became the regime's official aesthetic idiom, Futurism and its aesthetic amalgamation of popular culture and avant-garde modernism had penetrated deeply into the fabric of state-sponsored culture, and had lost none of its creativity, vitality, or humour for artists such as Carlo Cocchia and Enrico Prampolini. These belonged to two different generations of Futurists, but still could collaborate fruitfully in the celebration of 'Mediterranean-ness' in a special section of the exhibition dedicated to this theme. The exhibition juxtaposed different aesthetics in a ludic, ironic, theme-park spirit unimaginable in contemporary Germany. One fruit of this was the Marco Polo Tower designed by Vittorio Calza Bini, which has more than a hint of Gaudi's Catalan biomorphism about it in its deconstruction of the rectilinear and affirmation of the sinuous (see Figure 10). Another was Prampolini's 'futuro-cosmic' mural evoking the spirit of Africa, the only extant decoration of the exhibition.[42]

As a result of this logic, the *Gleichschaltung* of the arts that took place under Mussolini did not lead to the ritual destruction of books and paintings or the official persecution of artists for the alleged decadence of their aesthetics for which the Third Reich became infamous – though, as we shall see, the 'racist turn' of the regime after 1938 had the effect of encouraging unofficial witch-hunts against modernist artists in some quarters. Instead, as the architectural historian Richard Etlin puts it:

> The entire point of Fascist cultural politics was to embrace all aspects of Italian intellectual and artistic life as vital signs of a full flowering of Italian creative genius

under the aegis of Fascism. In all phases of intellectual, cultural, artistic, and social life, Fascism was like a voracious amoeba: it swallowed everything around it in order to proclaim that it was all a Fascist achievement.[43]

The result, however improvized and chaotic it seems in its outcome, was informed by a certain rationale which Marla Stone has neatly termed 'hegemonic pluralism', a Third Way between the laissez-faire ethos of the arts encouraged by liberalism and what under Stalin became a totally planned culture purged of avant-garde, 'formalist' innovations. As a result, Italy became a vast 'Patron State'.[44] It poured public money into sponsoring or commissioning public works, exhibitions, competitions, civic art and buildings, and projects of town planning or urban renewal conceived on an unprecedented scale to embody the

Figure 10 'Marco Polo Tower' designed by Vittorio Calza Bini for the Mostra delle terre d'oltremare, Naples 1940, in a style that flagrantly renounces any hint of the 'monumentalist' neo-classicism generally identified with the regime's architecture by the outbreak of the Second World War.

Source: *Illustrazione Italiana*, Vol. 67, No. 22 (2 June 1940). Photograph of original plate kindly supplied by Claudio Fogu.

ethos of the new state and stimulate cultural production. The organization of the Venice Biennale and Milan Triennale, the enormous *Enciclopedia Italiana* project overseen by Giovanni Gentile, the building of the Rome University complex, the creation of the Italian Royal Academy, and the ultra-modern film studios of Cinecittà are just some examples among many. This state largesse was backed up by a powerful propaganda machine instilling the idea that, thanks to the visionary qualities of the ultimate political artist, Mussolini himself,[45] Italy was undergoing a cultural renaissance, the concomitant of its allegedly spectacular growth, after centuries of decline and decay, in economic and military power, social cohesion, and international prestige. Underpinning this idea was the organic conception of the nation that assumed an axiomatic relationship between cultural and political power, the same mythic logic that caused British fascists to attribute so much importance to the Elizabethan Age.[46] By adopting this totalitarian version of laissez-faire policy on cultural matters, Fascist Italy thus manoeuvred itself into the position to bathe in the reflected glory of the considerable dynamism imparted to the regime by Italy's highly creative and overwhelmingly Fascistized artistic elite, many of whom now saw themselves, if not on the bridge then at least in the engine room of the gigantic liner that Italy had become.

No matter how much the original spirit of modernism was bound to be compromised once it was state-sponsored, there is no doubt that in the pioneering years of the 1920s and early 1930s the mobilizing myth of the 'Fascist revolution' had considerable impact on artists in every sphere of activity,

Figure 11   Mario Palanti's 1933 entry for the competition for the Palazzo del Littorio to be built near the Colosseum blends 1930s architectural modernism with the evocation of a Roman trireme in a particularly striking way. (The project was eventually abandoned as too intrusive for such an important site of classical antiquity.)

Source: *Architettura* (1934), special competition issue with 43 projects (Milan: Fratelli Treves Editors, Rome), p. 69.

Figure 12   Entry for the Palazzo del Littorio competition by Mario Ridolfi, Vittorio Cafiero, Ernesto la Padula, Ettore Rossi. The sinuous curves of the wall-like structure are another bold experiment in merging the neoclassical with the modernist.

Source: *Architettura* (1934), special competition issue with 43 projects (Milan: Fratelli Treves Editors, Rome), p. 25.

one that directly parallels the appeal exerted on the Russian avant-garde by the Bolshevik Revolution before Stalinist walls started coming in to crush them. When in 1933 the Fascist Syndicate of the Fine Arts of Sicily planned an exhibition intended to 'welcome with the broadest vision every possible Artistic expression and to accept all inspirations and techniques'[47] it could count on numerous participants keen to heed the call, all convinced that their form of art was the one most in tune with the revolutionary spirit of the New Italy.

What resulted from this situation was an extraordinary profusion of different modernist styles. These George Mosse attempts to reduce to some sort of order by distinguishing between two Fascist aesthetics, 'one dynamic and fully accepting of technology, the other more traditional in its desire to anchor nationalism in the organicist and auratic aestheticism outlined by [Walter] Benjamin'.[48] Similarly Mark Antliff talks of a 'polarity machine' allowing Fascism's palingenetic ideology to address both the past and the future by declaring the present to be decadent, and thus in need of regenerative 'cultural renewal'.[49] Jeffrey Schnapp paints an even more kaleidoscopic picture when he talks of Fascism's 'aesthetic overproduction' as neither 'monolithic nor homogeneous', instead relying on 'the ability of images to sustain contradiction and to make of paradox a productive principle'. This he sees as explaining 'the rhetorical figure that lurks at the core of every analysis of the Fascist phenomenon: oxymoron'.[50] Claudio Fogu too stresses Mussolini's polarization of the 'historical' (past) and 'historic' (present) which 'resonated with Nietzsche's famous opposition between the "historical" and the "supra-/un-historical" and, along this path with a whole series of dichotomies between literary modernism and historicism, spatial form and linear time, and speech acts and narrative writing'.[51]

All such observations are made by highly scholarly cultural historians trying to find a theoretical framework that accommodates the heterogeneous practice of Fascist aesthetics, rather than editing the practice to fit a preconceived, *a priori* notion of what they *should* be. They are also fully in tune with 'our' ideal type of modernism that embraces both attempts to sever all ties with the past represented by Futurism, and the cultivation of mythic appropriations of the past conceived as a source of regeneration typified by *romanità* and *strapaese*. However, the theory we have developed accounts for the fact that the relationship between the 'two aesthetics', 'two poles', and 'dichotomies' was one of constant synergy and interplay which could even be lived out within the same artist. In practice this meant that the regime was able to exert its hegemony over a wide gamut of attempted syntheses between several different mythicized pasts (regional, Renaissance, Baroque, Risorgimento, Classical Roman, pre-Roman) and several differently conceived futures (hyper-technological and dynamic, cosmopolitan, or rural idylls in which the balance with nature has been restored). Even the most belligerently futural of all, Marinetti's nationalist variant of Futurism, celebrated Italy as a timeless, primordial, organic entity, so that his movement was not as resolutely 'anti-pastist' as his rhetoric suggested. Common to all such syntheses, however, is the assumption that the role of art under Mussolini – in total contrast to art in the Giolittian era – is to act as a source of the regenerative myths needed to forge a vital new *communitas*, the national community, out of a moribund society, to inform the 'spirit' of Fascism's 'spiritual government'.

Considerable insight into the deep divisions between fellow Fascists over artistic principles that arose from this situation is afforded by the series of articles written by proponents of different aesthetics and published in Giuseppe Bottai's *Critica Fascista* between 1926 and 1927.[52] Another fault-line was revealed a decade later by the contrasting criteria applied for the Cremona Prize and the Bergamo Prize. The first was instituted by the fiercely anti-Semitic, anti-cosmopolitan, and pro-Nazi Roberto Farinacci in 1938 in the oppressive climate of the Race Laws. The second was created by the extreme modernizer Giuseppe Bottai a year later to promote precisely the type of internationalist aesthetic modernism that the Farinacci faction believed was contaminating the purity and heroism of Italian life under Mussolini.

In all these cases the hallmark of both their Fascism and their social, if not aesthetic, modernism is the pursuit of national renewal and the belief in the transcendent power of art to operate beyond the confines of aesthetics, leisure, and market forces.[53] To this extent Farinacci was as much a cultural modernist as Bottai, despite his animus against cosmopolitan art. It is consistent with this line of analysis that Fascist art is capable of displaying a degree of genuine originality, artistry, and visionary passion that refutes Norberto Bobbio's verdict on Fascist culture that we cited in Chapter 1: 'Where there was culture, there wasn't Fascism, where there was Fascism there wasn't culture. There never was a Fascist culture.'[54] There *was* a Fascist culture, but a highly heterogeneous and instrumentalized one which, whatever its formal aspects, was shaped by a *modernist* socio-political ethic. Its artistic expressions are thus impossible to judge without considerable distortion if critical criteria and canons of taste are used based on the Western cultural tradition that Fascism was trying to overthrow.

CULTURAL MODERNISM UNDER FASCISM

An outstanding example of the exceptional artistic talent and originality that could flower under the Patron State is Mario Sironi, whose sustained effort to create a Fascist aesthetic has been analysed in depth by Emily Braun in an impressive display of synergy between art history, political history, and comparative fascist studies. In a manner that has tantalizing points of both affinity and deep contrast with the primitivism of other modernists such as Pablo Picasso, Paul Gauguin, and Igor Stravinsky, Sironi executed didactic decorations for Fascism's highly modern state buildings that drew not just on Roman classicism, but on other examples of indigenous art such as Etruscan tomb sculpture, the mosaics of Ravenna, and the Romanesque. In returning to the earliest sources of Italian civilization he believed he was symbolically injecting the nation's eternal creative genius into the regeneration of modern Italy. It was a thus a 'rooted' modernism entirely in keeping with the 'Dionysian' cult of *romanità*.

Braun's analysis reveals that Sironi saw his work as a contribution to Fascism's 'ideological revolt against nineteenth-century materialism and democracy'. He thus undertook with extraordinary zeal and productivity the task of transforming civic spaces into sites for exposing the public to plastic expressions of the mythic consciousness of the Fascist new era, much as the stained glass windows and frescoes of medieval cathedrals served to reinforce the hegemony of the Catholic Church. His premise in doing so was that with its recourse to primitive forms of expression (that is, its own imaginary origins), aesthetic modernism could move and inspire the masses. Fascist modernism and modernist primitivism were thus founded on complementary myths of origins and rebirth, their revolutions predicated on radical cultural renewal.[55]

Sironi thus intended that in the act of looking at his mosaics and murals, 'ordinary Italians' would become conscious of the mysterious nexus between the ephemerality of the individual's life and the sacrality of the supra-individual nation being inaugurated by Mussolini. Through the metaphorical, transcendent power of art an individual life in the thrall of Cronus would undergo a secular transfiguration, suffused with the *aevum* of Fascism.

Ardengo Soffici exemplifies another form of 'modernist primitivism', one that projected Italians into an *imaginaire* quite different from that of a modernized Classical Rome. It brings out the deep tension between aesthetic and political modernism that could be generated once the signifier attached to the experimentalism and innovation of modernist aesthetics was transposed from 'cultural renewal' to 'cultural degeneration'. Walter Adamson traces Soffici's parabola from the celebration of *toscanità* (Tuscanness) in 1906, via the magic realism of Picasso's Cubism in 1910, and Futurism of the interventionist journal *Lacerba* in 1913, back to Tuscan Impressionism after the war. What determined his final orientation was mounting concern at the degenerative impact of Americanism and cosmopolitanism on the Italian avant-garde and Italian society in general, and a growing sense of the urgency of finding an aesthetic able to provide fellow-countrymen with a religious sense of community. Thereafter he campaigned for Fascism to give primacy to what Adamson calls 'a new, re-auratized art',[56] one that celebrated the organic rootedness of Italians in terms far closer to Barrès' nationalism of 'soil and the dead' than to Marinetti's Futurism.

A parallel situation of extreme diversity existed in architecture, where the regime's ambitious programmes for urban renewal attracted a significant number of the country's most passionate and gifted modern architects. The modernist ethos of the regime's large-scale rebuilding programmes and town-planning schemes is eloquently expressed both in the four towns built from scratch[57] – Le Corbusier himself unsuccessfully submitted a project for the new town of Pontinia in the reclaimed Pontine Marshes – and in the ambitious projects for transforming the 'Empire's' colonial capitals of Tripola and Addis.[58] It was also expressed in the interweaving of past and present in the total transformation of the Palazzo delle Esposizioni in Rome for the Exhibition of the Fascist Revolution (1932–33). The exhibition attracted nearly 4 million visitors, a major cultural event by any standards, and provides an outstanding example of the way propaganda, aesthetics, and politics could merge in the attempt to 'make Italians' and 'make history'. It also demonstrates the way the regime contrived to erect a sacred canopy over the heads of all its citizens and not just a chosen few. Jeffrey Schnapp argues in his analysis of the Exhibition that it deliberately manipulated the aesthetics of architecture, exhibits, symbols, space, and song, to contrive for the visitor the experience of passing from the chaos of the immediate post-war years to the sublime harmony of the Fascist era. The last room, the climax of the 'total experience' through which visitors passed, simulated a Fascist rally, but no ordinary rally. It was

> a rally of the living dead, a rally taking place in some indeterminate secular otherworld, 'immortal' yet of this world, where history's victims are forever present to each other.[59]

It was a rally taking place within the secular transcendence and temporalized utopia of the reborn nation.

Charged with the mission to 'challenge Time', the most creative architects under Fascism rejected the styles of civic building and conceptions of urban space associated with Giolittianism to experiment in permutations of what can broadly be seen as two contrasting aesthetic currents – leaving aside the numerous Futurist fantasy projects that never got off the drawing board. These were the 'International Style' associated with architectural Rationalism (but also termed 'Modern' and 'Modernist'), and the deliberate hybridization of classicist or Mediterranean traditions with modern(ist) elements – even Cubist – to produce the classicizing, 'monumentalist' style known as 'stile Littorio'.

The pioneers of Italianate variants of rationalism were the Novecento Movement based in Milan and the 'Group of Six' in Turin. The Patron State's munificence in funding grandiose projects while refusing to impose a particular aesthetic meant that Giuseppe Terragni's bold experiment in the symbolic use of rationalist (Modernist) design and modern building techniques, the Casa del Fascio, which we encountered in Chapter 1, could be completed in Como between 1932 and 1936 (see Figure 13). Terragni's visionary modernism is expressed equally powerfully in his design for the vast Danteum which was never built.[60] Meanwhile, Giuseppe Pagano was designing the main building of the Luigi Bocconi University in Milan. It was directly inspired by the plan of Walter Gropius' Bauhaus School in Breslau – recently closed down by Hitler – and proved to be an eloquent showcase for European rationalism.

In the same period Marcello Piacentini was also at work constructing the 'Palazzo del rettorato' for the Vice-Chancellor of the University of Rome in the 'stile Littorio'. He went on to be appointed chief architect for Mussolini's EUR project, the Exhibition of the Universality of Rome, the summmum of Fascism's modernist assault on history and the apogee of *romanità* (see Figure 14).

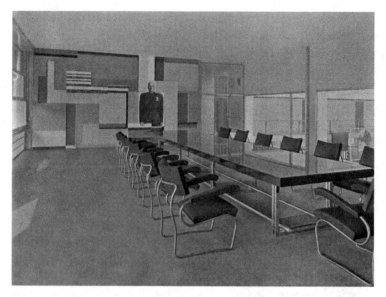

Figure 13   Meeting room in Giuseppe Terragni's Casa del Fascio, Como. Note the modernist design of the chairs and the equally modernist stylization of *Il Duce*'s image overseeing proceedings against the background of an abstract mural.

© Centro Studi Giuseppe Terragni, Como. Reproduced with the kind permission of Centro Studi Giuseppe Terragni.

Cancelled because of the war, it was intended to mark the twentieth anniversary of Mussolini's rule in what was conceived in the Fascist imaginary both as an 'Olympic Games of Civilization' surpassing all previous world fairs, and as the nerve-centre of the revived Roman Empire. In semiotic terms it was thus imagined as the ancient capital of Rome translated into the discourse of aesthetic modernism. Hence its civic buildings are built either in the Rationalist style or the 'stile Littorio'. The modernist élan towards the future embodied in both styles is symbolized iconographically in the arch projected for the entrance to the exhibition designed by the Rationalist architect Adalberto Libera (see Figure 15), and featured on the exhibition poster which adorns the front cover of this book. It is notable that the original poster gives the year of EUR both as 1942 and as the Fascist year XX, the Roman numerals indicating the years that would have elapsed since the clock of Italy's new *aevum* started ticking in 1922, the year of the March of Rome which inaugurated the Fascist Era of History.

It was not just in art and architecture that the avant-garde succumbed to the prospect of playing a key role in transforming society. A number of

Figure 14   Model of the projected EUR '42 complex showing the siting of Adalberto Libera's arch.

© EUR S.p.A, Rome. Reproduced with the kind permission of EUR S.p.A.

Figure 15   Artist's impression of the perspective through Adalberto Libera's arch designed for the EUR '42 exhibition, a blend of neoclassical, baroque, and modernist styles.

© EUR S.p.A, Rome. Reproduced with the kind permission of EUR S.p.A.

writers attempted, without signal success, to take literature out of the 'ivory tower' and make the modern novel an agent of ethical transformation.[61] In the theatre a more productive attempt was made by some avant-garde producers, directors, and writers to turn into an instrument of Fascistization an art form whose standard bourgeois or escapist fare was widely held to be 'un-Fascist'. In 1929 the Futurist director Anton Bragaglia expressed sentiments widely expressed in avant-garde theatre circles when he attacked the fundamentally 'anti-revolutionary' nature of contemporary productions, and called on the theatre to play a major role in the Fascist regeneration of the spiritual life of the masses. A number of visionary projects for the construction of vast open-air theatres were planned in the attempt to translate such high principles into reality. These principles were officially endorsed in April 1933 when Mussolini gave a speech calling for a Fascist theatre designed to be enjoyed by 20,000 spectators at a time.

After this, numerous productions of classics from the dramatic and operatic repertoires were performed to mass audiences at subsidized prices under the auspices of the Dopolavoro leisure organization, and these reached as many as 3 million Italians a year, thanks to the travelling motorcades of the 'Carri di tespi' (or Travelling Thespian Theatre) that made a point of venturing into the most remote areas. One moment where this current of social modernism merged with aesthetic modernism occurred in April 1934 when *18 BL* was performed on the left bank of the Arno in Florence. This was an elaborately choreographed mass spectacle centred on the life-cycle of a Fiat truck used in the First World War and later by *squadristi* in their anti-communist expeditions, and involved enough actors, vehicles, and military equipment to form a small army. One of the major theoretical influences on the project was Massimo Bontempelli, the major ideologue of Novecento aesthetics in architecture and design.

Bontempelli's rationale for creating a theatre in the form of a mass liturgical spectacle has an unmistakable resonance with the ideal type of modernism proposed in Part One. According to him, the First World War had swept away a decadent age. In its wake a 'primordial atmosphere' now pervaded the West in which Dionysian energies were stirring that would finally allow the lost metaphysical dimension of life to be recaptured. He thus looked forward to the emergence of a new mass spectacle which would establish a 'synergy linking Fascist politics to Fascist dramaturgy', both of which were efforts to 'reinvent the category of the sacred and re-establish the values of sacred rituality within resolutely secular confines'.[62] For Bontempelli, then, Fascism was identified with the task of re-embedding time and space and re-enchanting a world ravaged by the anomy and materialism of a spiritually bankrupt liberal era.

In the 1930s parallel attempts at Fascistization occurred in the cinema, the most popular art form of all, which was cryptically dubbed by Mussolini in 1922 as 'the strongest weapon of the State'. In the 1930s the regime deliberately set about – notably through the creation of the Centro Sperimentale di Cinematografia in 1935 – turning the cinema from a medium of entertainment and escapism into a vehicle for the 'organic reordering of society' and of the 'human reclamation' (*bonifica umana*) encountered earlier.[63] Furthermore, a handful of films were made – notably Raffaello Matarazzo's *Treno popolare*, Mario Camerini's *Gli uomini, gli mascalzoni!* and *Rotaie*, Alessandro Blasetti's *La Terra Madre* and *Sole*, Walter Ruttmann's *Accaio* – that can be seen as serious attempts to make popular films which at the same time explored the 'alternative modernities' resulting from Fascism's projects of social transformation.[64] It is thus no coincidence if some of them showed the unmistakable influence of the Soviet avant-garde cinema.[65] Yet, in the main the cinema remained firmly populist in the sense of offering a steady supply of films devoid of modernist elements not just aesthetically, but in their socio-political function. This was either to normalize Fascism by offering entertainment – the bulk of which was imported from the US or cloned in Italy from US models – or to corroborate the propaganda function of the LUCE newsreels and documentaries by celebrating the achievements of Fascism.[66] However, the wider significance of such thinly veiled propaganda only becomes apparent once we have considered its role within more direct attempts to transform society.

THE MODERNIST DYNAMIC OF FASCISM'S SOCIAL TRANSFORMATION

Exclusive concentration on the arts and architecture and popular culture of Fascist Italy creates a misleadingly 'culturalist' perspective on its relationship to modernism. It is thus important to see them as a correlative to the social modernism informing all the main policies undertaken by Fascism as a totalitarian 'gardening state' in order to reverse the decadence of liberalism and create renewal in every sphere of human activity, from cradle to tomb. A glimpse into the 'primordial' aspect that underlay the will to social renewal propounded by even the most modernizing of the regime's 'hierarchs' (*gerarchi*) is afforded by Giuseppe Bottai. A war veteran who before converting to Fascism had been drawn to political Futurism, he went on to incarnate the technocratic, managerial dimension of the 'new Italy' as Minister of Corporations, President of the National Institute for Social Welfare, Governor of Rome, and Minister of Education.

In a speech given in Milan February 1923, two years before Fascism was able to embark on its totalitarian experiment, he presented Fascism as the solution to 'the Spiritual Crisis of Italy'. By promulgating faith in the cause of national reawakening Mussolini's regime was providing a way out from the agnosticism and ethical indifference of modern society. For decades positivism, scepticism, and materialism had destroyed the organic link that once existed between words and deeds and hence undermined spiritual values. The result of this moral decline had been a period of 'total crisis' which bred the permanent restlessness and the mindless hyperactivity of a modern soul tormented by the 'horror of the void'.[67] However, true to the logic of what we have called the 'dialectic of the liminoid', modernity had, in the very process of creating anomy, also brought forth its own solution, namely 'the man of crisis', the Fascist, whose task it was to internalize the torments of the age and so create the possibility of 'rebirth'.[68] Quoting Mazzini's dictum that 'only religious thought is capable of transforming politics and men', Bottai presents Fascism in this speech as a primarily moral rather than political revolution made possible by 'the youth who have passed through the purification of the trenches'.[69] It is the primordial logic of war, hygiene, and sacrifice to a transcendent cause that will redeem Italy and make her new.

A similar mythic structure underlies the myriad initiatives of social transformation undertaken by the regime that together constitute the attempted 'Fascist Revolution'. It set up mass organizations to inculcate Fascist values in the youth in all stages of development and regiment the leisure of the masses.[70] It created an apparatus of state propaganda and censorship, as well as structures, including a secret police, for regimenting society and silencing or physically removing vociferous opposition.[71] It destroyed the threat to national rebirth allegedly posed by an independent labour movement and the spectre of Bolshevism.[72] It encouraged rapid industrialization and modernization. In a piecemeal, *ad hoc* manner it worked towards the construction of a corporatist economic system which in theory would eradicate the ills of laissez-faire capitalism – class conflict, high unemployment rates, and mass poverty – while retaining its productive dynamism.[73]

The new state also implemented a raft of measures to promote the family ethic in a way that reflected the deeply patriarchal spirit in which masculinity was celebrated both in its rhetoric[74] and in the educational system it devised for boys.[75] It repressed the rights of women in key areas such as abortion, divorce, and employment,[76] took as much control as possible of their reproductive functions,[77] and promoted large families.[78] To increase the health of the population and boost birth rates it introduced measures to eradicate disease and improve social welfare provision – especially in the area of maternity services.[79] In line with the prevailing stress on health and hygiene we saw in Chapter 5[80] was a central component of modernism, it also took radical measures to enhance Italy's 'racial hygiene' by promoting sport, physical exercise, and contact with nature to the point where the body itself became the locus of historical transformation in much of its 'political religion' – for example in the 'duce cult' which fetishized Mussolini's masculine body.[81]

To realize its deeply patriarchal and militaristic concept of national greatness, the new regime also built up the armed forces, militarized the youth,[82] and actively prepared Italians for imperialist campaigns and participation in European conflicts where it was in the 'national interest' to do so. It pursued an aggressive foreign policy to establish Italy as one of Europe's Great Powers, eventually leading to the occupation of Ethiopia as the jewel in the crown of the new Roman Empire.[83] It was a policy that made intervention in the Spanish Civil War and the Axis with Hitler all the more inevitable.[84]

At the same time the regime sponsored initiatives to stimulate a scientific and technological renaissance to underpin its industrial revolution, while also celebrating the virtues of rural life and regional traditions. Through its promotion of measures to 'reclaim' and 'purify' the Italian race, combined with the demographic campaign,[85] the drive for 'autarky',[86] and the heightened sense of a unique Italian genius nurtured through the cult of *romanità*,[87] Fascism developed a home-grown tradition of racism. This formed a vital precondition to the anti-Semitic legislation enacted in 1938 that brought Italy more in line with the Third Reich's racial policies.[88]

All these initiatives acquired a dimension of what we have called 'nationalist modernism' through the way they were associated in the mindset of at least the most idealistic Fascists with realizing the myth of Italianism and the Great Italy. To take just one example, it is the ethos of social modernism rather than rational economic thinking that infuses the rival concepts of the corporatism propounded by the former revolutionary left-wing syndicalist Sergio Panunzio[89] and by Ugo Spirito,[90] whose corporatism was based on a Gentilean concept of the 'transcendent Ego'. In their very different ways both saw the Corporate State not just as a new economic system, but as the basis of the social and ethical revolution vital to producing a whole human being, the 'homo novus' or 'homo corporativus', a project neatly summed up in the title of Peter Drucker's classic study of Soviet and Nazi society, *The End of Economic Man*.

It is this 'economic modernism'[91] that informs the speech given in November 1933 by Panunzio, by then head of the Fascist Faculty of Political Sciences at Perugia University, to the Assembly of the National Council for Corporations. In it he stressed the need for Fascist corporatism to keep alive the 'myth' – a term he specifically uses in the mass mobilizing and palingenetic sense that Georges Sorel gave it – which he claims originally inspired the corporatist project. This was not the myth of economic efficiency, but 'the myth of the nation for whom millions and millions of men sacrifice themselves, and in whose religious cult we make the whole of our people live as a single man, redeemed from the illness and poison of historical materialism and social hedonism'.[92] Once again the modernist ethos has melded the technocratic with the mythic, the ultramodern with the primordial.

THE PURSUIT OF A 'CRYSTALLINE MODERNITY'

The social modernism of Fascism is equally evident in the regime's sustained attempt to use demographic and welfare policies to reverse, not just the rise in physical degeneracy, but the moral decline of the West.[93] In this context, the career of Corrado Gini provides an illuminating case-study in the degree of pragmatic compromise, careerism, and genuine ideological commitment involved in the collusion that so often took place between Italy's modern scientific community and Fascism's 'gardening state'. Not only did his brilliant *curriculum vitae* as an internationally renowned sociologist, statistician, demographer, and eugenicist blossom even further under the regime, but he enjoyed a good personal relationship with Mussolini, whom he obviously looked on as a radical modernizer despite posing publicly in the guise of a latter-day Roman emperor.

In 1927 Gini published an article in English in the prestigious *Political Science Quarterly* in which he set forth 'the scientific basis of Fascism', and the underlying premise of his proposals for the Senate's reform under the new regime. This, he explained, was the nationalist concept of society as a 'true and distinct organism of a rank superior to that of the individuals who compose it, an organism endowed with a life of its own and with interests of its own'. These interests are 'given effect' by a 'state sacrificing, wherever necessary, the interests of the individual and operating in opposition to the will of the present generation'. Within this organic concept of modern politics government thus becomes 'an agency to which is entrusted a mission of a historical character, a mission which summarizes its very reason for existence'.[94] On 26 May of the same year, Mussolini delivered his notorious Ascension Day Speech, emphasizing the need for increasing the birth rate to arrest the nation's physical and moral decline, the official inauguration of the regime's demographic campaign.

The link between these two facts is not as oblique as it might appear. The roots of Gini's organic nationalism lay in a thriving Italian eugenicist tradition pioneered by Cesare Lombroso and subsequently refined by Herbert Spencer, Ernst Haeckel, and Francis Galton. The link between his passion for population and income distribution statistics, demography, sociology, and eugenics lay in an essentially *modernist* drive to use positivist knowledge and technology for the creation of a new state purged of the decadence and anarchic individualism bred by liberal democracy. There is thus an underlying link between the key role Gini played in setting up a School of Statistics in 1928 at Rome University and the Italian Committee for the Study of Population Problems in 1929, his appointment as President of the Central Institute of Statistics in Rome the same year, his organization of the first Population Congress held in Rome in 1931, his appointment as president of the Italian Genetics and Eugenic Society in 1935, and as president of the International Federation of Eugenics Societies in Latin-language Countries in 1936, the same year he created the Faculty of Statistical, Demographic and Actuarial Sciences.

As personal advisor to Mussolini since the late 1920s Gini helped prepare the scientistic ground – the cult of *romanità* and Axis with Hitler's Germany were the determining factors – for the 'Aryanization' and 'biologicization' of Fascist nationalism which exploded into Italian life with the Manifesto of Racist Scientists of 14 July 1938, with its infamous declaration of the Aryan origins of Italian civilization and the extraordinary claim that 'There exists by now a pure "Italian race".'[95] Both Panunzio and Gini illustrate the ease with which an elective affinity could grow up between the 'latest' economic or demographic theories and the New Italy in the mind of those bent on transforming Italy into a modern nation. It resulted in an overtly *modernist* symbiosis between Fascism and technocracy which grew up far from the 'oceanic assemblies' thronging the piazzas of major cities whenever Mussolini spoke which have left such an indelible imprint on the popular 'image' of Fascism as a primitive phenomenon of mass hysteria and mass hypnosis.

Practical expression of this collaboration was not only the rapid construction of the institutional and legislative apparatus of the new state, but the largely abortive attempt to restructure the entire economic system on Corporatist principles. A far more successful intervention was the creation in January 1933 of the Istituto per la Ricostruzione Industriale (IRI) to deal with the severe effects of the Depression on Italy's financial sector – effects never acknowledged, of course, in the Fascist press. Under the regime a modernist spin was imparted to all the achievements in the spheres of improvements to infrastructure, industrial capitalism, heavy industry, technological innovation, consumerism, and the battle of agricultural and economic autarky, all expressions of the national palingenesis that was allowing Italy to escape the fate of a dying liberal world.

This modernist ethos fostered the spiritualization of technology itself, recoding the dehumanizing force portrayed in Charlie Chaplin's *Modern Times* as a product of the Roman spirit – the Italian counterpart of the Faustian spirit in Spengler's metanarrative – and, as such, integral both to the nation's palingenesis and its autarky. One telling episode in the incorporation of technology into the modernist re-enchantment of the world is the shimmering

symbolic microcosm spun around rayon. Jeffrey Schnapp has shown how
Fascist propaganda encouraged a cultic celebration of the wonders of this
'regenerated cellulose fibre', organic yet man-made. He illustrates this with the
way it was treated in Marinetti's 'simultaneous poem' entitled *A Dress Made of
Milk*. This related 'a characteristically Futurist creation myth' which depicted
'a hard-edged new world of redeemed, spiritually charged materials' arising
out of 'the primordial nothingness represented by the inchoate materiality of
mother's milk'.[96] In the propaganda campaigns promoting public awareness
of Italy's achievements in perfecting artificial fibre technology, rayon – which
originated in the powerhouse of technological modernity, the US – became
the symbol of an alternative technological progress, identified with neither
capitalism nor socialism, but with national rebirth and a respiritualized
Western civilization. Because of rayon's natural translucence it also became the
emblem of 'a *crystalline modernity* that had emerged out of the dark shadows
of decadence',[97] picking up on the cult of crystal of the earliest modernist
architects, notably Bruno Taut.[98]

A parallel 'mystification'[99] – a fetishization based not on capitalism but on
a modernist 're-auratization' – of technological achievement in the key of the
transcendent organic nation could be documented in the case of motorway
construction,[100] the electrification of the railways, the 'integral reclamation'
(*bonifica* again) and resettlement of marshlands, the construction of new
towns, or hydro-electrical power schemes. In every case the subtext was that
Fascism was not just modernizing, but pioneering a healthy, *rooted* modernity
by reawakening the dormant creative genius of the race. The technocratic,
Promethean elements of Fascism therefore saw themselves not pitted against
modernity, but only against the *decadent* aspects of modernity allegedly
manifested most clearly in the moral degeneracy of the US, which it otherwise
longed to emulate.[101]

If this is 'reactionary modernism' then, it is not of the paradoxical sort
postulated by Jeffrey Herf, but instead the one we saw analysed by Peter
Osborne in Chapter 6 where 'reactionary' acquires as much a *futural* charge
as 'modernism'. It was the ethos of a new temporality that enabled a nexus to
grow up spontaneously in the minds of millions of Italians connecting the New
Italy with the pioneering achievements of Guglielmo Marconi in communications technology, a nexus externalized when he was appointed president of the
Italian Academy and a member of the Fascist Grand Council of Italy. The same
'globalizing' spirit that transformed Marconi into an icon of Fascist modernism
is reflected in the decision of the authorities planning the EUR exhibition to
integrate aspects of the utopian project set out in meticulous detail in his book
A World Centre of Communications (1913) by the Norwegian artist, Hendrik
Christian Andersens.[102] A friend of William James – who dismissed his scheme

for a 'world city' as megalomania – Andersens had lived in Rome for nearly four decades perpetuating the heady modernist spirit of turn of the century art, and bequeathed his home, studio, papers and more than 400 pieces of his work to the Fascist Government when he died in 1940, two years before EUR was supposed to open.

As we saw in Chapter 1, another exhibition, *Anni Trenta. Arte e Cultura in Italia*, was held in Milan in 1982. Though there was no allusion to Fascism in the title, it was held on the fiftieth anniversary of the Exhibition of the Fascist Revolution. What must have impressed many of its 300,000 visitors about the abundance of artefacts and images on view was the cumulative sense of vitality, productivity, unfettered creativity, stylishness, and technical sophistication they exuded, of the sheer *modernity* and *futurity* of life under Mussolini.[103] It was possible to imagine Fascist Italy being enjoyed by millions of 'ordinary Italians' unaware of the catastrophe that was about to engulf many of their lives with the outbreak of the Second World War at the end of the decade, somewhat like the Roman citizens of Pompeii or Herculaneum before Vesuvius erupted. The only exhibits to cast a dark shadow over the general mood of nostalgia and celebration were those that bore silent witness to the virulence of the official anti-Semitic campaign and the rapidity with which a new breed of 'racial experts' eagerly adapted their disciplines within the human and social sciences to the Italian's newly discovered 'Aryanness'. Yet even before its latent racism became official policy in 1938 and the New Italy became inextricably caught up in the machinations of the Third Reich a year later, Fascism had already revealed the fundamental contradictions of the modernist state that doomed its attempt to realize a temporalized utopia.

THE 'TRUE FACE' OF FASCIST MODERNISM

Fascism's gardening project, when compared to that pursued by Hitler's Germany, Stalin's Russia, or Pol Pot's Cambodia, was hardly draconian. The 'surgical operation' it undertook in the 'human reclamation' of Italian society initially required little more than the local anaesthetic provided by Fascism's elaborate political religion to assure that an adequate measure of popular consensus for its revolution would form once the storm of *squadrismo* had abated. The 'destruction' it carried out dialectically as part of the creative process of building a new order took the form of systematically dismantling the institutional and social basis of political liberalism and revolutionary socialism rather than the physical elimination of the cultural and human incarnations of alleged decadence or what George Orwell called 'Thoughtcrime'. Until 1938 Fascist racism was, with few exceptions, of a historical and cultural variety more akin to the variety ingrained in the chauvinism and imperialism displayed by all the Great Powers which fought in the First World War than to the biological and genocidal variety perfected by the Nazis. Even after 1938 the racial laws were incomprehensible to most Italians.

Yet even in its moderate form, the fate of the Fascist regime reveals the fundamental inviability of the modernist state. There were structural flaws in its dependency on charismatic forms of politics that cannot be indefinitely sustained, certainly beyond the death of its leader, and in a foreign policy with an in-built expansionist momentum. This predisposed Mussolini to commit economic and military resources the nation could ill afford to support Franco's civil war against the government, and then to play his part in the Berlin–Rome Axis which was to have such devastating consequences for the Italian nation.

One of the root causes of the failure, however, was the unrealizability of the Fascist 'anthropological revolution'. Symptoms of this were the ineffectuality of the demographic campaign, the failure to Fascistize most Italians beyond 'nationalizing' them, and the conspicuous absence of 'New Italians' as international conflict approached, even after two decades of intensive social engineering and state intervention. The gradual transformation of the *gerarchia* into a 'gerontocracy', the inexorable ageing process which turned Mussolini himself from an energetic *homo novus* to a neurotic, isolated figure with no-one to succeed him, the growing gulf between rhetoric and reality in every sphere of intended transformation, the degeneration of both the Fascist educational system and the National Fascist Party into authoritarian systems that encouraged conformism and corruption rather than the production of new elites,[104] the increasing hollowness of new political rituals, including the *duce* cult: everything points to the fact that even before Mussolini was dismissed by his own Fascist Council and King in July 1943 his regime was bankrupt politically, materially, and morally on a scale even more total than that of the Giolittian system it was supposed to replace.

The inner decay of the Fascist revolution as a mobilizing myth was not lost on some Fascists. Michael Ledeen has documented the futile struggle of idealistic Fascists to bring about a 'second revolution' which would fulfil the original regime's radical aspirations.[105] Ardengo Soffici, one of the original protagonists of modernist nationalism, was also able to break out of the state of denial in which others, such as Marinetti, Farinacci, and Gentile, remained immured. Having run through a wide gamut of aesthetics in his quest to revitalize Italy, he eventually 'came to believe that his prewar modernist vision was seriously flawed', and 'that the project of "cultural renewal" or a "transvaluation of values" through a revolution in art had failed and *would never succeed*'.[106] Even Giuseppe Bottai, the most zealous and capable of the regime's technocratic modernizers, was eventually forced to recognize the impossibility of creating the cornerstone of the New Italy, namely the fully internalized 'political religion' so vital to the social cohesion of the national community and the erection of a new sacred canopy. In 1942 he wrote:

> The failure of every official religion of the State, or State art and the like, like all attempts to revive religion (and not only revealed religion) on scientific and rational grounds, stems from the inability to appreciate the intrinsic and irreplaceable character of every genuine belief and faith.[107]

Bottai proceeded to put his finger on the ultimate aporia of political modernism: Fascism had been forced to create a viable collective myth to legitimize the regime precisely at a time when modernity was destroying the habitat in which such myths could survive. Not only can a modernist, totalitarian state, as David Kertzer argued, 'never eliminate all vestiges of alternative symbolic systems',[108] but it can never successfully impose from above an artificial state religion. The modernity that has shattered the hegemony of revealed religion will also undermine any substitute for it. The total nomos or total community cannot be socially engineered, since the body politic – or rather the millions of individuals who compose it – will always eventually reject the ideological skin-graft. By the time Mussolini was ousted from power by his own Fascist Grand Council on 25 July 1943 his aura of *propheta* had evaporated as a populist myth and lingered on only for a small nucleus of 'intransigents' who would form the backbone of the Salò Republic. The Fascistization of all Italians had been a mission impossible.

The fate of several architectural modernists under Fascism illustrates the regime's rapid moral dissolution as a cohesive force of social renewal after the regime's supreme act of 'making history': the evening of 18 May 1936 when Mussolini announced from his balcony in Rome that Ethiopia was finally 'Italian'. In the wake of the anti-Semitic race laws set out in the Declaration on Race – signed by King Victor Emmanuel III, Benito Mussolini, and Giuseppe Bottai on 5 September 1938 – Italy's Rationalist architects became particularly vulnerable to attacks on aesthetic modernism. The most important of these was mounted by the Farinacci circle, which accused their buildings of displaying signs of decadent Jewish cosmopolitanism. Rather than defend Italian Jews or attack the race laws as a betrayal of original Fascist principles – not to mention basic human rights – a number of architects unwittingly colluded with the new ethos instead by launching a counterattack which consisted in extolling the 'Mediterranean qualities' of indigenous Rationalist architecture, and insisting on the Aryan pedigrees of colleagues accused of being Jews, both concessions to the discourse of racism.

It was in this corrupt atmosphere that the debate within elite cultural circles over the Fascist or anti-Fascist properties of architectural modernism came to a head. It had been raging since 1934 when a bitter dispute broke out over the appropriateness of Rationalist aesthetics for the design of the Palazzo del Littorio, the Fascist Party National headquarters, in Rome for which Mario Palanti had proposed his 'Ship of State' (see Figure 11 above). However it now began to be overlaid by issues of Aryanism and racial purity. Given what was happening in the enforcement of Nazi cultural and racial policy north of the Alps this was far from a solely 'academic' matter. The situation degenerated further once the Second World War broke out. Giuseppe Terragni, the prolific champion of Rationalist experimentalism, was sent to the Russian front, from which he returned 17 months later a broken man.

Within six months he was dead, leaving it to his wife to communicate to his former colleagues his confession: 'For himself, for us, even for the executioners, whom he had joined without realizing it, *having first seen their mask rather than the true face*; he asked forgiveness after he discovered that face in all its horror.'[109] After the armistice and the creation of the Salò Republic, several fellow-modernists saw through the mask of Fascism and joined the resistance, notably Ernesto Rogers, Raffaello Giolli, Gian Luigi Banfi, and Ludovico Belgiojoso. It was in this broader context of Fascism's accelerating moral decadence, political, social, and military collapse, and renewed lease of life as a Nazi puppet regime that Giuseppe Pagano, once the hero of Fascist modernist architecture, met the unspeakable end we referred to in Chapter 1.

After the Manifesto of Fascist Racism was published he came under vicious attack by the flourishing anti-Semitic press which accused him of Jewish origins – his original family name was the Slav (not Jewish) Pogatschnig – and of spreading cultural decadence through his modernist style of architecture. Pagano's first reaction was to fight a long rear-guard action to defend modernism from its critics, staying a member of the School of Fascist Mysticism and Party member. But in late 1942 he left both, and in the summer of 1943 joined the Resistance, becoming an active partisan under the Salò Republic. He was captured twice, the second time in September 1944. This time he was tortured by the infamous Koch Gang, and ended his days in Mauthausen, where he died in unimaginable circumstances of collective inhumanity and personal suffering. His fellow modernist architects Giolli and Banfi met a similar fate in the same Mauthausen-Gusen group of extermination camps.

Such men rebelled against the increasingly sordid human realities spawned by Fascism as it degenerated ever further from the 'ethical state' postulated by Giovanni Gentile's actualism in the *Enciclopedia Italiana*. The incorporation of Mussolini's shrinking fiefdom into the Third Reich meant that they fell victims to the far more radical 'gardening state' created by the Nazis, prepared, in the words of Hitler himself, 'brutally and ruthlessly to prune off the wild shoots and tear out the weeds', extracting as much labour and suffering from its victims as possible.

...AND THE 'LOOK' OF NAZISM

Another victim of the self-destructive involution of Fascism's modernist state once utopian social engineering and attempted 'enracination' gave way to social control and eradication, was the Jewish Italian, Primo Levi. When the Salò Republic was created he attempted to join the liberal Giustizia e Libertà partisan movement, but was arrested by the militia of the GNR (Guardia Nazionale Repubblicana).

When it was discovered that he was Jewish, he was sent to an internment camp for Jews at Fossoli near Modena, from which he was transported to Auschwitz in cattle trucks in February 1944. He owed his survival to a surreal moment in mid-November 1944 when he found himself standing emaciated in the office of Dr Alex Pannwitz in the Auschwitz camp complex. There he underwent an impromptu *viva voce* examination in industrial chemistry on whose outcome his life literally depended: working on the Buna artificial rubber project in Pannwitz's laboratory considerably raised the chances of him surviving the merciless Polish winter. After the war Levi often pondered how his examiner 'really functioned as a man; how he filled his time, outside of the Polymerization and the Indo-Germanic conscience'. The way Pannwitz had looked at him held a particular fascination:

> That look was not one between two men; and if I had known how completely to explain the nature of that look, which came as if across the glass window of an aquarium between two beings who live in different worlds, I would also have explained the essence of the great insanity of the third Germany.[110]

The following chapters on the Third Reich will try to shed light on the 'great insanity' driving the policies and actions of the Nazis' 'different world' by approaching them as a function of the modernist dynamics of the Third Reich. The interpretation that emerges suggests that Primo Levi had in fact intuitively understood the 'look' on Pannwitz's face: lurking behind its inability to meet him eye to eye was what Modris Eksteins calls the 'irrationalism crossed with technicism' which made Nazism 'yet another offspring of the modernist impulse'.[111] Primo Levi had been staring at the face of Nazi modernism when confronted by someone who embodied for it the forces of decadence it set out to eliminate in the process of creating a new national community based on racial strength and advanced technology.

9
Nazism as a Revitalization Movement

There were overwhelming demonstrations of the new community spirit, mass oaths under floodlit cupolas, bonfires on the mountains, [...] choral singing in the churches in honour of the Nazi seizure of power. [...] Something genuinely new seemed beginning.

Rüdiger Safranski, *Martin Heidegger* (1999)[1]

This Age must be called, not the decline of the West, but the resurrection of the peoples of this West of ours! Only that which was old, decayed and evil perishes; and let it die! But new life will spring up. Faith can be found if the will is there.

Adolf Hitler, May Day Speech, 1 May (1935)[2]

JOSEPH: A GERMAN DESTINY

On 12 December 1933 the Third Reich's Minister for Propaganda sent a telegram to Edvard Munch, famed for several canvases epitomizing revelatory states of *Zerrissenheit* experienced in a 'modern mind' torn between madness and a higher sanity. In it Goebbels congratulated him on his seventieth birthday and on his outstanding achievement as an artist, highlighting the way his paintings displayed a powerful, wilful spirit inherited from a Nordic-Germanic heritage in its utter disregard for formal academic criteria, and in the struggle to grasp the naked truth of nature by returning to the basic principles of *völkisch* creativity.[3] Yet in 1937 the Reich Propaganda Minister, now toeing the Party line on aesthetic modernism, personally oversaw Germany's wholesale purge of 'degenerate art', which led to the removal of some eighty of Munch's paintings from modern art galleries, most of them subsequently sold to international buyers.[4] Probing further into Goebbels' fawning appreciation of the man who painted *The Scream* leads to the heart of Nazism's profound, and profoundly paradoxical, relationship with modernism in the 'maximalist' sense we have given the term.

250

This was not the only example of Goebbels' efforts on Munch's behalf. He almost certainly had a hand in ensuring that the Norwegian was awarded Germany's silver Goethe medal for services to art in 1932, and that a decade later the Quisling regime made overtures for him to become the figurehead of its Honorary Board of Norwegian Artists. The painter, now seriously ill, was adamant in his refusal, and rejected proposals for a major exhibition sponsored by the Nazis to be held in Oslo to mark his eightieth birthday. Goebbels' string-pulling can be detected here too, as well as in the puppet government's successful 'hi-jacking' of the funeral arrangements on Munch's death in January 1944. As a result, the last public act of this deeply private giant of aesthetic modernism, on whom the anathema had long since fallen in Nazi Germany, was to lie in a coffin bedecked with an enormous wreath 'swathed in silk ribbons covered in swastikas', with tributes signed personally by Reichkommissar Josef Terboven and representatives of Quisling's Culture Department.[5]

This Nazi apotheosis of a major modernist painter flouted official cultural policy at home, but was consistent with the passage in Goebbels' 1926 auto-biographical novel, *Michael: A German Destiny in Diary Pages*,[6] which, as we saw in Chapter 1, celebrates Van Gogh while implicitly portraying Nazism as a vast undertaking to translate into historical reality the 'mad idea' of self-sacrifice to the nation born of the modern search for God. The roots of such an idiosyncratic 'take' on Nazism are to be found in Goebbels' intense preoccupation with the spiritual dilemma of modernity documented by his PhD on Wilhelm von Schütz, an early nineteenth-century dramatist and poet drawn to Catholic conservatism. A revealing passage of the doctorate, successfully defended in 1921, claims that an analogy exists between contemporary history and the Romantic period. Both are pervaded by a 'flat, unspiritual atheism' that provokes the metaphysical revolt of 'a young generation of God-seekers, mystics, and Romantics' who long for a great man to lead them into a world which corresponds to their 'religious fervour'.[7]

In Weimar Germany inchoate longings for transcendence[8] were more likely than anywhere else to find an outlet in political projects of renewal rather than the purely artistic or metaphysical ones cultivated by Romantics and fin-de-siècle poets. It is consistent with this pattern that after his conversion to Nazism, Goebbels portrayed Adolf Hitler as the 'preacher' of a 'new political belief born of the despair induced by a collapsing, secularized world', and his followers as 'standing at the turning point of history'.[9] Having found his nomos, his community, and his *propheta*, he immediately set about doing everything he could to transform the NSDAP into the midwife of a new historical era that would expunge anomy from the modern world. However, he was yet to conceive this new era primarily in terms of the supremacy of the

'Aryan'.[10] In the late 1920s he could still picture Germany in almost Mazzinian terms as leading the vanguard of 'young peoples' whose unfolding destiny was contributing to the 'regeneration of the world and life itself'. The mission of National Socialism was to establish a classless, racially integrated, 'socialist national state' that would finally bring coherence and direction to a world dominated by spiritual chaos and bourgeois decadence, thus reversing the devastating impact of modern civilization and the machine age on traditional society.[11]

It is to trivialize the issue of Goebbels' modernism, then, if it is discussed solely in terms of his alleged taboo-breaking love of Jazz. In any case, it turns out that, though Goebbels might have tapped his foot to the dance rhythms of the Jack Hylton Band,[12] and created Charlie and his Orchestra to provide a racist variant of Swing for 'Aryan' ears only,[13] he may well have shared the Nazi contempt for its more abstract or frenetic forms as the epitome of degenerate music. Far more significant was Goebbels' conspicuous support for the campaign launched by the National Socialist Students Association in June 1933 to have German modernists such as Emil Nolde, Ernst Barlach, Erich Heckel, and Karl Schmidt-Rottluff officially acknowledged to be incarnations of the 'culture-creating mission of National Socialism'.

This was a deliberate act of defiance against the radical rejection of aesthetic modernism both by Alfred Rosenberg, newly appointed by Hitler to a major position in Nazi cultural policy,[14] and by the activists of the Militant League for German Culture (Kampfbund für deutsche Kultur) which Rosenberg had founded in 1929 to fight for the 'Aryanization' of German art. Goebbels used his position as Reichsminister for Propaganda and National Enlightenment to endorse both German Expressionism and 'New Objectivity' in a speech made to theatre directors in May 1933. This was the same month that the pro-Nazi art critic Bruno Werner claimed that it was the 'New Art that had paved the way for the national revolution', citing such artists as Ernst Nolde, Max Pechstein, Franz Marc, August Macke, Paul Klee, and Lyonel Feininger in painting, Ernst Barlach in sculpture, and Ludwig Mies van der Rohe in architecture.[15] Ten months later Goebbels made a conspicuous display of his opposition to Rosenberg in this debate when he formed part of the committee of honour to welcome the renowned Futurist poets Filippo Marinetti and Ruggero Vasari at the opening of an exhibition of Fascist 'aeropittura', the aviation painting that demonstrated how well aesthetic modernism was flourishing under Mussolini.

It was Hitler's personal intervention that put an abrupt end to the growing divisions within the Nazi art world over the status of German Expressionism. He pointedly used the occasion of the Nuremberg rally in September 1934 to attack both aesthetic modernism and any attempts by *völkisch* pressure groups to 'impose on the National Socialist revolution, as a binding heritage for the future a "Teutonic art" sprung from the fuzzy world of their romantic conceptions'.[16] However, the 'reflexive metanarrative' unfolding in this book suggests that to construct the dispute between Goebbels and Rosenberg as a conflict between modernism and anti-modernism is to distort the central issue. It was not Goebbels' aesthetics that mark him out as a modernist. Rather it was his deep-seated belief that the institutional and organizational might of the modern state could be used to create a new national culture and a new historical era. The reborn Germany would be a total culture, not just expressing the genius of the race, but embodying the sacred canopy and underpinning the organic community required to solve the problems of modernity.

Central to his vision of how to achieve this was the power of the latest technology of mass communications to coordinate and channel the creative energies of a modern, highly pluralistic nation into a 'spiritual' force providing the cohesion of an organic national community, the *Volksgemeinschaft*. Far from deliberately pursuing nihilistic policies of cultural vandalism, Goebbels seems genuinely to have believed, at least in his early years as propaganda minister, that the systematic 'corporatization' of all Germany's cultural and intellectual production within the 'Reichkulturkammer' he founded in 1933 would enable the nation to be purged of decadence and anarchy and enter a period of cultural renaissance. In Gramscian terms, he saw such an act of coordination as the precondition for the Third Reich to gain 'cultural hegemony', thereby minimizing the recourse to coercion, brainwashing, and social control ('dominion') in carrying out the Nazi revolution. Goebbels made a specific reference to this belief in the speech he made at the 1934 Nuremberg Rally 'immortalized' in Leni Riefensthal's *The Triumph of the Will*: 'May the bright flame of enthusiasm never be extinguished. It alone gives light and warmth to the creative art of modern political propaganda. [...] It is well and good to possess power based upon guns; it is however better and more gratifying to win and also to champion the hearts of the people.'

The German New Right intellectual Rüdiger Safranski, well known for his perceptive biography of Martin Heidegger, corroborates this interpretation of Goebbels as a political modernist in the primordialist, Cronus-defying sense when he claims that National Socialism originally represented for him 'the catechism of a new political faith amid the despair of a godless world that is falling apart', a way of 'finding a home', a 'community', and redemption from his 'dark feelings of meaninglessness, his social misery, his fear of abandonment'.[17] However, by the time Goebbels spoke in Nuremberg his vision of 'the people' had long since been purged of any residual elements of 'Christ-socialism' and solidarity with other 'young nations' discernible in more innocent times. His interpretation of the 'propaganda' and 'enlightenment' for which he had ministerial responsibility now conformed entirely to the perverse logic of 'truth' once it falls under the thrall of the 'gardening state' and becomes a tool of social engineering and surgical intervention of the most draconian type carried out by politicians in the 'higher interests of society'. As the war started to go against the Third Reich, the megamachine of social control he had created largely abandoned its projects for championing the hearts of the people to concentrate on reinforcing the power achieved through the guns and bombs of the armed forces, and on abetting the regime's apparatus of repression and state murder in sustaining the war effort.

As a result, Joseph Goebbels, the former admirer of Van Gogh and Munch, helped institutionalize an Orwellian 'doublethink' in the Reich in which cultural hegemony and coercion often became practically indistinguishable. Emblematic of this perversion of his original ideal of basing the Nazi revolution on the ideological mobilization of all 'Aryans' was the sinister 'Pst!' poster campaign conducted in the latter stages of the war designed to spread a paranoid state of fear.[18] The millions who, like Goebbels, had turned to Nazism as a refuge from the terror of anomy now found themselves confronting terror of a far less abstract and more immediate kind. The Third Reich, instead of creating a new canopy of meaning for them, now resorted to spreading fear of the nameless 'other' to psychologically enforce their conformity with the *Volksgemeinschaft*, which after Stalingrad was further travestied into the *Schicksalsgemein-schaft*, a 'community of destiny' plunging headlong to communal extinction while unspeakable crimes against humanity continued to be committed with accelerating momentum.

The distortions in 'reality' that resulted are reflected in *Kolberg*, a film commissioned by Goebbels to dramatize the 'heroic' (i.e. futile) last stand of a German community during the Napoleonic Wars. The genuine crown and orb of the Holy Roman Emperors were used as props and 187,000 soldiers were removed from the war front to be used as extras in the film's battle scenes. The idea that such a film could alter the outcome of the war – especially given the grim circumstances of film distribution in a carpet-bombed Reich on the brink of destruction – can be seen as the ultimate perversion of the fascist drive to 'make history' by enlisting the power of the 'historic imaginary'. By the same token it marked the uttermost degradation of the avant-garde's liberating belief in the capacity of art to shape from within a society revitalized through the transformative power of vision.

As for Goebbels himself, the trajectory on which he was launched by his personal search for transcendence in the aftermath of the war, though not racially motivated at the outset, eventually led him to argue for the unconditional extermination of Jews and Gypsies at a meeting with Otto Thierack, the Reich's 'Minister of Justice', in September 1942. In the famous

Sport Palast speech made five months later he promised the packed audience and the millions more listening on their People's Receiver ('Volksempfänger') the prospect of 'total war'. In doing so he rationalized not just the continued destruction of Germany by the Allies to the bitter end, but personally helped ensure that the campaigns of genocide, mass murder, and enslavement carried out under the cover of war would be stopped only by the total military defeat and occupation of Germany.

Through extraordinary quirks of happenstance, a PhD student exploring anomy through the medium of German literature came to find himself in a unique position to experiment with the cultural transformation of an entire nation, the ultimate dream of programmatic modernism. The parabola of his 'Dionysian adventure' in creating an alternative modernity was abruptly terminated in Hitler's bunker on 1 May 1945. There, by now a totally Gorgonized Gorgon, he poisoned his six children with cyanide, and then shot his wife and himself, while in the streets and tenement blocks a few metres above their heads nearly half a million Germans and Russians, civilians and soldiers, suffered more anonymous, and often more terrible fates in the Battle for Berlin.[19] The 'new era' on which he had gambled his life had turned into the nation's 'Stunde Null', 'zero hour', where the arrow of historical time stood agonizingly suspended for millions of human beings even after it had finally stopped for him.

RECONNECTING FORWARDS

It would be misleading to portray Goebbels, or any other Nazi leader – even Hitler himself – as the incarnation of some homogeneous 'Nazi ideology', let alone the even more chimerical 'Nazi personality'.[20] A detailed comparative analysis of Nazi thought – which this book seeks to show is no oxymoron – as expressed in the writings of the highest echelons of the party leadership reveals just how idiosyncratic it was on all key issues, such as the socialist contents of Nazism's 'national socialism', the virulence of the anti-Semitism, the degree to which racism was 'scientized' in terms of eugenics and racial hygiene, and the role played by *völkisch* currents of anti-industrialization and anti-technology. In any case, not all leading Nazis were initially ideologically motivated, let alone inspired by a modernist hankering for renewal – the dissolute and corrupt Hermann Goering being a notorious example. Even those that were, pursued remarkably disparate visions of the new Germany. Some, notably Robert Ley,[21] Fritz Todt, and Albert Speer,[22] converged on an overtly *technocratic* vision of the New Order, in marked contrast to Walter Darré's bucolic fantasies of an 'Aryan' aristocracy bred from sound peasant stock rooted in blood and soil,[23] or Heinrich Himmler's Ariosophical obsessions with the occult 'Aryan' roots of the German race.[24] His esoteric reading of Nazism, aberrant even by the standards of the rest of the leadership, would eventually lead to the bizarre research projects carried out by the SS Ahnenerbe – or, to give it its full name *German Ancestry – Research Society for the Primordial History of the Spirit*, jointly founded with Hermann Wirth and Walter Darré – some of which would be simply ludicrous if they were not bound up with the industrialization of state terror and murder.[25]

Meanwhile, Alfred Rosenberg concocted a total history of culture based on a *völkisch* idealization of the existence of a powerful pre-Judeo-Christian Germanic culture, an elaborate act of mythopoeia that drew extensively on the 'New Religions' that thrived in the Second Reich. These disseminated powerful *anti*-technocratic forms of organic nationalism blended with ingredients taken from a variety of religious, mystic, and occult traditions.[26] Under scrutiny, Hitler himself reveals a complex, ambivalent attitude to Western modernity, venting his spleen both on the degenerate minds of some modernist artists and on 'mystically-minded occult folk with a passion for exploring the secrets of the cosmos'.[27]

In his study of 'the end of utopianism', prompted by the comparative lack of palingenetic fervour that accompanied the 1989 revolutions in Europe, Joachim Fest comments on the surreal blend of archaism with modernity at the core of Nazism's 'aggressive utopia'. Its spokesmen promised to restore the 'world-order' that existed before it was 'perverted by Christianity, the Enlightenment, and the process of industrialization and emancipation', hence the 'flag consecrations, Thing dramas, and death cult'. Yet the Nazi 'longing to return to a primordial state of culture' constantly intersected with 'a future-directed' ambition to make Germany the most advanced technological nation on earth, and repeated claims that it 'had overtaken all other nations'.[28] It is precisely in this blend of the primordial with the hypermodern that, as we have seen, Modris Eksteins identifies National Socialism's fundamental *modernism*: 'National Socialism was yet another offspring of the hybrid that has been the modernist impulse: irrationalism crossed with technicism. [...] The intention of the movement was to create a new type of human being from whom would spring a new morality, a new social system, and eventually a new international order.'[29]

Such generalizations may seem hazardous given the extreme heterogeneity of Nazi ideology at an individual level. Yet they are borne out by the conclusion that the German historian Frank-Lothar Kroll reaches after a detailed comparison of the world-views of Adolf Hitler, Joseph Goebbels, Walter Darré, Alfred Rosenberg, and Heinrich Himmler on the basis of substantial primary-source research. One important conclusion he draws is that Nazi ideology is not to be dismissed either as cynical camouflage for the heinous deeds of the regime or as a mere tool for the manipulation of the masses: 'All the leading ideologues of the regime believed in their respective *Weltanschauung* and worked for its enactment.'[30] Another is the existence of a common matrix underlying the extreme divergence of their thinking on a number of key issues. This he identifies as 'the category of *renewal* manifested through the deliberate intention to inaugurate a fundamental turning-point in history through the establishment of National Socialism, and culminating in the related vision of the demiurgic act of creating a "new man" and a "new world"'. It is this 'category of renewal' that in Kroll's assessment makes National Socialism a 'concrete utopia' conditioned by the drive towards '*possibility* and *realization*', and a 'genuine concern [...] to transcend and transform the material conditions of the existing order into a substantively "different" future world'.[31]

Kroll sees as integral to the realization of this project and the ideological legitimation of the Third Reich 'the invocation of "history"', in other words turning elements of a mythicized German or 'Aryan' past into the mythic template for the transformation of Germany, and thereby developing a peculiarly Nazi variant of what Claudio Fogu terms the 'historic imaginary'. This process is fully consistent with Peter Osborne's theory of the modernism of Nazism as a 'conservative revolutionary' project affirming the 'temporality of the new' however much 'its image of the future may derive from the mythology of some lost origin or suppressed national essence'. Both academics emphasize in different ways the tendency of fascist political modernism to use history, or rather a mythicized past, as a source of historicized transcendent values which are projected into a 'rigorously futural' temporality. It is a principle articulated lucidly in a speech on the premises of Nazi culture made at the Party Rally of September 1938 where the Führer states that 'at the present moment the expression of a new view of the world which is determined by the conception of race will return to those ages which in the past have already possessed a similar freedom of the spirit, of the will, and of the mind'.[32]

Kroll's detailed analysis of Nazi ideology is thus a cogent, and thoroughly documented, refutation of both empirical and theoretical assumptions made by a number of scholars[33] in the past that Nazism embodied a backward-looking, reactionary 'anti-modernity'. His work underlines the importance of approaching the Nazi cult of the past – in the context of Moeller van den Bruck's concept of 'reconnection forwards' we encountered in Chapter 5.[34] This meant retaining whatever was healthy or redeemable of the present in a new ideological synthesis with what could be retrieved from the (mythic) greatness of the past in the creation of a new nomos and community. The mazeway that resulted would be based on the conception of the German nation as an organic homogeneous *race* – a people with a unique set of historically, culturally, and biologically determined faculties and gifts – destined to 'make history' for itself and the 'whole world'. The Nazis saw the advent of their movement in history as a cosmological act of creating a new society with a new *Weltanschauung* through the intervention of an inspired *propheta* in a national act of self-creation (Giovanni Gentile's *autoctisi*) performed within a temporalized history: a *modernist* cosmogony.

NAZISM'S ALTERNATIVE MODERNITY

Such considerations are important when evaluating the apparently anti-modern thrust of some elements which Nazism absorbed from the radically neo-pagan sphere of *völkisch* nationalism, and in particular from the arcane Ariosophical racism out of which the Nazism of the Deutsche Arbeiterpartei, itself was originally distilled.[35] It is consistent with our approach that Karla Poewe's extensively documented investigation of the links between Nazi ideology and the 'New Age' religious movements in the 1920s and 30s stresses how Weimar inherited a sprawling pre-war counterculture obsessed with reviving ancient traditions of spirituality, both Christian and pagan. The aim was not, however, to dwell on the past as a refuge from the present, but to transfuse elements of the healthy knowledge and values that thrived before the coming of modernity into a Germany seen as on the brink of total spiritual bankruptcy. In doing so the advocates of a spiritual revival assumed that 'symbols used by one's ancestors in antiquity had the power to impact and steer people today',[36] and help bring about 'a new beginning (Anfang)'.[37] (It is worth noting that Poewe's analysis underscores the fallacy of accepting at face value Nazi claims to represent 'positive Christianity', since the principle of redemption of all humanity through the blood of Christ alone was abandoned by Nazism in all its variants, and grotesquely travestied in those that claimed to represent a 'German' faith.)

Poewe's analysis bears out in impressive empirical detail the heuristic value of seeing both the European occult revival that produced Theosophy and Anthroposophy, and the 'life reform movement'[38] which cultivated alternative medicine, neo-paganism, and yoga, not as symptoms of a peculiarly German malaise, but as local manifestations of pan-European forms of social modernism bent on resolving the spiritual crisis of the West created by materialism and rationalism.[39] Her work also highlights the role played in creating a constituency for Nazism by the proliferation of associations, groups, and circles known as the *Bünde* (literally 'leagues') that sprang up in the 1920s exploring alternative world-views, life-styles, and politics, in particular the ultranationalist, anti-Semitic youth groups known as *bündische Jugend*. There is a clear link between this chapter in the origins of Nazism and the regime's subsequent promotion of alternative medical traditions such as herbalism and homeopathy, notably by the leader of the Reich Physicians Chamber, Gerhard Wagner. In 1934 he set up a teaching hospital in Dresden in order to disseminate the 'holistic' theory and practice of the 'New German Healing',[40] just one symptom of the 'Aryanization' of the many New Age currents of alternative medicine which arose as part of the social modernist reaction against decadence. At one point the Nazification of herbalism also led to the proposal put in all seriousness to Heinrich Himmler that extracts of a South American plant, *Dieffenbachia seguine*, should be used for the mass sterilization of racially undesirable war prisoners.[41]

In the event the Nazi authorities selected more 'advanced' scientific methods for the sterilization campaign, whose victims between 1933 and 1945 eventually numbered around 400,000 (compared with 64,000 in the US between 1930 and 1970). In addition, 'New Age' medicine remained as marginalized under Hitler as it is by mainstream Western medicine today. Nevertheless, it is curious to see the seriousness with which Himmler evaluated the report sent to him by the obscure army captain Emmerich von Moers, an expatriate German who had apparently lived for months in Amazonia with the medicine men of various tribes whom he claimed shared their pharmacological secrets with him before he returned to Germany to fight for his fatherland.[42] The SS Reichsführer took seriously his claim that rain-forest plants could be used to make powerful herbal sweeteners and aphrodisiacs, as well as cures for malaria, syphilis, and serious skin conditions, especially since the 'Americans and English' had apparently already offered von Moers 'enormous sums to reveal his secrets'. He thus ordered the Ahnenerbe to purchase all the books von Moers referred to in his report on the medicinal properties of Amazonian plants, and to maintain close links with him, declaring it 'one of the first tasks to be undertaken in peace time' to organize an SS expedition to accompany von Moers back to Amazonia in order to reconstitute the huge pharmacopeia he had collected, and so carry out a scientific assessment of its potentially 'enormous' economic significance for the New Germany.[43] It was an undertaking made necessary ever since the ship transporting 30 crates of samples to Germany had been intercepted by a British vessel and the entire collection stolen.

It is not being claimed here that the occultist creeds and practices that prospered under Nazism legitimate counter-cultural conspiracy theories concerning the 'true history' of the Third Reich ignored by orthodox historians.[44] Nazism was an alliance of *different* revolts against 'actually existing modernity', the bulk of which fully embraced orthodox science and the values of the modern technocracy as long they could be harnessed by the forces of national rebirth. Whatever interest he might have had in Ariosophy before the war, Hitler himself was perhaps the ultimate 'Nazi modernizer', proactively recruiting the most powerful technocrats of his day, and adamantly refusing to allow Nazism to be turned into a *völkisch* religion in which the Bhagavad Gita sat on the shelves alongside *Mein Kampf*. As he told his serried ranks of listeners assembled at the Nuremberg Rally of 1938: 'We have no religious retreats, but arenas for sports and playing-fields, and the characteristic feature of our places of assembly is not the mystical gloom of a cathedral, but the brightness and light of a room or hall which combines beauty with fitness for its purpose.'[45]

MEIN KAMPF AS A MODERNIST MANIFESTO

The primordialist reading of modernism that we are applying to Nazism suggests that, far from being symptomatic of its fundamental irrationalism, its regressive flight from the twentieth century, or the aporias of a fundamentally self-contradictory, irrational, or 'insane' political system, the interpenetration and symbiosis of modernity and culture with 'barbarism' and destructiveness in the Third Reich reveals something perhaps more disturbing still. This is its deadly serious attempt to realize an *alternative* logic, an *alternative* modernity, and an *alternative* morality to those pursued by liberalism, socialism, or conservatism. At its core lay a 'will' to renew the nation and revitalize not the 'body politic' of liberal theory, but rather the *Volkskörper*, the 'ethnic body' conceived as a living organism that transcends the plane of individual mortality. This in turn was rooted in the instinctive desire to create a new nomos and a new community as solutions to the pandemic of anomy produced in Weimar by the extreme liminoid conditions of inter-war German and European history. Nazism thus translated into a doctrine of radical political revolution, the same cosmological syndrome that had created the cult of war, the 'will to sacrifice', and the desire to regenerate the organic nation that enabled the German war effort to be maintained despite the horrendous toll of casualties between 1914 and 1918.[46]

Within the myth-framed horizon created by Nazism, the German people ('Volk') underwent a temporalized apotheosis as the collective embodiment of transcendence and sacrality, an apotheosis that demanded rituals of consecration and cleansing sanctioned by an all-pervasive political religion. This is the aspect of Nazism to which Ian Kershaw alludes – despite his profound scepticism about the concept 'political religion' – when he refers to its 'politics of national salvation – redemption brought about by purging the impure and the pernicious evil within'.[47] In his 'Afterthought' to a volume on the relationship between 'genocide and religion in the twentieth century' Kershaw enlarges on this idea by emphasizing the powerful role played in the causation of Nazi genocide by 'pseudo-religion' in comparison to the one committed by Pol Pot and the mass murder carried out by Mao and Stalin, all of whom pursued more overtly secular utopias. It is consistent with our construction of totalitarianism in all its forms as the attempt to realize a palingenetic, anti-anomic, *modernist* vision of a new society, that Kershaw refers to these atrocities as 'perpetrated under the aegis of a type of "crusading," exclusivist modern ideology aiming at the renewal of society'. In the same text he unwittingly refers to the role of Hitler as a *propheta* figure born of a liminoid situation in Germany which at the height of its intensity after 1929 created the political space for the Nazis to seize power.

> [T]he mass of his fanatical following increasingly depicted Hitler as a national saviour or redeemer, *which is certainly how he saw himself*.[...]
>   The demonization of the Jews fitted perfectly into the countervailing vision of national salvation, a utopia to be attained through stamping out the sources of 'disease' in a presumed 'decadent' society, eradication of the 'enemies of the people' and creation of an ethnically pure 'national community'. *The depth and extent of the crisis in German society opened the way to the radicality of the presumed solution to that crisis and the readiness to accept it*.[48]

As for the precise attitude of Hitler to his own Catholicism and revealed religion in general, it is a matter of intense debate which has been brought to a head by Richard Steigmann-Gall's claim in *The Holy Reich*[49] that the Führer represented a genuine form of the 'positive Christianity' that Nazi propaganda claimed for the spiritual and theological credentials of the movement. A conclusion that resonates more fully with our own line of argument is the one drawn by the US journalist Timothy Ryback after a close scrutiny of the books in Hitler's library: 'Hitler was the classic apostate. He rebelled against the established theology in which he was born and bred, while seeking to fill the resulting spiritual void.' His search for a personal mazeway with which to exit from the labyrinth of modern life led him to read a wide range of works which address metaphysical issues. According to the interpretative framework offered in this book it is highly revealing that Hitler sidelined a section in Ernst Schertel (1923) *Magic: History, Theory, and Practice* which stated in Nietzschean tones: 'He who does not carry demonic seeds within him will never give birth to a new world.'[50]

If we follow through the intuition that Hitler felt driven to find an antidote to the breakdown of society's nomos, and accept that the redemptive aspect of Nazism recognized by many conventional historians is to be located within the conception of modernity we developed in Part One, we are led to a radical reading of Adolf Hitler's *Mein Kampf* and of Nazi ideology in general.

Once widely dismissed as no more than a particularly turgid expression of the 'vast system of bestial Nordic nonsense' that constituted Nazi ideology for some eminent historians,[51] *Mein Kampf* underwent a radical re-reading by Eberhard Jäckel in his groundbreaking analysis of it as a 'blueprint for power', an interpretative strategy that helped launch an entire tradition of 'intentionalist' interpretations of Nazism.[52] The present analysis stresses another aspect of the text which is still widely neglected, and yet is consistent with an interpretation of the work as something much more than propaganda or logorrheic ranting. This is the way it affords insight into what we are arguing constitutes the mythic substratum of Nazism's political goals and actions, namely a rigorously futural, *modernist* drive to prevent the German nation being engulfed by decadence by creating the preconditions for it to enjoy a vitalistic, healthy future.

In Chapter 3 we considered a brief passage in *Mein Kampf* that suggested that Hitler intuitively understood the anthropological significance of a nomos ('philosophy of life', *Weltanschauung*) as the basis of a (national) community's suprapersonal meaning and cohesion.[53] It is consistent with this interpretation that other sections of the book reveal the tell-tale signs that Hitler conceives of himself as fighting a political modernist crusade to transcend the decadence and anomy of existing modernity. An outstanding example is chapter 10, 'Causes of the Collapse'. Here Hitler stresses the need to look beyond economic reasons for the crisis of 1918–19 so as to consider the primary role played by 'politics, ethics, morality, and blood'. He then portrays Germany as the *Volkskörper* which forms both subject and object of the Nazi revolution, claiming it is an organism suffering from a disease whose virulent symptoms should have aroused concern even before the First World War. Among these he lists the growing gap between rich and poor, the domination of society by materialism, utilitarianism, and the capitalist ethos, the internationalization of German economic life through the stock market, and the spinelessness of the ruling elites.

Hitler presents the dysfunctions of Weimar as expressions of the deeper process of decay caused by the 'semitization' ('Verjudung') of German spiritual life, the 'mammonization' of the mating instinct, the neglect of racial hygiene manifested in the spread of syphilis, prostitution, pornography, and the general corruption of metropolitan life. Another symptom of decay is the infiltration into German culture of degenerate forms of art deriving from a Bolshevik – and hence Jewish – anti-culture, notably 'the morbid excrescences of insane and degenerate men, with which, since the turn of the century, we have become familiar under the collective concepts of Cubism and Dadaism'.[54] The enthusiasm for them shown in Bolshevik Russia allows him to equate aesthetic modernism with the political modernism of Soviet Russia, prompting his use of what would become a key term of Nazi cultural criticism: 'Kultur-bolschewismus'.

Hitler singles out as the most graphic symbols of cultural decay the way modern cities no longer clearly demarcate the public from the private sphere with civic buildings conceived on a monumental scale such as the Acropolis, the Pantheon, or the Gothic cathedral. To reverse the decline Hitler proposes proceeding in the spirit of 'reactionary modernism' as Peter Osborne *redefines* it in *The Politics of Time*, drawing on the healthy elements of the national past in order to accelerate, not reverse, the 'rigorously futural' momentum of the Nazi assault on the status quo: 'The meaning and purpose of revolutions is not to tear down the whole building, but to remove what is bad or unsuitable and to continue building on the sound spot that has been laid bare.' In line with the prevailing modernist concern with social health we noted in Fascism, Hitler calls for radical educational reform to ensure that intellectual instruction is complemented by physical training through sports and gymnastics – obviously he wants fit 'Aryans', not Nordau's muscular Jews.[55] The seed of the major reorientation of the German educational system that occurred under the Third Reich is contained in this paragraph of *Mein Kampf*.[56]

To reinforce the process of *ethical* and moral convalescence, he then announces from his temporary headquarters in the prison of Landsberg Castle plans to 'clear away the filth of the moral plague of big-city "civilization"': 'Theatre, art, literature, cinema, press, posters, and window displays must be cleansed of all manifestations of our rotting world and placed in the service of a moral political, and cultural idea.' The measures of racial hygiene taken in the social sphere must be backed up by eugenics: a programme of mass sterilization is needed to ensure that the incurably sick are 'prevented from propagating equally defective offspring'. This is described as a measure that 'systematically executed, represents the most humane act of mankind', since 'the passing pain of a century can and will redeem millenniums from sufferings'.

At the end of his chapter Hitler once again returns to the need for a communal nomos, seeing as the root cause of the all-consuming decadence 'the absence of a definite, uniformly acknowledged *Weltanschauung*'. This has allowed 'humanitarian drivel' to take over, with the result that, 'by weakly yielding to cankers and sparing individuals, the future of millions is sacrificed'. With its programme of drastic measures to create a physically strong, morally healthy nation, to cleanse the ethnic body politic of cultural and genetic degeneracy, and to impose a unifying cosmology, National Socialism promises to 'halt the decline of the German people' and lay 'the granite foundation' for a state that is no longer 'an alien mechanism of economic concerns and interests', but a 'national organism': 'A German State of the German *Volk*'.

Such passages clearly show that long before the 'seizure of power' in 1933, Hitler had a consistent vision of the NSDAP's mission to transcend the decadence of contemporary history by inaugurating a new era. It would be an era of cultural, physical, and spiritual health lived by individual Germans as members of an organic, rooted national community under a new sacred canopy erected to replace the one torn to pieces by modern history. Though it has nothing aesthetically modernist in style or form, *Mein Kampf* has claims to be one of the most important manifestos of *political* modernism of the twentieth century. Conceptualizing modernism in explicitly primordialist terms highlights the causal relationship between *Mein Kampf* as a manifesto of political modernism and the particular form which Nazism assumed as a historical force before it seized power. Hitler came away from his first Deutsche Arbeiterpartei meeting on 12 September 1919 with a deep empathy for what had brought the four other men to that dingy back-room. He saw this as 'the longing for a new movement which should be more than a party in the previous sense of the word'.[57] The insistence in subsequent Nazi rhetoric that the NSDAP was a 'national uprising' ('nationale Erhebung'), or simply 'the *movement*' ('die Bewegung'), rather than a conventional political party, was crucial to its self-definition and popular appeal, and has obvious parallels with Mussolini's insistence on the 'anti-party' nature of early Fascism we saw in Chapter 7.

By this point in our argument it is hopefully self-evident what inference we wish to draw from Hitler's detailed description in *Mein Kampf* of the organization, goals, and tactics of the NSDAP which he construed as combining in a single entity political party, paramilitary formation, and populist social movement. After the abject failure of the putsch as a strategy to achieve power on 9 November 1923, Hitler deliberately set about transforming the reformed NSDAP on his release from prison into a 'revitalization movement' which would, like Mussolini's Fascism before 1922, serve as the vehicle for achieving the conquest of state power needed for a socio-political revolution. The 'new' NSDAP was conceived in modernist terms no longer as the basis for a military coup, but as a mass movement for social and political regeneration to be brought about by a broad, transclass segment of the population mobilized by myths of a 'holy war' against decadence and national decline fought in the spirit of creative destruction and active nihilism. The NSDAP would have to operate in a society vastly more populous, heterogeneous, technologically advanced, and rich in industrial and human resources than the societies of any premodern era, its temporality far more secularized and historicized than that of any of the major religions. Nevertheless, it retained the basic feature of all revitalization movements as described by the social anthropologist Victor Turner. New recruits to the Nazi cause sought 'the glow of *communitas* among those with whom they share[d] some *cultural or biological* feature they [took] to be their most signal mark of identity'.[58] Fortified by their communal Germanness which was rooted in a primordial 'Aryanness', Nazis could be pulled free from what Oswald Spengler called the 'quagmire' ['Sumpf'] of the Weimar Republic, secure in the knowledge they would soon be forcing their way into the temporalized utopia of a reborn Germany and start *making* history, instead of being its victims, by laying the foundations of a Thousand Year Reich.

It should be obvious that approaching the dynamics of Nazism from the perspective of modernism is offered not as a 'single-point' perspective on such an enormously complex and multilevel phenomenon, and that it is proposed as a way of complementing, not supplanting conventional historical accounts of the events of the rise of Nazism. There is certainly no shortage of factual knowledge about the Third Reich as an episode of modern history. The last six years alone have seen the publication of five major contributions in English by Ian Kershaw,[59] Michael Burleigh,[60] and Richard Evans.[61] Where much work still remains to be done, however, is on refining the generic terms and 'synoptic interpretations' needed to address some of the major issues left unresolved within the ongoing debate over the nature of Nazism as a phenomenon.[62] It is in this context that the maximalist definition of modernism elaborated in Part One of this book may make a significant contribution. It has a particular bearing on such questions as what mobilized its leaders and followers at an affective and socio-psychological level, what historical conditions account for the DAP's formation in 1918 and the NSDAP's breakthrough to take power in 1933, how far Nazism was an exclusively German phenomenon, what relationship it has to modernity and other forms of totalitarianism, and what led it to commit crimes against humanity on such an unimaginable scale.

NAZI MODERNIZATION REVISITED

A concrete example of how the present perspective may help clarify a thorny historiographical issue relating to Nazism concerns the controversy raised some years ago by Rainer Zitelmann, an academic, like Rüdiger Safranski, close to German New Right circles. In making his case for Hitler's credentials as 'modernizer' and 'social revolutionary' in the fields of technocracy, the consumer society, and the welfare state,[63] he correctly argued that the concept of modernization should be shorn of its prevailing connotations of progress in the liberal humanist sense. He nevertheless exposed himself to criticisms by the likes of eminent historians such as Norbert Frei and Ian Kershaw on the grounds that the effect of attributing to Hitler a modernizing 'social vision' is to marginalize the central component of his *Weltanschauung*, namely the Social Darwinist striving to create living space for the Germans and purge them of racial enemies, particularly the Jews. It also tends to relativize the heinous crimes committed by the Nazi terror state and its programmes of persecution and mass murder by metaphorically putting them in one scale to be weighed against the socio-political advantages that Nazism afforded to 'Aryan' members of the *Volksgemeinschaft* in the opposite scale, as if the one could partially compensate for or balance out the other.[64]

Such subtle perversions of the historiography of Nazism and of the moral yardsticks by which to assess its ideological objectives and achievements can be avoided if we take on board the argument put forward by the American academic Peter Fritzsche. His pointed response to Zitelmann's approach was to stress the need to 'eschew the Federal Republic as a model for assessing Nazism', and a call for historians to desist from approaching the Nazis simplistically in terms of being 'modernizers' of 'anti-modern'. He urged them instead to focus on 'the degree to which Nazism was invested in the renovative or therapeutic traditions of western civilizations', which means approaching them as '*modernists*'.[65] In substantiating this argument, one whose affinity with our own is self-evident, Fritzsche characterizes modernism as a force that 'breaks with the past, manufactures its own historical traditions, and imagines alternative futures'.[66] When this criterion is applied, the Nazis 'emerge as modernists because they made the acknowledgement of the discontinuity of history the premise of their fantastic political and racial designs'.[67] The programme of radical change they promoted thus made them widely identified, not with nostalgia for the mists of 'Aryan' time, but with 'a new national mood that emphasized national integration, social reform, and economic reform'[68] and with a radicalness that involved 'the wholesale renovation of the body of the people'.[69]

In an earlier article Fritzsche had shown how, in the hands of the Nazis, the wide-spread fears of an imminent age of air warfare directed against civilian populations were turned into a 'social myth, which described the dangerous crisis and opportune redemption of the German nation'.[70] Fritzsche saw this process as symptomatic of how Nazism constructed the ideal ethnic community in terms of 'crisis and reclamation', an example of what Claudio Fogu calls the 'historic imaginary' in action under Hitler which is not only, in our terms too, deeply modernist, but has obvious structural links with the *topos* of '*bonifica*' ('reclamation') that we saw in the last chapter served as a key metaphor in Fascist policies to bring about national rebirth. Constructing Nazism as the pursuit of an alternative modernity, or, in Osborne's terminology, an alternative temporality, rather than modernity in itself avoids using an equivocal discourse about Nazism that lends itself to revisionist interpretations. It underscores the way Nazism's attempt to create a new Germany, technocratically, economically, and militarily powerful as well as physically healthy and demographically strong, was rooted not in an Enlightenment myth of progress, but the anti-Enlightenment war against decadence.

The Third Reich was thus, like Fascist Italy and Bolshevik Russia – but unlike all other European countries such as liberal Britain or Franco's Spain – a totalitarian *modernist* state, one that based its deployment of technocratic power, its retooling of society, and its coordination of culture on a horizon resolutely fixed and framed by the myths of organic nationalism and race. Integral to the new nomos imposed by Nazism was the moral right and historical duty, not only to create a European empire through conquest, but also, as events unfolded, to commit genocide both against its racial enemies and the dysgenic members of its own population. War, persecution, and the application of Fordist principles to the enslavement and extermination of racial enemies and the mass-production of human suffering by a terror state were thus inscribed into the Nazi revolution. The resulting crimes against humanity were thus not incidental, but *integral* to Nazism's version of modernity.

Mass murder was not the primary goal of the Third Reich, but it was nonetheless the inevitable 'by-product' of what Richard Etlin called the 'perverse logic' of its war on biological and moral decadence, of the resolution to turn the rhetoric of racial palingenesis into 'political will', leading to state policies, official and unofficial, whose purpose was to redeem and purify the nation. This did not just demand a broad consensus among Nazi leaders in pivotal positions within the Reich's polycratic power structure on the allocation of the bureaucratic, military, and technocratic resources needed for systemic mass murder. It also demanded the internalization of the logic of the 'war' by enough *Nazified* Germans – but certainly not 'the Germans' – at every level of the hierarchy for the orders implementing its dictates to be carried out in many cases *proactively*. What was internalized was not necessarily 'racial hatred', but the premise that the sustained act of 'ruthless weeding' being carried out by the Third Reich in the German garden was a vital precondition for the 'progress' towards establishing the new order that was destined to supersede Western, liberal-capitalist modernity in securing the salvation of Western civilization.

The alternative modernity of the Third Reich that resulted dictated that its medical profession launched an aggressive anti-smoking campaign to save 'Aryan' lungs from cancer (though the *Sturm* brand continued to sell well),[71] while some within its ranks were keen to perform unspeakable experiments on 'subhumans', such as deliberately bursting non-Aryan lungs in order to further research into the effects of high altitude flying.[72] The new temporality that the Nazis aspired to realize was one in which the Minister of Labour could zealously promote 'the Beauty of Work' for 'Aryan' hands[73] and a healthy diet for 'Aryan' stomachs,[74] while colleagues in neighbouring ministries drew up meticulous plans for slowly starving millions to death while extracting the maximum work. In the Nazi new order the latest IBM information technology was used to track the movements and fates of its slaves.[75] The Reich's bureaucratic and executive resources were applied to institutionalizing cruelty on a scale unparalleled in history, deploying a sophisticated train network,[76] or the latest oven technology,[77] to resolve the logistical and technical problems posed by genocide.[78] This was socio-political modernism at its most radical.

THE WEIMAR REPUBLIC AS A 'STRESSED' SOCIETY

Recognizing the NSDAP's function as a modern revitalization movement also casts fresh light on its genesis and its eventual success in forming a government by highlighting the 'liminoid' conditions in which it made its assault on power. The precondition for the party's formation in the immediate aftermath of the First World War was the protracted liminality of the Second Reich which had produced Germany's luxuriant modernist aesthetic, social, and political culture and politics well before 1914 depicted so vividly by Modris Eksteins. The liminality common to all Western nations since the breakdown of feudal structures was intensified in the case of Germany by its belated unification under Bismarck in conjunction with the extraordinarily rapid process of industrialization and urbanization, following what even before 1871 had already been a dysfunctional progress to statehood and social modernization: the famous German *Sonderweg*. This created a situation in which the embryonic forces of aesthetic, philosophical, and socio-political modernism expressed in German Romanticism, German idealism, and liturgical nationalism in reaction to modernity were fuelled by a powerful surge of collective anomy in the period 1870–1914.[79] It was the generalized reaction against this protracted cultural and *ontological* crisis in national identity that turned Germany into what Eksteins calls 'the modernist nation *par excellence* of our century'.[80]

On the eve of the First World War Germany was therefore teeming with modernist energies: the deep longing for national identity expressed in ritualized patriotism[81] and *völkisch* literature and organizations,[82] the cult status achieved by Julius Langbehn and Paul Lagarde,[83] Richard Wagner,[84] and Friedrich Nietzsche, the spread of various forms of monism,[85] occultism, and neo-paganism, the rise of modern dance, the 'free body culture' movement, and movements for 'life reform', physical health and sexual emancipation,[86] the spread of youth and back-to-nature movements, the rise of politicized anti-Semitism and pan-Germanism, the emergence of various forms of scientistic modernism, especially 'racial hygiene' and eugenics, and of aesthetic modernism, notably Expressionism. In a parallel universe, the decaying Hapsburg Empire generated unique anomic conditions of its own in the two decades before its collapse in 1918, producing the pervasive mood of 'unreality' reflected in the work of Franz Kafka, Robert Musil, Hermann Broch, and the philosophy of Ludwig Wittgenstein.[87] This helps explain the rise of ultranationalism and political anti-Semitism[88] among ethnic Germans outside the Second Reich and the massive popular support that they would give to Hitler's policies to integrate them within the New Germany in the 1930s and thereby bring closure to decades of transition.

The first conspicuous explosion of populist modernist energies was the eagerness of so many hundreds of thousands of Germans to 'sacrifice themselves' in the First World War in what was widely constructed in Germany as a battle between healthy 'culture' and a decadent, soft 'civilization'.[89] The modernist dynamics of this episode of mass psychosis, what Carl Jung called a 'psychic epidemic', have already been considered in Chapter 5. Germany's subsequent defeat, the simultaneous loss of the monarchy, the Empire, and territory, the humiliating terms of the Versailles peace treaty, the threat, both real and imagined, posed by Bolshevism, and the profound socio-economic chaos that ensued, combined to intensify further the extreme liminoid conditions in which the Weimar Republic was created, fanning the flames of popular longings for national redemption and rebirth. Even more than Italy – which at least was on the winning side in the war – Germany hosted rising 'apocalyptic expectations about the end of time',[90] prompting thinkers on both left and right to 'grope for a new totality'.[91]

It is this situation of acute social abnormality and existential disorientation that Hermann Broch evokes in *The Sleepwalkers*. Though located in post-Hapsburg Vienna, the decay of values and breakdown of reality he depicts was also being lived out *en masse* in the Weimar Republic, predisposing even some naturally moderate citizens to subliminal longings for a 'Healer' who would 'begin time anew'. George Mosse adds a new element to this analysis of the particular 'mood' of Weimar after 1918 by documenting how in the wake of the defeat the cult of the war dead was appropriated by the right rather than the left. As a consequence, 'the Myth of the War Experience' that emerged spontaneously as a mechanism for transcending the horror of war, at the same time fed nationalist utopias projected onto the future *'as an alternative to the reality of postwar Germany'*.[92]

The account of Nazism's genesis given here underlines the futility of searching for the origins of 'its' ideology in any one particular thinker or movement. Its world-view does not derive principally from Paul Lagarde, Houston Stewart Chamberlain, Friedrich Nietzsche, or Richard Wagner, any more than it does from the *völkisch* movement, the Pan-Germans, political anti-Semitism, or male chauvinism. In fact, Nazism lacked a homogeneous world-view. Rather it was a broad alliance of different, and even conflicting schemes for Germany's regeneration both at the level of the leadership – as Frank-Lothar Kroll has documented – and at the level of the mass of followers. Like the Fascist state, the Nazi state accommodated, in a spirit of 'hegemonic pluralism' administered by an inner sanctum of party leaders often at loggerheads over major policy issues, any number of world-views and value systems as long as they contained a central component of 'modernist nationalism' in its German idiom. These ranged from Walter Darré's mission to reconnect modern citizens with the healing properties of the German soil, to Fritz Todt's celebration of the 'Aryan' technocratic power that created an ethos in which the Autobahn system was constructed with a wondrous blend of efficiency and style. The Nazi project was thus a far more contested and pluralistic one than the propaganda machine would admit. Again the anthropological concept of revitalization movement as conceived by Victor Turner and Anthony Wallace is illuminating here. As we have seen, it anticipates that its ideology and ritual will be created through an ongoing 'mazeway resynthesis', a process that in the context of a modern mass movement allows for many dynamically changing, kaleidoscopic combinations of past with future, and for competing visions of renewal to provide the different mobilizing myths needed by different constituencies of followers and 'believers' within the same party.

Understanding the social dynamics of revitalization movements in premodern societies also adds a new element to understanding the Nazis' conquest of power. In the first decade of its existence the new nomos offered by the NSDAP's *Weltanschauung* left most Germans cold. Though the party propaganda machine urged all those disaffected with the modernity of Weimar to channel diffuse longings for a new temporality into 'the Hitler movement', the NSDAP remained profoundly marginalized in all national elections, garnering only 2.6 per cent of the total vote in May 1928. The public mood was nationalistic, but still not revolutionary. Soon after this its fortunes dramatically changed. Ian Kershaw notes that after the Wall Street Crash Hitler's 'language of national renewal and rebirth' suddenly cast an 'intoxicating' spell on '[t]hose not firmly anchored in an alternative political ideology, social milieu, or denominational sub-culture'.[93]

Joachim Fest confirms this interpretation. He claims that conditions in Weimar created 'a general sense of disorientation that engendered a mass longing for radical change'. But it was the dramatic intensification of this sense after 1929 – when the nation's economic collapse occurred against the background of the global breakdown of capitalism and the deepening paralysis of Weimar's political system – that enabled Nazism to crystallize and channel those longings into a revolution against the liberal state. It was now that Nazism came to be looked to as a source of hope *en masse*:

> And in the distance, standing out against a depressing reality, loomed, no matter how vague in its contours, the counter-image, shrouded in the transfiguring mist rising from a cleansed world, of the New Man as well as of a closed system which, whatever its deficiencies and anomalies, promised to realise the new order.[94]

The Nazi pledge to bring about national renewal within a *post-liberal* new order was able to cast this 'spell' because the Depression had triggered not just an economic and political crisis but a *nomic* crisis, intensifying liminoid conditions in Germany to a point where millions now felt compelled to 'jump ship' from a Weimar now perceived as sinking fast. In the July 1932 elections over 50 per cent of voters opted for a revolutionary, anti-democratic party, whether of the left (the KPD) or the right (the NSDAP). In the process the Nazis won 37.3 per cent, turning the 'Bewegung' almost overnight into a powerful 'anti-structure', a revolutionary *communitas* welded together within a totalizing *Weltanschauung*, and able for the first time to mount a serious challenge for the state power it needed to erect a new sacred canopy.

THE SACRALIZATION OF POLITICS UNDER NAZISM

Another empirically documented aspect of Nazism consistent with the interpretation of the NSDAP as a modern revitalization movement is the prominent role played in its dynamics by ritual and spectacle aimed at sacralizing the entire socio-political process of national transformation and hence creating what is referred to by some historians as a 'political religion'. According to Ian Kershaw, the uniqueness of Nazism lay in 'the explosive mixture of "charismatic" politics of national salvation and the apparatus of a highly modern state'. However, he dismisses as the 'voguish revamping of an age-old notion' attempts to apply to the Third Reich the concept 'political religion', even though he himself observes that, while 'the quest for national rebirth lay, of course, at the heart of all fascist movements, [...] only in Germany did the striving for national renewal adopt such strongly pseudo-religious tones'.[95] In contrast, the present approach posits an intimate relationship between the 'redemptive nationalism' at the core of Nazi ideology, its comprehensive attempt to 'remould the German psyche and rebuild the German character' through a 'cultural revolution',[96] and the liturgical style of politics it displayed both as a revitalization movement before January 1933 and a totalitarian regime thereafter. It is a relationship that is illuminated by Emilio Gentile's theory of the synergic relationship between these elements considered in Chapter 8,[97] and our interpretation of Nazism as a form of fascism.[98]

Some of the most perceptive research into this aspect of Nazism was carried out over three decades ago by Klaus Vondung, whose investigation of the 'ideological cult' and 'political religion' of Nazism includes an exegesis of the elaborate ceremony enacted in Munich to commemorate the 'martyrs' of the failed Putsch of 9 November 1923. Citing Mircea Eliade, he argues persuasively that the rite, which combined a secular religious Cantata written by Herbert Böhme with a carefully choreographed liturgy, was deliberately designed to transfigure Munich's Feldherrnhalle into a sacred space and time, the steps of the building symbolically transformed into the 'altar' of a temple. Shaped by archetypal matrices of human consciousness, the commemoration thus became the locus for a ritual drama in which the deaths of Hitler's followers could be experienced as 'martyrdoms' vital to Germany's rebirth from decadence. Vondung comments that 'the religious symbols used in the liturgy were freed from their original context and transposed onto political events' in a way calculated to mark out 9 November 1923 as 'a historical turning point' and a 'metamorphosis of the human condition'. However, he notes that, whereas the 'Judeo-Christian apocalyptic tradition expects the *metastasis* [palingenesis] of the old world to take place through divine intervention, in modern speculation it is meant to be brought about through this-worldly human action'. Thus metaphysical immortality is replaced by 'symbolic immortality', a theologically conceived new heaven and new earth by a 'secular utopia', the immortal Christian *ecclesia* of the spiritual elect by the 'immortal *Volksgemeinschaft* of the racial elite.'[99]

Vondung's account of Nazism's 'ideological cult' thus dovetails neatly with the emphasis which our theory of modernism places on the 'temporalization of utopia' as a precondition to bids to create a new temporality, and the resulting drive to turn the fabric of history itself into the sacred canopy needed to ward off the threat of anomy, a process that involves not the aestheticization of politics but their ritualization. It is significant in this respect that he is convinced that such rites are no cynical manipulation of the masses, but stem from an essentially 'magical' view of the power of ritual to bring about social and historical renewal. Though no less sceptical than Kershaw of the value of 'political religion theory' to Nazism, Richard Evans nevertheless corroborates this line of interpretation when he writes that the Nazis 'wanted a new man, for that matter a new woman, to emerge out of the ashes of the Weimar Republic, re-creating the fighting unity and commitment of the front in the First World War'. This involved bringing about 'a change in people's spirit, their way of thinking, and their way of behaving', much of which 'was to be achieved by symbols, rituals, and rhetoric',[100] in other words by what Emilio Gentile calls the 'sacralization of politics'.

HITLER AS A MODERN *PROPHETA*

The focal point of Nazism's political religion was, of course, the Führer cult. The ceremony at the Feldherrnhalle typically portrayed Hitler as a 'messianic figure' stylized through myth and liturgy into a 'death transcending hero', able to become the redeemer of the *Volk* because, in the words of Böhme's Cantata, 'he is himself gripped by fanatical faith'. This dramatization of Hitler's charisma cannot be dismissed simply as brainwashing or a manipulative aestheticization of politics. The symbiotic relationship between believer and redeemer it implies fully corresponds to the personal testimonies of how his most fanatical followers actually experienced his presence. In the course of Kershaw's meticulous documentation of the Hitler cult as a source of 'secular salvation', he cites as typical one follower who claimed the Führer was 'the fulfilment of a mysterious longing' who 'worked a miracle of illumination and belief in a world of scepticism and despair'.[101]

The primordialist perspective on the essential modernism of such a longing suggests, however, that Hitler is not to be seen as the Messiah of a pseudo-Christian 'millenarian' religious movement[102] – nor as the embodiment of 'positive Christianity' in a sense compatible with Christianity as a revealed religion.[103] Rather, such ecstatic testimonies reflect the success with which in the course of the *Kampfzeit* (the Party's 'struggle for power'), Hitler adopted the archetypal role of the *propheta* leading a new *communitas* into the new order. Christianity conditioned the religious discourse, symbology, and ritual adopted by this movement and the way the powerful affective response to Hitler's prophetic persona was articulated, but the psycho-dynamics of his charismatic leadership were not Christian. This line of interpretation conflicts with that of both Richard Steigmann[104] and Claus-Ekkehard Bärsch who take Nazism's Christian linguistic and ritual discourse at greater face value.[105] However, it is consistent with Richard Fenn's speculations on the way fascism is born of the instinctive recourse to ceremonies of symbolic renewal when a society is gripped by the sensation of 'running out of time', a ritual response to the breakdown of reality that long predates Christianity.[106]

At this point a particular significance is assumed by Anthony Stevens' general observations in the passage of his 'Guide to the Symbols of Humankind', we referred to in Chapter 4, on 'the liminoid state of society'. Recapitulating Victor Turner's theory of how 'social anti-structures' may arise within societies in crisis to form a new one, he stresses the crucial role of the leader for the act of secession from the dying old order to be completed successfully by the embryonic new society: 'the leader has to inspire the departing group with its sense of mission and purpose, so that it can win against all the odds and find its own Promised Land'. The charismatic leaders needed to do this 'are thrown up at crucial moments in the history of all societies', many of them displaying 'a schizoid, paranoid, or schizotypal disposition'.[107] What enables them to inspire the followers to perform their collective ritual act of revolutionary *Aufbruch* is thus their 'shamanic quality'.

Stevens highlights the significance of the fact that the term 'shaman' originates in the 'Tungus noun *saman*' meaning 'one who is excited, moved, raised. As a verb it means to know in an ecstatic manner', which certainly applies to the *duce* as much as *der Führer*, and, for that matter to many of the leaders of twentieth-century totalitarian movements or states. He also stresses the intense *liminality* of the shaman's relationship to society, using language which evokes Hitler's public persona much more than Mussolini's:

> The inspired figure is always one who stands apart, completely focussed on his inner vision. This sets him on a level above ordinary humanity. He is seen to be in the liminoid state, halfway between Heaven and Earth. It means that he speaks with the conviction of higher authority, which puts his followers in awe of him.[108]

Stevens proceeds to portray Nazism as 'new religion born out of social disintegration and the compensatory emergence of a charismatic leader'. The enormous power that Hitler accumulated demonstrates 'the power of liminoid symbolism arising from the unconscious of a charismatic leader to inspire his people to collective action with incalculable consequences'.[109] It was a power that, in the context of the devastating impact the Wall Street Crash had on Weimar's economic, social, and *ontological* viability, was no longer to be confined to 'leading a subgroup', the fate of the NSDAP in the 1920s. Instead, 'he took over the host group, completely displacing the old guard'. He adds that this radicalness is not unique to Nazism but is common to all *political* movements driven by the intrinsically revolutionary vision of history's total regeneration.

Stevens concludes by drawing attention to the way the new religion travestied, parodied even, the key components of Christianity:

> Thus Nazism had its Messiah (Hitler), its Holy Book (*Mein Kampf*), its cross (the Swastika), its religious processions (the Nuremberg Rally), its ritual (the Beer Hall Putsch Remembrance Parade), its anointed elite (the SS), its hymns (the 'Horst Wessel Lied'), excommunication for heretics (the concentration camps), its devils (the Jews), its millennial promise (the Thousand-Year Reich), and its Promised Land (the East).[110]

If documentary evidence were required for Hitler's 'shamanic' style of leadership it is worth studying the scene in *The Triumph of the Will* where Rudolf Hess declares to literally 'ecstatic' cheers: 'The Party is Hitler! Hitler however is

Germany, just as Germany is Hitler!' Leni Riefenstahl's canny montage ensures that this statement of total symbiosis between a leader and his new *communitas* comes just after we have heard the Führer himself state in the last words of his closing speech to the Party Congress: 'the Movement is a living expression of our people, and therefore, a symbol of eternity'. Hitler embodied the promise of becoming *part of* a revitalization movement that would turn the nation into a source of secular immortality, of transcendence, of a new nomos, and a new community. He thus enabled millions of those who after 1929 became what Broch calls 'time's outcasts' to escape the clutches of Cronus and enter a new *aevum*. The primordialist concept of political modernism thus adds an extra explanatory and causal layer to the multi-level phenomenon familiar to historians as 'the rise of Nazism'.

GERMANY'S NEW BEGINNING

The key features of Nazism highlighted by analysing it as a modernist revitalization movement have now been established. Nazism was a form of fascism, no more or less unique than any individual variants of the species. It was a product of the intense liminoid cultural climate that arose in Germany before the First World War, and which was radicalized and 'democratized' in the aftermath of the war, and further radicalized after the Wall Street Crash. These conditions created a habitat conducive to the appearance of a number of revitalization movements, one of which, the NSDAP, hosted an alliance of unique blends of nationalism, racism, anti-Semitism, anti-Marxist socialism, technocratic and anti-urban thought harnessed to the vision of a national palingenesis within a new order. The world-views of even high-ranking Nazis diverge in detail, but converge in the project of a reborn Germany. The Party was led by a man onto whom widespread popular longings for redemption and a new sacred canopy could be projected, Adolf Hitler, who only in the exceptional conditions of crisis created by the Depression finally attracted enough popular support to be able to engineer his election to the Chancellorship with the collusion of conservatives fearful of the growing power of the left.

Within this perspective the constant stream of ritual events generated by Nazism – the Nuremberg rallies, the Nazi May Day celebrations,[111] the state funerals arranged for Nazi leaders, the open air Thing Plays,[112] the ceremonial opening of the House of German Art, or the annual Harvest Thanksgiving Festivals held in Bückeberg in Lower Saxony attended by hundreds of thousands of the rural and provincial faithful – are not to be seen merely as aestheticized politics, or forms of political liturgy cynically created to make the masses 'believe' in the regime. Instead they constitute modern examples of archaic 're-centring' and cleansing ceremonies, such as those held in premodern societies in which the *axis mundi*, the metaphysical centre of society symbolized in a cosmic tree or magic mountain – was ritually reconsecrated, thereby renewing the bond between human beings and the cosmos.[113] The recurrent obsession in Nazi culture with 'Heimat'[114] – homeland, heartland – can be interpreted in this perspective not simply as a longing for communal belonging in the sociological sense familiar from the pioneering critiques of modernity carried out by Émile Durkheim and Ferdinand Tönnies. It also stems from archaic longings for enracination and re-embedding more mythic than geographical, the longing for a primordial shelter from what Broch called in *The Sleepwalkers* modernity's 'icy hurricane'.

The heuristic value of this line of interpretation is corroborated by the extensive research carried out by Jost Hermand into the symbolic significance of the 'Third Reich' as a utopian project. In the flood of *völkisch* literature that preceded the Nazi 'seizure of power' the imminent Reich was portrayed in such tropes as 'the Heimat of the Strong', 'the Cultural Land of the New Man', 'the Beautiful Land of the Future'. It was to be 'a new and purified reality' in which the racially purged and revitalized Germans once again would become 'organic as a *Volk*, a society, and a race', bringing 'light and salvation to the world'.[115] The link between Nazism's longing for transcendence and a historicized immortality expressed in such tropes, and the NSDAP's role as a revitalization movement emerges clearly from Hitler's proclamation which was read to the Party Congress of September 1938 by the Gauleiter of Bavaria, Adolf Wagner. One passage in particular articulates clearly the inner connection between its discrete functions as a vehicle for secular transcendence, for the re-embedding of society, for national regeneration, and for the cultural and ethnic cleansing that would eventually lead to genocide:

> Perhaps in the future one may speak of a miracle that destiny worked on us. Be that as it may, at the beginning of this miracle stood belief – the belief in the eternal German nation. [...] The creative bearer of this rebirth is the National Socialist Workers Party. [...] It had to cleanse Germany of all parasites from whom the distress of the Fatherland and of the people was a source of personal enrichment. It had to recognize the eternal values of blood and soil and raise them to the level of the governing laws of our life. It had to begin to fight against the greatest enemy that threatened to destroy our people: the international Jewish world enemy. [...] Its task was to purge the German nation, our race and our culture from this enemy.[116]

It was the projection onto Hitler of this temporalized utopia of a purified society created within historical time that lay at the heart of the Hitler cult, and allowed him to assume the role of the *propheta* leading his new community through its collective rite of passage into the new world beyond decadence and decay. Thus Otto Dietrich, the Third Reich's Press Chief, declared on the occasion of the *Führer*'s birthday in April 1935 that 'Just as Adolf Hitler has raised the German people to new life in heroic struggle, so we find incorporated in his own path of life the eternal rebirth of the German nation.'[117] In another outburst of adulation one ardent fan wrote a small book entitled *The German Hitler-Spring*. It was prefaced by a piece of doggerel that Kershaw translates thus: 'Now has us the Godhead a saviour sent/ Distress its end has passed./ To gladness and joy the land gives vent/ Springtime is here at last'.[118]

This mythic springtime may reverberate with echoes of 'Christian' or 'millenarian' expectations, but it also activates a *topos* of the primordial human cosmological imagination: the longing for transcendence of *chronos*, of Cronic time. In the context of mass meetings the experience of sudden release from the terror of anomy when the Hitler cult was at its height could be overwhelming, generating primordial communal energies that are the constituents of all human culture. This can be sensed from Guido Kopp's statement that 'Hundreds of thousands experienced [Hitler's] speeches as a collective trance that put them in a whirl of expectation, satisfaction and sense of community. [...] They wanted to believe in the new beginning that was promised, in an end to economic distress, in the redemption of a humiliated nation.'[119] It is a generalization borne out by individual testimonies collected after the war. One woman recollects that, when as an 18-year-old she approached Hitler with her friends at yet another Nazi event, 'we were in a trance. We did not know what was happening to us.' Another who succumbed to 'Hitler-mania' attributed the public's susceptibility to the 'messianic image of Hitler' to the 'cosmological vacuum that prevailed in Germany'.[120] Ian Kershaw independently confirms the importance to Nazis of the *temporal* dimension of their revolution when he states '30 January 1933 was the day they had all dreamed about, the triumph of what they had fought for, *the opening of the portals to a brave new world*'.[121] Even some devout Protestants could convince themselves that 'It was as if the wing of a great turn of fate was fluttering above us. There was to be a new start.'[122]

The next chapter will explore the dialogic that arose between the archaic and the modernizing, 'cultural hegemony' and 'dominion', destruction and creation in the Nazis' attempt to transform the wilderness of Weimar's culture into an immaculately landscaped garden with all weeds removed, and all ugliness tidied away out of sight. However, the semblance of aesthetic harmony and hygiene that was contrived, for example, in the curiously inanimate blend of the Romantic and the Classical found in one school of Nazi painting was belied by the growing stench of acrid smoke in the air wafting for all who cared to see across from bonfires kept out of sight behind high walls. In the background could also be heard the dull, steady beat of a drum.

In 1922 Hitler told the conservative revolutionary Moeller van den Bruck: 'You are providing the spiritual armament needed for Germany's renewal. I am merely a drummer and a rallier.'[123] Scholars agree that in the Landsberg prison Hitler decided to change his role within the NSDAP from 'drummer for the national cause' to '*Führer*'.[124] But in making the transition he did not abandon drumming. Instead, the military drum was swapped for the shaman's drum, its rhythms forming the backbeat of a revolution still to be achieved through the force of arms, but allied to the transformative power of culture and the regenerative energies of collective trance.[125] The 'mass oaths under floodlit cupolas', 'choral singing', and 'bonfires lit on mountains' to celebrate the Nazi seizure of power on 30 January 1933 were signs that his tactic had been successful, that Hitler's promises of a new order resonated profoundly with populist longings for metamorphosis. What this meant for the transformation of German culture is the subject of the next chapter.

Figure 16   One of Albert Speer's 'Cathedrals of Light', partly inspired by the artist Paul Scheerbart who had a major impact on the modernist architectural projects of Bruno Taut.[126] It was created over the Olympic Stadium in Berlin by using some 60 searchlights. The pretext for this dramatic display of Nazism's transformative technological and cultural power was the visit of Mussolini to Germany on 28 October 1937.

10
The Modernism of Nazi Culture

When Hitler's national Socialists came to power in January of 1933, they believed they stood at the very edge of history, poised to redirect the nation to fit the grooves of an envisioned Aryan future.

Peter Fritzsche, 'Nazi Modern' (1996)[1]

Even in art, where Hitler ensured that every product of the leading modernist movements of the day was swept off the walls of German galleries and museums, the massive, muscular figures sculpted by Arno Breker and his imitators spoke not of traditional human forms, but of a new type of man, physically perfect and ready for violent action.

Richard Evans, *The Third Reich in Power* (2005)[2]

GRADUATING FROM FIN-DE-SIÈCLE VIENNA

'Vienna was and remained for me the hardest, though most thorough school of my life',[3] Hitler asserted in *Mein Kampf* as he took stock of the four years he spent there as a down-and-out on the eve of the First World War. Ian Kershaw confirms that 'the Vienna "schooling" did indeed stamp its lasting imprint on his development', stressing the way the city 'epitomized tension – social, cultural, political – that signalled the turn of an era, the death of the nineteenth century world'. The backcloth to his daily existence was one of dissolution: 'The mood of disintegration and decay, anxiety and impotence, the sense that the old order was passing, the climate of a society in crisis was unmistakable.'[4] But were a fanatical nationalism and an undying hostility to modernity, modernism, and Jews all that the young Adolf learnt from his apprenticeship there? An extreme ethnic and cultural heterogeneity thrived in the dying embers of the ancien régime in Europe where archaic tradition and hypermodernity constantly intersected, and the passing of an old order opened up unexpected vistas onto new ones. The intensely liminoid social climate that resulted made turn-of-the-century Vienna not only a cultural maelstrom, but a powerful incubator of experimentation and innovation in every sphere of cultural production. It thus became home to scores of prominent cultural and social modernists, notably Arnold Schoenberg, Otto Wagner, Adolf Loos, Josef Hoffmann, Karl Kraus, Arthur Schnitzler, Robert Musil, Gustav Klimt, Egon Schiele, Oskar Kokoschka, Otto Weininger, Sigmund Freud, and Ludwig Wittgenstein.[5] It also provided the ideal habitat for propagating, not just the political ultranationalism and anti-Semitism of Georg von Schönerer's Pan-German League, Karl Lueger's Christian Social Party, and Karl Wolf's German-Radical Party, but the Zionism of Theodor Herzl, as well as a powerful sub-culture of left-wing radicalism, all movements bent on removing the root causes of decadence in a radically new type of society; all forms of *political* modernism.[6]

As Brigitte Hamann makes clear in her *Hitler's Vienna*, the future Führer's response to the prevailing atmosphere of programmatic modernism that he encountered was not one of wholesale rejection but of selective osmosis. He virulently attacked 'Jewish modernism',[7] yet had the 'greatest admiration' for Gustav Mahler because of the 'perfection' with which he performed Wagner, despite attacks on the 'crooked-nose Mahlerians' in the anti-Semitic press.[8] (This admiration was too short-lived to protect Mahler's niece, the violinist Alma Mahler, who died in Auschwitz after her uncle's music had been banned as 'degenerate' by the Third Reich.) Paul Reitter suggests that Hitler's support for Mahler shows he 'not only learned to hate Modernism in Vienna but also learned from it', in particular from 'the Viennese Modernists' push for social redemption through art'.[9] However, this line of argument is difficult to sustain with respect to Mahler, since it was not his own music, on the cusp aesthetically between Romanticism and Modernism, but his brilliant performances of Wagner as conductor that filled the young Hitler with enthusiasm. More to the point, art was to play a subordinate role to power politics in his redemptive scheme for the Germans set forth in *Mein Kampf*.

The thesis that Hamann's book does sustain, however, is that Hitler's four years of material hardship and psychological anomy were lived out within a counter-cultural intellectual and political milieu rife with virulent cultural, political, *and racial* critiques of the existing system, expressed in fanatical certainties about which way the era should 'turn'.[10] He thus entered the profoundly radicalizing experience of the First World War, to which he was to be exposed for four long years, already seething with contempt for the decadence of 'actual existing modernity', as well as committed to the cause of national and racist renewal. A variant of modernism was thus gestating in him in which cultural, social, nationalist, racial, and political symptoms of decay merged into a single 'organic' experience of decadence whose reversal was beyond the power of any established form of party politics, whether conservative, liberal, or socialist. Regeneration thus demanded the transformation of the DAP into precisely what, as we argued in the last chapter, it became under his leadership after 1923: a political *revitalization movement* led by a *propheta* armed with a totalizing *mazeway* and committed to inaugurating a radical new temporality beyond decadence. Hamann intuits this in the conclusion she draws about the chief legacy of Hitler's time in Vienna. When he finally appeared in public, it was

> expressly not with a party programme but as the leader of a movement, as a herald of his Weltanschauung. He wanted to arouse *in the hearts* of his *supporters the holy conviction that with* his movement *political life was to be given, not to a new election slogan, but to a new philosophy of fundamental significance.*[11]

'IN THE MIND OF THE FÜHRER'

We have seen that Mussolini gravitated from the politics of revolutionary socialism towards a form of national modernism concerned with cultural renewal, but initially devoid of either the anti-Semitism or the eugenics that his own regime would eventually come to host officially. By contrast, Hitler progressively rationalized and politicized an obsession with socio-cultural and racial decay which were at least *partially* influenced by both scientistic – principally Social Darwinian – and occultist – mainly Ariosophical – notions of a historical conflict between 'Aryans' and Jews. Their incorporation within an ideology of change was nourished by a milieu that predisposed him to conceive revolution in biopolitical and cultural rather than party-political terms, but simultaneously as a mission that met his psychological need for a vague 'religious' or 'spiritual' sense of higher reality.

What perhaps encouraged the politicization of the young Hitler's sense of mission was the example set by the more radical *völkisch* thinkers active in pre-war Vienna, notably Georg Ritter von Schönerer, Karl Lueger, and Karl Wolf. But at its core resided the energy of the fin-de-siècle revolt against decadence in its most programmatic, mythic, and 'apocalyptic' varieties with which he brushed shoulders in the capital's sprawling artistic, intellectual, and political subculture which he daily frequented. In contrast to the *duce*, it was only after the war that Hitler developed a sense of being the *propheta* demanded by the new community of a disintegrating age. However, again in marked contrast to Mussolini, whose *Weltanschauung* would remain in a permanent and notorious state of flux, the basic principle of the highly syncretic 'mazeway' that would determine how Hitler fulfilled his mission had already hardened before 1914. It was a relatively coherent and stable vision of the Germans as a *Volk* territorially divided by history, betrayed by politicians, threatened by inner racial and political enemies, and demanding unification and regeneration through a total process of renewal. It assumed the nexus between society, culture, history, and race in a spirit that was not just anti-liberal but profoundly anti-humanist, a mindset utterly alien to the young Mussolini when he first felt called to 'announce a new era' in 1909.

It is thus one of the less mendacious passages in *Mein Kampf* when Hitler states in the chapter 'Years of Study and Suffering in Vienna' that 'in this period there took shape within me a world picture and a philosophy (*Weltanschauung*) which became the granite foundation of all my acts'.[12] The key principle of this nomos is revealed a few paragraphs later: 'social activity must never and on no account be directed toward humanitarian drivel, but rather toward the elimination of the basic deficiencies in the organization of our economic and cultural life.' The premise for change was 'the deepest sense of social responsibility for the creation of better foundations for our development, coupled with brutal determination in breaking down incurable tumours (*Auswüchslinge*)'.[13] In contrast to Mussolini, Hitler envisaged the regeneration of society in terms that demanded a far more radical process of 'creative destruction', a revolution conceived in the discourse of biopolitical and bio-cultural purging and as the outcome of an epic struggle between the forces of total decadence and total renewal long preceding modern times. The concept of history as a Manichaean battle between light and dark, between destruction and rebirth, 'Untergang' and 'Wiedergeburt', was to remain the constant of Hitler's world-view from his earliest rants as a new recruit to the DAP to the 'political testament' dictated to his secretary Traudl Junge the day before his suicide in the bunker.[14] It was a battle to be fought out not just in the sphere of socio-economic engineering, eugenics, re-militarization, and imperialism, but also in the sphere of culture, 'philosophy of life', and 'faith', which Hitler saw as the premise to all other aspects of human existence.[15]

We saw in Chapter 6 that one of the metaphors that came naturally to Hitler when formulating this 'struggle' against decadence was that of the gardener with the self-confidence and strength needed 'brutally and ruthlessly to prune off the wild shoots and tear out the weeds'.[16] Enthusiastic recruits to Nazism found themselves automatically enlisted in the brutal and ruthless battle to turn Germany into the perfect garden, not through blind obedience or submission to terror, but by internalizing Hitler's value-system, his *Weltanschauung*, in the process of ideological assimilation that Ian Kershaw has called, in a somewhat awkward translation, 'working towards the Führer'. The speech by Werner Willikens, State Secretary in the Prussian Agricultural Ministry, in which he came across this telling phrase, talks of striving to work always 'im Sinne des Führers', and hence in a way that is true to what he means, what he has in mind, his way of thinking, his purpose, his 'spirit'.[17] Phenomenologically, this meant not just responding passively to Hitler's charisma, but proactively partaking in his mission. This secular version of *participatio mistica* is integral to the psychological mechanisms at work in Hitler's infamous 'charisma', turning the *Volksgemeinschaft* when the leader cult was at its height in the 1930s into a 'charismatic community' of Germans spontaneously channelling their creativity and productivity into the new Reich as a *modernist* state. As one convert put it, who was 20 years old when Hitler became Chancellor:

> He radiated a charisma (*Ausstrahlung*) that *he seemed to transfer onto us*. We not only felt addressed personally, but believed that we were in the presence of someone who had to fulfil a mission that went beyond the merely political.[18]

The implications for Germany's cultural transformation of the vast process of ideological osmosis that initially took place under the Third Reich were enormous. Much scholarly activity has understandably focused on the attempt to socially engineer through coercion a new German culture from above, notably through purges of decadent art and thought, and the incorporation and coordination of all areas of cultural production through the agency of Goebbels' tentacular Reich Cultural Chambers. Less attention has been accorded to the *cultural* concomitant of the synergy between leader and followers which forms the basis of the pervasive hegemony generated by Nazism for as long as the regime appears to be fulfilling its goals. This is the spontaneous creation of art and thought which, at least in the mind of the artist and thinker, gave verbal or plastic form to what Broch called society's 'ideal centre of values',[19] embodied for millions in the Führer. 'Working towards the leader' meant assimilating the cosmology that he embodied and proactively expressing it as praxis in a way familiar to anyone who has studied a traditional charismatic religious community or movement.

Richard Etlin has made a significant contribution to understanding this 'ideal centre of values' provided by the regime by analysing the 'perverse logic of Nazi thought' as a function of its 'base-metaphors'. He suggests that the base-metaphor of Nazi myth is 'Blood and Soil', in which 'the deep psychic appeal of blood is conjoined with the base-metaphor of rootedness, whereby all that seems vital in life is considered as growing from the ground'.[20] Our investigation of fascism as a form of political modernism would suggest that this compound metaphor is, in the case of Nazi culture, bound up with two other no less fundamental ones: first, the conception of the nation or people as a living organism, not just the 'body politic' central to the Hobbesian concept of the state, but a literal bio-historical entity, the 'Volkskörper'; second, the archaic myth of palingenesis, of decay, death, and destruction as the necessary prelude to regeneration, rebirth, and renewal. A close reading of Nazi ideological texts[21] will show that they are often informed by one or other of these base-metaphors or their combination. Together they form the animating logic – the 'ideal centre of values' – of the Nazi 'new order', providing the affective power of such recurrent themes as 'national redemption', cultural and racial 'cleansing', and 'sacrifice'.

For example, this is how Dietrich Loder, destined to be a minor official under the Third Reich, explained the relationship between race and culture to readers of the *Völkischer Beobachter* four months before the 'seizure of power':

> Culture is an organism like any other. An organism that lives, grows, thrives, but which can also fall sick and needs to be healed. And modern German culture is suffering today from countless parasites. Since culture is born of the essential being of the people, from the totality of its living conditions and vital manifestations, so the whole people suffers when its culture becomes sick.

Loder then warned 'the parasites' that the anti-bodies of the German nation would soon fight off the infection, and, in a seamless shift of metaphor, that 'the vultures should start looking for a new place to wait for their prey'.[22]

Etlin himself provides a graphic illustration in the way such organic metaphors, with their lethal implications for living human beings, also structure Nazi thinking on aesthetics. He cites the rejection of the Bauhaus conception of architecture by the pro-Nazi architectural expert Karl Straub on the grounds that its asymmetrical constructions lacked 'Wurzelgefühl', a feeling of rootedness.[23] But Straub's concern with the degenerative effects of 'rootless' architectural modernism on German life also points to an organicist 'imagining' of the nation, and is indissociable from a palingenetic myth of its imminent renewal. This point is underlined by the fact that the book where Straub made these comments, *The Architecture of the Third Reich*, was published in 1932, *before* the Third Reich existed, and thus not under pressure from the state.[24] However, Etlin's exploration of the 'logic' of Nazism arguably needs supplementing in another respect, in case Straub's verdict on the International Style is taken as proof of Nazism's animus against aesthetic modernism in all its forms.

Certainly there is no shortage of powerful images or texts which indicate this animus existed, such as the pillorying of modernist paintings in the Exhibition of Degenerate Art[25] and the hysterical verbal attacks on 'modern art' and 'cultural Bolshevism' made by Hitler, Rosenberg, Goebbels, and scores of lesser 'art experts' even before the NSDAP came to power.[26] It is therefore understandable that the documentary-maker Peter Adam, who grew up in Berlin in the Hitler era, sees in Nazi culture no more than 'the artistic expression of a barbaric ideology', declaring that 'one can only look at the art of the Third Reich through the lens of Auschwitz'.[27] However, hindsight can be a particularly distorting lens in historiography, and Adam's reductionist precept obscures the complexity of the causal relationship that links the Third Reich's efforts to bring about a 'cultural revolution', to the mass crimes it committed against humanity.

Doubtless, the crimes against culture and humanity committed by the regime on such an unimaginable scale were partly driven by the vandalism of the conqueror who relishes laying waste the culture of the defeated enemy in an orgy of nihilism at least as old as the Vandals themselves. This helps explain the Nazis' wholesale pillaging and looting of Europe's cultural heritage, legitimated by the conviction that the Germans were an 'Aryan' people engaged in a war against racial inferiors incapable of true culture. Greed and vanity were also factors, for the 'rape of Europa' contained extraordinary episodes of personal corruption on the part of certain Nazi leaders, notably Hermann Goering.[28] On *one* level it was also the ritualistic and age-old iconoclasm exemplified in the Protestant crusade against 'graven images' at the height of the Reformation, and more recently in the Taliban's destruction of the two gigantic Buddhas of Bamiyan.[29]

Yet the Nazis' devastating 'war on culture' was also bound up paradoxically with the modernist logic of the Third Reich as a whole. This was directed towards establishing solid foundations for a cultural Renaissance that would flourish in defiance of the decadence spawned by a time out of joint, a flowering of creativity produced by healthy minds which would make the reborn Germany the cultural power-house of European civilization which at the last minute Hitler had saved from collapsing into cosmopolitanism and spiritual anarchy.[30] This interpretation is corroborated by the art historian Eric Michaud. He draws particular attention to the passage in *Mein Kampf* where Hitler divides humanity into three groups, 'the founders of culture, the bearers of culture, the destroyers of culture'.[31] It is a categorization that leads to the assumption that the corollary of founding a new nomos (an 'incontrovertible religion') must be the ruthless elimination of the enemy's culture:

> Christianity could not content itself with building up its own altar: it was absolutely forced to undertake the destruction of the heathen altars. Only from this fanatical intolerance could the apodictic [incontrovertible] faith take form: this intolerance is, in fact, an indispensable condition for the growth of such a faith.[32]

This Michaud takes to mean that 'destroying the culture of another people carried with it the destruction of the people themselves by suppressing its "moral right to exist"'.[33] In this reading of Hitler's text, he too has sensed the central importance that the Führer attached to the *Weltanschauung* as the basis of physical and racial existence.

THE MODERNISM OF NAZI ART

The thesis we have outlined opens up a radical perspective on the aesthetics of those works of art which the Third Reich considered 'artgemäß' as opposed to 'entartet' ('generate', racially healthy, as opposed to degenerate), and hence promoting cultural health rather than decadence. It fully accepts that the official Nazi art now so familiar to historians – whether the sinister serenity of Arcadian idylls or bucolic landscapes, the curiously de-eroticized nudes of an Aryanized neo-classicism, the statues embodying a 'muscular Germanness' pitted against a dysgenic humanity, or the Titanic proportions of civic buildings whose neo-classicism has been stripped of humanizing proportion and grace – may well represent a form of 'kitsch'[34] when Renaissance or Enlightenment criteria are applied. It certainly expresses a disdain for the ethos of 'modern art' in the form in which it has come to be celebrated by the liberal, individualistic, capitalist West for over a century, and is thus in a restricted sense indeed 'anti-modern'. However, the perspective we are exploring suggests that – leaving aside the thorny issue of establishing firm criteria for such value-judgements – all cultural artefacts sanctioned by the Nazi brand of political religion are simultaneously expressions of its fundamental socio-political modernism, and hence its *cultural* modernism, *whatever the particular school of aesthetics they employ.*

The clash between Goebbels and Rosenberg over the 'Aryan' credentials of Expressionism referred to in the last chapter is in this sense to be seen not as a conflict between modernism and anti-modernism, but as a clash over which signifier was to be attached to the aesthetics of Expressionism, 'healthy' or 'diseased', *artgemäß* or *entartet*. Even the most 'pastist', anti-modernist manifestations of Nazi aesthetics on closer inspection reveal a futural, time-defying dynamic, the will to embody a new transcendent temporality. The German historian Ulrich Schmidt intuitively recognizes this as a trait of generic fascism when he states that it was 'engaged in a constant rivalry with other forms of modernism', and produced art in which 'future and past were amalgamated into a timeless present'. This it did in tune with cultural theories that 'went back to mythological roots and wanted to reinstate these cultural models *in a radiant present which at the same time anticipated the future*'.[35] However, Peter Osborne, who has done so much pioneering work on the relationship between the rightist flank of the avant-garde, modernity, and alternative temporalities, takes the argument a stage further, once again bringing much needed conceptual lucidity to a tangled aesthetic and historical issue.

In *Philosophy in Cultural Theory* he warns against assuming there is a universal aesthetic formula for expressing the values of cultural modernism, arguing that 'an adequate theoretization of socialist modernity as a cultural-historic form' is still lacking. In fact, 'Soviet-style Socialist Realism is a far more credible candidate for the role of an inaugural modernism in Chinese painting than any extension of the formalism of its traditional visual culture'.[36] In other words, the 'realism' which in Western eyes expresses the values of anti-modernism when juxtaposed with Chagall or Picasso is, in the context of Maoism and the traditional Chinese culture it was seeking to transcend, charged with revolutionary connotations of breaking with the past. It is thus imbued with a *modernist* ethos.

By the same token, academia still lacks an adequate theoretization of fascist modernity as a cultural-historic form. By going against the grain of deeply accultured liberal responses to Nazi art, it is possible to see each artefact on display in the House of German Art in the first exhibition held there in 1937 – no matter how unoriginal, grotesque, regressive, or kitsch in 'our' eyes – as the equivalent of the equally 'inauthentic' products of heroic realism used in the 'revolutionary art' promoted by Maoism. Both the heroic postures of liberated peasants and the idealized bodies of 'Aryan' manhood (and womanhood) are tokens of a new age, acts of creation wilfully purged of 'decadent' experimentalism, self-expression, and a fanatical cult of innovation. By ruthlessly persecuting and 'rooting out' those products of aesthetic modernism identified with degenerate forms of humanity, Nazi iconoclasm asserted the regenerative power of art to bring about the new era, a profoundly modernist assertion of *iconopoesis*.

The *futural* drive to transcend the decadence of modernity is a subtext, for example, in Oskar Martin-Amorbach's *The Sower* (1937), a Nazi painting which it is tempting to identify with the longing to return to a pre-industrial world where peasants lived in harmony with the soil. Yet, not only is the farmer hand-sowing next year's crop framed by a rainbow suggesting cosmological renewal, but it originally hung in the Bayreuth House of German Education, 'where it was meant to encourage teachers to "sow" National Socialist values among the German youth'.[37] The subtext of the painting was thus not nostalgia for a mythicized past, but longing for the future Reich. Richard Evans underlines the futural aspect of 'blood-and-soil' art as a whole when he states that 'idyllic country scenes [...] spoke not of a return to a rural order mired in the hierarchical and hidebound past, but rather a new order where the peasant would be independent, prosperous and proud, delivering food that would sustain Germany in the conflicts to come'.[38] In short 'Nazism did not try to turn the clock back, for all its talk of reinstating the hierarchies and values of a mythical Germanic past'.[39]

Though the *Gleichschaltung* of Nazi culture was taken much further than it was under Mussolini, there was no one formula for the aesthetic 'objective correlative' of German rebirth. It was thus no aberration if artists with strong *aesthetic* modernist tendencies such as Emil Nolde, Ernst Barlach, Gottfried Benn, Ernst Jünger, and Hanns Johst could be attracted to the prospect of total cultural renewal promised by the Third Reich. Nor should it surprise us to find that an overtly modern ethos occasionally emanates even from the small sample of the Third Reich's cultural artefacts on which historians have based their interpretation of Nazi art to date, namely the 700 or so works of the Reichsbesitz der Kunst [Reich Art Holdings] housed, since 2002, in the Spandau depot of Berlin's German Historical Museum. This was a collection created in the immediate aftermath of the war not by cultural historians, but by US Army personnel at art collection points in Munich, Frankfurt, and Wiesbaden with the express purpose of removing National Socialist 'propaganda art' from public view. Nevertheless, it contains works which challenge deeply engrained stereotypes.

There is little that is 'nostalgic' or 'reactionary' in Nazi paintings portraying Olympic oarsmen, soldiers, bombing raids, tank assaults, motor-way bridges, or quarries. Likewise, the hundreds of samples of 'Autobahnkunst' on display at the 1936 exhibition 'The Roads of Adolf Hitler in Art' demonstrated in their different ways the symbiosis of modernity with the 'eternal' that lay at the heart of the Nazis' *alternative* modernist aesthetics in the fine arts. Nor were the artists who produced such images 'working against the Führer'. In *Hitler and the Power of Aesthetics*, the cultural historian Frederic Spotts highlights the 'sleek, even Modernist' design of Autobahn overpasses.[40] He also asserts that 'when it came to his autobahns, Hitler was a Modernist'.[41] However, he makes no link between his use of the term as an aesthetic category and the portrait of Hitler that he has painted in his book, someone 'for whom culture was not only the end to which power should aspire but also a means of achieving and keeping it'. Unwittingly evoking our primordialist and existentialist theory of modernism, he then cites Eric Gombrich's observation that Expressionism 'sprang from the fear of "that utter loneliness that would reign if art were to fail and each man [sic] were to remain immured in himself"'. He continues:

This fear was deeply felt by Hitler personally, even though he considered Expressionism the disease it sought to cure. Perceiving the anomie of twentieth-century life may have been his most precocious intuition. To replace the German feeling of defeat and isolation with self-confidence and pride was the aim he set himself and a critical element in his political appeal. Culture, which historically defined German identity in the face of disunity and ambiguous borders, played a vital role.[42]

In terms of our reflexive metanarrative, this passage highlights the fact that it was not just with respect to autobahns that Hitler was a modernist: his vision of culture, history, society, and power was also modernist, leading him towards to an 'aestheticization', or rather a *metapoliticization* of his own concept of politics that goes far beyond the creation of beguiling spectacles staged to conceal reactionary intents. His conviction that it was possible for the 'will' to triumph over defeat, for the base matter of historical reality to be melted down, purified, and recast into a new form through the power of a total *Weltan-schauung* sprang from a *modernist* diagnosis of the crisis of twentieth-century modernity.[43] There is thus a subterranean passageway linking Kandinsky's *Concerning the Spiritual in Art* to Hitler's belief that art was the source of 'the eternal, magic strength [...] to master confusion and restore a new order out of chaos',[44] just as there is a passageway linking the realm of what Kermode called the 'harmless' fictions of renewal to lethal myths of political revolution. More than even for Mussolini, a culture purged of decadence represented for Hitler the crucible for the white-hot energy that would transform Germany, a vision which after 1929 gained an enormous resonance not just within the avant-garde but within broad swathes of the German public.

AESTHETIC MODERNISM UNDER NAZISM

However, it is not just the subject matter of Nazi painting that could be overtly and uncompromisingly 'modern'. The US scholar Gregory Maertz has spent several years cataloguing some 10,000 paintings produced, exhibited, and traded quite openly under the Third Reich. They have languished in crates in the US and Germany since 1945, silent witnesses of the Nazi cataclysm whom neither government were anxious to call to the stand. Some of these canvases provide irrefutable evidence that in the hands of many hundreds of Nazi or Nazified painters an intensely *aesthetic* modernism continued to be practised uncompromisingly – at least as far as painterly style and technique were concerned – till the very end. Maertz's stupendous discoveries promise, if not a 'new era', then at least a highly productive phase in the cultural history of the Third Reich, one in which it will in all likelihood become common sense to acknowledge a hitherto unsuspected continuity between the explosion of aesthetic modernism under Weimar and Nazi cultural production even at a formal stylistic level. Contrary to what had been assumed, not all aesthetic modernism was removed from the public domain, only artefacts with a 'decadent' subject matter or excessively distorted, or unintelligible formal qualities that smacked of the pathological.[45]

Once the process of re-evaluation is complete, historians may cease to be surprised by the Expressionist use of colour in this depiction of the 'Mountain of Redemption' (see Figure 17), or by or the elements of Japanese art and Turneresque technique discernible in this remarkable evocation of Mount Olympus being enveloped by a rainstorm (Figure 18).

Figure 17 One of approximately 10,000 paintings openly produced, exhibited, bought and sold under the Third Reich, but which until recently remained unavailable to art and cultural historians researching Nazi culture. Ulrich Ertl, 'Erlöserberg' [Mountain of Redemption], watercolour and chalk on paper. My thanks go to Gregory Maertz for generously ceding me the permission to use his original photos of this painting.

Staffel der bildenden Künstlern, German War Art Collection, Deutsches Historisches Museum, Berlin (Munich number 50873, Gilkey number 2111). The ambiguities surrounding the legal ownership and copyright issues relating to this painting remain unresolved at the time of going to press.

Figure 18 Another 'lost' Nazi painting held by the Deutches Historiches Museum. 'Der Olymp im Regen' [Mount Olympus in Rain], signed Otto Meister, 1943, watercolour on paper. My thanks go to Gregory Maertz for generously ceding me the permission to use his original photos of this painting.

Staffel der bildenden Künstlern, German War Art Collection, Deutsches Historisches Museum, Berlin (Munich number 51315, Gilkey number 4588). The ambiguities surrounding the legal ownership and copyright issues relating to this painting remain unresolved at the time of going to press.

A MODERNIST CLASSICISM

Once Nazi aesthetics are re-imagined along these radical lines, the links between apparently anti-modern Nazi art and contemporary forms of social modernism are thrown into relief. In particular, the Third Reich's official promotion of neo-classicism after 1935 as one of the acceptable aesthetics in which painters and sculptors can be seen as anything but a flight from modernity. Instead, the de-eroticized, athletic nudes that gaze beyond the onlooker to a distant horizon in allegories, portraits, heroic poses, or sporting scenes invoke classicism as the repository of the 'eternal' values of the culture-creating 'Aryan'. They are also redolent of the cult of health, wholeness, and reconnection with nature that informed such currents of social modernism of the early twentieth century as the naturism of the 'Free Body Culture' movement,[46] the growing international passion for athleticism and spectator sport, the modern dance movement, the 'back-to-nature' and 'life reform movement', the cult of the body,[47] the youth movement, philosophical, literary, and scientist forms of vitalism, monism, eugenics, and racial hygiene.[48]

Hitler's insistence that every work of art should look 'completed' and that sculpture should have 'clean' lines and avoid distorting human perspective – except in the scale on which it was reproduced – is an aspect of what we saw Francis Saunders call the imperative 'to clean up, to sterilize, to re-order, to eliminate chaos and dirt'[49] that is both an integral part of modernism, social and aesthetic, and essential to the psychodynamics of the gardening state. In this respect Leni Riefenstahl's two-part documentary of the 1936 Berlin Olympics, *Olympiade* (1938), or the 'Aryan' colossi that formed Josef Thorak's project for a 'Monument to Work' (see Figure 19) designed to rise up from the central reservation of the motorway near Salzburg[50] are both outstanding examples of Nazi aesthetic modernism, exhibiting the link between classicism, body culture, and eugenics within the Nazis' project for an 'Aryan' anthropological revolution.

A similar picture emerges when we consider Nazi building projects, widely treated as the paradigm of architectural anti-modernism.[51] Yet in his study of the Nazis' building schemes for Berlin Ian Boyd Whyte warns against reading their predilection for a monumentalizing Graeco-Roman style in civic architecture and public spaces solely in terms of the celebration of 'Aryan' creativity and racial purity promoted in the regime's own propaganda.[52] He argues that it also carries the semiotic connotations of the widespread use of 'stripped neoclassicism' in the inter-war period as an emblem of modern state authority, not just in Fascist Italy or Communist Russia but throughout the 'liberal world'. Those still tempted, like Peter Adam, to dismiss Nazi classicism, along with all other products of Nazi culture, as 'the expression of a barbaric

Figure 19   Maquette of the colossal sculpture 'Denkmal der Arbeit' [Monument to Work] that Josef Thorak designed to grace the central reservation of the newly built motorway near his birth place, Salzburg.

Source: Nazi art magazine, *Die Kunst im Dritten Reich* (1938).

ideology'[53] would also do well to consider Brandon Taylor's observation that the symmetrical use of massive blocks of polished stone under Nazism evoked not an 'Aryan' past, but the supposedly 'eternal' qualities of smoothness, geometry, and proportion, central features of international modernism. In the Nazified mindset all these properties were symbols of the health of the reborn organic society that produced them, and hence can be seen as inextricably bound up with the modernism, both social and aesthetic, expressed in the striving to overcome the amorphous, anomic, dysgenic qualities of contemporary culture and create a sense of eternity.[54] Hitler was thus expressing one of the core principles of Nazi *modernism* when at the opening of the House of German Art, referred to in Chapter 1, he explained the significance of Troost's design now widely identified with the conservatism and regressiveness of Nazi culture. He claimed it represented a major step towards the 'cultural cleansing of the life of the *Volk*', 'a turning point, the first new building to take its place in the ranks of the immortal creations of our German artistic life'. It was a work of art created not for the artist, but for the people, a building marking the symbolic end of the age of cultural Bolshevism, and betokening the start of a cultural renaissance.[55]

The variety of formal qualities used in Nazi building also challenges widely held preconceptions. The 'Modern Style' was not condemned as such except for civic buildings. It was widely used in large housing estates, factories, and power-stations, while an updated version of vernacular German architecture was common in rural contexts.[56] Paul Bonatz showed considerable flair in using an uncompromisingly modern aesthetic in the design of the suspension bridge built over the Rhine between Cologne and Rodenkirche as part of his search for a 'contemporary monumental style'.[57] The 'International Style', albeit in an oppressively dehumanizing version, was also employed in the two-and-a-half mile long apartment block constructed to accommodate 20,000 post-war 'Aryan' holiday-makers at Prora on the Baltic island of Rügen. It was built under the auspices of Strength through Joy, the typical mass organization spawned by a 'gardening state' to resolve the problem posed by leisure in the age of the ('Aryan') working masses. Whyte casts light on the background to such projects when he refers to the tussle between the visceral rejection of aesthetic modernism within *völkisch* groups and the modified aesthetic modernism enthusiastically espoused by the technocratic faction led by Robert Ley, Fritz Todt, and Albert Speer. These, he claims, nurtured 'visions of a Modernist National Socialist state almost American in its commitment to technology and industrial rationalization'. Hitler occupied a 'necessarily ambiguous' middle-ground, giving some 'encouragement to both groups, but identified solely with neither'.[58] Despite lambasting modern buildings in *Mein Kampf*, he was even capable of wooing Germany's most progressive architects on occasion with such surprising pronouncements as: 'The development from now on takes place deploying new building materials, such as steel, iron, glass, and concrete, and is necessarily shaped by the purposes of the construction and the properties of the materials used.'[59]

The fact that Hitler welcomed technocrats into his entourage helps resolve into a simple paradox one of the apparent contradictions of fascism's relationship to modernism encountered in Chapter 1. Within months of taking power the regime closed down the Bauhaus, which it saw as a hotbed of 'cultural Bolshevism'. Yet, as we saw in Chapter 1, the same year the authorities short-listed competition entries by both Walter Gropius, the Bauhaus' founder and Mies van der Rohe, its former director. This was no blip. They were both encouraged to contribute to the 1934 'German Volk, German Work' exhibition, and Mies went on to have a hand in designing service stations for the new Autobahn network. Such paradoxes evaporate altogether in the light of Werner Durth's essay on Nazi architecture and town planning. This shows how the Nazis 'attempted to exploit to their own ends many of the scientific and artistic, formal and material innovations of modern architecture and urban planning'. They did so wherever they could be used 'one-dimensionally for technical processes of modernization, but without reference to the political, social, and cultural intentions that had been associated with them before'.[60]

By the same token, van der Rohe's willingness to stay on in the hope of winning some major contracts from the very regime that had closed down his institute was symptomatic of reciprocity between the regime and the nation's creative elite that went well beyond the sphere of architecture. As Durth explains: 'In the expectation that the demands for an "art of blood and soil" and a *völkisch* architectural climate would die down in the context of the new tasks the government faced, and hence open the way to an uncompromising development of the technical possibilities offered by modern architecture and town planning, many of the denounced representatives of the cultural avant-garde even supported Nazism.'[61]

This mindset helps explain why van der Rohe was a signatory of the 'Declaration of the Creators of Culture' published on 18 August 1934 in the *Völkischer Beobachter*, an oath of loyalty to the Führer also signed by Ernst Barlach and several lesser figures. In fact, a number of Bauhaus architects went on to hold important positions within the Nazi state, notably Hanns Dustmann, Gropius' office manager till 1933, who was promoted to Reichs-architeckt of the Hitler Youth and planned a nationwide network of Youth and Leisure Centres, and Ernst Neufert, a colleague of Gropius, who became one of Speer's adjutants. It was only in 1938, after the official climate had turned decidedly hostile for architectural innovation and both racial persecution and international conflict were in the air, that van der Rohe migrated to the United States to re-launch himself on a career that paradoxically turned his skyscrapers into icons of modern architecture in the Free World,[62] the conqueror of 'barbaric' Nazism.

However, to focus on the persistence of elements of the 'Modern Movement' in Nazi architecture as evidence of its debt to modernism is to miss the point. As in the case of painting, closer inspection reveals that even the most seemingly anti-modern building fantasies of the Third Reich yield a futural, palingenetic dimension disclosed by a primordialist definition of modernism. This is clear from Eric Michaud's analysis of 'The Law of the Monumental' formulated by one the Third Reich's many cultural pundits, Friedrich Tamms. It dictated that the architecture of the new national community 'must have within it the measure "of what touches the heavens"', go 'beyond human scale', and be built 'as if it were for eternity'.[63] Michaud shows that the 'Law' implied a leap towards an imaginary space of temporalized transcendence beyond the reach of Cronus, thereby signifying a radical change in the conventional function of the monument. It is metamorphosized into the symbol of 'a messiah for an impatient community, the heralded new man who came when summoned to liberate the community from time, who came to put an end to its waiting'. The temples associated with the remains of the 'November martyrs', and the chain of necropolises for dead Nazi soldiers planned by the architect Wilhelm Kreis to stretch 'from the Urals to the Atlantic and from Norway to Greece' had no commemorative function in the conventional sense. They were to act as temporal 'accelerators', tools of social engineering meant 'to propel the German people to its common destiny' which could only be lived out in a mythic future.[64] In this sense they gave a sinister meaning to Franz Kafka's cryptic observation that 'Art is a mirror which goes fast, like a watch, sometimes.'[65]

THE MODERNISM OF NAZI MUSIC

Given the outstanding contribution made by German music to the classical tradition in Europe since the Baroque, and its highly public, communal nature as a form of cultural production, music was of immense practical and symbolic significance to the Third Reich as the expression of Nordic creativity and racial health. Indeed 'Aryan' musicians thrived under the Third Reich, with a constant flow of performances of acceptable classical and popular music in theatres, churches, festivals, rallies, and on the radio, not to mention the countless musical events sponsored by Ley's German Work Front (DAF) and the Hitler Youth, or the 170 new operas and many more symphonic works to be premièred.

Prevailing stereotypes are confirmed by the fact that the Reich's crusade against cultural Bolshevism in this area led to the censorship of the 'spiritless', 'unnatural' experimentalism epitomized in atonal music, and the attempted purge of both the music industry and the classical repertoire of 'Jewishness', whether genetic or aesthetic. It also brought about the removal of left-wing composers, critics, and conductors, and the enforced 'incorporation' of all musical artists, performers, and producers within Goebbels' Reich Music Chamber, a move which inhibited genuine creativity and effectively imposed over a decade of cultural isolation from European developments. Predictably, full-blown New Orleans Jazz was also placed on the Nazi Index and broadcasting it became illegal in 1935. Accordingly Jazz was pilloried in the 'Degenerate Music Exhibition' of 1938 as epitomizing the anti-culture and anti-civilization of Blacks, who, like the Jews and Gypsies, were regarded as a rootless, dysgenic, and congenitally uncreative people. Towards the end of the war the Gestapo persecuted members of the 'Swing youth' movement who defiantly perpetuated a residue of Germany's flourishing pre-Nazi Jazz scene and risked deportation to a concentration camp in order to listen to and dance to Allied broadcasts of 'genuine' American Swing and Jazz. This was an act considered treasonable in the context of the Anglo-American onslaught on Germany.[66]

Yet, as with painting and architecture, the issue of musical modernity under Hitler is more complex than generally assumed. The musicological problems of defining 'Jewish' and distinguishing healthy innovation from degenerate experimentation, compounded by genuine differences of musical taste between leaders and experts alike, meant that '[c]ontrary to conventional interpretations of the nature and function of totalitarian dictatorship, German musicians in the Nazi era had a surprising degree of latitude in the creation and performance of their works'.[67] This allowed an undercurrent of aesthetic modernism not only to survive under the Nazis, but occasionally to break the surface in a number of successful public performances of music that could only incur disgust among those in the Rosenberg's NS-Kulturgemeinde [Cultural Community]. Highlights of experimentalism under the noses of the Reich's cultural censors were Paul von Klenau and Winifried Zillig's experiments in serial techniques inspired by the exiled 'Jew', Arnold Schoenberg; Paul Hindemith's opera on the life of Matthias Grünewald, an Expressionist icon, in 1934; Karl Orff's first performance of *Carmina Burana* in 1937, a piece unmistakably influenced by Stravinsky; and in 1938, Werner Egk's opera *Peer Gynt*, whose modernist elements so appropriate to a drama by Henrik Ibsen aroused a furore; apparently it was spared because Hitler personally liked it. The NS-Kulturgemeinde also sponsored Ludwig Maurick's attempt to create a modern Nazi form of *Gemeinschaftsoper* [community opera] in *The Homecoming of Jörg Tilman*. Though a resounding flop at the box-office, the initiative indicates a genuine desire in some quarters to create a healthy *Nazi* modernism in opera to supplant the decadent 'Western'/American one.[68]

It is also symptomatic of the confused situation of Nazism's relationship to musical modernism that in the first years of the regime foreign innovators such as Béla Bartók and Stravinsky were still performed. The case of Richard Strauss blurs the picture even further. As one of the world's most famous pioneers of musical modernism in the classical tradition, both his appointment by Goebbels as president of the Reich Music Chamber and his acceptance of it were not exactly 'on the cards'. Normal service resumed soon enough when he was forced to resign for refusing to remove from the handbill of his new comic opera *Die schweigsame Frau* the name of the liberal Jewish writer Stefan Zweig, whose novel formed the basis of the libretto. The opera was banned in 1935. Nevertheless, before he withdrew into 'inner emigration', Strauss was still allowed to produce another opera *Friedenstag* [Day of Peace], a thinly veiled pacifist critique of Nazi militarism and the cult of war.

The Nazi ban on Jazz does not tell the whole story either. As everywhere else in the modern West, from the mid-1930s, when the craze for dancing the Lindy Hop and the Jitterbug took off among the young, there was an insatiable public appetite in Germany's night-life for Swing, a big-band variant of Jazz synonymous with dance-halls, night-clubs, variety shows, and light entertainment. Despite its American origins and the conspicuous role played in its performance abroad by Black and Jewish performers, Swing's limited room for improvisation and the upbeat mood of 'Lebensfreude' it generated made it acceptable to the Goebbels faction within the Third Reich, which recognized the need of the 'Aryan' masses to be entertained in their increasingly rare leisure moments. This explains the use of Swing in the soundtrack of some Nazi films, why major foreign Swing bands like Jack Hylton and his Orchestra were performing to rapturous receptions right up to the war, and why a – by Nazi standards – 'wild' Jazz-scene continued to flourish under the cover provided by Swing in war-time Hamburg, its dedicated aficionados even arranging for one of the hottest bands from Holland to play a season in the Alsterpavillon till the Gestapo intervened.

Just as some Germans experienced no conflict between their Christian faith and their commitment to Hitler – whose 'positive Christianity' made a mockery of everything that Christ's sacrifice on the cross stood for[69] – some Germans managed to reconcile their love of Jazz with their loyalty to the Third Reich. A notable example in this paradoxical phenomenon was provided by Luftwaffe Oberleutnant Dietrich 'Doktor Jazz' Schulz-Köhn, Germany's foremost Jazz impresario before 1933. His passion for this taboo art-form was undimmed by his conversion to Nazism. During the war he circulated clandestine Jazz briefings ('Mitteilungen'), and in late 1942 was photographed in full uniform standing outside the famous Parisian Jazz-venue, La Cigale, together with six Swing musicians: four negroes, a Jew, and the Gypsy guitarist Django Reinhardt, all officially embodiments of racial degeneracy.[70]

Yet merely listing such tensions between official policy and practice is to stay on the surface of Nazism's musical modernism. Michael Kater himself reminds us that '[s]ince the Nazis conceived of themselves as political, social, and cultural revolutionaries, they expected changes, not to say revolutions, to take place in the arts in conformity with all the other changes they might cause'.[71] The attempt to purge German music of what Hitler called 'tumorous excrescences' should not prevent us from recognizing the futural, culture-renewing thrust of their attitude to music as a communal source of 'artgemäß', 'racially correct', sublimity. Nor should we overlook the central importance which the regime attached to the arts in general as the life-blood of a culture-creating people, and not just something associated with entertainment, leisure, money, or an ethereal, 'unrooted' sense of the beautiful. It was in this spirit that the Third Reich was prepared to enlist into the service of its cultural renaissance all music, past and present, that could be deemed compatible with its project of renewal. No wonder so many established composers, players, conductors, music critics, and musicologists[72] felt able to continue their business under the new management, even figures of the talent of Richard Strauss, Paul Graener, Gustav Havemann, Wilhelm Furtwängler, and Peter Raabe. After all, the Third Reich promised to accord the German artist a more central role in the communal and national life than Weimar ever could.

In this context the equation of cult Wagnerian music sponsored by Hitler himself with reactionary *anti*-modernism is surely long overdue for revision.[73] We have already seen that in fin-de-siècle Europe Wagnerism was widely identified with movements of anti-decadence and social revitalization such as Nietzscheanism, Freudianism, and Monism. Thus when Nordau sought to persuade his readers in *Degeneration* that Wagnerism was Germany's contribution to the 'modern mysticism' which he equated with modern decadence, he was indirectly paying tribute to its essential *modernism*.[74] This lay in its systematic bid to use the combined power of myth and art to regenerate a Germany being ravaged by the forces of disenchantment and re-centre a spiritually deracinated society. It was this *anti-decadent* aspect of Wagner that caused the archetypal cultural modernist, Nietzsche – also rejected as degenerate by Nordau, this time for his 'egomania', and also subject of an official Nazi cult – to write a paean to the redemptive power of Wagnerian operas in *The Birth of Tragedy*.

Robert Gooding-Williams shows how the early Nietzsche saw in them the expression of 'the Dionysian "root" and essence of the German spirit', their performance at Bayreuth marking 'that spirit's "return to itself" through the purifying power of myth'.[75] Even in his pointed retraction of his earlier position in *The Case of Wagner* (1888), Nietzsche could write: 'Wagner sums up modernity. There is no way out, one must first become a Wagnerian.'[76] It is consistent with this that the musicologist Walter Frisch treats Wagner as 'the most important figure' of German modernism in music in the last quarter of the nineteenth century. His operas were seen by contemporaries 'as advanced in technique and expression', providing 'the acknowledged inspiration for countless works recognized and perceived as "modern" at the time'.[77]

However, Frisch qualifies this assertion by arguing that Wagner embodies the way the modernism that emerged in the Second Reich 'took on a particular profile, a *Sonderweg* or special path' that made it 'ambivalent in admiring and fostering the new, at the same time as clinging fervently to the past out of a sense that the past (especially the German past) was an essential part of the German character that could not be abandoned'.[78] According to our ideal type he has put his finger precisely on the pulse of the *futural* relationship to the past which is the *norm* of all cultural modernism: the radically '*anti-pastist*' neophilia of the Italian and Russian futurists, of Wyndham Lewis, or of Ernst Jünger was the exception rather than the rule.

What Frisch terms 'ambivalent modernism'[79] is thus modernism *tout court*! This point is underscored when he accepts Kevin Repp's thesis that the wholesale rejection of *die Moderne* by artists and thinkers such as Richard Wagner and Paul Lagarde in the late nineteenth century was not anti-modernism as such. Instead, it is to be seen as integral to the search for 'alternative modernities' as a solution to the perceived decadence of the '*Gründerzeit*' when the newly unified Germany was hit by the full force of modernization.[80] It was not Wagner's aestheticization of *völkisch* nationalism or his anti-Semitism that explains his extraordinary impact on early European modernism,[81] particularly in France and Russia.[82] Rather it was his aspiration towards a 'total' synthesis of all the arts, fusing classical with modern elements of tonality, aestheticism with programmatic aspirations towards social and national renewal, to bring different elements together within a world-view saturated with nostalgia for *Heimat*, for community, for roots, and reveal a primordial German past as the basis of the new nomos.

Operas such as *Tristan and Isolde* summoned the products of a disenchanted modern society to engage once more with the archetypal forces of *eros* and *thanatos*[83] being explored by his contemporary Sigmund Freud, who by no coincidence also became the focus for a modernist cult of social renewal. As one cultural historian puts it, 'Wagner's legacy to modernism was above all a new way of understanding myth, which was regarded no longer as "mythology", [...] but as a way of explaining reality' – and, I would add, not just explaining reality but *revitalizing* it.[84] His description of myth in *Opera and Drama* (1851) as the 'concentrated image of reality' anticipates the concept of myth as a set of mobilizing images developed subsequently by the social modernist Georges Sorel. It also points to a deep but neglected kinship between Wagner and Igor Stravinksy, whose modernist credentials as the composer of *The Rite of Spring* are never questioned by historians even though the piece evokes the dark primordial forces of natural awakenings and ritual sacrifice in a spirit akin to the Wagnerian *imaginaire*.[85]

Wagner thus lent himself to being canonized by the Third Reich. Similarly, all the German composers welcomed into the Nazi repertoire, whatever their ethics or politics, were also given a 'spin' to coordinate them with qualities deemed essential to the national reawakening, whether it was Bach's 'Faustian drive to create' or the 'rootedness' of Schubert's Lieder[86] – some of the most famous of which had actually been written by the 'rootless' Jew, Heinrich Heine. Whatever the original artists might have thought of it, large sections of the vast back catalogue of classical German music were appropriated in the Third Reich's equivalent of 'hegemonic pluralism' and recoded to become exemplars of the organic, healthy, community-building qualities of 'Aryan' creativity in recording studios and concert halls. This cultural heritage was augmented by the work of an impressive number of living German composers and performers who were enlisted with varying degrees of enthusiasm or reluctance to make music for the new Germany. Meanwhile, in some extermination camps some non-'Aryan' musicians were permitted to suffer a little longer in a human hell because their professional skills served to take the torturers' mind off their work, or to distract the tortured for a few moments from their fate.[87] The title of the piece written and performed by the modernist musician Olivier Messiaen in Stalag VIIIA, bore the pregnant title 'Quartet for the End of Time'.

RACIALLY ACCEPTABLE LITERATURE AND DANCE

The complex process of music's Nazification has some parallels with the *Gleichschaltung* of German literature. Here too the goal in theory was to restore the 'organic' relationship between artists and the *Volksgemeinschaft* which made their work creative, vitalistic expressions of the eternal 'Aryan' nomos, rather than pathological symptoms of the agonies and ecstasies of atomized 'modern man'. By 1937 Helmut Langenbucher felt able to report in his introduction to an anthology of 'national' (*volkhaft*) literature that the task of 'cleansing German cultural life from all distortions alien to its racial essence (*artfremd*) was complete': the political revolution of 1933 had 'created in the sphere of literary life those lucid, healthy relationships which alone make it possible for the work of everyone active in the creation or mediation of art to be meaningful'.[88]

What this meant in reality was that the bulk of the rich treasure store of German literature from Middle High German through to the late nineteenth century could be read as before, but purged of 'Jewishness' and available in editions which emphasized allegedly Aryan qualities or the emergence of the national identity promoted by the regime. The rich canonical literature of German Classicism and Romanticism lent itself to this purpose practically intact. As for 'modern literature', the public burning of 'un-German' fiction and non-fiction orchestrated by Goebbels in May 1933 had issued a stark warning to any writer tempted to produce something whose form or contents was open to the charge of undermining the values of the new 'national community'. *Völkisch* novels and poetry, some of it of execrable mediocrity judged by non-nationalist criteria, enjoyed an only partially artificial boom, while all new fiction, both 'native' and foreign, was subject to special scrutiny for signs of decadence before publication. In any case, nearly all the most prominent liberal, communist, and Jewish writers were now in exile, their works inaccessible in their homeland: the German and Jewish Intellectual

Émigré Collection established in 1976 at the University at Albany in New York provides a record of just a fraction of the vast cultural resources that had haemorrhaged from Germany as a result of Nazi policies.[89] The handful of genuinely gifted writers sympathetic to the regime remaining, who included Gottfried Benn and Ernst Jünger, had been forced into inner emigration by the outbreak of war.[90] Perhaps in literature more than in any other cultural sphere the modernist *élan* of German culture had been effectively crushed in line with the stereotypes of a totalitarian society.[91]

In the theatre,[92] there unfolded another convoluted drama of cultural cleansing, the 'corporatization' of all dramatic and theatrical creativity, and the semiotic recoding of 'healthy' plays, ripped from their original cultural context and re-sited within the 'immortality' of the new Germany. The insidious way artists of considerable talent could be lured into collaboration with this process was brilliantly explored in the 1936 novel *Mephisto*,[93] written by Thomas Mann's son, Klaus Mann, based on the life of his brother-in-law, the outstanding theatre actor of the day, Gustaf Grundgens. Nor was the Nazi theatre simply a matter of crude *Gleichschaltung*. A revealing case study in the way the aesthetic theories of a dramatist could put him on a 'collusion course' with Nazism is offered by Hanns Johst, who experimented in both non-naturalist and naturalist techniques to articulate his vision of the 'new man' whom he clothed first in Expressionist, then in *völkisch*, and finally in Nazi garb.

It was Johst who dramatized the 'martyrdom' of a young Nazi in *Schlageter* (1933) which bequeathed the quote misattributed to Goebbels about reaching for a revolver at the word 'culture'. As president of the Reich Chamber for Literature from 1935 to 1945, he oversaw the purging of the nation's literary canon and launched initiatives to promote healthy art. That this was not simply an act of opportunism is clear from the theory of drama he was expounding in 1928, when Nazism was still a marginalized political force. Four years before he joined the NSDAP Johst postulated the existential function of drama as providing 'the last refuge for an unprejudiced, elementary, living community', by inducing a 'primitive psychic state' that has regained a 'fundamental significance today'. It was thus theatre's role to put modern Germans once more 'into contact with a *Weltanschauung*, with the metaphysical substance of the world'.[94] Here again, we are not dealing with 'ambivalent modernism', but an unambiguously *futural* modernism or 'reconnection forwards' driven by the need to transcend Cronus, a drive which in Johst's case can be traced back to his formative phase as the writer of the Expressionist drama *The Young Man: An Ecstatic Scenario*[95] at the height of the First World War. Nor was Johst a voice crying in the wilderness in calling for a 'rooted', communal theatre.

Even before 1933, the longing in some *völkisch* circles for a 'transformative' drama able to infuse the national community with primordial mythopoeic energies had given rise to the *Thingspiel*.[96] This was an experimental drama whose main protagonist was not an individual character but the *Sprechchor* [speaking choir], whose liturgical and choreographic qualities aimed to engender a collective experience of catharsis by enacting the possibility of individual redemption through subordination to the higher destiny of the *Volk*. It was a conception of drama that deliberately marked a radical break with the traditions of the bourgeois theatre and with the classics of Goethe and Schiller. In a typical act of modernist syncretism it managed to be both ancient and futuristic simultaneously, drawing on a variety of influences: Richard Wagner, Expressionism, callisthenics, the supposed lineage of 'Aryan' Germans from Graeco-Roman ancestors, the spectacles and ceremonies of Nazism's political religion. It even contained echoes of Nietzsche's impassioned call for the reawakening of myth in *The Birth of Tragedy*.[97]

The *Thing* movement also has tantalizing parallels with contemporary attempts to create a mass theatre in Fascist Italy which, as we saw in Chapter 7, culminated in the performance of the 'truck drama' *18 BL* on a vast site outside Florence. Until 1935, when the movement fell victim to the strident hostility to aesthetic modernism whipped up by the Rosenberg camp, a number of elaborate experiments in staging the *Thingspiel* were held in specially adapted open-air auditoria or constructed 'sacred sites' in natural settings throughout Germany. Despite their minimal appeal to the public, they provide an outstanding example of the seriousness with which some convinced Nazis took the search for an *alternative* modernist aesthetic in drama, one in which the impulse to go back to the mythic origins in order to go forward is particularly apparent.

In other areas of Nazi culture the futural ethos of modernism was even more pronounced, at least till the outbreak of war. Predictably, the Reich's cultural authorities initially promoted folk-dancing, generally performed with clinical but joyless precision. When this failed to capture the popular imagination – though only after some soul-searching – the waltz was declared an authentic German dance, and even the tango was tolerated as long as it was executed without any hint of eroticism. To prevent the waltz from being tarred with the brush of Cultural Bolshevism, Johann Strauss' birth certificate in St Stephen's Cathedral in Vienna was falsified by the *Reichssippenamt* (Reich Office of Genealogy) in Berlin to airbrush out the embarrassing fact that his father was a Jew.[98] It was at a time when cultural censorship had been relaxed to make the Olympic Games a show-case for the Third Reich, a move that had the unintended consequence that the cult of Swing dance hit Nazi Germany with full force.

The response of the authorities to the passion of the young for Swing was to domesticate it to the point where it became a harmless outlet for youthful exuberance, associated not with the excesses of the 'decadent' Jazz scene, but with the vitalism and *Lebensfreude* to be enjoyed by all healthy 'Aryans' out to have fun. However, from 1940 a series of decrees issued by the Ministry of Propaganda effectively prohibited any form of exuberant dancing as a legal form of entertainment, thereby turning even restrained Swing dance into a form of resistance, let alone the wild goings-on at Hamburg's Alsterpavillon. After that a Cromwellian Puritanism reigned once more, while fun was driven underground.[99]

It was in the realm of Modern Dance – another influence on the *Thingspiel* – that we again see the readiness of the arbiters and watchdogs of Nazi culture to assimilate any form of modernism that could become a signifier of moral and racial regeneration. As we saw in Chapter 5, the international Modern Dance movement pioneered by such figures as Isadora Duncan, Emil Jaques-Dalcroze, Rudolf von Laban, and Mary Wigman in the first decades of the twentieth century, manifested deeply modernist longings to reconnect modern humanity with nature, the body, and primordial experiential truths. It had thrived in Wilhelmine and Weimar Germany in the form of 'Expressive Dance', and was looked on benignly by modernizing factions within Nazi cultural politics as an acceptable form of aesthetics, both 'Aryan' and German, the kinetic equivalent of classicism in sculpture. Certainly, it was a far cry from the decadent eroticism of the dances of urban night-life.

Many practitioners of the far-flung New Dance community in Germany responded by enthusiastically placing their art in the service of the new regime. The sustained collusion this led to was epitomized in the career of Rudolf Laban, the supreme modernist choreographer of the inter-war years. Already ballet director of the Berlin State Opera when the Nazis came to power, he convinced himself the new regime could be persuaded to make 'Expression Dance' the vehicle of cultural rebirth, and zealously set about 'Aryanizing' his ballet school. The high-point of the Nazification of modernist dance in this period was the collaboration between Laban and Wigman, his former student at Mount Verity, whose school, opened in 1920, had earned Dresden the reputation of 'City of Dance'. The pair became responsible not only for choreographing the lavish dance spectacles at the Berlin Olympics (subsequently filmed for *Olympiade* by Riefenstahl), but for organizing an international dance competition to run parallel to the sporting competition. The festival dance *Olympic Youth*, which formed part of the opening ceremony on 1 August 1936, employed the services of Carl Orff and Werner Egk, both composers with unmistakable modernist elements in their style, and was 'designed to bind dance and athletic achievement into the new Nazi body culture'.[100] The Games closed with a performance of Wigman's *Hero's Fight and Death's Lament* in which wailing women mourned for fallen heroes in a deliberate synthesis of the classical and the modern, a piece that displayed a marked, and courageous, ambivalence to the Nazi cult of war.

The artistic event that would have been a major aesthetic event, forming the climax of the dangerous liaison that Laban had initiated between modernist dance and Nazism, was *Of the Warm Wind and the New Joy*, a four-part 'choric consecration play' to be performed by a cast of 1,000 in Berlin's newly constructed Dietrich-Eckhart Amphitheatre. However, it was 'pulled' by Goebbels at the last minute, perhaps anticipating the displeasure of Hitler who presided over the Games and who was known to be no fan of 'Ausdruckstanz'.[101] Thereafter genuinely innovative Modern Dance, even in its 'Aryanized' version, fell from grace to the point where Laban emigrated in 1938 and propagated his movement in Britain (where it still thrives as a form of contemporary dance). Wigman's school in Dresden was closed in 1942, but she went on to have a major impact on European dance through the academy she ran in Berlin from 1950 till 1967. The possibility for genuine aesthetic modernism to survive within the German Dance Movement was finally extinguished by Goebbels' decree of January 1942 banning any form of dance drama or dramatic ballet with a conceptual or experimental component.

THROUGH THE LENS OF NAZISM

Nazi cinema reflects a tension parallel to the one found in music and dance between the need to provide entertainment for the hard-working *Volksgemein-schaft*, and the attempt to use it as a vehicle for cultural and social renewal. The stereotype of the Third Reich as a regime concerned only with brainwashing citizens in the spirit of George Orwell's *1984* is borne out by films with an overt propagandistic purpose, such as the documentary *Triumph of the Will* (1935), the full-length feature *Ich klage an* (1941) – made deliberately in order to 'sell' the euthanasia programme to the public[102] – and the notorious 'public information film', *The Eternal Jew* (1940), which, in an outstanding example of Doublethink, implicitly provided the rationale for the Final Solution even though the genocide of the Jews was never declared an official policy and took place with the same secrecy as that enforced by the 'Night and Fog Directive' or the 'disappearing' of political prisoners. (The title of Alain Resnais' 1955 film on the Nazi extermination programme, *Nuit et Brouillard*, is an allusion to this directive.)

Other Nazi films dramatize the notion of sacrifice to one's nation or the great leader who saves it in a time of need. The bulk were, however, apparently anodyne, 'escapist' films, many of them comedies of contemporary life (e.g. *Lucky Kids*, 1936) whose 'brainwashing' function consisted largely in presenting dramas, crime-stories, romances, or domestic situations of 'everyday life' against a backcloth of an entirely normalized and *sanitized* Third Reich in which any allusion to the atrocities being committed had been rigorously expurgated. The link of propaganda and escapist films to modernism exists only in so far as they were both integral to the social engineering of the Third Reich as a gardening state and hence to the implementation of *political* modernism.

There was a third category of Nazi film, however, where echoes of the cultural rebellion of modernism as a palingenetic *movement* are still audible. Several were produced of an overtly propagandistic nature whose subtext was the need to turn back the tide of decadence and anomy. In his analysis of *Hitler Youth Quex* (1933), the dramatization of the conversion to Nazism and martyrdom of a working-class teenager, Eric Rentschler reminds the reader that

> Nazi cinema originated as a site of transformation, an art and technology implemented to engineer emotion, to create a new man – and to recreate woman in the service of the new man and the new order. The different being here was an amalgam of vitalism and irrationality, a creature longing for spiritual rebirth, for ecstatic life undaunted by cerebration.[103]

He traces the roots of *Quex* in the 'transformation dramas' of German Expressionists such as Ernst Toller, Georg Kaiser, and Ernst Barlach, and the portrayal of meaningless individual life being merged into a communal, transcendent whole by Gottfried Benn and Ernst Jünger.

Rentschler's chapter on the genre of the 'Heimat' film – exemplified in *A German wants to Go Home* (1934) – brings out another aspect of the thematic modernism of Nazi cinema integral to the regime's pursuit of an 'anthropological revolution'. The home where anomic Germans wished to return was less a geographical home than a mythic one embodying the nomos and *communitas* destroyed by Western modernity and the catastrophic events in Germany since 1917. In even the most apparently escapist Romantic dramas made in the Third Reich there bubbled just below the surface the theme of existential security (*Geborgenheit*) and bondedness (*Gebundenheit*), whether to one's 'natural' gender role, family, social roots, native land, history, landscape, or the *Volk*, all of which assume primordial connotations of belonging and restored wholeness.[104] Thousands of talented script-writers, film technicians, directors, and actors adapted effortlessly, often with no coercion or official directives, which suggests a wave of spontaneous inner alignments to the spirit of the Nazis' cultural revolution. The result was an extraordinary *variety* of films in different genres – over 1,200 premiered between 1933 and 1945 – which together constitute a 'home-grown', and largely 'autarkic' cinema.

While a film such as the obscenely anti-Semitic historical drama *Jud Süss* (1940) sticks indigestibly in the mind, the bulk of the box-office hits seemed on the surface 'modern' and apolitical, and hence even more insidiously effective in drawing a euphemistic veil over the unspeakable suffering the regime was inflicting while cinema-goers sat in a state of controlled reverie. However, two films, both made after the wheels had started falling off the Nazi Juggernaut of destruction emphasize the importance of seeing the cinema of the Third Reich as a complex product of cultural and political *modernity* rather as the state-controlled 'propaganda' of Big Brother. *Paracelsus* (1943) was a historical drama using conventional aesthetics and production values, yet it introduced a subtextual criticism of the fiction at the heart of the Hitler Myth whose subtlety would probably be more liable to delight today's postmodern intellectuals than it did the audiences of the time. Even more extraordinary, the colour film *Münchhausen* (1943) manages to confirm anti-Semitic stereotypes while at the same time exploring the bottomless pits of madness and nihilism that were breaking open in what had seemed the bedrock of reality directly under the feet of all Germans, Nazis or not. Moreover, it used an aesthetic deeply indebted to Surrealism that would be instantly recognized as modernist were it not for its Nazi origins and racial subtext.

These were followed by the unintentionally bizarre *Kolberg* (1945), which, as we saw in the last chapter, was the ultimate expression of the aesthetization of politics under totalitarianism. Yet by finding a historical correlative in the Napoleonic Wars to Germany's imminent defeat, Goebbels' film epitomized the highly modern reflexivity integral to the regime's self-conscious 'will to transcendence', even when it meant trying to find immortality within annihilating military defeat rather than victory. The resulting 'point of view' is reminiscent of the voyeuristic, 'scopophiliac' murderer in Michael Powell's 1960 film *Peeping Tom* who spends his final moments trying to film his own death.[105]

THE 'DESTRUCTIVE CREATION' OF NAZI MODERNISM

George Mosse was swimming against powerful currents within studies of the Third Reich when in 1966 he published an anthology of primary source materials culled from the artistic and social history of the Third Reich. At the time its title, *Nazi Culture*,[106] still smacked of a contradiction in terms, if not a sick joke. Thanks to the maturing of the discipline there is little that should strike the reader as groundbreaking or heretical about the conclusion we propose to draw from our whistle-stop tour of this vast topic, where so much work still needs to be done.

First, in terms of sheer quantity of output the cultural production of the first decade of the regime was as impressive as the parallel explosion in industrial production after the Depression years. Such a 'Cultural Renaissance' would have been utterly impossible to engineer from above, and depended on many thousands of artists and intellectuals supported by scores of thousands of technicians and performers all of whom with varying degrees of conviction and originality worked 'in the spirit' of the new Reich and 'in the mind' of its Führer.

Second, what is revealed in every sphere of culture is not the workings of a monolithic 'megamachine', or a human ant colony in which all activity is perfectly coordinated through a 'group mind' whose compliance to official norms and directives is reinforced by fear. Instead, in every branch of the arts Nazism presided over a complex cultural habitat hosting pockets of genuine aesthetic variety and artistic creativity, as well as ongoing tensions between reducing art to a tool of mass manipulation and authentic poetic impulses to bring into being the new world that the Nazis wanted to create beyond liberal decadence.

Third, the criteria for academic evaluations of Nazi culture have to take into account the 'paradigm shift' the regime wanted to bring about in the way culture itself was conceived. The new nomos of organic and racist nationalism in Germany dictated that art was no longer to be evaluated using Romantic criteria in terms of genius, originality, and the breakthrough to new ways of seeing and expressing reality, but as the manifestation of the unique historical and racial identity of the *Volk* and its 'eternal' values. After January 1933, art was held to be neither a deeply personal activity nor a commercial activity, but a primary constituent of national identity and racial health, intimately bound up with the social and the political spheres of life. To Nazi cultural theorists the proliferation of different movements, aesthetics, and 'isms' in early twentieth-century Europe was a sign not of vitality and progress, but the morbidity and decay that resulted from modernity's destructive power to sever the living roots and tendrils connecting artists to their people and 'life'. The Nazi revolution in art was thus inseparable from the attempted anthropological revolution that lay at the core of its totalitarianism. To create an alternative modernity demanded an alternative modernism.

Fourth, even if much Nazi art invokes the aesthetics of classical antiquity or of German Romanticism, this is not anti-modern nostalgia, but the evocation of the 'eternal' values needed to regenerate the future. In its utopian aspirations Nazi culture is a futural culture, a culture charged with the 'temporality of the new' in which even non-modernist *aesthetics* – and it seems much more modernist aesthetics survived under Hitler than has been generally recognized to date – serve modernist socio-political, and *racist* ends. As such the modernist ethos they embody has been purged of individualism and experimentalism, and healed of the 'morbid' urge to explore repressed instincts and drives the Nazis identified with the creativity of a 'decadent' age. Even the most crudely propagandistic forms of art were in Nazi eyes not 'brainwashing', but integral to the process of cultural cleansing.

It would thus be facile to dismiss as pure propaganda or philistinism the speech Hitler made at the ceremonial opening of the House of German Art referred to earlier. In it he asserted that the purpose of art was 'not to retreat backwards from the development of a people: its sole function must be to symbolise that living development'. Expanding on the biopolitical implications of this function, he explained 'The new age of today is at work on a new human type. Men and women are to be healthier and stronger. There is a new feeling of life, a new joy in life. Never was humanity in its external appearance and in its frame of mind nearer to the ancient world than it is today.' He then rhetorically addresses aesthetic modernists – most of whom, if German citizens, had long since disappeared into exile, inner emigration, or concentration camps. He calls them 'prehistoric daubers', and, having evoked the eternal qualities of healthy 'Aryan' men and women that the Reich sought to revive, asks: 'What do you manufacture? Malformed cripples and cretins, women who inspire only disgust, men who are more like wild beasts, children who, were they alive, would have to be seen as cursed by God.'[107]

However, to create the new human type was not just a matter of awarding prizes to healthy paintings and selling off or burning degenerate ones, ensuring all civic buildings expressed eternal values of proportion and scale, or making inspiring speeches about 'Aryan' values. The new race of Germans had to be reared mentally and physically by new institutions as members of an ethnic community united within a country purged of all sources of mental and physical decay and all threats to the new order. Their lives had to become individual cells of a new type of nation, the fusion of the modern state with the regenerated *Volkskörper*, a politico-cultural-racial entity previously unknown to history. The frantic gardening of the resulting regime aimed to place its inhabitants in the heartland of a vast continental empire in which all social, political, and racial enemies had been defeated, and which would provide the economic resources needed to make the Third Reich the world's supreme industrial, technocratic, military, and cultural power.

Our investigation of Nazi culture thus leads 'organically' to a consideration of the Nazi technocracy which within months of the 'seizure of power' had set to work on realizing a revolution which was not just political, but *anthropological*. It aimed to use the power not just of the modern state and of German culture, but of 'Technik' to create a *Gesamtkunstwerk* with the raw materials of human minds, bodies, and machines, and so erect a sacred canopy able to provide millennial protection for the regenerated *Volk*. The new German race would, in the words of Gottfried Benn, be 'neither gods, nor mediocre human beings', but would 'issue forth from the purity of a new people'.[108] In *Der Arbeiter* (1932) Ernst Jünger announced in high flown metapolitical prose the emergence of a new type of human being, born of the 'mother soil of the race', who would express the principles of 'total mobilization' and 'the total character of work' in the coming state.[109] In this highly influential essay, Jünger articulated what for many Nazis who were not artists or intellectuals but technocrats by training and profession was a vital precondition to this evolutionary, profoundly *modernist* act of creation.

In the words of his Italian admirer, Julius Evola, what had been revealed to Ernst Jünger in the mechanized slaughter of the First World War was that modern technology represented an 'elemental force combined with the "material" in an array of technologies of extreme destructive potential'.

> Technology in its elemental aspect operated like a non-human force awakened and set in motion by Man. He must face up to this force, become the instrument of the machine, and yet at the same time master it, not just physically, but spiritually. This is only possible if human beings make themselves capable of a new form of existence, forging themselves into a new type of human being, who, precisely in the midst of situations which are lethal to anyone else, is able to derive from them an absolute sense of being alive. To this end it is, however, necessary to transcend entirely the way of being, the ideals, the values, and, the whole world view cultivated by the bourgeoisie.[110]

In such a passage we arrive at the heart of Julius Evola's fascination with Ernst Jünger, of that extraordinary confluence between Traditionalist and hypermodernity dubbed by the New Right French intellectual, Guillaume Faye 'archeofuturism'.[111] It was in this spirit that the ex-Dadaist turned occultist called for 'a more radical Fascism, more fearless, a really absolute Fascism, made of pure force, impervious to any compromise'.[112] It is when we consider Nazi technocracy as a modernist phenomenon in the primordialist sense that we also arrive at the heart of the Third Reich's alternative modernity.

11
The Third Reich's Biopolitical Modernism

By building a defensive barrier of peasant protection well to the east in order to seal this land off once and for all from the storm floods of Asia, [...] we will slowly lay down one German wall after another, so that, working eastwards, German people of German blood can carry out German settlement.

Reinhardt Heydrich, Reich Protector of Bohemia-Moravia, (September 1941)[1]

Faust: A swamp lies there below the hill,
Infecting everything I've done:
My last and greatest act of will
Succeeds when that foul pool is gone.
Let me make room for many a million,
Not wholly secure, but free to work on.
Green fertile fields, where men and herds
May gain swift comfort from the new-made earth.[...]

Wolfgang Goethe, *Faust Part II*

NAZI *LEBENSFREUDE*

'Can machines think?' a headline asks intriguingly in the 18 May 1941 issue of *Koralle*,[2] a weekly magazine for 'Knowledge, Entertainment, and *Lebensfreude*' (joie de vivre) published by the Nazis for 'Aryan' households throughout the life of the regime (see Figure 20). The article beneath it describes the rapid progress being made towards making robots to carry out human functions. One is a calculator for solving within seconds problems in electronics and quantum physics which would have taken a human brain months. Another is a sophisticated punch card machine which had enabled the last census to be carried out 'in a fraction of the time needed before'. It goes on to pose the issue raised in the title, the basic cognitive issue that the Cambridge mathematician

Alan Turing would attempt to resolve in his groundbreaking paper 'Computing Machinery and Intelligence' published in *Mind* in 1950. This was partly the fruit of his work to break the code of another outstanding product of German computing technology, the Enigma Machine.[3]

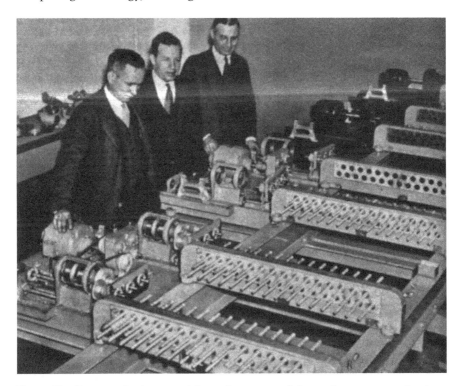

Figure 20 German scientists examining a forerunner of electronic computer technology. The calculator was used to 'draw the solution curve for problems of electronics and quantum physics'.

Source: Nazi general interest magazine, *Koralle*, Vol. 9, No. 20 (18 May 1941), p. 531.

If Allied students of the Third Reich might have been tempted to dismiss such an article during wartime as an anomaly in a society dominated by the cult of a bygone 'Aryan' golden age, a minor incident at the end of the war should have disabused them. In 1945 advancing Anglo-British forces discovered hidden in the cellar of a house in the small Bavarian village of Hinterstein a large mechanical device code-named 'V4'. The vast assembly of mechanical bits and bobs turned out to be not the fourth of Hitler's 'Wonder Weapons', but Versuchsmodell 4 ('Prototype 4'), a programme-controlled calculator with an electromechanical memory and arithmetical unit, made in 1941 by Konrad Zuse as the result of a project funded by the Third Reich's

Aerodynamic Institute. It was the first fully operational modern computer, and earned its keep working out complex mathematical calculations associated with the mechanics of vibrating airframes under stress.

The openness of the Third Reich to the latest technology is further illustrated by its extensive use of IBM punch card and card sorting equipment, this time less a census than a logistics exercise to keep track of a considerably more mobile and unstable population than 'Aryan' citizens. The SS used machines custom-designed by IBM's German subsidiary Dehomag to monitor the movements and deaths of the millions condemned to be prisoners, forced labourers, and slaves in the service of the Reich. (It did so with the full collaboration of the New York headquarters of IBM, which made a healthy profit on the vast quantity of specially printed punch cards – 1.5 billion in 1943 alone – consumed by the New Germany. In the summer of 1943 all non-Germans at Auschwitz were tattooed with five-digit IBM Hollerith numbers.[4]) By 1947 New York had secured nearly all the equipment belonging to Dehomag (now called IBM Germany), along with the 7.5 million Reichsmarks it had amassed for helping ensure the machinery of slave labour and extermination functioned 'like clockwork'.

Such facts sit awkwardly with Henry Turner's once widely touted thesis that Nazism, in contrast to 'pro-modernist' Fascist Italy, was a form of 'utopian anti-modernism' pursuing 'a fanatical and ultimately suicidal pursuit of an unattainable, archaic utopia'.[5] This final chapter in our exploration of modernism's relation to fascism will focus on the way the Third Reich's determination to create a 'healthy' alternative to existing modernity involved not just a new artistic culture, but a new type of society created by a professional cultural and technocratic elite inspired by the essentially modernist vision of 'designing a new world'[6] both in terms of core values and overall 'plan'. It was a task which in the extreme conditions created by the First World War suddenly seemed eminently feasible. War and military defeat eventually intervened to truncate the Nazi experiment in laying the foundation on which an 'Aryanized' Western civilization and culture was to have been based. It would have had tantalizing points of correspondence to and contrast with the 'heroic', constructivist ethos of Fascist, US, and Soviet modernization at the time. It is this prevailing ethos, both nationalistic and palingenetic, that makes the Third Reich both unique *and* part of the family of generic fascism as we have defined it.

As we saw in the case of architecture, one of the key features of the Nazi technocracy was the importance it attached to cultural, historical, and biological rootedness to guarantee all 'Aryans' a sense of belonging, and allow technology to be geared exclusively to the needs of the *Volk* as interpreted by the leader. There is thus nothing contradictory about a technologically advanced 'racial state'[7] constantly evoking images of nature, rural idylls, premodern traditions, and the mythical German *Heimat*.[8] Such apparently anti-modern idealizations of the past dominate a propaganda film such as *Blühendes Land*. This showed healthy Dirndl-clad maidens, bursting with feigned *Lebensfreude*, picking grapes on the banks of a 'Romantic' German river. In another sequence evoking Germany as a now 'blossoming land' a latter-day peasant girl gaily feeds chickens and goats in an embarrassingly staged communion with nature.[9] However, to focus on such images to characterize the ethos of the New Germany is to overlook the flood of counter-images of uncompromising modernity, such as a cinema short advertising the efficiency of the Nazi railway system, the Deutsche Reichsbahn. The film employed modern montage techniques to evoke the power of steam to transport the new generation of 'Aryan' Germans to their destinations, producing sequences which the 2003 documentary *Hitler's Hit Parade* intercuts with shots of train transports to concentration camps.[10] Another public information film celebrated the advanced technology of the Reich in a different sphere of efficiency by showing off the latest scientific method for killing pests in warehouses. When the camera zooms in to provide a close-up of the canisters containing the pesticide, the trade-name is horribly familiar: Zyklon B.[11]

Such extreme instances underline the importance of approaching apparent evidence of the Nazi flight from modernity with caution. For example, the Dirndl revival promoted by the regime never caught on at a popular level. In fact, the average young 'Aryan' woman living an urban life-style proved to be no less fashion-conscious than her French or American counterparts. As a result, the regime poured considerable resources into setting up the German Fashion Institute with the explicit goal of creating a 'Nazi chic' that would replace New York, Hollywood, and Paris – all designated epicentres of racial degeneracy – as the arbiters of dress-style for 'genuinely' German women, as well as earning some hard foreign currency.[12] As Irene Guenther points out in her revealing study of this neglected topic, alongside the much touted Blood and Soil or 'Bubo' (*Blut und Boden*) current of the Third Reich, Nazism 'had another countenance, one that was intensely modern, technologically advanced, supremely stylized, and fashionably stylish'.[13]

Some of the unique flavour of Nazi modernity has been captured by the documentaries *Eternal Beauty*[14] and *Hitler's Hit Parade*,[15] both ingenious collages of excerpts taken from the newsreel, film, and musical output of the Third Reich. Alongside their weightier subtexts, they vividly evoke the sense that a vital aspect of the popular consensus that the regime enjoyed in the years 1933–39 was the sheer relief felt by a significant proportion of the generation who had spent its youth in the turmoil, poverty, and instability of the Weimar years to find itself finally in a society which offered the opportunity to enjoy a modern life-style. By the mid-1930s young city-dwelling 'Aryan' women still not performing their duties to the race as mothers – in which they would be supported by a rapidly expanding welfare state – might work in a modern office building during the day and then on the occasional night out watch a 'Nordified' ('aufgenordet') version of a Hollywood comedy or dance to sanitized Swing.

The privileged few who had the financial means – Nazism did little to erode class differences economically – might wear the latest Nordic variant of Paris male and female fashion, drive a product of 'Aryan' engineering on the new motorway, and use the latest domestic appliances in modern living spaces incorporating aesthetics uncannily resembling 'American' or Bauhaus notions of style.[16] In 1936 some could even watch an outside broadcast of Hitler attending the Berlin Olympics on the latest triumph of German advances in communications technology: television.[17] In 1939 the Fernseh-Volksemp-fänger – the equivalent of the extremely successful radio-receiver built for mass consumption, the Volksempfänger – was displayed at the 16th Grosse Deutsche Rundfunkausstellung (Great German Wireless Exhibition), at a target price of 650 Mark. Two years earlier the exhibition had demonstrated the possibility of colour TV transmission. Only the war prevented the rapid development of TV as a mass-medium. That some Nazi leaders saw in the medium of television not just another tool of manipulative propaganda is suggested by Hitler's immediate reaction to being shown one of the latest cine cameras: 'Every German family must have one. Every aspect of the nation's growth would be captured.'[18] Such a response implies a profound belief that 'Aryan' Germans equipped with such a recording device would spontaneously document the achievements of the reborn nation, the very process of 'making history' being carried out reflexively in the intimate lives of the *Volksgemeinschaft*.

The Nazi vision of an alternative modernity embraced a technological Land of Cockaigne, not only supplying unprecedented industrial and military power to the new Germany, but also improving the fabric of urban life. The latest gadgets and inventions were celebrated and advertised in a media machine and press apparently driven as much by the autonomous logic of consumer capitalism and the cult of material progress as by the Ministry of Propaganda. Even if the social inequalities and enduring poverty of the post-Depression years placed 'the modern life-style' far beyond the reach of most Germans considered members of the *Volksgemeinschaft*, the regime did not suppress the seductive images of a technocratic modernity in films and magazines now recoded to express the creativity of a superior race. In recognizing this, however, it is important, as was pointed out in Chapter 9, to see the futural thrust of the Third Reich as neither 'progressive' nor 'reactionary' but 'modernist', a term which should by now have long since shed connotations of 'good' or 'rational'.

Figure 21   A model of the proposed headquarters of the Nazi radio broadcasting centre planned for Berlin (but never built).

Photo © 1978 Bison Books Ltd. Reproduced in Ward Rutherford, *Hitler's Propaganda Machine* (London: Bison Books, 1978, reprinted 1985). Source: Bison Picture Library. Bison Books and Bison Picture Library are no longer extant.

THE 'OTHERNESS' OF NAZI MODERNITY

What this means in practice is that we need to abandon analyses of Nazism carried out in dichotomous terms of simultaneous 'anti-modern' and 'modern' tendencies implied by Irene Guenther. Nazi modernity was not a two-headed Janus, but a three-headed Chimaera. Intertwined into the plait of a mythicized past with intense modernization was a third element, the systematic purge of everything considered excrescent or detrimental to the process of national regeneration. By being harnessed to the programme of racial purification carried out by Germany as a 'gardening state' and to a massive campaign of territorial expansion embarked on by it as an imperial state, the technocratic, overtly modernizing impulses within Nazism to 'design a new world' involved designing *out* everything unhealthy, dysfunctional, decadent, or dysgenic.

As a result, ruthless military campaigns, state terror, and systemic cruelty became an integral part of Nazi modernity. A strand of inhumanity ran through the entire weft and woof of the new society, even if it was only when the Nazis' plans for foreign conquest began to be implemented – and then encounter major obstacles in their realization – that the full scale on which that inhumanity could be conceived and executed began to reveal itself. If the 'devil is in the small-print', then the chilling nexus between Nazi modernity and atrocity is revealed in the detail. To take two examples: in the spring of 1935 an exhibition was held in Berlin devoted to 'The Miracle of Life', a theme conceived in the uncompromisingly 'modern' way expressed in the advanced design of its poster and catalogue.[19] Yet the entire ethos of the exhibition was shaped by a concern with 'racial hygiene', and even as good 'Aryans' admired the information and exhibits on display, compulsory sterilizations were being carried out on the state's 'dysgenic' citizens under the Law for the Prevention of Genetically Diseased Offspring of July 1933. Nazi *haute couture* and Nazi chic flourished long into the war despite escalating supply problems of raw materials, yet did so by becoming increasingly dependent on the skills of Jews, prisoners of war, and other 'racial degenerates'.[20] There was even a 'sewing room' in Auschwitz producing hand-tailored fineries for SS wives and female guards.[21]

Preconceptions about Nazism's essential nostalgia for premodernity may be one reason for the comparative dearth of texts studying what Joachim Fest called the 'breathtaking' technological modernity of the Third Reich, except, that is, in terms of its '*reactionary* modernism'.[22] Another could be the lack of a substantial body of theoretical pronouncements by Hitler or other leading Nazis setting out the basic principles of the new economy and new technocracy on which the reborn Germany would depend. Such major planks of Nazi doctrine and policy as the destruction of cultural Bolshevism and the creation of German art, the destruction of Judaism and Communism and the creation of an empire in Eastern Europe, or the destruction of a dysgenic society and creation of a healthy *Volksgemeinschaft* were regularly promulgated, but not the axioms of Nazism's vision of an alternative *technocracy*. These have to be gleaned from primary sources, such as the idea of the 'German' as builder and technocrat touched on in the brief section of Hitler's reflections on 'Nation and Race' in *Mein Kampf*. Here he outlines the distinction between founders, bearers, and destroyers of culture referred to in the last chapter, and portrays the 'Aryans' as the sole race representing the first category:

> All the human culture, all the results of art, science, and technology that we see before us today, are almost exclusively the creative product of the 'Aryan'. [...] He is the Prometheus of mankind from whose bright forehead the divine spark of genius has sprung at all times, forever kindling anew that fire of knowledge which illumined the night of silent mysteries and thus caused man to climb the path to mystery over the other beings of this earth.[23]

There were also occasional statements in Nazi propaganda that portrayed the Reich as a vast undertaking to construct a new reality out of the raw materials, both physical and spiritual, of history, thereby expressing the unique 'Aryan' constructive will embodied in the Führer. The last stanza of a hagiographic poem published in *Der Völkische Beobachter* of July 1926 (when Nazism was still extremely marginalized in Weimar politics) sums up this idea:

'He points to a dawn breaking in the distance/and all hearts are enflamed. / The fist shakes and the spirits too – / Now build your people, oh master, / a new, great Fatherland!'[24]

However, if we leave aside Ernst Jünger's *Der Arbeiter*, the most revealing insights into the technocratic aspect of Nazism's Brave New World have to be inferred from such sources as the autobiography of Albert Speer[25] or the biography of Robert Ley, head of the German Labour Front.[26] What emerges from such sporadic first-hand testimonies, but especially from the *praxis* of Nazism itself, is the *biopolitical* nature of the Nazi revolution. Here the term is not just referring in its conventional meaning to the application of biological racism, eugenics, and racial hygiene to state policies. Instead it denotes the marked degree to which the Nazis conceived the creation of the Third Reich as the product of a new form of politics shaped by and grounded *in the forces of life itself*, by a revolution conceived biologically. The many permutations of the Nazi *Weltanschauung* were all simultaneously a totalizing 'life-philosophy', for even when they did not base themselves on life sciences such as biology or anthropology, they invoked a more nebulous, non-scientific, 'Dionysian' spirit of vitalism or 'Lebensphilosophie' that, as we saw in Chapter 5, became so prevalent in late nineteenth-century Europe, particularly in Germany, during the revolt against decadence. It was a spirit which could be expressed in a wide array of registers whether occultist, religious, mystical, Romantic, Wagnerian, Nietzschean, militaristic, scientistic, or technocratic. It is this '*vitalistic*' political vision that historian Robert Pois analysed extensively in terms of Nazism's 'Religion of Nature'.[27]

Within Nazism this protean, essentially 'pagan' cult of the life-force as a primordial source of value and meaning effectively replaced both traditional Enlightenment and revealed religion as the rationale for science, technology, and modernity itself. At the same time it provided the basis of a form of humanism which axiomatically assumed the application to history and society of the 'laws of life' in a broadly Social Darwinian, or rather 'monistic' – though not necessarily Haeckelian[28] – sense which axiomatically branded as 'decadent', and hence anti-life, principles of human equality and human rights. This biopolitical morality is expressed with chilling terseness in Franz Pfeffer von Salomon's internal Party memorandum circulated at Christmas 1925 which accused Gregor Strasser of promoting a 'German socialism' which flouted the fundamentally elitist principle that 'all Germans are unequal'. For von Salomon egalitarianism, even when applied to 'Aryans', was a poisoned fruit of 'the Jewish-liberal-democratic-Marxist-humanitarian mentality': 'As long as there is even a single minute tendril which connects our programme with this root then it is doomed to be poisoned and hence to wither away to a miserable death.'[29]

Within a few years of the 'seizure of power' the Nazis had created an entire state system and set of policies based on the assumption that the *Volk* was a living organism to be healed of disease and purged of parasites, even if they were found among 'Aryan stock'. This was only possible because of the prior absorption into the Nazi *Weltanschauung* of 'biopolitics' in the primary, non-scientific – though frequently *scientized* – sense we are postulating here. It is a line of interpretation entirely consistent with Richard Etlin's recognition of the importance of blood and rootedness as the base-metaphors of the Nazis' mythic universe.[30] Under the Third Reich a political discourse established itself as the norm that melded biopolitical fictions and myths with the language of political power, a fusion exemplified in the sequence of speeches made by Hitler almost every year on 1 May throughout his political career. In them the natural cycle of decay and renewal is repeatedly linked to the process of German rebirth, an equation that found ritualistic expression in the elaborate May Day celebrations held in Berlin in 1936 referred to in Chapter 3.[31]

What follows from this approach is that the teams of specialists in every field of the human and natural science who under the Third Reich pursued the advancement of knowledge in their discipline, worked on technological projects, or planned society on eugenic principles were encouraged to feel they were enacting the principle of 'reconnecting forwards', of reconnecting the future with *life*. They were charged with creating a modern state based no longer on the outdated abstractions of liberal individualism and reason, but on the eternal forces of race and biology. Their enthusiasm for the new world being forged in a collective, synergic burst of Promethean, 'Aryan' creativity enabled Nazism to complete such extraordinary projects of national reconstruction before the outbreak of war, and deploy such a highly effective fighting machine after it. Some contemporaries abroad were deeply impressed by the radical modernity of the New Germany and the efficiency with which it dealt with the threat posed by communism.

Yet, the familiarity and 'normality' of the technological achievements and artefacts of Nazi modernity are specious: they are imbued with an ethos of 'otherness' emanating from the harnessing of the latest technology by a modernist project to change a nation's history at the cost of millions of lives and unspeakable suffering. The resulting 'alterity' is perhaps less the province of the historian than of the creative writer. It is powerfully conveyed, for example, in the moment to which we referred at the end of Chapter 8 when Primo Levi saw Nazism's 'great insanity' in the eyes of Dr Pannwitz. Pannwitz was an industrial chemist leading a team of researchers in the sanctuary of Birkenau, an annex to the Auschwitz main camp built to service the nearby IG Farben industrial complex, which was taking advantage of slave labour to advance its cutting-edge work on the production of synthetic rubber and fuel. In practical terms, the realization of the Nazi new order depended far more on the daily routine of thousands of well trained German scientists, experts, and technicians, like Pannwitz, quietly going about their business in the countless fields of applied science, technology, and administration that make up technocratic modernity than it did on the theoretical writings of high-profile ideologues such as Carl Schmitt, Martin Heidegger, and Ernst Jünger.

Winston Churchill seems to have intuited this when writing the speech delivered to the House of Commons on 18 June 1940 which bequeathed the phrase 'their finest hour'. Now that the 'Battle of France' had been lost and the 'Battle of Britain' was about to begin, he had no doubt that Christian civilization itself was at a crossroads, representing a challenge to liberal democracy from a force invisible at the time, namely an ultranationalist form of political modernism that had unleashed a mass-mobilization last seen in German, French, and British commitment to defeating the enemy in the First World War. Significantly, his own account of what is at stake in fighting Hitler contains no trace of the palingenetic fervour about epic 'rebirths' and glorious 'new beginnings' that was the staple of fascist rhetoric at the time:

> If we can stand up to him, all Europe may be free and the life of the world may move forward into broad, sunlit uplands. But if we fail, then the whole world, including the United States, including all that we have known and cared for, will sink into the abyss of a new Dark Age made more sinister, and perhaps more protracted, by the lights of perverted science.[32]

CONVERTING TO HITLER

If the Third Reich was able to become such an enormously powerful industrial-military complex in so few years after a devastating economic and political collapse, it was at least *partly* because of the modernist ethos of its revolution. This encouraged millions of Germans with education, skills, expertise, and specialist training to 'work towards the Führer', and develop their skills and personalities 'with the mind of the Führer'. They did not do so only in the sense of responding to his personal 'charisma', but also in the technocratic sense that they believed they were helping to realize his vision of a Germany that would not only be a Great Power once again, but a *modern* society in which men and women would, as Hitler put it, be 'healthier and stronger', their work and leisure imbued with 'a new feeling for life, a new joy in life'. Events between

1929 and 1933 had largely undermined or destroyed any residual existential attachment Germans had developed to the Weimar Republic, hollowing out their core social, cultural, and historical identity to produce the acute – though extensively denied and repressed – sense of disorientation, anxiety, and anomy explored by Hermann Broch in *The Sleepwalkers*.

Once in power Nazism effectively filled this vacuum for millions, at least in the early years. It encouraged 'Aryan' Germans of an older age group to resume the external functions of their former jobs and professions. It persuaded younger Nazis to take up employment in what they had been trained for often for the first time, and do so with a heightened sense of communal identity, purpose, and future inconceivable under Weimar. The flames of enthusiasm were also fanned by the supercharged dynamism of the German economic, political, and social recovery after 1933. If citizens of the new Reich lacked profound moral or existential anchorage elsewhere, the human survival instinct, combined with a craving for transcendence, for nomos and *communitas*, ensured that their inner world thus automatically accommodated the 'new order', their language and behaviour conforming to the realities of life in the Third Reich even if they resisted full acknowledgment of what was happening to them and what they were doing. Every personal instance of Nazification told its own story of accommodation, collusion, and denial.

While it is right to stress the degree of resistance and opposition that survived under Hitler,[33] it is also important to acknowledge that broad swathes of highly educated 'Aryan' Germans with professional skills essential to the creation and functioning of the Third Reich collaborated with the Reich, though with markedly varying degrees of bad conscience, simulated conformism, and 'inner emigration'.[34] The statistics showing over a quarter of Germans were members of the NSDAP or affiliated associations are perhaps less impressive than the more subtle forms of social, economic, and moral collusion revealed by painstaking historical research in such works as *Biologists under Hitler*, *The Faustian Bargain*, and *Hitler's Volksstaat*.[35] While 'the Germans' were never collectively 'Hitler's willing executioners' in the way Goldhagen so simplistically maintains, millions certainly became accomplices in the creation and maintenance of the regime's alternative modernity in its crucial formative years. The pain of cognitive dissonance, not to mention the utterly justified fear of suffering as the consequence of non-compliance, exerted intense psychological pressure on 'Aryan' Germans to buy into the myth that a new world was being constructed, and to take the euphemisms and rhetoric[36] of propaganda at face value. The result was that only an unquantifiable minority resisted creating a complex accommodation between their personal world-view and the new *Weltanschauung*. It was a compromise uniquely configured within the contours of each 'Aryan' German's life, but aggregated within the population it guaranteed the Third Reich the possibility of proceeding on the basis not just of 'dominion' but extensive 'cultural hegemony' till deep into the Second World War.

The basic mechanism of ideological collusion and assimilation that took place within Nazi academic, natural scientific, and technocratic circles – which from the earliest days of the Third Reich meant endorsing its openly promulgated and pursued anti-Communist, anti-Semitic, and racial policies – can be illuminated by considering one *cause célèbre*. It involved a high-profile academic with a deep interest in what Ernst Jünger identified as the central task of modern man, namely to master the machine 'not just physically but spiritually', and who for a time convinced himself that the Nazis would create the basis for an ontologically grounded technical civilization.

NAZISM'S MARRIAGE OF TECHNOLOGY WITH BEING

In 1933, several years after abandoning his Catholic faith, Martin Heidegger used his position as an internationally acclaimed academic philosopher to embrace Nazism in the most public possible manner. It is significant for our 'primordialist' account of such dramatic conversions to a totalizing ideology in the modern era, that in his biography of Heidegger, Rüdiger Safranski portrays him as a child of the same age of radical cosmological upheaval that produced the philosophical modernism of Nietzsche and the cultural modernism of Hugo von Hofmansthal, Stefan George, Hermann Bahr, Franz Werfel, and Wilhelm Dilthey. His outlook was also decisively shaped by the climate of vitalism or 'Lebensphilosophie' so prevalent in pre-1914 Germany.[37] Little wonder that a constant in Heidegger's philosophical career from the outset was his wish, as he put it in his autobiographical *Denkerfahrungen*, 'to open himself up to the vastness of the sky and at the same time be rooted in the dark of the earth'.[38] It is a phrase that epitomizes the longing for transcendence, the search for a new firmament that we argued in Part One is the existential driving force behind all modernism.

Though the war-fever of 1914 left Heidegger untouched, by 1916 he had succumbed to the lure of 'phenomenology', a philosophical concern with the experience of reality which Safranski presents as emanating 'the aura of a new dawn, which made it popular at a time when moods fluctuated between the extremes of doomsday despair and the euphoria of a new beginning'.[39] It was by dedicating himself with extraordinary intellectual and linguistic tenacity to analysing the distortions of consciousness wrought by the rise of modern anomy that he refined his unique form of 'existentialist' phenomenology. His was a sustained act of philosophical mountaineering at the extremes of language and thought that places him on a par with Friedrich Nietzsche, Ludwig Wittgenstein, William James, and Giovanni Gentile as one of the outstanding modernist philosophers of the twentieth century. In their own way all turned philosophy into a vehicle for affirming what Peter Osborne calls 'the temporality of the new', a way of analysing and *transcending* the contemporary crisis.[40]

Safranski emphasizes that the context in which Heidegger undertook this Herculean intellectual task was the climate of 'revolutionary excitement' that dominated the first years of the Weimar Republic, spawning countless 'interpretations of the world in the spirit of the "last day" and of radical new beginning':

> Fanatical anti-Semitism and racial ideas were rampant, the Bolshevization of the German Communist Party was starting, Hitler was writing *Mein Kampf* in Landsberg prison, millions were seeking salvation in sectarian movements – occultism, vegetarianism, nudism, theosophy and anthroposophy – there were countless promises of salvation and offers of a new road.[41]

It was an age of 'charismatics and prophets' preaching their own versions of 'millennium and apocalypse', as well as of 'decisionists of the renewal of the world, raving metaphysicians, and profiteers'. Meanwhile in politics 'messianism and redemption doctrines flourished on the left and the right'. The supercharged palingenetic climate prompted the philosopher Eduard Spranger to observe that 'full of faith, the younger generation is awaiting an inner rebirth', and that the mood of the times expressed 'a drive towards wholeness', a 'religious yearning', and 'a groping back from artificial and mechanical circumstances to the eternal spring of the metaphysical'.[42] In short, Heidegger's philosophical quest cannot be understood without reference to the hothouse climate of cultural and social modernism of early twentieth-century Germany.

In the last phase of the war Heidegger had already experienced solidity turning into air: 'the "spirit" that imbued the culture of the prewar years no longer has any reality'.[43] True to the dialectic of Dionysian pessimism, he saw 'a new beginning has to be found'.[44] By the mid-1920s, when the last ties of his attachment to Catholicism had finally been severed, he felt 'the old heaven ha[d] fallen'. The world, now cut off from its metaphysical taproot, had relapsed into total 'worldliness' and was crying out for metaphysical renewal.[45] What finally showed Heidegger the path to completing his intellectual rite of passage to a new world-view was his intellectual encounter with Ernst Jünger, an encounter made against the background of the paralysis of Weimar and the dramatic rise of Nazism. Richard Wollin argues that the two works by Jünger in which he set out his vision of the technocratic New Man, the essay 'Total Mobilization' (1930) and *The Worker* (1932), had 'an indelible impact on Heidegger's understanding of modern politics'. He ascribes the philosopher's 'option' for National Socialism in the early 1930s to the fact that he had convinced himself that 'Nazism was the legitimate embodiment of the *Arbeitergesellschaft* (society of workers) that had been prophesied by Jünger and which, as such represented the heroic overcoming of Western nihilism as called for by Nietzsche and Spengler'.[46]

On the basis of this revelation about the possibility of the West's imminent rebirth, both metaphysical and technological, Heidegger formulated his own mazeway synthesis from two main components: first his Nietzschean analysis of contemporary decadence and nihilism refracted through German idealist philosophy. This highlighted the erosion by modernity of the powerful sense of metaphysical 'Being' that he believed had sustained the heroic phase of classical Greek culture. Second, a 'conservative revolutionary' celebration of the birth of a new metaphysically grounded but technocratically powerful race of Germans. This new development had first been made possible by the total mobilization of man and machine in the First World War, its potential fulfilled by the process of national rebirth launched by the Nazi movement.

It was a diagnosis that imbued Heidegger with a missionary sense that his philosophical interpretation of history had placed him in a unique position to recognize the potential of the Third Reich to solve the crisis of modernity. Moreover, fate seemed to have charged him with the heroic task of using his influence as rector of Freiberg University to promote the understanding of the metaphysical revolution that was the precondition to the successful social and political transformation of Germany under the Third Reich. 'To lead the leaders'.[47] This explains the cryptic reference that he makes in his *Introduction to Metaphysics* (1935) to 'the inner truth and greatness' of National Socialism, of which most Nazis were themselves oblivious, namely the way it represented 'the encounter [*Begegnung*] of a globally determined technology with modern man'.[48] In this cryptic phrase he was alluding to his vision of Nazism creating a new synthesis between a globalizing technocracy and the human need for rootedness and metaphysical life.

Safranski comments that '[t]o Heidegger the National Socialist seizure of power was a revolution. It was far more than politics; it was a new act of the history of Being, the beginning of a new epoch. Hitler, to him, meant a new era.'[49] Gradually it dawned on him that the Nazi leadership had not grasped the fact that the 'inner' purpose of their revolution was not to purge the West racially[50] but heal it *spiritually*. He thus withdrew his support, but only after he had seized every opportunity afforded by his privileged academic position to deliver erudite pronouncements on the higher spiritual and historical purpose of the Third Reich, and to ensure the smooth enforcement of its racial policies in his university – i.e. the removal of Jews from the academic departments under his authority. For two years he had thus zealously dedicated his professional expertise and idealism not to 'working towards the Führer', but towards the metaphysical rebirth of Germany.[51]

THE NAZI CULT OF TECHNOCRATIC MODERNISM

Whatever its fascination for professional philosophers, the main significance of Heidegger's conversion to Nazism in the context of this book is that the same reason that led him to believe the regime was fulfilling Ernst Jünger's prophecy of the Worker endowed the Third Reich with an irresistible appeal to many academics working in the natural and applied sciences: the prospect that a new, spiritually and vitalistically grounded technocracy was being born. It was a prospect that generated an even stronger gravitational pull on the technocrats themselves, a modern caste which enjoyed special status in a country that, even after the ravages of the Weimar years and the Wall Street Crash, was in terms of tradition, human resources, and potential still Europe's greatest industrial power.

On a human level, German scientists and technocrats were no less vulnerable to the nomic crisis of modernity than their compatriots in the 'arts', and in many cases their career prospects must have seemed even more devastated than theirs by the Depression following the Wall Street Crash. The Nazi Revolution could seem to offer them a way of reconciling positivist knowledge and technological know-how with a powerful sense of identity and the 'spiritual'. It embedded their professional work in the living communal and historical reality of the immortal *Volk* while actively encouraging them to contribute to the shaping of a new future, of a new civilization. On a more pragmatic level the Third Reich's ambitious plans for the new Germany opened up an unlimited horizon for major innovative projects in areas such as town planning, civil engineering, industrial production, and technological innovation. These would be undertaken by both a private and public sector energized and resourced by the ongoing process of Germany's reconstruction as the Third Reich.

An eloquent example of the technocratic and *Promethean* modernism that resulted is provided by the schemes to transform vast tracts of Polish territory now occupied by the Third Reich into productive 'Aryan' farm land for the New Reich. They included the reclamation of the immense stretches of wetland formed by the Pripet Marshes on the border with Russia. David Blackbourn offers an impressively detailed analysis of this single episode in the attempted realization of the Third Reich's plans for an Eastern Empire stretching to the Urals. It reveals heated infighting between conservationists warning about the risks of desertification and technocrats proposing radical schemes for exploiting the agricultural and human resources of the area.[52] All such debates were framed in the prevailing Nazi biopolitical discourse both in the wider and narrow technical sense of the term where initiatives to improve society draw on elements of racial anthropology, Social Darwinism, and eugenics. This element adds an entirely new dimension to the otherwise equivalent metaphorical discourse of *bonifica* that, as we saw in Chapter 8, came to crystallize the palingenetic ambitions of the Fascist state when it drained the Pontine Marshes for farmland and new cities. It imbued 'reclamation' with a specifically *biological* ethos of the clash of Aryan with non-Aryan cultures and their struggle to the death for existence. Goethe's importance as the jewel in the crown of the literary canon also assured that such undertakings had a peculiarly *Faustian* ring to Germans, since in *Faust II* the redeemed hero dies blind and frail, but his spirit is still borne up by the delusion that the sound of digging means that work has begun on his scheme for vast earthworks to reclaim land from the sea and from marshland. It is a vision that endows technological imperialism with Cronus-defying ethos. Faust's last wish is to gaze upon:

> Free earth: where a free race, in freedom, stand.
> Then, to the Moment I'd dare say:
> 'Stay a while! You are so lovely!'
> Through aeons, then, never to fade away.

The Nazis' land reclamation also had a racial purpose, but one where not just an innocent old couple but an indigenous population was to be 'sacrificed' to the fulfilment of the mission.[53] The engineering problems of drainage in the Polish marshes were inseparable from the task of creating new farmland for 'Aryan' settlers to supplement the thousands of square kilometres of land already seized from Polish farmers. But for some 'racial experts' the task was also, as Reinhardt Heydrich stated in the epigraph to this chapter, to erect a 'defensive wall' of German peasants to act as a bulwark against 'the storm floods of Asia'. The wetlands also caught the eye of the planners of genocide for their potential contribution to solving the 'Jewish problem', offering both a site for the 'natural' decimation of slaves through the severe working conditions and as a site for 'disappearing' the victims of massacres. The East thus became the Third Reich's 'Wild West'.[54] It offered unprecedented scope for pioneers trying out techniques of colonization and resettlement, for exploitation, and for mass murder appropriate to the post-liberal age that Hitler had brought to Europe.

In the brief 'window' between the launching of Barbarossa in June 1941 and the Russians' decisive victory at Stalingrad in February 1943, technocrats were in their element. Konrad Meyer, the Nazi official responsible for the General

Plan for the East, waxed lyrical about the 'work of art' to be created out of the topographical chaos of the marshes as the new landscape took shape through the agency of Aryan creators of civilization. To realize this vision his office engaged the services of engineers, architects, regional planners, geographers, sociologists, demographers, soil specialists, foresters, botanists, and plant geneticists. With such a concentration of expertise at the disposition of technocrats, 'there was virtually no limit to their visions of the modern east':

> Autobahnen would anchor German settlements from Leningrad to the Caucasus, with rural electrification to power their milking machines. Institutes of tropical medicine would test new means of eradicating malarial mosquitoes, while a programme of planting and water management created modern means of 'climate control'.[55]

Once more, the three strands from which Nazism's alternative modernity was woven are apparent. The Nazis were simultaneously going 'back to the land' while realizing a technocratic dream-world that could only be created through a process of purging destruction, the ruthless subjugation and 'resettlement' of indigenous Slav races, the eradication of their culture, the annihilation of Jews, communists, prisoners of war, and everything that smacked of the subversive or dysgenic. The insinuation of a modern, biopolitical, and ultimately genocidal logic into every aspect of the Nazi technocracy can be seen in all the areas where sectors of capitalism and industrial production were aligned to the interests of the state through such resolutely 'modern' economic entities as the Todt Organization, the Hermann Goering Works, the agencies enforcing the Four Year Plan, and the firms and large corporations such as Krupp,[56] Daimler Benz,[57] Opel, BMW, IG Farben,[58] and AEG, all eager to have access to the unlimited pool of forced and slave labour created by the Nazi terror state, a work-force numbering some 7.6 million by 1945.

The same perverted ethos conflating technological advance with a lethal biopolitical agenda conditioned the nature of the modernity involved in work on the atom bomb[59] as well as the development of jet technology. Conditions for slave labourers in the factories underneath the Harz mountains where the V-2 was being constructed, were so grotesquely inhuman that even Albert Speer was appalled when he inspected the results of the implementation of his own orders in December 1943. A concomitant of the extraordinary expansion of German industry in the 1930s was first the smashing of independent labour organizations and the persecution of their communist leaders, and then, during the war, the rapid increase in the use of foreign, forced, and slave labour to a point where the productivity of the Nazi war economy actually increased after Speer took over from Fritz Todt as Minister of Armaments and War Production in 1942. Under the Nazis' 'apartheid system' – which in contrast to the pale imitation by the Republic of South Africa after the war was not reactionary and conservative but futural and *modernist* – 'non-Aryans' were routinely worked to death in marshes, quarries, and industrial complexes.

An insight into the 'human' side of Nazi technocratic modernism is afforded by the Deutsche Arbeitsfront (DAF), which together with its two sister organizations *Kraft durch Freude* (Strength through Joy) and *Amt für Schönheit der Arbeit* (Office for the Beauty of Work), worked to apply the principles of social modernism to improving the lot of ordinary 'Aryans' at work and play. Its visionary leader, Robert Ley, sought on their behalf to realize a Taylorist vision of utopia: maximum productive efficiency would be delivered by a racially pure workforce enjoying hygienic factory conditions, an equal-opportunity work market and employment rights (for men), regular retraining and continuous education, an extensive welfare and benefits system, a comprehensive scheme of social insurance, pension rights, and an access to health care which combined preventive, alternative, and hi-tech medicine. While slaves went to their excruciating, anonymous deaths, their heroic 'Aryan' counterparts would be housed on new estates in green suburbs in dwellings designed to encourage sound principles of social and ecological health.[60]

It is significant in the context of our primordialist theory of modernism that Ley's biographer, Ronald Smelser, attributes his tireless devotion to the revolution of 'Aryan' working-class life in the Third Reich – which meant total indifference to the suffering of other categories of human being – to what he describes as the 'millenarian' (palingenetic) temperament exhibited in his dramatic conversion to Hitler in 1924. Overnight this solved his profound existential crisis, transforming the 'hopelessness' and 'Godlessness' he had experienced throughout the First World War into the sense that (literally) through the intercession of Adolf Hitler 'a God in heaven' now 'led', 'steered', and 'protected' him. It was the same God who 'blessed Adolf Hitler's work with success', and who apparently looked to the Führer and not Christ, his 'only-begotten' Son, to represent him on earth.[61] Though lacking the philosophical sophistication of Heidegger's far more ephemeral enthusiasm for the Nazi regime, Ley was clearly motivated 'phenomenologically' by a similar drive to anchor his existence in the sacred and metaphysical dimension provided by the regenerated *Volk*.

PLANNING THE THIRD REICH

The inter war period was the Golden Age of planners if they could secure the funds to realize their projects. The manifest 'crisis of civilization' encouraged a general abandonment of the laissez-faire capitalism and the minimalist, night-watchman state which had been the ideals of nineteenth-century liberalism. The belief in the need for 'strong government' taking radical decisions in hard times in the best interests of its citizens ('dirigisme') links the Soviet five-year plans, the Fascist corporatist system, Keynsian economic theory, the New Deal in the US, and the 'planism' of the Belgian political thinker, first left-wing then right-wing, Hendrik de Man.[62] The future was painted in many contrasting political colours, but it was *planned*. The Third Reich enthusiastically embraced the new ethos and gave it a specifically modernist dimension by conceiving planning in terms of maximizing the health of a community defined as a homogeneous racial unit in order to overcome the crisis of Modernity.[63]

Symptomatic of the forward thinking that resulted were the mass housing projects drawn up by Hans Reichow to implement his concept of 'Organic Town Planning' and published during the war in the Reich's main periodical for planning theory.[64] Reichow was one of a generation of town planners who continued their profession under capitalist or communist regimes after the war, helping to create the foundations of a very different sort of society. But Nazi forward planning did not just involve housing. An entire section of German bureaucracy dedicated its energies till late in the war to finalizing the blueprint for the New European Order soon to result from the 'inevitable' victories of the Wehrmacht.[65] Even before 1939 other departments of Nazi 'macro-planning' had been drawing up detailed plans for the modernization of the Reich itself that was to start in earnest only after the projected end of the war in 1942. These envisioned a sophisticated infrastructure designed to support 9 million private cars and vast urban agglomerations, and addressed the environmental problems resulting from such rapid developments in what the historian Michael Prinz calls a 'staggeringly modern way'. The pedestrian zones in inner cities, cycle-lanes, and nature-sensitive routing of motorways that Nazi planners envisaged were decades ahead of their time, all symptoms of a concerted effort to establish a new harmony in the relationship of technological modernity to the forces of 'nature' and 'life'.

Prinz draws attention to the paradox that such an advanced urban life and 'a modern, popular leisure culture' would coexist after the war with Thing-Dramas, *Heimat* poetry, and a 'back to the soil' movement.[66] Yet such a paradox is resolved in the Nazi concept of a *rooted* modernity, an *organic* modernity based on a *biopolitical* concept of the value of life. Nor was this synthesis new. Two years before the Englishman Ebenezer Howard postulated his vision of the Garden City as a source of social regeneration in *To-morrow: A Peaceful Path to Real Reform* (1898), blueprints for fostering the symbiosis of nature with urban civilization had been already published in *Die Stadt der Zukunft* (*The City of the Future*) published by Theodor Fritsch.[67] Unlike Le Corbusier, whose reciprocal relationship with fascist town planners was born of architectural modernism,[68] Fritsch had arrived at his vision of the new city via his keen interest in *völkisch* communes, the back-to-nature movement, and racial hygiene. As owner of the notoriously anti-Semitic Hammer press, he went on to become Germany's most prolific writer and publisher of vitriolic attacks on Jews long before it became possible for the Nazis to take power. In 1944 *The Handbook of the Jewish Question*, which he also published in 1896, reached its 49th edition, having sold over a million copies, one of the thousands of racist diatribes that helped prepare the ground for the creation of the world's first 'racial state' in 1933.

THE MODERNIST RACIAL STATE

Fritsch's biopolitical thinking was informed by a vague cult of 'life' combined with intense racial prejudice. It was when biopolitics was shaped by scientistic currents of Social Darwinism, Monism, physical anthropology, eugenics, and racial hygiene that the modernist dynamic of the Third Reich was to have such devastating consequences. We established in Part One that by the turn of the century biopolitics in this sense was rapidly growing into an international phenomenon, part of the reaction by elites within the scientific, technocratic, and political community to a mythic cultural decadence recoded as a problem of mounting physical and biological degeneracy. The impact of this strand of modernism on political thinking was so powerful that in the course of the twentieth century sterilization programmes were adopted at some stage by the US, Peru, Panama, the Soviet Union, India, China, Australia, Canada, Sweden, Estonia, Finland, Iceland, Norway, Slovakia, and Switzerland. Even before the First World War had made concerns about the physical and demographic health of the nation endemic to the West, Winston Churchill, in his term as Home Secretary, had introduced a bill that included enforced sterilization. Previously he had written a memorandum to Prime Minister Henry Asquith in which he stated:

> The unnatural and increasingly rapid growth of the feeble-minded and insane classes, coupled as it is with a steady restriction among all the thrifty, energetic and superior stocks, constitutes a national and race danger which it is impossible to exaggerate. [...] I feel that the source from which the stream of madness is fed should be cut off and sealed up before another year has passed.[69]

The bill was rejected.

When Nazism came to power on the basis of a racial concept of the organic nation, a virulent anti-Semitism, and a totalitarian vision of the role of the state, it was integral to its 'perverse' logic that it would pass legislation designed to deal with its own 'race danger' and to 'cut off' and 'seal up' its own 'stream of madness'. It would also implement it with a systematic ruthlessness, bureaucratic efficiency, and technological modernity impossible in liberal democracies. The biopolitical rationale for the legislation was a complex mesh of the rigorously scientific with fantasies born of both scientistic and non-scientific mythopoeia, but it shared the same primordial *topoi* of pollution and cleanliness that inspired the Rwandan genocide of 1994.[70] According to research into the anthropological principles on which the regime based their efforts to establish a 'pure race',[71] the dominant influence was the confluence of the quest of *völkisch* thinkers such as Paul Lagarde for racial *purity* with the eugenicist obsession with racial *hygiene* which led Alfred Ploetz to found the German Society for Racial Hygiene in 1905.

The two currents of racism were able to converge largely because the Nuremberg Race Laws applied a blend of criteria drawn from *both völkisch* nationalism *and* eugenic racism in classifying the 'Aryan' community and its racial enemies. This created a composite juridical and bureaucratic – but also mental – framework for the state's subsequent biopolitical measures. They were also reconciled in the nebulous metaphor of the organic body politic, the *Volkskörper*,[72] as when Hitler declared in a speech of 27 January 1934:

> My movement encompasses every aspect of the entire *Volk*. It conceives of 'Germany' as a corporate body, as a single organism. There is no such thing as non-responsibility in this organic being, not a single cell which is not responsible, by its very existence, for the welfare and well-being of the whole.[73]

In *Mein Kampf*, he had already spoken prophetically of the man 'who profoundly understands the distress of his people and, having attained the ultimate clarity with regard to the disease, seriously tries to cure it'.[74] Such seer-like pronouncements from the Saviour, Artist, Warlord, Protector, Healer and *Physician* of Germany constituted a licence for racial hygienists and eugenicists 'working towards' the new Reich to adopt whatever measures they saw appropriate to improve the biological health of the nation, and believe they had *carte blanche* for removing any perceived threats to its purity and fitness. Nevertheless, their separate rationales for racial persecution produced ideological tensions that could still be detected in the discussions at the Wannsee Conference and during the execution of the Final Solution.[75]

However simplistic this account of Nazi racism, what stands out in the context of the present book is that both the currents of ethnic hatred it subsumes have a built-in component of social modernism. We have already seen that the *völkisch* movement was a manifestation of wide-spread populist and avant-garde longings for rootedness and embeddedness. We have also seen that eugenics originated in calls for the modern state both to eradicate degeneracy and for humanity's biological existence to be given a new *religious*, nomic basis by the spectacular progress of science in unravelling its mysteries. Michael Schwarz's article on the euthanasia debate in Germany between 1895 and 1945 assumes particular significance in this context. It throws into relief the way the advocates of euthanasia under the Third Reich saw themselves as the vanguard of the nation's modernization, but also highlights their zealous sense of *mission* in bringing about a healthy society in which the biological causes of degeneration had been eradicated.[76] Underlying their scientific zeal is the palpable *metaphysical* longing for a process of ritual catharsis that guarantees the health and immortality of the Volk, sacralized into the sole source of transcendence and redemption in the modern age. It is an act of sacralization symbolized in the toned bodies of Aryan workers showering in the washrooms of newly built hygienic factories or playing football on a KdF sportsground, their camaraderie and zest for life expressing the hope for the future of a young, healthy nation.[77]

It is this *modernist* aspect of Nazi racism that emerges whenever scholarly attention focuses on its modernity rather than its barbarity. Thus Christian Pross, in his introduction to *Cleansing the Fatherland*, highlights the intimate connection within the eugenics programme 'between destruction and modernization', stressing that 'Auschwitz cannot be seen without the Volkswagen plant in Wolfsburg, nor the SS regime of terror without the social security, health, and recreation programme provided by the Nazi trade union Deutsche Arbeitsfront'.[78] When the depth of field of the 'lens of Auschwitz' through which Peter Adam asked us to consider Nazi culture is modified to take in the hygienic housing estates, improved sports facilities, and subsidized holidays within the same panorama as the mass murder of racial enemies then it starts to become clear just how radical the Nazis' alternative to liberal modernity was, and how fanatical their modernist zeal to create a new order.

THE 'ECOLOGY' OF GENOCIDE

What has emerged from the application of our primordialist ideal type of modernism to the Third Reich is that it was created as a totalitarian 'gardening state' by a modern revitalization movement to implement a wide-ranging modernist programme of radical cultural, social, political, and military policies in order to purge Germany of decadence and create a healthier society. It is a portrait of the regime – painted with a consciously 'anti-revisionist' stress on the crimes against humanity it committed in the realization of this programme – which is deeply compatible with Zygmunt Bauman's *Modernity and the Holocaust*, his magisterial analysis of the nexus between Nazi genocide and the forces of modernization.[79]

It is a portrait also broadly corroborated by Enzo Traverso's investigation into the deeper rationale of the Holocaust in *The Origins of Nazi Violence*. Independently of Peter Osborne, but convergent with his argument, he stresses the intense *futural* dynamic of the Conservative Revolution which informed the ethos of Nazism. For him too it was the disembedding impact of modernity that by the first part of the nineteenth century had created a situation in which all radical attempts to restore the values allegedly destroyed by 'progress' were forced to assume a revolutionary rather than a conservative guise. At this point 'nostalgia for the traditional community was converted into a utopian aspiration toward a new community, a *Volksgemeinschaft* of the future'.[80]

Traverso also corroborates our analysis by interpreting the National Socialist drive for transcendence not as the travesty of allegedly Christian articles of faith and redemptive patterns of belief emphasized by some historians,[81] but a primordial and deeply *pagan* vitalism. In addition, he emphasizes the essentially syncretic nature of the Nazi *Weltanschauung* that we have interpreted as integral to its nature as the mazeway of a revitalization movement. Nazism was the product of the confluence of factors that had made Germany 'the laboratory of the West, one that synthesized a collection of elements – nationalism, racism, anti-Semitism, imperialism, anti-Bolshevism, anti-humanism – all of which existed throughout Europe but which elsewhere either remained muted or else never entered into toxic combination'.[82]

What stands out for Traverso in this lethal ideological cocktail, as it did for Modris Eksteins and Joachim Fest before him, was the conflation of the mythic with the scientistic, of the historical with the historic, of archaism with technicism:

> The crusading spirit of the old religious anti-Judaism was combined with the coldness of 'scientific' anti-Semitism, hence the horrifying World War II mixture of pogroms and industrial extermination, eruptions of brute violence and administrative massacre. *The revolt against the decadence of modernity appropriated the means of that very modernity.*[83]

The ultimate fruit of this ideological compound was what Traverso calls Nazism's 'redemptive violence',[84] a phrase redolent with palingenetic connotations of the quest for a secular transcendence. He quotes the assertion of Hans Kohn made in 1938 that the Nazi racial theory 'amounts to a new naturalistic religion for which the German people are the *corpus mysticum* and the army the priesthood'. In this ethos anti-Semitism became inseparable from a 'religion of nature' based on blind faith in biological determinism to the point where genocide itself came to represent *both* 'a disinfection, a purification – in short an "ecological" measure', *and* a ritual act of sacrifice performed to redeem history from chaos and decadence.[85]

Anecdotal evidence for the cogency of Traverso's argument comes from an interview given to the distinguished BBC reporter John Simpson by a veteran member of the Red Cross who in 1944 made an unofficial inspection of Nazi death camps. Asked why he did not attempt to confront the commandant of Auschwitz, Rudolf Höss, with the moral enormity of what was taking place under his authority, he was visibly shocked by the question. The very idea of challenging them was preposterous.

> These people were proud of their work. They were convinced of being engaged in an act of purification. They called Auschwitz the anus of Europe. Europe had to be cleansed. They were responsible for the purification of Europe. If you cannot get your head round that you will understand nothing at all.[86]

Such sentiments are echoed in the testimony of Dr Ella Lingens-Reiner, medical doctor and Auschwitz survivor, who on one occasion was able to ask the SS Doctor, Fritz Klein, employed to perform experiments on camp inmates, how he could reconcile his work with his Hippocratic oath. His reply was that it was precisely his Hippocratic Oath that legitimized his work: 'I am cutting out a festering appendix. The Jews are the festering appendix in the body of Europe. And this is why they must be cut out.'[87]

This chapter has presented one interpretive strategy for 'getting our head round' the apparently obscene proposition that, for most convinced Nazis working towards the new Reich, Auschwitz was a 'site' not for the enactment of sadistic fantasies and pathological hatreds, but for the purification of Europe, both literal and metaphorical. This is to see it 'ultimately' – though for purposes of historiographical reconstruction not *primarily* – as the product of *modernist* projects for a new, better, cleaner world. Primo Levi captured this thought with characteristic visionary precision when he called Auschwitz 'the ultimate drainage point of the German universe'.[88] Within the Nazi mindset, this camp was not just built to punish Jews and many other categories of alleged racial or moral degeneracy for being enemies of the Reich. It also was designed to act as a vast biopolitical sewage works, a technocratic installation where human waste products were disposed of once anything of value, their work capacity, their possessions, their hair, had been extracted for recycling to help the Nazi war effort. Genocide had become a matter of radical ecology.

The hell of Auschwitz and the many other death camps so scrupulously manufactured in the Third Reich was the anti-image of the ordered, efficient, *modern* villages and cities planned for the post-war Reich, teeming with healthy, productive citizens each one of whom had been deemed to have a 'life worthy of life' because of their potential contribution to the 'Aryan' gene pool and to realizing the goals of the national community. To destroy this life with technocratic efficiency was simultaneously, in cosmological terms, a 'holy act' paralleled by the Aztecs' ritual slaughter of their enemies to placate the Sun God.

Richard Evans has stated that: 'The Third Reich was engaged in a vast experiment in human engineering, both physical and spiritual, that recognized no limits in its penetration of the individual's body and soul, as it tried to configure them into a co-ordinated mass, moving and feeling as one.'[89] But this technocratic experiment was carried out for a higher purpose, a redemptive purpose, a transcendent, Cronus-defying purpose. It was an experiment carried out under a primordial sign of regeneration, the Swastika, perverted by Nazi cosmology into the symbol of an exclusively 'Aryan' rebirth based on the mysticism of good blood and bad blood. But it could only be a botched experiment.

In Franz Kafka's *The Penal Colony*, one of the most chilling fruits of the modernist literary (and Jewish)[90] imagination, the explorer who has arrived on the island witnesses an execution that also goes disastrously wrong, one that blends ancient ritual, hi-tec murder, and a mechanized process of redemption. The condemned are killed on an elaborate contraption, the Harrow, supposed to allow victims to understand the nature of their crime through the words it engraves in their flesh as they die, and so achieve a macabre transfiguration. But it starts to malfunction gruesomely:

> The machine was obviously going to pieces; its silent working was a delusion. [...] The Harrow was not writing, it was only jabbing, and the Bed was not turning the body over but bringing it up quivering against the needles. The explorer wanted to do something, if possible, to bring the whole machine to a standstill, for this was no exquisite torture such as the officer desired, this was plain murder [...] No sign was visible of the promised redemption.[91]

In December 1925, at a low point in the NSDAP's fortunes, another Franz, Franz Pfeffer von Salomon, had already placed himself on the other side of the 'aquarium glass' that separated him from Franz Kafka, Primo Levi and other alleged enemies of *homo Aryanus*. In his internal memorandum attacking Georg Strasser's 'socialism', he left no doubt about the fate that in his utopia of a reborn Germany would await those who were 'asocial', had 'lives unworthy of life', or were otherwise unfit to participate in the rebirth of the national community. He called them 'weighed and found wanting', a sardonic allusion to the phrase in Jewish scripture '*mene tekel*',[92] the Aramaic words written on the wall by an irate Jehovah to announce the imminent collapse of Belshazzar's

Empire. The judgement of von Salomon was equally final: 'Trees which do not bear fruit should be cut down and thrown into the fire.'[93]

Two decades later the emaciated bodies of *Fremdopfer* – the term used when *others* are sacrificed to a transcendent cause – would be burnt in their hundreds of thousands in the hi-tech crematoria of Auschwitz using ovens specially constructed by Topf & Söhne of Erfurt to SS specifications so as to be able to incinerate up to 4,765 corpses a day when used efficiently.[94] By then the vast Nazi megamachine of cultural metamorphosis and anthropological revolution was being smashed to pieces by the superior fire power of the Allies. *Wiedergeburt* had turned to *Untergang*. *Aufbruch* to another *Zusammenbruch*.[95] Rebirth to abortion. Hitler, the Healer, the *propheta*, the embodiment of 'redemptive nationalism', had failed to erect a new sacred canopy for the millions of Weimar's sleepwalkers, to 'rebuild the house', or 'start time anew'. Instead, by April 1945 entire German cities had been reduced to millions of tons of rubble. The promised renewal of history, the supposed new *aevum* had ended in *Stunde Null*. This was the 'zero hour' of the Third Reich's surrender, but also the zero hour when the arrow of Nazi historic time stopped, the sense of new beginning overwhelmed by the sense of an ending. Here too there was no sign of the promised redemption.

12
Casting Off

The first row of any knitting project is the 'cast-on' row. This provides the foundation for the stitches. The last row, which finishes the loops so they don't unravel, is called the 'bind-off' or 'cast-off' row.

Anon., Beginning to Knit (2006)[1]

My aim is not to dispute the existence of a connection between modernism and fascism: it is to think where that connection leaves us.

Reed Way Dasenbrock, 'Slouching towards Berlin' (1995)[2]

ENDING WITHOUT CLOSING

The 630-foot-high St Louis Gateway Arch was submitted as a competition entry by the distinguished Finnish-American architect Eero Saarinen in 1947. Finally opened to the public six years after his death, it was practically a replica[3] of the 590 foot arch which was designed by Adalberto Libera, one of Fascism's outstanding modernist architects, to provide the time-defying monument to EUR '42, the Esposizione Universale di Roma, had the Second World War not intervened. In 1933 the head of the Fascist air force, Italo Balbo, put in a triumphal appearance at Chicago's 'A Century of Progress' world fair after his successful formation flight across the Atlantic. The poet Marinetti composed an ode to the translucence of rayon as a metaphor to express Italy's regeneration. Le Corbusier submitted a project for building the new city of Pontinia on marshland newly drained by the Fascists. A Fascist doctrine of race was submitted to Mussolini by the Traditionalist thinker, Julius Evola, formerly Italy's leading Dadaist painter, admirer of Ernst Jünger, and praised to the skies in his turn by Gottfried Benn. Ernst Haeckel, one of the most scientific thinkers of his day, founder of the Monist League, and pioneer of the new disciplines of eugenics and ecology in Germany, joined the Ariosophically oriented Thule Society in 1918, just before it metamorphosized into the Deutsche Arbeiterpartei. Goebbels identified with the spirit of Vincent van Gogh's canvases and behind the scenes arranged the state funeral of Edvard Munch. A section of the SS intended to evaluate the medicinal properties of Amazonian plants immediately the war was finished, while other state departments fought an anti-smoking campaign, or planned pedestrian precincts and bicycle lanes in city centres.

Adolf Hitler had a genuine passion for Richard Wagner, one of the supreme musical modernists of the age, and took a personal interest in the building of the Autobahn system, an outstanding expression of modernist principles in aesthetics, design, engineering, regional and macro-planning, building technology, civil engineering, social engineering, and the gardening state: symbol of an 'alternative modernity' under construction. The car designed to turn the motorway into a mass transportation system, the Volkswagen, was so advanced in its technology and sleek in its design that it earned a place in the exhibition Modernism: Designing a New World held in London in the spring of 2006. Both Mies van der Rohe and Walter Gropius, two luminaries of the left-wing Bauhaus, submitted designs for major building projects under the Third Reich. Mies's co-designer of New York's Seagram Building, an iconic modernist architectural statement, was Philip Johnson, who had helped organize a US fascist party in the 1930s and followed Nazi troops into Poland. In 1978 Albert Speer donated Johnson a copy of his new book on architecture[4] with the dedication: 'For Philip Johnson, a fellow architect. With sincere admiration of his most recent designs. Best regards, Albert Speer.'[5] Speer created 'cathedrals of light' inspired by modernist aesthetics 70 years before searchlights were used in a similar way to mark Ground Zero, the sacralized space that was created where the World Trade Center Twin Towers stood till the morning of 9/11.[6] Ezra Pound took time out from writing some of the most important modernist poetry of the age to broadcasting pro-Fascist propaganda to the US and Britain and to supplementing his *Cantos* with a homage to the Salò Republic.[7] If readers find nothing disconcerting or anomalous in such *faits divers* it is because they (now) sense the profound elective affinity that can exist between the impulse of cultural modernism to create a new fictional nomos, the aspirations of social modernists to transcend an age of decadence and ill-health, and the rigorously futural mission of right-wing political modernists to build a *revolutionary*, but securely tap-rooted, society framed once more by a fixed mythic horizon.

No attempt will be made in this chapter to give our metanarrative a 'well-rounded' conclusion, for closure is impossible in such an empirically vast and methodologically complex field of studies, especially after the 'cultural turn' sensitized us to the fictitiousness of all neat endings. It will focus instead on 'casting off'. This can be taken in the technical sense given it by the knitting community of producing a 'bind-off' row which 'finishes the loops' of the argument to prevent them from unravelling. Simultaneously, it is being used with the nautical connotations both of leaving the temporary intellectual moorings provided by this synoptic interpretation of Western modernity, and of 'changing direction', of setting off on another tack. The reader will hopefully be left with a sense of having completed one exhausting but fulfilling journey, but also with the prospect of heading out from the jagged coastline and treacherous shallows we have explored in this book towards new intellectual and historiographical destinations, now liberated from my services as acting captain for the duration of the voyage. What follows are some tentative inferences, further considerations, and possible future research itineraries based on our findings with respect to three broad topics: modernism, fascism, and the historiography of both under the conditions of 'late modernity'.

MAXIMALIZING MODERNISM

Part One of this book constructed an ideal type of the term 'modernism' which contrasts in several important respects with the 'minimalist' one still prevalent in cultural history. This conventional usage, even when it refrains from delivering a concise definition of the term, tends to confine its remit in practice to avant-garde artistic and literary phenomena, which have furthermore often been endowed with left-wing connotations of socially progressive and anti-right wing political values, even though 'modernism' is not applied to political activism itself. In the maximalist sense we have given it, 'cultural modernism' acquires a significantly wider resonance by applying to projects conceived as contributions to the war against Modernity – modernity equated with a historical force or cultural ethos fostering decadence, ambivalence, anomy, the decay of values – that can be fought not just in art, but on the printed page and in lecture halls in a wide range of human sciences, such as philosophy, sociology, cultural anthropology, jurisprudence, economic, and political theory, freelance social criticism, cultural commentary, and journalism.

At this point *cultural* modernism morphs into *social* modernism, which embraces areas of academic endeavour and social activism rarely associated with modernism, such as the efforts of natural scientists to improve or regenerate society, and reformist projects or utopian movements working for radical social change of every description – expressed more corporeally and physically in action rather than verbally or through aesthetic form – whose sole common denominator is the aspiration to bring health and a renewed idealism about the future to a particular segment of society. Here it overlaps with the third aspect of modernism within its generously extended semantic boundaries, political modernism, which applies to vanguard or (would-be) mass movements of radicalism which work towards creating an entirely new form of society, envisaged metaphorically as 'a new world', by replacing a system of government experienced as spiritually bankrupt and chronically inadequate for the physical, social, and spiritual needs of human beings under actually existing modernity.

A number of propositions concerning this maximalist definition of modernism are to be drawn from Part One. Taken together they invite experts still applying the minimalist, predominantly literary or aesthetic usage to consider whether it enriches rather than dilutes the value of the term as a forensic tool for investigating aspects of Western modernity once its scope is deliberately widened in this manner – a process parallel in some respects to negotiating an enlargement of the European Union to admit new, culturally 'alien' societies.

One inference is the usefulness of distinguishing between on the one hand 'epiphanic modernism', where the artist or thinker makes no attempt to go beyond the comprehension and poetic articulation of what Frank Kermode calls 'fictions' of fallen and renewed metaphysical states of being, and on the other 'programmatic modernism' where they see in their *sustained* apprehension of a transcendent reality or higher values the basis for transforming aspects of, or even the whole of society. At this point literary tropes of decadence and renewal become palingenetic 'myths' that give inner cohesion and an ideological rationale to actions performed in external reality to inject new values and meaning into a spiritually dying modern world. The journal *La Voce* produced by the Florentine avant-garde to disseminate 'modernist nationalism' as the basis of a new Italy, and Ernst Jünger's promulgation of the new era being pioneered by technocratic German Man in *The Worker* are outstanding examples of programmatic modernism in the cultural sphere, as are the many Nietzschean announcements of an imminent 'transvaluation of values', such as the *Blue Rider Almanac* of 1911 or the plethora of Futurist manifestos on a wide range of creative activity.

We have already stressed in Part One that the pair of terms do not represent mutually exclusive positions, but two poles of sentiment or levels of optimism about the prospects of transforming Modernity and healing the damage inflicted on the sense of identity and transcendence by its 'storm' (Benjamin) or 'hurricane' (Broch). Many artists – W. B. Yeats and Ernst Jünger are just two examples – spent years working on the cusp between one and the other, while others, like Aleksandr Blok or Hanns Johst, moved to different positions on the spectrum according to the objective historical conditions in which they found themselves. Used sensitively within modernist studies as ideal types rather than rigid categories, the paired terms may help scholars make sense of a phenomenon that, reconceptualized as we have suggested, embraces at one extreme Frank Kafka, an artist who shunned publicity and became increasingly absorbed in his 'dreamlike inner world', and at the other Walter Gropius, an extrovert architect intent on 'changing the world' through design, whatever the regime in power at the time; at one extreme Virginia Woolf's painfully sensitive literary exploration of her intensely anomic experience of modernity occasionally suspended by diaphanous moments out of time, and at the other the fanatical dedication of Adolf Hitler and Joseph Stalin to 'making history' and forcing it on a straighter path.

Another challenge to conventional approaches to modernism posed by this book is the 'primordialist' perspective we have constructed, which is based on the premise that the double-edged sword of reflexivity predisposes human beings to be engulfed by terror if they are stripped of culture's 'sacred canopy'. At a purely metaphorical level this deliberately suggestive, speculative rather than scientific hypothesis concerning the dynamics of cultural formation and production has an affinity with the findings of the latest scientific research into the function of 'black holes' in the creation of the cosmos. Once entirely speculative entities or 'mathematical possibilities', and then considered an astronomical rarity, black holes now turn out to be not only banally common cosmic objects, but primary constituents of the universe as we know it, and do not know it – since as much as 96 per cent of the universe may consist of black matter and black energy whose presence is only inferable to human beings. Some leading astro-physicists postulate that many millions of the 80 billion galaxies or so thought to exist contain a 'supermassive black hole' which 'by churning up the gas around it' triggers 'the birth of stars, planets and life itself'. If this is true then the process of creative destruction is not just a metaphysical principle, but a literal cosmic and *cosmogonic* one: 'Despite being the most destructive thing in the Universe, scientists now think our supermassive black hole could be crucial in creating the galaxy as we know it'[8] (see Figure 22).

Our account of modernism postulates that our primal terror of the void has a similarly paradoxical function. Thus, when Marshall Berman talks of the 'maelstrom' driving contemporary utopianism, he is referring to the modern variant of the existential vacuum eternally abhorred by human consciousness. From an objective secular standpoint, this void has always provided the bookends of our brief existence as living organisms since the first dawning of human self-awareness and human temporality. But for the sake of sanity and survival it has always had to be denied and overcome through elaborate psychological ploys, mythopoeic illusionism, ritual mirrors, and cultural 'tricks of the light'. Such a bleak vision of the human condition is not to be dismissed simply because it smacks of modern existentialism. It has a deep kinship with much older philosophical traditions, such as Buddhism, Hinduism, and

Figure 22   Artist's impression of the supermassive black hole at the centre of a galaxy which imparts momentum and hence structure to the space around it and hence makes the creation of stars possible.[9]

Artist credit: © Gabriel Pérez Díaz (Instituto de Astrofisica de Canarias). Reproduced here with the kind permission of IAC.

Stoicism, as well as the 'negative epiphanies' of many individuals, most destined to go unrecorded. Perhaps the fascination of Edvard Munch's *The Scream* lies in its power as a wordless evocation of primitive terror and the ambivalent, crepuscular nature of modern experience. A lucid glimpse into the nihilistic substratum of all human existence was provided by Blaise Pascal when he refers in his *Pensées* of 1660 to the 'eternal abyss' at the core of Being. It is no coincidence that he devoted a section of his reflections to analysing the role of 'diversion' in providing a refuge from the 'pain' and 'nothingness' of the present which make it impossible for most of us to live solely within the moment without being overcome by acute restlessness and panic.[10]

The relevance of this primordial reflexive consciousness of the void to modernism[11] is underscored by the doyen of Modernist poets, Charles Baudelaire. The first stanza of his poem *Le Gouffre* (The Abyss) in *The Flowers of Evil* reads:

> Pascal had his abyss that moved along with him
> Alas! All is abyss – action, desire, dream,
> Word! And over my hair which stands on end
> I feel the wind of Fear pass again and again.

Here we are at the heart of darkness which he referred to in the poem *The Irremediable* as what he called 'la conscience dans le mal'. This has been translated 'the consciousness of doing evil', but our theory of modernism's primordial dynamics suggests instead that it expresses the dilemma of a human consciousness trapped in an infinite reflexivity without illusion, a bottomless fall from the grace of transcendence:

> Somber and limpid tête-à-tête –
> A heart becomes its own mirror!
> Well of Truth, clear and black,
> Where a pale star flickers.[12]

Considered from this gloomy perspective, the elaborate cosmologies and rituals of human 'culture' can be seen as elaborately systematized, and often extremely beautiful, but ultimately vain 'diversions'. It is the black hole of existential self-awareness in all of us, our fear of the 'eternal silence of infinite spaces' that so alarmed Pascal, which produces culture. Once the 'givenness' of the culture that has been handed down by tradition is eroded or shattered under the impact of modernity to a point where contemporary history is experienced as 'decaying', and the fabric of the world is 'rent asunder', it is this primordial black hole that 'churns up' the human psyche, causing our mythopoeic consciousness to swirl around the vortex until it either exhausts itself or triggers the principle of hope once again, engendering new mythic meanings projected onto the 'world'. It is the resulting palingenetic epiphanies and utopian programmes for change under modernity that are collectively familiar to historians as forms of 'modernism'. They are fruit of a dynamic, 'world-creating' process of the sort alluded to in Nietzsche's cryptic aphorism in the Prologue to *Thus Spoke Zarathustra*: 'One must still have chaos inside, in order to give birth to a dancing star.' (Zarathustra adds that the 'last men' will be so attuned to decadence and nihilism that 'the time will come when the human will give birth to no more stars'.)[13]

Such a highly speculative, though empirically grounded, thesis about the archaic dynamics of the modern creation of nomos under the conditions of modernity clearly invites further discussion and refinement. It calls upon those in the academic community who tend to treat modernism as an exclusively *modern* phenomenon to allow for the possibility that its widely acknowledged relationship to modernity of 'creative destruction' has adventitious roots extending into *archetypally* human responses to being alive in the world, notably the subliminal need to access a transcendent temporality, to feel in the presence of 'the numinous'. It urges cultural historians to give more weight to the accounts of the 'human condition' provided by modernists themselves whenever they take the form of programmatic texts that summon a new world to arise phoenix-like out of the decadence of the present. No less important for understanding the phenomenological aspect of twentieth-century social realities are the countless testimonies to profound but fleeting epiphanic experiences that explore the problem of sustaining flashes of suprapersonal meaning under the heartless, soulless dispensation of Modernity.

One such text that is worth many pages of dispassionate cultural analysis of the nature of modernity from our perspective is Lucky's sudden *Aufbruch* from muteness into logorrhoea in Samuel Beckett's *Waiting for Godot*. His soliloquy dramatizes the failure of our diversions, science, technology, religion, and even of 'panenhenic' moments of happiness[14] to secure meaning in a secularized world. Sporting activities, holidays, progress in medicine, 'the public works of Puncher and Wattmann', 'the labours left unfinished crowned by the Acacacacademy of Anthropopopmetry',[15] fragmentary images of 'a personal God with a white beard outside time,' or a this-worldy 'heaven so blue still and calm so calm with a calm which even though intermittent is better than nothing' ultimately fail in their primary aestheticizing and anaesthetizing function, namely to make us forget 'the skull, the skull, the skull, the skull'.

Beckett's play can be seen as a tragic-comic exposure, both devastating and cathartic, of the flimsy, threadbare veil we spin over the void in everyday life to 'give ourselves the illusion we exist'. It exposes through the power of dramatized metaphor the ploys and mind-games with which we delude ourselves momentarily into thinking that aeval time can be accessed and Cronus can be outwitted in a world where 'down in the hole, lingeringly, the grave-digger puts on the forceps'. Of course, *Waiting for Godot* is itself an example of countervailing, anti-nihilistic modernism which takes down to the wire the power of aesthetic creativity to give Apollonian form to human outrage against a Dionysian sense of cosmic absurdity and futility. But Beckett is a symptom of a much vaster cultural syndrome. Modernity has produced countless examples of epiphanic and programmatic modernism, of unique blends of Romantic with Dionysian pessimism in necessarily idiosyncratic cultural, social, and political visions of alternative worlds. There is thus no shortage of test cases with which to assess in considerable empirical detail the cogency of the 'big picture' we have drawn of modernism from our specially constructed vantage point, should the vista it offers strike a chord with experts in the field.

A FOOTNOTE ON POSTMODERNITY

Max Horkheimer once famously remarked that 'Someone not prepared to talk about capitalism should keep quiet about fascism.'[16] Less dogmatically, this book has argued that anyone not prepared to talk about modernity or modernism may by all means speak of fascism, but risks remaining oblivious of important aspects of its dynamics, and incapable of resolving the many paradoxes posed by its relationship to liberal capitalist modernity. In particular, it means underestimating the causal significance in its genesis and its appeal attributable to the crucial role played by the 'disembedding', anomy-generating impact of modernization in fuelling countless revolts against 'decadence' of which fascism was but one example – albeit one which changed the course of modern history in a way that cost millions of lives. It is a position that behoves us not to remain entirely silent about *postmodernity* either.

The high-altitude reconnaissance mission we have carried out over the terrain of modernity suggests that it can be ideal-typically periodized within the following phases of development: the 'pre-Revolutionary' (1730–89) and 'post-Revolutionary' (1790–1850) phases of 'early modernity'; followed by 'high modernity' starting around 1850 in some urbanized, cosmopolitan milieux of the West and coterminous with the rise of modernism. The importance of the caesura marked by the First World War suggests that 'high modernity' can in turn be usefully divided into fin-de-siècle (1850–1914) and inter-war phases (1918–39), followed by 'late modernity' (1945–2001), the two world wars creating exceptional conditions of their own. It should be noted that this schema does not accommodate such a thing as 'postmodernity'.[17] Late modernity may still be with us, but further into the twenty-first century the long-term repercussions of 9/11 and the responses of the international community to the threat of global warming may with hindsight come to be considered by cultural historians as marking the inauguration of a new phase in the evolution of modernity of as yet uncertain terminology.

A feature of 'late modernism' is the general retreat of modernism from its more programmatic and totalizing forward positions in the permanent war with anomy. In the decades after 1945 a mood of profound existential disillusionment, and of disaffection with utopian schemes of renewal, swept though the European intelligentsia, so helping to spawn yet another polysemic 'ism', namely 'postmodernism'. What the primordialist perspective on modernism developed in this book suggests is that postmodernism does not betoken a general shift in the *Zeitgeist*, let alone herald a whole new stage in the evolution of Western culture. Instead, it is to be treated as a particular current or 'school' of contemporary speculative thought and academic methodology which coexists with countless *modernist* responses to Modernity still seeking palingenetic solutions to the continuing (perceived) cultural crisis of the sort familiar from the first decades of the century, the majority of which have renounced totalizing ambitions. Given the age that produced it, it is hardly surprising if it is possible to detect within postmodernism a modernist dynamic of its own.

Some schools of postmodernism have stigmatized socio-political modernism as a source of methodologically naïve intellectual practice and of totalitarian ('fascistoid') projects for the transformation of society whose attempted realization has catastrophic consequences. This has diverted attention from the degree to which 'postmodernism' is in some respects *itself* a manifestation of a totalizing war against decadence, in other words a paradoxical form of modernism. An intellectual current that belligerently declares war against 'metanarratives' is liable to spawn grand narratives of its own with which to combat them. This can be seen particularly clearly in the case of Jean-François Lyotard who announced the death of 'grands récits' in *The Postmodern Condition. A Report on Knowledge.*[18] As Gary Browning has shown,[19] he nevertheless absolutizes his own interpretation of Marx and Hegel 'through the back door', thereby betraying in his own work the presence of an unacknowledged metanarrative that is integral to all abstracted configurations of reality in the human battle with Cronus.[20]

In short, postmodernists have developed their own cultural revitalization movement with its own rites and cultic discourse presided over by 'major' thinkers, luminaries who assume the guise of *prophetae* weaving intellectual spells with their ludic and ironic recombinations of Western thought. Some of their 'petits récits' of modern history intended to dethrone master narratives themselves have thinly veiled delusions of grandeur. Meanwhile millions of their fellow human beings continue to inhabit not postmodernity, but high modernity, and thus retain non-postmodern worlds of cognition, experience, and belief within mental horizons framed by myths, and thus remaining stubbornly impervious to the efforts of deconstruction and demystification performed by mere intellectuals.

The thesis of this book is that the condition of modernity and its countervailing modernism has not been – and will never be – collectively or comprehensively superseded by a total era of postmodernity and postmodernism. Once these are seen as no more than countercultural sub-currents within late modernity, and hence forms of late modernism, it clears the way for academic attention to focus on the continued historical repercussions of a now *globalizing* modernity on traditional societies both inside and outside the West. Thus modernist political studies in the maximalist and primordialist sense proposed in this book promise to illuminate neglected aspects of the totalizing forms of sacralized politics that emerged in the twentieth century in non-Europeanized societies such as twentieth-century China[21] and Cambodia that became exposed to the anomic, disembedding forces of modernization that earlier ravaged the Europeanized world.

One contemporary phenomenon illuminated by this perspective is the growth in 'religious extremism'. The perpetual nomic crisis generated by an ever intensifying process of modernization precipitates in some believers on whose society it impacts the Manichaean vision of a traditional faith community 'running out of time', the victim of an alien Modernity of the West that has become a lethal enemy in the name of 'progress'. Following a primordial existential logic, those with a sufficiently intact faith in a religious tradition – especially those who feel personally or vicariously oppressed by the acute socio-economic or political problems of their spiritual fellow-countrymen – may thus resolve to protect *at all costs* the (imagined) wellsprings of *their* culture and religion. By doing so they hope to stave off the collapse of the sacred canopy peculiar to their tradition, so protecting from inner decay a society once (mythically) united by a shared cosmology. This approach is fully corroborated by the detailed work on the mindset of 'religious' terrorism already carried out by some experts. Thus in his seminal work on the subject, *Destroying the World to Save It* – written *before* 9/11 – Robert Lifton argues that it is the anomy experienced in all rapidly secularizing societies that has bred movements such as the Aum Shinrikyo sect in Japan or the now globalized al-Qaeda, all of them mobilized by the belief that moral regeneration can only be brought about by acts of cathartic terrorism directed at mainstream society. True to the principle of 'creative destruction' we have encountered throughout this study of modernism, such surgical violence aims to purge the corruption of a decadent modernity and inaugurate a new historical dispensation with restored metaphysical foundations.[22]

The radicalization of religious politics into anti-liberal creeds is not always socio-political modernism in the way we have defined it or explored in this book. The operational premise of 'religious fundamentalism' is that the historical link with the sacred tradition or 'base' – the literal meaning of 'al-Qaeda' – of society has *not* yet been severed or irrevocably damaged. Acts of violence committed in order to protect an ancient religious culture thus stem from a modern permutation of an *ultra-conservative*, and *reactionary* response to the terror of anomy, even if it has absorbed many new elements into the traditional faith, such as heterodox readings of Scripture and the deployment of Western technology such as the internet and mobile phone.[23]

Such a line of interpretation thus sheds light both on the politicization of non-European religions into illiberal political creeds,[24] and on the growth in religiously motivated 'terrorism' which, at least *on one level*, can be seen as the ritualized expression of a *palingenetic* war on Modernity. In this perspective it becomes particularly significant that at a structural level 'religious extremism' displays parallels with the 'fanaticism' of inter-war Bolshevism and fascism – for example in the obsession with decadence and society's purification, and with the need to eliminate 'racial' enemies. It also accounts for the role played in its ideological rationalization by elements of ludic recombination in tailoring the traditional religious world-view into a mazeway appropriate to believers condemned to live within Western modernity. This phenomenon is epitomized not only in the sophisticated use of globalized technology by some Islamist groups to realize their vision of a resurrected caliphate, but also in instances of symbiosis of the neo-fascist extreme right with ultra-religious Islamism.[25] Such developments are consistent with a theory of modernism that predicts the ongoing formation process of unlikely ideological alliances and hybrids in the quest for a new 'mazeway' as a reaction to globalization.

No less significant are those within minority faith communities in Western societies who attempt to create a new synthesis between their traditional religious culture and the secular pluralism of their host 'First World' culture in a way that embraces pluralism rather than the demonization of imaginary enemies of the 'true' faith. This is a benign modernist reaction to the threat of anomy, since it generates new hybrid forms of culture. The results exemplify the 'cultural mongrelization' which Salman Rushdie has celebrated for its role in ensuring that 'newness enters the world'. This approach to culture abhors the 'absolutism of the Pure', and welcomes the way different cultural identities and cosmologies 'leak into each other' under modernity 'like flavours when you cook'. It is a spirit that marries a postmodern awareness of cultural relativism with the ability to assert a strong identity.[26] Clearly such issues are of enormous complexity. Nevertheless, the progressive refinement and empirical 'fleshing out' of a maximalist definition of modernism along the lines we have suggested may contribute eventually to the emergence of a 'bigger picture' of modernity, one which highlights common patterns in the psychological and social dynamics conditioning how traditional societies all over the world are responding to an increasingly globalized late modernity within an ever more stressed planetary habitat.

FASCISM: NEITHER MODERN NOR ANTI-MODERN

In his classification of fundamental ideological positions assumed by historians on the nature of fascism, Adrian Hewitt – one of a handful of cultural historians to have explored in depth its relationship to modernism – identifies a 'crucial axis of distinction'. This is 'between those who regard fascism as one of the forms taken by political and cultural modernity, and those who view it as a more or less overt reaction *against* modernity'.[27] If the perspective offered in this book is applied not just to Fascism and Nazism but to generic fascism 'as a whole', then the dichotomy between these two camps of opinion is transcended (*aufgehoben*) in almost Hegelian fashion within a higher synthesis.

Fascism is one of the forms taken by political and cultural modernity, but it is simultaneously a radical reaction *against* the political forms of 'actually existing modernity' that emerged from the organized bloodshed of the First World War, whether that of liberal capitalist (e.g. in France) or purely authoritarian military dictatorship (e.g. in Primo de Rivera's Spain). It equally strongly rejected other alternatives to this modernity, such as the one offered by Bolshevism in Russia, or the modernized authoritarian nationalism embodied in Austria's 'Corporate State' under Engelbert Dollfuss. Instead, it sought a new temporality, or rather it sought to actualize 'the temporality of the new'. Even when it welded elements of the past – many also valued by conservatives – into the new ideological synthesis (mazeway), fascism was an expression of modernism in the political, maximalist sense we have proposed, and hence imbued with its own distinctive futurity.

The important feature of this approach is not the recognition of the 'connection between modernism and fascism' in itself, but as Dasenbrock points out, 'where that connection leaves us'. In formulating its own anti-conservative, revolutionary variant of organic nationalism each fascism generated a unique ideological position attuned to local historical conditions on such issues as the health or degeneracy of aesthetic modernism, biological racism and anti-Semitism, economics, technology, imperialism, and the Church. However, despite considerable differences on specific issues even within the same movement, the hallmark of fascism compared with liberal or less radical forms of nationalism is that it operated as a political form of modernism in the maximalist, primordialist sense, both as a movement (a 'revitalization movement') and regime (a 'modernist state'), based explicitly on an organic conception of the nation.

There are several inferences to be drawn from this model which require considerable road-testing before they can be said to make a significant contribution to the historicization of fascism in general, and to the reconstruction of specific episodes in its history by specialists working 'idiographically'. First, it proposes that it is the modernist revolt against Modernity that provides the historical context and causal explanation for the palingenetic aspect of fascism's ideology, policies, and *praxis* – its drive to construct a new type of society and a new type of national character ('Man'). As I pointed out in Chapter 6, its vital role in shaping fascism which I postulated in *The Nature of Fascism* has been recognized implicitly or explicitly by a number of eminent historians working in this area over the last decade, whatever faults they find with the concept of fascism I have elaborated from this recognition. The theory of modernism presented in this book adds a new dimension to the argument put forth there. It maintains that the differently constituted 'modernist' component of both Fascism and Nazism means that their common theme of national rebirth, of 'cleansing' the nation of decadence, their ritual form of politics ('political religion'), and their charismatic leader cult – so often associated in the past with travesties of Christian millenarianism – are to be located within archetypally human instincts to project a canopy of meaning and of communal belonging onto the 'world' when confronting the spectres of chaos and anarchy. Works that focus on the religious dimension of the two fascist regimes, such as Emilio Gentile's seminal *The Sacralization of Politics in Fascist Italy*, and Michael Burleigh's *The Third Reich: A New History* and *Sacred Causes*[28] are provided by the theory of modernism constructed here with a *primordial* and 'anthropological' rather than narrowly Christian and Eurocentric framework. It is a theory profoundly compatible with the insistence of both authors that the regime under investigation is not to be construed as a form of Christianity, 'positive' or otherwise, but as one that compulsively created its own cultic form of politics.

Second, my approach suggests that 'modernism', 'the revitalization movement', and (in the case of the two regimes) 'the gardening state' should be considered definitional components of generic fascism. To be more precise, they should be inserted into a cluster of generic concepts which, as Emilio Gentile has argued,[29] intersect and interact in characterizing fascism, notably 'totalitarianism', 'political religion', 'charismatic politics', 'palingenetic myth', 'anthropological revolution', and 'organic nationalism'. A third feature of treating fascism as a form of modernism is that it encourages more emphasis to be placed on its policies and *praxis* than the abstract reconstructions of its 'nature',[30] and thus discourages the wild-goose chase for the 'fascist minimum' that scholars such as myself have sometimes been accused of encouraging. The pursuit of the 'ultimate ideal type' of fascism – as numerous historians have pointed out – does indeed risk becoming sterile and static from an idiographic perspective if it detracts attention from 'what actually happened'. It also diverts precious intellectual resources from considering fascism's evolution as a living historical force in its unique permutations. However, the reflexive metanarrative we have offered here will hopefully provide comparative fascist studies with the intellectual exit velocity needed to move out of the rather stagnant phase into which debate seems to have settled at present.

THE MODERNIST CAUSALITY OF GENERIC FASCISM

How an emphasis on the modernist aspect of fascism encourages such a reorientation can be illustrated by briefly considering the relevance of this book to the 'five stages' in its development that form the subject of Robert Paxton's *The Anatomy of Fascism* (2004). What it throws particularly into relief are important aspects of the material preconditions to both the first and second stages of fascism's development that he identifies, 'the creation of movements' and 'their rooting in the political system'.[31] It highlights the fact that the first wave of fascist movements emerged in the acutely liminoid conditions of high modernity then prevailing in inter-war Europe. They all originated as attempts to create the nucleus of a new national *communitas* that would be capable of 'seceding' from an existing society seen as in its death throes and beyond repair, so as to form a new order on the basis of a new, highly syncretic nomos (world-view, programme) embodied in a leader who was, at least to his most fanatical followers, 'charismatic'.

Such a generic conceptual framework arguably offers a useful heuristic perspective within which to analyse the specific configuration of crisis prevailing in each national context where a fascist movement emerged, and how far the counter-revolutionary forces, whether liberal, conservative, or communist, closed off or opened up the political space needed for it to thrive. The most salient value of the modernist perspective, however, is the way it interprets the syncretic nature of fascism's ideology as the product of a primordial process of mazeway resynthesis. It thus encourages historians to study the way each movement acted as a point of convergence or a lingua franca for a host of *diverse* currents of cultural, social, and political modernism that were, in circumstances of exceptional instability, able to be loosely allied by the common cause of a reborn nation under a leader who assumed the guise of a *propheta*.

As for the crucial third stage, 'the seizure of power', or fascism's *Aufbruch* into what it saw as a new era in the form of a totalitarian regime, this occurred only in Giolittian Italy, Weimar Germany, and to a very limited extent in authoritarian Romania and Hungary. Despite Paxton's best efforts to demonstrate the contrary, two case studies are an inadequate empirical basis for a generic ideal type of fascism's 'life-cycle' beyond the movement stage. However, one common feature does stand out among the profound differences between the two national contexts of the fascist breakthrough: a nomic crisis of national proportions. In Italy this was the result of a constellation of factors which created a sense of state emergency intense enough to convince Victor Emmanuel III that Mussolini was a suitable head of a coalition government in October 1922 after the March on Rome had demonstrated the vulnerability of the government. A second constellation of such factors which emerged in late 1924 after the ambiguous outcome of the Matteotti Crisis legitimized Fascism's totalitarian experiment with personal dictatorship in the eyes of millions of active supporters and passive fellow travellers. Similarly, the collapse of

Weimar after 1929 created a unique window of opportunity for Hitler by turning Nazism for the first time into a genuine mass movement rallied by the prospect of a new Germany. It is important to stress, however, that in each case, it was the collusion or acquiescence of political elites prepared to lever the fascist leader into power that played the decisive role in the success of their movement. This points to a contingency that defies the formulation of 'laws of evolution' governing fascism's metamorphosis from revitalization movement into modernist state.

The present approach also draws attention to two causal aspects of Paxton's stages four and five, 'the exercise of power' and 'the long duration'. These he sees involving 'entropy' and inner collapse in the case of Fascism, and a catastrophic 'radicalization' in the case of Nazism that hastened military defeat. First, by envisaging a future based on perpetual charismatic rule, continuous dynamism, ceaseless territorial expansion, and permanent revolution, both the Fascist and Nazi regimes gave themselves no hypothetical way out of the second, liminal phase of the triadic process involved in all rites of passage. Unlike Bolsheviks who theoretically could look forward to the eventual withering away of the state, inter-war fascist movements had no exit strategy, no way of turning off the *perpetuum mobile* they had created, no prospect of closure even in the long term. They were bound eventually to become bogged down in their own dynamism, moribund in their vitalism. There could be no stabilization, no viable routinization of the charismatic legitimacy of the state, no social or military peace, no institutional procedures for passing on power to a non-charismatic leader, or for reinvesting it in the party. Nor could power even on paper be one day entrusted to the people itself in a gradual process of democratization without abandoning the first principles of fascism as a process of permanent palingenesis. Had Mussolini and Hitler managed to cling on to power, growing old 'gracefully' and slipping into senility, then both regimes may have gone the way of Salazar's Portugal and Franco's Spain, charismatic power draining away to a point where the renewal of autocracy after their deaths was impossible, and rapid democratization ensued. However, such an atrophy of modernist energies would have been the ultimate betrayal of the core fascist world-view, a betrayal neither leader could contemplate.

The ultimate 'failure' of fascism as the praxis of a regime emphasized by our approach, however, lies in its ultimate aspiration – the 'anthropological revolution'. The goal of producing a generation of 'new men' and 'new women' incarnating national rebirth – was intrinsically unrealizable. This is because the modernist state sets itself objectives which have not been conceived within the 'art of the possible', but through the faculty of metaphysical mythopoeia and the idealist cult of the 'will'. It refuses to be constrained by pragmatic evaluations of what is feasible within the resources available, and proceeds to pursue policies dictated by projections of future mythic states of transcendent perfection onto three-dimensional human reality which can only be realized in the fourth dimension of fiction, art, or religious myth. The sheer complexity of the psychological and social forces shaping human nature and behaviour is beyond the ken and control of any state, no matter how powerful. No amount of social engineering, social control, and state terror can resolve this aporia, especially in a pluralistic, atomized, modern society.

As Richard Evans observes, 'a society cannot be totally transformed in a mere six years without huge, murderous violence of the kind that occurred in Russia' in red terror and purges. As the decline and fall of the Soviet Empire in the 1980s demonstrated, even this was not enough to create the New Soviet Man.[32] As a result, even the more radical of the two regimes, the Third Reich, found that 'in one area after another [...] the totalitarian impulse was forced to compromise with the intractability of human nature'.[33] No matter how much energy Mussolini and Hitler had been able to pour into rooting out decadence at home as well as abroad, human nature would have continued to remain 'intractable' under their regimes. Even given more decades in which to pursue its scheme for the rebirth of the West, the Nazi state, by far the more ruthless in eradicating the weeds and pests in its garden, would have failed just as much to make the 'new German' in its image as the Fascist efforts to 'complete the Risorgimento' failed to make 'the new Italian'. Had historical circumstances enabled Speer to realize his project for Germania's 'Große Halle' – the Great Dome of the new Berlin to be built on a scale so vast that clouds would have formed near its ceiling – it would have been no more than an empty mausoleum for the still-born 'New German' (see Figure 23). The slaves completing its obscenely proportioned cupola would have been granted a vista over killing fields stretching as far as the eye could see from which no authentic human life, individual or communal, could ever spring forth as long as the Nazis were in power.

Yet the main value of the account we have given of the role of modernism in the regimes created by Fascism and Nazism for historians hopefully lies less in the realm of the counter-factual, than in understanding what they actually achieved in the few years allotted to them. Seeing them as different permutations of the 'modernist state' reveals the 'perverse' *logic* of the doctrines and policies they applied to social reality, their thrust towards establishing an *alternative* modernity based on a preliminary process of regeneration, cleansing, or palingenesis. In whatever sphere they considered worthy of their horticultural or surgical attention, their efforts were directed towards bringing into being a new *future*, even if the utopian vision was formulated in the apparently 'pastist' discourse of 'reconnecting forwards'. This has considerable importance not just for the (once) highly contested existence of a 'fascist culture', but also for

Figure 23   Still of actors from the German docu-drama *Speer und Er* showing Hitler in the last days of the Reich discussing details of the Große Halle with its architect, Albert Speer. The building, whose proportions deliberately dwarfed any other domed edifice in existence, was conceived as the centrepiece of the transformation of Berlin into Germania, the capital of a world empire that now existed only in the Führer's head.

an appreciation of how quickly the two fascist states could count on sufficient consensus among the population to undertake radical renewal in every major area of society. By feeling enthusiasm for what was happening in their nation, millions of 'ordinary' Italians and Germans became *de facto* cultural, social, and political *modernists* working towards the new nation and new era. Their sympathy for a regime adopting radical solutions to the perceived anomy and decadence of a society 'running out of time' created the basis for a profound receptiveness to draconian solutions. This in turn provided the basis for the proactive collaboration of millions with the regimes in their years of consensus (c. 1929–36 in Italy, 1933–41 in Germany). Particularly in the Third Reich it was a tacit or explicit collaboration which often had catastrophic personal consequences for the lives of all those who projected their hopes and fears for the future onto Nazism, not to mention those inflicted on the lives and deaths of their demonized enemies.

A further advantage of this approach is that focusing on the common denominator of modernism both *within* the ideological currents that constituted Fascism and Nazism and *between* them supplies a methodological basis for comparing the two regimes that is more heuristically valuable than one based on 'an "outside in" perspective'.[34] Rather than mechanically note external parallels and contrasts (leader cult, demographic policy, cult of violence etc.), it encourages the researcher to investigate their inner rationale and common palingenetic dynamic and to understand, using methodological empathy, the goals, utopias, and *dreams* of convinced fascists so as to make greater sense of their *actions*.[35]

THE ROLE OF MODERNISM IN ABORTIVE FASCISMS

This book has focused on the implications of fascism's modernist dynamics for the ideology and praxis of Fascism and Nazism, two fascisms that successfully made the transition from 'social anti-structure' to a regime that through a blend of hegemony and coercion implemented programmes designed to regenerate the nation. However, the thesis we have constructed also has considerable repercussions for the study of fascisms that never reached this stage, as well as for comparative fascist studies in general. In particular, it suggests that the individual histories of these 'abortive' fascisms[36] need further scrutiny to establish their unique relationships to modernity in the light of the new ideal type. An example of the innovative interdisciplinary scholarship, both empirically rich and theoretically sophisticated, that could result is the growing corpus of groundbreaking articles and monographs already published by Mark Antliff on the relationship between modernism, modernity, and several varieties of French ultranationalism and fascism.[37] Cumulatively, these complement the extensive empirical work on French fascism carried out by Zeev Sternhell while significantly modifying his thesis concerning the nature of fascism. This they achieve by exploring the multiple interconnections and synergies that arose in fin-de-siècle and inter-war France between cultural modernists, organic nationalists, Sorelian socialists, and various types of home-grown and mimetic fascist. In the process all became active in promoting currents of modernism in such areas as aesthetics, philosophy, social criticism, social hygiene, welfare theory, eugenics, or town planning, a natural response to the crisis of inter-war France at a time when the national obsession with decadence and renewal was at its height and the end of liberal civilization palpably nigh.[38]

In other cases, too, research into fascist modernism can build on valuable foundations already in place. The British Union of Fascism's commitment to a technocratic vision of national rebirth is well documented, and some important research has been undertaken on the palingenetic, anti-decadent thrust of its cultural politics which underlay its increasing tendency after 1933 to look on Nazism rather than Fascism as its role model for the new order,[39] and on the highly modern way it conceived politics and the use of the media to create support.[40] A major monograph remains to be written on the common modernist matrix that links the support the BUF received from a motley set of high-profile ideologues represented by such figures as Arthur Chesterton (an avant-garde writer and anti-Semite obsessed with cultural decadence),[41] Alexander Raven Thomson (former communist, Spenglerian historian of civilization, and theoretician of a British corporate state), Henry Williamson (who harboured fantasies of the 're-greening' of Britain and establishing its historical entente with Germany now that it was under Hitler), William Joyce (later Lord Haw-Haw, a proponent of the crudest Nazi anti-Semitism), and Ezra Pound. This is not to forget Oswald Mosley himself, whose proposed mazeway resynthesis for the Greater Britain blended elements of bowdlerized Nietzsche, Spengler, a secularized Christianity, and Keynesian economics with increasingly virulent cultural and economic anti-Semitism.[42]

Elsewhere there is little to go on as far as Anglophone publications about the relationship between modernism and fascism are concerned, but trial borings indicate several deposit-rich terrains waiting to be explored in greater detail. For example, the absorption of cultural modernism into Portugal's 'parafascist'[43] Estado Novo and into Rolão Preto's abortive Blue Shirt fascist movement invite further investigation in the light of an article by José Zúquete. This documents the failed attempt of the intellectual António Ferro to use his role as director of propaganda to inject into Salazar's regime elements of the radical vision of the new Portugal he had previously articulated as editor of *Orpheu*, an organ of cultural and nationalist modernism reminiscent of what was being produced in pre-war Florence.[44] In Franco's Spain fascism was again marginalized, the Falange reduced to playing a largely propagandistic role despite the official hero cult of its leader José Antonio Primo de Rivera. However, the social modernism of its 'national syndicalist' vision of the new Spain and the futural thrust of the only apparently 'pastist' aesthetics exemplified in its cultural journal *El Escorial* may well prove worth revisiting in the context of the theory expounded in this book.

Research into the Brazilian Integralists promises to reveal an even more powerful synergy of aesthetic, social, and political modernism. In national conditions of extreme socio-economic upheaval, this movement, which in 1934 numbered some 180,000 members, celebrated the unique synthesis of races which formed the basis of 'Brazilianness', staged elaborate political rituals of communal integration and organic renewal, and adopted as its equivalent of the Swastika the Greek letter Sigma (Σ), the mathematical symbol for summation. Moreover, its leader, Plínio Salgado, wrote visionary tracts announcing the advent of the 'fourth era of humanity' to overcome the contemporary age of dissolution.[45] In doing so he was exploring ways to implement the totalizing metanarrative he had generated in response to an acute sense of living on the threshold of a new era. It was his sense of mission to act as the *propheta* of the nation that had earlier inspired him to lead the nationalist, anti-cosmopolitan faction in the 'Week of Modern Art' of February 1922 which launched cultural modernism in Brazil.[46]

A MODERNIST IRON GUARD?

Just how radically revisions carried out in this vein might challenge still well-entrenched assumptions about fascism's essential reactionariness can be illustrated by the Romanian Iron Guard. This movement is still generally assumed to be both radically anti-modern,[47] and so aberrantly 'religious' in its politics that its credentials as a member of the fascist family are sometimes questioned.[48] Yet, seen through the lens of our ideal type of modernism, a radically different reading suggests itself. Radu Ioanid has argued persuasively that the Iron Guard made a concerted attempt to appropriate and transform Romanian Orthodox Christianity into a political instrument in a spirit that made it 'the enemy of genuine Christian values and spirituality'. As a result religious belief was subtly stripped of its metaphysical dimension so as to be enlisted in the mythic construction of 'Romanianness' and the creation of *Omul Nou*, the New (Romanian) Man, *within* historical time.[49] Thus when Eugen Weber stressed the similarities of its revivalist ethos and that of an African cargo cult,[50] he was picking up, not on its religious orthodoxy, but on its nature as a modern revitalization movement based on charismatic politics, one which extensively mythicized Romania's past and its religion in a bid to create an alternative future.

This interpretation is entirely consistent with the active involvement of some its leading members with biopolitical currents cultivated in Romania's more technocratic academic and political circles.[51] These in turn formed an integral part of a flourishing Eastern European academic and technocratic culture of social modernism concerned with promoting racial hygiene in the inter-war period.[52] Indeed, some of the most influential Romanian eugenicists were members of Codreanu's movement, notably Iordache Fǎcǎoaru, Traian Herseni, and Sabin Manuilǎ, who headed the 'Bioanthropological Section' of the Central Institute of Statistics in Bucharest where Iordache worked. Had the Iron Guard come to power it may well have developed its own technocracy pursuing an active programme of modernization and modernist social engineering, including eugenics, within its idiosyncratic variant of the totalitarian state.[53]

In this context links between the Iron Guard's charismatic politics[54] and elements of cultural modernism, so widely ignored in Anglophone scholarship, assume a fresh significance. The Romanian scholar, Maria Bucur, has identified two of the formative influences on the organic nationalism and extreme xenophobia embraced by the post-war generation of students from which the movement's leader and *propheta*, Corneliu Codreanu, emerged. One was the cultural journal *Cuvântul* ('The Voice', a name reminiscent of the Florentine periodical of modernist nationalism, *La Voce*). The second was the charismatic professor of philosophy Nae Ionescu, whose call for a new ethical basis for modern existence was 'in line with the modernist reconstruction of spiritual renewal'.[55] Even before the war a powerful anti-Semitic *völkisch* culture had grown up embodied in the poet Mihai Eminsecu, the political economist Alexandru Cuza, and the historian Nicolae Iorga. In the extreme liminoid conditions of inter-war Romania one interpretation of the crisis of contemporary civilization that gained currency in avant-garde circles held that the collapse of the Newtonian cosmology resulting from the work of Albert Einstein and Max Planck signalled the transition from the era of physics to the era of metaphysics, where the forces of mythopoeia and 'the dream' would regain their primacy over the decadent forces of rationalism and materialism.[56]

Such ideas, whose resonance with the primordialist theory of modernism is obvious, had a deep impact not only on Codreanu's sacralization of politics, but on intellectual modernists such as Mircea Eliade, Emil Cioran, and Constantin Noica. All three embarked on idiosyncratic quests for sources of cultural renewal before being drawn to the Iron Guard. The culmination of this trend was December 1937 when Eliade, while still a professor at the University of Bucharest, ran for Parliament as the candidate of *Totul pentru Ţarǎ* ('Everything for the Fatherland'), the party-political formation of the Iron Guard. He went on to become Director of the History of Religions Department at the University of Chicago after the war. Here he pursued his passionate interest in the universality of cultural constructions of sacred and profane time, producing the seminal texts incorporated into our analysis in Chapter 3. He also remained the life-long intellectual companion of Julius Evola.

A further symptom of the synergy between the Iron Guard and intellectuals promoting nationalism as a remedy to modernity's ills, was its appointment of Emile Cioran to cultural attaché in Paris when it briefly shared power with General Ion Antonescu to form the Legionary Regime (1940–41). The inspiration for Eugène Ionescu's absurdist (and highly modernist) play, *Rhinoceros* (1974), was the way so many of the Romanian avant-garde, which included his friends Cioran and Eliade, were succumbing to the epidemic of organic, anti-Semitic racism in front of his eyes in the mid-1930s. Further research into other apparently anti-modern forms of inter-war fascism, such as those in Hungary, Croatia, Finland, Belgium, South Africa, and Ireland, may also reveal similarly modernist dynamics at work in the sudden appearance of so many political rhinos in European politics, each able to take refuge from mounting anomy by associating themselves with a uniformed movement of national revitalization and national *cleansing*.

MODERNIST INTELLECTUALS AND FASCISM

The involvement of the two outstanding European intellectuals Cioran and Eliade in the apparently atavistically 'religious' Iron Guard points to another important area of specialist studies where the recognition of fascism's political modernist dynamics promises to have considerable heuristic value. A significant secondary literature has grown up over the last three decades seeking to unravel the paradox posed by the involvement of individual modernist writers and intellectuals with fascism, generally assumed by the researcher not to be a revolutionary force, but an essentially anti-modern, backward-looking, reactionary movement in which no self-respecting avant-garde artist or intellectual would feel comfortable.

The list of 'usual suspects' includes W. B. Yeats, Ezra Pound, Wyndham Lewis, Ernst Jünger, Carl Schmitt, Gottfried Benn, Filippo Marinetti, Louis Ferdinand Céline, Pierre Drieu la Rochelle, and even extends to D. H. Lawrence and T. S. Eliot. Martin Heidegger's involvement with Nazism has created an academic industry in its own right. Particularly among Marxist or 'Marxian' cultural historians – and here Peter Osborne is a notable exception – the rarely questioned premise is that fascism is capable of producing only grotesque travesties of a radically *futural* explosion in the continuum of history.[57] Thus Charles Ferrall is going with the flow when he argues that Yeats, Pound, Eliot, and Lawrence 'combined a radical aesthetic modernity with an almost outright rejection of even the emancipatory aspects of bourgeois modernity'. This resulted in these figures experiencing an affinity to fascism whose ideologies 'provided a kind of parody of "revolution" which reflected their own ambivalence towards modernism'.[58]

The reconstruction of modernism offered here provides a radically different conceptual framework, one in which such paradoxes and parodies simply evaporate. It suggests that the many acts of 'betrayal' by the clerks of humanism in its liberal or socialist permutations have to be seen in the context of its abandonment by countless more obscure artists and intellectuals, and by a large proportion of educated, 'politically' aware citizens. These also succumbed to the temptation of believing they could contribute to the new era being inaugurated by the Bolshevik, Fascist, and Nazi Revolutions. It is no more a contradiction that Picasso was a modernist painter fascinated by 'primitive' art and drawn to anarchism, than that Jünger was a modernist prose-writer fascinated by the 'primitive', and hence *regenerative*, emotions unleashed by the mechanized war and drawn to Nazism. Fortunately, as this book has shown repeatedly in the sources it has cited, a number of works are already available that lay the basis for such a radical process of 'revision'. It is a process which must obviously be carried out in a way that avoids 'revisionism', by refusing to mitigate, or to simply elide from discussion, the crimes against humanity committed by fascism with which intellectual or artistic fellow-travellers colluded in their quest for transcendence.

However, while stressing the potential for convergence between aesthetic, intellectual and political modernism both left and right, the thesis we have explored has also underlined how simplistic it is to postulate any *direct* lineage between cultural modernism and those crimes. Paul Virilio's assertion that Marinetti's slogan '*War is the world's only hygiene*' led 'to the shower block of Auschwitz-Birkenau', may have produced a personal moment of intellectual catharsis when he wrote it, but it has minimal empirical content. It misrepresents in the language of tabloid journalism the complex causal nexus that relates the strands of modernism concerned with aesthetic and social hygiene to the regime that attempted to enact the Nazis' eugenic and genocidal projects of Europe's 'purification'. It is an act of reductionism similar to the one which prompted Georg Lukács to attribute the paternity of fascism to the 'destruction of reason' embodied in Nietzschean philosophy and Expressionism.[59] As we saw earlier, a parallel simplification led Jean-François Lyotard to equate fascism with the 'totalizing' narratives imputed to modernism as a whole.[60]

By contrast, the ideal type we have expounded stresses that fascism only has highly mediated connections to the 'epiphanic' modernism of Franz Kafka, Virginia Woolf, or Vincent van Gogh – however lyrically Josef Goebbels waxed about him as a 'seer' with method in his madness. Even its linkages to a particular variant of *programmatic* modernism, whether cultural or social, can only be multi-causal and 'rhizomic'[61] rather than 'arborial', precluding direct lineages of influence and responsibility. Not even the most ecstatic 'proto-fascist' prose of Filippo Marinetti or Ernst Jünger can be blamed for Fascism or Nazism, any more than Aleksandr Blok, Vladimir Mayakovsky, or Vladimir Tatlin can be held accountable for Stalin's Purges.

LOCATING FASCISMS IN 'SOMETHING LARGER'

The fallacy of treating the Futurist Manifesto as a direct causal factor in the genocide committed at Auschwitz might be taken as a warning of the traps awaiting historians whenever they stray from a narrow idiographic focus on uniqueness. Instead, it should be construed as an example of the contrast between cultural journalism and genuine historiography. As was made clear in the preface, the historiography of this book is based on the premise articulated by Detlef Peukert: 'If experience is to be understood at all, it cannot do without synoptic interpretation.'[62] This observation is congruent with that of Karl Popper, an intellectual who in his day exerted considerable impact on the way specialists in the human sciences understand their methodology: 'There can be no history of the "past as it actually did happen"; there can only be historical interpretations, and none of them final; and every generation has a right to frame its own.'[63] Anticipating the more absurdly reductionist postmodernist critiques of historical objectivity being made 40 years later, he also stressed that 'this does not mean that all interpretations are of equal merit'.[64] Both these principles unfortunately still need reasserting, since the quest for synoptic, historical interpretation based on locating facts within overarching analytical frameworks using generic concepts is in bad odour in some quarters of the profession. This is true not just in postmodernist circles, but particularly in the specialist field of comparative fascist studies.

Some of the most eminent historians of Fascism and Nazism choose to ignore the existence of the specialism, or make scathing or ill-informed comments about it when they do refer to it. Thus Richard Bosworth asks 'Why opt for a long list of factors or a paragraph of rococo ornateness when Mussolini, on a number of occasions, informed people he regarded as convertible to his cause that Fascism was a simple matter.' Yet the patent shortcomings of his own – impeccably documented but conceptually impoverished – narrative of Fascism provide an answer to this question in itself. The *duce*'s advice to General Franco in October 1936 that he should aim at creating a regime that was 'simultaneously "authoritarian", "social" and "popular"' which was 'the basis of universal fascism'[65] was not just simple, but simplistic. The definition both of Fascism and of fascism this implies is utterly inadequate to probe into the gap between what Fascism set out to achieve and what it accomplished, or to provide a comparative framework for examining Fascism's relationship to the other nationalist forms of authoritarianism that abounded in inter-war Europe. Bosworth assumes that citing it somehow reveals the irrelevance of attempts to give generic fascism heuristic value for historiography, an assumption that leads in practice not to a history of Fascism, but an extended chronicle of events studded with anecdotes that cumulatively trivialize it as a phenomenon. It precludes incisive conclusions being drawn about it as a *historical* – as opposed to a *lived* – phenomenon.

It was precisely the realization that dispensing with comparative frameworks and generic terms stunts historical understanding and impoverishes research that led Tim Mason to remind his colleagues at a conference on the Third Reich that 'If we can now do without much of the original contents of the concept of fascism, we cannot do without comparison.'[66] He went on to warn them that '[h]istoricization may easily become a recipe for provincialism' if it fails to recognize that 'fascism was a continental phenomenon, and that Nazism was a peculiar part of something much larger'.[67] This 'something' has been variously identified by different specialists as political religion, totalitarianism, fascism, and now political modernism, the common denominator of all of which is the bid to create an alternative modernity. Emilio Gentile's many publications cumulatively vindicate Mason's insight with respect to Fascism as well, by using a combination of thorough archival scholarship and conceptual rigour to demonstrate that it too was a 'peculiar part of something much larger'. In fact Mussolini's regime becomes effectively *de-historicized* if it is not located within wider processes at work shaping modern history, notably modernist nationalism, generic fascism, totalitarianism, and political religion.

Historians of Fascism or Nazism who continue to experience a knee-jerk reaction against the very idea that generic terms and comparative frameworks may be relevant to their research, seem to be clinging on to the same methodologically naïve conception of 'pure empiricism' which has been exposed to such sustained – and in this case fully justified – critiques by postmodernists. There is much more than irrational invective in the passage in *The Will to Power* where Nietzsche rails against the self-deception of those who think that understanding can be objectively derived from data without the intervention of an interpreting, meaning-creating mind:

> There are no 'facts-in-themselves', for a sense must always be projected into them before there can be 'facts'.[68] [...] Against positivism, which halts at phenomena – 'There are only facts' – I would say: No, facts is precisely what there is not, only interpretations. We cannot establish any fact 'in itself': perhaps it is folly to want to do such a thing.[69]

What this book has attempted to do is provide a remedy to such folly in a relatively well delimited area of modern history. It offers the prototype of a synoptic interpretation of fascism based on the concept of modernism. It constructs and applies a conceptual framework within which to project 'sense' into the pure empirical data relating to the ideology and praxis of Fascism and Nazism so that they can be seen like Russian dolls fitting into a larger doll called fascism, which in turn fits into modernism which is a subcategory of modernity. Furthermore, by repeatedly drawing attention to the constructed nature of this framework and the existence of others with which it conflicts or harmonizes, my argument has sought to avoid being misconstrued as an *unreflexive* grand narrative, no matter how broad its brushstrokes. In fact, closer scrutiny reveals that at least two levels of mythopoeia have been at work in its construction. The first is intrinsic to the process of 'idealizing abstraction' required to construct an ideal type. Max Weber himself describes this as a 'thought-picture' which in its 'conceptual purity [...] cannot be found empirically anywhere in reality, it is a utopia'.[70] The imprint of this strictly academic and heuristic genus of utopianism is to be found on every page of this book.

THE MODERNISM OF HUMANISTIC RESEARCH

The second level of mythopoeia that this book subsumes is highlighted by the primordialist theory of modernism we have developed. It suggests that in miniature – and sometimes on a nano-scale of scholarly detail – each act of synoptic historical interpretation of an established topic by an academic, no matter how meticulous in its execution, can be seen as a symbolic gesture towards closure, towards resolving the liminoid element intrinsic to any protracted debate where consensus seems to be a mirage. Each 'original thesis' attempts to offer a fresh vision, a fixed horizon, a new sky within the microcosm of the specialism, however evanescent and 'contested' when the 'conceptual purity' of the original project in the head of the researcher is exposed to the sobering, 'sullying' process of peer evaluation and critique by colleagues.

This implies that secret 'messianic' agendas lurk within the theses being constantly formulated and documented within the human sciences which ostensibly pursue the strictly rational goal of transforming the dominant paradigm. All ambitious, speculative, 'original' acts of synoptic interpretation require researchers to complete a personal act of 'mazeway resynthesis' in formulating the innovative hypothesis, ideal type, or methodology within a particular scholarly tradition known as 'the discipline'. Each reference to a previously published book or article which corroborates the argument represents, to invoke Walter Benjamin's metaphor, the leap of a now fully house-trained Tiger into past scholarship or archival sources. The aim is not to go 'back', but to 'reconnect forward' so as to establish a solid foothold from which to jump to more 'advanced' (i.e. futural) understanding and 'explode the continuum' of the dominant paradigm. The subliminal purpose is to form a break-away minority of like-minded rebels prepared to secede from old ways of seeing, routinized thoughts, and superseded paradigms so as to form a new 'current' or 'school' of thought. Until superseded in its turn – as Cronus dictates it eventually will be – any new intellectual *communitas* that forms will operate like a team of energetic gardeners busily tidying up an overgrown corner of their 'field', clearing the paths for new avenues of inquiry, and propagating new varieties of expertise, sometimes with an aggressive animus against the weeds or dead wood they see as obstructing clear understanding.

In short, there is a *modernist* dynamic at work in all attempts to create definite – never definitive – knowledge in a world deluged by an increasing flood of data, information, theories, and approaches. Academia provides the ideal habitat for non-heroic, Lilliputian quests for nomos, for transcendence, for community. In extreme cases the prospect of metaphysical immortality available in some premodern societies has been traded in for that of surviving death as a corroborating endnote in someone else's analysis. The subtitle of this book, *The Sense of a Beginning*, thus refers not only to the futural temporality of Fascism and Nazism, but also on a subtextual level to the revitalizing impact its publication aspires – however unrealistically – to have on the disciplines on which it touches, especially comparative studies of modernity, modernism, and fascism. However, this is not an age in which historians can afford to indulge in such narcissistic delusions about the ultimate importance of carrying out Zarathustran transvaluations of their specialism writ small, of inscribing new tablets of academic Truth in 10pt Sabon Roman. Sting exhorts us in the song that serves as the epigraph to this book to 'climb down from our ivory tower', and claim our 'stake in the world'. So perhaps there is just time for the principle of hope to be let off the leash once more before the formal closing ceremony of this reflexive metanarrative which takes the form, not of a lavishly staged and brilliantly choreographed spectacle performed to the twinkling of camera-flashes, but of the more sombre procession of appendix, notes, bibliography, and index. At the very last gasp there is perhaps just time for a *coup de théâtre*.

Postscript: A Different Beginning?

THE GREENING OF DIONYSUS

On 17 September 1998 BBC News made the following announcement under the headline 'The sky is falling': 'The height of the sky has dropped by 8km in the last 38 years, according to scientists from the British Antarctic Survey. Greenhouse gases like carbon dioxide are believed to be responsible for creating the effect.'[1] This is not a metaphysical lapsus of the sort that caused Adam and Eve to be ejected from the Garden of unreflexive consciousness. It is one of myriad physical and terrestrial processes and events which have been occasioned by the cumulative impact of human action on the ecosystem, and whose long-term repercussions will be felt, not only in the meteorological atmosphere, but in the spiritual and ethical atmosphere of human society as well, the *Zeitgeist*. For as Ernest Becker stated perceptively at a time when global warming was no more than an anxious twinkle in the eye of some 'zany' scientists:

> One of the terrifying things about living in the late decades of the twentieth century is that the margin that nature has been giving to cultural fantasy is suddenly being narrowed down drastically. The consequence is that for the first time in history man [sic], if he is to survive, has to bring down to near zero the large fictional element in his hero-systems. This is the critical challenge of our time.[2]

It was in a similar spirit that some commentators reacted to the terrible events of 9/11, arguing that they had created an *ideological* ground zero. For them the disaster was a valuable wake-up call to Western civilization to 'get real' after decades of collective somnambulism. Thus Michael Mehaffy and Nikos Salingaros wrote:

> And so we are left with a world after the modern towers, and after modernism. We will surely destroy al Qaeda and the Taliban [sic!]. But even more important, we need to destroy the festering conditions in which men like these are made. To do that, we will have to re-examine the kind of modern world we have imposed upon the

365

planet – economic, technological, artistic. We will have to re-examine, and rebuild, the decaying foundations of our own modern culture.[3]

But if modernism is, as we have repeatedly argued, an instinctive counter-vailing reaction to the decadence of modernity and the catastrophes it causes, then this heart-felt plea for humankind to move collectively beyond modernism to a planetary perspective is itself quintessentially modernist, just as Becker's idea of a fictionless hero-system is itself a fiction striving to become a myth. Their arguments are to be seen as the recognition of the increasingly urgent *practical* need for the community, not the national, but the international one, to move beyond the delusions of 'postmodernity' to a renewed *modernism* based on a *new* modernity upholding the principles of ecological sustainability and global social justice.

In the run up to the mythic millennial watershed of what was (only in Christian reckoning) the year 2000, Fay Weldon wrote a radio play, *The Hole at the Top of the World*, which dramatized the need for a radical new 'Gestalt' of contemporary history. One speech stands out for its concise indictment of the fatal flaw in the anthropocentric, ideocentric schemes to improve society that have dominated Western history under high and late modernity:

> We used to think that Marxism or feminism held the answers to all our problems. We thought, 'If only we can get rid of racism, change capitalism and educate people, everything will be different'. But now we know those hopes and aspirations left out something fundamental. They failed because they failed to take account of the earth we walk on. Without the earth we have nothing. Our Utopian concepts are flying out of the sky. So we have to rethink all our ideas in a new framework.[4]

Had Nietzsche been philosophizing at the beginning of the twenty-first century instead of the end of the nineteenth, amidst Swiss glaciers shrivelling under skies where the abstract art of vapour trails punctures illusions of transcending Good and Evil, maybe he would have 'rethought all his ideas' in a different, greener 'framework'. Instead of railing against the advent of 'nihilism', decadence', and 'the Last Men', he might have realized that the time for any sort of 'eternal return' is rapidly running out in a literal, not a symbolic sense. His own attempt at the transvaluation of values was posited on the absence of any sort or higher reality or metaphysical realm 'behind' existence, and the vision of the world as 'a monster of energy, without beginning, nor end; a firm, iron magnitude of force that does not grow bigger or smaller, that does not expend itself but only transforms itself'.[5] He had thus placed himself in an ideal vantage point from which to understand the interconnectedness of all life processes, and re-imagine the *Übermensch*, the 'superior human being', as someone of either gender and of any race who abandons the in-built hubris of our species so as to become truly 'all-too-human', finally renouncing the right to create what Francis Bacon called in *Novum Organon* (1620) the 'Empire of Man'. What is needed in the early twenty-first century is not the end of modernism, since any rebellion against the status quo becomes impregnated with a modernist ethos, but a better, *ecologically grounded* civilization in which both Dionysian and Promethean modernism has been greened, thus providing the 'base-metaphors' and 'myths' by which to live in a *really* new age of sustainability, which means not going 'backwards' but developing the most advanced form of technocracy possible.

A DIFFERENT BEGINNING?

Even this *grounded* utopia of an alternative modernity can be perverted by some intellectuals before it has left the drawing board. This is eloquently demonstrated by one of the cultural pundits of the German New Right, Gerd Bergfleth. His essay 'Earth and Homeland. On the End of the Age of Desolation' ostensibly addresses the need to overcome the nihilism that underlies modern 'homelessness' through the 'paradigm change' to an 'earth-based' world-view, a 'return to the source' which will be simultaneously 'a renewal'.[6] He presents this as involving a 'turn of thought which leads from the superficiality of the Enlightenment back to the primordial knowledge of myth'. Yet the authorities cited to underpin his analysis are not ecologists and green humanists, but Carl Schmitt, Martin Heidegger, and Ernst Jünger, the founding fathers of the German 'Conservative Revolution', and one-time fellow travellers of Nazism. In line with this deeply anti-ecocentric train of thought, Bergfleth attributes the craving for communion with nature displayed in the philosophy and poetry of the German Romantics to the fact that his fellow-countrymen are a 'metaphysically homeless' *Volk* , but, since they long for roots, an *organic* one. As 'a people of the centre' – a phrase borrowed from Heidegger – they are spiritually 'open to the world' in a way that fosters a powerful sense of 'homesickness'. In fact their heightened need for 'belonging' and 'roots' makes them paradoxically 'xenophobic *out of principle*' [sic].[7]

On the basis of such dubious axioms Bergfleth argues that 'the Germans' are uniquely placed to transcend the contemporary ecological crisis, which he presents as the outward symptom of modernity's spiritual desolation. Their national, *Nordic* character predisposes them to discover the spiritual *Heimat* they long for in 'bondedness with the earth', and to find 'redemption' through an ecstatic filial reunion with Mother Nature. Their metaphysical, Romantic temperament means that the 'coming total collapse' will produce (at least in Germany) a 'religion of the earth', a 'return to a geocentric worldview' based on the realization that 'our world is not the universe, but a single earth held by the sky'. This collective epiphany will, he claims, mark what Heidegger looked forward to as 'der andere Anfang', 'the other beginning', a 'different beginning'. The era in which the earth was taken for granted will come to an end, and human beings will awaken from their 'obliviousness of Being'.[8]

It is clear from Bergfleth's text that, like his mentors, he still craves a *German* remembrance of things past enacted under a *German* sky. The concrete physical demands that flow from the goal of achieving an ecologically sustainable human civilization have been translated through the intellectual acrobatics and conjuring tricks of New Right thinking first into nationalistic metaphysics and then into racist metapolitics. 'Blood and soil' has been surreptitiously recoded as 'earth and homeland'. Such texts demonstrate the fascist pedigree of the European New Right's brand of political modernism – another topic demanding thorough scholarly investigation elsewhere.[9] Nevertheless, Bergfleth's essay can be treated as a fine example of 'teaching by negative example', a warning about the dangers of slipping into the quagmire of un-ecological, *anthropocentric* thinking even when ostensibly promoting ecological awareness. Perhaps an increasingly globalized West *is* finally reaching a point where those who hear the trumpets sounding are becoming inwardly prepared – but mainly by calamitous *outward* events – for an *Aufbruch* into the sustainable human society. Walter Benjamin talks in his *Theses on the Philosophy of History* of the need 'to seize hold of a memory as it flashes up at a moment of danger'.[10] The present generation is perhaps approaching a compound 'moment of danger' in which to seize hold of an epiphanic moment of global consciousness experienced not by Heidegger, but by another philosopher who was active over 22 centuries ago. It is 'immortalized' as one of the reflections and aphorisms of Diogenes of Oinoanda carved into now fragmented blocks of stone which once stood proudly in the centre of the market place of his home town and are now known as the 'Epicurean Inscription'. In a passage that reaches out across more than two millennia in a way that nothing from the ruins of Hitler's Thousand Year Reich ever could, it states that this public display of timeless wisdom was intended not just for local inhabitants but for 'those who are called "foreigners"'. It wastes no time in explaining why there is no such thing:

> For, while the various segments of the earth give different people a different country, the whole compass of this world gives all people a single country, the entire earth, and a single home, the world.[11]

Perhaps a juncture of serious, but not annihilating, ecological, demographic, economic, and political crises may yet be reached in time for the mythic power deriving from visions of the Earth as the *Heimat* of *all* humanity to suddenly crystallize as a mass-mobilizing myth and all-embracing new nomos. In such a scenario – one admittedly among many far bleaker ones and blatantly shaped by the logic of palingenetic myth – the modern era so far dominated by examples of the unsustainable social transformation that Immanuel Kant called 'palingenesis' could within a few generations give way to one of sustainable 'metamorphosis'.[12] It would not be a symbolic event occurring in a metaphysical realm outside time, but a real regenerative process that takes place within our own history and our own time: the time of earthly existence. This time, this earthly *aevum*, after all, is the precondition for all human life, whether or not it subsequently submits to further transfiguration in a sacred dimension posited by revealed religion.

This is not the ultimate destination dreamt of in the many variants of political and social modernism of earlier decades, and there are doubtless many more harbours out there to reach. Yet the premise to the realization of any of them is not a utopia, but a material and biological necessity: the end of one history in which the planet became increasingly unable to bear the ecological burdens imposed on it by our species' colonization of the globe, and the *Aufbruch* – perhaps protracted over several generations but a twinkling of an eye in geological terms – to a *different* beginning 'away from here', to a new history of sustainable, viable, stabilized human life on earth. At that point Western civilization ceases to be the *Titanic*, as Bob Dylan depicts it in one of his most famous songs, doomed to sink on its maiden voyage.[13] Instead it makes it through against the odds to become the ship that sails triumphantly into the harbour at dawn in another of his early songs.[14] In such a new order the abundant provisions of natural resources and of human time itself once again become available to our species for what Kafka called a 'truly immense journey', a species not ending, but just beginning: *homo incipiens*.

In the last lines of his allegorical drama about the innate goodness or evil of human beings, Bertolt Brecht, an artistic and political modernist from an earlier 'Age of Desolation', addresses the audience with a string of questions. These have acquired even more urgency today, when the medium-term option for our race may be no longer between palingenesis and nihilism, but between metamorphosis and annihilation:

> Where's the solution that we can trust?
> *We* could find none for love nor money.
> Shall new men, or new worlds end confusion?
> Perhaps new gods? Or *no* gods – that would be funny. [....]
> Dear public, come on and find your own conclusion!
> There must be a good one somewhere, must, must, must![15]

Appendix: More on Methodology

Over the years my first monograph, *The Nature of Fascism* (1991), has been charged by some academic colleagues with essentialism, reductionism, 'revisionism', a disinterest in praxis or material realities, and even a philosophical idealism which trivializes the human suffering caused by Hitler's regime. It is thus worth offering the more methodologically self-aware readers, inveterately sceptical of the type of large-scale theorizing ('metanarration') that forms the bulk of Part One of this book, a few more paragraphs to substantiate my approach and give it some sort of intellectual pedigree. It can be thought of as deriving from three lines of methodological inquiry – and there are doubtless others that are complementary to them.

One is the sophisticated (but inevitably contested) model of concept formation through 'idealizing abstraction'[1] which was elaborated piece-meal by Max Weber when wrestling with a number of the dilemmas which plagued the more epistemologically self-aware academics engaged in the late nineteenth-century '*Methodenstreit*'. This was a conflict over methodology within the German human sciences that anticipated many themes of the late twentieth-century debate over how humanities disciplines should respond to postmodernism and the critical turn.[2] The upshot of this line of thinking is that researchers must take it upon themselves to be as self-conscious as possible in the process of constructing the premises and 'ideal types' which shape the investigation of an area of external reality. Nor should they ever lose sight of the purely heuristic nature of their inquiry, and hence its inherently partial, incomplete nature. One important inference to be drawn is that, instead of insisting on the superiority of their interpretation over 'rival' approaches, they should proactively seek out its potential for complementing those based on other empirical research, premises, and concepts.

The second source of insight – again BCT (Before the Cultural Turn) – is offered by the deceptively simple advice which Karl Popper gave for solving the problems posed by, first, the intrinsic open-endedness of the historical process, and, second, the irreducible complexity of all human reality, and, third, the consequent element of arbitrariness or 'subjectivity' intrinsic to the attempt to analyse any segment of it. Popper's proposed strategy for resolving the first dilemma is for all researchers – and ideally political ideologues as well – to firmly resist the urge to mistake the patterns and trends they have detected in phenomena for historical 'laws', particularly the predictive ones that generate what he terms (confusingly, given its conflicting connotations) 'historicism', or what in 'postmodernese' would be called 'totalizing discourses' or 'metanarratives'. Furthermore, Popper recommends that academics speculating nomothetically – in the search for basic patterns or generic features in phenomena – should be on their guard against confusing corroborative evidence with the 'proof' or 'verification' of a hypothesis, especially since its formulation in the context of the human sciences can rarely conform to the criterion of falsifiability which he regarded as crucial to the experimental sciences. The prospect of providing closure to any fundamental issue of disputed interpretation in the human sciences is thus a mirage.

However, Popper did not see such restrictions on objective knowledge or definitive interpretation as delegitimizing historiography as such, even of the most speculative variety. This is demonstrated by his own metanarrative on the history of progress, and the obstacles to progress, in human knowledge, *The Open Society and its Enemies*, published within months of the end of the Second World War. As for the thorny issue of objectivity raised by the proliferation of possible perspectives, Popper suggests that 'The only way out of this difficulty is, I believe, consciously to introduce a *preconceived selective point of view* into one's history; that is, to write *that history which interests us*',[3] and, I would add, to present our findings in such a way that they are likely to interest others working in the same field. Objectivity thus reveals itself as a methodology for producing useful knowledge, the way a theory is formulated and applied, and not the inherent property of 'facts', let alone a spuriously 'theory-less', or 'personality-free' state achieved by the mind that seeks them.

The third line of thinking congruent with the concept of 'reflexive metanarrative' that I have so deliberately and *self-consciously* introduced is to be found, appropriately enough, in works by specialists concerned with repelling the perceived threat posed by the cultural turn to their discipline. One example is the defiant conclusion of Richard Evans' robust, both stylistically trenchant and *empirically* argued defence against the vehement criticisms that some of the more fundamentalist upholders of postmodernist relativism – the irony is intentional – have laid at the door of 'traditional' historiography in general, and of his concept of historiography in particular:

I will look humbly at the past and say despite them all: it really happened, and we really can, *if we are very scrupulous and careful and self-critical*, find out how it happened and reach some less than final conclusions about what it all meant.[4]

The tack that Evans adopts in order to negotiate the murky and choppy waters of post-CT academia is broadly consistent with the conclusions which Marjorie Levinson drew from her attempt to 'rethink historiography' a decade earlier.[5] These were summarized by the anthropologist Joan Vincent as 'reconstructing the historicist project' as one 'conceived and conducted as a reflexive affair'.[6] In fact, the cultivation of heightened methodological reflexivity as the precondition, if not for a 'new beginning' in the human sciences, then at least for a fairly normal service to be resumed in them without a debilitating sense of the illegitimacy of all interpretation and theorizing is a theme common to a number of works symptomatic of the post-positivist age.[7] Given the emphasis on anthropological insights encountered in Chapter 3, it is appropriate that it is one account of anthropology's response to postmodernism that perhaps provides the neatest formulation of the methodological spirit in which the metanarrative that unfolds in *Modernism and Fascism* has been conceived. In his contribution to the collective effort to 'recapture anthropology', Graham Watson situates the 'reflexive anthropology' he is advocating 'near the middle' of a continuum between 'an ontology-cum-epistemology according to which our accounts of reality *mirror* reality', and a diametrically opposed postmodern one where the very act of investigating reality actually *constitutes* it.[8] It is in this intermediate zone, somewhere between a naïve objectivity and a paralysing subjectivism, that this book operates. It is a sustained exercise in the speculative interpretation of a relationship between two vast areas of data subsumed within two highly contested generic concepts or 'isms'. The speculation is not arbitrary but controlled by attested empirical data and reflexive theorizing that extensively takes account of and draws on the work of other scholars. It has no pretensions of providing a definitive picture of modernism's relationship to fascism, but neither can it be dismissed as an elaborate 'fiction'.

This extensive 'caveat lector' assumes particular significance in the context of the rampant syncretism that characterizes this book. It is in the nature of the hypothesis it is exploring that it seeks to synthesize and produce synergies between theories and insights culled from a wide range of disciplines in which, as a specialist in comparative fascist studies, I can claim no professional expertise. These include social psychology, social and cultural anthropology, the sociology of modernity, the theory and history of modernism, the history of art, modern (Western) intellectual, cultural, and social history, and the historiography of Fascism and Nazism. When researchers raid any neighbouring discipline for insights and data which lend themselves to being integrated within their argument there is a natural temptation to treat it as a homogeneous field of studies, and to present any apparently corroborative data or theory that suits their case as if it were *the* authoritative take of that discipline on the issue. Given the contested nature of every position adopted within every branch of the humanities this is patently not the case. To take one example, the cohabitation of several schools of thought within social anthropology – structuralist, poststructuralist, constructivist, and so forth – means that all its key concepts and theories are highly contested, producing a proliferation of debates intensified by the fact that, as we have seen, the discipline has gone through its own epistemological crisis under the impact of postmodernism.

Again a judicious dose of reflexivity comes to the rescue here. The appropriation of a particular anthropological argument by a historian is legitimate as long as it is treated as no more than one component in the construction of an analytical framework, and not as 'proof' of that framework's objective validity or 'truth'. The resulting theoretical edifice, no matter how lofty and imposing in the knowledge it subsumes, the linguistic and stylistic register in which it is expressed, or the number of endnotes deployed and books cited in its validation, cannot be, and has no intention of being, 'true'. Instead, its highest aim is to be found heuristically *useful* by other scholars in advancing knowledge and understanding in the specialist area on which it provides a perspective. It resembles the moving platforms that TV companies install to follow golf competitions, both substantial and temporary, and to be judged by what can be seen from them when a particular game is played, in this case investigating 'modernism's' relationship to 'fascism'.

These methodological observations seek not to excuse but to *legitimize* ambitious exercises such as the one undertaken here in formulating overarching hypotheses and syncretizing elements from a variety of disciplines, on condition that they are carried out in a non-totalizing spirit. As such they appear to be entirely consistent with the ethos and goals of the Study Group launched by UNESCO in 1992 to promote what it terms 'transdisciplinarity'. The report of the Philosophy and Ethics division produced after the seminar held in 1998 was that the purpose of transdisciplinarity was to 'stimulate synergies and integrate knowledge' by creating 'the "intellectual space" where the nature of the manifold links among isolated issues can be explored and unveiled, the space where issues are rethought, alternatives reconsidered, and interrelations revealed'.[9] It highlighted as one of the central points to arise from the meeting the need for reflexivity:

> The way to attain an integrated concept and practice of knowledge, and consequently to address many crucial issues of our age through a transdisciplinary approach, does not lie in applying ready-made, 'mechanical' procedures based on automatic, stereotyped formulas and standardized recipes; but rather, in establishing various complex, integrative processes to be *mindfully and cautiously implemented in the light of manifold criteria*.[10]

This book makes no claim to have discovered buried truths or triumphantly resolved issues that have baffled other experts. No matter how single-mindedly and tenaciously I develop and affirm its central thesis, I am mindful of its limitations and cautious in the inferences I draw from it, especially since its chapters are not the specialist essays resulting from a symposium of experts, but the results of a series of expeditions by the same researcher into the alien terrain of other disciplines from a base-camp in fascist studies. The resulting book is to be evaluated as a work of speculative syncretism rather than of specialist scholarship, carried out to fashion a new 'intellectual space' where 'new interrelationships' can be revealed between modernism and fascism. It is obviously for *readers* to judge whether, as they penetrate further into the complex argument and empirical texture of this book, the more these inter-relationships emerge in a convincing, increasingly 'self-evident' way, so that they acquire a deeper insight into linkages between a whole range of twentieth-century phenomena whose affinities with the work of familiar aesthetic modernists such as Baudelaire and Kandinsky have been generally ignored. Of course, they may arrive at a point – one perhaps long since reached so that these lines are destined to remain unseen by them – where the conceptual 'Gestalt' behind this book fails to reconstitute itself in their minds through the magic of language and the entire heuristic device it is constructing crumbles like a jerry-built high-rise block, making the text simply unreadable.

However, I would almost prefer to be found unintelligible than be responded to as if this whole book was simply an invitation to play an elaborate game of conceptual chess or ping-pong about modernism's relationship to fascism, oblivious of the questions it should raise at a visceral level about such 'cosmological' issues as the nature of modernity, progress, the state, the origins of mass belief and mass violence, human rationality and culture, or the source of 'higher purpose' and the 'sacred' in a globalizing social reality. This book aims, despite the intrinsic 'difficulty' and even abstruseness of its topic, to break down the artificial barriers Western society has tended to erect between thought and experience, intellect and feeling. While written in an academic register and with an academic methodology, it has an inner resonance, at least in intent, with the rejection of abstract thought found posthumously among the unpublished notes of the outstanding incarnation of philosophical modernism, Friedrich Nietzsche:

> I have at all times thought with my whole body and my whole life. I do not know what purely intellectual problems are. [...] You know these things as thoughts, but your thoughts are not your experiences, they are an echo and after-effect of your experiences: as when your room trembles when a carriage goes past. I however, am sitting in the carriage and often I am the carriage itself.[11]

Franz Kafka, the archetypal literary modernist, could be even more vehement in his scorn for the type of reading in which the intellect (the neo-cortex) does not bond with 'gut emotions' (the limbic brain). In 1904 he declared in a letter to his friend Oskar Pollack:

> I think we ought to read only the kind of books that bite and stab us. If the book we are reading doesn't wake us up with a blow on the head, what are we reading it for? [...] A book must be the axe for the frozen sea inside us.[12]

This is no easy book. Its argument is highly theoretical and conceptual while being at the same time brimming with 'facts'. It was demanding to write and will doubtless be even more demanding to read. Like all other works of academic synthesis and speculation, its success is to be judged not only by the accuracy and rigour with which an individual theory has been summarized, a particular episode reconstructed, or a theoretical model applied but, as Kafka suggests, by its capacity to 'wake up' the reader with startling new insights and leaps of understanding.

Clearly *Modernism and Fascism* cannot hope to deliver a series of mind-curdling, life-enhancing punches, or precipitate a permanent paradigm shift in the way academics approach the phenomenon of avant-garde cultural 'production' and ideological extremism under the dispensation of Western modernity. Nor is there any suggestion that it can deliver the 'Big Picture' of modernism. However, according to my own criteria, it is 'working' as a monograph if it occasionally produces in a reader a heady sensation that new vistas of comprehension are opening up into the mythopoeic mechanisms capable of turning the disorienting *experience* of modernity into a source of fanaticism both religious and secular. If it does not leave some readers able to *experience* more directly the creative and destructive matrices that for long periods turned the first half of twentieth-century Europe into vast killing fields, *and which continue to shape our social and inner lives today*, then it has failed in one of its primary tasks.

Notes

Short titles are used within the endnotes for each chapter.

INTRODUCTION: AUFBRUCH

1. Paul Raabe (ed.), *Franz Kafka. Sämtliche Erzählungen* (Frankfurt: Fischer, 1975), p. 321. This story, part of his '*Nachlass*', i.e. works not published in his lifetime, is known in German under the title *Der Aufbruch*, usually translated as *My Destination* (sometimes as *Sudden Departure*). However, the suitability of the title I propose here is corroborated by the suggestion of a translation website that the phrase 'Begeisterung für Aufbruch' be translated in a managerial context as 'enthusiasm for new beginnings': the translator, Mats Wiman, comments '*Aufbruch* does not refer to anything specific like innovation, reform, reorganization or the like: it is a question of mental attitude or personality trait, i.e. *to be willing/positive/enthusiastic about making a new start or accepting new challenges*'. http://www.proz.com/kudoz/15886 (accessed 11/01/06). My emphasis.
2. Frank Kermode, *The Sense of an Ending. Studies in the Theory of Fiction* (1967) (New York: Oxford University Press, 2000), p. 98.
3. Julius Petersen, *Die Sehnsucht nach dem Dritten Reich in deutscher Sage und Dichtung* (Stuttgart: Metzlersche Verlagsbuchhandlung, 1934), p. 1. Cited in Jost Hermand, *Old Dreams of a New Reich: Volkish Utopias and National Socialism* (Bloomington: Indiana University Press, 1992), p. 163. Hermand's book is crucial for understanding the powerful archaizing, mythic dimension of Nazi ideology so often dismissed as 'nostalgic' or anti-modern, but which we will argue is both futural and an integral component of Nazi modernism.
4. Roger Griffin, *The Nature of Fascism* (London: Pinter, 1991), p. 47. My emphasis.
5. The metaphorical significance of the sinking of the *Titanic* and the huge impact it had on contemporaries as a symbol of the fragility of Western 'progress' is referred to frequently in Stephen Kern, *The Culture of Time and Space 1880–1918* (2nd edition Cambridge, MA: Harvard University Press, 2003). Bob Dylan famously used the image of the *Titanic* as a metaphor for modern civilization in the song 'Desolation Row' on the album *Highway 61 Revisited* (1965).
6. This 'mythic' aspect of the French Revolution has been brilliantly explored in Lynn Hunt, *Politics, Culture, and Class in the French Revolution* (Berkeley: California University Press, 1984); Mona Ozouf, *L'Homme régénéré. Essai sur la Révolution française* (Paris: Gallimard, 1989).
7. The context of this self-characterization is a passage that reads as follows: 'I know my fate. One day my name will be associated with the memory of something tremendous – a crisis without equal on earth, the most profound collision of conscience, a decision that was conjured up *against* everything that had been believed, demanded, hallowed so far. I am no man, I am dynamite' (Friedrich Nietzsche, *Ecce Homo* (New York: Vintage, 1967), p. 326). Part 1, par. 4: 'Why I am Destiny'.
8. Filippo Marinetti, 'The Founding Manifesto of Futurism', in Umbro Apollonio, *Futurist Manifestos* (London: Thames and Hudson, 1973), pp. 21–2.

9. This association is made in particular by the postmodernist theorist Jean-François Lyotard. See Reed Dasenbrock, 'Slouching toward Berlin: Life in a Postfascist Culture', in Richard Golsan (ed.), *Fascism's Return* (Lincoln: University of Nebraska Press, 1998), pp. 247–50.

10. Friedrich Nietzsche, *Unzeitgemäße Betrachtungen*, published as *Unmodern Observations* (New Haven, CT: Yale University Press, 1990).

11. Jack Hexter popularized this distinction in his criticism of Raymond Carr in *On Historians* (Cambridge, MA: Harvard University Press, 1979), pp. 241–2. It is invoked in endnote 2 of Richard Etlin's excellent introduction to *Art, Culture, and Media under the Third Reich* (Chicago: University of Chicago Press, 2002) which presents his essay on the 'logic' of Nazi thought as a deliberate act of 'lumping'.

12. Detlef Peukert, *Inside Nazi Germany* (Harmondsworth: Penguin, 1982), p. 245. My emphasis.

13. Karl Popper, *The Poverty of Historicism* (1957) (London: Routledge and Kegan Paul, 1974), p. 151.

14. W. B. Yeats, *The Second Coming* (1921) in (no ed.) *The Collected Poems of W. B. Yeats* (London: Macmillan, 1982), p. 211.

15. Kermode, *The Sense of an Ending*, p. 108. My emphasis.

16. There are, of course, deep affinities between communism and nationalism as totalitarian ideologies. Moreover, communist states in practice fostered powerful currents of nationalism and ethnocentrism which gave it elements of kinship with fascism which contradicted Marxist theory. The polarization between left and right in this passage is thus a simplification.

17. 'Palingenesis', and its adjective 'palingenetic', are terms connoting rebirth, new birth, regeneration. In English it used to be regarded an archaism used mainly in religious and biological contexts, though in the last decade it has gained currency as a term of political analysis. It is recurrently used in translations of works by the Italian historian Emilio Gentile for whom it is a key analytical term of political discourse connoting the characteristic utopian fantasy of political and social revolutionaries that they are inaugurating a radically new age.

18. Siegfried Kracauer, *From Caligari to Hitler. A Psychological History of the German Film* (1947) (Princeton, NJ: Princeton University Press, 1970), p. 38.

1   THE PARADOXES OF 'FASCIST MODERNISM'

1. Frank Kermode, *The Sense of an Ending. Studies in the Theory of Fiction* (1967) (New York: Oxford University Press, 2000), pp. 110–11.

2. Hayden White, 'Historical Emplotment and the Problem of Truth', in Saul Friedländer (ed.), *Probing the Limits of Representation. Nazism and the Final Solution* (Cambridge, MA: Harvard University Press, 1992), pp. 52–3.

3. Paul Virilio, *Art and Fear* (London: Continuum, 2003), pp. 29–30.

4. The passage is taken from the website 'Report to Himmler on Julius Evola' at http://thompkins_cariou.tripod.com/id6.html (accessed 15/11/05). The text is taken from Renato del Ponte's 'Weisthor-Wiligut Dossier', *Arthos*, 4.7–8 (2000), pp. 241–65.

5. See Hans-Jürgen Lange: *Weisthor – Karl Maria Wiligut – Himmlers Rasputin und seine Erben* (Engerda: Arun-Verlag, 1998). For more on Wiligut in English see the chapter 'Karl Maria Wiligut. The Private Magus of Heinrich Himmler' in Nicolas Goodrick-Clarke, *The Occult Roots of Nazism* (Wellingborough, Northamptonshire, UK: Aquarian Press, 1985), which also contains a fleeting reference to Evola's lectures to the SS (p. 190). On the convoluted relationship of orthodox and 'alternative' science in the projects undertaken by Himmler's Ahnenerbe see Heather Pringle, *The Master Plan: Himmler's Scholars and the Holocaust* (New York: Viking, 2006).

6. Julius Evola, *Erhebung wider die moderne Welt* (Stuttgart: Deutsche Verlagsanstalt, 1935), new translation *Revolte gegen die moderne Welt* (Interlaken: Ansata-Verlag, 1982).

7. The racist and philo-Nazi aspects of Evola's thought have been explored in Francesco Germinario, *Razza del Sangue, razza dello Spirito. Julius Evola, l'antisemitismo e il nazionalsocialismo (1930–1945)* (Torino: Bollati Boringhieri, 2001).

8. For the material impact that occultism did have on Nazism see Goodrick-Clarke, *The Occult Roots of National Socialism*, a scholarly investigation that indirectly refutes New Ageist delusions that the NSDAP was 'really' an esoteric organization.

9. See Mark Sedgwick, *Against the Modern World. Traditionalism and the Secret Intellectual History of the Twentieth Century* (Oxford: Oxford University Press, 2004).

10. See Julius Evola, 'Il mito Marcuse', *Gli uomini e le rovine* (Rome: Volpe, 1967), pp. 263–9. For more on the background to Almirante's remark see Roger Griffin, 'Revolts against the Modern World. The blend of literary and historical fantasy in the Italian New Right', *Literature and History* 11.1 (Spring 1985), pp. 101–24. Also at http://www.rosenoire.org/articles/revolts.php (accessed 15/05/06).

11. On Evola's Dadaism see Jeffrey Schnapp, 'Bad Dada (Evola)', in Leah Dickerman and Matthew S. Witkovsky (eds.), *The Dada Seminars* (CASVA seminar papers 1, National Gallery of Art, Washington, 2005), pp. 30–55.

12. E.g. in the essays 'Kunst und Staat', in Dieter Wellerhoff (ed.), *Gottfried Benn. Gesammelte Werke in acht Bänden* (Wiesbaden: Limes, 1968), volume 3, pp. 603–13; 'Der neue Staat und die Intellektuellen' (1933), in Wellerhoff, *Gottfried Benn*, volume 4, pp. 1004–13.

13. Walter Adamson, *Avant-Garde Florence: From Modernism to Fascism* (Cambridge, MA: Harvard University Press, 1993).

14. See Günter Berghaus, *Futurism and Politics. Between Anarchist Rebellion and Fascist Reaction, 1909–1944* (Oxford: Berghahn, 1996).

15. The *sagra* is a local festivity celebrating a local speciality such as potatoes or anchovies. On Fascist regionalism see Stefano Cavazza, *Piccole Patrie. Feste popolari tra regione e nazione durante il fascismo* (Bologna: Il Mulino, 1997).

16. The swastikas on the Ara Pacis are referred to on the website on the Swastika run by the US neo-Nazi organization Stormfont at http://www.stormfront.org/archive/t-4817.html (accessed 27/10/06).

17. For more images of the building see http://www.greatbuildings.com/buildings/Casa_del_Fascio.html (accessed 30/11/06).

18. For a detailed history of the project see Orietta Rossini, *Ara Pacis Augustae* (Rome: Electa, 2006).

19. David Crowley, 'Nationalist Modernisms', in Christopher Wilk (ed.), *Modernism 1914–1939. Designing a New World* (London: V&A Publications, 2006), p. 351.

20. Remark made in an interview with *L'Espresso*, 26 December 1982, cited in Richard Bosworth, *The Italian Dictatorship* (London: Arnold, 1998), p. 155.

21. Dan Cruickshank, *Marvels of the Modern Age*, 4 part documentary series, 1st part, at approx 42 minutes. First shown on BBC 2, 9 May 2006, 9.00–10.00 pm, in association with the exhibition 'Modernism: Designing a New World 1914–1939' held at the Victoria and Albert Museum, London, in the spring of 2006.

22. Walter Benjamin launched this prolific school of interpretation with his famous 1937 essay 'The Work of Art in the Age of Mechanical Reproduction'. See Russell Berman, 'The Aestheticization of Politics: Walter Benjamin on Fascism and the Avant-Garde', in Russell Berman, *Modern Culture and Critical Theory: Art, Politics, and the Legacy of the Frankfurt School* (Madison: University of Wisconsin Press, 1989), pp. 27–41.

23. Igor Golomstock, *Totalitarian Art in the Soviet Union, the Third Reich, Fascist Italy and the People's Republic of China* (London: HarperCollins, 1990).

24. Virilio, *Art and Fear*, pp. 41–2.

25. Frederic Jameson (ed.), *Aesthetics and Politics: The Key Texts of the Classic Debate within German Marxism. Adorno, Benjamin, Bloch, Brecht, Lukács.* (New York: Verso, 1977).

26. Andrew Hewitt, *Fascist Modernism: Aesthetics, Politics, and the Avant-Garde* (Stanford, CA: Stanford University Press, 1993), p. 17.

27. Michael Ledeen, *Fascism. An Informal Introduction to its Theory and Practice* (New Brunswick, NJ: Transaction Books, 1976), pp. 55–7. My emphasis.

28. The vitalistic ethos of the exhibition is captured well in its catalogue: Anty Pansera (ed.), *Anni Trenta. Arte e Cultura in Italia* (Milan: Mazotta, 1981).

29. Peter Adam, *The Arts of the Third Reich* (New York: Harry N. Abrams, 1992), p. 9.

30. On the alleged nexus between the kitsch of Nazi art and the genocide committed by the Nazi state, see Saul Friedlaender, *Reflections of Nazism. An Essay on Kitsch and Death* (New York: Harper & Row, 1984).

31. Adolf Hitler, *Liberty, Art, Nationhood. Three Addresses by Adolf Hitler* (published in English) (Berlin: M. Müller & Son, 1935), p. 45.

32. The strikingly modernist design of the eight-storey-high extension that Mies proposed (his entry among the six designs awarded final prizes none of which were built) is reproduced in the web article 'Modernism: How Bad was it?' at http://pc.blogspot.com/2006/04/modernism-how-bad-was-it.html (accessed 30/11/06).

33. 'Mies's life' at http://www.moma.org/exhibitions/2001/mies/ (webpage of Museum of Modern Art, New York) (accessed 13/12/05).

34. Cruickshank's TV documentary omits reference to the elements of continuity between Bauhaus and Nazi design or to the intense interest shown by French fascists in Le Corbusier and the close relationship this equally iconic representative of architectural modernism enjoyed with the Vichy regime. Fortunately, these topics are dealt with extensively by Mark Antliff in his chapter 'La Cité française: George Valois, Le Corbusier, and Fascist Theories of Urbanism' in Mark Antliff and Matthew Affron (eds.), *Fascist Visions: Art and Ideology in France and Italy* (Princeton, NJ: Princeton University Press, 1997). See also Mark Antliff, *Avant-Garde Fascism. The Mobilization of Myth, Art and Culture in France, 1909–1939* (Durham, NC: Duke University Press, 2007).

35. Tim Dyckhoff, 'Mies and the Nazis', *Guardian*, 30 November 2002. See http://arts.guardian.co.uk/features/story/0,,850738,00.html (accessed 29/09/06).

36. Anecdote recounted by Maureen Potter for the BBC Radio 4 programme on the history of Jazz entitled 'Painting the Clouds with Sunshine' broadcast 12 November 2005, 10.30–11.00. For the full 'story' of the complex and tortuous relationship between Jazz and Nazism, which mirrors Nazism's paradoxical relationship with artistic modernism as a whole, see Michael Kater, *Different Drummers* (Oxford: Oxford University Press, 1982).

37. Joseph Goebbels, *Michael. Ein deutsches Schicksal* (Munich: Franz Eher Press, 1931), p. 124.

38. Hitler's speech on the opening of the House of German Art, 17 July 1937, excerpted in Raoul de Roussy de Sales (ed.), *Adolf Hitler. My New Order* (London: Angus and Robertson: 1942), pp. 335–6.

39. Henry A. Turner, 'Fascism and Modernization', in Henry A. Turner (ed.), *Reappraisals of Fascism* (New York: Franklin Watts, 1976), p. 131.

40. Raoul de Roussy de Sales (ed.), *Adolf Hitler. My New Order*, pp. 335–6.

41. Christina Lodder, 'Searching for Utopia', in Wilk, *Modernism 1914–1939*, pp. 23–70.

42. Crowley, 'Nationalist Modernisms', p. 352.

43. Ibid., p. 358.

44. Malcolm Bradbury and James McFarlane (eds.), *Modernism 1890–1930* (Harmondsworth: Penguin, 1976), pp. 30–1.

45. Christopher Wilk, 'Introduction: What was Modernism?', in Wilk, *Modernism 1914–1939*, pp. 12–13.

46. To take just two examples, A. James Gregor, *Phoenix* (New Brunswick, NJ: Transaction, 1999); Michael Mann, *Fascists* (New York: Cambridge University Press, 2004).

47. E.g. Robert Paxton, *The Anatomy of Fascism* (New York: Alfred A. Knopf, 2004); Roger Griffin with Matt Feldman, *Fascism: Critical Concepts in Political Science* (London: Routledge, 2004), volume 1: 'The Nature of Fascism'.

48. E.g. A. James Gregor's introduction to *Interpretations of Fascism* (2nd edn) (New Brunswick, NJ: Transaction, 1997); Roger Griffin, Werner Loh, and Andreas Umland (eds.), *Fascism Past and Present, East and West. An International Debate and Concepts and Cases in the Comparative Study of the Extreme Right* (Stuttgart: Ibidem, 2006).

49. Clifford Geertz, *The Interpretation of Cultures* (New York: Basic Books, 1973), p. 29. My emphasis.

50. Two important books on this topic are Frederic Jameson, *The Cultural Turn. Selected Writings on the Postmodern, 1983–1998* (Verso: London and New York, 1998); Victoria E. Bonnel and Lynn Hunt (eds.), *Beyond the Cultural Turn* (Berkeley: University of California Press, 1999). See also the Cultural Turn website at http://www.soc.ucsb.edu/ct/ (accessed 12/05/06).

51. Richard Evans, *In Defence of History* (London: Granta Books, 2000).

52. Richard Fox (ed.), *Recapturing Anthropology. Working in the Present* (Santa Fe, NM: School of American Research Press, 1991). For an eloquent sample of the tone of methodological caution, modest claims for the discipline, and the wariness of metanarratives that characterizes contemporary social anthropology, while offering a panoramic view of the sheer range of contemporary phenomena it embraces, see Wendy James, *The Ceremonial Animal. A New Portrait of Anthropology* (Oxford: Oxford University Press, 2003).

53. Evans, *In Defence of History*, p. 102.

54. Virginia Woolf, *The Waves* (1931) (London: Penguin, 2000), p. 183.

55. I recommend to those with a reading knowledge of German and who are interested in the methodological issues touched on here the periodical *Erwägen Wissen Ethik* (Deliberation, Knowledge, Ethics) whose mission is to create a more reflexive, methodologically sophisticated, and collaborative ethos in the human sciences, or what it calls an 'Erwägungskultur' ('deliberative culture'). Its website is http://iug.uni-paderborn.de/ewe/ (accessed 12/05/06).

56. Callum Brown, *Postmodernism for Historians* (London: Pearson Education, 2005), p. 134.

57. Ibid., p. 149.

58. Julius Evola, *Il Cammino del Cinabro* (Milan: Vanni Scheiwiller, 1972), p. 22.

59. Evola's introduction to *La tradizione ermetica nei suoi simboli, nella sua dottrina e nella sua 'Arte regia'* (Bari: Gius. Laterza & Figli, 1931) is significantly entitled 'La realtà della palingenesi' ('The reality of palingenesis'). The text is reproduced on the website of the Centri Studi La Runa at http://www.centrostudilaruna.it/realtapalingenesi.html (accessed 13/05/06). It will become obvious that 'palingenesis' (from the Greek 'palin' again and 'genesis' birth) and its derivative 'palingenetic' are crucial terms in my formulation of the modernist and fascist thrust towards renewal and regeneration.

60. Evola, *Il Cammino del Cinabro*, p. 60.

61. Evola's visceral racism and profound philo-Nazism, which so many thinkers of the European New Right tend to pass over in silence, has been thoroughly documented in Germinario, *Razza del sangue, razza dello Sprito*.

62. Schnapp, 'Bad Dada (Evola)', p. 36.

63. Ibid., p. 39.

64. Julius Evola, *L 'operaio' nel pensiero di Ernst Jünger* (Rome: Armando Armando Editore, 1960).

65. My emphasis. The text was viewed at http://www.y-land.net/juliusevola/revolte_rez1.php (accessed 20/01/06).

66. On the intimate link between the Nazis' 'monumental building project economy' and the concentration camp system see Paul Jaskot, *The Architecture of Oppression* (London: Routledge, 2000).

67. See the memorial website at http://www.remember.org/camps/mauthausen/mau-list.html (accessed 12/11/06).

2 TWO MODES OF MODERNISM

1. Friedrich Nietzsche, *Thus Spoke Zarathustra. A New Translation by Graham Parkes* (Oxford: Blackwell, 2005), p. 100.

2. Marshall Berman, *All that is Solid Melts into Air. The Experience of Modernity* (London: Verso, 1982), p. 15.

3. Jürgen Habermas, *The Philosophical Discourses of Modernity* (Cambridge, MA: The MIT Press, 1987), p. 6.

4. Susan Friedman, 'Definitional Excursus: The Meanings of Modern/ Modernity/ Modernism', *Modernism/Modernity*, 8.3 (2001), p. 510.

5. Ibid.

6. Christopher Wilk, 'Introduction: What was Modernism?', in Christopher Wilk (ed.), *Modernism 1914–1939. Designing a New World* (London: V&A Publications, 2006), p. 12. Recent examples are David Ayers, *Modernism. A Short Introduction* (Oxford: Blackwell, 2004); Jane Goldman, *Modernism. 1910–1945* (London: Palgrave Macmillan, 2004).

7. Vassiliki Kolocotroni, Jane Goldman, and Olga Taxidou (eds.), *Modernism: An Anthology of Sources and Documents* (Edinburgh and Chicago: Edinburgh University Press and Chicago University Press, 1998), p. xvii.

8. For an excellent discussion of the weaknesses of the term 'modernization' as a 'master-narrative' applied to totalitarianism which has much relevance to the thesis of this book (especially in the insistence that fascism and Bolshevism pursued 'alternative modernities') see David Roberts, *The Totalitarian Experiment in the Twentieth-Century* (New York: Routledge, 2006), pp. 31–9.

9. For a recent and fairly unreflexive metanarrative on this topic see C. A. Bayly, *The Birth of the Modern World, 1780–1914: Global Connections and Comparisons* (Oxford: Blackwell Publishers, 2004).

10. In contrast to the interpretive strategy being developed here, Marxists would naturally tend to focus on the rise of capitalism and its social and material consequences as the principal driving force of change and of modernism itself, as well as being the progenitor of fascism. In fact Marxist and non-Marxist historians can be seen as engaged in an endless dispute over the appropriate discourse for the construction of the narrative of modernity and its associated concepts.

11. An allusion to the 'law of combined and uneven development' that plays an important part in the theory of capitalism's development under modernity elaborated by Marxists (for whom the term 'modernization' retains suspiciously liberal-bourgeois connotations).

12. The title of the new translation by Rodney J. Payton and Ulrich Mammitzsch, *The Autumn of the Middle Ages* (Chicago: University of Chicago Press, 1996) is more faithful to that of the original Dutch edition of 1919 than *The Waning of the Middle Ages* under which it became famous.

13. David Harvey, *The Condition of Postmodernity* (Oxford: Basil Blackwell, 1989), p. 111. This passage is taken from the chapter devoted to 'modernization' in the context of modernity.

14. A statement by Theodor Adorno, cited in Peter Osborne, *The Politics of Time. Modernity and the Avant-garde* (London: Verso, 1995), p. 9. It is taken from Theodor Adorno, *Minima Moralia* (Frankfurt: Suhrkampf, 1951), volume 3, aphorism 140 (no page no.).

Adorno's work is available in English (translated by Dennis Redmond) as a web resource at http://www.efn.org/~dredmond/MinimaMoralia.html (accessed 02/10/06). A useful overview of the history of the term 'modern' is offered by Osborne on pp. 9–13 of *The Politics of Time*.

15. Zygmunt Bauman, *Modernity and Ambivalence* (Cambridge: Polity, 1991), p. 3, fn. 1.

16. The timing of modernity as a period concept is the main focus of Koselleck's investigations in his *Critique and Crisis. Enlightenment and the Pathogenesis of Modern Society* (Oxford: Berg, 1988), and in *The Practice of Conceptual History. Timing History, Spacing Concepts* (Stanford, CA: Stanford University Press, 2002).

17. E.g. David Harvey in *The Condition of Postmodernity* (Oxford: Blackwell, 1990).

18. Bauman, *Modernity and Ambivalence*, pp. 3–4.

19. Cf. Jean-Luc Marion, *Being Given. Towards a Phenomenology of Givenness* (Palo Alto, CA: Stanford University Press, 2002).

20. Bauman, *Modernity and Ambivalence*, p. 9.

21. Themes addressed in Anthony Giddens, *The Consequences of Modernity* (Cambridge: Polity Press, 1990), and *Modernity and Self-identity* (Cambridge: Polity Press, 1991).

22. Fredric Jameson, *The Seeds of Time* (New York: Columbia Press, 1994), p. 84.

23. Stephen Kern, *The Culture of Time and Space 1880–1918* (2nd edition Cambridge, MA: Harvard University Press, 2003), chapter 4, 'The Future'.

24. This theme is reflected in the title of several investigations of modernity such as Erich Heller, *The Disinherited Mind. Essays in Modern German Literature and Thought* (Philadelphia: Dufour & Saifer, 1952); Hans Holthusen, *Der unbehauste Mensch* ['Homeless/unhoused Man'] (Munich: Piper, 1952). Particularly relevant to our thesis is Peter Berger, Brigitte Berger, and Hansfried Kellner, *The Homeless Mind. Modernization and Consciousness* (Harmondsworth: Penguin, 1974).

25. Max Weber, 'The Social Psychology of the World's Religions' (1915) in Hans Gerth and C. Wright Mills (eds.), *From Max Weber. Essays in Sociology* (New York: Oxford University Press, 1946), p. 282. For a major attempt to develop a new synoptic interpretation of Weber's orginal thesis see Marcel Gauchet, *The Disenchantment of the World: A Political History of Religion* (Princeton, NJ: Princeton University Press 1997). There are tantalizing points of congruity and divergence between Gauchet's master narrative of the human drive to reinvent secularized forms of religion in a 'post-religious' society and the theory of modernism I am developing, but which 'time and space' preclude from pursuing here. For an important 'historiographic review' of the topic see Michael Saler, 'Modernity and Enchantment', *American Historical Review* 111.3 (June 2006), pp. 692–716. In his conclusion Saler endorses the contention of Mark Schneider in *Culture and Enchantment* (Chicago: University of Chicago Press, 1993), p. x, that '[e]nchantment [...] is part of our normal condition, and far from having fled with the rise of science, it continues to exist (though often unrecognized) where neither science nor practical knowledge seem of much utility'.

26. Émile Durkheim, *The Division of Labour in Society* (1893) (New York: The Free Press 1972).

27. Ferdinand Tönnies, *Gemeinschaft und Gesellschaft* (Leipzig: Fues, 1887).

28. Georg Simmel, *The Metropolis and Mental Life* (1903) (New York: Free Press, 1950).

29. Sigmund Freud, *Das Unbehagen in der Kultur* (Vienna: Internationaler Psychoanalytischer Verlag, 1930), translated as *Civilization and its Discontents* (London: Hogarth Press and Institute of Psycho-Analysis, 1930).

30. Carl G. Jung, *Modern Man in Search of a Soul* (New York: Harcourt, Brace & World, 1933).

31. For a fascinating exegesis of the importance for a Marxist analysis of society of the modern sense of time being 'out of joint' (a phrase taken from William Shakespeare's *Macbeth*), see Jacques Derrida's *Specters of Marx, the State of the Debt, the Work of Mourning, & the New International* (London: Routledge, 1994), chapter 4, 'In the name of the revolution,

the double barricade', pp. 95–124. (The allusions to *Macbeth* remind us that there have been many situations before modernity when time seemed 'out of joint', so that the modern experience of anomy is the permutation of a recurrent social phenomenon.)

32. Hans Blumenberg, *Lebenszeit und Weltzeit* (Frankfurt: Suhrkampf, 1986), p. 240.
33. See, for example, Anthony Giddens, *Modernity and Self-identity. Self and Society in the Late Modern Age* (Cambridge: Polity Press, 1991). See too Martin O'Brien, Sue Penna, and Colin Hay, *Theorising Modernity. Reflexivity, Environment and Identity in Giddens' Social Theory* (London: Longman, 1999).
34. Bauman, *Modernity and Ambivalence*, p. 5.
35. Reinhardt Koselleck, 'The Eighteenth Century as the Beginning of Modernity', in Koselleck, *The Practice of Conceptual History*, p. 165.
36. Ibid.
37. Ibid., 'The Temporalization of Utopia', p. 85.
38. Ibid., 'Remarks on the Revolutionary Calendar and "Neue Zeit"', p. 152. My emphasis.
39. Helga Nowotny, *Time. The Modern and Postmodern Experience* (1989) (Cambridge: Polity Press, 1994), p. 48.
40. Ibid., p. 51.
41. Osborne, *The Politics of Time*, p. 12.
42. Harvey, *The Condition of Postmodernity*, chapter 16, pp. 260–83.
43. Morse Peckham, 'Toward a Theory of Romanticism', *PMLA* 66.2 (March 1951), pp. 5–23. See also Mario Praz's classic text written at the height of the inter-war period, *The Romantic Agony* (1933) (Oxford: Oxford University Press, 1970).
44. Friedrich Nietzsche attacks 'Romantic pessimism' in the Preface to the 'First Sequel' to *Human, All Too Human: A Book for Free Spirits*, published as 'Mixed Opinions and Maxims' in 1879, and reprinted in Friedrich Nietzsche, *Human, All Too Human* (1986) (Cambridge: Cambridge University Press, 1996), p. 213. In *The Gay Science* (1887) he returns to this theme, contrasting Romantic pessimism with *Dionysian* pessimism in Section 370: see Friedrich Nietzsche, *The Gay Science* (New York: Vintage, 1974), pp. 327–31.
45. As in the case of modernity itself, a mythic point, though a number of scholars have agreed that a *symbolic* starting point for modernism is Charles Baudelaire's publication of his essay 'The Painter of Modern Life' in 1863. We will see that there are also arguments for seeing the Communist Manifesto of 1848 as a no less historic moment in the genesis of modernism.
46. H. Stuart Hughes, *Consciousness and Society. The Reorientation of European Social Thought. 1890–1930* (New York: Vintage Books, 1977).
47. Harvey, *The Condition of Postmodernity*, p. 98.
48. Bauman, *Modernity and Ambivalence*, p. 4.
49. Frank Kermode, *The Sense of an Ending. Studies in the Theory of Fiction* (1967) (New York: Oxford University Press, 2000), p. 93. Cf. p. 108. His crucial distinction between 'fiction' and 'myth' is explored in depth in chapter 4, 'The Modern Apocalypse', pp. 93–124.
50. Malcolm Bradbury and James McFarlane, 'The Name and Nature of Modernism', in Malcolm Bradbury and James McFarlane (eds.), *Modernism 1890–1930* (Harmondsworth: Penguin, 1976), p. 46.
51. Peter Childs, *Modernism* (London: Routledge, 2000), p. 17.
52. Goldman, *Modernism*, p. 3.
53. Ibid., pp. 239–43.
54. Walter Adamson, *Avant-Garde Florence: from Modernism to Fascism* (Cambridge, MA: Harvard University Press, 1993), pp. 7–9. Adamson builds on the classic account of modernism given in Stephen Spender's *The Struggle of the Modern* (London: Methuen, 1963), pp. 71–97, which has several important points of congruity and contrast with the ideal type I am constructing here.
55. Berman, *All that is Solid Melts into Air*, p. 16. My emphasis. For a trenchant criticism of Berman's cavalier depiction of modernism see Gladys M. Jiménez-Muñoz's review of the

book in *PROUD FLESH: A New Afrikan Journal of Culture, Politics & Consciousness*, 1.1 (2002). We will later see that Osborne too has grave misgivings about how Berman has 'constructed' the term.

56. Modris Eksteins, *Rites of Spring* (1989) (Boston: Houghton Mifflin, 2000), p. xvi.
57. Osborne, *The Politics of Time*, p. 142.
58. Peter Fritzsche, 'Nazi Modern', *Modernism/modernity* 3.1 (1996), p. 12.
59. Ronald Schleifer, *Modernism and Time. The Logic of Abundance in Literature, Science, and Culture* (Cambridge: Cambridge University Press, 2000), pp. 4–7.
60. Ibid., pp. 10–11.
61. Schleifer elaborates his subtle and intricate argument in the course of chapter 1 of *Modernism and Time*, 'Post-Enlightenment Modernism and the experience of time', ibid. pp. 1–31.
62. An allusion to the Wilhelmine (Second) Reich that had been formed three years earlier with the enthusiastic support of the bulk of Germany's educated elite.
63. Friedrich Nietzsche, 'Schopenhauer as Educator', in Friedrich Nietzsche, *Unmodern Observations* (New Haven, CT: Yale University Press, 1990), p. 185.
64. Ibid.
65. Friedrich Nietzsche, Preface to *The Case of Wagner* (New York: Vintage Books, 1967), p. 155.
66. Friedrich Nietzsche, *The Will to Power. Notes written 1883–1888* (London: Weidenfeld and Nicolson, 1967), Book I, 23 (Spring–Fall 1887), pp. 18–19. My emphasis.
67. Friedrich Nietzsche, *Ecce Homo* (1908) (New York: Vintage, 1967), Part 1, par. 4: 'Why I am Destiny'. For an important essay on the prevalence of this principle in modernist economics see Hugo Reinert and Erik Reinert, 'Creative Destruction in Economics: Nietzsche, Sombart, Schumpeter', in Jürgen Backhaus and Wolfgang Drechsler (eds.), *Friedrich Nietzsche. Economy and Society* (Heidelberg: Springer, 2006).
68. Nietzsche, *The Will to Power*, Preface, pp. 3–4. My emphasis.
69. Robert Gooding-Williams, *Zarathustra's Dionysian Modernism* (Stanford, CA: Stanford University Press, 2001), pp. 4–5. Chapter 1, 'The Possibility of Modernism', paints a vivid picture of the confusions and conundrums that have arisen for academics attempting to locate Nietzsche within modernism or postmodernism.
70. Ibid., p. 7.
71. Ibid., p. 274.
72. Friedrich Nietzsche, *Dithyrambs of Dionysus* (London: Anvil Press, 1984), p. 41.
73. This occurs in the section 'At Noontide' in Nietzsche, *Thus Spoke Zarathustra*, Part IV, pp. 286–9.
74. Friedrich Nietzsche, *Sils-Maria*, poem printed in the appendix to *Fröhliche Wissenschaft* (1882), this translation by Adrian del Caro, in Friedrich Nietzsche, *The Gay Science* (Cambridge: Cambridge University Press, 2001), p. 258.
75. Rudolf Zaehner, *Mysticism Religious and Profane* (Oxford: Oxford University Press, 1961), pp. 28–9. For an eloquent description of such a moment see Virginia Woolf, 'A Sketch of the Past', in Jeanne Schulkind (ed.), *Moments of Being* (New York: Harcourt Brace, 1985), pp. 71–3.
76. Nietzsche, *Thus Spoke Zarathustra*, Prologue, p. 52.
77. Ibid., Part 2, 'Of Great Events', p. 154.
78. Gooding-Williams, *Zarathustra's Dionysian Modernism*, p. 274.
79. Kermode, *The Sense of an Ending*, pp. 93–104.
80. T. S. Eliot, 'The Dry Salvages', *The Four Quartets*, III (1941), in *The Complete Poems & Plays. T. S. Eliot* (London: Faber and Faber, 2004), p. 190.
81. An allusion to Milan Kundera's novel, *The Unbearable Lightness of Being* (London: Faber and Faber, 1984).
82. James Joyce uses this term in the novel *Stephen Hero* (1944).

83. Kermode, *The Sense of an Ending*, p. 47. The distinction between *chronos* (linear, entropic) and *kairos* (special, revelatory) time, and the attempts of modern (epiphanic) artists to access or conjure up *kairos* and break out of *chronos* is one of the main themes of the chapter entitled 'Fictions', pp. 35–64.

84. Marcel Proust, *À la recherche du temps perdu* (Paris: Gallimard, 1945), volume 3, p. 871.

85. Zaehner, *Mysticism Religious and Profane*, p. 55. Chapter 4 (pp. 50–83) is devoted to a discussion of the natural mystic experiences of Proust and Arthur Rimbaud, and has a deep relevance to the theme of 'epiphanic modernism' being developed here, and especially to the peculiar concept of transcendence it cultivates which stands in such marked contrast to the ambitions of programmatic modernists to inaugurate an entirely new era of society within historical time.

86. Virginia Woolf, 'A Sketch of the Past', in Schulkind, *Moments of Being*, pp. 70–2. *Moments of Being* was also the title of Woolf's autobiography published posthumously in 1941.

87. Nicole Urquhart, 'Moments of Being in Virginia Woolf's Fiction', http://writing.colostate. edu/gallery/matrix/urquhart.htm (accessed 21/07/05).

88. Bauman, *Modernity and Ambivalence*, p. 183.

89. Kafka Project, *Diaries and Travel Diaries*, volume 12, diary entry for 13 January 1922, 'He could have left the cage, since the bars were yards apart. He was not even a prisoner.' http://www.kafka.org/index.php?h12 (accessed 21/07/05).

90. Remark made in conversation with Gustav Janouch after 1920 and 1924, cited in Gustav Janouch, *Gespräche mit Kafka. Aufzeichnungen und Erinnerungen* (Frankfurt am Main: Fischer, 1968), p. 38.

91. Kafka Project, *Diaries and Travel Diaries*, volume 12, diary entry for 19 January 1922. http://www.kafka.org/index.php?h12 (accessed 21/07/05).

92. Franz Kafka, 'Betrachtungen über Sünde, Leid, Hoffnung und den wahren Weg' [Reflections on Sin, Suffering, Hope, and the True Way], in Max Brod (ed.), *Franz Kafka. Hochzeitsvorbereitungen auf dem Lande und andere Prosa aus dem Nachlaß* (Frankfurt am Main: Fischer, 1980), p. 40.

93. Malcolm Bradbury and James McFarlane, 'Movements, Magazines and Manifestos: The Succession from Naturalism', in Bradbury and McFarlane, *Modernism 1890–1930*, p. 192.

94. Hugo von Hofmansthal, *The Lord Chandos Letter and Other Writings* (New York: New York Review Books Classics, 2005).

95. Richard Sheppard, 'The Crisis of Language', in Bradbury and McFarlane, *Modernism 1890–1930*, p. 324.

96. Kafka Project, *Diaries and Travel Diaries*, volume 12, diary entry for 16 January 1922, http://www.kafka.org/index.php?h12 (accessed 21/07/05).

97. Ibid.

98. Walter Gropius, 'Ja! Stimmen des Arbeitrates für Kunst in Berlin' (Berlin, 1919), cited in Wilk, 'Introduction: What was Modernism?', p. 11.

99. Franz Kafka, Diary Entry, 1917–1918, Heinz Politzer (ed.), *Das Kafka-Buch* (Frankfurt am Main: Fischer, 1965), p. 247.

100. See Introduction.

101. Nietzsche, 'Schopenhauer as Educator', p. 169.

102. Cf. Nietzsche, *Thus Spoke Zarathustra*, Prologue, p. 46: 'The earth has become small, and on it hops the Ultimate Man, who makes everything small. His species is inexterminable as the flea; the Ultimate Man lives longest.'

103. Wilk, 'Introduction: What was Modernism?', p. 14.

104. Christina Lodder, 'Searching for Utopia', in Wilk, *Modernism 1914–1939*, p. 24.

105. See note 3.

3   AN ARCHAEOLOGY OF MODERNISM

1. The term 'archaeology' in this context obviously comes with considerable intellectual baggage thanks to Michel Foucault's pioneering works *The Order of Things. An Archaeology of the Human Sciences* (New York: Vintage Books, 1970) and *The Archaeology of Knowledge* (London: Tavistock, 1972). I should thus stress that the term is being used here metaphorically without technical Foucauldian connotations.

2. Frank Kermode, *The Sense of an Ending* (1967) (Oxford: Oxford University Press, 2000), p. 9.

3. Arthur Koestler, *The Act of Creation* (1964) (London: Pan Books, 1975), p. 391.

4. Anthony Stevens, *Ariadne's Clue. A Guide to the Symbols of Humankind* (London: The Allen Press, 1998), p. 170.

5. Herbert W. Schneider, *Making the Fascist State* (New York: Oxford University Press, 1928), p. 229.

6. See particularly Emilio Gentile, *The Sacralization of Politics in Fascist Italy* (Cambridge, MA: Harvard University Press, 1996); Mabel Berezin, *Making the Fascist Self* (Ithaca, NY: Cornell University Press, 1997).

7. Anglophone Nazi studies still lacks a comprehensive monograph in English on the political religion of Fascism on the scale of Klaus Vondung's *Magie und Manipulation – Ideologischer Kult und politische Religion des Nationalsozialismus* (Göttingen: Vandenhoeck and Ruprecht, 1971), or Gentile's *The Sacralization of Politics in Fascist Italy*. Nevertheless the images of Leni Riefenstahl's *Triumph of the Will* are worth many thousand words of academic analysis of Nazism's ritual dimension.

8. On the debate on the relevance of the concept 'political religion' to fascist studies see *Totalitarian Movements and Political Religion* 5.3 (Winter 2004) and 6.2 (Summer 2005).

9. E.g. Sharon Stockton, 'Aesthetics, Politics and the Staging of the World: Wyndham Lewis and the Renaissance-author', *Twentieth Century Literature* 20.2 (Winter 1996), pp. 494–515.

10. Guy Debord, *Society of the Spectacle* (Detroit: Black and Red, 1983), p. 110. Original emphasis.

11. For a vivid account of the Nazi May Day see Iain Boyd Whyte, 'Berlin, 1 May 1936' in Dawn Ades et al. (eds.), *Art and Power. Europe under the Dictators, 1930–45* (London: Hayward Gallery, 1995), pp. 43–9.

12. David Kertzer, *Ritual, Politics and Power* (New Haven: Yale University Press, 1988), p. 13.

13. Ibid., p. 4.

14. Anthony Smith, *Nations and Nationalism in a Global Era* (Cambridge: Polity, 1995), p. 159. For a discussion of 'modernist' compared with several variants of 'primordialist' approaches to nationalism see ibid., pp. 30–41, and the chapter 'Primordialism and Perennialism', in Anthony Smith, *Nationalism and Modernism. A Critical Survey of Recent Theories of Nations* (London: Routledge, 1998), especially pp. 145–59. It should be noticed that Smith is critical of the one-sided application of *both* approaches.

15. See Appendix: Move on Methodology.

16. Peter Berger, *The Sacred Canopy. Elements of a Sociological Theory of Religion* (London: Doubleday, 1967), pp. 4, 22, 27. A child of his age, Berger uses throughout male-gendered language typical of the human sciences of the time.

17. Ibid., pp. 22, 27.

18. Kertzer, *Ritual, Politics and Power*, p. 4.

19. Berger, *The Sacred Canopy*, p. 54.

20. Ibid., p. 23. Berger's use of 'anomy' (usually spelt in English 'anomie') is deeply indebted to Émile Durkheim's analysis of modernity.

21. Two graphic examples of this metaphorical projection of existential rootedness onto the sky are the imagery associated with the Egyptian god Shu, the 'holder of the sky', e.g. http://www.touregypt.net/featurestories/shu.htm (accessed 01/12/06), and the sixteenth-century Hindu Bhugola or Earth-Ball held on the backs of three elephants, on display at the Oxford History of Science Museum, http://www.mhs.ox.ac.uk/images/, image no. 156048, inventory no. 51703 (accessed 09/11/06).

22. Cited in Matthew Feldman, *Aporetics: An empirical study on philosophical influences in the development of Samuel Beckett's writing* (Oxford: unpublished PhD Thesis, Dept of Arts and Humanities, Oxford Brookes University, 2004), pp. 394–5. For more on the sustained ontological crisis that drives Beckett's unique brand of epiphanic modernism see Matthew Feldman, *Beckett's Books: A Cultural History of Samuel Beckett's 'Interwar Notes'* (London and New York: Continuum, 2006).

23. Berger, *The Sacred Canopy*, pp. 79–80.

24. Stevens, *Ariadne's Clue*, p. 17.

25. Ibid., p. 20.

26. See Richard Noll, *The Jung Cult* (New York: Simon & Schuster, 1994).

27. For a sustained hypothesis about the persistence of processes of re-enchantment which countervail the 'disenchantment of the world' under modernity postulated by Max Weber see Jane Bennet, *The Enchantment of Modern Life: Attachments, Crossings, and Ethics* (Princeton, NJ.: Princeton University Press, 2001).

28. See Roger Griffin, *The Nature of Fascism* (London: Pinter, 1991), pp. 186–8.

29. See Richard Fenn, *Time Exposure. The Personal Experience of Time in Secular Societies* (Oxford: Oxford University Press, 2000), chapter 3.

30. Ibid., p. 115.

31. For a scholarly attempt to recuperate what might be of value to professional social anthropologists and comparative religion experts in Eliade's highly contested theses on the perennial patterns in human religions, cosmologies, and rituals, see Bryan Rennie, *Reconstructing Eliade. Making Sense of Religion* (New York: State University of New York Press, 1996).

32. Mircea Eliade, *The Myth of the Eternal Return, or Cosmos and History* (1954) (Princeton, NJ: Princeton University Press, 1971), chapter 4, 'The Terror of History', pp. 139–62.

33. Mircea Eliade, *The Sacred and the Profane. The Nature of Religion. The Significance of Religious Myth, Symbolism, and Ritual within Life and Culture* (San Diego, CA: Harcourt Brace & Co, 1959), pp. 205–6.

34. T. S. Eliot, 'Burnt Norton', *The Four Quartets* (1935), in *The Complete Poems & Plays. T. S. Eliot* (London: Faber and Faber, 2004), p. 172.

35. Cf. Paul Bowles, *The Sheltering Sky* (1949) (Harmondsworth: Penguin, 1990), p. 79: '"You know, the sky here's strange. I often have the sensation when I look at it that it's a solid thing up there, protecting us from what's behind." Kit shuddered slightly as she said: "From what's behind?" "Yes" "But what *is* behind?" Her voice was very small. "Nothing, I suppose. Just darkness. Absolute night."'

36. At this point it is important to spell out a premise of this account of the human condition which will be blatantly obvious to the members of any faith community. It assumes an 'absolute night' lurking behind the myriad artificial skies or sacred canopies erected to shield us from nothingness. There may well be readers who believe passionately in some form of divinity or suprahuman reality, and who are thus convinced of the metaphysical meaningfulness or createdness of human life. I invite them nonetheless to bear with my secular argument in the hope that the account of modernity and modernism that emerges may contribute to their own understanding of modern history and the extreme pressures it exerts on faiths both religious and secular.

37. Blaise Pascal, *Pensées* (Harmondsworth: Penguin, 1966), no. 201, p. 95.

38. See Terence Deacon, *The Symbolic Species* (London: Allen Lane/The Penguin Press, 1997).

39. See, for example, Wendy James, *The Ceremonial Animal. A New Portrait of Anthropology* (Oxford: Oxford University Press, 2003).

40. Giorgio Agamben, *Homo Sacer: Sovereign Power and Bare Life* (Stanford, CA: Meridian, 1998).

41. Cosimo Quarta, 'Homo utopicus sive transcendens', *Utopian Studies* 12.2 (2001), pp. 174–87. More disturbing species-defining attributes have been be ascribed to 'man' by those linking humankind's need to create an artificial world to its unique capacity for annihilating other cultures (*homo pathologicus*) and destroying our own ecological habitat (*homo destructivus*: the term used by the apocalyptic 'ecofascist' Pentti Linkola).

42. See Andrew Tengan, *The Search for Meaning as the Basic Human Motivation. A Critical Examination of Viktor Emil Frankl's Logotherapeutic Concept of Man* (Frankfurt am Main: Peter Lang, 1999).

43. See Viktor Frankl, *Man's Search for Meaning* (London: Simon & Schuster, 1959), written in 1945 soon after his liberation from the camp.

44. Viktor Frankl, *Homo Patiens. Versuch einer Pathodizee* (Vienna: Deuticke, 1950).

45. The theme of the metaphysical and cultural 'disinheritance' of human beings under modernity is expressed in the famous poem of Gérard de Nerval, 'El Desdichado' (literally 'the disinherited one') published in 1854. Cf. Erich Heller, *The Disinherited Mind. Essays in Modern German Literature and Thought* (Philadelphia: Dufour & Saifer, 1952).

46. Gustav Janouch, *Gespräche mit Kafka. Aufzeichnungen und Erinnerungen* (1954) (Frankfurt am Main: Fischer, 1968), pp. 98–9.

47. Ernest Becker, *The Birth and Death of Meaning. An Interdisciplinary Perspective on the Problem of Man* (Harmondsworth: Penguin, 1962), p. 143.

48. Ibid.

49. Ernest Becker, *Escape from Evil* (New York: The Free Press, 1975), pp. 125–6.

50. Ibid., p. xvii. The post-WWII consensus among several major sociological thinkers on a 'primordial terror of the void' may betray the contemporary influence of the existentialist analysis of the human condition found, for example, in the works of Jean-Paul Sartre, Albert Camus, and Samuel Beckett.

51. This innocent 'animal' state of unreflexive being is contrasted with the torments of human reflexivity in the Eighth Elegy of Rainer Maria Rilke's deeply modernist cycle of poems, *The Duino Elegies*, completed in 1922.

52. Zygmunt Bauman, *Mortality, Immortality and Other Life Strategies* (Stanford, CA: Stanford University Press, 1992), pp. 3–4. My emphasis.

53. See above Chapter 2, p. 64.

54. Kermode, *The Sense of an Ending*, p. 47.

55. Ibid., p. 72.

56. For a dualistic scheme of human time which plays on these confusingly homophonic mythological figures see the essay 'Cronus and Chronos' in Edmund Leach, 'Two Essays concerning the Symbolic Representation of Time', in Edmund Leach, *Rethinking Anthropology* (Monographs on Social Anthropology, no. 22), (London: Athlone Press, 1971), pp. 124–32. Leach's theory of time is subjected to a withering critique in Alfred Gell, *The Anthropology of Time* (Oxford: Berg, 1992), pp. 30–53.

57. Gell, *The Anthropology of Time*, p. 315.

58. See ibid., Part II, 'Time-maps and Cognition'.

59. Maurice Bloch and Jonathan Parry (eds.), *Death and the Regeneration of Life* (Cambridge: Cambridge University Press, 1982), p. 15. The introduction contains a valuable overview of how the significance of mortuary rites has been interpreted by academics in the past.

60. Angela Hobart, *Healing Performances of Bali. Between Darkness and Light* (Oxford: Berghahn, 2003), p. 204.

61. Ibid.

62. Ibid., p. 5.

63. Herbert Read, *The Collected Works of C. G. Jung* (London: Routledge, 1953–78), Par. 50; cited in Stevens, *Ariadne's Clue*, p. 174.
64. Jeff Greenberg, Tom Pyszczynski, and Sheldon Salomon, 'The Causes and Consequences of a Need for Self-Esteem. A Terror Management Theory', in Roy Baumeister (ed.), *Public and Private Self* (New York: Springer, 1986), p. 198.
65. Ibid., p. 196. My emphasis.
66. Emanuele Castano and Mark Dechesne, 'On Defeating Death. Group reification and social identification as immortality strategies', *European Review of Social Psychology* 6 (2005), pp. 231–65.
67. Amin Maalouf, *Les Identités Meurtrières* (Paris: Grasset, 1998), p. 128.
68. Cited in Castano and Dechesne, 'On Defeating Death', p. 233. For a study of anaesthetizing strategies to 'kill time' see Stanley Cohen and Laurie Taylor, *Escape Attempts. The Theory and Practice of Resistance to Everyday Life* (New York: Penguin Books, 1978).
69. Richard Fenn, *Time Exposure*, p. 77.
70. Berger, *The Sacred Canopy*, pp. 79–80.
71. Castano and Dechesne, 'On Defeating Death', p. 254.
72. Ibid., p. 255.
73. Bauman, *Mortality, Immortality and Other Life Strategies*, pp. 104–9.
74. Smith, *Nations and Nationalism in a Global Era*, pp. 158–9.
75. David Ulansey, 'Cultural Transition and Spiritual Transformation. From Alexander the Great to Cyberspace', in Thomas Singer (ed.), *The Vision Thing. Myth, Politics and Psyche in the World* (New York: Routledge, 2000), pp. 213–31.
76. See Robert Kinsman (ed.), *The Darker Vision of the Renaissance. Beyond the Fields of Reason* (Berkeley, CA: University of California Press, 1974).
77. See Graeme Garrard, *Rousseau's Counter-Enlightenment. A Republican critique of the Philosophes* (New York: State University of New York Press, 2003).
78. See above, Chapter 2, p. 61.
79. Heinrich Heine, *Reisebilder*. Dritter Teil. 'Die Bäder von Lucca', in Klaus Briegleb (ed.), *Heinrich Heine. Sämtliche Schriften in sechs Bänden. Volume 2* (Munich: Carl Hanser, 1968–76), p. 405.
80. See Elissa Marden, *Dead Time. Temporal Disorders in the Wake of Modernity (Baudelaire and Flaubert)* (Stanford, CA: Stanford University Press, 2001).
81. Ibid., p. 130.
82. Walter Benjamin, 'Theses on the Philosophy of History', IX, in *Illuminations* (London: Fontana, 1992), p. 249.
83. Ibid., pp. 253–5.
84. Malcolm Bradbury and James McFarlane, 'The Name and Nature of Modernism', in Malcolm Bradbury and James McFarlane (eds.), *Modernism 1890–1930* (Harmondsworth: Penguin, 1976), p. 46. My emphasis.
85. David Harvey, *The Condition of Postmodernity* (Oxford: Basil Blackwell, 1989), p. 206.
86. Karsten Harries, 'Building and the Terror of Time', *Prospecta. The Yale Architectural Journal* 19 (1982), p. 60.
87. Eliade, *The Myth of the Eternal return, or Cosmos and History*, p. 76.
88. Harries, 'Building and the Terror of Time', p. 64–5. My emphasis.
89. Charles Baudelaire, 'The Painter of Modern Life' (1863), cited in P. E. Charvet (ed.), *Baudelaire: Selected Writings on Art and Literature* (New York: Viking 1972), pp. 395–422.
90. Draft epilogue for the second edition of *Les Fleurs du mal*. Published in Charles Baudelaire, *Les Fleurs du Mal* (1861) (Paris: Gallimard, 1964), p. 212.
91. See above, Chapter 2, p. 63.
92. 'L'Albatros', Baudelaire, *Les Fleurs du Mal*, p. 20.
93. Marden, *Dead Time*, p. 24.

94. Fredric Jameson, *The Seeds of Time* (New York: Columbia University Press, 1994), pp. 84–5. My emphasis. Cited in Marden, *Dead Time*, p. 189.
95. Friedrich Nietzsche, *The Birth of Tragedy* (Oxford: Oxford University Press, 2000), section 23, pp. 122–3.
96. Friedrich Nietzsche, 'History in the Service and Disservice of Life', in Friedrich Nietzsche, *Unmodern Observations* (1874) (New Haven, CT: Yale University Press, 1990), p. 138.
97. Ibid., p. 142.
98. E.g. in Friedrich Nietzsche, *Thus Spoke Zarathustra. A New Translation by Graham Parkes* (Oxford: Blackwell, 2005), pp. 98–101.
99. Ernst Bloch, *Geist der Utopie* (Frankfurt/Main: Suhrkampf, 1991), p. 216. 1st edition 1918, passage written 1916. The passage is on p. 171 in the English edition, Ernst Bloch, *The Spirit of Utopia* (Stanford, CA: Stanford University Press, 2000).
100. 'The new life begins'. Ibid., p. 248.
101. Ernst Bloch, *The Principle of Hope* (1953) (Cambridge, MA: MIT Press, 1995), volume 3, pp. 175–6.
102. Norman Cohn, *The Pursuit of the Millennium. Revolutionary Millenarians and Mystical Anarchists of the Middle Ages* (1957) (London: Granada, 1970), p. 286. Like most Western historians of millenarianism and political religion, Cohn applies a secular, but Christiano-centric historical perspective to his study. For refreshingly non-ethnocentric accounts of Judaic Messianism and Christian millenarianism as two manifestations of a universal pattern of shamanism, see Gershon Winkler, *Magic of the Ordinary. Recovering the Shamanic in Judaism* (Berkeley, CA: North Atlantic Books, 2003); Carl McColman, *Embracing Jesus and the Goddess. A Radical Call for Spiritual Sanity* (Gloucester, MA: Fair Winds Press, 2001).
103. Eliade, *The Sacred and the Profane*, pp. 206–7.
104. Becker, *Escape from Evil*, pp. 148–51.
105. Adolf Hitler, *Mein Kampf*, trans. Ralph Mannheim (London: Pimlico, 1992), volume 2, pp. 345–6.
106. Joanne Rowling, *Harry Potter and the Philosopher's Stone* (London: Bloomsbury, 1997), p. 212.

4   A PRIMORDIALIST DEFINITION OF MODERNISM

1. Friedrich Nietzsche, *Thus Spoke Zarathustra. A New Translation by Graham Parkes* (Oxford: Blackwell, 2005), p. 24.
2. David Weir, *Decadence and the Making of Modernism* (Amherst: University of Massachusetts, 1996), p. 203.
3. Norman Cohn, *The Pursuit of the Millennium* (1957) (London: Granada, 1970), p. 274.
4. Ibid., p. 282.
5. Ibid., p. 284.
6. Frank Kermode, *The Sense of an Ending. Studies in the Theory of Fiction* (1967) (New York: Oxford University Press, 2000), p. 12.
7. Ibid., p. 99.
8. Ibid., p. 12.
9. Ibid,. p. 28.
10. Jürgen Habermas, *Theorie und Praxis. Sozialphilosophische Studien* (Neuwied/Berlin: Luchterhand, 1963), p. 294.
11. Bloch also emphasizes the importance of the Joachite tradition to the Nazi vision of history. See Ernst Bloch, *The Heritage of our Times* (1962) (Cambridge: Polity, 1991), pp. 122–8.

12. Arnold van Gennep, *The Rites of Passage* (1909) (London: Routledge & Kegan Paul, 1960).
13. Cited in Victor Turner, *The Forest of Symbols. Aspects of Ndembu Ritual* (Ithaca, NY: Cornell University Press, 1967), p. 94.
14. Mathieu Deflem, 'Ritual, Anti-structure, and Religion: A discussion of Victor Turner's processual symbolic analysis', *Journal for the Scientific Study of Religion* 30.1 (1991), p. 9.
15. See above Chapter 3, p. 84.
16. Maurice Bloch, *Prey into Hunter* (Cambridge: Cambridge University Press, 1992), p. 3.
17. Ibid., pp. 4–6.
18. Ibid., pp. 46–7.
19. Richard Fenn, *The End of Time. Religion, Ritual, and the Forging of the Soul* (Cleveland, OH: Pilgrim Press, 1997). See in particular chapter 4, 'Rituals of Purification: Renewing Time'. In the introduction and chapter 6, 'Ritual and the Elementary Forms of Fascism', Fenn relates the proliferation of ritual politics under fascism to the experience that society was 'running out of time', a sensation deeply related to what Peter Berger saw as 'the terror of anomy'.
20. Deflem, 'Ritual, Anti-structure, and Religion', p. 9.
21. Victor Turner, *Dramas, Fields and Metaphors. Symbolic Action in Human Society* (Ithaca, NY: Cornell University Press, 1979), pp. 237–8.
22. Victor Turner, 'Variations on a Theme of Liminality', in Sally Moore and Barbara Myerhoff (eds.), *Secular Ritual. Forms and Meaning* (Assen, Netherlands: Van Gorcum, 1977), p. 48.
23. See Anthony Wallace, 'Revitalization Movements' (first published 1956), in Robert Grumet (ed.), *Anthony Wallace. Revitalization & Mazeways. Essays on Cultural Change, Volume 1* (Lincoln: University of Nebraska Press, 2003), pp. 9–29. Victor Turner makes the link between liminal situations and the revitalization movements in Victor and Edith Turner, 'Religious Celebrations', in Victor Turner (ed.), *Celebration. Studies in Festivity and Ritual* (Washington, DC: Smithsonian Institution Press, 1982), pp. 33–57.
24. Anthony Wallace, 'Mazeway Disintegration', in Grumet, *Anthony Wallace*, p. 181.
25. This is the summary of Turner's thesis offered by Kenneth Tollefson in his article 'Titus: Epistle of religious revitalization', *Biblical Theology Bulletin* 30.4 (Winter 2000), p. 146. The article provides an excellent overview of the relevance of revitalization movements and their six-stage syndrome to religious phenomena encountered in the Bible.
26. Turner, *Dramas, Fields and Metaphors*, p. 212.
27. Anthony Wallace, 'Mazeway Resynthesis: A biocultural theory of religious inspiration', (first published 1956), Grumet, *Anthony Wallace*, p. 170.
28. Tollefson, 'Titus', p. 146.
29. John Price, 'Anthropology and Psychiatry', *The British Journal of Psychiatry* 186 (2005), pp. 168–9.
30. In the light of this analysis, an expert on modern millenarianism is surely putting the cart before the horse when he states 'apocalypticism creates structural liminality'. See David Bromley, 'Constructing Apocalypticism. Social and Cultural Elements of Radical Organization', in T. Robbins and Susan Palmer (eds.), *Millennium, Messiahs, and Mayhem: Contemporary Apocalyptic Movements* (New York: Routledge, 1997), p. 33.
31. There are obvious links between the concept of the revitalization movement and both Max Weber's concept of 'charismatic political movements' and Jacob Talmon's concept of 'political messianism'. See Douglas Madsen and Peter Snow, *The Charismatic Bond. Political Behavior in Time of Crisis* (Cambridge, MA: Harvard University Press, 1996); Jacob Talmon, *Political Messianism. The Romantic Phase* (London: Secker and Warburg, 1960). It is significant that both books stress the link between crisis (i.e. liminoid conditions) and the rise of the archetypal *propheta* leading the new *communitas*, a syndrome whose

literally epoch-making exemplification in the West is to be found in the figure of Jesus Christ as the Messiah of a new historical and metaphysical dispensation.

32. Victor and Edith Turner, 'Religious Celebrations', in Victor Turner (ed.), *Celebration. Studies in Festivity and Ritual* (Washington, DC: Smithsonian Institution Press, 1982), pp. 211–12.

33. Ibid.

34. Ibid., p. 214.

35. Kermode, *The Sense of an Ending*, p. 28. Cf. p. 101.

36. Zygmunt Bauman, *Modernity and Ambivalence* (Cambridge: Polity, 1991).

37. Richard Fenn, *Time Exposure. The Personal Experience of Time in Secular Societies* (Oxford: Oxford University Press, 2000), p. 107. Fenn's *The End of Time: Religion, Ritual, and the Forging of the Soul* illuminates an important aspect of fascism's relationship to modernism by exploring the crucial role of ritual in generating the experience of purification, sacrifice, resacralization, and time renewal, and relating the proliferation of ritual politics under fascism to the experience that society is 'running out of time'. See in particular the introduction, chapter 4 'Rituals of Purification: Renewing Time', and chapter 6 'Ritual and the Elementary Forms of Fascism'.

38. See above Chapter 2, p. 50.

39. Jiří Karásek ze Lvovic, *Renaissanční touhy v umění. Kritické studie* (1902) (Prague: Aventinum, 1926), p. 165. Cited in Robert Pynsent (ed.), *Decadence and Innovation. Austria-Hungary in the fin-de-siècle.* (London: Weidenfeld & Nicolson), p. 151.

40. Preface to *Miss Julie*, cited in Malcolm Bradbury and James McFarlane (eds.), *Modernism 1890–1930* (Harmondsworth: Penguin, 1976), p. 47.

41. Friedrich Nietzsche, *Unmodern Observations [Unzeitgemäße Betrachtungen]* (New Haven, CT: Yale University Press, 1990), p. 138.

42. See Roger Griffin, *The Nature of Fascism* (London: Pinter, 1991), p. 33.

43. David Weir, *Decadence and the Making of Modernism* (Amherst: University of Massachusetts, 1996), p. 203.

44. Ernst Bloch, *The Spirit of Utopia* (1923) (Stanford, CA: Stanford University Press, 2000), p. 171. The passage originated in 1916.

45. Joseph Goebbels, *Michael: Ein deutsches Schicksal* (Munich: Franz Eher Press, 1931), p. 124.

46. In *Reflexive Historical Sociology* (London: Routledge, 2000), pp. 218–19, the 'reflexive sociologist' Arpad Szakolczai argues that liminality as understood by Victor Turner, 'is potentially one of the most general and useful terms in the social sciences'. However his subsequent exposition of its importance, despite obvious parallels with the one presented here, is arguably flawed in its failure to recognize the crucial distinction between *liminal* situations in which an existing society is regenerated and *liminoid* ones which generate initiatives to create a new order. In our analysis it is precisely the protracted 'liminoidality' of European society between 1880 and 1945 induced by high modernity that has such significant consequences for the rise of new forms of totalitarian politics and the destructiveness of human life they eventually precipitated. Szakolczai himself implies this when he claims that 'the central task' of modern society is 'an actual search for order, with all the existential anxiety this entails', and observes that the absence of 'the masters of ceremonies' of traditional societies and 'the frightening presence of the dissolution of all stable frameworks' means that 'no effective control is put against the dark forces that are liberated in the "situation"'.

47. This use of the term 'shaman' would be contested by many anthropologists, for whom it has specialized connotations inappropriate in this context.

48. Anthony Stevens, *Ariadne's Clue. A Guide to the Symbols of Humankind* (London: The Allen Press, 1998), p. 86.

49. Bradbury and McFarlane, *Modernism 1890–1930*, pp. 51, 36.

50. Walter Benjamin, 'Theses on the Philosophy of History', in *Illuminations* (London: Fontana, 1992), pp. 245–55.
51. Ronald Schleifer, *Modernism and Time. The Logic of Abundance in Literature, Science, and Culture* (Cambridge: Cambridge University Press, 2000), pp. 10–11.
52. Modris Eksteins, *Rites of Spring* (1989) (Boston: Houghton Mifflin, 2000), p. 257.
53. Peter Osborne, *The Politics of Time. Modernity and the Avant-Garde* (London: Verso, 1995), p. 142.
54. Eksteins, *Rites of Spring*, p. xvi.
55. 'A pervasive, indispensable structure of human understanding by means of which we figuratively comprehend our world.' See Richard Etlin, 'Introduction. The *Perverse* Logic of Nazi Thought', in Richard Etlin (ed.), *Art, Culture, and Media under the Third Reich* (Chicago: The University of Chicago Press, 2002), p. 8. The philosopher Mary Midgley introduces a similar concept of the powerful role of these 'base-metaphors' in shaping entire cultures in her *The Myths We Live By* (London: Routledge, 2003), p. 2.
56. Guillaume Apollinaire, *The Cubist Painters* (1913) (New York: George Wittenborn, 1962), pp. 14–15.
57. Though the principal focus for the liminoidality that bred modernism was late nineteenth-century Europe, important 'hot spots' of modernist energy emerged later in some parts of the US and Latin America (e.g. Mexico, Brazil, and Argentina) in the twentieth century, where the urban intelligentsia were extensively Europeanized. See for example: Townsend Ludington, Thomas Fahy, and Sarah Reuning (eds.), *A Modern Mosaic. Art and Modernism in the United States* (Chapel Hill: University of North Carolina Press, 2000); Daryle Williams, *Culture Wars in Brazil. The First Vargas Regime, 1930–1945* (Durham, NC: Duke University Press, 2001); Mauro F. Guillén, 'Modernism Without Modernity. The Rise of Modernist Architecture in Mexico, Brazil, and Argentina, 1890–1940', *Latin American Research Review* 39.2 (Summer 2004), pp. 6–64.
58. Carl Schorske, *Fin-de-Siècle Vienna. Politics and Culture* (New York: Vintage Books, 1981); Pynsent (ed.), *Decadence and Innovation.* (London: Weidenfeld, 1989).
59. Hermann Broch, *The Sleepwalkers* (New York: Grosset and Dunlap, 1964), p. 373.
60. Ibid., p. 374.
61. Ibid., p. 446.
62. Ibid., p. 447.
63. Ibid., pp. 480–1.
64. Ibid., p. 486.
65. Ibid., p. 642.
66. Ibid., p. 559.
67. Ibid., p. 642.
68. Ibid., p. 448. My emphasis.
69. Ibid., pp. 640–2.
70. Ibid., p. 646.
71. Ibid., p. 647.
72. Ibid., p. 375.
73. A concept used in helicopter terminology.
74. Broch, *The Sleepwalkers*, pp. 644–5.
75. Ibid., p. 647.
76. Ibid., p. 648.
77. It is significant that though the definition of modernism offered by Stephen Spender in his highly influential *The Struggle of the Modern* (London: Methuen, 1963), pp. 71–97, does not extend the concept beyond the parameters of art, he nonetheless identifies as one of its definitional components (pp. 84–6) 'the invention through art of a *pattern of hope*' based on the artists' belief that the new vision of reality expressed in their work might 'transform the contemporary environment' and 'revolutionize the world', a theme he illustrates with quotations from *Der Blaue Reiter* and Wyndham Lewis.

78. An image introduced in T. S. Eliot's poem *Burnt Norton* (1935).

79. Roger Shattuck, *The Banquet Years. The Origins of the Avant-garde in France 1885 to World War I* (London: Faber and Faber, 1958), p. 271.

80. See Maurice Tuchman, 'Hidden Meanings in Abstract Art', in Edward Weisberger (ed.), *The Spiritual in Art. Abstract Painting 1890–1985* (New York: Abbeville Press, 1986), pp. 17–61.

81. Rose-Carol Long, 'Occultism, Anarchism, and Abstraction: Kandinsky's Art of the Future', *Art Journal* 46.1 (Spring 1987), p. 41, part of a special issue on 'Mysticism and Occultism in Modern Art'.

82. Edward Tiryakian, 'Towards the Sociology of Esoteric Culture', in Edward Tiryakian (ed.), *On the Margins of the Visible. Toward the Sociology of Esoteric Culture* (New York: Wiley, 1974), pp. 274–5, cited in Linda Henderson, 'Editor's Statement: Mysticism and Occultism in Modern Art', *Art Journal* 46.1 (Spring 1987), p. 7. My emphasis.

83. Wassily Kandinsky, *Concerning the Spiritual in Art* (1914) (New York: Dover Publications, 1977), p. 20. My emphasis.

84. An allusion to a line in the first of Rainer Maria Rilke's *Duino Elegies* (1912–22).

85. Timothy Benson, 'Mysticism, Materialism, and the Machine in Berlin Dada', *Art Journal* 41.6 (Spring 1987), pp. 47, 53.

86. This influence has been brilliantly explored by Mark Antliff's *Inventing Bergson. Cultural Politics and the Parisian Avant-Garde* (Princeton, NJ: Princeton University Press, 1993). For the profound interconnections between Bergsonianism, illiberal politics, and the quest for an alternative temporality and modernity, see in particular the last chapter 'The Politics of Time and Modernity', pp. 169–84.

87. Patrick Waldberg, *Surrealism* (London: Thames and Hudson, 1965), p. 41.

88. Ibid., p. 50.

89. Richard Sonn, *Anarchism and Cultural Politics in Fin de Siècle France* (Lincoln: University of Nebraska Press, 1989), p. 263.

90. Ibid., pp. 265–7.

91. Ibid., pp. 269–70.

92. For a penetrating study of Picasso's peculiarly aesthetic brand of anarchism see Patricia Leighten, *Re-ordering the Universe: Picasso and Anarchism, 1897–1914* (Princeton, NJ: Princeton University Press, 1989).

93. Robert Short, 'Dada and Surrealism', in Bradbury and McFarlane, *Modernism 1890–1930*, p. 295.

94. Sonn, *Anarchism and Cultural Politics*, p. 284.

95. Cited, ibid., p. 285.

96. Douglas Kellner, 'Expressionist Literature and the Dream of the "New Man"', in Stephen Bronner and Douglas Kellner (eds.), *Passion and Rebellion. The Expressionist Heritage* (London: Croom Helm, 1983), p. 167.

97. Apollinaire, *The Cubist Painters*, p. 23. The association of 'conflagration' with the birth of the New Man is yet another manifestation of the archaic syndrome of 'creative destruction' and cognate to the deep structure linking iconoclasm to ritual purification. For the way this archetype expresses itself in episodes of 'libricide' and 'biblioclasm' in both Europeanized and non-Europeanized cultures see Rebecca Knuth, *Burning Books and Leveling Libraries* (New York: Praeger, 2006).

98. Françoise Gilot and Carlton Lake, *Life with Picasso* (London: Nelson, 1965), pp. 248–9. It is significant that Wassily Kandinsky experienced a similar epiphany on encountering the vitality of folk art when, while still a law student, he took part in an ethnographic project on tribal law among the pagan Zyrian tribe in Siberia.

99. Ananda Coomaraswamy, 'Rajput Painting and its Artistic Sisterhood to "Modernist Art"', *Vanity Fair* 7 (July 1916), p. 69; cited in Allan Antliff, *Anarchist Modernism. Art, Politics,*

and the First American Avant-Garde (Chicago: The University of Chicago Press, 2001), p. 137.

100. Ibid., p. 128.

5   SOCIAL MODERNISM IN PEACE AND WAR 1880–1918

1. Friedrich Nietzsche, *Thus Spoke Zarathustra. A New Translation by Graham Parkes* (Oxford: Blackwell, 2005), p. 10.
2. Ernst Jünger, *Der Kampf als inneres Erlebnis* (1922) (Berlin: E. S. Mittler & Sohn, 1929), p. 1.
3. It is generally held that the existence of a *philosophia perennis* underlying different world religious and mystic traditions was first postulated by the neo-Platonist thinker Marsilio Ficino (1433–1499).
4. For a general history of the Theosophy movement see Bruce Campbell, *Ancient Wisdom Revived. A History of the Theosophical Movement* (Berkeley: University of California Press, 1980).
5. Friedrich Nietzsche, *The Birth of Tragedy* (Oxford: Oxford University Press, 2000), section 23, pp. 122–3.
6. See Arthur Moeller van den Bruck, *Das Dritte Reich* (1923) (Hamburg: Hanseatische Verlagsanstalt, 1931), p. 163, where he talks of a 'Wiederanknüpfung nach vorwärts'.
7. See Christopher McIntosh, *Éliphas Lévi and the French Occult Revival* (London: Rider, 1972); Ruth Brandon, *The Spiritualists. The Passion for the Occult in the Nineteenth and Twentieth Centuries* (New York: Alfred Knopf, 1983).
8. Eric Hobsbawm's phrase for the liberal and industrial revolutions of the eighteenth to nineteenth centuries.
9. This dynamic has been studied perceptively by David Weir in *Decadence and the Making of Modernism* (Amherst: University of Massachusetts, 1996). See particularly p. 203.
10. Some latter-day right-wing occultist conspiracy theorists believe 'vril' may have supplied the power for Nazi-piloted flying saucers allegedly deployed in the closing stages of the war. See Nicholas Goodrick-Clarke, *Black Sun* (New York: New York University Press, 2002), pp. 164–7.
11. Frances Saunders, *Hidden Hands* (London: Channel 4, 1995), p. 6. My emphasis.
12. See the special issue of *Architronic*, 8.1 (Jan 1999) on architecture and theosophy edited by Susan Henderson, especially her article 'J. M. L. Lauweriks and K. P. C. de Bazel: Architecture and Theosophy', pp. 1–12.
13. For more on the role of esotericism in the deeply modernist curriculum of the early Bauhaus see Ludger Busch, 'Das Bauhaus und Mazdaznan', in Rolf Bothe, Peter Hahn, and Hans Christoph von Tavel (eds.), *Das frühe Bauhaus und Johannes Itten* (Weimar: Kunstsammlungen, 1995), pp. 83–90.
14. See Allan Antliff, *Anarchist Modernism. Art, Politics, and the First American Avant-Garde* (Chicago: The University of Chicago Press, 2001).
15. Richard Noll, *The Jung Cult* (New York: Simon and Schuster), p. 30.
16. R. Hinton Thomas, *Nietzsche in German Politics and Society 1890–1918* (Manchester: Manchester University Press, 1983), chapter 9, pp. 112–24.
17. See especially Mark Antliff, *Inventing Bergson. Cultural Politics and the Parisian Avant-Garde* (Princeton, NJ: Princeton University Press, 1993).
18. Colin Campbell, 'The Cult, the Cultic Milieu, and Secularization', in Michael Hill (ed.), *A Sociological Yearbook of Religion in Britain 5* (London: SMC Press, 1972), pp. 119–36. For a case-study of one such cultic milieu where leftist social modernism flourished in pre-war New York see the chapter 'Nietzschean Matrix' in Allan Antliff, *Anarchist Modernism. Art, Politics, and the First American Avant-Garde* (Chicago: The University of Chicago Press, 2001), pp. 146–66.

19. Karla Poewe, *New Religions and the Nazis* (London: Routledge, 2006), p. 3.
20. Leon Poliakov, *The Aryan Myth* (London: Sussex University Press, 1974), p. 313. Cited in Noll, *The Jung Cult*, p. 71.
21. The apolitical but tendentially left-wing nature of the avant-garde was affirmed, for example, in Renato Poggioli's influential book *The Theory of the Avant-Garde* (New York: Harper & Row, 1968).
22. Paradigmatic of this tendency is Jeffrey Herf, *Reactionary Modernism. Technology, Culture, and Politics in Weimar and the Third Reich* (London: Cambridge University Press, 1986).
23. Mark Sedgwick, *Against the Modern World. Traditionalism and the Secret Intellectual History of the Twentieth Century* (Oxford: Oxford University Press, 2004), pp. 109–17.
24. The authoritative study of this particularly murky and easily sensationalized area of cultural and political history is Nicholas Goodrick-Clarke, *The Occult Roots of Nazism* (Wellingborough, Northamptonshire, UK: Aquarian Press, 1985).
25. Arthur Rosenberg, *Der Mythus des 20. Jahrhunderts* (Munich: Hoheneichen, 1924), pp. 21–35.
26. Paul Lagarde, 'Die graue Internationale', *Deutsche Schriften* (1878) (Jena: Eugen Diederichs, 1944), p. 337.
27. Julius Langbehn, *Rembrandt als Erzieher* (Leipzig: C. L. Hirschfeld, 1890), p. 329.
28. See George Mosse, *The Crisis of German Ideology. Intellectual Origins of the Third Reich* (New York: Howard Fertig, 1998), chapter 2, 'A Germanic Faith', pp. 31–51.
29. Ibid., p. 51.
30. Saunders, *Hidden Hands*, p. 11.
31. Poewe, *New Religions and the Nazis* brings out this nexus between esotericism and the concern with biopolitical health in Weimar Germany particularly well.
32. Robert Gooding-Williams, *Zarathustra's Dionysian Modernism* (Stanford, CA: Stanford University Press, 2001), pp. 127, 129.
33. See Mosse, *The Crisis of German Ideology*, chapter 6, 'Germanic Utopias', pp. 108–25.
34. Christina Lodder, 'Searching for Utopia', in Christopher Wilk (ed.), *Modernism 1914–1939. Designing a New World* (London: V&A Publications, 2006), pp. 23–70. H. G. Wells' *A Modern Utopia* was published in 1905.
35. Christopher Wilk, 'The Healthy Body Culture', in Wilk, *Modernism 1914–1939*, p. 250.
36. Hitler's reputation for being a vegetarian is apparently a folk myth: see Ryan Berry, *Hitler Neither Vegetarian nor Animal Lover* (New York: Pythagorean Publishers, 2004).
37. For a contemporary account of the centrality of vegetarianism to yoga see http://www.jivamuktiyoga.com/inspr/veg2.html (accessed 06/10/06).
38. Wolfdietrich Rasch, 'Aspekte der deutschen Literatur', in Wolfdietrich Rasch, *Zur deutschen Literatur der Jahrhundertswende* (Stuttgart: J. B. Metzlersche, 1967), pp. 1–48.
39. On this aspect of the 'Healthy Body Culture' and its links with Expressionist drama and dance see Modris Eksteins, *Rites of Spring* (1989) (Boston: Houghton Mifflin, 2000), pp. 80–9.
40. Stuart Hughes, *Consciousness and Society. The Reorientation of European Social Thought 1890–1930* (Brighton: Harvester Press, 1979), pp. 338–9. The point made here is amply corroborated by Robert Wohl's *The Generation of 1914* (London: Weidenfeld and Nicolson, 1980).
41. The article appeared in Lanz von Liebenfels (ed.), *Nackt- und Rassenkultur im Kampf gegen Mucker- und Tschandkultur*, No. 66 in the *Ostara* Pamphlet series (Rodaun, 1913).
42. Karl Toepfer, *Empire of Ecstasy. Nudity and Movement in German Body Culture, 1910–1935* (Berkeley: University of California Press, 1997), p. 37.
43. Ibid., p. 382. Another book that deals with the nexus between nudism, body cult, nationalism, and racial hygiene in the German context is Chad Ross, *Naked Germany* (Oxford: Berg, 2005).
44. Manfred Kuxdorf, 'The New German Dance Movement', in Stephen Bronner and Douglas Kellner (eds), *Passion and Rebellion. The Expressionist Heritage* (London: Croom Helm, 1983), pp. 350–62.

45. See Brigitte Peuker, 'The Fascist Choreography: Riefenstahl's Tableaux', *Modernism/ modernity* 11.2 (2004), pp. 279–97.
46. See above, Chapter 4, p. 119.
47. Cf. Hannah Arendt, *The Origins of Totalitarianism* (London: George Allen and Unwin, 1967), p. 346, who cites Eric Voeglin's 1948 essay 'The Origins of Scientism': 'science has become an idol that will magically cure the evils of existence and transform the nature of man'. For an exploration of the rise of the catastrophic human consequences of scientism for twentieth-century politics see Tzvetan Todorov, *Hope and Memory. Lessons from the Twentieth Century* (Princeton, NJ: Princeton University Press, 2004).
48. Noll, *The Jung Cult*, p. 46. The degree to which Freudianism assumed elements of a revitalization movement is charted in John Kerr, *A Most Dangerous Method. The Story of Jung, Freud and Sabina Spielrein* (New York: Alfred Knopf, 1993).
49. Sigmund Freud, *Das Unbehagen in der Kultur* (1930) [The Malaise in [our/modern] Culture] translated as *Civilization and its Discontents* (1930).
50. Noll, *The Jung Cult*, p. 188.
51. Ibid., chapters 10–13.
52. Ernst Haeckel, *The Riddle of the Universe* (New York: Harper & Bros., 1900), p. 337.
53. Georges Vacher de Lapouge, *L'Aryen* (Paris: Albert Fontemoing, 1899).
54. Daniel Gasman, *Haeckel's Monism and the Birth of Fascist Ideology* (New York: Peter Lang, 1998), p. 144.
55. Noll, *The Jung Cult*, p. 49.
56. Francis Galton, 'Eugenics, its Definition, Scope, and Aims', *The American Journal of Sociology* 10.1 (July 1904), pp. 1–25.
57. E.g. Laura Doyle, *Bordering on the Body. The Racial Matrix of Modern Fiction and Culture* (New York: Oxford University Press, 1994); Donald Childs, *Modernism and Eugenics. Woolf, Eliot, Yeats, and the Culture of Degeneration* (Cambridge, New York: Cambridge University Press, 2001).
58. David Bradshaw (ed.), *A Concise Companion to Modernism* (Oxford: Blackwell, 2003) is particularly interesting in this context. Each of its 12 chapters spotlights 'ideas emanating from a particular field which helped to shape Modernism, including eugenics, primitivism, Freudianism, and Nietzscheanism'. Within my 'synoptic interpretation' all these 'ideas' are themselves manifestations of social modernism, which explains the elective affinity between cultural modernists and the different 'fields' of modern society considered.
59. G. W. Harris, 'Bio-Politics', *The New Age* 10.9 (28 December 1911), p. 197.
60. Laputa was described in a newspaper article published in *Macmillan's Magazine*, No. 12, 1865.
61. G. Clayes, 'Introducing Francis Galton, "Kantsaywhere" and "The Donoghues of Dunno Weir"', *Utopian Studies* 12.2 (2001), pp. 188–90.
62. For an overview see Daniel Pick, *Faces of Degeneration. A European Disorder c. 1848–1918* (Cambridge: Cambridge University Press, 1989).
63. See Alan Sykes, *The Radical Right in Britain* (London: Palgrave Macmillan, 2005), chapter 1, 'Social Imperialism and Race Regeneration'. See too Dan Stone, *Breeding Superman. Nietzsche, Race and Eugenics in Edwardian and Interwar Britain* (Liverpool: Liverpool University Press, 2002).
64. See Marius Turda, *The Idea of National Superiority in Central Europe, 1880–1918* (New York: Edwin Mellen Press, 2005); Marius Turda and Paul Weindling (eds.), *'Blood and Homeland'. Eugenics and Racial Nationalism in Central and Southeast Europe, 1900–1940* (Budapest: Central European University Press, 2006).
65. Elizabeth Darling, *Re-forming Britain. Narratives of Modernity before Reconstruction* (London: Routledge, 2006), p. 53. My emphasis.
66. Ibid., p. 55.
67. On the eugenicist climate that informed progressive social policy in early twentieth-century Britain see Geoffrey Searle, *The Quest for National Efficiency* (Oxford: Basil Blackwell,

1971); Greta Jones, *Social Hygiene in Twentieth Century Britain* (London: Croom Helm, 1986).

68. See Arthur Herman, *The Idea of Decline in Western History* (New York: The Free Press, 1997), pp. 109–44.

69. Todd Samuel Presner, '"Clear Heads, Solid Stomachs, and Hard Muscles": Max Nordau and the Aesthetics of Jewish Regeneration', *Modernism/modernity* 10.2 (2003), pp. 285–6.

70. Wilk, 'The Healthy Body Culture', p. 251.

71. Eksteins, *Rites of Spring*, p. 30.

72. See Paul Weindling, *Health, Race, and German Politics* (Cambridge: Cambridge University Press, 1993), p. 144. Also Paul Weindling, 'The Medical Publisher J. F. Lehmann and Racial Hygiene', in Sigrid Stöckel (ed.), *Die 'rechte Nation' und ihr Verleger. Politik und Popularisierung im J. F. Lehmanns Verlag 1890–1979* (Berlin: Lehmanns Media, 2002), pp. 159–70.

73. Eksteins, *Rites of Spring*, p. 30.

74. *Die Jüdische Turnzeitung* 6 (1908), p. 112, cited in Presner, '"Clear Heads, Solid Stomachs, and Hard Muscles"', p. 286.

75. Paul Scheerbart, *Glasarchitektur* (Berlin: Geb. Mann, 1914), translated in Ulrich Conrads, *Programs and Manifestos on 20th Century Architecture* (Cambridge, MA: MIT Press, 1975), p. 32.

76. Jack Roth, *The Cult of Violence. Sorel and the Sorelians* (Berkeley: University of California Press, 1980).

77. Giovanni Amendola, 'La Guerra', *La Voce*, cited in Emilio Gentile, 'The Myth of National Regeneration in Italy. From Modernist Avant-garde to Fascism', in Matthew Affron and Mark Antliff, *Fascist Visions* (Princeton, NJ: Princeton University Press, 1997), p. 29.

78. Gentile, 'The Myth of National Regeneration', p. 36. On premodern cosmological myths of universal conflagration and renewal see Mircea Eliade, *The Myth of the Eternal Return, or Cosmos and History* (1954) (Princeton, NJ: Princeton University Press, 1971), pp. 87–8, 134–6.

79. Pádraic H. Pearse, 'The Coming Revolution', in Pádraic Pearse, *Political Writings and Speeches* (Dublin: Phoenix Publishing, 1924), p. 99.

80. See above, Chapter 1, p. 15.

81. Eksteins, *Rites of Spring*, p. 10. The whole of Part One, pp. 1–54, is a brilliant exposition of the symbolic significance of Stravinsky's *The Rite of Spring* for an understanding of modernism's relationship to the cultural crisis manifested in the First World War.

82. Roland Stromberg, *Redemption by War. The Intellectuals and 1914* (Kansas: The Regents Press of Kansas, 1982), p. 5. Other important works documenting the currency of palingenetic mythopoeia projected onto war are Daniel Pick, *War Machine. The Rationalization of Slaughter in the Modern Age* (New Haven, CT: Yale University Press, 1993); John Horne (ed.), *State, Society, and Mobilization in Europe during the First World War* (Cambridge: Cambridge University Press, 1997).

83. Michael Burleigh, *Earthly Powers. Religion and Politics in Europe from the French Revolution to the Great War* (London: HarperCollins, 2005), p. 440.

84. Angelo Ventrone, *Le seduzione totalitarian. Guerra, modernità, violenza politica (1914–1918)* (Rome: Donzelli, 2003), p. 6. See too Angelo Ventrone, *Piccola storia della Grande Guerra* (Rome: Donzelli, 2005), chapter 1. 'L'avvento della società di massa', pp. 3–30.

85. James Joll, *The Origins of the First World War* (London: Longman, 1992), pp. 199–233, 'The mood of 1914'.

86. Stromberg, *Redemption by War*, p. 40. The image of a 'thunderstorm' breaking is also used by Eric Hobsbawm, *The Age of Empire, 1875–1914* (London: Abacus, 1994), p. 326.

87. Eksteins, *Rites of Spring*, pp. 63–4.

88. Stromberg, *Redemption by War*, p. 198.

89. See below, Chapter 6, pp. 175–7.

90. Cited in Stromberg, *Redemption by War*, p. 43.
91. This account of the Great War as a 'modernist event' has some affinity with Hayden White's thesis that it was experienced as a 'modernist event', but also significant differences which time does not allow us to go into. See Hayden White, 'The Modernist Event', in Vivian Sobchack (ed.) *The Persistence of History: Cinema, Television, and the Modernist Event* (New York: Routledge, 1996), pp. 21–2. See also Claudio Fogu, *The Historic Imaginary. Politics of History in Fascist Italy* (Buffalo, NY: University of Toronto Press, 2003), pp. 34–5.
92. Robert Wohl, Introduction to Tim Cross (ed.), *The Lost Voices of World War I* (London: Bloomsbury Publishing, 1988), p. 1.
93. Ibid., p. 5.
94. Eric Leed, *No Man's Land. Combat and Identity in World War 1* (Cambridge: Cambridge University Press, 1979), p. 15.
95. Ibid., pp. 12–17.
96. Allen Frantzen, *Bloody Good. Chivalry, Sacrifice, and the Great War* (Chicago: University of Chicago Press, 2004), p. 261.
97. May Sinclair, *The Tree of Heaven* (London: Cassell and Company, 1917), pp. 330–1.
98. Burleigh, *Earthly Powers*, p. 453.
99. Babak Rahimi, 'Sacrifice, Transcendence and the Solider', *Peace Review* 17.1 (January–March 2005) (special issue on 'The Psychological Interpretation of War'), p. 18 . The quote is from Leo Braudy, *From Chivalry to Terrorism. War and the Changing Nature of Masculinity* (New York: Alfred A. Knopf, 2003). No page reference given.
100. See Patrick Porter, 'War and the Religious Will to Sacrifice', *Peace Review* 17.1 (January–March 2005), pp. 17–24; Norman Steinbart, 'Group Psychology, Sacrifice and War', *Peace Review* 17.1 (January–March 2005), pp. 9–16. On the interpenetration of Catholic discourse with the construction of death in battle as sacrifice to the nation see too Annette Becker, *War and Faith. The Religious Imagination in France, 1914–1930* (Oxford: Berg, 1998).
101. Richard Koenigsberg, 'Aztec Warfare, Western Warfare, The Soldier as Sacrificial Victim', http://home.earthlink.net/~libraryofsocialscience/aztec.htm (accessed 26/10/05). For his many papers on this topic in public domain see http://home.earthlink.net/~libraryofsocialscience/index.html (accessed 06/10/06).
102. Rahimi, 'Sacrifice, Transcendence and the Solider', p. 5.
103. Richard Koenigsberg, 'As the soldier dies so does the nation come alive', http://home.earthlink.net/~libraryofsocialscience/as_the_soldier.htm (accessed 26/10/05).
104. 'Metanoia' is an epiphanic moment of sudden spiritual conversion and illumination.
105. Gentile, 'The Myth of National Regeneration', p. 38.
106. Ibid.
107. Niall Ferguson, *The Pity of War* (London: Allen Lane, 1998), p. 358.
108. Deborah Buffton, 'Memorialization and the Selling of War', *Peace Review* 17.1 (January–March 2005), p. 27.
109. Paul Fussell, *The Great War and Modern Memory* (Oxford: Oxford University Press, 1977), p. 115.
110. George Mosse, *Fallen Soldiers. Reshaping the Memory of the World Wars* (New York: Oxford University Press, 1990), p. 111.

6 THE RISE OF POLITICAL MODERNISM 1848–1945

1. Peter Fritzsche, 'Nazi Modern', *Modernism/Modernity* 3.1 (1996), p. 12.
2. Mark Antliff, 'Fascism, Modernism, and Modernity', *The Art Bulletin* 84.1 (March 2002), p. 164.

3. Stanley Payne, *A History of Fascism 1914–45* (London: University College London Press, 1995), pp. 78–9.
4. David Harvey, *The Condition of Postmodernity* (Oxford: Basil Blackwell, 1989), p. 278.
5. Ibid., p. 279.
6. Fritzsche, 'Nazi Modern', p. 13.
7. Modris Eksteins, *Rites of Spring* (1989) (Boston: Houghton Mifflin, 2000), p. 257.
8. See above Chapter 4, p. 120.
9. See Richard Fenn, *The End of Time. Religion, Ritual, and the Forging of the Soul* (Cleveland, OH: Pilgrim Press, 1997).
10. See above, Chapter 4, p. 120.
11. Fritzsche, 'Nazi Modern', p. 13.
12. Eksteins, *Rites of Spring*, p. 257.
13. See John Barry, *The Great Influenza. The Story of the Deadliest Pandemic in History* (London: Penguin, 2005). Barry cites as evidence of the psychological impact of the pandemic (p. 393) the observation of one of the US's leading philosophers, John Dewey, who wrote in 1923: 'It may be doubted if the consciousness of sickness was ever so widespread as it is today. [...] The interest in cures and salvations is evidence of how sick the world is.'
14. For the primal theological resonance of this palingenetic concept see Catherine Keller, *The Face of the Deep. A Theology of Becoming* (London: Routledge, 2003).
15. Quoted in C. Harrison and P. Wood (eds.), *Art in Theory 1900–1990* (Oxford: Blackwell, 1992), pp. 244–5.
16. Virginia Woolf, *The Waves* (1931) (London: Penguin, 2000), p. 228. This passage comes a few lines before the final words of the novel.
17. Ernst Jünger, *Der Kampf als inneres Erlebnis* (Berlin: E. G. Mittler and Son, 1929), pp. xi–xv. The title means 'Battle as an inner experience'.
18. Eric Leed, *No Man's Land. Combat and Identity in World War 1* (Cambridge: Cambridge University Press, 1979), p. 213.
19. Ibid., p. 146.
20. Ibid., p. 141.
21. The archetypal association between the blacksmith and tool-making is preserved in the Italian for blacksmith: 'il fabbro', the term also used by T. S. Eliot to refer to Ezra Pound.
22. For examples of this phase of Beckmann's art see his painting 'Night' at http://www.bethel.edu/~letnie/BeckmannNight.jpg (accessed 01/12/06).
23. Richard Sheppard, 'German Expressionism', in Malcolm Bradbury and James McFarlane (eds.), *Modernism 1890–1930* (Harmondsworth: Penguin, 1976), p. 289.
24. See Allan Antliff, *Anarchist Modernism. Art, Politics, and the First American Avant-Garde* (Chicago: The University of Chicago Press, 2001), chapter 6, 'The New Internationalism', p. 126.
25. Ananda Coomaraswamy, *The Dance of Shiva. Fourteen Indian Essays*, with an Introduction by Romain Rolland (New York: The Sunwise Turn, 1924), pp. i, v–vi.
26. Ibid., pp. v–vi.
27. Ibid., p. i.
28. T. S. Eliot, 'Burnt Norton' (1935), subsequently published as the first of the Four Quartets in 1943.
29. Cited in Frances Saunders, *Hidden Hands* (London: Channel 4, 1995), p. 12.
30. Ibid., p. 11. Two books that evoke the powerful palingenetic ethos of art and technology in the inter-war period particularly effectively, are Robert Hughes, *The Shock of the New. Art and the Century of Change* (London: Thames & Hudson, 1981); Christopher Wilk (ed.), *Modernism 1914–1939. Designing a New World* (London: V&A Publications, 2006).

31. Arthur Penty, *Tradition and Modernism in Politics* (London: Sheed and Ward, 1937), p. 183.
32. Charles Harrison and Paul Wood (eds.), *Art in Theory. 1900–1990* (Oxford: Blackwell, 1992), p. 145.
33. For more on this 'decadent' phase of Blok's poetic career see Simon Morrison, *Russian Opera and the Symbolist Movement* (Berkeley and Los Angeles: The University of California Press, 2002).
34. Cited in Nina Berberova, *Aleksandr Blok. A Life* (Manchester: Carcanet Press, 1996), p. 127.
35. Isaak Steinberg, *In the Workshop of the Revolution* (New York: Rinehart, 1953), pp. 44–5. Cited in Richard Stites, *Revolutionary Dreams. Utopian Vision and Experimental Life in the Russian Revolution* (New York: Oxford University Press, 1989), p. 39.
36. The website http://rubymatt.backpackit.com/pub/657103 (accessed 08/10/06) reproduces numerous photos published in the periodical which bring out its constructivist ethos.
37. On the powerful synergy between cultural modernism and Bolshevism see Boris Groys, *The Total Art of Stalinism. Avant-Garde, Aesthetic Dictatorship, and Beyond* (Princeton, NJ: Princeton University Press, 1992).
38. Sergei Tretyakov, 'From where to where (Futurism's perspectives)', *Lef* 1 (1923), pp. 192–203, cited in Anne Lawton and Herbert Eagle (eds.), *Russian Futurism through its Manifestoes, 1912–1918* (Ithaca, NY: Cornell University Press, 1998), pp. 206–7.
39. Ibid., p. 211.
40. Ibid., p. 216.
41. Bernice Rosenthal, *New Myth, New World. From Nietzsche to Stalin* (Pennsylvania: Pennsylvania State University Press, 2002), p. 148.
42. Ibid., chapter 9, pp. 246–65.
43. Ibid., p. 323.
44. See above, Chapter 2, p. 57.
45. Peter Osborne, *The Politics of Time. Modernity and the Avant-Garde* (London: Verso, 1995), p. 142. The quest for an alternative modernity is central to the sustained analysis of the palingenetic logic of totalitarianism in David Roberts, *The Totalitarian Experiment in Twentieth-Century Europe* (London: Routledge, 2006).
46. Peter Osborne, *Philosophy in Cultural Theory* (London: Routledge, 2000), p. 58.
47. Ibid., p. 61. Of course the revolutionaries themselves cannot admit that the new order they wish to establish will be only 'temporary'.
48. Ibid., p. 73. Osborne shows how the manifesto is also an early example of *aesthetic* modernism in its montage of no less than six literary forms.
49. Ibid., p. 63.
50. Tom Stoppard, *Salvage*, Part 1 of *The Coast of Utopia Trilogy* (London: Faber and Faber, 2002), pp. 117–18.
51. Karl Marx, 'Speech at anniversary of the People's Paper', *The People's Paper*, 19 April 1856. Reprinted in David McLellan, *Karl Marx. Selected Writings* (Oxford: Oxford University Press, 2000), pp. 338–9.
52. Notably Norman Cohn, *The Pursuit of the Millennium* (London: Granada, 1970), pp. 285–6.
53. E.g. Jean-Pierre Sironneau, *Sécularisation et religions politiques* (La Haye: Mouton, 1982); Klaus-George Riegel, 'Marxism-Leninism as a Political Religion', *Totalitarian Movements and Political Religions* 6.1 (2005), pp. 97–126.
54. Namely Eric Voegelin, *The Political Religions* (1938) (Lewiston, NY: E. Mellen Press, 1986).
55. See Rosenthal, *New Myth, New World*, pp. 127–36, 'Lenin: A Closet Nietzschean?'
56. See Georgii Gloveli, '"Socialism of science" and "socialism of feeling". Bogdanov and Lunacharsky', *Studies in East European Thought* 42.1 (July 1991), pp. 29–55.
57. Osborne, *Philosophy in Cultural Theory*, p. 57.

58. Claude Levi-Strauss, *Tristes tropiques* (New York: Washington Square Press, 1977).
59. George Mosse, *The Nationalization of the Masses* (New York: Howard Fertig, 1975), pp. 211–12.
60. James Billington, *Fire in the Minds of Men: Origins of the Revolutionary Faith* (New York: Basic Books, 1980). On the longing for transcendence at the core of ultranationalism see especially chapter 6, 'National vs. Social Revolution', pp. 146–90. The book also throws into relief the palingenetic mindset at work in Russian anarchism, revolutionary syndicalism, and Leninism (pp. 367–481). It highlights too the role played by creative destruction and longings for transcendence in revolutionary processes, both of which are symbolized in the flame, a recurrent topos of the revolutionary imagination (see p. 5).
61. Koenraad Swart, *The Sense of Decadence in Nineteenth-Century France* (The Hague: M. Nijhoff, 1964).
62. Zeev Sternhell, *Maurice Barrès et le nationalisme français* (Paris: Fayard, 2nd edition 2000), p. 82. Sternhell's biography provides an illuminating account of Barrès' paradigmatic journey from aesthetic to political modernism.
63. Maurice Barrès, *Scènes et doctrines du nationalisme* (Paris: F. Juven, 1902) 1, pp. 85–6. My emphasis. Cited in Sternhell, *Maurice Barrès*, pp. 315–16.
64. This emerges clearly from Mark Antliff, *Inventing Bergson. Cultural Politics and the Parisian Avant-Garde* (Princeton, NJ: Princeton University Press, 1993).
65. See Zeev Sternhell, *La droite révolutionnaire* (Paris: Fayard, 2000).
66. Paul Mazgaj, *The Action Française and Revolutionary Syndicalism* (Chapel Hill, NC: University of North Carolina Press, 1979).
67. Osborne, *The Politics of Time*, p. 142.
68. Ibid., p. 116.
69. Osborne specifically describes Heidegger as 'an example of philosophical modernism', ibid., p. 166.
70. Ibid., p. 164.
71. Ibid.
72. Ibid., pp. 163–5.
73. Ibid., p. 166. My emphasis.
74. See Werner Loh, Roger Griffin, and Andreas Umland (eds.), *Fascism Past and Present, East and West. An International Debate and Concepts and Cases in the Comparative Study of the Extreme Right* (Stuttgart: Ibidem, 2006).
75. Roger Eatwell, *Fascism* (London: Chatto & Windus, 1995), p. 11.
76. Stanley Payne, *A History of Fascism, 1914–1945* (London: University College London Press, 1995), p. 14.
77. James Gregor, *Phoenix. Fascism in our Time* (New Brunswick: Transaction, 1999), pp. 162, 166.
78. Martin Blinkhorn, *Fascism and the Right in Europe 1918–1945* (London: Longmans, 2000), pp. 115–16.
79. Stephen Shenfield, *Russian Fascism. Traditions, Tendencies, Movements* (Armonk, NY: M. E. Sharpe, 2001), p. 17.
80. Philip Morgan, *Fascism in Europe, 1919–1945* (London: Routledge, 2003), pp. 13–14.
81. Robert Paxton, *The Anatomy of Fascism* (New York: Alfred Knopf, 2004), p. 218.
82. Michael Mann, *Fascists* (Cambridge: Cambridge University Press, 2004), p. 13.
83. Zeev Sternhell, 'Fascist Ideology', in Walter Laqueur (ed.), *Fascism. A Reader's Guide* (Harmondsworth: Penguin, 1976), pp. 325–406.
84. Roger Griffin, *The Nature of Fascism* (London: Pinter, 1991), pp. 44–5.
85. The definition is written in the present tense, because, no matter how withered on the vine of history since 1945, it is still an active form of politics, especially when post-war derivatives are considered such as the New Right.
86. For a dissenting view see A. James Gregor, *The Faces of Janus. Marxism and Fascism in the Twentieth Century* (New Haven, CT: Yale University Press, 2000) which stresses the kinship between fascism and communism. Gregor also denies Nazism fascist status.

87. John Passmore, *The Philosophy of History* (Oxford: Oxford University Press, 1974), p. 152.

88. Karl Popper, *The Poverty of Historicism* (1957) (London: Routledge and Kegan Paul, 1974), p. 150. For more on this topic see Appendix: More on Methodology.

89. Along with the bulk of modern historians, I claim that Nazism is to be regarded as a form of fascism. For my rationale see *The Nature of Fascism*, pp. 106–10. Chapters 9–11 of the present book provide further corroboration of the heuristic value of classifying it within this generic category when defined in the terms I have outlined, for all its undeniable uniqueness (which is, of course a feature of *all* fascisms).

90. Mark Antliff, *Avant-Garde Fascism. The Mobilization of Myth, Art and Culture in France, 1909–1939* (Durham, NC: Duke University Press, 2007).

91. Zygmunt Bauman, *Modernity and Ambivalence* (Cambridge: Polity, 1991), p. 15.

92. Pierre Riberette, *Les bibliothèques françaises pendant la révolution 1789–1795; recherches sur un essai de catalogue collectif* (Paris: Bibliothèque Nationale, 1970), p. 46.

93. Bauman, *Modernity and Ambivalence*, p. 27, footnote. Significantly, Roberts in *The Totalitarian Experiment* also makes use of Bauman's concept.

94. Ibid., p. 7.

95. Ibid., p. 29.

96. Luis Borges, 'Deutsches requiem', *Labyrinths* (New York: New Directions, 1964), p. 144, cited in Claudia Koonz, *The Nazi Conscience* (Cambridge, MA: The Belknap Press, 2003), p. 16, one of the few works to explore in depth the ethical implications of the alternative nomos proposed by Nazism, i.e. the existence of an *alternative* morality as a function of the new nomos (*Weltanschauung*).

97. Adolf Hitler, *Mein Kampf*, trans. Ralph Mannheim (London: Pimlico, 1992), p. 28.

98. David Gellner, 'Religion, Politics, and Ritual. Remarks on Geertz and Bloch', *Social Anthropology* 7.2 (1999), pp. 135–53.

99. David Kertzer, *Ritual, Power, and Politics* (New Haven, CT: Yale University Press, 1988), pp. 176–7.

100. This concept was explored in Gilles Deleuze and Felix Guattari, *A Thousand Plateaus. Capitalism and Schizophrenia* (Minneapolis: University of Minneapolis Press, 1988); *Anti-Oedipus. Capitalism and Schizophrenia* (Minneapolis: University of Minneapolis Press, 1989).

101. Frank Kermode, *The Sense of an Ending. Studies in the Theory of Fiction* (1967) (New York: Oxford University Press, 2000), p. 111.

102. Tony Harrison, *The Gaze of the Gorgon* (Highgreen Tarset: Bloodaxe Books, 1992), p. 72.

7 THE BIRTH OF FASCISM FROM MODERNISM

1. Filippo Marinetti, 'Manifesto of Futurism', in Umbro Apollonio, *Futurist Manifestos* (London: Thames & Hudson, 1973), pp. 21–2.

2. Giovanni Gentile, 'The Transcending of Time in History', in *Philosophy and History. Essays presented to Ernst Cassirer* (Oxford: Clarendon Press, 1936), p. 104.

3. See the article by Bruno Gravagnuolo, 'Chi voleva morto Giovanni Gentile?' *L'Unità*, 24 February 2000.

4. Upper-case 'Fascism' will be used for Italian Fascism and lower-case 'fascism' for generic fascism, and the spelling in quotations 'harmonized'.

5. Cited in Emilio Gentile, 'The Conquest of Modernity. From Modernist Nationalism to Fascism', in Emilio Gentile, *The Struggle for Modernity. Nationalism, Futurism, and Fascism* (Westport, CT: Praeger, 2003), p. 53.

6. Walter Adamson, *Avant-garde Florence. From Modernism to Fascism* (Cambridge, MA: Harvard University Press, 1993).

7. The essay 'Politics and Philosophy' was published in Giovanni Gentile, *Dopo la vittoria. Nuovi frammenti politici* (Rome: Edizioni La Voce, 1920).

8. Claudio Fogu, *The Historic Imaginary. Politics of History in Fascist Italy* (Buffalo, NY: University of Toronto Press, 2003), p. 46.

9. Claudia Lazzaro and Roger J. Crum (eds.), *Donatello Among the Blackshirts. History and Modernity in the Visual Culture of Fascist Italy* (Ithaca, NY: Cornell University Press: 2005), p. 34.

10. Fogu, *The Historic Imaginary*, p. 40.

11. Ibid., p. 42.

12. Giovanni Gentile, *Genesis and Structure of Society* (Urbana: University of Illinois, 1966), p. 215.

13. The most comprehensive account is still Jost Hermand, *Old Dreams of a New Reich. Volkish Utopias and National Socialism* (Bloomington: Indiana University Press, 1992).

14. Zeev Sternhell, *Neither Right Nor Left. Fascist Ideology in France* (Berkeley: University of California Press, 1986).

15. Norma Bouchard, 'Introduction. Risorgimento as an Unfinished Story', in Norma Bouchard (ed.), *Risorgimento in Modern Italian Culture. Revisiting the 19th-century Past in History, Narrative, and Cinema* (Madison, NJ: Fairleigh Dickinson University Press, 2005).

16. Luisa Mangoni, *Una crisi di fine secolo. La cultura italiana e la Francia fra Otto e Novecento* (Turin: Einaudi, 1985), pp. 216–28, 'La rinascita dell'idealismo'.

17. Emilio Gentile, 'The Myth of National Regeneration in Italy. From Modernist Avant-garde to Fascism', in Matthew Affron and Mark Antliff, *Fascist Visions* (Princeton, NJ: Princeton University Press, 1997), p. 25.

18. This aspect of Fascism's genesis is thoroughly explored in Adamson, *Avant-garde Florence.*

19. In *Futurism and Politics. Between Anarchist Rebellion and Fascist Reaction, 1909–1944* (Oxford: Berghahn, 1995), Günter Berghaus stresses the importance of not equating Futurism with Fascism and the importance of the anarchist component that is often neglected by scholars.

20. Emilio Gentile, *La Grande Italia. Ascesa e declino del mito della nazione nel ventesimo secolo* (Milan: Mondadori, 1997), p. 102. On national syndicalism see the seminal work by David Roberts, *The Syndicalist Tradition and Italian Fascism* (Chapel Hill: University of North Carolina Press, 1979).

21. A. James Gregor, *Giovanni Gentile. Philosopher of Fascism* (New York: Transaction, 2001), p. 33. On the ANI see Alexander De Grand, *The Italian Nationalist Association and the Rise of Fascism* (Lincoln: University of Nebraska Press, 1978).

22. Gentile, *La Grande Italia*, pp. 85–7.

23. Giovanni Giolitti was prime minister five times between 1892 and 1921 and his name became a short-hand for the variant of parliamentary liberalism that dominated Italy socially and politically from the fin-de-siècle to the advent of Fascism.

24. See Giovanni Bardelli, *Il mito della 'Nuova Italia'. Gioacchino Volpe tra guerra e fascismo* (Rome: Lavoro, 1988).

25. This is the central theme of Emilio Gentile, *Il mito dello Stato nuovo Dall'antigiolittismo al fascismo* (Bari: Laterza, 1982).

26. Emilio Gentile, 'Conflicting Modernisms: *La Voce* against Futurism', in Emilio Gentile, *The Struggle against Modernity* (Westport, CT: Praeger, 2003), p. 29.

27. For Filippo Marinetti's doubts about the genuineness of D'Annunzio's conversion to Italianism, see Gentile, *Il mito dello Stato nuovo*, pp. 135–7.

28. Cited Gentile, *La Grande Italia*, p. 101.

29. Cited ibid., p. 103.

30. Adamson, *Avant-garde Florence*, pp. 7–9. Adamson builds on the classic account of modernism given in Stephen Spender's *The Struggle of the Modern* (London: Methuen, 1963), pp. 71–97, which, as we have seen, also contains themes that anticipate our 'own' ideal type.

31. Georges Bataille, 'The Psychological Structure of Fascism', in Georges Bataille, *Visions of Excess. Selected Writings 1927–1939* (Minneapolis: University of Minnesota Press, 1985), pp. 137–60. Bataille's own intellectual and spiritual trajectory provides yet another case study in the intense syncretism of programmatic modernism in the inter-war period: among his main sources were Hegel, Freud, Marx, Nietzsche, Marcel Mauss, the Marquis de Sade, Alexandre Kojève, Surrealism, and rituals of human sacrifice. In 1936, in a bid to found a new religion, he set up his own secret society, Acéphale (the headless), the symbol of which was a decapitated man.

32. Fogu, *The Historic Imaginary*, pp. 18–19.

33. Ibid., p. 51.

34. Ibid., p. 48.

35. Claudio Fogu, 'Actualism and the Fascist Historic Imaginary', *History and Theory* 42 (May 2003), pp. 208–9.

36. Richard Bosworth reveals considerable confusion about Emilio Gentile's intellectual pedigree when he identifies him, utterly misleadingly, as one of the 'culturalist historians' who since the 1980s 'began to reflect the "linguistic turn" associated with Michel Foucault and other French critical theorists'. See Richard Bosworth, *The Italian Dictatorship* (London: Arnold, 1998), pp. 234–5.

37. Gentile, *La Grande Italia*, p. 95. My emphasis.

38. See especially Gentile, 'Conflicting Modernisms', pp. 27–40.

39. Giovanni Amendola, 'La Guerra', *La Voce* (28 December 1928).

40. Gentile, 'The Conquest of Modernity,' p. 44. In the English original Berman uses the term 'maelstrom' for 'vortex'.

41. Ibid., p. 55.

42. Ibid., p. 46.

43. Ibid., p. 53.

44. A good example of this is the claim that 'Fascism's aim to respiritualize politics unfolded from a position of absolute self-referentiality that inevitably led the regime to privilege the claims of aesthetic worth over claims of any other nature'. Simonetta Falasca-Zamponi, *Fascist Spectacle. The Aesthetics of Power in Fascist Italy* (Berkeley: University of California Press, 1997), p. 14.

45. Gentile, 'The Conquest of Modernity', p. 43.

46. Zeev Sternhell, with Mario Sznajder and Maia Asheri, *The Birth of Fascist Ideology: From Cultural Rebellion to Political Revolution* (Princeton, NJ: Princeton University Press, 1995).

47. The most comprehensive Anglophone source on the eventual input of Italian and European social science into Fascism is A. James Gregor, *The Ideology of Fascism* (New York: Free Press, 1969).

48. Corrado Gini, 'Contributi statisici ai problemi dell'eugenica', *Rivista Italiana di sociologia* 3–4 (May–August 1912), pp. 64–71.

49. Giuseppe Sanarelli continued his career under Fascism and wrote the pamphlet *L'igiene nella vita pubblica e privata dell'antica Roma* (Rome: Istituto di Studi Romani, 1940).

50. Cited in Adrian Lyttelton, *Italian Fascisms. From Pareto to Gentile* (London: Jonathan Cape, 1973), pp. 102–3. Published in Giovanni Papini, *Vecchio e nuovo nazionalismo* (Rome: Giovanni Volpe, 1967).

51. Ibid., p. 119.

52. Renzo De Felice, *Mussolini il rivoluzionario 1883–1920* (Turin: Einaudi, 1965), pp. 65–7. The article was not published. The impact of Vocian modernist nationalism on Mussolini's concept of revolution is independently attested by A. James Gregor in *Young Mussolini and the Intellectual Origins of Fascism* (Berkeley: University of California Press, 1979), pp. 87–9; also in Emilio Gentile, *Il mito dello Stato nuovo*, pp. 103–34; Emilio Gentile, *Le origini dell'ideologia fascista* (1975) (Bologna: Il Mulino, 1996), pp. 61–110.

53. Gentile, *Il mito dello Stato nuovo*, p. 105.

54. Gentile, *La Grande Italia*, p. 141.
55. Richard Bosworth typically trivializes the importance of Mussolini's subscription to *La Voce* and correspondence with its editor Prezzolini in his biography of Mussolini, treating it as little more than sign of his desire 'to go beyond Trento to some more exciting and important spot: perhaps Florence, perhaps Milan, perhaps Rome'. See Bosworth, *Mussolini* (London: Arnold, 2002), pp. 71–2.
56. Gentile, *La Grande Italia*, p. 141.
57. Gentile, 'The Conquest of Modernity', p. 58. On the contribution of modernists to the myth of the Great War see Mario Isnenghi, *Il mito della grande guerra. Da Marinetti a Malaparte* (Bologna: Il Mulino, 1989).
58. For the wider Italian context see Vincenzo Calì, Gustavo Corni and Giuseppe Ferrandi (eds.), *Gli intellettuali e la Grande guerra* (Bologna: Il Mulino, 2000); Angelo Ventrone, *La seduzione totalitaria. Guerra, modernità, violenza politica (1914–1918)* (Rome: Donzelli, 2003).
59. Marinetti, 'Manifesto of Futurism', p. 22.
60. *L'avvenire*, 23 February 1915, cited in Berghaus, *Futurism and Politics*, p. 79.
61. Filippo Marinetti, 'Guerra sola igiene del mondo', in *Teoria e invenzione* (Milan: Arnaldo Mondadori, 1968), p. 284, cited in Gentile, *Il mito dello Stato nuovo*, p. 146.
62. Cited in Gentile, 'The Conquest of Modernity', pp. 58–9.
63. On *Lacerba*'s relationship to cultural and political modernism see Adamson, *Avant-garde Florence*, pp. 155–80.
64. *Lacerba*, 1 October 1914, p. 1.
65. Roberts, *The Syndicalist Tradition in Italian Fascism*, pp. 122–3.
66. Ibid., p. 111.
67. On the attempted appropriation of Mussolini as the 'new man' by *vociani* in this period see Gentile, *Il mito dello Stato nuovo*, pp. 118–31.
68. Ventrone, *La seduzione totalitaria*, pp. 47–52.
69. On this neglected phase in the development of Mussolini's Fascism see Paul O'Brien, *Mussolini in the First World War. The Journalist, the Soldier, the Fascist* (Oxford: Berg, 2005).
70. The final statistics were 275,000 prisoners taken, 40,000 killed, 20,000 wounded, and staggering material losses, while Austro-German forces advanced more than 60 miles towards Venice in a few days.
71. Elvio Fachinelli, 'Il fenomeno fascista' in *La freccia ferma. Tre tentative di annullare il tempo* [The arrow stops: three attempts to annul time] (Milan: Feltrinelli, 1979), pp. 147, 166.
72. Benito Mussolini, 'Trincerocrazia', *Il Popolo d'Italia*, 15 December 1917. Reprinted in E. Susmel and D. Susmel (eds.), *Omnia Opera di Benito Mussolini* (Florence: La Fenice, 1951–63), volume 10, pp. 140–3.
73. Excerpts of this article are reprinted in Roger Griffin, *Fascism* (Oxford: Oxford University Press, 1995), pp. 28–9. My emphasis.
74. Kenneth Tollefson, 'Titus. Epistle of Religious Revitalization', *Biblical Theology Bulletin* 30.4 (Winter 2000), p. 146.
75. Adrian Lyttelton, *The Seizure of Power* (London: Taylor & Francis, 2004).
76. For a useful overview of the impact of the First World War and its aftermath on the rise of authoritarianism and fascism in Europe see Juan Linz, 'Totalitarian and Authoritarian Regimes', in F. I. Greenstein and N. W. Polsby (eds.), *Handbook of Political Science. Macropolitical Theory*, volume 3 (Massachusetts: Addison-Wesley, 1975), pp. 313–21; Stanley Payne, *A History of Fascism, 1914–45* (London: University College London Press, 1995), chapter 3, 'The Impact of World War I', pp. 71–9.
77. Mussolini, *Omnia Opera*, volume 8, p. 144, cited in Gentile, *Le origini dell'ideologia fascista*, p. 207.

78. My emphasis. The text is reprinted in Roger Griffin, *International Fascism. Theories, Causes, and the New Consensus* (London: Arnold, 1998), pp. 248–9. The second section of the original article, 'Fundamental Ideas', was written by Giovanni Gentile and offers his neo-Hegelian, 'actualist' interpretation of Fascism as the basis of the totalitarian ethical state.

79. See Michael Ledeen, *The First Duce. D'Annunzio at Fiume* (Baltimore: Johns Hopkins University Press, 1977); George Mosse, 'The Poet and the Exercise of Political Power: Gabriele d'Annunzio', *Yearbook of Comparative and General Literature* 22 (1973), pp. 32–3.

80. For an interpretation of Fascism that stresses the contribution of the role of paramilitarism in 'cleansing' the nation see Michael Mann, *Fascists* (New York: Cambridge University Press, 2004), pp. 93–137.

81. Roberto Farinacci, *Squadrismo* (Rome: Edizioni Ardita, 1934); *Storia della rivoluzione fascista* (Cremona: Cremona Nuova, 1937).

82. Umberto Banchelli, *Memorie di un fascista* (Florence: Edizioni della Sassaiola fiorentina, 1922); Mario Piazzesi, *Diario di uno squadrista toscano 1919–22* (Rome: Bonnaci, 1980).

83. Roberta Valli, 'The Myth of *Squadrismo* in the Fascist Regime', *Journal of Contemporary History* 35.2 (2000), pp. 140–4.

84. See above Chapter 6, p. 165.

85. David Roberts, 'How not to think about Fascism and Ideology, Intellectual Antecedents and Historical Meaning', *Journal of Contemporary History* 35.2 (2000), p. 208.

86. Adamson cites this metaphor in 'Modernism and Fascism', p. 389.

87. An allusion to Zeev Sternhell's groundbreaking *Neither Right nor Left: Fascist Ideology in France*, (University of California Press, Berkeley and Los Angeles, 1986).

88. Alfredo Rocco, *Scritti e discorsi politici* (Milan: Dott. A. Giuffrè Editori, 1928), volume 3, pp. 984–5, cited in Gentile, *Il mito dello Stato nuovo*, p. 198.

89. Sergio Panunzio, 'Stato e sindacato', *Rivista internazionale di filosofia del diritto* 3.1 (Jan–March, 1923), pp. 4–9. The article was written in November 1922, the month after the March on Rome.

90. The underlying hostility of the Vatican and of Catholic culture in general to Fascism's attempt to establish itself as a political religion is explored in Emilio Gentile, 'New Idols. Catholicism in the Face of Fascist Totalitarianism', *Journal of Modern Italian Studies* 11.2 (2006), pp. 143–70. The distance that monarchism retained from Fascism was crucial to Mussolini's downfall in July 1943 when King Victor Emmanuel III endorsed the decision of the Fascist Grand Council to remove him as head of state and put him under arrest.

91. For examples of this spectacularly modernist form of painting see the web exhibition of *aeropittura* at http://www.fdabisso.com/aero/aeropittura.html (accessed 02/12/06).

92. See Tim Redman, *Ezra Pound and Italian Fascism* (Cambridge: Cambridge University Press, 1991).

93. Michael Golston, *Rhythm and "Race" in Twentieth Century Poetry and Poetics: Pound, Yeats, Williams, and Modern Sciences of Rhythm* (New York: Columbia University Press, 2007).

94. Cited in William Cookson (ed.), *Ezra Pound. Selected Prose 1909–1965* (New York: New Directions, 1973), p. 300.

8   THE FASCIST REGIME AS A MODERNIST STATE

1. Emilio Gentile et al., 'Manifesto of Fascist Intellectuals', in Jeffrey Schnapp (ed.), *A Primer of Italian Fascism* (Lincoln: University of Nebraska Press, 2000), pp. 297–303.

2. For example, in his article 'Modernism and Fascism: The Politics of Culture in Italy, 1903–1922', *American Historical Review* 9.2 (1900), p. 360, Walter Adamson argues that

'it was from the *vociani* that Mussolini took the essence of his cultural politics', and that 'his fascism might therefore be characterized in important respects as the politicization of Italian modernism'.

3. The basic argument in Zeev Sternhell, with Mario Sznajder and Maia Asheri, *The Birth of Fascist Ideology: From Cultural Rebellion to Political Revolution* (Princeton, NJ: Princeton University Press, 1995).

4. Claudio Fogu, *The Historic Imaginary. Politics of History in Fascist Italy* (Buffalo, NY: University of Toronto Press, 2003), p. 6. My emphasis.

5. Notably Denis Mack Smith, *Mussolini. A Biography* (New York: Vintage Books, 1983).

6. Alexander De Grand, 'Cracks in the Façade. The Failure of Fascist Totalitarianism in Italy, 1935–9', *European History Quarterly* 21 (1991), pp. 515–35.

7. The autobiography was published with a glowing endorsement of his political achievements to date from Richard Washburn Child, the former US Ambassador to Italy. Until November 1936 when Fascist Italy declared itself as forming an 'Axis' with the Third Reich, Mussolini was so popular in some anti-communist sections of the US and British public that for the 1935 London production of *Anything Goes* P. G. Wodehouse changed the original lyric of a verse from the 1934 Cole Porter song *You're the Top* to 'You're the top! You're the Great Houdini! You're the top! You are Mussolini!'

8. Benito Mussolini, *My Autobiography* (New York: Charles Scribner, 1928), pp. 68–9.

9. Angelo Ventrone, *La seduzione totalitaria. Guerra, modernità, violenza politica (1914–1918)* (Rome: Donazelli, 2003), pp. 133–51.

10. Ibid., p. xii.

11. Ibid., p. 192.

12. Emilio Gentile, *The Struggle for Modernity. Nationalism, Futurism, and Fascism* (Westport, CT: Praeger, 2003), pp. 61–2.

13. Pier Giorgio Zunino, *L'Ideologia del fascismo* (Bologna: Il Mulino, 1985), p. 164.

14. Ibid., pp. 123–35.

15. See Romke Visser, 'Fascist Doctrine and the Cult of the *Romanità*', *Journal of Contemporary History* 27.1 (1992), pp. 5–22.

16. Cited in Emilio Gentile, 'The Conquest of Modernity. From Modernist Nationalism to Fascism', in *The Struggle for Modernity*, p. 60.

17. Giuseppe Bottai, 'Roma e Fascismo', *Roma* 15.10 (1937), p. 351.

18. Ibid., p. 352.

19. For the mythic function intended to be performed by the Ara Pacis project see Spiro Kostof, 'The Emperor and the Duce: The Planning of Piazzale Augusto Imperatore di Roma', in Henry Millon and Linda Nochlin (eds.), *Art and Architecture in the Service of Politics* (Cambridge, MA: The MIT Press, 1978), pp. 270–325.

20. Joshua Arthurs, *A Revolution in the Idea of Rome: The Archaeology of Modernity in Fascist Italy* (History Dept., University of Chicago) unpublished PhD, 2006 draft version, p. 6.

21. Cited ibid. My emphasis.

22. Cited in Fogu, *The Historic Imaginary*, p. 44.

23. Walter Benjamin, *Illuminations* (London: Fontana, 1992), pp. 252–5.

24. See Gentile 'The Conquest of Modernity', p. 61.

25. The year was divided into ten months with poetic new names, the most famous being Thermidor and Brumaire for historic events that occurred within them; the day into ten hours of a hundred minutes of a hundred seconds to make exactly 100,000 seconds per day. In the city in Fritz Lang's profoundly modernist evocation of a future both utopian and dystopian in *Metropolis* (1927), the workers' lives are regulated by a decimal clock with digits running counter-clockwise on the face. The apocryphal tale that Joseph Goebbels offered Lang the chance to become head of the Nazi film industry on the strength of this film contains a profound intuition about Nazi modernism.

26. Cited in Gentile, 'The Conquest of Modernity', p. 62. Original emphasis.

27. See above, Chapter 6.
28. Ruth Ben-Ghiat, *Fascist Modernities. Italy 1922–1945* (Berkeley: University of California Press, 2001), pp. 5–6. The quotation is taken from Omar Bartov, *Murder in our Midst. The Holocaust, Industrial Killing, and Representation* (Oxford: Oxford University Press, 1996), p. 5. On 'human reclamation' see too the section 'bonifica umana' in Zunino, *L'Ideologia del fascismo*, pp. 269–81.
29. Ben-Ghiat, *Fascist Modernities*, p. 6.
30. Emilio Gentile, 'The Sacralisation of Politics: Definitions, Interpretations and Reflections on the Question of Secular Religion and Totalitarianism', *Totalitarian Movements and Political Religion* 1.1 (2000), pp. 18–55. The article is taken from a chapter of Gentile's book *Le religioni della politica. Fra democrazie e totalitarismi* (Rome-Bari: Laterza, 2000), published in English as *Politics as Religion* (Princeton, NJ: Princeton University Press, 2006).
31. The best overview of the formative period in the establishment of the regime is Stanley Payne, *A History of Fascism, 1914–45* (London: University College London Press, 1995), chapter 4, 'The Rise of Italian Fascism, 1919–1929', pp. 80–128, which also provides a useful bibliography.
32. Tracy Koon, *Believe, Obey, Fight. Political Socialization of Youth in Fascist Italy, 1922–1943* (Chapel Hill: University of North Carolina Press, 1985).
33. Doug Thompson, *State Control in Fascist Italy. Culture and Conformity* (Manchester: Manchester University Press, 1991).
34. Marla Stone, *The Patron State. Culture and Politics in Fascist Italy* (Princeton, NJ: Princeton University Press, 1998)
35. Emilio Gentile, *The Sacralization of Politics in Fascist Italy* (Cambridge, MA: Harvard University Press, 1996).
36. Mabel Berezin, *Making the Fascist Self: The Political Culture of Inter-War Italy* (Ithaca, NY: Cornell University, 1997).
37. See Emilio Gentile, 'Mussolini's Charisma', in Emilio Gentile, *The Struggle for Modernity. Nationalism, Futurism, and Fascism* (Westport, CT: Praeger, 2003), pp. 127–44.
38. Simonetta Falasca-Zamponi, *Fascist Spectacle. The Aesthetics of Power in Fascist Italy* (Berkeley: University of California Press, 1997), p. 28.
39. Lidia Santarelli, 'Muted Violence. Italian War Crimes in Occupied Greece', *Journal of Modern Italian Studies* 9.3 (2004), pp. 280–99.
40. Emily Braun, 'The Visual Arts. Modernism and Fascism', in Adrian Lyttleton (ed.), *Liberal and Fascist Italy* (Oxford: Oxford University Press, 2002), p. 197.
41. See above, Chapter 1, p. 24.
42. For more on both these highly 'un-Fascist' exhibits, which refute simplistic notions of Fascist culture being an oxymoron, see Claudio Fogu, 'Mussolini's Mare Nostrum', in Roberto Dainotto and Eric Zakim (eds.), *Mediterranean Studies* (New York: MLA Books, forthcoming) in the series World Literatures Reimagined.
43. Richard Etlin, *Modernism in Italian Architecture, 1890–1940* (London: MIT Press, 1991), p. 387.
44. Marla Stone, 'The State as Patron. Making Official Culture in Fascist Italy', in Matthew Affron and Mark Antliff (eds.), *Fascist Visions* (Princeton, NJ: Princeton University Press, 1997), pp. 205–38. This important thesis is explored at length in Marla Stone, *The Patron State. Culture and Politics in Fascist Italy* (Princeton, NJ: Princeton University Press, 1998).
45. On Mussolini as an artist or sculptor reshaping the 'masses' into the nation see Falasca-Zamponi, *Fascist Spectacle*, pp. 15–28.
46. See Roger Griffin, '"This Fortress Built against Infection." The BUF Vision of Britain's Theatrical and Musical Renaissance', in Tom Linehan and Julie Gottlieb (eds.), *Cultural Expressions of the Far Right in Twentieth Century Britain* (London: Macmillan, 2003), pp. 45–65.

47. Ibid., p. 210.
48. Cited in Affron and Antliff, *Fascist Visions*, p. 13.
49. Ibid., p. 11.
50. Jeffrey Schnapp, 'Epic Demonstrations. Fascist Modernity and the 1932 Exhibition of the Fascist Revolution', in Richard Golsan (ed.), *Fascism, Aesthetics, and Culture* (Hanover and London: University Press of New England, 1992), p. 3.
51. Fogu, *The Historic Imaginary*, p. 34.
52. For a full English translation of some of the most important of these articles see Jeffrey Schnapp and Barbara Spackmann, 'Selections from the Great Debate on Fascism and Culture: *Critica Fascista* 1926–1927', *Stanford Italian Review*, special issue on 'Fascism and Culture', 8.1–2 (1990), pp. 235–72.
53. See Roger Griffin, 'The Sacred Synthesis. The Ideological Cohesion of Fascist Cultural Policy', *Modern Italy* 3.1 (1998), pp. 5–23.
54. Interview with *L'Espresso*, 28 (26 December 1982), cited in Richard Bosworth, *The Italian Dictatorship* (London: Arnold, 1998), p. 155.
55. Emily Braun, *Mario Sironi and Italian Modernism. Art and Politics under Fascism* (Cambridge: Cambridge University Press, 2000), pp. 188–9.
56. Walter Adamson, 'Ardengo Soffici and the Religion of Art', in Affron and Antliff, *Fascist Visions*, p. 66.
57. These were Littoria (founded 1932), now Latina, Pontinia (1934), Aprilia (1936), and Pomezia (1938). See Henry Millon, 'Some New Towns in Italy in the 1930s', in Millon and Nochlin, *Art and Architecture in Service of Politics*, pp. 326–41; Diane Ghirardo, *Building New Communities. New Deal America and Fascist Italy* (Princeton, NJ: Princeton University Press, 1989).
58. See Mia Fuller, *Moderns Abroad. Italian Colonial Architecture and Urbanism* (London: Routledge, 2006). For a fascinating insight into the modernism of the aesthetics employed in the regime's colonial civic architecture see Jobst Welge, 'Fascism Triumphans: Modernism, "Romanitas", and Architectural Form', in Claudia Lazarro and Roger Crum (eds.), *Donatello Among the Blackshirts: History and Modernity in the Visual Culture of Fascist Italy* (Ithaca, NY: Cornell University Press, 2004), pp. 83–94. The essays in this book cumulatively offer a penetrating insight into the complexities of Fascism's aesthetic modernism while also underlining the nexus between its culture and its attempted modernist social, political, and 'anthropological' revolutions.
59. Schnapp, 'Epic Demonstrations', p. 30. For other illuminating accounts of the exhibition see Fogu, *The Historic Imaginary*, pp. 132–64; Etlin, *Modernism in Italian Architecture*, pp. 407–17.
60. Thomas Schumacher, *The Danteum. Architecture, Poetics, and Politics Under Italian Fascism* (Princeton, NJ: Princeton Architectural Press; 1993); Etlin, *Modernism in Italian Architecture*, pp. 517–68.
61. Ben-Ghiat, *Fascist Modernities*, pp. 46–69.
62. Quoted in Jeffrey Schnapp, *Staging Fascism. 18BL and the Theatre of Masses for Masses* (Stanford, CA: Stanford University Press, 1996), pp. 41–2. For a penetrating exploration of the sacralizing dimension of fascist theatre alluded to by Bontempelli and which indirectly corroborates our 'primordialist' theory of modernism, see the important essay by Günter Berghaus, 'The Ritual Core of Fascist Theatre. An Anthropological Perspective', in Günter Berghaus (ed.), *Fascist Theatre. Comparative Studies on the Aesthetics and Politics of Representation in Europe, 1925–1945* (Oxford: Berghahn, 1996).
63. Schnapp, *Staging Fascism*, pp. 91–2.
64. See ibid., pp. 80–8.
65. Piero Garofalo, 'Seeing Red', in J. Rice and P. Garofalo (eds.), *Re-viewing Fascism Italian Cinema 1922–1943* (Bloomington and Indianapolis: Indiana University Press, 2002), pp. 223–49.

66. For an overview of Fascist commercial cinema see James Hay, *Popular Film Culture in Fascist Italy. The Passing of the Rex* (Bloomington: Indiana University Press, 1987); Marcia Landy, *Fascism in Film. The Italian Commercial Cinema, 1931–1943* (Princeton, NJ: Princeton University Press, 1986).

67. Giuseppe Bottai, *Il Fascismo e L'Italia Nuova* (Rome: Giorgio Berlutti, 1923), p. 71.

68. Ibid., p. 54.

69. Ibid., p. 74.

70. Koon, *Believe, Obey, Fight*; Victoria De Grazia, *The Culture of Consent. Mass Organisation of Leisure in Fascist Italy* (Cambridge: Cambridge University Press, 1981).

71. Michael Robert Ebner, 'The Fascist Archipelago. Political Internment, Exile, and Everyday Life in Mussolini's Italy, 1926–1943' (Unpublished PhD, Columbia University, 2005).

72. E.g. Tobias Abse, 'The Rise of Fascism in an Industrial City. The Case of Livorno 1919–1922', in David Forgacs (ed.), *Rethinking Italian Fascism* (London: Wishart, 1986).

73. See David Baker, 'The Political Economy of Fascism. Myth or Reality, or Myth and Reality?' *New Political Economy* 11.2 (June 2006), pp. 227–50.

74. Barbara Spackman, *Fascist Virilities. Rhetoric, Ideology, and Social Fantasy in Italy* (Minneapolis: University of Minnesota Press, 1996).

75. See Ben-Ghiat, *Fascist Modernities*, chapter 4, 'Class Dismissed: Fascism's Politics of Youth', pp. 93–122.

76. Victoria De Grazia, *How Fascism Ruled Women. Italy 1922–1945* (Berkeley: University of California Press, 1992).

77. David Horn, *Social Bodies. Science, Reproduction, and Italian Modernity* (Princeton, NJ.: Princeton University Press, 1994).

78. Carl Ipsen, *Dictating Demography. The Problem of Population in Fascist Italy* (Cambridge: Cambridge University Press, 1996).

79. Maria Quine, *Italy's Social Revolution. Charity and Welfare from Liberalism to Fascism* (New York: Palgrave Macmillan, 2002).

80. See above, Chapter 5, pp. 152–3.

81. Gigliola Gori, 'Model of Masculinity. Mussolini, the "New Italian" of the Fascist Era', in James Mangan (ed.), *Shaping the Superman. Fascist Body as Political Icon – Global Fascism* (London: Cass, 1999).

82. See Koon, *Believe, Obey, Fight*.

83. Ruth Ben-Ghiat (ed.), *Italian Colonialism* (London: Palgrave Macmillan, 2005).

84. Aristotle Kallis, *Fascist Ideology. Territory and Expansionism in Italy and Germany, 1922–1945* (New York: Routledge, 2000); Ben-Ghiat, *Italian Colonialism*.

85. Carl Ipsen, *Dictating Demography*.

86. The principle of securing Italy's economic independence from international trade and imports, a goal closely bound up with putting the nation on a war footing.

87. See Visser, 'Fascist Doctrine and the Cult of the *Romanità*'.

88. Ben-Ghiat, *Fascist Modernities*, chapter 5, 'Aryans and Others. The Fascist War against the Jews', pp. 123–70.

89. For a detailed account of how the radical socialism of syndicalists such as Sergio Panunzio morphed into leftist Fascism see David Roberts, *The Syndicalist Tradition and Italian Fascism* (Chapel Hill: University of North Carolina Press, 1979).

90. James Gregor devotes a chapter to Ugo Spirito in *Fascist Intellectuals: Fascist Social and Political Thought* (Princeton, NJ: Princeton University Press, 2005).

91. This phrase is not being used in the technical sense it has acquired within economic theory: see Deirdre N. McCloskey, *The Rhetoric of Economics* (Madison: University of Wisconsin Press, 1998).

92. Sergio Panunzio, *Riforma Costitutionale. Le Corporzaioni; il Consiglio delle Corporazioni, il Senato* (Florence: La Nuova Italia, 1934), p. 15.

93. Horn, *Social Bodies*.

94. Corrado Gini, 'The Scientific Basis of Fascism', *Political Science Quarterly* 42 (1927), pp. 102–3.
95. For the text of the Manifesto see Schnapp, *A Primer of Italian Fascism*, 'Three Documents on Race', pp. 172–84.
96. Jeffrey Schnapp, 'The Fabric of Modern Times', *Critical Inquiry* 24 (Autumn 1997), pp. 192.
97. Ibid., p. 202. My emphasis.
98. On the importance of glass, light, and crystal as metaphors for the modernist spirit see Christina Lodder, 'Searching for Utopia', in Christopher Wilk (ed.), *Modernism 1914–1939. Designing a New World* (London: V&A Publications, 2006), pp. 25–7.
99. In 1931 an elite school was set up in Milan to elaborate Fascist ideology with the name 'School of Fascist Mysticism': see Daniel Marchesini, *La scuola dei gerarchi. Mistica fascista. Storia, problemi, istituzioni* (Milan: Feltrinelli, 1976). The winner of the prize for the best essay in 1941 was Enzo Leone, who published it as *La mistica del razzismo fascista* (Milan: Quaderni della 'Scuola di Mistica Fascista', No. 3, 1941), another sign of the nexus between cultural and social modernism within the Fascist regime.
100. L. Bortolotti and G. De Luca, *Fascismo e autostrade. Un caso di sintesi. La Firenze-mare* (Milan: F. Angeli, 1994).
101. See Emilio Gentile, 'Impending Modernity: Fascism and the Ambivalent Image of the United States', *Journal of Contemporary History* 28.1 (1993).
102. Etlin, *Modernism in Italian Architecture*, pp. 395–403.
103. Some impression of this vitality can be gleaned from the lavishly produced catalogue: Anty Pansera (ed.), *Anni Trenta. Arte e Cultura in Italia* (Milan: Mazzotta, 1982).
104. See Emilio Gentile, *La via italiana al totalitarismo* (Rome: Carocci, 2002), particularly Part Two, 'Il cesarismo totalitario'.
105. Michael Ledeen, *Universal Fascism* (New York: Howard Fertig, 1972).
106. Walter Adamson, *Avant-Garde Florence: From Modernism to Fascism* (Cambridge, MA: Harvard University Press, 1993), p. 250. My emphasis.
107. Giuseppe Bottai, 'I miti moderni', 15 February 1942.
108. David Kertzer, *Ritual, Politics and Power* (New Haven, CT: Yale University Press, 1988), pp. 176–7.
109. Etlin, *Modernism in Italian Architecture*, p. 378. The section 'Italian rationalism and anti-Semitism' (pp. 569–97) provides important insights into the ideological contortions forced on aesthetic and social modernists previously working enthusiastically under Fascism by its 'racial turn' towards anti-Semitism, and into the complex weave of freedom and constraint created by 'hegemonic pluralism' in practice.
110. Primo Levi, *If this is a Man* (Harmondsworth: Penguin, 1987), pp. 111–12.
111. Modris Eksteins, *Rites of Spring* (1989) (Boston: Houghton Mifflin, 2000), p. 303.

9 NAZISM AS A REVITALIZATION MOVEMENT

1. Rüdiger Safranski, *Martin Heidegger. Between Good and Evil* (Cambridge, MA: Harvard University Press, 1998), p. 229.
2. Adolf Hitler, *My New Order* (London: Angus and Robertson, 1942), p. 241.
3. The full text is reproduced in Hans Buderer, *Entartete Kunst. Beschlagnahmeaktionen in der Städtischen Kunsthalle Mannheim 1937. Kunst und Dokumentation* (Mannheim: Städtische Kunsthalle Mannheim, 1991), p. 42.
4. Some of the buyers were Norwegian, so that part of Munch's work actually found its way back home as a result of the purge. One of them, *Summer Day*, became part of the private collection of Hermann Goering, and was auctioned in February 2006 for £6.17 million.
5. For a full account of this grotesque episode see Sue Prideaux, *Edvard Munch. Behind the Scream* (New Haven, CT: Yale University Press, 2005), pp. 150–1.

6. The name alludes to 'der deutsche Michel' or 'the German Michael', a sort of German Everyman. For the passage referred to see above Chapter 1, p. 30.

7. Claus-Ekkehard Bärsch, *Die politische Religion des National-Sozialismus* (Munich: Wilhelm Fink, 1998), pp. 172–8. The 'conservative revolutionary' and Nazi jurist, Carl Schmitt, used the term 'Romanticism' in an analogous way to 'religion' in his *Politische Romantik* (Berlin: Duncker & Humblot, 1919).

8. It should be noted that the term 'transcendence' is being used here with the specific anthropological significance given to it in Chapter 3, which conflicts with the connotations given it by Ernst Nolte in the famous definition of fascism identifying it with *resistance* to 'practical and theoretical' transcendence formulated in *The Three Faces of Fascism* (1965: German edition, *Der Faschismus in seiner Epoche* 1963).

9. Bärsch, *Die politische Religion des National-Sozialismus*, p. 178.

10. See Léon Poliakov, *The Aryan Myth* (London: Sussex University Press, 1974).

11. Frank-Lothar Kroll, *Utopie als Ideologie. Geschichtsdenken und politisches Handeln im Dritten Reich* (Paderborn: Ferdinand Schöningh, 1999), pp. 291–5.

12. Michael Kater, *Different Drummers. Jazz in the Culture of Nazi Germany* (Oxford: Oxford University Press, 1992), p. 35.

13. See Horst Bergmeier and Rainer Lotz, *Hitler's Airwaves. The Inside Story of Nazi Radio Broadcasting and Propaganda Swing* (New Haven, CT: Yale University Press, 1997).

14. His formal title was 'Director of the Office for the Supervision of the Entire Cultural and Ideological Education and Training of the NSDAP'.

15. Bruno Werner, *Deutsche Allgemeine Zeitung*, Berlin, 12 May 1933. For the context of the article see Georg Bussmann, '"Degenerate Art". A Look at a Useful Myth', in Christos Joachimides et al., *German Art of the Twentieth Century* (London: Royal Academy, 1985), p. 117; also Brandon Taylor, 'Post-Modernism in the Third Reich', in Brandon Taylor and Wilfried van der Will (eds.), *The Nazification of Art* (Winchester: The Winchester Press, 1990), p. 131.

16. Hildegaard Brenner, 'Art in the Political Power Struggle of 1933 and 1934', in Jao Holborn (ed.), *Republic to Reich. The Making of the Nazi Revolution. Ten Essays* (New York: Random House, 1972), p. 423.

17. Rüdiger Safranski, *Wieviel Wahrheit braucht der Mensch? Über das Denkbare und das Lebbare* (München: Hanser, 1990), pp. 143–4.

18. See Andreas Fischer and Frank Kämpfer, 'The Political Poster in the Third Reich', in Taylor and van der Will, *The Nazification of Art*, pp. 183–203. Several examples of these posters for the year 1943 can be seen on the German Propaganda Archive website at http://www.calvin.edu/academic/cas/gpa/posters2.htm (accessed 14/10/06).

19. The Russians lost 80,000 men killed and 275,000 wounded; 150,000 Germans were killed.

20. Cf. Eric Zillmer, Molly Harrower, and Barry Ritzler, *The Quest for the Nazi Personality. A Psychological Investigation of Nazi War Criminals* (Hillsdale, NJ: Lawrence Earlbaum Associates, 1995).

21. Ronald Smelser, *Robert Ley* (Oxford: Berg, 1988).

22. Albert Speer's own blend of technocracy with nationalism emerges clearly from his autobiographical *Inside the Third Reich. Memoirs* (New York: Macmillan, 1970). These paper over his own official and moral responsibility for the atrocities committed as a direct result of the measures he adopted to maintain the productivity of the Nazi war-machine after the death of Fritz Todt in 1942.

23. For an overtly 'revisionist' and 'apologetic' biography of Darré see Anna Bramwell, *Blood and Soil. Richard Walther Darré and Hitler's 'Green Party'* (Bourne End, Buckinghamshire: Kensal Press, 1985).

24. Nick Goodrick-Clarke, *The Occult Roots of Nazism* (Wellingborough, UK: Aquarian Press, 1985).

25. Christopher Hale, *Himmler's Crusade* (New York: Bantam Books, 2003).

26. See especially Karla Poewe, *New Religions and the Nazis* (New York and London: Routledge 2006).

27. Speech made by Hitler at the Nuremberg Party Rally on 6 September 1938 and archived at http://www.hitler.org/speeches/09-06-38.html (accessed 05/07/06).

28. Joachim Fest, *Der zerstörte Traum. Das Ende des utopistischen Zeitalters* (Munich: Siedler Verlag, 1991), pp. 50–1. Fest's reconstruction of the last days of Hitler, *Der Untergang*, became the main basis for the highly controversial film of the same name which dramatizes the ultimate consequences of Hitler's bid to make history whose principles were set forth in *Mein Kampf*.

29. Madris Eksteins, *Rites of Spring* (1989) (Boston: Houghton Mifflin, 2000), p. 303.

30. Kroll, *Utopie als Ideologie*, p. 312.

31. Ibid., pp. 311–12. Original emphasis. Kroll cites Karl Mannheim's *Ideologie und Utopia* (1929) in support of this pragmatic, praxis-oriented definition of utopianism. 'Matrix' here is my translation for the IT expression *Leitgröße* or 'command variable'.

32. Speech made by Hitler at the Nuremberg Party Rally on 6 September 1938 and archived at http://www.hitler.org/speeches/09-06-38.html (accessed 05/07/06).

33. Notably Henry Turner, 'Fascism and Modernization', *World Politics* 24 (1972), pp. 547–64; Michael Ledeen and Renzo de Felice, *Fascism. An Informal Introduction to its Theory and Practice* (New Brunswick, NJ: Transaction Books, 1976); Jeffrey Herf, *Reactionary Modernism. Technology, Culture, and Politics in Weimar and the Third Reich* (New York: Cambridge University Press, 1984).

34. Arthur Moeller van den Bruck, *Das Dritte Reich* (1923) (Hamburg: Hanseatische Verlagsanstalt, 1931), p. 163.

35. Goodrick-Clarke, *The Occult Roots of Nazism.*

36. Poewe, *New Religions and the Nazis*, pp. 84–5.

37. Ibid., p. 3.

38. On the assimilation and Nazification of the German life reform movement by the Third Reich, see Wolfgang Krabbe, '"Die Weltanschauung der Deutschen Lebensform-Bewegung ist der Nationalsozialismus". Zur Gleichschaltung einer Alternativströmung im Dritten Reich', *Archiv für Kulturgeschichte* 71.2 (1989), pp. 431–61.

39. See above Chapter 5, p. 142.

40. Michael Kater, *Doctors under Hitler* (Chapel Hill: University of North Carolina Press, 1989), pp. 111–20.

41. Michael Kenny, 'A Darker Shade of Green: Medical Botany, Homeopathy, and Cultural Politics in Interwar Germany', *Social History of Medicine* 15.3 (December 2002), pp. 481–504; see also Mary Seeman, 'Psychiatry in the Nazi Era', *The Canadian Journal of Psychiatry* 50.1 (2005), pp. 218–25.

42. The correspondence relating to this bizarre episode is to be found in the archives of the former Dachau concentration camp (now the KZ-Gedenkstätte Dachau), in file DaA 29.597. My thanks to Tudor Georgescu and to the archivist Dirk Riedel for this information.

43. 'Himmler an Ahnenerbe betr. Tätigkeit Moers', 9.10.1942, DaA 29.597.

44. A major role in establishing the currency of such theories was played by Louis Pauwels and Jacques Bergier, *The Morning of the Magicians* (1960) (London: Mayfair, 1971).

45. Speech made by Hitler at the Nuremberg Party Rally on 6 September 1938 and archived at http://www.hitler.org/speeches/09-06-38.html (accessed 05/07/06).

46. See above, Chapter 5.

47. Ian Kershaw, 'Hitler and the Uniqueness of Nazism', *Journal of Contemporary History* 39.2 (2004), pp. 245–6.

48. Ian Kershaw, 'Reflections on Genocide and Modernity', in Omer Bartov and Phyllis Mack (eds.), *In God's Name. Genocide and Religion in the 20th Century* (Oxford: Berghahn, 2001), pp. 381–2. My emphasis.

49. See Richard Steigmann-Gall, *The Holy Reich. Nazi Conceptions of Christianity, 1919–1945* (Cambridge: Cambridge University Press, 2003).

50. Timothy Ryback, 'Hitler's Forgotten Library: The Man, His Books, and His Search for God', *The Atlantic Monthly* 291.4 (May 2003), p. 88. Ryback's findings are broadly consistent with the extensive analysis of Hitler's conception of God in Michael Rißmann, *Hitlers Gott. Vorsehungsglaube und Sendungsbewußtsein des deutschen Diktators* (Zurich: Pendo, 2001), which is revealed as the essentially pagan – and certainly un-Christian – one of a providential force who had charged him with the mission to bring about the rebirth of the German race.

51. Hugh Trevor-Roper, 'The Phenomenon of Fascism', in Stuart Woolf (ed.), *European Fascism* (London: 1968), p. 55.

52. Eberhard Jäckel, *Hitler's World View. A Blueprint for Power* (Cambridge, MA: Harvard University Press, 1981).

53. See above Chapter 3, p. 98.

54. Adolf Hitler, *Mein Kampf* (London: Pimlico, 1992), volume I, chapter 10, 'The Causes of the Collapse', p. 235.

55. See Wolfgang Weber and Paula Black, 'Muscular *Anschluss*. German Bodies and Austrian Imitators', in Joseph Mangan (ed.), *Shaping the Superman. Fascist Body as Political Icon. 'Aryan' Fascism* (Portland: Frank Cass, 1999), pp. 62–81.

56. For a penetrating overview of what this school reform meant in practice in the context of the Nazi attempt to create a new type of German see particularly Richard Evans, *The Third Reich in Power 1933–1939* (London: Allen Lane, 2005), pp. 220–320.

57. Hitler, *Mein Kampf*, volume 1, chapter 9, 'The "German Workers' Party"', pp. 197–204.

58. Victor Turner, 'Variations on a Theme of Liminality', in Sally F. Moore and Barbara G. Myerhoff (eds.), *Secular Ritual: Forms and Meaning* (Assen, Netherlands: Van Gorcum, 1977), p. 48. My emphasis.

59. Ian Kershaw, *Hitler. 1889–1936: Hubris* (New York: W.W. Norton, 1998); *Hitler 1936–1945. Nemesis* (New York: W.W. Norton, 2000).

60. Michael Burleigh, *The Third Reich. A New History* (London: Macmillan, 2000).

61. Richard Evans, *The Coming of the Third Reich* (London: Allen Lane, 2004); *The Third Reich in Power 1933–1939* (London: Allen Lane, 2005). These are the first two volumes of a trilogy.

62. For an overview of these debates see Ian Kershaw, *The Nazi Dictatorship* (London: Arnold, 2000).

63. Rainer Zitelmann, *Hitler. Selbstverständnis eines Revolutionärs* (Stuttgart: Klett-Cotta, 1986).

64. For Kershaw's summary of the debate and his own summing up see Kershaw, *The Nazi Dictatorship*, pp. 243–8.

65. Peter Fritzsche, 'Nazi Modern', *Modernism/Modernity* 3.1 (1996), p. 3.

66. Ibid., p. 12.

67. Ibid., p. 11.

68. Ibid., p. 6.

69. Ibid., p. 14.

70. Peter Fritzsche, 'Machine Dreams. Airmindedness and the Reinvention of Germany', *The American Historical Review* 98.3 (June 1993), pp. 707–9.

71. Robert Proctor, *The Nazi War on Cancer* (Princeton, NJ: Princeton University Press, 2000).

72. Robert Proctor, *Racial Hygiene. Medicine under the Nazis* (Cambridge, MA: Harvard University Press, 1988).

73. Anson Rabinbach, 'The Aesthetics of Production in the Third Reich', *Journal of Contemporary History* 11.4 (1976), pp. 43–74.

74. Proctor, *The Nazi War on Cancer*.

75. Edwin Black, *IBM and the Holocaust* (New York: Crown Publishers, 2001).

76. Alfred Mierzejewski, *Hitler's Trains. The German National Railway and the Third Reich* (Chapel Hill: University of North Carolina Press, 2000).

77. Franciszek Piper, 'Gas Chambers and Crematoria', in Yisrael Gutman and Michael Berenbaum (eds.), *Anatomy of the Auschwitz Death Camp* (Bloomington: Indiana University Press, 1994).

78. Such crimes were, of course, paralleled in the totalitarian societies established in initially less industrially developed non-Western societies elsewhere in the twentieth century, namely Russia, Japan, China, and Cambodia, in the pursuit of other perverted utopias of national renewal.

79. Eksteins, *Rites of Spring*, pp. 80–90.

80. Ibid., p. xvi. Eksteins is writing in the twentieth century.

81. George Mosse, *The Nationalization of the Masses* (New York: Howard Fertig, 1975).

82. George Mosse, *The Crisis of German Ideology. Intellectual Origins of the Third Reich* (New York: Howard Fertig, 1964).

83. See Fritz Stern, *The Politics of Cultural Despair* (California: University of California Press, 1974).

84. Max Nordau devotes a chapter to portraying the Wagner cult as a symptom of moral decay in *Degeneration* (1892).

85. In *The Scientific Origin of National Socialism* (New York: American Elsevier, 1971), Daniel Gasman rightly sees the roots of both Haeckel's monism and Nazi ideology in the late nineteenth-century revolt against decadence and positivism, but is deeply misleading in his monocausal insistence that Nazism is to be largely understood as the implementation of Monism, the same reductionism that mars its companion volume *Haeckel's Monism and the Birth of Fascist Ideology* (New York: Peter Lang, 1998).

86. On the sexual emancipation fostered by the Third Reich as a continuation of this aspect of Weimar Germany see Dagmar Herzog, 'Sex and Secularisation in Nazi Germany', in Angelica Fenner and Eric Weitz (eds.), *Fascism and Neofascism. Critical Writings on the Radical Right in Europe* (New York: Palgrave Macmillan, 2004), pp. 103–23. The article focuses on the role of Nazism in encouraging sexual liberation as part of a general celebration of bodily pleasure and vitalism, so that the majority of the 'Aryan' population experienced life under the Third Reich as a time when the 'general liberalization of heterosexual mores' was 'progressing further and accelerating' (p. 117). In defending the principle of giving illegitimate offspring the same rights as legitimate ones, the jurist Dr Rudolf Bechert wrote a celebration of sexual love in an article for the law periodical where he states 'Love is the only true religious experience in the world'. *Deutsches Recht*, nos. 23/24 (15 December 1936), p. 106.

87. See Carl Schorske, *Fin-de-Siècle Vienna. Politics and Culture* (New York: Vintage Books, 1981); Robert Pynsent (ed.), *Decadence and Innovation. Austria-Hungary in the Fin-De-Siècle* (London: Weidenfeld, 1989).

88. See Peter Pulzer, *The Rise of Political Anti-Semitism in Germany and Austria* (London: Peter Halban, 1987).

89. See Roland Stromberg, *Redemption through War. The Intellectuals and 1914* (Lawrence: Regents Press of Kansas, 1982); George Mosse, *Fallen Soldiers. Reshaping the Memory of the World Wars* (New York: Oxford University Press, 1990), chapter 4, 'Youth and the War Experience', pp. 53–69; Eksteins, *Rites of Spring*, pp. 90–4.

90. Fritzsche, 'Nazi Modern', p. 13.

91. Ibid., p. 15. Fritzsche cites Ernst Bloch and Carl Schmitt.

92. Mosse, *Fallen Soldiers*, p. 106. My emphasis.

93. Kershaw, *Hitler. 1889–1936: Hubris*, p. 317.

94. Fest, *Der zerstörte Traum*, pp. 42–3. See also Detlev Peukert, *The Weimar Republic. The Crisis of Classical Modernity* (New York: Hill and Wang, 1989).

95. Kershaw, 'Hitler and the Uniqueness of Nazism', p. 247. For a recent overview of the debate on the relevance of the concept 'political religion' to Nazism see Klaus Vondung, 'National Socialism as a Political Religion. Potentials and Limits of an Analytical Concept', *Totalitarian Movements & Political Religions* 6.1 (2005). Kershaw surely underestimates

the strength of 'pseudo-religious elements' in other forms of fascist nationalism, notably the Romanian Iron Guard. He also presents Nazism's 'modern state system' based on ideas of a 'mission' (*Sendung*) to bring about 'salvation' (*Rettung*) or 'redemption' (*Erlösung*) as unique to Germany. This is to ignore its significant parallels to the no less 'modern' and *modernist* states being created in contemporary Fascist Italy and Bolshevik Russia.

96. See Richard Evans, *The Coming of the Third Reich*, chapter 6, 'Hitler's Cultural Revolution', p. 461. Cf. Kershaw, *The Nazi Dictatorship*, pp. 172–82.

97. See above, Chapter 8, p. 225.

98. See above, Chapter 6, p. 180. An example of a major 'empirical' history of the Third Reich which does emphasize the relevance of the concept 'political religion' is Burleigh, *The Third Reich*. See pp. 9–14; 252–67.

99. Klaus Vondung, *Magie und Manipulation. Ideologischer Kult und politische Religion des Nationalsozialismus* (Göttingen: Vandenhoeck & Ruprecht, 1971), pp. 159–71. The thrust of Vondung's argument is summarized in, 'Spiritual Revolution and Magic: Speculation and Political Action in National Socialism', *Modern Age* 23.4 (1979).

100. Evans, *The Third Reich in Power 1933–1939*, p. 503.

101. Ian Kershaw, *The Hitler Myth* (Oxford: Oxford University Press, 1987), p. 26. For further first-hand testimonies of the power of the Hitler cult see Guido Kopp and Peter Hartl, 'Der Verführer', in Guido Kopp (ed.), *Hitler. Eine Bilanz* (Berlin: Siedler, 1995), pp. 31–90.

102. The argument of James Rhodes, *The Hitler Movement: A Modern Millenarian Revolution* (Stanford, CA: Hoover Institute Press, 1980).

103. Steigmann-Gall, *Holy Reich*.

104. Ibid.

105. Bärsch, *Die politische Religion des National-Sozialismus*.

106. Richard Fenn, *The End of Time* (Cleveland, OH: Pilgrim Press, 1997), pp. 7–10.

107. Anthony Stevens, *Ariadne's Clue. A Guide to the Symbols of Humankind* (London: Penguin, 1998), p. 85.

108. Ibid., p. 86.

109. Ibid.

110. Ibid.

111. Ian Boyd Whyte, 'Berlin, 1 May 1936', in Dawn Ades (et al.), *Art and Power: Europe under the Dictators 1930–45*, exhibition catalogue to 23rd Council of Europe Exhibition (Hayward Gallery, London, 1996), pp. 43–9.

112. William Niven, 'The Birth of Nazi Drama? *Thing* Plays', in John London (ed.), *Theatre under the Nazis* (Manchester: Manchester University Press, 2000), pp. 54–95.

113. See the section on the Galungan ceremony on Bali in Chapter 3, p. 84.

114. Jost Hermand and James Steakley, *Heimat, Nation, Fatherland (The German Sense of Belonging)* (New York: Peter Lang, 1996).

115. Jost Hermand, *Old Dreams of a New Reich. Volkish Utopias and National Socialism* (Bloomington: Indiana University Press, 1992), pp. 171–207.

116. Speech made by Hitler at the Nuremberg Party Rally on 6 September 1938 and archived at http://www.hitler.org/speeches/09-06-38.html (accessed 05/07/06).

117. Cited in Kershaw, *The Hitler Myth*, p. 72.

118. Kershaw, *The Hitler Myth*, p. 53.

119. Ibid., p. 66.

120. Kopp, *Hitler*, pp. 71, 67.

121. Kershaw, *Hitler. 1889–1936: Hubris*, p. 433. My emphasis.

122. Ibid., p. 432.

123. Statement attributed to Hitler after giving a speech to the conservative revolutionary Juni-Klub in 1922, when suggesting to Moeller van den Bruck they should join forces in the struggle for a new Germany. Quoted by Kershaw, *Hitler. 1889–1936: Hubris*, p. 168.

124. Albrecht Tyrell, *Vom ‚Trommler' zum ‚Führer'. Der Wandel von Hitlers Selbstverständnis zwischen 1919 und 1924 und die Entwicklung der NSDAP* (Munich: Fink, 1975). See also Kershaw, *Hitler. 1889–1936: Hubris*, chapter 6, pp. 167–219: 'The Drummer'.

125. On the connection between drumming, trance-states, and shamanism see, for example, Tim Hodgkinson, 'Improvised Music and Siberian Shamanism', *Contemporary Music Review* 14.1–2 (1996), pp. 59–66.

126. On the impact of Scheerbart's modernist theories of architecture on Speer's cathedral of light see the doctorate by Anne Krauter, *Die Schriften Paul Scheerbarts und der Lichtdom von Albert Speer – 'Das große Licht'* (Heidelberg University, 1997, URN: urn:nbn:de: bsz:16-opus-49031), available at http://www.ub.uni-heidelberg.de/archiv/4903/ (accessed 30/11/06).

10 THE MODERNISM OF NAZI CULTURE

1. Peter Fritzsche, 'Nazi Modern', *Modernism/modernity* 3.1 (1996), pp. 1–21.
2. Richard Evans, *The Third Reich in Power 1933–1939* (London: Allen Lane, 2005), p. 708.
3. Adolf Hitler, *Mein Kampf*, trans. Ralph Mannheim (London: Pimlico, 1992), p. 114.
4. Ian Kershaw, *Hitler. 1889–1936: Hubris* (New York: W. W. Norton, 1998), pp. 30–1.
5. On Vienna's remarkable contribution to European modernism see Allan Janik and Stephen Toulmin, *Wittgenstein's Vienna* (Chicago: Ivan R. Dee, 1996).
6. Carl Schorske, 'Politics in a New Key. An Austrian Trio', in *Fin-de-Siècle Vienna. Politics and Culture* (New York: Vintage Books, 1981).
7. Brigitte Hamann, *Hitler's Vienna* (Oxford: Oxford University Press, 2000), pp. 78–82.
8. Ibid., p. 66.
9. Paul Reitter, 'Hitler's Viennese Waltz', *The Nation* (9 August 1999).
10. See particularly Hamann, *Hitler's Vienna*, chapter 7, 'Theoreticians of Race and Explainers of the World'; chapter 8, 'Political Role Models'.
11. Ibid., p. 406. Original emphasis: used to indicate phrases cited from Hitler, *Mein Kampf*, volume 2, chapter 1, p. 339.
12. Ibid., p. 21.
13. Hitler, *Mein Kampf*, pp. 27–8.
14. The 'scene' is dramatized in Oliver Hirschbiegel's film *Der Untergang* (2004), adapted from Joachim Fest's book of the same name.
15. See above Chapter 3, p. 98.
16. Hitler, *Mein Kampf*, p. 28.
17. Kershaw refers to the speech in *Hitler. 1889–1936: Hubris*, p. 529. The reference he gives is Niedersächsisches Staatsarchiv, Oldenburg, Best. 131, Nr. 303, Fol. 131v.
18. Cited in Guido Knopp and Peter Hartl, 'Der Verführer', in Guido Knopp (ed.), *Hitler. Eine Bilanz* (Berlin: Siedler, 1995), p. 76. My emphasis.
19. There are intriguing parallels between Broch's concept of the 'ideal centre' of a culture and the role attributed to the 'Absolute Centre' in the dynamics of cultural hegemony by Louis Althusser's 'Lacanian' theory of ideology. See his *Essays on Ideology* (London, New York: Verso, 1971), p. 54.
20. Richard Etlin, 'Introduction. The *Perverse* Logic of Nazi Thought', in Richard Etlin (ed.), *Art, Culture, and Media under the Third Reich* (Chicago: The University Press of Chicago, 2002), p. 9.
21. For readers without a reading knowledge of German, Detlef Mühlberger's two-volume thematic anthology of texts, *Hitler's Voice. Der völkische Beobachter. 1920–1933* (Bern: Peter Lang, 2004) offers an important introduction to the ideological dynamics of Nazism as a transclass *movement* of national renewal, emphasizing how fallacious it would be to reduce Nazi thought to the ideology of its principal leaders, let alone solely to Hitler's.
22. Dietrich Loder, 'Die Krankheit der deutschen Kultur', *Völkischer Beobachter*, issue 269/270, 25/26 September (1932).
23. Etlin, 'The *Perverse* Logic of Nazi Thought', pp. 11–12.

24. Karl Willy Straub, *Die Architektur im Dritten Reich* (Stuttgart: Akademischer Verlag Wedekind, 1932).

25. Stephanie Barron, *Degenerate Art. The Fate of the Avant-garde in Nazi Germany* (Los Angeles: Los Angeles County Museum, 1991).

26. This is borne out by the numerous articles on art, aesthetics, and culture that appeared in the *Völkischer Beobachter* during the '*Kampfzeit*', e.g. 3 March 1921; 28 Jan. 1928; 27 April 1929; 11 April 1930; 22 Oct. 1930; 3 June 1931; 21 Feb. 1931; 7 Oct. 1931; 14 July 1932; 25–26 Sept. 1932; 4 Nov. 1932. My thanks to Detlef Mühlberger for generously providing this data.

27. Peter Adam, *Arts of the Third Reich* (New York: Harry N. Abrams, 1992), p. 9.

28. The extraordinary scale of the Third Reich's systematic pillage of occupied Europe's artistic legacy has been painstakingly documented in Lynn Nicholas, *The Rape of Europa* (New York: Vintage Books, 1995), and by Jonathan Petropoulos, *Art as Politics in the Third Reich* (Chapel Hill: University of North Carolina Press, 1996). Both underline the endemic greed and corruption of the Third Reich which is integral to the gap between the ideals of the Nazi *Weltanschauung* and the personal morality of many Nazis, another aspect of the impossibility of realizing its utopia that doomed the enterprise from the outset.

29. See David Freedberg, *The Power of Images. Studies in the History and Theory of Response* (Chicago: The University of Chicago Press, 1989).

30. A major expression of the Nazis' image of themselves as the cultural purifiers not just of Germany but of Aryan Europe is to be found in Christoph Steding, *Das Reich und die Krankheit Europas* (Hamburg: Hanseatische Verlagsanstalt, 1938).

31. Hitler, *Mein Kampf*, p. 263.

32. Ibid., pp. 412–13. It is worth noting that 'fanatical' has exclusively positive connotations in *Mein Kampf* and derives from the Latin 'fanum', temple, which gives the word 'profane' (outside the temple). The faith in the rebirth of the organic nation that Hitler calls thus has elements of a 'holy war'.

33. Eric Michaud, 'National Socialist Architecture as an Acceleration of Time', *Critical Enquiry* 19 (Winter 1993), p. 224. For a more sustained exposition of his analysis of the Nazis' aestheticized concept of temporalized immortality see Eric Michaud, *The Cult of Art in Nazi Germany* (1996) (Stanford, CA: Stanford University Press, 2004). Here the author offers a highly sophisticated 'synoptic interpretation' of the Nazi project to transform German society through the power of art and its 'political theology' of redemption from decadence, examined through the lens of cultural history. It contains intriguing points of convergence and contrast with the thesis of fascist modernism developed in this book (which space precludes from discussing here), revealing fascinating resonances between the 'cleansing', palingenetic function of Nazi art, ritual, and eugenics. It also offers extensive independent corroboration of the thesis that Nazism sought to use the power of art and culture to mediate the experience of a transcendent *aevum*, an 'eternal present' which would liberate Germans from the clutches of Cronus.

34. Saul Friedländer, *Reflections of Nazism. An Essay on Kitsch and Death* (New York: Harper & Row, 1984).

35. Ulrich Schmid, 'Towards a Conceptualisation of Fascist Aesthetics', *Totalitarian Movements and Political Religions* 6.1 (June 2005), p. 139. My emphasis.

36. Peter Osborne, *Philosophy in Cultural Theory* (London: Routledge, 2000), pp. 60–1.

37. Mark Antliff, 'Fascism, Modernism, and Modernity', *The Art Bulletin* 84 (2002), pp. 150–1.

38. Evans, *The Third Reich in Power*, p. 708.

39. Ibid., p. 501.

40. Frederic Spotts, *Hitler and the Power of Aesthetics* (London: Pimlico, 2000), p. 387.

41. Ibid., p. 393.

42. Ibid., p. xii.

43. See Michaud, *The Cult of Art in Nazi Germany*, pp. 4–5, 34–5, where Hitler is portrayed in the persona of the Christ-artist moulding Germans into a new race. Cf. also Simonetta Falasca-Zamponi, *Fascist Spectacle. The Aesthetics of Power in Fascist Italy* (Berkeley: University of California Press, 1997), p. 13, which describes Mussolini as a 'sculptor-leader' making the new Italians.

44. Michaud, *The Cult of Art in Nazi Germany*, p. 15. The source of Hitler's remark is not given.

45. Gregory Maertz's radical major re-evaluation of Nazi art history on the basis of the wealth of new paintings he has discovered will be published in his *Hitler's List and the Real Canon of Nazi Art* (New Haven, CT: Yale University Press, forthcoming).

46. See above Chapter 5, p. 145.

47. The essays in Joseph Mangan (ed.), *Shaping the Superman. Fascist Body as Political Icon – Aryan Fascism* (Portland, OR: Frank Cass, 1999) provide a valuable survey of the centrality of the cult of the body to all fascist movements.

48. Wilfried van der Will, 'The Body and the Body Politic as Symptom and Metaphor in the Transition of German Culture to National Socialism', in Brandon Taylor and Wilfried van der Will (eds.), *The Nazification of Art* (Winchester: The Winchester Press, 1990), pp. 14–52.

49. See above, Chapter 5, p. 145.

50. An artist's impression of how the sculpture would have appeared once constructed in the median at the southern entrance to the Autobahn at Salzburg is to be found at http://www. thirdreichruins.com/ThorakDenkmalAutobahn.jpg (accessed 30/11/06). The sculpture thus expresses no nostalgia for the past, but the heroization of German construction workers, whom it transforms into modern incarnations of the reborn Aryan race with its innate capacity for creating culture and civilization. It is thus no coincidence if a 1940 poster for the latest Mercedes-Benz limousine with the slogan 'Expression of powerful beauty' appears against the background image of Thorak's maquette. See Berthold Hinz, *Art in the Third Reich* (Oxford: Basil Blackwell, 1974), p. 164.

51. E.g. Michael Kaplan, '*Degenerate Art* and the New Corporate Style', *University of Tennessee Journal of Architecture* 16 (1995), pp. 29–34.

52. Ian Boyd Whyte, 'Berlin Architecture. National Socialism and Modernism', in Dawn Ades et al., *Art and Power. Europe under the Dictators 1930–45* (London: Hayward Gallery, 1996).

53. Adam, *Art of the Third Reich*, p. 9.

54. Brandon Taylor, 'Post-modernism in the Third Reich', in Taylor and van der Will, *The Nazification of Art*, pp. 135–41.

55. Norman Baynes (ed.), *The Speeches of Adolf Hitler, April 1922–August 1939*, 2 vols (London: Oxford University Press , 1942), volume 1, pp. 587–91.

56. On the plurality of styles used in Nazi building see Adam, *Art of the Third Reich*, pp. 206–99.

57. Hartmut Frank, 'Bridges: Paul Bonatz's Search for a Contemporary Monumental Style', in Taylor and van der Will, *The Nazification of Art*, pp. 144–57.

58. Whyte, 'Berlin Architecture', p. 261.

59. Cited in Werner Durth, 'Architektur und Stadtplanung im Dritten Reich', in Michael Prinz and Rainer Zitelmann (eds.), *Nationalsozialismus und Modernisierung* (Darmstadt: Wissenschaftliche Buchgesellschaft, 1991), p. 139.

60. Ibid., p. 151.

61. Ibid.

62. See Elaine S. Hochman, *Architects of Fortune. Mies van der Rohe and the Third Reich* (New York: Fromm International Publishing Corporation, 1990).

63. Friedrich Tamms expounds his 'Law of the Monumental' in 'Das Große in der Baukunst', *Die Baukunst* (supplement to *Die Kunst des Deutschen Reichs*), No. 8 (March 1944), p. 60.

64. Michaud, 'National Socialist Architecture as an Acceleration of Time', pp. 226–31.
65. Gustav Janouch, *Conversations with Kafka* (London: Quartet Books, 1985), p. 143.
66. Michael Kater, *Different Drummers. Jazz in the Culture of Nazi Germany* (Oxford: Oxford University Press, 1992); Mike Zwerin, *Swing under the Nazis. Jazz as a Metaphor for Freedom* (New York: Cooper Square Press, 2000).
67. Michael Kater, *The Twisted Muse. Musicians and their Music in the Third Reich* (Oxford: Oxford University Press, 1997), p. 189.
68. Erik Levi, 'Opera in the Nazi Period', in John London (ed.), *Theatre under the Nazis* (Manchester: Manchester University Press, 2000), pp. 136–86.
69. In *Holy Reich. Nazi Conceptions of Christianity, 1919–1945* (Cambridge: Cambridge University Press, 2003), Richard Steigmann-Gall attempts to substantiate the thesis that there was considerable substance to Nazi claims to represent a 'positive Christianity'. However, his arguments have been exposed to detailed scholarly critique in four articles published in the issue of *The Journal of Contemporary History* 42.1 (January 2007) devoted to a debate on 'Nazism, Christianity and Political Religion', all of which employ scrupulous documentation to show that at its core Nazism was profoundly hostile to and incompatible with Christian metaphysics, ethics, and soteriology. It strove towards representing to 'Aryanized' Germans not a 'positive' Christianity, but an alternative religion to Christianity.
70. See http://www.djangomontreal.com/doc/Pictures.htm (accessed 17/10/06).
71. Kater, *The Twisted Muse*, p. 177.
72. See Erik Levi, 'Music and National Socialism. The Politicization of Criticism, Composition, and Performance', in Taylor and van der Will, *The Nazification of Art*, pp. 158–82.
73. E.g. one reviewer of Brigitte Hamann, *Winifred Wagner. A Life at the Heart of Hitler's Bayreuth* (London: Granta Books, 2005) called his piece 'A Window on Despotism and the Mind of the Reactionary'.
74. Max Nordau, *Degeneration*, Vol. 2 (New York: D. Appleton, 1895), Chapter 5, 'The Richard Wagner Cult', p. 171
75. Robert Gooding-Williams, *Zarathustra's Dionysian Modernism* (Stanford, CA: Stanford University Press, 2001), pp. 103. On the celebration of Wagner's music as a vehicle of Germany's redemption from decadence and Bayreuth as 'the site of artistic regeneration' see Walter Frisch, 'Ambivalent Modernism. Perspectives from the 1870s and 1880s', in *German Modernism. Music and the Arts* (Berkeley: University of California Press, 2005), pp. 15–28.
76. Friedrich Nietzsche, Preface to *The Case of Wagner* (New York: Vintage Books, 1967), p. 156.
77. Walter Frisch, 'Ambivalent Modernism', p. 9.
78. Ibid., p. 8.
79. Frisch takes this concept from Marion Deshmukh, 'Cultural Migration. Artists and Visual Representation between Americans and Germans during the 1930s and 1940s', in David Barclay (ed.), *Transatlantic Images and Perceptions. Germany and America since 1776* (London: Cambridge, 1997).
80. Kevin Repp develops this theory in *Reformers, Critics, and the Paths of German Modernity. Anti-Politics and the Search for Alternatives, 1890–1914* (Cambridge, MA: Harvard University Press, 2000).
81. David Large and William Weber (eds.), *Wagnerism in European Culture and Politics* (Ithaca, NY: Cornell University Press, 1984).
82. Rosamund Bartlett, *Wagner and Russian Modernism* (Cambridge: Cambridge University Press, 1995).
83. The twin polarity of the human psyche postulated by Freudian psychoanalysis.
84. Dieter Borchmeyer, *Drama and the World of Richard Wagner* (Princeton, NJ: Princeton University Press, 2003), p. 312.

85. In his *Rites of Spring* (1989) (Boston: Houghton Mifflin, 2000), Modris Eksteins treats *Le Sacre du printemps* as the epitome of modernism and the adumbration of the cataclysmic events to follow soon after its first performance.

86. Kater, *The Twisted Muse*, p. 76.

87. See Fania Fénélon with Marcelle Routier, *Playing for Time* (New York: Atheneum, 1977). The Viktor Ullmann Foundation preserves the memory of the music performed in Theresienstadt Concentration Camp and of the musicians who performed it. Ullmann himself, a student of Schoenberg, was deported to Poland and gassed in Auschwitz in October of 1944, along with a large number of the other musicians who performed at Theresienstadt.

88. Helmut Langenbucher, *Volkhafte Dichtung der Zeit* (Berlin: Junker und Dünnhaupt, 1937), p. 11.

89. See the website at http://library.albany.edu/speccoll/emigre.htm (accessed 17/10/06).

90. On the complex relationship of these two outstanding authors with Nazism and post-war fascism see Russell A. Berman, 'Gottfried Benn. A Double Life in Uninhabitable Regions', in Richard Golsan (ed.), *Fascism, Aesthetics and Culture* (Hanover, NH: University Press of New England, 1992), pp. 67–80; Elliot Neaman, 'Ernst Jünger's Millennium. Bad Citizens for the New Century', in Richard Golsan (ed.), *Fascism's Return: Scandal, Revision, and Ideology since 1980* (Lincoln, NE: University of Nebraska Press, 1998).

91. The vast and complex topic of the Nazi appropriation and retooling of German literature is covered by such works as Ernst Loewy, *Literatur unterm Hakenkreuz. Das Dritte Reich und seine Dichtung. Eine Dokumentation* (Frankfurt am Main: Europäische Verlagsanstalt, 1966); Hans Sarkowicz and Alf Mentzer, *Literatur in Nazi-Deutschland. Ein biografisches Lexikon* (Hamburg: Europa, 2002). See also George Mosse, *Masses and Man. Nationalist and Fascist Perceptions of Reality* (New York: Howard Fertig, 1980), chapter 3, 'What Germans Really Read'.

92. On Nazi theatre see Günter Berghaus (ed.), *Fascism and Theatre* (Oxford: Berghahn, 1996), chapters 2, 8, 9, 10; John London (ed.), *Theatre under the Nazis* (Manchester: Manchester University Press, 2000).

93. Not legally published till 1981, the novel formed the basis of István Szabó's 1982 film of the same name.

94. Hanns Johst, *Ich glaube! Bekenntnisse* (Munich: A. Langen, 1928), p. 73, in Günter Berghaus's 'The Ritual Core of Fascist Theatre', in Berghaus, *Fascism and Theatre*, p. 52. The essay is important for its exploration of the anthropological dimension of the fascist concept of theatre which has profound analogies with the theory of modernism developed here.

95. Hanns Johst, *Der junge Mensch. Ein ekstatisches Szenarium* (Munich: Delphin, 1916).

96. William Niven, 'The Birth of Nazi Drama?: Thing Plays', in London, *Theatre under the Nazis*, pp. 54–95.

97. This lineage is analysed in Manfred Frank, 'Vom Bühnenweihefestspiel zum Thingspiel. Zur Wirkungsgeschichte der neuen Mythologie bei Nietzsche, Wagner und Johst', in W. Haug and R. Warning (eds.), *Das Fest* (Munich: Fink, 1989), pp. 573–601.

98. This episode is related in Peter Kemp, *The Strauss Family: Portrait of a Musical Dynasty* (Tunbridge Wells: Baton Press, 1985).

99. Marion Kant, 'The Nazi Attempt to Suppress Jazz and Swing', in Lilian Karina and Marion Kant (eds.), *Hitler's Dancers. German Modern Dance and the Third Reich* (Oxford: Berghahn, 2003), part III, pp. 167–90.

100. Karina and Kant, *Hitler's Dancers*, p. 118.

101. Ibid., pp. 117–121. Cf. Karl Topfer, *Empire of the Senses* (Berkeley: University of California Press, 1997), p. 315.

102. On the place of this film in the 'euthanasia' programme see Mark Mostert, 'Useless Eaters. Disability as Genocidal Marker in Nazi Germany', *The Journal of Special Education* 36.3 (1 October 2002), pp. 157–70.

103. Eric Rentschler, *The Ministry of Illusion. Nazi Cinema and its Afterlife* (Cambridge, MA: Harvard University Press, 1996), p. 57.

104. In *Entertaining the Third Reich* (Durham, NC: Duke University Press, 1996), Linda Schulte-Sass explores the way Nazi films used cinematic techniques to create the aesthetic illusion of wholeness. Such an illusion was crucial to articulating and normalizing its vast project to construct an alternative modernity, and drew on an artistic and technical creativity manifested throughout the cinema industry that could never have been simply 'dictated' from above.

105. Reflexivity's deep structural link to high modernity is a theme developed in Anthony Giddens, *The Consequences of Modernity* (Cambridge: Polity Press, 1991).

106. George Mosse (ed.), *Nazi Culture. Intellectual, Cultural and Social Life in the Third Reich* (New York: Grosset and Dunlap, 1966).

107. Speech of 18 July 1937, Baynes, *The Speeches of Adolf Hitler*, volume 1, pp. 584–92. The German original appeared in *Völkischer Beobachter*, 19 July 1937.

108. Gottfried Benn, 'Züchtung I' (1933), in Dieter Wellerhoff (ed.), *Gottfried Benn. Gesammelte Werke in acht Bänden* (Wiesbaden: Limes, 1968), volume 3, p. 784.

109. Ernst Jünger, *Der Arbeiter*, in *Ernst Jünger. Sämtliche Werke*, Essays. volume 2 (1932) (Stuttgart: Klett-Cotta, 1981), pp. 249–50.

110. Julius Evola, *Il Cammino del Cinabro* (Milan: Vanni Scheiwiller, 1972), p. 192.

111. Guillaume Faye, *L'Archéofuturisme* (Paris: L'Æncre, 1998).

112. Evola, *Il Cammino del Cinabro*, p. 100.

11 THE THIRD REICH'S BIOPOLITICAL MODERNISM

1. Cited in David Blackbourn, *The Conquest of Nature. Water, Landscape and the Making of Modern Germany* (London: Jonathan Cape, 2006), p. 262.

2. Dr Paul Karlson, 'Können Maschinen denken?', *Koralle. Zeitschrift für Unterhaltung, Wissen, Lebensfreude* 9.20 (18 May 1941), pp. 528–30.

3. David Kahn, *Seizing the Enigma. The Race to Break the German U-boat Codes 1939–1943* (London: Arrow Books, 1996).

4. Edwin Black, *IBM and the Holocaust. The Strategic Alliance between Nazi Germany and America's Most Powerful Corporation* (New York: Crown Books, 2001), pp. 352–3.

5. Henry Turner, 'Fascism and Modernization', in H. A. Turner (ed.), *Reappraisals of Fascism* (New York: Franklin Watts, 1976), p. 131.

6. See Christopher Wilk (ed.), *Modernism 1914–1939. Designing a New World* (London: V&A Publications, 2006).

7. This is the term applied to the Third Reich in Michael Burleigh and Wolfgang Wippermann, *The Racial State* (Cambridge: Cambridge University Press, 1991). The authors see Nazi racial policies as 'anti-modern', and question the heuristic value to their analysis of 'existing theories, whether based upon modernisation, totalitarianism, or global theories of Fascism'. Hopefully this book will encourage them to rethink their position on both counts.

8. Eric Rentschler, *The Ministry of Illusion. Nazi Cinema and its Afterlife* (Cambridge, MA: Harvard University Press, 1996), chapter 3, 'Home Sweet *Heimat*', pp. 73–96.

9. Oliver Axer and Susanne Benze, *Hitler's Hit Parade* (Bad Schwartau: C. Cay Wesnigk Filmproducktion, 2003). The sequence runs from 1'53" to 2'52".

10. Ibid. The sequence runs from approximately 49 to 52 minutes. On the role of the Reichsbahn under Nazism see Alfred Miercejewski, *Hitler's Trains. The German National Railway and the Third Reich* (Chapel Hill: University of North Carolina Press, 2000).

11. Axer and Benze, *Hitler's Hit Parade*, approximately 66 to 68 minutes. When the trade name comes into view the voice-over claims that 'With hydrocyanic acid you can gas even big factories without any damage to man or material.' On Zyklon B's part in the extermination

programme see Paul Weindling, *Epidemics and Genocide in Eastern Europe, 1890–1945* (New York: Oxford University Press, 2000), pp. 111–38.

12. Irene Guenther, *Nazi Chic. Fashioning Women in the Third Reich* (Oxford: Berg, 2004), chapter 6, 'Germany's National Fashion Institute', pp. 167–210. The semiotic recoding of the potentially decadent as healthy that this involved is a phenomenon familiar in the history of modern architecture, where the International Style of architecture flourishing under liberal capitalism was nationalized by Fascism to express the values of the Third Rome. Similarly Stalin saw to it that New York's Municipal Building became the template for the Moscow University, a key institution in producing the new technocratic and political class of Soviet Russia. See Vladimir Paperny, *Architecture in the Age of Stalin* (Cambridge: Cambridge University Press, 2002), which offers a reappraisal of Stalin's abandonment of avant-garde architecture which shows that he retained modernist elements in his view of culture.

13. Guenther, *Nazi Chic*, p. 265.

14. Marcel Schwierin (director), *Ewige Schönheit* (Good Morning/New Vision, EAN 878658, 1993).

15. Axer and Benze, *Hitler's Hit Parade*.

16. John Heskett, 'Modernism and Archaism in Design in the Third Reich', in Brandon Taylor and Wilfried van der Will (eds.), *The Nazification of Art* (Winchester: The Winchester Press, 1990), pp. 110–27.

17. See the documentary Michael Kloft (director), *Television under the Swastika. The History of Nazi Television* (Chicago: International Historic Films Inc., 2001).

18. One of numerous snippets of Hitler's conversations with his entourage made in 'home movies' filmed at his retreat at the Berghof in the Bavarian Alps and deciphered by new lip-reading software. They were first made known to the English-speaking public in the documentary *Hitler's Private Life Revealed*, shown on the UK's Channel 5 on 29 November 2006.

19. They were the work of Herbert Bayer, who in the 1920s had taught design at the Bauhaus in Dessau and been art director for *Vogue* in Paris. The inclusion of his work in the 'Degenerate Art Exhibition' of 1937 prompted his emigration to the US in 1938. The striking poster can be seen at http://www.ikg.uni-karlsruhe.de/projekte/exilarchitekten/architekten/bilder/bayer_2gross.jpg (accessed 30/11/06).

20. See Guenther, *Nazi Chic*, pp. 252–63.

21. Ibid., pp. 4–6.

22. A phrase popularized by Jeffrey Herf in his *Reactionary Modernism. Technology, Culture, and Politics in Weimar and the Third Reich* (New York: Cambridge University Press, 1984).

23. Adolf Hitler, *Mein Kampf*, trans. Ralph Mannheim (London: Pimlico, 1992), p. 263.

24. Otto Bangert, no title, *Der Völkischer Beobachter* 150 (3 July 1926), in Detlef Mühlberger (ed.), *Hitler's Voice. The Völkischer Beobachter, 1920–1933*, 2 vols. (Bern: Peter Lang, 2004), vol. 1, p. 243.

25. Albert Speer, *Inside the Third Reich* (New York: Simon & Schuster, 1970).

26. Ronald Smelser, *Robert Ley. Hitler's Labour Front Leader* (Oxford: Berg, 1988), pp. 305–6.

27. Robert Pois, *National Socialism and the Religion of Nature* (London: Croom Helm, 1986). See also Chapter 5, p. 143.

28. Daniel Gasman drastically exaggerates the direct influence on Nazism of Ernst Haeckel's philosophy of Monism in *The Scientific Origins of National Socialism* (New York: American Elsevier, 1971). However, as we argued in Chapter 5, the this-worldly, philosophically monist life-mysticism that informed it was certainly an all-pervasive ingredient in the multi-faceted European revolt against positivism, materialism, and decadence between 1880 and 1945, and played a central role in the Nazi *Weltanschauung* independently of the philosophy of any one thinker. On the erroneous tendency to equate National Socialism with Social

Darwinism, see Paul Weindling, 'Dissecting German Social Darwinism. Historicizing the Biology of the Organic State', *Science in Context* 11 (1998), pp. 619–37.

29. Franz Pfeffer von Salomon, '"Zucht". Eine Forderung zum Programm', memorandum for 'top leaders of the NSDAP', Christmas 1925, NSDAP Hauptarchiv, (Hoover Institution Microfilm Collection), Reel, 44, Folder 896, p. 11. An excerpt of the memorandum is reproduced in Roger Griffin, *Fascism* (Oxford: Oxford University Press, 1995), pp. 118–19.

30. See Chapter 10, p. 283.

31. Iain Boyd Whyte, 'Berlin, 1 May 1936', in Dawn Ades et al. (eds.), *Art and Power. Europe under the Dictators, 1930–45* (London: Hayward Gallery, 1995), pp. 43–9.

32. F. W. Heath (ed.), *A Churchill Anthology* (London: Odhams Books, 1962), p. 679.

33. E.g. Frank McDonough, *Opposition and Resistance in Nazi Germany* (Cambridge: Cambridge University Press, 2001).

34. Gitta Sereny, *Albert Speer. His Battle with the Truth* (New York: Vintage, 1995) is a sustained investigation into what she constructs as a leading Nazi's extraordinary battle with himself to 'confess' the enormity of the crimes against humanity he had committed in his service to the regime. More case studies in the moral dilemmas posed by collaboration with the regime are provided by Gitta Sereny, *The German Trauma* (London: Allen Lane, 2000). The case of Hans Münch, the 'man who said no' (pp. 262–5), would be particularly revealing of the potential of individuals to resist oppression under appalling pressure to conform, if there were not the suspicion that Münch was disingenuous in the claim he made to Sereny that he defied Nazi authority. See Weindling, *Epidemics and Genocide*, pp. 248, 253, 259, 365–7, 410.

35. Ute Deichmann, *Biologists under Hitler* (Cambridge, MA: Harvard University Press, 1996); Jonathan Petropoulos, *The Faustian Bargain. The Art World in Nazi Germany* (Oxford: Oxford University Press, 2000); Götz Aly, *Hitlers Volksstaat* (Frankfurt am Main: Fischer, 2005).

36. For an incisive account of the Nazi discourse (or Newspeak) in which it expressed its modernist projects, see Victor Klemperer, *The Language of the Third Reich: LTI, Lingua Tertii Imperii* (London: Martin Brady, Athlone, 2000).

37. Rüdiger Safranski, *Martin Heidegger. Between Good and Evil* (Cambridge, MA: Harvard University Press, 1998), p. 51.

38. Martin Heidegger, *Denkerfahrungen* (Frankfurt am Main: Vittorio Klostermann, 1983), p. 38, cited in Safranski, *Martin Heidegger*, p. 3.

39. Safranski, *Martin Heidegger*, p. 71.

40. See above Chapter 4, p. 115.

41. Safranski, *Martin Heidegger*, p. 153.

42. Ibid., pp. 91–3.

43. Ibid., p. 86.

44. Ibid., p. 146.

45. Ibid., p. 93.

46. Richard Wollin, *The Heidegger Controversy* (Cambridge, MA: The MIT Press, 1993), p. 121.

47. Cited in Matthew Feldman, 'Between *Geist* and *Zeitgeist*. Martin Heidegger as Ideologue of "Metapolitical Fascism"', *Totalitarian Movements and Political Religion* 6.2 (September 2005), p. 187.

48. Martin Heidegger, *Einführung in die Metaphysik* (Tübingen: Max Niemeyer Verlag, 1935), pp. 151–2.

49. Safranski, *Martin Heidegger*, p. 228.

50. Cf. Heidegger's post-war observation about his commitment to Nazism, namely that: 'I accepted the social and national (not national-socialist) component, but rejected its intellectual and metaphysical underpinnings in the biologism in Party doctrine, because the social and national component, as I saw it, had no essential connection with the ideological

doctrine of biological racialism.' Cited in Günther Neski and Emil Kettering (eds.), *Martin Heidegger and National Socialism* (New York: Paragon House, 1990), pp. 53–4.

51. The 'case' of Heidegger's Nazism is notoriously complex. I have drawn extensively on Safranski's interpretation of Heidegger's relationship to Nazism because of the stress it places on its cultural, non-philosophical preconditions for the philosopher's conversion is congruent with my own theory of modernism. However, some excellent works exist that supplement and qualify this account, or provide precious documentation of his thought processes, notably Hugo Ott, *Martin Heidegger: A Political Life* (New York: Basic Books, 1993); Hans Sluga, *Heidegger's Crisis: Philosophy and Politics in Nazi Germany* (Cambridge, MA: Harvard University Press, 1993); Wollin, *The Heidegger Controversy*; Tom Rockmore, *On Heidegger's Nazism and Philosophy* (Hemel Hempsted: Harvester Wheatsheaf, 1992).

52. Blackbourn. *The Conquest of Nature*. The campaign to settle the marshes also reveals the deep nexus that existed between the concerns of so-called 'green' Nazis with nature and ecology, their pursuit of racial supremacy, and their promotion of racial persecution, all of which indicate that they were devoid of ecological principles or understanding of any depth. They were thus more interested in 'blood' than in 'soil', and had no concept of the need for the biosphere to be conserved for the sake of all humankind. On this see Franz-Josef Brüggemeier et al., *How Green were the Nazis? Nature, Environment, and Nation in the Third Reich* (Ohio: Ohio University Press, 2005). For a contrasting (and explicitly revisionist) assessment of Nazism's green credentials see Anna Bramwell, *Blood and Soil: Richard Walther Darré and Hitler's 'Green Party'* (Bourne End, Buckinghamshire: Kensal Press, 1985).

53. In Goethe's play Mephistopheles makes sure the old couple, Philemon and Baucis, along with an innocent stranger, die as a direct result of Faust's action.

54. See Blackbourn, *The Conquest of Nature*, pp. 280–96: 'The Mystique of the Frontier and the "Wild East"'.

55. Ibid., p. 276.

56. See Peter Batty, *The House of Krupp* (London: Secker & Warburg, 1961).

57. See Neil Gregor, *Daimler-Benz in the Third Reich* (New Haven, CT: Yale University Press, 1998).

58. See Peter Hayes, *Industry and Ideology. IG Farben in the Nazi Era* (New York: Cambridge University Press, 1987).

59. Thomas Powers, *Heisenberg's War. The Secret History of the German Bomb* (London: Cape, 1993).

60. Smelser, *Robert Ley*, pp. 305–6.

61. Ibid., p. 22.

62. On de Man's 'planism' see Zeev Sternhell, *Neither Right nor Left* (Princeton, NJ: Princeton University Press, 1995), pp. 119–41.

63. Rolf Messerschmidt, 'Nationalsozialistische Raumforschung und Raumordnung', in Michael Prinz and Rainer Zitelmann (eds.), *Nazionalsozialismus und Modernisierung* (Darmstadt: Manfred Weißbecker, 1991), p. 138.

64. Reichow's projects were published in *Raumforschung und Raumordnung. Monatschrift der Reichsarbeitsgemeinschaft für Raumforschung* 5.3–4 (1941).

65. For an account of the advanced stage reached by the middle of the war in Nazi forward planning of a post-war European Union based on 'Aryan' principles see Robert Herzstein, *When Nazi Dreams Come True. The Third Reich's Internal Struggle over the Future of Europe after a German Victory* (London: Sphere/Abacus, 1982).

66. Michael Prinz, 'Moderne Elemente in der Gesellschaftspolitik', in Prinz und Zitelmann, *Nazionalsozialismus und Modernisierung*, pp. 315–16.

67. See Dirk Schubert, 'Theodor Fritsch and the German (völkisch) version of the Garden City. The Garden City invented two years before Ebenezer Howard', *Planning Perspectives* 19 (January 2004).

68. We saw in Chapter 8 that Le Corbusier submitted a project for Pontina. For his impact on French fascist modernizers see Mark Antliff, *Avant-Garde Fascism. The Mobilization of Myth, Art and Culture in France, 1909–1939* (Durham, NC: Duke University Press, forthcoming), chapter 3, 'La Cité française: Georges Valois, Le Corbusier and Fascist Theories of Urbanism', pp. 134–70.

69. Cited in Clive Ponting, *Winston Churchill* (London: Sinclair-Stevenson, 1994), p. 102. The original memo is in the Asquith Papers, MS 12, f. 224–8. Asquith Papers Bodleian Library, Oxford.

70. Christopher Taylor, *Sacrifice as Terror. The Rwandan Genocide of 1994* (Oxford: Berg, 1999), p. 145.

71. Édouard Conte and Cornelia Essner, *La Quête de la Race. Une Anthropologie du Nazisme* (Paris: Hachette, 1995).

72. Peter Fritzsche stresses 'the central role played in National Socialism' by the concept of the *Volkskörper* in his pivotal article 'Nazi Modern', *Modernism/Modernity* 3.1 (1996), p. 9.

73. Cited in Richard Koenigsberger's on-line essay 'Genocide as Immunology. The Psychosomatic Source of Culture', at http://home.earthlink.net/~libraryofsocialscience/ gi.htm (accessed 09/01/07). The literalness with which Hitler and Nazism took the biological implications of an organic imagining of the nation is central to Koenigsberger's thesis about the dynamics of the Holocaust. He develops this thesis in 'Ideology, Perception, and Genocide. How Fantasy Generates History' at http://ideologiesofwar.com/papers/rk_ipg.htm (accessed 22/01/06).

74. Hitler, *Mein Kampf*, volume II, chapter 8, 'The Strong Man is Mightiest Alone', p. 466.

75. Conte and Essner, *La Quête de la Race*, pp. 360–8.

76. Michael Schwarz, '"Euthanasie"-Debatten in Deutschland (1895–1945)', *Vierteljahreshefte für Zeitgeschichte* 46 (1998), pp. 617–65.

77. Memorable images of these themes are included in Peter Adam's television documentary shown by the BBC in 1989, *Art in the Third Reich. The Orchestration of Power.*

78. Christian Pross, 'Introduction', in Aly Götz, Peter Chroust, and Christian Pross, *Cleansing the Fatherland. Nazi Medicine and Racial Hygiene* (Baltimore, MD: Johns Hopkins University Press, 1994), p. 14.

79. Zygmunt Bauman, *Modernity and the Holocaust* (Cambridge: Polity Press, 1989). There is a tendency on the part of some eminent historians to neglect the 'deeper' levels of causation explored by social and cultural historians such as Bauman and Modris Eksteins. Thus Christopher Browning, a leading expert on the Final Solution, makes only a fleeting allusion to the 'modernization crisis' and 'reactionary modernism' (and none to the work of either expert) in his chapter on the background to Nazi Jewish Policy 1939–42, in *The Origins of the Final Solution* (London: William Heinemann, 2004).

80. Enzo Traverso, *The Origins of Nazi Violence* (London: The New Press, 2003), p. 137.

81. Notably in Claus-Ekkehard Bärsch, *Die politische Religion des Nationalsozialismus* (Munich: Wilhelm Fink, 1998), who does, however, concede the 'modern', non-Christian aspect of Nazi political religion.

82. Traverso, *The Origins of Nazi Violence*, p. 148.

83. Ibid., p. 143. My emphasis.

84. Ibid., p. 136.

85. Ibid., p. 144.

86. Quote from an interview in Beth Holgate (producer), *Crossing the Lives. The History of the International Red Cross Committee* (London: BBC2 [Timewatch], 1998).

87. Saskia Baron (producer/director), *Science and the Swastika* (London: Darlow Smithson Productions, 2001), TV documentary series, episode 2, 'The Deadly Experiment', approximately 29 to 30 minutes.

88. Primo Levi, *Moments of Reprieve. A Memoir of Auschwitz* (New York: Penguin, 1987), p. 124. Cited in Blackbourn, *The Conquest of Nature*, p. 264.

89. Richard Evans, *The Third Reich in Power 1933–1939* (London: Allen Lane, 2005), p. 708.

90. The thesis that the 'high modernism' of Kafka's literary world is on one level a reaction to the anti-Semitism endemic to fin-de-siècle European society is evaluated in Sander L. Gilman, *Franz Kafka. The Jewish Patient* (New York: Routledge, 1995).

91. Nahum Glatzer, *The Complete Short Stories of Franz Kafka* (London: Minerva, 1992), pp. 165–6. The fact that the officer or 'commandant' dies as the victim of the execution system he has created is a situation that acquires a palingenetic twist in the inscription on his gravestone, an eerie adumbration of the post-war Hitler cult among neo-Nazis: 'It is prophesied that after a given number of years the commandant will rise again, and will lead out his followers from this house to reconquer the colony. Have faith and watch!'

92. Book of Daniel, 5:27 where 'mene tekel' is translated 'Thou art weighed in the balances, and art found wanting'.

93. Griffin, *Fascism*, pp. 118–19.

94. See Weindling, *Epidemics and Genocide* pp, 266, 317–20.

95. 'Zusammenbruch' means 'collapse', 'breakdown', and is the term used to refer to the aftermath of Germany's military defeat in 1918.

12   CASTING OFF

1. http://www.wonderful-things.com/newknit1.htm (accessed 02/03/06).

2. Reed Dasenbrock, 'Slouching towards Berlin', in Richard Golsan (ed.), *Fascism's Return. Scandal, Revision, and Ideology since 1980* (Lincoln: University of Nebraska Press, 1995), p. 250.

3. For the visual affinity between the two arches see http://flickr.com/photos/raimist/tags/arch/ (accessed 02/03/06). For a discussion of the degree of plagiarism involved in Saarinen's project, see http://flickr.com/photos/raimist/91076910/ (accessed 02/03/06). Apparently Libera contemplated suing Saarinen for the flagrant act of intellectual property theft his project involved. For a fascinating study of the significance of the arch in the Fascist *imaginaire* see Johst Welge, 'Fascism *Triumphans*: On the Architectural Translation of Rome', in Claudia Lazzaro and Roger Crum (eds.), *Donatello among the Black Shirts* (Ithaca, NY: Cornell University Press, 2005), pp. 83–96.

4. Albert Speer (et al.), *Albert Speer. Architektur. Arbeiten 1933–1942* (Frankfurt/M: Ullstein/ Propylaen, 1978).

5. Robert Hughes, 'Of Gods and Men', *Guardian*, Saturday 1 February 2003, pp. 7, 20.

6. Photos of the commemorative use of searchlights at Ground Zero can be seen on the Web, e.g. at www.smwa.org (accessed 01/12/06).

7. See Tim Redman, *Ezra Pound and Italian Fascism* (Cambridge: Cambridge University Press, 1991), chapters 7 and 8, pp. 191–274.

8. http://www.bbc.co.uk/science/horizon/2000/massivebholes.shtml (accessed 14/07/06).

9. For more on the astrophysical science of the black hole invoked here for its metaphorical potency see the website of the Instituto de Astrofisica de Canarias (IAC) in the Canary Islands, Spain at http://www.iac.es/gabinete/noticias/2001/nov20i.htm (accessed 01/12/06).

10. Blaise Pascal, *Pensées* (1660) (London: Penguin, 1966), part 8, 'Diversion', pp. 66–72.

11. For another perspective (this time that of a clinical psychologist) on the profound link between modern reflexivity, exacerbated time consciousness, acute anomy, a subjectivity torn between bottomless angst and epiphany, and the longing for transcendence see Louis Sass, *Madness and Modernism. Insanity in the Light of Modern Art, Literature, and Thought* (Cambridge, MA: Harvard University Press, 1992), especially pp. 28–39 on the nature of modernity and modernism, and pp. 154–64 on the need of human beings under high modernity to 'escape from chronology'.

12. William Aggeler, *The Flowers of Evil* (Fresno, CA: Academy Library Guild, 1954). Cited at http://fleursdumal.org (accessed 23/10/06).
13. Friedrich Nietzsche, *Thus Spoke Zarathustra. A New Translation by Graham Parkes* (Oxford: Blackwell, 2005), p. 15.
14. See above Chapter 2, p. 61.
15. 'Caca' is an infantile expression for faeces in French (Italian 'cacca'), and 'popo' evokes English 'poo', in Italian 'popo'. 'Popo' is also baby German for 'bottom'.
16. 'Wer aber vom Kapitalismus nicht reden will, sollte auch vom Faschismus schweigen', Max Horkheimer, Die Juden in Europa, in H. Dubiel and A. Söllner (eds.), *Wirtschaft, Recht und Staat im Nationalsozialismus. Analysen des Instituts für Sozialforschung 1939–1942* (Frankfurt am Main: Suhrkampf, 1984), p. 33.
17. For a powerfully argued counter-thesis that there has been, see David Harvey, *The Condition of Postmodernity. An Enquiry into the Origins of Cultural Change* (Oxford: Blackwell, 1990).
18. Jean-François Lyotard, *The Postmodern Condition. A Report on Knowledge* (1979) (Minneapolis: University of Minnesota, 1993).
19. See Gary Browning, *Lyotard and the End of Grand Narratives* (Cardiff: University of Wales, 2000), pp. 165–71.
20. See especially Paul Ricoeur, *Time and Narrative* (Chicago: University of Chicago Press, 3 volumes, 1984, 1985, 1988).
21. See Rana Mitter 'Maoism in the Cultural Revolution: a Political Religion?', in Robert Mallett, John Tortorice, and Roger Griffin (eds.), *The Sacred in Politics. A Festschrift for Stanley Payne* (London: Palgrave, forthcoming).
22. Robert Lifton, *Destroying the World to Save It: Aum Shinrikyo, Apocalyptic Violence, and the New Global Terrorism* (New York: Metropolitan Books, 1999). Similarly, in *The Enemy of My Enemy. The Alarming Convergence of Militant Islam and the Extreme Right* (Lawrence, KS: University Press, 2006), p. 36, George Michael attributes the genesis of the Islamist movement to a 'backlash against Westernization and modernization'. He compares the quest for 'moral renewal' that has mobilized the spread of the Muslim Brotherhood throughout the Muslim world to the 'various Great Awakenings that have punctuated American history', bequeathing a legacy of apocalypticism that still informs mainstream US politics today.
23. In *Islamic Government. Governance of the Jurist*, a key Islamist text, for example, Imam Khomeini states in section 3, 'The Form of Islamic Government', that 'Now that we are in the time of the Occultation of the Imâm, it is still necessary that the ordinances of Islam relating to government be preserved and maintained, and that anarchy be prevented' (Tehran: The Institute for Compilation and Publication of Imam Khomeini's Works, no date), at http://al-islam.org/islamicgovernment (accessed 29/10/06). In the article 'What is Islamism?', *Totalitarian Movements and Political Religions* 8/1 (2007), p. 30, Mehdi Mozaffari argues that the aim of Islamism is to 'reinstate its fallen caliphate and regain its lost glory', a phrase attributed to Ayman Zawahiri, Osama Bin Laden's deputy, reportedly killed in an American air-strike in January 2006.
24. See Robert Frykenberg, 'Hindutva as a Political Religion: A Historical Perspective', in Robert Mallett, John Tortorice, and Roger Griffin (eds.), *The Sacred in Politics. A Festschrift for Stanley Payne* (London: Palgrave Macmillan, forthcoming). This essay not only brings out extraordinary parallels between the construction of the (Muslim) 'Other' in radical Hinduism and of the (Jewish) 'Other' in Nazism, but suggests the presence of universal patterns in the way modernity's corrosive impact on traditional society can produce a countervailing xenophobia combined with palingenetic aspirations for the 'stressed' community to be led into a new political order purged of decadence. In this way it will be able to maintain its fixed horizon 'framed by myth'.
25. Just such a process is the central theme of George Michael's, *The Enemy of My Enemy*.
26. Salman Rushdie, *Imaginary Homelands* (London: Penguin, 1992), p. 394.

27. Adrian Hewitt, 'Ideological Positions', in Angelica Fenner and Eric Weitz (eds), *Fascism and Neofascism. Critical Writings on the Radical Right in Europe* (London: Palgrave Macmillan, 2004), p. 24.

28. Michael Burleigh, *Sacred Causes: Religion and Politics from the European Dictators to al-Qaeda* (London: HarperCollins, 2006).

29. See above Chapter 8, pp. 225.

30. An allusion to my *The Nature of Fascism* (London: Pinter, 1991).

31. Robert Paxton, *The Anatomy of Fascism* (New York: Alfred A. Knopf, 2004).

32. Richard Evans, *The Third Reich in Power 1933–1939* (London: Allen Lane, 2005), p. 500.

33. Ibid., p. 709. Evans points out that, in contrast to Bolshevik Russia, the Third Reich reserved its main violence for people outside the country in acts of state terror and genocide committed under the cover of war.

34. This is the approach deliberately applied by Alexander de Grand. See his *Fascist Italy and Nazi Germany: The Fascist Style of Rule* (New York: Routledge, 1995), p. 3.

35. See George L. Mosse, 'The Genesis of Fascism', *Journal of Contemporary History* 1.1 (1966), pp. 19–20. See too his introduction to *The Fascist Revolution* (New York: Howard Fertig, 1999), p. x.

36. See Stanley Payne, *A History of Fascism 1914–45* (London: UCL Press, 1995), pp. 245–327; Roger Griffin, *The Nature of Fascism* (London: Pinter, 1991), chapter 5, 'Abortive Fascist Movements in Inter-war Europe', pp. 116–45.

37. Mark Antliff's key works on this topic, written with a conceptual framework profoundly congruent with that used in this book, are: *Inventing Bergson. Cultural Politics and the Parisian Avant-Garde* (Princeton, NJ: Princeton University Press, 1993); 'La Cité française. George Valois, Le Corbusier, and Fascist Theories of Urbanism', in Mark Antliff and Matthew Affron (eds.), *Fascist Visions: Art and Ideology in France and Italy* (Princeton, NJ: Princeton University Press, 1997), pp. 134–70; 'The Jew as Anti-Artist. Georges Sorel. Antisemitism, and the Aesthetics of Class-Consciousness', *Oxford Art Journal* 20.1 (1997), pp. 50–7; 'Modernism and Fascism: French Fascist Aesthetics between the Wars', in Oystein Hjort (ed.), *Re-thinking Images between the Wars: New Perspectives in Art History* (Copenhagen: Museum Tusculanum, 2000), pp. 13–45; 'Machine Primitives. Philippe Lamour, Germaine Krull, and the Fascist Cult of Youth', *Qui Parle* 13.1 (Fall/Winter 2001), pp. 57–102; *Avant-Garde Fascism: The Mobilization of Myth, Art and Culture in France, 1909–1939* (Durham, NC: Duke University Press, 2007). Antliff's 'Fascism, Modernism and Modernity', *The Art Bulletin* 3.2 (March 2002), pp. 148–69, is a seminal essay on the intimate relationship between fascism and modernism.

38. Koenraad Swart, *The Sense of Decadence in Nineteenth-century France* (The Hague: International Archives of the History of Ideas, 1964).

39. See Thomas Linehan, *British Fascism 1918–39. Parties, Ideology and Culture* (Manchester: Manchester University Press, 2000); Julie Gottlieb and Thomas Linehan (eds.), *The Culture of Fascism. Visions of the Far Right in Britain* (London: I. B. Tauris, 2004).

40. Julie Gottlieb, 'The Marketing of Megalomania. Celebrity, Consumption and the Development of Political Technology in the British Union of Fascists', *Journal of Contemporary History* 41.1 (2006), pp. 45–65.

41. See David Baker, *Ideology of Obsession. A. K. Chesterton and British Fascism* (London and New York: I. B. Tauris & Co. Ltd., 1996), which brings out Chesterton's conversion to fascism and anti-Semitism as a way of resolving his personal struggle with anomy.

42. See Oswald Mosley, *My Life* (London: Nelson, 1968), pp. 316–35, 'The Ideology of Fascism. Science and Caesarism'.

43. For the use of this term to describe forms of inter-war regime outwardly modelled on fascism (in this case Mussolini's Italy) but lacking its revolutionary aspirations, see Griffin, *The Nature of Fascism*, pp. 120–8.

44. José Zúquete, 'In Search of a New Society. An Intellectual between Modernism and Salazar', *Portuguese Journal of Social Science* 4.1 (2005), pp. 61–81.

45. Plinío Salgado, *A Quarta Humanidade* (San Paolo: José Olympio Press, 1934).

46. The intensely modernist flavour of Brazilian Integralism can be gleaned from Helgio Trindade, 'Fascism and Authoritarianism in Brazil under Vargas (1939–1945)', in Stein Larsen (ed.), *Fascism outside Europe. The European Impulse against Domestic Conditions in the Diffusion of Global Fascism* (Boulder: Social Science Monographs; New York: Columbia University Press, 2001), pp. 491–52.

47. E.g. the Romanian Iron Guard is described as having 'the most radical anti-modern discourse of inter-war Romania' in Constantin Davidescu, 'Totalitarian Discourse as a Rejection of Modernity', in Mihaela Czobor-Lupp and Stefan Lupp (eds.), *Moral, Legal and Political Values in Romanian Culture. Romanian Philosophical Studies, IV* (Washington, DC: The Council for Research in Values and Philosophy, 2002), p. 150.

48. To take one example, in his seminal chapter, 'The Concept of Fascism', in Stein Larsen, *Who were the Fascists.* (Oslo: Universitetforlaget, 1980), p. 22, Stanley Payne describes the Iron Guard as a 'mystical, kenotic form of semi-religious fascism that represented the only notable movement of this kind in an Orthodox country and was also marginal to the species'.

49. Radu Ioanid, 'The Sacralised Politics of the Romanian Iron Guard', *Totalitarian Movements and Political Religions* 5.3 (Winter 2004), pp. 419–53.

50. Eugen Weber, 'Romania', in Hans Rogger and Eugen Weber (eds.), *The European Right* (Berkeley and Los Angeles: University of California Press, 1965). He subsequently wrote a panoramic study of what we have called revitalization movements: *Apocalypses. Prophesies, Cults, and Millennial Beliefs through the Ages* (Cambridge, MA: Harvard University Press, 1999).

51. Marius Turda, 'Fantasies of Degeneration. Some Remarks on Racial Antisemitism in Interwar Romania', *Judaic Studies* 3 (2003), pp. 336–48.

52. See Marius Turda and Paul Weindling (eds.), *'Blood and Homeland'. Eugenics and Racial Nationalism in Central and Southeast Europe, 1900–1940* (Budapest: Central European University Press, 2006).

53. Maria Bucur, *Eugenics and Modernization in Interwar Romania* (Pittsburgh: University of Pittsburgh Press, 2002).

54. See Constantin Iordachi, *Charisma, Politics and Violence. The Legion of the Archangel Michael in Interwar Romania* (Trondheim: Trondheim Studies on East European Cultures and Societies no. 15, 2004), a perceptive study of the Iron Guard which corroborates several aspects of the interpretation of the movement presented here that makes it not 'marginal', but central to generic fascism.

55. Maria Bucur, 'Fascism and the New Radical Movement in Romania', in Angelica Fenner and Eric D. Weitz (eds.), *Fascism and Neofascism. Critical Writings on the Radical Right in Europe* (New York: Palgrave Macmillan, 2004), p. 164.

56. Eugen Weber, 'Romania', pp. 535–6.

57. Examples are Frederic Jameson, *Fables of Aggression. Wyndham Lewis, the Modernist as Fascist* (Berkeley: University of California Press, 1979); Tim Redman, *Ezra Pound and Italian Fascism* (Cambridge: Cambridge University Press, 1991); Andrew Hewitt, *Fascist Modernism. Aesthetics, Politics, and the Avant-Garde* (Stanford, CA: Stanford University Press, 1993); Vincent Sherry, *Ezra Pound, Wyndham Lewis and Radical Modernism* (New York: Oxford University Press, 1993).

58. Charles Ferrall, *Modernist Writing & Reactionary Politics* (Cambridge: Cambridge University Press, 2001), p. 2.

59. Georg Lukács, *The Destruction of Reason* (1952) (London: Merlin, 1980).

60. Useful introductions to this, for the uninitiated, intensely esoteric topic are Dasenbrock, 'Slouching towards Berlin', and Hewitt, 'Ideological Positions'.

61. For the concept of the rhizome as a way of avoiding simplistic concepts of causation see Felix Guattari and Gilles Deleuze, *A Thousand Plateaus. Capitalism and Schizophrenia* (Minneapolis: University of Minnesota Press, 1987).

62. Detlef Peukert, *Inside Nazi Germany* (Harmondsworth: Penguin, 1982), p. 245.

63. Karl Popper, *The Open Society and its Enemies* (1950) (London: Routledge, 2002), 'Conclusion: Has history any meaning?', p. 297.

64. Ibid., p. 295.

65. Richard Bosworth, *Mussolini's Italy* (London: Allen Lane, 2005), p. 564.

66. For a direct correlative in anthropology to Mason's remark see Edmund Leach's defence of the value of generalization (which he contrasts with 'taxonomic comparison'): 'Generalization is inductive; it consists of perceiving possible general laws in the circumstances of special cases; it is guesswork, a gamble, you may be wrong or you may be right, but if you happen to be right you have learnt something altogether new.' Edmund Leach, 'Rethinking Anthropology', in *Rethinking Anthropology* (London: Athlone Press, 1966), p. 5.

67. Tim Mason, 'Whatever Happened to "Fascism"?', in Jane Caplan (ed.), *Nazism, Fascism and the Working Class. Essays by Tim Mason* (Cambridge: Cambridge University Press, 1995), p. 331.

68. Friedrich Nietzsche, *The Will to Power* (London: Weidenfeld & Nicolson, 1967), Book Three: Principles of A New Evaluation, volume 1, Methods of Inquiry, 9: 'Thing-in-itself and Appearance', note 556, p. 301.

69. Ibid., 3: 'Belief in the "Ego". The Subject', note 481, p. 267.

70. Cited in Thomas Burger, *Max Weber's Theory of Concept Formation, History, Laws, and Ideal Types* (Durham, NC: Duke University Press, 1976), pp. 127–8.

POSTSCRIPT: A DIFFERENT BEGINNING?

1. http://news.bbc.co.uk/1/hi/sci/tech/173351.stm (accessed 13/01/06).

2. Ernest Becker, *The Birth and Death of Meaning* (New York: The Free Press, 1962), p. 132.

3. Michael Mehaffy and Nikos Salingaros, 'The End of the Modern World', 27/02/02, on Open Democracy website: http://www.opendemocracy.net/articles/ViewPopUpArticle.jsp?id=10&articleId=173 (accessed 14/11/05). See Etien Santiago's spirited reply 'Misrepresenting Modernism' of 23/11/02, http://www.opendemocracy.net/forums/thread.jspa?forumID=111&threadID=41473&tstart=0 (accessed 14/11/05).

4. Fay Weldon, *The Hole at the Top of the World* (dir. Shaun McLoughlin: L.A. Theatre Works/ BBC, 1995).

5. Friedrich Nietzsche, *The Will to Power*, Book Four: Discipline and Breeding, section 3, The Eternal Recurrence, note 1067 (1885), pp. 549–50.

6. Gerd Bergfleth, 'Erde und Heimat. Über das Ende der Ära des Unheils', in Heimo Schwilk and Ulrich Schacht (eds.), *Die selbstbewußte Nation. 'Anschwellender Bockgesang' und weitere Beiträge zu einer deutschen Debatte* (Berlin: Ullstein, 1996), p. 107.

7. Ibid., p. 116.

8. Ibid., pp. 117–23.

9. As a contribution to this topic see Roger Griffin, 'Plus ça change!: The Fascist Pedigree of the Nouvelle Droite', in Edward Arnold (ed.), *The Development of the Radical Right in France 1890–1995* (London: Routledge, 2000), pp. 217–52.

10. Walter Benjamin, 'Theses on the Philosophy of History', in Walter Benjamin, *Illuminations* (London: Fontana, 1992), p. 247.

11. Diogenes of Oinoanda (c. 200 BC), taken from *The Epicurean Inscription* (Abridged), fragment 30, translated by Martin Smith, reproduced at http://www.epicurus.info/etexts/tei.html#ethics (accessed 20/03/06).

12. Howard Williams, 'Metamorphosis or Palingenesis? Political Change in Kant', *Review of Politics* 63.4 (Fall 2001), pp. 693–722.
13. Bob Dylan, *Desolation Row* on the album *Highway 61 Revisited* (1965). The song portrays Ezra Pound and T. S. Eliot as 'fighting in the captain's tower' aboard the *Titanic*.
14. Bob Dylan, *When the Ship Comes In* on the album *The Times They are A'Changing* (1964).
15. Bertolt Brecht, Epilogue to *The Good Person of Szechuan* (1943) (my translation).

APPENDIX: MORE ON METHODOLOGY

1. See Thomas Burger, *Max Weber's Theory of Concept Formation. History, Laws, and Ideal Types* (Durham, NC: Duke University Press, 1976).
2. See Basit Koshul, *The Postmodern Significance of Max Weber's Legacy* (London: Palgrave Macmillan, 2005).
3. Karl Popper, *The Poverty of Historicism* (1957) (London: Routledge and Kegan Paul, 1974), p. 150. Original emphasis.
4. Richard Evans, *In Defence of History* (London: Granta Books, 2000), p. 253. My emphasis.
5. Marjorie Levinson, 'The New Historicism. Back to the Future', in *Rethinking Historicism. Critical Readings in Romantic History* (Oxford: Basil Blackwell, 1989).
6. Joan Vincent, 'Engaging Historicism', in Richard Fox (ed.), *Recapturing Anthropology. Working in the Present* (Santa Fe, NM: School of American Research Press, 1991), p. 46.
7. E.g. Pierre Bourdieu and Loic Wacquant, *An Invitation to Reflexive Sociology* (Chicago: University of Chicago Press, 1992); Arpad Szakolczai, *Reflexive Historical Sociology* (London: Routledge Studies in Social and Political Thought, 2000); Ido Oren, 'Political Science as History. A Reflexive Approach', in Dvora Yanow and Peregrine Schwartz-Shea (eds.), *Interpretation and Method. Empirical Research Methods and the Interpretive Turn* (New York: M. E. Sharpe, 2006).
8. Graham Watson, 'Rewriting Culture', in Fox, *Recapturing Anthropology*, p. 81. Watson also calls reflexive anthropology 'interpretive anthropology'.
9. Massimiliano Lattanzi (ed.), *Transdisciplinarity* (Paris: UNESCO, 1998), p. 3. Downloadable at http://unesdoc.unesco.org/images/0011/001146/114694eo.pdf (accessed 22/05/06).
10. Ibid., p. 13. My emphasis.
11. Friedrich Nietzsche, *Gesammelte Werke* (Munich: Musarion, 1926–29), volume 21, p. 81.
12. Letter from Franz Kafka to Oskar Pollack, 27 January 1904, in Gerhard Neumann, Malcolm Pasley, and Jost Schillemeit (eds.), *Franz Kafka. Briefe 1900–1912* (Frankfurt am Main: Fischer, 1999), p. 36.

Bibliography

PRINTED SOURCES

Abse, Tobias. 'The Rise of Fascism in an Industrial City. The Case of Livorno 1919–1922', in David Forgacs (ed.), *Rethinking Italian Fascism* (London: Wishart, 1986), pp. 52–82.

Adam, Peter. *The Arts of the Third Reich* (New York: Harry N. Abrams, 1992).

Adamson, Walter. *Avant-Garde Florence. From Modernism to Fascism* (Cambridge, MA: Harvard University Press, 1993).

——. 'Modernism and Fascism. The Politics of Culture in Italy, 1903–1922', *The American Historical Review*, Vol. 95, No. 2 (1990), pp. 359–90.

——. 'Ardengo Soffici and the Religion of Art', in Matthew Affron and Mark Antliff (eds.), *Fascist Visions. Art and Ideology in France and Italy* (Princeton, NJ: Princeton University Press, 1997), pp. 46–72.

Adorno, Theodor. *Minima Moralia* (Frankfurt: Suhrkampf, 1951).

Amendola, Giovanni. 'La Guerra', *La Voce*, 28 December 1928.

Antliff, Allan. *Anarchist Modernism. Art, Politics, and the First American Avant-Garde* (Chicago: The University of Chicago Press, 2001).

Antliff, Mark. *Inventing Bergson. Cultural Politics and the Parisian Avant-Garde* (Princeton, NJ: Princeton University Press, 1993).

——, Matthew Affron (eds.). *Fascist Visions. Art and Ideology in France and Italy* (Princeton, NJ: Princeton University Press, 1997).

——. 'La Cité française. George Valois, Le Corbusier, and Fascist Theories of Urbanism', in Mark Antliff and Matthew Affron (eds.), *Fascist Visions. Art and Ideology in France and Italy* (Princeton, NJ: Princeton University Press, 1997), pp. 134–70.

——. 'The Jew as Anti-Artist. Georges Sorel, Antisemitism, and the Aesthetics of Class-Consciousness', *Oxford Art Journal*, Vol. 20, No. 1 (1997), pp. 50–7.

——. 'Modernism and Fascism. French Fascist Aesthetics between the Wars', in Oystein Hjort (ed.), *Re-thinking Images Between the Wars. New Perspectives in Art History* (Copenhagen: Museum Tusculanum, 2000), pp. 13–45.

——. 'Machine Primitives. Philippe Lamour, Germaine Krull, and the Fascist Cult of Youth', *Qui Parle*, Vol. 13, No. 1 (Fall/Winter 2001), pp. 57–102.

——. 'Fascism, Modernism, and Modernity. The State of Research', *The Art Bulletin*, Vol. 84, No. 1 (March 2002), pp. 148–69.

——. *Avant-Garde Fascism. The Mobilization of Myth, Art and Culture in France, 1909–1939* (Durham, NC: Duke University Press, 2007).

Aly, Götz. *Hitlers Volksstaat* (Frankfurt am Main: Fischer, 2005).

Apollinaire, Guillaume. *The Cubist Painters* (Harrogate: Broadwater House, 2000).

Arendt, Hannah. *The Origins of Totalitarianism* (London: George Allen and Unwin, 1967).

Axer, Oliver, Susanne Benze. *Hitler's Hit Parade* (Bad Schwartau: C. Cay Wesnigk Filmproduktion, 2003).

Ayers, David. *Modernism. A Short Introduction* (Oxford: Blackwell, 2004).

Bärsch, Claus-Ekkehard. *Die politische Religion des National-Sozialismus* (Munich: Wilhelm Fink, 1998).

Baker, David. *Ideology of Obsession. A.K. Chesterton and British Fascism* (London and New York: I. B. Tauris & Co. Ltd., 1996).

——. 'The Political Economy of Fascism. Myth or Reality. Or Myth and Reality?', *New Political Economy*, Vol. 11, No. 2 (June 2006), pp. 227–50.

Banchelli, Umberto. *Memorie di un fascista* (Florence: Edizioni della Sassaiola fiorentina, 1922).

Bardelli, Giovanni. *Il mito della 'Nuova Italia'. Gioacchino Volpe tra guerra e fascismo* (Rome: Lavoro, 1988).

Barrès, Maurice. *Scènes et doctrines du nationalisme* (Paris: F. Juven, 1902).

Barron, Stephanie. *Degenerate Art. The Fate of the Avant-garde in Nazi Germany* (Los Angeles: Los Angeles County Museum, 1991).

Bartlett, Rosamund. *Wagner and Russian Modernism* (Cambridge: Cambridge University Press, 1995).

Bartov, Omer. *Murder in our Midst. The Holocaust, Industrial Killing, and Representation* (Oxford: Oxford University Press, 1996).

Bataille, Georges. 'The Psychological Structure of Fascism', in Georges Bataille, *Visions of Excess. Selected Writings 1927–1939* (Minneapolis: University of Minnesota Press, 1985), pp. 137–60.

Batty, Peter. *The House of Krupp* (London: Secker & Warburg, 1961).

Baudelaire, Charles. *Les Fleurs du Mal* (1861) (Paris: Gallimard, 1964).

——. 'The Painter of Modern Life' (1863), cited in P. E. Charvet (ed.), *Baudelaire. Selected Writings on Art and Literature* (New York: Viking, 1972), pp. 395–422.

Bauman, Zygmunt. *Modernity and the Holocaust* (Cambridge: Polity Press, 1989).

——. *Modernity and Ambivalence* (Cambridge: Polity, 1991).

——. *Mortality, Immortality and Other Life Strategies* (Stanford, CA: Stanford University Press, 1992).

Bayly, C. A. *The Birth of the Modern World, 1780–1914. Global Connections and Comparisons* (Oxford: Blackwell Publishers, 2004).

Baynes, Norman (ed.). *The Speeches of Adolf Hitler, April 1922–August 1939* (London: Oxford University Press, 1942).

Becker, Annette. *War and Faith. The Religious Imagination in France, 1914–1930* (Oxford: Berg, 1998).

Becker, Ernest. *The Birth and Death of Meaning. An Interdisciplinary Perspective on the Problem of Man* (Harmondsworth: Penguin, 1962).

——. *Escape from Evil* (New York: The Free Press, 1975).

Ben-Ghiat, Ruth. *Fascist Modernities. Italy, 1922–1945* (Berkeley and Los Angeles: University of California Press, 2001).

—— (ed.), *Italian Colonialism* (London: Palgrave Macmillan, 2005).

Benjamin, Walter. *Illuminations* (London: Fontana, 1992).

——. 'Theses on the Philosophy of History', in Walter Benjamin, *Illuminations* (London: Fontana, 1992), pp. 245–55.

Benn, Gottfried. 'Der neue Staat und die Intellektuellen' (1933), in Dieter Wellerhoff (ed.), *Gottfried Benn. Gesammelte Werke in acht Bänden* (Wiesbaden: Limes, 1968), volume 4, pp. 1004–13.

——. 'Kunst und Staat', in Dieter Wellerhoff (ed.), *Gottfried Benn. Gesammelte Werke in acht Bänden* (Wiesbaden: Limes, 1968), volume 3, pp. 603–613.

——. 'Züchtung I' (1933), in Dieter Wellerhoff (ed.), *Gottfried Benn. Gesammelte Werke in acht Bänden* (Wiesbaden: Limes, 1968), volume 3, pp. 776–84.

Benson, Timothy. 'Mysticism, Materialism, and the Machine in Berlin Dada', *Art Journal*, Vol. 46, No. 1 (Spring 1987), pp. 46–55.

Berberova, Nina. *Aleksandr Blok. A Life* (Manchester: Carcanet Press, 1996).

Berezin, Mabel. *Making the Fascist Self* (Ithaca, NY: Cornell University Press, 1997).

Berger, Peter. *The Sacred Canopy. Elements of a Sociological Theory of Religion* (London: Doubleday, 1967).

——, Brigitte Berger, Hansfried Kellner. *The Homeless Mind. Modernization and Consciousness* (Harmondsworth: Penguin, 1974).

Bergfleth, Gerd. 'Erde und Heimat. Über das Ende der Ära des Unheils', in Heimo Schwilk and Ulrich Schacht (eds.), *Die Selbstbewußte Nation. ‚Anschwellender Bockgesang' und weitere Beiträge zu einer deutschen Debatte* (Berlin: Ullstein, 1996), pp. 101–23.

Berghaus, Günter (ed.). *Fascism and Theatre* (Oxford: Berghahn, 1996).

——. *Futurism and Politics. Between Anarchist Rebellion and Fascist Reaction, 1909–1944* (Oxford: Berghahn, 1996).

——. 'The Ritual Core of Fascist Theatre. An Anthropological Perspective', in Günter Berghaus (ed.), *Fascist Theatre. Comparative Studies on the Aesthetics and Politics of Representation in Europe, 1925–1945* (Oxford: Berghahn, 1996), pp. 39–71.

Bergmeier, Horst, Rainer Lotz. *Hitler's Airwaves. The Inside Story of Nazi Radio Broadcasting and Propaganda Swing* (New Haven, CT: Yale University Press, 1997).

Berman, Marshall. *All that is Solid Melts into Air. The Experience of Modernity* (London: Verso, 1982).

Berman, Russell. 'The Aestheticization of Politics. Walter Benjamin on Fascism and the Avant-Garde', in R. A. Berman (ed.), *Modern Culture and Critical Theory. Art, Politics, and the Legacy of the Frankfurt School* (Madison: University of Wisconsin Press, 1989), pp. 27–41.

——. 'Gottfried Benn. A Double Life in Uninhabitable Regions', in Richard Golsan (ed.), *Fascism, Aesthetics and Culture* (Hanover, NH: University Press of New England, 1992), pp. 67–80.

Berry, Ryan. *Hitler: neither Vegetarian nor Animal Lover* (New York: Pythagorean Publishers, 2004).

Black, Edwin. *IBM and the Holocaust* (New York: Crown Publishers, 2001).

Blackbourn, David. *The Conquest of Nature. Water, Landscape and the making of Modern Germany* (London: Jonathan Cape, 2006).

Blinkhorn, Martin. *Fascism and the Right in Europe 1918–1945* (London: Longmans, 2000).

Bloch, Ernst. *Geist der Utopie* (Frankfurt/Main: Suhrkampf, 1991).

——. *The Heritage of Our Times* (1962) (Cambridge: Polity, 1991).

——. *The Principle of Hope* 3 vols (1953) (Cambridge, MA: MIT Press, 1995).

——. *The Spirit of Utopia* (1923) (Stanford, CA: Stanford University Press, 2000).

Bloch, Maurice, Jonathan Parry (eds.). *Death and the Regeneration of Life* (Cambridge: Cambridge University Press, 1982).

——. *Prey into Hunter* (Cambridge: Cambridge University Press, 1992).

Blumenberg, Hans. *Lebenszeit und Weltzeit* (Frankfurt: Suhrkampf, 1986).

Borchmeyer, Dieter. *Drama and the World of Richard Wagner* (Princeton, NJ: Princeton University Press, 2003).

Bonnel, Victoria E., Lynn Hunt (eds.). *Beyond the Cultural Turn* (Berkeley: University of California Press, 1999).

Borges, Luis. 'Deutsches requiem', in Luis Borges, *Labyrinths* (New York: New Directions, 1964), pp. 173–9.

Bortolotti, L., G. De Luca. *Fascismo e autostrade. Un caso di sintesi: la Firenze-mare* (Milan: F. Angeli, 1994).

Bosworth, Richard. *The Italian Dictatorship* (London: Arnold, 1998).

——. *Mussolini's Italy* (London: Allen Lane, 2005).

Bottai, Giuseppe. *Il Fascismo e L'Italia Nuova* (Rome: Giorgio Berlutti, 1923).

Bouchard, Norma. 'Introduction. Risorgimento as an Unfinished Story', in Norma Bouchard (ed.), *Risorgimento in Modern Italian Culture. Revisiting the 19th-century Past in History, Narrative, and Cinema* (Madison, NJ: Fairleigh Dickinson University Press, 2005), pp. 9–22.

Bourdieu, Pierre, Loic Wacquant. *An Invitation to Reflexive Sociology* (Chicago: University of Chicago Press, 1992).

Bosworth, R. J. B. *The Italian Dictatorship* (London: Arnold, 1998).

Bowles, Paul. *The Sheltering Sky* (1949) (Harmondsworth: Penguin, 1990).

Bradbury, Malcolm, James McFarlane (eds.). *Modernism 1890–1930* (Harmondsworth: Penguin, 1976).

——, James McFarlane. 'The Name and Nature of Modernism', in Malcolm Bradbury and James McFarlane (eds.), *Modernism 1890–1930* (Harmondsworth: Penguin, 1976), pp. 19–55.

——, James McFarlane. 'Movements, Magazines and Manifestos. The Succession from Naturalism', in Malcolm Bradbury and James McFarlane (eds.), *Modernism 1890–1930* (Harmondsworth: Penguin, 1976), pp. 192–205.

Bradshaw, David (ed.). *A Concise Companion to Modernism* (Oxford: Blackwell, 2003).

Bramwell, Anna. *Blood and Soil. Richard Walther Darré and Hitler's 'Green Party'* (Bourne End, Buckinghamshire: Kensal Press, 1985).

Brandon, Ruth. *The Spiritualists. The Passion for the Occult in the Nineteenth and Twentieth Centuries* (New York: Alfred Knopf, 1983).

Braudy, Leo. *From Chivalry to Terrorism. War and the Changing Nature of Masculinity* (New York: Alfred A. Knopf, 2003).

Braun, Emily. *Mario Sironi and Italian Modernism. Art and Politics under Fascism* (Cambridge: Cambridge University Press, 2000).

——. 'The Visual Arts. Modernism and Fascism', in Adrian Lyttleton (ed.), *Liberal and Fascist Italy* (Oxford: Oxford University Press, 2002), pp. 196–215.

Brenner, Hildegaard. 'Art in the Political Power Struggle of 1933 and 1934', in Hajo Holborn (ed.), *Republic to Reich. The Making of the Nazi Revolution. Ten Essays* (New York: Random House, 1972), pp. 395–432.

Briegleb, Klaus (ed.). *Heinrich Heine. Sämtliche Schriften in sechs Bänden. Vol. 2* (Munich: Carl Hanser, 1968–76).

Broch, Hermann. *The Sleepwalkers* (New York: Grosset and Dunlap, 1964).

——. *Essays on Ideology* (London, New York: Verso, 1971).

Bromley, David. 'Constructing Apocalypticism. Social and Cultural Elements of Radical Organization', in T. Robbins and Susan Palmer (eds.), *Millennium, Messiahs, and Mayhem. Contemporary Apocalyptic Movements* (New York: Routledge, 1997), pp. 31–46.

Brown, Callum. *Postmodernism for Historians* (London: Pearson Education, 2005).

Browning, Christopher. *The Origins of the Final Solution* (London: William Heinemann, 2004).

Browning, Gary. *Lyotard and the End of Grand Narratives* (Cardiff: University of Wales Press, 2000).

Brüggemeier, Franz-Josef (et al.). *How Green were the Nazis? Nature, Environment, and Nation in the Third Reich* (Ohio: Ohio University Press, 2005).

Bucur, Maria. *Eugenics and Modernization in Interwar Romania* (Pittsburgh, PA: University of Pittsburgh Press, 2002).

——. 'Fascism and the New Radical Movement in Romania', in Angelica Fenner and Eric D. Weitz (eds.), *Fascism and Neofascism. Critical Writings on the Radical Right in Europe* (New York: Palgrave Macmillan, 2004), pp. 159–74.

Buderer, Hans. *Entartete Kunst. Beschlagnahmeaktionen in der Städtischen Kunsthalle Mannheim 1937; Kunst und Dokumentation* (Mannheim: Städtische Kunsthalle Mannheim, 1991).

Buffton, Deborah. 'Memorialization and the Selling of War', *Peace Review*, Vol. 17, No. 1 (January–March 2005), pp. 25–31.

Burger, Thomas. *Max Weber's Theory of Concept Formation, History, Laws, and Ideal Types* (Durham, NC: Duke University Press, 1976).

Burgio, Alberto (ed.). *Nel nome della razza. Il razzismo nella storia d'Italia 1870–1945* (Bologna: Il Mulino, 1999).

Burleigh, Michael. *Sacred Causes: Religion and Politics from the European Dictators to al-Qaeda* (London: HarperCollins, 2006).

——, Wolfgang Wippermann. *The Racial State* (Cambridge: Cambridge University Press, 1991).

——. *The Third Reich – A New History* (London: Macmillan, 2000).

——. *Earthly Powers. Religion and Politics in Europe from the French Revolution to the Great War* (London: HarperCollins, 2005).

Busch, Ludger. 'Das Bauhaus und Mazdaznan', in Rolf Bothe, Peter Hahn, and Hans Christoph von Tavel (eds.), *Das frühe Bauhaus und Johannes Itten* (Weimar: Kunstsammlungen, 1995), pp. 83–90.

Bussmann, Georg. '"Degenerate Art". A Look at a Useful Myth', in Christos Joachimides et al., *German Art of the Twentieth Century* (London: Royal Academy, 1985), pp. 113–34.

Calì, Vincenzo, Gustavo Corni, Giuseppe Ferrandi (eds.). *Gli intellettuali e la Grande guerra* (Bologna: Il Mulino, 2000).

Campbell, Bruce. *Ancient Wisdom Revived. A History of the Theosophical Movement* (Berkeley: University of California Press, 1980).

Campbell, Colin. 'The Cult, the Cultic Milieu, and Secularization', in Michael Hill (ed.), *A Sociological Yearbook of Religion in Britain* (London: SMC Press, 1972), pp. 119–36.

Caplan, Jane (ed.). *Nazism, Fascism and the Working Class. Essays by Tim Mason* (Cambridge: Cambridge University Press, 1995).

Castano, Emanuele, Mark Dechesne. 'On Defeating Death. Group reification and social identification as immortality strategies', *European Review of Social Psychology*, No. 6 (2005), pp. 231–65.

Cavazza, Stefano, *Piccole Patrie. Feste popolari tra regione e nazione durante il fascismo* (Bologna: Il Mulino, 1997).

Childs, Peter. *Modernism* (London: Routledge, 2000).

——. *Modernism and Eugenics. Woolf, Eliot, Yeats, and the Culture of Degeneration* (Cambridge, New York: Cambridge University Press, 2001).

Clayes, G. 'Introducing Francis Galton, "Kantsaywhere" and "The Donoghues of Dunno Weir"', *Utopian Studies*, Vol. 12, No. 2 (2001), pp. 188–90.

Cohen, Stanley, Laurie Taylor. *Escape Attempts. The Theory and Practice of Resistance to Everyday Life* (New York: Penguin Books, 1978).

Cohn, Norman. *The Pursuit of the Millennium. Revolutionary Millenarians and Mystical Anarchists of the Middle Ages* (1957) (London: Granada, 1970).

Coomaraswamy, Ananda. *The Dance of Śiva. Fourteen Indian Essays*, with an Introduction by Romain Rolland (New York: The Sunwise Turn, 1924).

Conrads, Ulrich. *Programs and Manifestos on 20th Century Architecture* (Cambridge, MA: MIT Press, 1975).

Conte, Édouard, Cornelia Essner. *La Quête de la Race. Une Anthropologie du Nazisme* (Paris: Hachette, 1995).

Cookson, William (ed.). *Ezra Pound. Selected Prose 1909–1965* (New York: New Directions, 1973).

Crowley, David. 'Nationalist Modernisms', in Christopher Wilk (ed.), *Modernism 1914–1939. Designing a New World* (London: V&A Publications, 2006), pp. 341–73.

Dasenbrock, Reed. 'Slouching toward Berlin. Life in a Postfascist Culture', in Richard Golsan (ed.), *Fascism's Return. Scandal, Revision, and Ideology since 1980* (Lincoln: University of Nebraska Press, 1998), pp. 244–59.

Davidescu, Constantin. 'Totalitarian Discourse as a Rejection of Modernity', in Mihaela Czobor-Lupp and Stefan Lupp (ed.), *Moral, Legal and Political Values in Romanian Culture. Romanian Philosophical Studies, IV* (Washington, DC: The Council for Research in Values and Philosophy, 2002), pp. 149–60.

Deacon, Terence. *The Symbolic Species* (London: Allen Lane/The Penguin Press, 1997).

Debord, Guy. *Society of the Spectacle* (Detroit: Black and Red, 1983).

Deflem, Mathieu. 'Ritual, Anti-structure, and Religion. A discussion of Victor Turner's processual symbolic analysis', *Journal for the Scientific Study of Religion*, Vol. 30, No. 1 (1991), pp. 1–25.

De Grand, Alexander. *The Italian Nationalist Association and the Rise of Fascism* (Lincoln: University of Nebraska Press, 1978).

——. 'Cracks in the Façade. The Failure of Fascism. Totalitarianism in Italy, 1935–9', *European History Quarterly*, No. 21 (1991), pp. 515–35.

——. *Fascist Italy and Nazi Germany. The Fascist Style of Rule* (New York and London: Routledge, 1995).

De Grazia, Victoria. *The Culture of Consent. Mass Organisation of Leisure in Fascist Italy* (Cambridge: Cambridge University Press, 1981).

——. *How Fascism Ruled Women. Italy 1922–1945* (Berkeley: University of California Press, 1992).

Deichmann, Ute. *Biologists under Hitler* (Cambridge, MA: Harvard University Press, 1996).

Deleuze, Gilles, Felix Guattari. *A Thousand Plateaus. Capitalism and Schizophrenia* (Minneapolis, MN: University of Minneapolis Press, 1987).

——. *Anti-Oedipus. Capitalism and Schizophrenia* (Minneapolis, MN: University of Minneapolis Press, 1989).

Derrida, Jacques. *Specters of Marx, the State of the Debt, the Work of Mourning, & the New International* (London: Routledge, 1994).

Deshmukh, Marion. 'Cultural Migration. Artists and visual representation between Americans and Germans during the 1930s and 1940s', in David Barclay (ed.), *Transatlantic Images and Perceptions. Germany and America since 1776* (London: Cambridge, 1997), pp. 265–83.

Doyle, Laura. *Bordering on the Body. The Racial Matrix of Modern Fiction and Culture* (New York: Oxford University Press, 1994).

Durkheim, Émile. *The Division of Labour in Society* (1893) (New York: The Free Press, 1947).

Durth, Werner. 'Architektur und Stadtplanung im Dritten Reich', in Michael Prinz and Rainer Zitelmann (eds.), *Nationalsozialismus und Modernisierung* (Darmstadt: Wissenschaftliche Buchgesellschaft, 1991), pp. 139–71.

Dyckhoff, Tim. 'Mies and the Nazis', *Guardian*, 30 November 2002.

Eatwell, Roger. 'Towards a New Model of Generic Fascism', *Journal of Theoretical Politics*, Vol. 4, No. 2 (1992), pp. 161–94.

—— *Fascism* (London: Chatto & Windus, 1995).

Ebner, Michael Robert. 'The Fascist Archipelago. Political internment, exile, and everyday life in Mussolini's Italy, 1926–1943' (Unpublished PhD, Columbia University, 2005).

Eksteins, Modris. *Rites of Spring* (1989) (Boston: Houghton Mifflin, 2000).

Eliade, Mircea. *The Sacred and the Profane. The Nature of Religion. The Significance of Religious Myth, Symbolism, and Ritual within Life and Culture* (San Diego, CA: Harcourt Brace & Co, 1959).

——. *The Myth of the Eternal Return, or Cosmos and History* (1954) (Princeton, NJ: Princeton University Press, 1971).

Eliot, T. S. *The Complete Poems & Plays. T. S. Eliot* (London: Faber and Faber, 2004).

Ericksen, Robert. *Theologians under Hitler* (New Haven, CT: Yale University Press, 1985).

Etlin, Richard. *Modernism in Italian Architecture, 1890–1940* (London: MIT Press, 1991).

——. 'Introduction. The Perverse Logic of Nazi Thought', in Richard Etlin (ed.), *Art, Culture, and Media under the Third Reich* (Chicago: The University of Chicago Press, 2002), pp. 1–39.

Evans, Richard. *In Defence of History* (London: Granta Books, 2000).

——. *The Coming of the Third Reich* (London: Allen Lane, 2003).

——. *The Third Reich in Power 1933–1939* (London: Allen Lane, 2005).

Evola, Julius. 'Introduzione: La realtà della palingenesi', in Julius Evola, *La tradizione ermetica nei suoi simboli, nella sua dottrina e nella sua 'Arte regia'* (Bari: Gius. Laterza & Figli, 1931).

——. *Erhebung wider die moderne Welt* (Stuttgart: Deutsche Verlagsanstalt, 1935).
——. 'Il mito Marcuse', in Julius Evola, *Gli uomini e le rovine* (Rome: Edizioni dell'Ascia, 1953), pp. 263–9.
——. *L 'operaio' nel pensiero di Ernst Jünger* (Rome: Armando Armando Editore, 1960).
——. *Il Cammino del Cinabro* (Milan: Vanni Scheiwiller, 1972).
Fachinelli, Elvio. *La freccia ferma. Tre tentative di annullare il tempo* (Milan: Adelphi, 1979).
Falasca-Zamponi, Simonetta. *Fascist Spectacle. The Aesthetics of Power in Fascist Italy* (Berkeley: University of California Press, 1997).
Farinacci, Roberto. *Squadrismo* (Rome: Edizioni Ardita, 1934).
——. *Storia della rivoluzione fascista* (Cremona: Cremona Nuova, 1937).
Felice, Renzo De. *Mussolini il rivoluzionario. 1883–1920* (Turin: Einaudi, 1965).
Fénélon, Fania, Marcelle Routier. *Playing for Time* (New York: Atheneum, 1977).
Fenn, Richard. *The End of Time. Religion, Ritual, and the Forging of the Soul* (Cleveland, OH: Pilgrim Press, 1997).
——. *Time Exposure. The Personal Experience of Time in Secular Societies* (Oxford: Oxford University Press, 2000).
Fenner, Angelica, Eric D. Weitz (eds.). *Fascism and Neofascism. Critical Writings on the Radical Right in Europe* (New York: Palgrave Macmillan, 2004).
Ferrall, Charles. *Modernist Writing and Reactionary Politics* (New York: Cambridge University Press, 2001).
Fest, Joachim. *Der zerstörte Traum. Das Ende des utopistischen Zeitalters* (Munich: Siedler Verlag, 1991).
Fischer, Andreas, Frank Kämpfer. 'The Political Poster in the Third Reich', in Brandon Taylor and Wilfried van der Will (eds.), *The Nazification of Art* (Winchester: The Winchester Press, 1990), pp. 183–203.
Foucault, Michael. *The Order of Things. An Archaeology of the Human Sciences* (New York: Vintage Books, 1970).
——. *The Archaeology of Knowledge* (London: Tavistock, 1972).
Fox, Richard (ed.). *Recapturing Anthropology. Working in the Present* (Santa Fe, NM: School of American Research Press, 1991).
Frank, Hartmut. 'Bridges. Paul Bonatz's Search for a Contemporary Monumental Style', in Brandon Taylor and Wilfried van der Will (eds.), *The Nazification of Art* (Winchester: The Winchester Press, 1990), pp. 144–57.
Frank, Manfred. 'Vom Bühnenweihefestspiel zum Thingspiel. Zur Wirkungsgeschichte der Neuen Mythologie bei Nietzsche, Wagner und Johst', in W. Haug and R. Warning (eds.), *Das Fest* (Munich: Fink, 1989), pp. 573–601.
Frankl, Viktor. *Homo Patiens. Versuch einer Pathodizee* (Vienna: Deuticke, 1950).
——. *Man's Search for Meaning* (London: Simon & Schuster, 1959).
Frantzen, Allen. *Bloody Good. Chivalry, Sacrifice, and the Great War* (Chicago: University of Chicago Press, 2004).
Freedberg, David. *The Power of Images. Studies in the History and Theory of Response* (Chicago: The University of Chicago Press, 1989).
Freud, Sigmund. *Das Unbehagen in der Kultur* (Vienna: Internationaler Psychoanalytischer Verlag, 1930); English translation: *Civilization and its Discontents* (London: Hogarth Press and Institute of Psycho-Analysis, 1930).
Friedlaender, Saul. *Reflections of Nazism. An Essay on Kitsch and Death* (New York: Harper&Row, 1984).
Friedman, Susan. 'Definitional Excursus: The Meanings of *Modern/Modernity/Modernism*', *Modernism/Modernity*, Vol. 8, No. 3 (2001), pp. 493–513.
Frisch, Walter. 'Ambivalent Modernism. Perspectives from the 1870s and 1880s', in *German Modernism. Music and the Arts* (Berkeley: University of California Press, 2005), pp. 15–28.
Fritzsche, Peter. 'Machine Dreams. Airmindedness and the reinvention of Germany', *The American Historical Review*, Vol. 98, No. 3 (June 1993), pp. 685–709.

——. 'Nazi Modern', *Modernism/modernity*, Vol. 3, No. 1 (1996), pp. 1–22.

Ferguson, Niall. *The Pity of War* (London: Allen Lane, 1998).

Fogu, Claudio. 'Actualism and the Fascist Historic Imaginary', *History and Theory*, Vol. 42, No. 2 (May 2003), pp. 196–221.

——. *The Historic Imaginary. Politics of History in Fascist Italy* (Buffalo, NY: University of Toronto Press, 2003).

——. 'Mussolini's Mare Nostrum', in Roberto Dainotto and Eric Zakim (eds.), *Mediterranean Studies* (New York: MLA Books, forthcoming).

Fuller, Mia. *Moderns Abroad. Italian Colonial Architecture and Urbanism* (London: Routledge, 2006).

Fussel, Paul. *The Great War and Modern Memory* (Oxford: Oxford University Press, 1977).

Galton, Francis, 'Eugenics, its Definition, Scope, and Aims', *The American Journal of Sociology*, Vol. 10, No. 1 (July 1904), pp. 10–11.

Garofalo, Piero. 'Seeing Red', in J. Rice and P. Garofalo (eds.), *Re-viewing Fascism: Italian Cinema 1922–1943* (Bloomington and Indianapolis: Indiana University Press, 2002), pp. 223–49.

Garrard, Graeme. *Rousseau's Counter-Enlightenment. A Republican Critique of the Philosophes* (New York: State University of New York Press, 2003).

Gasman, Daniel. *The Scientific Origins of National Socialism* (New York: American Elsevier, New York, 1971).

——. *Haeckel's Monism and the Birth of Fascist Ideology* (New York: Peter Lang, 1998).

Gauchet, Marcel. *The Disenchantment of the World. A Political History of Religion* (Princeton, NJ: Princeton University Press, 1997).

Geertz, Clifford. *The Interpretation of Cultures* (New York: Basic Books, 1973).

Gell, Alfred. *The Anthropology of Time* (Oxford: Berg, 1992).

Gellner, David. 'Religion, Politics, and Ritual. Remarks on Geertz and Bloch', *Social Anthropology*, Vol. 7, No. 2 (1999), pp. 135–53.

Gennep, Arnold Van. *The Rites of Passage* (1909) (London: Routledge & Kegan Paul, 1960).

Gentile, Emilio. *Il mito dello stato nuovo Dall'antigiolittismo al fascismo* (Bari: Laterza, 1982).

——. 'Impending Modernity. Fascism and the Ambivalent Image of the United States', *Journal of Contemporary History*, Vol. 28, No. 1 (1993), pp. 7–29.

——. *Le origini dell'ideologia fascista* (1975) (Bologna: Il Mulino, 1996).

——. *The Sacralization of Politics in Fascist Italy* (Cambridge, MA: Harvard University Press, 1996).

——. *La Grande Italia. Ascesa e declino del mito della nazione nel ventesimo secolo* (Milan: Mondadori, 1997).

——. 'The Myth of National Regeneration in Italy. From Modernist Avant-garde to Fascism', in Matthew Affron and Mark Antliff (eds.), *Fascist Visions* (Princeton, NJ: Princeton University Press, 1997), pp. 25–45.

——. *Le religioni della politica. Fra democrazie e totalitarismi* (Rome-Bari: Laterza, 2000).

——. 'The Sacralisation of Politics. Definitions, Interpretations and Reflections on the Question of Secular Religion and Totalitarianism', *Totalitarian Movements and Political Religion*, Vol. 1, No. 1 (2000), pp. 18–55.

——. *La via italiana al totalitarismo* (Rome: Carocci, 2002).

——. 'Conflicting Modernisms. *La Voce* against Futurism', in Emilio Gentile, *The Struggle against Modernity* (Westport, CT: Praeger, 2003), pp. 27–40.

——. 'Mussolini's Charisma', in Emilio Gentile, *The Struggle for Modernity. Nationalism, Futurism, and Fascism* (Westport, CT: Praeger, 2003), pp. 127–44.

——. 'The Conquest of Modernity. From Modernist Nationalism to Fascism', in Emilio Gentile, *The Struggle for Modernity. Nationalism, Futurism, and Fascism* (Westport, CT: Praeger, 2003), pp. 41–76.

——. 'New Idols. Catholicism in the Face of Fascist Totalitarianism', *Journal of Modern Italian Studies*, Vol. 11, No. 2 (2006), pp. 143–70.

——. *Politics as Religion* (Princeton, NJ: Princeton University Press, 2006).

Gentile, Giovanni. *Dopo la vittoria. Nuovi frammenti politici* (Rome: Edizioni La Voce, 1920).
——. 'The Transcending of Time in History', in Raymond Klibansky and H. J. Paton (eds.), *Philosophy and History. Essays Presented to Ernst Cassirer* (Oxford: Clarendon Press, 1936), pp. 91–105.
——. *Genesis and Structure of Society* (1946) (Urbana: University of Illinois Press, 1966).
——, et al. 'Manifesto of Fascist Intellectuals', in Jeffrey Schnapp (ed.), *A Primer of Italian Fascism* (Lincoln: University of Nebraska Press, 2000), pp. 297–303.
Germinario, Francesco. *Razza del Sangue, razza dello Spirito. Julius Evola, l'antisemitismo e il nazionalsocialismo (1930–1945)* (Torino: Bollati Boringhieri, 2001).
Ghirardo, Diane. *Building New Communities. New Deal America and Fascist Italy* (Princeton, NJ: Princeton University Press, 1989).
Giddens, Anthony. *The Consequences of Modernity* (Cambridge: Polity Press, 1990).
——. *Modernity and Self-identity* (Cambridge: Polity Press, 1991).
Gilman, Sander. *Franz Kafka, the Jewish Patient* (New York: Routledge, 1995).
Gilot, Françoise, Carlton Lake. *Life with Picasso* (London: Nelson, 1965).
Gini, Corrado. 'Contributi statisici ai problemi dell'eugenica', *Rivista Italiana di sociologia*, 3–4 (May–August 1912), pp. 64–71.
——. 'The Scientific Basis of Fascism', *Political Science Quarterly*, Vol. 42 (1927), pp. 99–115.
Glatzer, Nahum. *The Complete Short Stories of Franz Kafka* (London: Minerva, 1992).
Gloveli, Georgii. '"Socialism of Science" and "Socialism of Feeling." Bogdanov and Lunacharsky', *Studies in East European Thought*, Vol. 42, No. 1 (July 1991), pp. 29–55.
Goebbels, Joseph. *Michael. Ein deutsches Schicksal in Tagebuchblättern (1926)* (Munich: Franz Eher Press, 1931).
Golomstock, Igor. *Totalitarian Art in the Soviet Union, the Third Reich, Fascist Italy and the People's Republic of China* (London: HarperCollins, 1990).
Golsan, Richard (ed.). *Fascism, Aesthetics, and Culture* (Brandeis: University of New England Press, 1992).
Golston, Michael. *Rhythm and 'Race' in Twentieth Century Poetry and Poetics: Pound, Yeats, Williams, and Modern Sciences of Rhythm* (New York: Columbia University Press, 2007).
Gooding-Williams, Robert. *Zarathustra's Dionysian Modernism* (Stanford, CA: Stanford University Press, 2001).
Goodrick-Clarke, Nicolas. *The Occult Roots of Nazism* (Wellingborough, Northamptonshire, UK: Aquarian Press, 1985).
——. *The Occult Roots of Nazism, Secret Aryan Cults and Their Influence on Nazi Ideology* (New York: New York University Press, 1992).
——. *Black Sun* (New York: New York University Press, 2002).
Gori, Gigliola. 'Model of Masculinity. Mussolini, the "New Italian" of the Fascist Era', in James Mangan (ed.), *Shaping the Superman. Fascist Body as Political Icon – Global Fascism* (London: Cass, 1999).
Gottlieb, Julie. 'The Marketing of Megalomania. Celebrity, Consumption and the Development of Political Technology in the British Union of Fascists', *Journal of Contemporary History*, Vol. 41, No. 1 (2006), pp. 35–55.
——, Thomas Linehan (eds.). *The Culture of Fascism. Visions of the Far Right in Britain* (London: I.B. Tauris, 2004), pp. 45–65.
Grass, Günter. *The Tin Drum* (New York: Harcourt, Brace & World, 1965).
Gravagnuolo, Bruno. 'Chi voleva morto Giovanni Gentile?', *L'Unità*, 24 February 2000.
Greenberg, Jeff, Tom Pyszczynski, Sheldon Salomon. 'The Causes and Consequences of a Need for Self-Esteem. A Terror Management Theory', in Roy Baumeister (ed.), *Public and Private Self* (New York: Springer, 1986), pp. 189–212.
Gregor, A. James. *The Ideology of Fascism* (New York: Free Press, 1969).
——. *Young Mussolini and the Intellectual Origins of Fascism* (Berkeley: University of California Press, 1979).
——. *Phoenix. Fascism in our Time* (New Brunswick, NJ: Transaction, 1999).

——. *The Faces of Janus. Marxism and Fascism in the Twentieth Century* (New Haven, CT: Yale University Press, 2000).

——. *Giovanni Gentile. Philosopher of Fascism* (New York: Transaction, 2001).

——. *Fascist Intellectuals. Fascist Social and Political Thought* (Princeton, NJ: Princeton University Press, 2005).

Gregor, Neil. *Daimler-Benz in the Third Reich* (New Haven, CT: Yale, 1998).

Griffin, Roger. 'Revolts against the Modern World. The blend of literary and historical fantasy in the Italian New Right', *Literature and History*, Vol. 11, No. 1 (Spring 1985), pp. 101–24.

——. *The Nature of Fascism* (London: Pinter, 1991).

——. *Fascism* (Oxford: Oxford University Press, 1995).

——. *International Fascism. Theories, Causes, and the New Consensus* (London: Arnold, 1998).

——. 'The Sacred Synthesis. The Ideological Cohesion of Fascist Cultural Policy', *Modern Italy*, Vol. 3, No. 1 (1998), pp. 5–23.

——. 'Plus ça change! The fascist pedigree of the Nouvelle Droite', in Edward Arnold (ed.), *The Development of the Radical Right in France 1890–1995* (London: Routledge, 2000), pp. 217–52.

——. ' "This Fortress Built against Infection." The BUF vision of Britain's theatrical and musical Renaissance', in Tom Linehan and Julie Gottlieb (eds.), *Cultural Expressions of the Far Right* (London: Macmillan, 2003).

——, Matt Feldman. *Fascism. Critical Concepts in Political Science, vols 1–5* (London: Routledge, 2004).

——, Werner Loh, Andreas Umland (eds.). *Fascism Past and Present, East and West. An International Debate and Concepts and Cases in the Comparative Study of the Extreme Right* (Stuttgart: Ibidem, 2006).

Guenther, Irene. *Nazi Chic. Fashioning Women in the Third Reich* (Oxford: Berg, 2004).

Guillén, Mauro F. 'Modernism Without Modernity. The Rise of Modernist Architecture in Mexico, Brazil, and Argentina, 1890–1940', *Latin American Research Review*, Vol. 39, No. 2 (Summer 2004), pp. 6–64.

Habermas, Jürgen. *Theorie und Praxis. Sozialphilosophische Studien* (Neuwied/Berlin: Luchterhand, 1963).

——. *The Philosophical Discourses of Modernity* (Cambridge, MA: The MIT Press, 1987).

Haeckel, Ernst. *The Riddle of the Universe* (New York: Harper & Bros., 1900).

Hale, Christopher. *Himmler's Crusade* (New York: Bantam Books, 2003).

Hamann, Brigitte. *Hitler's Vienna* (Oxford: Oxford University Press, 2000).

——. *Winifred Wagner. A Life at the Heart of Hitler's Bayreuth* (London: Granta Books, 2005).

Harris, G. W. 'Bio-Politics', *The New Age*, Vol. 10, No. 9 (28 December 1911), pp. 59–69.

Harries, Karsten. 'Building and the Terror of Time', *Prospecta. The Yale Architectural Journal*, Vol. 19 (1982), pp. 58–69.

Harrison, Charles, Paul Wood (eds.). *Art in Theory 1900–1990* (Oxford: Blackwell, 1992).

Harrison, Tony. *The Gaze of the Gorgon* (Highgreen Tarset: Bloodaxe Books, 1992).

Harvey, David. *The Condition of Postmodernity. An Enquiry into the Origins of Cultural Change* (Oxford: Basil Blackwell, 1989).

Hay, James. *Popular Film Culture in Fascist Italy. The Passing of the Rex* (Bloomington: Indiana University Press, 1987).

Hayes, Peter. *Industry and Ideology. IG Farben in the Nazi Era* (Cambridge: Cambridge University Press, 1987).

Heidegger, Martin. *Einführung in die Metaphysik* (Tübingen: Max Niemeyer Verlag, 1935).

——. *Denkerfahrungen* (Frankfurt am Main: Vittorio Klostermann, 1983).

Heller, Erich. *The Disinherited Mind. Essays in Modern German Literature and Thought* (Philadelphia: Dufour & Saifer, 1952).

Henderson, Linda. 'Editor's Statement. Mysticism and Occultism in Modern Art', *Art Journal*, Vol. 46, No. 1 (Spring 1987), pp. 5–8.

Henderson, Susan. 'J. M. L. Lauweriks and K. P.C de Bazel. Architecture and Theosophy', *Architronic*, Vol. 8, No. 1 (January 1999), pp. 1–12.

Herf, Jeffrey. *Reactionary Modernism. Technology, Culture, and Politics in Weimar and the Third Reich* (New York: Cambridge University Press, 1984).

——. *Reactionary Modernism. Technology, Culture, and Politics in Weimar and the Third Reich* (London: Cambridge University Press, 1986).

Herman, Arthur. *The Idea of Decline in Western History* (New York: The Free Press, 1997).

Hermand, Jost. *Old Dreams of a New Reich. Volkish Utopias and National Socialism* (Bloomington: Indiana University Press, 1992).

——, James Steakley. *Heimat, Nation, Fatherland (The German Sense of Belonging)* (New York: Peter Lang, 1996).

Herzog, Dagmar. 'Sex and Secularisation in Nazi Germany', in Angelica Fenner and Eric Weitz (eds.), *Fascism and Neofascism. Critical Writings on the Radical Right in Europe* (New York and London: Palgrave Macmillan, 2004), pp. 103–23.

Herzstein, Robert. *When Nazi Dreams Come True. The Third Reich's Internal Struggle Over the Future of Europe After a German Victory* (London: Sphere/Abacus, 1982).

Heskett, John. 'Modernism and Archaism in Design in the Third Reich', in Brandon Taylor and Wilfried van der Will (eds.), *The Nazification of Art* (Winchester: The Winchester Press, 1990), pp. 110–27.

Hewitt, Adrian. 'Ideological Positions', in Angelica Fenner and Eric Weitz (eds.), *Fascism and Neofascism. Critical Writings on the Radical Right in Europe* (New York and London: Palgrave Macmillan, 2004), pp. 19–41.

Hewitt, Andrew. 'Fascist Modernism, Futurism, and Postmodernity', in Richard Glosan (ed.), *Fascism, Aesthetics, and Culture* (Hanover: University Press of New England, 1992), pp. 38–55.

——. *Fascist Modernism. Aesthetics, Politics, and the Avant-Garde* (Stanford, CA: Stanford University Press, 1993).

Hexter, Jack. *On Historians* (Cambridge, MA: Harvard University Press, 1979).

Hirsch, Emanuel. *Die gegenwärtige geistige Lage im Spiegel philosophischer und theologischer Besinnung* (Göttingen: Vandenhoeck und Ruprecht, 1934).

Hitler, Adolf. *Liberty, Art, Nationhood. Three Addresses by Adolf Hitler* (published in English) (Berlin: M. Müller & Son, 1935).

——. *My New Order* (London: Angus and Robertson, 1942).

——. *Mein Kampf*, trans. Ralph Mannheim (London: Pimlico, 1992).

Hobart, Angela. *Healing Performances of Bali. Between Darkness and Light* (Oxford: Berghahn, 2003).

Hobsbawm, Eric. *The Age of Empire, 1875–1914* (London: Abacus, 1994).

Hochman, Elaine S. *Architects of Fortune. Mies van der Rohe and the Third Reich* (New York: Fromm International Publishing Corporation, 1990).

Hodgkinson, Tim. 'Improvised Music and Siberian Shamanism', *Contemporary Music Review*, Vol. 14, Nos. 1–2 (1996), pp. 59–66.

Holthusen, Hans. *Der unbehauste Mensch* ['Homeless/unhoused Man'] (Munich: Piper, 1952).

Horkheimer, Max. 'Die Juden in Europa', in H. Dubiel and A. Söllner (eds.), *Wirtschaft, Recht und Staat im Nationalsozialismus. Analysen des Instituts für Sozialforschung 1939–1942* (Frankfurt am Main: Suhrkampf, 1984), pp. 33–53.

Horn, David. *Social Bodies. Science, Reproduction, and Italian Modernity* (Princeton, NJ: Princeton University Press, 1994).

Horne, John (ed.). *State, Society, and Mobilization in Europe during the First World War* (Cambridge: Cambridge University Press, 1997).

Hughes, Robert. *The Shock of the New. Art and the Century of Change* (London: Thames & Hudson, 1981).

——. 'Of Gods and Men', *Guardian*, 1 February 2003, pp. 7–20.

Hughes, Stuart. *Consciousness and Society. The Reorientation of European Social Thought 1890–1930* (Brighton: Harvester Press, 1979).

Hunt, Lynn. *Politics, Culture, and Class in the French Revolution* (Berkeley: California University Press, 1984).

Ioanid, Radu. 'The Sacralised Politics of the Romanian Iron Guard', *Totalitarian Movements and Political Religions*, Vol. 5, No. 3 (Winter 2004), pp. 419–53.

Iordachi, Constantin. *Charisma, Politics and Violence. The Legion of the Archangel Michael in Interwar Romania* (Trondheim: Trondheim Studies on East European Cultures and Societies, No. 15, 2004).

Ipsen, Carl. *Dictating Demography. The Problem of Population in Fascist Italy* (Cambridge, MA: Cambridge University Press, 1996).

Isnenghi, Mario. *Il mito della grande guerra. Da Marinetti a Malaparte* (Bologna: Il Mulino, 1989).

Jäckel, Eberhard. *Hitler's World View. A Blueprint for Power* (Cambridge, MA: Harvard University Press, 1981).

James, Wendy. *The Ceremonial Animal. A New Portrait of Anthropology* (Oxford: Oxford University Press, 2003).

Jameson, Frederic (ed.). *Aesthetics and Politics. The Key Texts of the Classic Debate within German Marxism. Adorno, Benjamin, Bloch, Brecht, Lukács* (New York: Verso, 1977).

——. *Fables of Aggression. Wyndham Lewis, the Modernist as Fascist* (Berkeley: University of California Press, 1979).

——. *The Seeds of Time* (New York: Columbia Press, 1994).

——. *The Cultural Turn. Selected Writings on the Postmodern, 1983–1998* (London and New York: Verso, 1998).

Janik, Allan, Stephen Toulmin. *Wittgenstein's Vienna* (Chicago: Ivan R. Dee, 1996).

Janouch, Gutsav. *Gespräche mit Kafka. Aufzeichnungen und Erinnerungen* (Frankfurt am Main: Fischer, 1968).

——. *Conversations with Kafka* (London: Quartet Books, 1985).

Jarausch, Konrad (ed.). *The Unfree Professions. German Lawyers, Teachers, and Engineers, 1900–1950* (New York: Oxford University Press, 1990).

Jaskot, Paul. *The Architecture of Oppression* (London: Routledge, 2000).

Johst, Hanns. *Der junge Mensch. Ein ekstatisches Szenarium* (Munich: Delphin, 1916).

——. *Ich glaube! Bekenntnisse* (Munich: A. Langen, 1928).

Joll, James. *The Origins of the First World War* (London: Longman, 1992).

Jones, Greta. *Social Hygiene in Twentieth Century Britain* (London: Croom Helm, 1986).

Jünger, Ernst. *Der Kampf als inneres Erlebnis* (Berlin: E. G. Mittler and Son, 1929).

——. *Ernst Jünger. Sämtliche Werke* (1932) (Stuttgart: Klett-Cotta, 1981).

Jung, Carl G. *Modern Man in Search of a Soul* (New York: Harcourt, Brace & World, 1933).

Kafka, Franz. 'Betrachtungen über Sünde, Leid, Hoffnung und den wahren Weg' in Max Brod (ed.), *Franz Kafka. Hochzeitsvorbereitungen auf dem Lande und andere Prosa aus dem Nachlaß* (Frankfurt am Main: Fischer, 1980), pp. 30–40.

Kahn, David. *Seizing the Enigma. The Race to Break the German U-boat Codes 1939–1943* (London: Arrow Books, 1996).

Kallis, Aristotle. *Fascist Ideology. Territory and Expansionism in Italy and Germany, 1922–1945* (New York: Routledge, 2000).

Kandinsky, Wassily. *Concerning the Spiritual in Art* (1914) (New York: Dover Publications, 1977).

Kant, Marion. 'The Nazi Attempt to Suppress Jazz and Swing', in Lilian Karina and Marion Kant (eds.), *Hitler's Dancers. German Modern Dance and the Third Reich* (Oxford: Berghahn, 2003), pp. 167–90.

Kaplan, Alice. *Reproductions of Banality. Fascism, Literature, and French Intellectual Life* (Minneapolis: University of Minnesota Press, 1986).

Kaplan, Michael. 'Revisiting Fascism: Degenerate Art and the New Corporate Style', *University of Tennessee Journal of Architecture*, No. 16 (1995), pp. 29–34.

Karlson, Paul. 'Können Maschinen denken?', *Koralle. Zeitschrift für Unterhaltung, Wissen, Lebensfreude*, Vol. 9, No. 20 (18 May 1941), pp. 528–30.

Kater, Michael. *Different Drummers* (Oxford: Oxford University Press, 1982).

——. *Doctors under Hitler* (Chapel Hill: University of North Carolina Press, 1989).

——. *Different Drummers. Jazz in the Culture of Nazi Germany* (Oxford: Oxford University Press, 1992).

——. *The Twisted Muse. Musicians and their Music in the Third Reich* (Oxford: Oxford University Press, 1997).

Keller, Catherine. *The Face of the Deep. A Theology of Becoming* (London: Routledge, 2003).

Kellner, Douglas. 'Expressionist Literature and the Dream of the "New Man"', in Stephen Bronner and Douglas Kellner (eds.), *Passion and Rebellion. The Expressionist Heritage* (London: Croom Helm, 1983), pp. 166–200.

Kemp, Peter. *The Strauss Family: Portrait of a Musical Dynasty* (Tunbridge Wells: Baton Press, 1985).

Kenny, Michael. 'A Darker Shade of Green. Medical botany, homeopathy, and cultural politics in interwar Germany', *Social History of Medicine*, Vol. 15, No. 3 (December 2002), pp. 481–504.

Kermode, Frank. *The Sense of an Ending. Studies in the Theory of Fiction* (1967) (New York: Oxford University Press, 2000).

Kern, Stephen. *The Culture of Time and Space 1880–1918* (Cambridge, MA: Harvard University Press, 2003).

Kerr, John. *A Most Dangerous Method. The Story of Jung, Freud and Sabina Spielrein* (New York: Alfred Knopf, 1993).

Kershaw, Ian. *The Hitler Myth* (Oxford: Oxford University Press, 1987).

——. *Hitler. 1889–1936: Hubris.* (New York: W. W. Norton, 1998).

——. *Hitler. 1936–1945: Nemesis* (New York: W. W. Norton, 2000).

——. *The Nazi Dictatorship* (London: Arnold, 2000).

——. 'Reflections on Genocide and Modernity', in Omer Bartov and Phyllis Mack (eds.), *In God's Name: Genocide and Religion in the 20th Century* (Oxford: Berghahn, 2001), pp. 373–83.

——. 'Hitler and the Uniqueness of Nazism', *Journal of Contemporary History*, Vol. 39, No. 2 (2004), pp. 239–54.

Kertzer, David. *Ritual, Politics and Power* (New Haven, CT: Yale University Press, 1988).

Kinsman, Robert (ed.). *The Darker Vision of the Renaissance. Beyond the Fields of Reason* (Berkeley: University of California Press, 1974).

Klemperer, Victor. *The Language of the Third Reich. LTI, Lingua Tertii Imperii.* (London: Martin Brady, Athlone, 2000).

Knopp, Guido, Peter Hartl. 'Der Verführer', in Guido Knopp (ed.), *Hitler. Eine Bilanz* (Berlin: Siedler, 1995), pp. 31–90.

Koenen, Andreas. *Der Fall Carl Schmitt. Sein Aufstieg zum 'Kronjuristen des Dritten Reiches'* (Darmstadt: Wissenschaftliche Buchgesellschaft, 1995).

Koestler, Arthur. *The Act of Creation* (London: Pan Books, 1975).

——. *The Ghost in the Machine* (London: Picador, 1976).

Kolnai, Aurel. *The War against the West* (New York: Viking Press, 1938).

Kolocotroni, Vassiliki, Jane Goldman, Olga Taxidou (eds.). *Modernism. An Anthology of Sources and Documents* (Edinburgh, Chicago: Edinburgh University Press, Chicago University Press, 1998).

Koon, Tracy. *Believe, Obey, Fight. Political Socialization of Youth in Fascist Italy, 1922–1943* (Chapel Hill: University of North Carolina Press, 1985).

Koselleck, Reinhardt. *Critique and Crisis. Enlightenment and the Pathogenesis of Modern Society* (Oxford: Berg, 1988).

——. *The Practice of Conceptual History. Timing History, Spacing Concepts* (Stanford, CA: Stanford University Press, 2002).

——. 'The Eighteenth Century as the Beginning of Modernity', in Reinhardt Koselleck, *The Practice of Conceptual History. Timing History, Spacing Concepts* (Stanford, CA: Stanford University Press, 2002), pp. 154–69.

Koshul, Basit. *The Postmodern Significance of Max Weber's Legacy* (London: Palgrave Macmillan, 2005).

Krabbe, Wolfgang. '"Die Weltanschauung der Deutschen Lebensform-Bewegung ist der Nationalsozialismus". Zur Gleichschaltung einer Alternativströmung im Dritten Reich', *Archiv für Kulturgeschichte*, Vol. 71, No. 2 (1989), pp. 431–61.

Kracauer, Siegfried. *From Caligari to Hitler. A Pyschological History of the German Film* (1947) (Princeton, NJ: Princeton University Press, 1970).

Kroll, Frank-Lothar. *Utopie als Ideologie. Geschichtsdenken und politisches Handeln im Dritten Reich* (Paderborn: Ferdinand Schöningh, 1999).

Kuxdorf, Manfred. 'The New German Dance Movement', in Stephen Bronner and Douglas Kellner (eds.), *Passion and Rebellion. The Expressionist Heritage* (London: Croom Helm, 1983), pp. 350–62.

Lagarde, Paul. *Die graue Internationale* (1878) (Jena: Eugen Diederichs, 1944).

Landy, Marcia. *Fascism in Film. The Italian Commercial Cinema, 1931–1943* (Princeton, NJ: Princeton University Press, 1986).

Langbehn, Julius. *Rembrandt als Erzieher* (Leipzig: C. L. Hirschfeld, 1890).

Lange, Hans-Jürgen. *Weisthor – Karl Maria Wiligut – Himmlers Rasputin und seine Erben* (Engerda: Arun-Verlag, 1998).

Langenbucher, Helmut. *Volkhafte Dichtung der Zeit* (Berlin: Junker und Dünnhaupt, 1937).

Lapouge, Georges Vacher de. *L'Aryen* (Paris: Albert Fontemoing, 1899).

Laqueur, Walter (ed.). *Fascism. A Reader's Guide* (Harmondsworth: Penguin, 1976).

Large, David, William Weber (eds.). *Wagnerism in European Culture and Politics* (Ithaca, NY: Cornell University Press, 1984).

Larsen, Stein. *Who were the Fascists?* (Oslo: Universitetforlaget, 1980).

Lazzaro, Claudia, Roger J. Crum (eds.). *Donatello Among the Blackshirts. History and Modernity in the Visual Culture of Fascist Italy* (Cornell, NY: Cornell University Press: 2005).

Leach, Edmund. 'Two Essays Concerning the Symbolic Representation of Time', in Edmund Leach, *Rethinking Anthropology* (London: Athlone Press, 1971), pp. 124–32.

Ledeen, Michael. *Universal Fascism* (New York: Howard Fertig, 1972).

——. *Fascism. An Informal Introduction to its Theory and Practice* (New Brunswick, NJ: Transaction Books, 1976).

——. *The First Duce. D'Annunzio at Fiume* (Baltimore, MD: Johns Hopkins University Press, 1977).

Leed, Eric. *No Man's Land. Combat and Identity in World War 1* (Cambridge: Cambridge University Press, 1979).

Leo, Nunzio. *Italo Balbo* (Predappio: Ufficio Propaganda, 1940).

Leone, Enzo. *La mistica del razzismo fascista* (Milan: Quaderni della 'Scuola di Mistica Fascista', No. 3, 1941).

Levi, Erik. 'Music and National Socialism. The Politicization of Criticism, Composition, and Performance', in Brandon Taylor and Wilfried van der Will (eds.), *The Nazification of Art* (Winchester: The Winchester Press, 1990), pp. 158–82.

——. 'Opera in the Nazi Period', in John London (ed.), *Theatre under the Nazis* (Manchester: Manchester University Press, 2000), pp. 136–86.

Levi, Primo. *If this is a Man* (Harmondsworth: Penguin, 1987).

——. *Moments of Reprieve. A Memoir of Auschwitz* (New York: Penguin, 1987).

Levinson, Marjorie. 'The New Historicism. Back to the Future', in Marjorie Levinson (ed.), *Rethinking Historicism. Critical Readings in Romantic History* (Oxford: Basil Blackwell, 1989), pp. 102–11.

Levi-Strauss, Claude. *Tristes tropiques* (New York: Washington Square Press, 1977).

Liebefels, Lanz von (ed.). *Nackt- und Rassenkultur im Kampf gegen Mucker- und Tschandkultur*, Ostara Pamphlet Series, No. 66 (Rodaun and Mödling, 1913).

Lifton, Robert. *Destroying the World to Save It: Aum Shinrikyo, Apocalyptic Violence, and the New Global Terrorism* (New York: Metropolitan Books, 1999).

Linehan, Thomas. *British Fascism 1918–1939. Parties, Ideology and Culture* (Manchester: Manchester University Press, 2000).

Linz, Juan. 'Totalitarian and Authoritarian Regimes', in F. I. Greenstein and N. W. Polsby (eds.), *Handbook of Political Science. Vol. 3: Macropolitical Theory*, (Reading: Addison-Wesley, 1975), pp. 313–21.

Linz, Juan. 'Political Space and Fascism as a Late-comer', in Stein Larsen et al. (eds.), *Who were the Fascists. Social Roots of European Fascism* (Bergen: Universitetsforlaget, 1980), pp. 153–89.

Lodder, Christina. 'Searching for Utopia', in Christopher Wilk (ed.), *Modernism 1914–1939. Designing a New World* (London: V&A Publications, 2006), pp. 25–69.

Loder, Dietrich. 'Die Krankheit der deutschen Kultur', *Völkischer Beobachter*, No. 269/270 (25/26 September 1932).

Loewy, Ernst. *Literatur unterm Hakenkreuz. Das Dritte Reich und seine Dichtung. Eine Dokumentation* (Frankfurt am Main: Europäische Verlagsanstalt, 1966).

Loh, Werner, Roger Griffin, Andreas Umland (eds.). *Fascism Past and Present, East and West. An International Debate and Concepts and Cases in the Comparative Study of the Extreme Right* (Stuttgart: Ibidem, 2006).

Long, Rose-Carol. 'Occultism, Anarchism, and Abstraction. Kandinsky's Art of the Future', *The Art Journal*, Vol. 46, No. 1 (Spring 1987), pp. 38–45.

Ludington, Townsend, Thomas Fahy, Sarah Reuning (eds.). *A Modern Mosaic. Art and Modernism in the United States* (Chapel Hill: University of North Carolina Press, 2000).

Lukács, Georg. *The Destruction of Reason* (1952) (London: Merlin, 1980).

Jiří Karásek ze Lvovic, *Renaissanční touhy v umění. Kritické studie* (1902) (Vinohrady, Prague: Aventinum, 1926).

Lyotard, Jean-François. *The Postmodern Condition. A Report on Knowledge* (1979) (Minneapolis: University of Minnesota, 1993).

Lyttleton, Adrian. *Italian Fascisms. From Pareto to Gentile* (London: Jonathan Cape, 1973).

——. *The Seizure of Power* (London: Taylor & Francis, 2004).

Maalouf, Amin. *Les Identités Meurtrières* (Paris: Grasset, 1998).

Mack Smith, Denis. *Mussolini. A Biography* (New York: Vintage Books, 1983).

Madsen, Douglas, Peter Snow. *The Charismatic Bond. Political Behavior in Time of Crisis* (Cambridge, MA: Harvard University Press, 1996).

Maertz, Gregory. *Hitler's List and the Real Canon of Nazi Art* (New Haven, CT: Yale University Press, forthcoming).

Makiya, Kanan. *The Monument. Art and Vulgarity in Saddam Hussein's Iraq* (1991) (New York: I. B. Tauris, 2004).

Mangan, Joseph (ed.). *Shaping the Superman. Fascist Body as Political Icon – Aryan Fascism* (Portland, OR: Frank Cass, 1999).

Mangoni, Luisa. *Una crisi di fine secolo. La cultura italiana e la Francia fra Otto e Novecento* (Turin: Einaudi, 1985).

Mann, Michael. *Fascists* (New York: Cambridge University Press, 2004).

Marchesini, Daniel. *La scuola dei gerarchi. Mistica fascista. Storia problemi, istituzioni* (Milan: Feltrinelli, 1976).

Marden, Elissa. *Dead Time. Temporal Disorders in the Wake of Modernity (Baudelaire and Flaubert)* (Stanford, CA: Stanford University Press, 2001).

Marinetti, Filippo. 'Guerra sola igiene del mondo', in Filippo Marinetti, *Teoria e invenzione futurista* (1915) (Milan: Arnaldo Mondadori, 1968), pp. 253–341.

——. 'The Founding Manifesto of Futurism', in Umbro Apollonio, *Futurist Manifestos* (London: Thames and Hudson, 1973), pp. 21–2.

Marion, Jean-Luc. *Being Given. Towards a Phenomenology of Givenness* (Palo Alto, CA: Stanford University Press, 2002).

Marx, Karl. 'Speech at Anniversary of the People's Paper', in David McLellan (ed.), *Karl Marx. Selected Writings* (Oxford: Oxford University Press, 2000), pp. 338–9.

Mason, Tim. 'Whatever Happened to Fascism?', *Radical History Review*, Vol. 49 (Winter 1991), pp. 89–98.

——. 'Whatever Happened to "Fascism"?', in Jane Caplan (ed.), *Nazism, Fascism and the Working Class* (Cambridge: Cambridge University Press, 1995), pp. 323–31.

Mazgaj, Paul. *The Action Française and Revolutionary Syndicalism* (Chapel Hill: University of North Carolina Press, 1979).

McCloskey, Deirdre N. *The Rhetoric of Economics* (Madison: University of Wisconsin Press, 1998).

McColman, Carl. *Embracing Jesus and the Goddess. A Radical Call for Spiritual Sanity* (Gloucester, MA: Fair Winds Press, 2001).

McDonough, Frank. *Opposition and Resistance in Nazi Germany* (Cambridge: Cambridge University Press, 2001).

McElligott, Anthony. 'Sentencing towards the Führer', in Anthony McElligott and Tim Lirk (eds.), *Working towards the Führer* (Manchester: Manchester University Press, 2003), pp. 153–85.

McIntosh, Christopher. *Éliphas Lévi and the French Occult Revival* (London: Rider, 1972).

Messerschmidt, Rolf. 'Nationalsozialistische Raumforschung und Raumordnung aus der Perspektive der "Stunde Null"', in Michael Prinz and Rainer Zitelmann (eds.), *Nazionalsozialismus und Modernisierung* (Darmstadt: Wissenschaftliche Buchgesellschaft, 1991), pp. 139–71.

Michael, George. *The Enemy of My Enemy. The Alarming Convergence of Militant Islam and the Extreme Right* (Lawrence, KS: University Press, 2006).

Michaud, Eric. 'National Socialist Architecture as an Acceleration of Time', *Critical Enquiry*, Vol. 19 (Winter 1993), pp. 220–33.

——. *The Cult of Art in Nazi Germany* (1996) (Stanford: Stanford University Press, 2004).

Midgley, Mary. *The Myths We Live By* (London: Routledge, 2003).

Millon, Henry, Linda Nochlin (eds.). *Art and Architecture in the Service of Politics* (Cambridge, MA: The MIT Press, 1978).

Miercejewski, Alfred. *Hitler's Trains. The German National Railway and the Third Reich* (Chapel Hill: University of North Carolina Press, 2000).

Moeller van den Bruck, Arthur. *Das Dritte Reich* (1923) (Hamburg: Hanseatische Verlagsanstalt, 1931).

Morgan, Philip. *Fascism in Europe, 1919–1945* (London: Routledge, 2003).

Morrison, Simon. *Russian Opera and the Symbolist Movement* (Berkeley, Los Angeles: The University of California Press, 2002).

Mosley, Oswald. *My Life* (London: Nelson, 1968).

Mosse, George. *The Crisis of German Ideology. Intellectual Origins of the Third Reich* (New York: Howard Fertig, 1964).

—— (ed.). *Nazi Culture. Intellectual, Cultural and Social Life in the Third Reich* (New York: Grosset and Dunlap, 1966).

——. 'The Genesis of Fascism', *Journal of Contemporary History*, Vol. 1, No. 1 (1966), pp. 14–26.

——. *The Nationalization of the Masses* (New York: Howard Fertig, 1975).

——. *Masses and Man. Nationalist and Fascist Perceptions of Reality* (New York: Howard Fertig, 1980).

——. *Fallen Soldiers. Reshaping the Memory of the World Wars* (New York: Oxford University Press, 1990).

——. *The Crisis of German Ideology. Intellectual Origins of the Third Reich* (New York: Howard Fertig, 1998).

——. *The Fascist Revolution* (New York: Howard Fertig, 1999).

Mostert, Mark. 'Useless Eaters. Disability as Genocidal Marker in Nazi Germany', *The Journal of Special Education*, Vol. 36, No. 3 (1 October 2002), pp. 157–70.

Müller, Ingo. *Hitler's Justice. The Courts of the Third Reich* (Cambridge, MA: Harvard University Press, 1991).

Mühlberger, Detlef. *Hitler's Voice. Der völkische Beobachter. 1920–1933* (Bern: Peter Lang, 2004).

Mussolini, Benito. *My Autobiography* (New York: Charles Scribner's Sons, 1928).

——. 'Trincerocrazia', [*Il Popolo d'Italia*, 15 December 1917] in E. Susmel and D. Susmel (eds.), *Omnia Opera di Benito Mussolini, Vol. 10* (Florence: La Fenice, 1951–63), pp. 140–3.

Neaman, Elliot. 'Ernst Jünger's Millennium. Bad Citizens for the New Century', in Richard Golsan (ed.), *Fascism's Return. Scandal, Revision, and Ideology since 1980* (Lincoln: University of Nebraska Press, 1998), pp. 218–43.

Neumann, Gerhard, Malcolm Pasley, Jost Schillemeit (eds.). *Franz Kafka. Briefe 1900–1912* (Frankfurt am Main: Fischer, 1999).

Nicholas, Lynn. *The Rape of Europa* (New York: Vintage Books, 1995).

Nietzsche, Friedrich. *Ecce Homo* (1908) (New York: Vintage, 1967).

——. *The Case of Wagner* (New York: Vintage Books, 1967).

——. *The Will to Power. Notes written 1883–1888* (London: Weidenfeld and Nicolson, 1967).

——. *Dithyrambs of Dionysus* (London: Anvil Press, 1984).

——. *Human, All Too Human. A Book for Free Spirits*, trans. R. J. Hollingdale (Cambridge: Cambridge University Press, 1986).

——. 'History in the Service and Disservice of Life' (1874), in Friedrich Nietzsche, *Unmodern Observations* (New Haven, CT: Yale University Press, 1990), pp. 87–145.

——. 'Schopenhauer as Educator', in Friedrich Nietzsche, *Unmodern Observations* (New Haven, CT: Yale University Press, 1990), pp. 147–226.

——. *Unmodern Observations* (New Haven, CT: Yale University Press, 1990).

——. *The Gay Science* (Cambridge: Cambridge University Press, 2001).

——. *Thus Spoke Zarathustra. A New Translation by Graham Parkes* (Oxford: Blackwell, 2005).

Niven, William. 'The Birth of Nazi Drama? Thing Plays', in John London (ed.), *Theatre under the Nazis* (Manchester: Manchester University Press, 2000), pp. 54–95.

Noll, Richard. *The Jung Cult* (New York: Simon & Schuster, 1994).

Nordau, Max. *Degeneration* (New York: D. Appleton, 1895).

Nowotny, Helga. *Time. The Modern and Postmodern Experience* (1989) (Cambridge: Polity Press, 1994).

O'Brien, Martin, Sue Penna, Colin Hay. *Theorising Modernity. Reflexivity, Environment and Identity in Gidden's Social Theory* (London: Longman, 1999).

O'Brien, Paul. *Mussolini in the First World War. The Journalist, the Soldier, the Fascist* (Oxford: Berg, 2005).

Oren, Ido. 'Political Science as History. A Reflexive Approach', in Dvora Yanow and Peregrine Schwartz-Shea (eds.), *Interpretation and Method. Empirical Research Methods and the Interpretive Turn* (New York: M. E. Sharpe, 2006), pp. 215–27.

Osborne, Peter. *The Politics of Time. Modernity and the Avant-garde* (London: Verso, 1995).

——. *Philosophy in Cultural Theory* (London: Routledge, 2000).

Ott, Hugo. *Martin Heidegger: A Political life* (New York: Basic Books, 1993).

Ozouf, Mona. *L'Homme régénéré. Essai sur la Révolution française* (Paris: Gallimard, 1989).

Pansera, Anty (ed.). *Anni Trenta. Arte e Cultura in Italia* (Milan: Mazotta, 1981).

Panunzio, Sergio. 'Stato e sindacato', *Rivista internazionale di filosofia del diritto*, Vol. 3, No. 1 (January–March, 1923), pp. 4–9.

——. *Riforma Costitutionale. Le Corporzaioni; il Consiglio delle Corporazioni, il Senato* (Florence: La Nuova Italia, 1934).

Paperny, Vladimir. *Architecture in the Age of Stalin* (Cambridge: Cambridge University Press, 2002).

Papini, Giovanni. *Vecchio e nuovo nazionalismo* (Rome: Giovanni Volpe, 1967).

Pascal, Blaise. *Pensées* (1660) (London: Penguin, 1966).

Passmore, Patrick. *The Philosophy of History* (Oxford: Oxford University Press, 1974).

Pauwels, Louis, Jacques Bergier. *The Morning of the Magicians* (1960) (London: Mayflower, 1971).

Payne, Stanley. 'The Concept of Fascism', in Stein Larsen (ed.), *Who were the Fascists?* (Oslo: Universitetforlaget, 1980), pp. 14–25.

——. *A History of Fascism, 1914–1945* (London: University College London Press, 1995).

Paxton, Robert. *The Anatomy of Fascism* (New York: Alfred A. Knopf, 2004).

Pearse, Pádraic H. 'The Coming Revolution', in Pádraig Pearse, *Political Writings and Speeches* (Dublin: Phoenix Publishing, 1924).

Peckham, Morse. 'Toward a Theory of Romanticism', *PMLA*, Vol. 66, No. 2 (March 1951), pp. 5–23.

Penty, Arthur. *Tradition and Modernism in Politics* (London: Sheed and Ward, 1937).

——. *Distributism. A Manifesto* (1937), *Distributist Perspectives*, Vol. I (Norfolk, VA: IHS Press, 2004), pp. 86–110.

Petersen, Julius. *Die Sehnsucht nach dem Dritten Reich in deutscher Sage und Dichtung* (Stuttgart: JB Metzlersche, 1934).

Petropoulos, Jonathan. *Art as Politics in the Third Reich* (Chapel Hill: University of North Carolina Press, 1996).

——. *The Faustian Bargain. The Art World in Nazi Germany* (New York: Oxford University Press, 2000).

Peukert, Detlev. *Inside Nazi Germany* (Harmondsworth: Penguin, 1982).

——. *The Weimar Republic. The Crisis of Classical Modernity* (New York: Hill and Wang, 1989).

Piazzesi, Mario. *Diario di uno squadrista toscano 1919–22* (Rome: Bonnaci, 1980).

Pick, Daniel. *Faces of Degeneration. A European Disorder c. 1848–1918* (Cambridge: Cambridge University Press, 1989).

——. *War Machine. The Rationalization of Slaughter in the Modern Age* (New Haven, CT: Yale University Press, 1993).

Piper, Franciszek. 'Gas Chambers and Crematoria', in Yisrael Gutman and Michael Berenbaum (eds.), *Anatomy of the Auschwitz Death Camp* (Bloomington: Indiana University Press, 1994), pp. 157–82.

Poewe, Karla. *New Religions and the Nazis* (New York: London, 2006).

Poggioli, Renato. *The Theory of the Avant-Garde* (New York: Harper & Row, 1968).

Pois, Robert. *National Socialism and the Religion of Nature* (London: Croom Helm, 1986).

Poliakov, Leon. *The Aryan Myth* (London: Sussex University Press, 1974).

Politzer, Heinz (ed.). *Das Kafka-Buch* (Frankfurt am Main: Fischer, 1965).

Ponte, Renato del. 'Weisthor-Wiligut Dossier', *Arthos*, Vol. 4, Nos. 7–8 (2000), pp. 241–65.

Ponting, Clive. *Winston Churchill* (London: Sinclair-Stevenson, 1994).

Popper, Karl. *The Poverty of Historicism* (1957) (London: Routledge and Kegan Paul, 1974).

——. *The Open Society and its Enemies* (1950) (London: Routledge, 2002).

Porter, Patrick. 'War and the Religious Will to Sacrifice', *Peace Review*, Vol. 17, No.1 (January–March 2005), pp. 17–24.

Powers, Thomas. *Heisenberg's War. The Secret History of the German Bomb* (London: Cape, 1993).

Praz, Mario. *The Romantic Agony* (1933) (Oxford: Oxford University Press, 1970).

Presner, Todd Samuel. '"Clear Heads, Solid Stomachs, and Hard Muscles." Max Nordau and the Aesthetics of Jewish Regeneration', *Modernism/modernity*, Vol. 10, No. 2 (2003), pp. 269–96.

Price, John. 'Anthropology and Psychiatry', *The British Journal of Psychiatry*, Vol. 186, No. 2 (2005), pp. 168–9.

Prideaux, Sue. *Edvard Munch. Behind the Scream* (New Haven, CT: Yale University Press, 2005).

Pringle, Heather. *The Master Plan. Himmler's Scholars and the Holocaust* (New York: Viking, 2006).

Prinz, Michael. 'Die soziale Funktion moderner Elemente in der Gesellschaftspolitik des Nationalsozialismus', in Michael Prinz and Rainer Zitelmann (eds.), *Nazionalsozialismus und Modernisierung* (Darmstadt: Wissenschaftliche Buchgesellschaft, 1991), pp. 297–327.

Proctor, Robert. *Racial Hygiene. Medicine under the Nazis* (Cambridge, MA: Harvard University Press, 1988).

——. *The Nazi War on Cancer* (Princeton, NJ: Princeton University Press, 2000).

Pross, Christian. 'Introduction', in Götz Aly, Peter Chroust, and Christian Pross, *Cleansing the Fatherland. Nazi Medicine and Racial Hygiene* (Baltimore, MD: Johns Hopkins University Press, 1994), pp. 1–21.

Proust, Marcel. *À la Recherche du Temps perdu* (Paris: Gallimard, 1945).

Pulzer, Peter. *The Rise of Political Anti-Semitism in Germany and Austria* (London: Peter Halban, 1987).

Pynsent, Robert (ed.). *Decadence and Innovation. Austria-Hungary in the Fin-De-Siècle* (London: Weidenfeld & Nicolson, 1989).

Quarta, Cosimo. 'Homo utopicus sive transcendens', *Utopian Studies*, Vol. 12, No. 2 (2001), pp. 174–87.

Quine, Maria. *Italy's Social Revolution. Charity and Welfare from Liberalism to Fascism* (New York: Palgrave Macmillan, 2002).

Raabe, P. (ed.). *Franz Kafka. Sämtliche Erzählungen* (Frankfurt: Fischer, 1975).

Rabinbach, Anson. 'The Aesthetics of Production in the Third Reich', *Journal of Contemporary History*, Vol. 11, No. 4 (1976), pp. 43–74.

Rahimi, Babak. 'Sacrifice, Transcendence and the Solider', *Peace Review*, Vol. 17, No. 1 (January–March 2005), pp. 1–8.

Rasch, Wolfdietrich. 'Aspekte der deutschen Literatur', in Wolfdietrich Rasch, *Zur deutschen Literatur der Jahrhundertswende* (Stuttgart: J. B. Metzlersche, 1967), pp. 1–48.

Read, Herbert. *The Collected Works of C. G. Jung* (London: Routledge, 1953–78).

Redman, Tim. *Ezra Pound and Italian Fascism* (Cambridge: Cambridge University Press, 1991).

Reinert, Hugo, Erik Reinert. 'Creative Destruction in Economics. Nietzsche, Sombart, Schumpeter', in Jürgen Backhaus and Wolfgang Drechsler (eds.), *Friedrich Nietzsche. Economy and Society* (Heidelberg: Springer, 2006).

Reitter, Paul. 'Hitler's Viennese Waltz', *The Nation*, 9 August 1999.

Rennie, Bryan. *Reconstructing Eliade. Making Sense of Religion* (New York: State University of New York Press, 1996).

Rentschler, Eric. *The Ministry of Illusion. Nazi Cinema and its Afterlife* (Cambridge, MA: Harvard University Press, 1996).

Repp, Kevin. *Reformers, Critics, and the Paths of German Modernity. Anti-Politics and the Search for Alternatives, 1890–1914* (Cambridge, MA: Harvard University Press, 2000).

Rhodes, James. *The Hitler Movement. A Modern Millenarian Revolution* (Stanford, CA: Hoover Institute Press, 1980).

Ricoeur, Paul. *Time and Narrative (Temps et Récit)*, 3 vols, (Chicago: University of Chicago Press, 1984, 1985, 1988).

Riegel, Klaus-George. 'Marxism-Leninism as a Political Religion', *Totalitarian Movements and Political Religions*, Vol. 6, No. 1 (2005), pp. 97–126.

Ringer, Fritz. *The Decline of the Mandarins. The German Academic Community, 1890–1933* (Cambridge, MA: Harvard University Press, 1969).

Roberts, David. *The Syndicalist Tradition and Italian Fascism* (Chapel Hill: University of North Carolina Press, 1979).

——. 'How not to Think about Fascism and Ideology, Intellectual Antecedents and Historical Meaning', *Journal of Contemporary History*, Vol. 35, No. 2 (2000), pp. 185–211.

——. *The Totalitarian Experiment in the Twentieth-Century* (New York: Routledge, 2006).

Rocco, Alfredo. *Scritti e discorsi politici* (Milan: Dott. A. Giuffrè Editori, 1928).

Rogers, Ernesto. 'L'esperienza degli architetti', in G. Cassinis (ed.), *Fascismo e antifascismo 1918–1936. Lezioni e testimonianze* (Milan: Feltrinelli, 1972), pp. 334–9.

Rosenberg, Arthur. *Der Mythus des 20. Jahrhunderts* (Munich: Hoheneichen, 1924).

Rosenthal, Bernice. *New Myth, New World. From Nietzsche to Stalin* (University Park: Pennsylvania State University Press, 2002).

Ross, Chad. *Naked Germany* (Oxford: Berg, 2005).

Roth, Jack. *The Cult of Violence. Sorel and the Sorelians* (Berkeley: University of California Press, 1980).

Roussy de Sales, Raoul de (ed.). *Adolf Hitler. My New Order* (London: Angus and Robertson, 1942), pp. 335–6.

Rowling, Joanne. *Harry Potter and the Philosopher's Stone* (London: Bloomsbury, 1997).

Rushdie, Salman. *Imaginary Homelands* (London: Penguin, 1992).

Safranski, Rüdiger. *Wieviel Wahrheit braucht der Mensch? Über das Denkbare und das Lebbare* (München: Hanser, 1990).

——. *Martin Heidegger. Between Good and Evil* (Cambridge, MA: Harvard University Press, 1998).

Salgado, Plinío. *A Quarta Humanidade* (San Paolo: José Olympio Press, 1934).

Santarelli, Lidia. 'Muted Violence. Italian War Crimes in Occupied Greece', *Journal of Modern Italian Studies*, Vol. 9, No. 3 (2004), pp. 280–99.

Sarkowicz, Hans, Alf Mentzer. *Literatur in Nazi-Deutschland. Ein biografisches Lexikon* (Hamburg: Europa, 2002).

Saunders, Frances. *Hidden Hands* (London: Channel 4, 1995).

Scheerbart, Paul. *Glasarchitektur* (Berlin: Geb. Mann, 1914).

Schleifer, Ronald. *Modernism and Time. The Logic of Abundance in Literature, Science, and Culture* (Cambridge: Cambridge University Press, 2000).

Schmid, Ulrich. 'Towards a Conceptualisation of Fascist Aesthetics', *Totalitarian Movements and Political Religions*, Vol. 6, No. 1 (June 2005), pp. 127–40.

Schmitt, Carl. *Politische Romantik* (Berlin: Duncker & Humblot, 1919).

——. *Der Begriff des Politischen* (Munich: Duncker & Humblot, 1932).

——. *Staat, Bewegung, Volk. Die Dreigliederung der politischen Einheit* (Hamburg: Hanseatische Verlagsanstalt, 1933).

——. 'Der Führer schützt das Recht', *Deutsche Juristen-Zeitung*, No. 39 (1934), p. 945.

——. 'Totaler Feind, totaler Krieg, totaler Staat' (1937), in Carl Schmitt, *Positionen und Begriffe im Kampf mit Weimar* (Hamburg: Hanseatische Verlagsanstalt, 1940).

——. *Der Nomos der Erde im Völkerrecht der Jus Publicum Europaeum* (1950) (Berlin: Duncker & Humblot, 1988).

Schnapp, Jeffrey, Barbara Spackmann. 'Selections from the Great Debate on Fascism and Culture. *Critica Fascista*', *Stanford Italian Review*, special issue on 'Fascism and Culture', Vol. 8, Nos. 1–2 (1990), pp. 235–72.

——. 'Epic Demonstrations. Fascist Modernity and the 1932 Exhibition of the Fascist Revolution', in Richard Golsan (ed.), *Fascism, Aesthetics, and Culture.* (Hanover and London: University Press of New England, 1992), pp. 1–32.

——. *Staging Fascism. 18BL and the Theatre of Masses for Masses* (Stanford, CA: Stanford University Press, 1996).

——. 'The Fabric of Modern Times', *Critical Inquiry*, Vol. 24, No. 1 (Autumn 1997), pp. 191–245.

——. 'Bad Dada (Evola)', in Leah Dickerman and Matthew S. Witkovsky (eds.), *The Dada Seminars* (CASVA seminar papers 1, National Gallery of Art, Washington, 2005), pp. 30–55.

Schneider, Herbert W. *Making the Fascist State* (New York: Oxford University Press, 1928).

Schorske, Carl. *Fin-de-Siècle Vienna. Politics and Culture* (New York: Vintage Books, 1981).

——. 'Politics in a New Key. An Austrian Trio', in Carl Schorske, *Fin-de-Siècle Vienna. Politics and Culture* (New York: Vintage Books, 1981), pp. 116–80.

Schubert, Dirk. 'Theodor Fritsch and the German (völkisch) Version of the Garden City. The Garden City invented two years before Ebenezer Howard', *Planning Perspectives*, Vol. 19, No. 1 (January 2004), pp. 3–35.

Schulte-Sass, Linda. *Entertaining the Third Reich* (Durham, NC: Duke University Press, 1996).

Schumacher, Thomas. *The Danteum. Architecture, Poetics, and Politics under Italian Fascism* (Princeton, NJ: Princeton Architectural Press, 1993).

Schwarz, Michael. '"Euthanasie" – Debatten in Deutschland (1895–1945)', *Vierteljahreshefte für Zeitgeschichte*, Vol. 46 (1998), pp. 617–65.

Sedgwick, Mark. *Against the Modern World. Traditionalism and the Secret Intellectual History of the Twentieth Century* (Oxford: Oxford University Press, 2004).

Searle, Geoffrey. *The Quest for National Efficiency* (Oxford: Basil Blackwell, 1971).

Seeman, Mary. 'Psychiatry in the Nazi Era', *The Canadian Journal of Psychiatry*, Vol. 50, No. 1 (2005), pp. 218–25.

Sereny, Gitta. *Albert Speer. His Battle with the Truth* (London: Macmillan, 1996).

——. *The German Trauma* (London: Allen Lane, 2000).

Shenfield, Stephen. *Russian Fascism. Traditions, Tendencies, Movements* (Armonk, NY: M. E. Sharpe, 2001).

Sheppard, Richard. 'German Expressionism', in Malcolm Bradbury and James McFarlane (eds.), *Modernism 1890–1930* (Harmondsworth: Penguin, 1976), pp. 274–91.

Sherry, Vincent. *Ezra Pound, Wyndham Lewis and Radical Modernism* (New York: Oxford University Press, 1993).

Shils, Edward, Henry Finch (eds.). *Max Weber. The Methodology of the Social Sciences* (New York: The Free Press, 1949).

Short, Robert. 'Dada and Surrealism', in Malcolm Bradbury and James McFarlane (eds.), *Modernism 1890–1930* (Harmondsworth: Penguin, 1976), pp. 292–308.

Simmel, Georg. *The Metropolis and Mental Life* (1903) (New York: Free Press, 1950).

Sinclair, May. *The Tree of Heaven* (London: Cassell and Company, 1917).

Sironneau, Jean-Pierre. *Sécularisation et religions politiques* (La Haye: Mouton, 1982).

Sluga, Hans. *Heidegger's Crisis: Philosophy and Politics in Nazi Germany* (Cambridge, MA: Harvard University Press, 1993).

Smelser, Ronald. *Robert Ley. Hitler's Labour Front Leader* (Oxford: Berg, 1988).

Smith, Anthony. *Nations and Nationalism in a Global Era* (Cambridge: Polity, 1995).

——. *Nationalism and Modernism. A Critical Survey of Recent Theories of Nations* (London: Routledge, 1998).

Sonn, Richard. *Anarchism and Cultural Politics in Fin de Siècle France* (Lincoln: University of Nebraska Press, 1989).

Spackman, Barbara. *Fascist Virilities. Rhetoric, Ideology, and Social Fantasy in Italy* (Minneapolis: University of Minnesota Press, 1996).

Speer, Albert. *Inside the Third Reich. Memoirs* (New York: Macmillan, 1970).

—— (et al.). *Albert Speer. Architektur. Arbeiten 1933–1942* (Frankfurt/M: Ullstein/Propylaen, 1978).

Spender, Stephen. *The Struggle of the Modern* (London: Methuen, 1963).

Spotts, Frederic. *Hitler and the Power of Aesthetics* (London: Pimlico, 2000).

Steding, Christoph. *Das Reich und die Krankheit Europas* (Hamburg: Hanseatische Verlagsanstalt, 1938).

Steigmann-Gall, Richard. *Holy Reich. Nazi Conceptions of Christianity, 1919–1945* (Cambridge: Cambridge University Press, 2003).

Steinbart, Norman. 'Group Psychology, Sacrifice and War', *Peace Review*, Vol. 17, No. 1 (January–March 2005), pp. 9–16.

Steinberg, Isaak. *In the Workshop of the Revolution* (New York: Rinehart, 1953).

Stern, Fritz. *The Politics of Cultural Despair* (California: University of California Press, 1974).

Sternhell, Zeev. 'Fascist Ideology', in Walter Laqueur (ed.), *Fascism. A Reader's Guide* (Harmondsworth: Penguin, 1976), pp. 325–406.

——. *Neither Right Nor Left. Fascist Ideology in France* (Berkeley: University of California Press, 1986).

——. *La droite révolutionnaire* (Paris: Fayard, 2000).

——. *Maurice Barrès et le nationalisme français, La droite révolutionnaire* (Paris: Fayard, 2000).

——. *Ni droite ni gauche* (Paris: Fayard, 2000).

——, Mario Sznajder, Maia Asheri. *The Birth of Fascism. from Cultural Rebellion to Political Revolution* (Princeton, NJ: Princeton University Press, 1994).

Stevens, Anthony. *Ariadne's Clue. A Guide to the Symbols of Humankind* (London: The Allen Press, 1998).

Stites, Richard. *Revolutionary Dreams. Utopian Vision and Experimental Life in the Russian Revolution* (New York: Oxford University Press, 1989).

Stockton, Sharon. 'Aesthetics, Politics and the Staging of the World. Wyndham Lewis and the renaissance-author', *Twentieth Century Literature*, Vol. 42, No. 4 (Winter 1996), pp. 414–515.

Stoppard, Tom. *Salvage, Part 1 of The Coast of Utopia Trilogy* (London: Faber and Faber, 2002).

Stone, Dan. *Breeding Superman. Nietzsche, Race and Eugenics in Edwardian and Interwar Britain* (Liverpool: Liverpool University Press, 2002).

Stone, Marla. 'The State as Patron. Making Official Culture in Fascist Italy', in Matthew Affron and Mark Antliff (eds.), *Fascist Visions* (Princeton, NJ: Princeton University Press, 1997), pp. 205–38.

——. *The Patron State. Culture and Politics in Fascist Italy* (Princeton, NJ: Princeton University Press, 1998).

Straub, Karl Willy. *Die Architektur im Dritten Reich* (Stuttgart: Akademischer Verlag Wedekind, 1932).

Stromberg, Roland. *Redemption by War. The Intellectuals and 1914* (Kansas: The Regents Press of Kansas, 1982).

Susmel, E., D. Susmel (eds.). *Omnia Opera di Benito Mussolini, Vols. 1–10* (Florence: La Fenice, 1951–63).

Swart, Koenraad. *The Sense of Decadence in Nineteenth Century France* (The Hague: M. Nijhoff, 1964).

Sykes, Alan. *The Radical Right in Britain* (London: Palgrave Macmillan, 2005).

Szakolczai, Arpad. *Reflexive Historical Sociology* (London: Routledge, 2000).

Talmon, Jacob. *Political Messianism. The Romantic Phase* (London: Secker and Warburg, 1960).

Tamms, Friedrich. 'Das Große in der Baukunst', *Die Baukunst* (supplement to *Die Kunst des Deutschen Reichs*), No. 8 (March 1944), pp. 47–60.

Taylor, Brandon. 'Post-modernism in the Third Reich', in Brandon Taylor and Wilfried van der Will (eds.), *The Nazification of Art* (Winchester: The Winchester Press, 1990), pp. 128–43.

Taylor, Christopher. *Sacrifice as Terror. The Rwandan Genocide of 1994* (Oxford: Berg, 1999).

Tengan, Andrew. *The Search for Meaning as the Basic Human Motivation. A Critical Examination of Viktor Emil Frankl's Logotherapeutic Concept of Man* (Frankfurt am Main: Peter Lang, 1999).

Thomas, Richard Hinton. *Nietzsche in German Politics and Society 1890–1918* (Manchester: Manchester University Press, 1983).

Thompson, Doug. *State Control in Fascist Italy. Culture and Conformity* (Manchester: Manchester University Press, 1991).

Tiryakian, Edward. 'Towards the Sociology of Esoteric Culture', in Edward Tiryakian (ed.), *On the Margin of the Visible. Toward the Sociology of Esoteric Culture* (New York: Wiley, 1974), pp. 257–80.

Todorov, Tzvetan. *Hope and Memory. Lessons from the Twentieth Century* (Princeton, NJ: Princeton University Press, 2004).

Tönnies, Ferdinand. *Gemeinschaft und Gesellschaft* (Leipzig: Fues, 1887).

Toepfer, Karl. *Empire of Ecstasy. Nudity and Movement in German Body Culture, 1910–1935* (Berkeley: University of California Press, 1997).

Tollefson, Kenneth. 'Titus. Epistle of Religious Revitalization', *Biblical Theology Bulletin*, Vol. 30, No. 4 (Winter 2000), pp. 145–57.

Topfer, Karl. *Empire of the Senses* (Berkeley: University of California Press, 1997).

Traverso, Enzo. *The Origins of Nazi Violence* (London: The New Press, 2003).

Tretyakov, Serget. 'From Where to Where (Futurism's perspectives)', *Lef* 1 (1923), pp. 192–203, in Anne Lawton and Herbert Eagle (eds.), *Russian Futurism through its Manifestoes, 1912–1918* (Ithaca, NY: Cornell University Press, 1998), pp. 205–16.

Trevor-Roper, Hugh. 'The Phenomenon of Fascism', in S. J. Woolf (ed.), *European Fascism* (London: Weidenfeld and Nicolson, 1968), pp. 19–38.

Trinidade, Hermino. 'Fascism and Authoritarianism in Brazil under Vargas (1930–1945)', in Stein Larsen (ed.), *Fascism outside Europe. The European Impulse against Domestic Conditions in the Diffusion of Global Fascism* (Boulder: Social Science Monographs; New York: Columbia University Press, 2001), pp. 491–528.

Tuchman, Maurice. 'Hidden Meanings in Abstract Art', in Edward Weisberger (ed.), *The Spiritual in Art. Abstract Painting 1890–1985* (New York: Abbeville Press, 1986), pp. 17–62.

Turda, Marius. 'Fantasies of Degeneration. Some Remarks on Racial Antisemitism in Interwar Romania', *Judaic Studies*, No. 3 (2003), pp. 336–48.

——. *The Idea of National Superiority in Central Europe, 1880–1918* (New York: Edwin Mellen Press, 2005).

——, Paul Weindling (eds.), *'Blood and Homeland'. Eugenics and Racial Nationalism in Central and Southeast Europe, 1900–1940* (Budapest: Central European University Press, 2006).

Turner, Henry A. 'Fascism and Modernization', *World Politics*, Vol. 24, No. 4 (1972), pp. 547–64.

——. 'Fascism and Modernization', in Henry A. Turner (ed.), *Reappraisals of Fascism* (New York: Franklin Watts, 1976), pp. 117–39.

Turner, Victor. *The Forest of Symbols. Aspects of Ndembu Ritual* (Ithaca, NY: Cornell University Press, 1967).

——. 'Variations on a Theme of Liminality', in Sally F. Moore and Barbara G. Myerhoff (eds.), *Secular Ritual. Forms and Meaning* (Assen, Netherlands: Van Gorcum, 1977), p. 36–52.

——. *Dramas, Fields and Metaphors. Symbolic Action in Human Society* (Cornell, NY: Cornell University Press, 1979).

——, Edith Turner. 'Religious Celebrations', in Victor Turner (ed.), *Celebration. Studies in Festivity and Ritual* (Washington, DC: Smithsonian Institution Press, 1982), pp. 211–12.

Tyrell, Albrecht. *Vom 'Trommler' zum 'Führer'. Der Wandel von Hitlers Selbstverständnis zwischen 1919 und 1924 und die Entwicklung der NSDAP* (Munich: Fink, 1975).

Ulansey, David. 'Cultural Transition and Spiritual Transformation. From Alexander the Great to Cyberspace', in Thomas Singer (ed.), *The Vision Thing. Myth, Politics and Psyche in the World* (New York: Routledge, 2000), pp. 213–31.

Valli, Roberta. 'The Myth of *Squadrismo* in the Fascist Regime', *Journal of Contemporary History*, Vol. 35, No. 2 (2000), pp. 131–50.

van der Will, Wilfried. 'The Body and the Body Politic as Symptom and Metaphor in the Transition of German Culture to National Socialism', in Brandon Taylor and Wilfried van der Will (eds.), *The Nazification of Art* (Winchester: The Winchester Press, 1990), pp. 14–52.

Ventrone, Angelo. *Le seduzione totalitarian. Guerra, modernità, violenza politica (1914–1918)* (Rome: Donzelli, 2003).

——. *Piccola storia della Grande Guerra* (Rome: Donzelli, 2005).

Vincent, Joan. 'Engaging Historicism', in Richard Fox (ed.), *Recapturing Anthropology. Working in the Present* (Santa Fe, NM: School of American Research Press, 1991), pp. 45–58.

Virilio, Paul. *Art and Fear* (London: Continuum, 2003).

Visser, Romke. 'Fascist Doctrine and the Cult of the *Romanità*', *Journal of Contemporary History*, Vol. 27, No. 1 (1992), pp. 5–22.

Voegelin, Eric. *The Political Religions* (1938) (Lewiston, NY: E. Mellen Press, 1986).

Vondung, Klaus. *Magie und Manipulation – Ideologischer Kult und politische Religion des Nationalsozialismus* (Göttingen: Vandenhoeck and Ruprecht, 1971).

——. 'Spiritual Revolution and Magic. Speculation and Political Action in National Socialism', *Modern Age*, Vol. 23, No. 4 (1979), pp. 394–402.

——. 'National Socialism as a Political Religion. Potentials and limits of an analytical concept', *Totalitarian Movements & Political Religions*, Vol. 6, No. 1 (2005), pp. 87–95.

Waldberg, Patrick. *Surrealism* (London: Thames and Hudson, 1965).

Wallace, Anthony. 'Mazeway Resynthesis. A biocultural theory of religious inspiration', *Transactions of the New York Academy of Sciences*, Vol. 18 (1956), pp. 626–38.

——. 'Revitalization Movements', *American Anthropologist*, No. 58 (1956), pp. 264–81.

Watson, Graham. 'Rewriting Culture', in Richard Fox (ed.), *Recapturing Anthropology. Working in the Present* (Santa Fe, NM: School of American Research Press, 1991), pp. 73–92.

Weber, Eugen. 'Romania', in Hans Rogger and Eugen Weber (eds.), *The European Right* (Berkeley, Los Angeles: University of California Press, 1965), pp. 501–74.

——. *Apocalypses – Prophesies, Cults, and Millennial Beliefs through the Ages* (Harvard, Cambridge, MA: Harvard University Press, 1999).

Weber, Max. 'The Social Psychology of the World Religions' (1915), in Hans Gerth and C. Wright Mills (eds.), *From Max Weber. Essays in Sociology* (New York: Oxford University Press, 1946), pp. 267–92.

Weber, Wolfgang, Paula Black. 'Muscular *Anschluss*. German Bodies and Austrian Imitators', in Joseph Mangan (ed.), *Shaping the Superman. Fascist Body as Political Icon – 'Aryan' Fascism* (Portland, OR: Frank Cass, 1999), pp. 62–81.

Weindling, Paul. *Health, Race, and German Politics* (Cambridge: Cambridge University Press, 1993).

——. 'Dissecting German Social Darwinism. Historicizing the Biology of the Organic State', *Science in Context* 11 (1998), pp. 619–37.

——. 'The Medical Publisher J. F. Lehmann and Racial Hygiene', in Sigrid Stöckel (ed.), *Die 'rechte' Nation und ihr Verleger. Politik und Popularisierung im J. F. Lehmanns Verlag 1890–1979* (Berlin: Lehmanns Media, 2002), pp. 159–70.

Weir, David. *Decadence and the Making of Modernism* (Amherst: University of Massachusetts, 1996).

Weldon, Fay. *The Hole at the Top of the World* (L.A. Theatre Works/BBC, 1995).

Welge, Jobst. 'Fascism Triumphans. Modernism, "Romanitas", and Architectural Form', in Claudia Lazarro and Roger Crum (eds.), *Donatello Among the Blackshirts. History and Modernity in the Visual Culture of Fascist Italy* (Ithaca, NY: Cornell University Press, 2004), pp. 83–94.

White, Hayden. 'Historical Emplotment and the Problem of Truth', in Saul Friedländer (ed.), *Probing the Limits of Representation. Nazism and the Final Solution* (Cambridge, MA: Harvard University Press, 1992), pp. 37–53.

Whyte, Iain Boyd. 'Berlin, 1 May 1936', in Dawn Ades et al. (eds.), *Art and Power. Europe under the Dictators, 1930–45* (London: Hayward Gallery, 1995), pp. 43–9.

——. 'Berlin Architecture. National Socialism and Modernism', in Dawn Ades et al. (eds.), *Art and Power. Europe under the Dictators 1930–45* (London: Hayward Gallery, 1995), pp. 258–69.

Wilde, Oscar. 'The Garden of Eros' (1881), in Robert Ross (ed.), *The Collected Works of Oscar Wilde* (London: Dawsons of Pall Mall, 1969), pp. 50–3.

Wilk, Christopher (ed.). *Modernism 1914–1939. Designing a New World* (London: V&A Publications, 2006).

——. 'Introduction. What was Modernism?', in Christopher Wilk (ed.), *Modernism 1914–1939. Designing a New World* (London: V&A Publications, 2006), pp. 11–21.

——. 'The Healthy Body Culture', in Christopher Wilk (ed.), *Modernism 1914–1939. Designing a New World* (London: V&A Publications, 2006), pp. 249–95.

Williams, Daryle. *Culture Wars in Brazil. The First Vargas Regime, 1930–1945* (Durham, NC: Duke University Press, 2001).

Williams, Howard. 'Metamorphosis or Palingenesis? – Political Change in Kant', *Review of Politics*, Vol. 63, No. 4 (Fall 2001), pp. 693–722.

Willrich, Wolfgang. *Die Säuberung des Kunsttempels* (Berlin: Lehmann, 1937).

Winkler, Gershon. *Magic of the Ordinary. Recovering the Shamanic in Judaism* (Berkeley, CA: North Atlantic Books, 2003).

Wohl, Robert. *The Generation of 1914* (London: Weidenfeld and Nicolson, 1980).

——. 'Introduction', in Tim Cross (ed.), *The Lost Voices of World War I* (London: Bloomsbury Publishing, 1988), pp. 1–10.

Wolin, Richard. *The Heidegger Controversy* (Cambridge, MA: The MIT Press, 1993).

Woolf, Virginia. 'A Sketch of the Past', in Jeanne Schulkind (ed.), *Moments of Being* (New York: Harcourt Brace, 1985), pp. 61–137.

Zaehner, Rudolf. *Mysticism Sacred and Profane* (Oxford: Oxford University Press, 1961).

Zillmer, Eric, Molly Harrower, Barry Ritzler. *The Quest for the Nazi Personality. A Psychological Investigation of Nazi War Criminals* (Hillsdale, NJ: Lawrence Earlbaum Associates, 1995).

Zitelmann, Rainer. *Hitler. Selbstverständnis eines Revolutionärs* (Stuttgart: Klett-Cotta, 1986).

Zunino, Pier Giorgio. *L'Ideologia del fascismo* (Bologna: Il Mulino, 1985).

Zúquete, José. 'In Search of a New Society. An intellectual between modernism and Salazar', *Portuguese Journal of Social Science*, Vol. 4, No. 1 (2005), pp. 61–81.

Zwerin, Mike. *Swing under the Nazis. Jazz as a Metaphor for Freedom* (New York: Cooper Square Press, 2000).

Documentaries

Axer, Oliver, Susanne Benze. *Hitler's Hit Parade* (Bad Schwartau: C. Cay Wesnigk Filmproduktion, 2003).

Baron, Saskia (dir.). *Science and the Swastika* (London: Darlow Smithson Productions, 2001).

Breloer, Heinrich. *Speer und Er* (Munich: Bavaria Film, 2004).

Holgate, Beth. *Crossing the Lives. The History of the International Red Cross Committee.* (BBC2, Timewatch, 1998).

Kloft , Michael (dir.). *Television under the Swastika. The History of Nazi Television* (Chicago: International Historic Films Inc., 2001).

Schwierin, Marcel (dir.). *Ewige Schönheit* (Berlin: Neue Visionen, 1993).

Online publications (with date accessed in brackets)

Hitler, Adolf. Untitled Speech at the Nuremberg Party Rally on 6 September 1938, http://www.hitler.org/speeches/09-06-38.html (05/07/06).

Koenigsberg, Richard. 'As the Soldier Dies so Does the Nation Come Alive', http://home.earthlink.net/~libraryofsocialscience/as_the_soldier.htm (26/10/05).

——. 'Aztec Warfare, Western Warfare, The Soldier as Sacrificial Victim', http://home.earthlink. net/~libraryofsocialscience/aztec.htm (26/10/05).

——. 'Genocide as Immunology. The psychosomatic source of culture', http://home.earthlink. net/~libraryofsocialscience/gi.htm (09/01/07).

——. 'Ideology, Perception, and Genocide. How Fantasy Generates History', http://ideolo-giesofwar.com/papers/rk_ipg.htm (22/01/06).

Kohout, Ed. 'Masonic Astronomy and Saint Louis' Gateway Arch', http://www.startiming.net/ cave/arch-1.html (03/3/06).

Lattanzi, Massimiliano (ed.). *Transdisciplinarity* (Paris: UNESCO, 1998), http://unesdoc.unesco. org/images/0011/001146/114694eo.pdf (22/05/06).

Mehaffy, Michael, Nikos Salingaros. 'The End of the Modern World', http://www.opendemocracy. net/articles/ViewPopUpArticle.jsp?id=10&articleId=173 (14/11/05).

Santiago, Etien. 'Misrepresenting Modernism', http://www.opendemocracy.net/forums/thread. jspa?forumID=111&threadID=41473&tstart=0 (14/11/05).

Smith, Martin (trans.). 'The Epicurean Inscription (Abridged), fragment 30', http://www.epicurus. info/etexts/tei.html#ethics (20/03/06).

Websites (with date accessed in brackets)

http://al-islam.org/islamicgovernment (29/10/06).

http://arts.guardian.co.uk/features/story/0,,850738,00.html (29/09/06).

http://fl eursdumal.org (23/10/06).

http://fl ickr.com/photos/raimist/tags/arch/ (2/03/06).

http://home.earthlink.net/~libraryofsocialscience/gi.htm (09/01/07).

http://iug.uni-paderborn.de/ewe/ (12/05/06).

http://library.albany.edu/speccoll/emigre.htm (17/10/07).

http://news.bbc.co.uk/1/hi/sci/tech/173351.stm (13/01/06).

http://rubymatt.backpackit.com/pub/657103 (08/10/06).

http://thompkins_cariou.tripod.com/id6.html (15/11/05).

http://writing.colostate.edu/gallery/matrix/urquhart.htm (21/07/05).

http://www.bbc.co.uk/science/horizon/2000/massivebholes.shtml (14/07/06).

http://www.bethel.edu/-letnie/BeckmannNight.jpg (10/12/06).

http://www.calvin.edu/academic/cas/gpa/posters2.htm (14/10/06).

http://www.centrostudilaruna.it/realtapalingenesi.html (13/05/06).

http://www.djangomontreal.com/doc/Pictures.htm (17/10/06).

http://www.efn.org/~dredmond/MinimaMoralia.html (02/10/06).

http://www.fdabisso.corn/aero/aeropittura.html (02/12/06).

http://www.flickr.com/photos/raimist/91076910/ (02/03/06).

http://www.greatbuildings.com/buildings/Casa_del_Fascio.html (30/11/06).

http://www.iac.es/gabinete/noticias/2001/nov20i.htm (01/12/06).

http://www.ikg.uni-karlsruhe.de/projekte/exilarchitekten/architekten/ bilder/bayer_2gross.jpg (30/11/06).

http://www.jivamuktiyoga.com/inspr/veg2.html (06/10/06).

http://www.kafka.org/index.php?h12 (21/07/05).

http://www.mhs.ox.ac.uk/images/image.no.156048 (09/11/06).

http://www.moma.org/exhibitions/2001/mies/ (13/12/05).

http://www.opendemocracy.net/forums/thread.jspa?forumID=111&threadID=41473&tstart=0 (14/11/05).

http://www.pc.blogspot.com/2006/04/modernism-how-bad-was-it.html (13/12/06).

http://www.thirdreichruins.com/ThorakDenkmalAutobahn.jpg (30/11/06).

http://www.proz.com/kudoz/15886 (11/01/06).

http://www.remember.org/camps/mauthausen/mau-list.html (12/11/06).

http://www.rosenoire.org/articles/revolts.php (15/05/06).

http://www.soc.ucsb.edu/ct/ (12/05/06).
http://www.stormfront.org/archive/t-4817.html (27/10/06).
http://wwwtouregypt.net/featurestories/shu.htm (01/12/06).
http://www.ub.uni-heidelberg.de/archiv/4903 (30/11/06).
http://www.wonderful-things.com/newknit1.htm (02/03/06).
http://www.y-land.net/juliusevola/revolte_rez1.php (20/01/06).

Index

Italic numbers indicate principal passages where topic is discussed.

461

CPSIA information can be obtained
at www.ICGtesting.com
Printed in the USA
LVHW082337220820
663924LV00003B/47